ARCHIVES
P⏻WER

Memory, Accountability,
and Social Justice

Randall C. Jimerson

SOCIETY OF
American
Archivists

Chicago

The Society of American Archivists

www.archivists.org

Printed in the U.S.A.

Library of Congress Cataloging-in-Publication Data

Jimerson, Randall C.
    Archives power: memory, accountability, and social justice / Randall C. Jimerson.
        p. cm.
    Includes bibliographical references and index.
    ISBN 1-931666-30-X (alk. paper)
    1. Archives--Social aspects. 2. Archives--Political aspects. 3. Archivists--
Professional ethics. 4. Social justice. 5. Public interest. I. Society of American
Archivists. II. Title.
    CD971.J56 2009
    025--dc22

                         2009025519

DESIGNED BY PAC1ONE VISUALS jim.pacione@gmail.com

ARCHIVES POWER

Dedicated to my mother
and the memory
of my father

TABLE OF CONTENTS

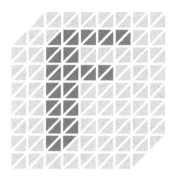

Foreword

Archivists conduct their work in a complex and changing ethical environment. Records-related controversies in recent years have surged to the forefront of national political and intellectual debates, and the profession has responded by taking more transparent and aggressive positions on a variety of public policy issues. The Society of American Archivists (SAA), which now boasts a "Position Statements and Resolutions" section on its website, has voiced its collective opinion on matters ranging from the repatriation of Iraqi records to presidential papers policies to the renewal of the USA Patriot Act. Professional associations regularly receive requests to file amicus briefs in controversial legal proceedings, archivists often testify before congressional committees, and members demand that their leadership speak out about significant public matters.

SAA's publications program and annual meetings in recent years have reflected this growing archival political consciousness. SAA has been proud to publish several especially influential books that have highlighted and broadened archival political discourse, including *Political Pressure and the Archival Record* (2005) edited by Margaret Procter, Michael G. Cook, and Caroline Williams, and *Archives and Justice: A South African Perspective* (2007) by Verne Harris with a foreword by Terry Cook. Other monographs by Trudy Peterson, Richard J. Cox, David Wallace, and Francis X. Blouin have also reminded archivists that such concepts as accountability, memory, social justice, and truth remain central to their everyday labors. Evan a casual perusal of recent SAA annual meeting programs reveals sessions on topics that range from whistle-blowing to cultural privacy to postcolonialism. Clearly, the level and intensity of this wide-ranging discourse has increased.

Randall Jimerson's book advances this discussion and enhances this literature in several important ways. As an archival educator and accomplished historian, Jimerson has long championed the power of archives as a force for good. His 2005 SAA presidential address, "Embracing the Power of Archives," called upon archivists to abandon their rhetoric of neutrality and instead embrace the power of records to promote social responsibility, democratic accountability, and community empowerment. Characteristically, Jimerson ranged broadly over the academic and cultural terrain in constructing his memorable argument, drawing on George Orwell, Claude Lévi-Strauss, George Lucas, and Harry Potter for illustration and inspiration. *Archives Power: Memory, Accountability, and Social Justice* builds on this influential address and introduces a variety of new themes and insights that will undoubtedly spark spirited professional debate. Three noteworthy features of this exciting new work especially deserve emphasis.

First, Jimerson grounds his analysis carefully and thoroughly in historical theory and method. He meticulously documents the ways in which North American archival institutions and recordkeeping practices have served the needs of social and political elites. Politicians, corporate leaders, and scientific historians have self-consciously constructed mythical notions of objectivity and factual accuracy around archives, legitimizing their own influence and fostering their institutional hegemony in the process. Archivists, following the lead of Sir Hilary Jenkinson, often embraced such perceptions as part of their own professional self-definitions and imagery. Jimerson's fresh insights into archival history and professionalization will surprise and stimulate many readers, while also demonstrating the need for all archivists to grapple seriously with the complex historical and intellectual foundations of their craft.

Second, Jimerson engages the growing body of academic literature that examines "the archive" from a variety of particularistic perspectives. Foucault and Derrida make their obligatory appearances here, but Jimerson also draws upon such influential theorists as Pierre Nora, Maurice Halbwachs, Jacques Le Goff, and Carolyn Steedman to develop his interpretations of social memory and power. For nearly a generation, North American archivists (excepting a few notable Canadians) largely have sat on the sidelines as historians, literary theorists, postmodernists, postcolonialists, and cultural studies enthusiasts have argued about archival theory and practice. Archives constitute the central spaces in which very diverse scholarly communities diverge and converge, yet archivists themselves too often appear reluctant to embrace the theoretical implications of their methodologies. Jimerson clearly has immersed himself in this cross-disciplinary conversation, and brings a fresh perspective to the proceedings. His work combines the rich analytical breadth of a fully engaged academician with the practical good sense of a seasoned archival practitioner. He accurately synthesizes and introduces this broader academic literature for archivists, but he also contributes a valuable perspective to theorists who too often write about "the archive" without really understanding the culture and history of people in the recordkeeping community.

Finally, Jimerson writes with passion about his profession. Social justice remains an integral component of his own personal background and life journey. He has devoted his career to archives not owing to a mere intellectual interest in information management, but rather because he believes that archives matter on a very fundamental human level. Not surprisingly, Jimerson spends considerable time analyzing the ethical implications of archival practice. He reminds archivists that their personal choices remain meaningful, and that they can serve either as passive tools of oppression or active forces for liberation. The controversies that have united and divided the profession over the past generation all receive their due attention, and Jimerson writes with conviction about their implications. Creating a useful framework for the future, rather than merely chronicling and reviewing past practice, informs his analysis throughout. And, he writes with the wry wit and the winning sense of humor that have characterized his entire life and career. *Archives Power* will no doubt attract a wide readership across a broad spectrum of academic disciplines. It eloquently testifies to the vitality and sophistication of the archival world as recordkeepers confront the considerable challenges of the early twenty-first century.

PETER J. WOSH
Chair, Publications Board, Society of American Archivists
Director, Archives/Public History Program, History Department, New York University
May 2009

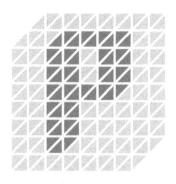

Preface

*What you can become is the miracle you were born to be
through the work that you do.*

- Kurt Vonnegut, *A Man Without a Country*[1]

I am both a historian and an archivist. At times these dual
professional identities have seemed closely interwoven, at other
times divergent and tangential. I am also an American citizen
concerned about the past injustices, present day inequalities,
and future possibilities of my society. This personal concern for
social issues at times seems disconnected from my professional
responsibilities as historian and archivist. There are many who
think that there should be no link between one's personal values
and conscience and one's professional duties—that historians and
archivists should be neutral, unbiased, and silent about social
issues. These concerns have led me to examine the professional
purposes served by archivists—and the rich documentary sources they
manage—and their connections to issues of supreme importance
to society. For me, these values center on historical knowledge and
understanding, legal evidence, conceptions of memory and how it
can be interrogated through documentary sources, accountability of
political, economic, and intellectual leadership, representations of
social diversity, and the search for social justice.

This book grew out of my repeated questions about the role of archivists in society. In my early years in the archival profession I focused mainly on what I needed to accomplish and how to do my work. As I became engaged in wider circles of professional activity and responsibility, I found it necessary to ask *why*. Why do archivists select some people and some organizations to document and not others? Why do they appraise (evaluate) certain types of records as significant and others as unimportant? Why do they establish security measures and reference room policies that may seem intrusive to researchers? Why do they take extraordinary measures to preserve some archival materials, but allow others to slowly rot or remain neglected and unorganized? Why do they provide full access to some records but restrict use of others? The list goes on.

This book is a result of this questioning, and my own search for answers that could unite my dual identities as archivist and historian, as concerned citizen and committed professional. In responding to these issues, I have looked to the ancient past to understand the fundamental purposes of archives, what I call the *archival imperative*. Only a small sliver of human experience can be documented through forms of evidence, deliberately created since the age of ancient cave paintings and, later, cuneiform tablets, the earliest known forms of written communication. From pictographs to YouTube videos, from clay tablets to e-mail and Twitter, people have sought to connect with others across distance and over time. Moving from oral cultures to written cultures, people have sought surrogates for memory, some means of conveying reliable information. Initially the province only of temple priests, lawmakers, and those with economic wealth to protect, written records now form one of the principal means by which citizens can hold their leaders accountable for their actions, protect their own rights, explore and share ideas and culture, and establish an authentic record of events and transactions, among other purposes.

If the incentives and purposes for documenting human experience have changed somewhat over time, they have remained relatively constant compared to the media used to record information. A brief and partial history of documentary media includes: cave paintings, clay tablets, cuneiform script, papyrus, parchment, codex books, maps and charts, printing presses, telegraphs, photographs, motion picture film, wire recordings, wax cylinders, vinyl records, magnetic tape recordings, microfilm, telex, mimeograph, photocopies, and a plethora of electronic and computer formats extending into the Internet and Web 2.0 eras. The new waves of media challenge archivists with problems of identification, selection, appraisal, preservation, description, and access. Some of the skills and techniques required are new and at times daunting, but the purpose and significance of such media can be understood best by reference to previous revolutions in communication, such as the emergence of literacy, printing, and nineteenth-century mass media.

My hope is that this discussion of archival concerns and contributions to society might prove interesting to a wider audience. Those who use or conduct research in archives—including historians, genealogists, administrators, legal researchers, community activists, and others—should understand how source materials reach the archives and how they are managed prior to public use. Scholars of memory, documentation, and communication should understand the legal, administrative, cultural, and symbolic values of archival documentation. Librarians, museum curators, information scientists, and technologists will find similarities and differences in the concerns they share with archivists. Because archival sources assist in protecting the rights of all citizens and in holding public leaders accountable for their actions, this discussion may be valuable for anyone concerned about social and political issues, or anyone interested in the cultural aspects of evidence and documentation.

For those who are not familiar with the basic functions and activities of archivists, the introduction includes a brief overview of archival responsibilities. These include: determining what documentary materials will be chosen and protected in the archives; evaluating or appraising the significance of these archival sources; ensuring their preservation from decay, neglect, media instability, and theft; organizing and describing the materials in order to make them accessible for future use; providing access and reference assistance; promoting knowledge of archival holdings through outreach and public programs; and conducting advocacy on behalf of archives and archival interests.

Above all archivists are concerned with the record—its purposes, origins, uses, and values. Their knowledge of records enables them to interpret these records, assist others in using them as evidence, preserve and organize them for use, protect their reliability and authenticity, and ensure their accessibility as either legal or administrative evidence or as conveyors and communicators of culture and human experience. In common with libraries, museums, and other cultural institutions, archives help us to know the past, to understand the present, and to prepare for the future. Although less well known than their information profession counterparts, archivists serve a vital function in society.

The roles archivists play date back more than two millennia, but archivists have identified themselves as a profession for only a little more than a century. In that time they have used several metaphors or concepts to define their contributions to society and the value of archives. These metaphors include history, the past, legal evidence, memory, democracy, and cultural heritage. In recent years some archivists have explored a more active role for their profession in responding to the challenges of modern society and a growing social conscience stemming from the social reform movements of the past generation. These archivists have added to the value of archives concepts including accountability, identity, diversity, and social justice. This is the context in which I approach the questions of the role of archivists in society, the power and value of archives, and the connection between professional ethics and social responsibility.

◆　　　◆　　　◆

Before entering this discussion, however, the reader has a right to know something about the author and his perspective on these issues. Like all authors, I am a product of my genetics, my upbringing, my personal experiences, and the times in which I live. My father, Norman C. "Jim" Jimerson, was a veteran of the Second World War, who then became ordained as an American Baptist minister, served as chaplain of a federal reformatory, and later worked as a college administrator and church minister. In 1961 he accepted a position as director of the Alabama Council on Human Relations, a state affiliate of the Southern Regional Council. For three years he worked behind the scenes as the only full-time paid civil rights worker in the state of Alabama. As a mediator between the moderates in the white power structure and black activists (mainly religious leaders), he worked with people such as Wyatt T. Walker, Andrew Young, Fred Shuttlesworth, Charles Morgan, Jr., David Vann, and Robert Zellner. He met and conferred with Martin Luther King, Jr., Robert Coles, Hubert Humphrey, Burke Marshall, and numerous journalists seeking background information about the civil rights movement in Birmingham and Alabama.[2] As a result of his civil rights work, our family was forced to leave the Southern Baptist church we attended and we received numerous telephone death threats and harassing calls. On several occasions my mother argued with those making such threats, but as a young teenager, I dreaded answering the telephone. My parents later became co-directors of a peace center in rural Virginia, and my mother worked as a legislative liaison for the Church of the Brethren in Washington, DC.

While attending high school in Kalamazoo, Michigan, I led a fundraising drive to build a Peace Corps school in Tanzania. I also opposed the escalating war in Vietnam and in 1966-67 took part in numerous classroom debates about the war, usually as the only vocal opponent of the war. When I turned eighteen in 1967, I registered for the draft as a conscientious objector and then headed to Earlham College, a Quaker institution. As a "baby boomer" I thus directly engaged in the two transformative political movements of my generation.

As a graduate student at the University of Michigan (1971–1977), I closely followed the Watergate investigations and hearings in 1973–74, learning the importance of documentation in ensuring accountability of government officials. In choosing a topic for my PhD dissertation, though, my experience having moved as a young boy from New England to Virginia and later Alabama led me to examine sectional consciousness as shown in personal letters and diaries of Civil War era soldiers and civilians, both northern and southern, men and women. This would be history from the bottom up, but focusing on ideas and popular thought.

My research experience in archives led me to a part-time job as an archives assistant, and then to a career as an archivist, at the University of Michigan, Yale University, and the University of Connecticut. Since 1981, part-time at UConn and, since 1994, full time at Western Washington University, I have taught graduate courses in archives and records management and undergraduate courses in American history. Along the way I have served as president of New England Archivists, Council member and president of the Society of American Archivists (SAA), and currently as chair of the SAA Committee on Ethics and Professional Conduct. (Although this volume is published by SAA, it is in no way an official statement of SAA policy, and I speak only for myself.)

As my professional career evolves, I have come to believe that archivists can contribute to a richer human experience of understanding and compassion. They can help to protect the rights of citizens, and to hold public figures in government and business accountable for their actions. Archivists provide resources for people to examine the past, to understand themselves in relation to others, and to deepen their appreciation of people with different backgrounds and perspectives. This is the essence of our common humanity. Combining my personal values with my responsibilities as an archivist offers a sense of professional purpose with a social conscience.

⬦ ⬦ ⬦

This is not the book I had planned to write. Beginning in 2000 I
conducted extensive archival research for a study of the historical
development of archives, and the importance of documents and
records, in American society from the Revolution to the Second
World War. I had published three articles based on this research,
with plans to complete a book manuscript. Then in 2003 I was
elected vice president/president-elect of the Society of American
Archivists (SAA), serving one year as vice president and, in 2004-
05, as president of SAA. This position gave me direct experience with
significant issues facing the profession—from the forced resignation
of Archivist of the United States John Carlin, to the George W. Bush
administration's efforts to shroud government activities in secrecy,
to the inadequate funding of the District of Columbia Archives, to
international perspectives on archives at the International Council of
Archives (ICA) meeting in Vienna in 2004.

This book grew from my involvement in the professional advocacy
and political implications of my role as SAA president. My final
responsibility as president was the opportunity to deliver an official
address at the 2005 SAA annual meeting in New Orleans—which
took place only ten days before Hurricane Katrina devastated the city.
For my presidential address I turned my attention to the fundamental
purposes of archives and the role of archivists in society. This talk,
"Embracing the Power of Archives," considered the impact of recent
writings about postmodern archives and efforts to infuse social justice
issues into the archival discourse. I was invited to elaborate my views
on these themes at the 2006 SAA annual meeting.

My search for answers to the *why* questions of the archival profession
became an obsession. Having used quotes from Orwell in my SAA
presidential address, I re-read six of George Orwell's books and
many of his essays, which examine totalitarianism, memory, and
written records, for a 2007 ICA conference paper. After publishing
my two SAA presentations in the *American Archivist,* I decided to couple
them with my research on American archival history and on Orwell,
along with a brief essay I had published on "Archives and Memory,"
for an extended study of these issues.[3] In spring 2007 I co-taught
a course on "History, Memory, and Documentation" with my
colleague Harry Ritter, which led me to an expanded perspective on
the concept of memory.

In combining ideas from a variety of topics, I have tried to present a
unified argument about archives and society, rather than a quilt of

distinct and separate pieces. This book is a personal effort to raise and grapple with some complex social, political, professional, and ethical questions, not an attempt to answer them with a simple, neat formula. These are issues at the heart of the roles and identity of the archival profession, and I do not expect consensus on these matters. Some of the ideas presented here are radical, both in the sense of challenging traditional concepts of archives and in the sense of examining the roots of why people create, preserve, and use archival documents. In making some of these arguments at the Congress of Brazilian Archivists in July 2008, I stirred up a lively debate on whether there was such a thing as "archival science" or only a reality of "archival politics." At a smaller conference in Vancouver, British Columbia, in February 2009 I made a few brief comments about the need to consider *why* archivists do things, as well as what and how, and said they should support diversity in archival collections, accountability, and even social justice. One panel member replied that it is "presumptuous" for an archivist to have an opinion about what the archives should acquire, and that he does what his employer—the government and the citizens—want him to do. I found that response appalling. It falsely assumes that archivists work in value-free settings and it abdicates responsibility for what archivists do.

This book is thus a very personal statement of my thoughts about the archival profession, its significance in modern society, and its impact on human history and culture. Perhaps in this respect I truly am presumptuous. As I was completing this project, I discovered the Kurt Vonnegut passage concerning the importance of one's work in helping to achieve one's purpose in life. Although I remain convinced that my personal and family connections are more important than my professional roles, Vonnegut's words speak to my search for meaning both in my professional calling and my personal life.

I hope this conversation will continue, that archivists and those who rely upon them—whether or not they know what archivists actually do—will continue to ask *Why?* and to explore the significance and meaning of documents and archival records. This is part of our human impulse to know who we are, to understand where we come from, and to anticipate who we will become. It is a journey of discovery well worth taking. I do not presume to be a tour guide or an expert on these matters, but I hope that you will find the questions embedded in the following chapters to be as intriguing and as significant as I do. Please join me, and the many authors already engaged in this conversation, as we seek to understand the power and the importance of archives of the people, by the people, and for the people.

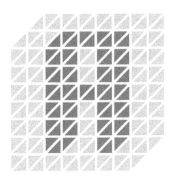

Acknowledgments

I can never adequately thank the many people who have contributed to my journey of exploration that I hope this book represents. Some friends and colleagues contributed directly to shaping my ideas on these topics and the form this book has taken, others have assisted me along the course of my professional career, but some of the most important contributions have come from family and friends who have helped me in my personal journey through life.

Those who have shaped my ideas for this book include the many authors cited in the text and notes. In addition, I am deeply grateful to colleagues and friends who have helped to shape my understanding and focus my ideas, through conversations and e-mail exchanges. Special thanks to Fran Blouin, Scott Cline, Terry Cook, Mark Greene, Verne Harris, Julie Herrada, Anthea Josias, Tom Nesmith, Gudmund Valderhaug, and David Wallace. Kate Theimer helped me to gain an understanding of Web 2.0 technology and its impact on archives, and Kevin Lindeberg and Rick Barry guided me through the complex legal and political tangles of the Heiner affair in Australia. I have also learned a great deal from my colleagues in the Western Washington University Department of History, particularly Cecilia Danysk, Peter Diehl, George Mariz, Johann Neem, and Harry Ritter.

Throughout the process of turning two articles and some related ideas into a book, I have received superb guidance, advice, and encouragement from Peter Wosh, the Society of American Archivists publications editor, and Teresa Brinati, SAA Director of Publishing. Two peer reviewers, Ciaran Trace and Bob Sink, provided superb suggestions for reorganizing chapters, tightening my arguments, and improving my presentation of these ideas. I also want to thank SAA Executive Director Nancy Perkin Beaumont and the members of the SAA Publications Board for valuable advice and suggestions along the way.

Special thanks also goes to John Ross, long a poetic voice for social justice, for permission to quote at length from his poem, "Against Amnesia." Verne Harris obtained permission for me to include the "Memory for Justice" report in the appendix.

My professional career as an archivist began at the Bentley Historical Library, University of Michigan, under the outstanding leadership of Dr. Robert M. Warner. My first mentors also included Tom Powers, Fran Blouin, and Mary Jo Pugh. At Yale University Larry Dowler helped me hone my archival skills. During fifteen years as archivist of the University of Connecticut, I learned a great deal from university librarian Norman D. Stevens, and my colleagues Daria D'Arienzo and Anne Ostendarp. My predecessor at Western Washington University, James B. Rhoads, provided generous advice and an example worthy of emulation. I am deeply grateful for archival colleagues at WWU and the Washington State Archives Northwest Region, past and present, including Beth Joffrion, Tony Kurtz, Scott Roley, Diana Shenk, and Ruth Steele.

One of the best ways to gain understanding of the archival enterprise is through professional associations. As a member of SAA since my graduate school days in 1976, I have collaborated with too many people and developed too many friendships to list fully. I hope you know who you are. Special appreciation goes to Elizabeth Adkins, Brenda Banks, Frank Boles, Tom Connors, Fynnette Eaton, Tim Ericson, John Fleckner, Beth Kaplan, Waverly Lowell, Bill Maher, Kathy Marquis, Richard Pearce-Moses, and Joel Wurl. Through New England Archivists, I had the opportunity to work closely with and learn from Diane Kaplan, Eva Moseley, Jim O'Toole, Helen Samuels, Bruce and Patty Stark, and many others. Thanks also to Northwest Archivists colleagues Jodi Allison-Bunnell, Terry Baxter, Jerry Handfield, Susan Karren, Deb Kennedy, Candace Lein-Hayes, Donna McCrea, and Karyl Winn.

As almost any teacher will tell you, we often learn more from our students than they do from us. I have been fortunate to collaborate with many students during almost thirty years teaching graduate students in archives and records management. Among those who have kept in touch through professional activities and personal contact, I am especially grateful to former UConn students Pam Hackbart-Dean, Leith Johnson, Hal Keiner, Narissa Ramdhani, and Nanci Young; and to former Western Washington students Terry Badger, Sharon Howe, David Keller, Rainbow Koehl, Gina Rappaport, Sarah Nelson Smith, Arlene Schmuland, Leslie Schuyler, Nancy Shader, Jason Viers, Erin Whitesel-Jones, Joshua Zimmerman, and many others. I am continually renewed by current graduate students, too many to name, who have likewise helped me learn to be a better archivist—and a better person.

Gratitude beyond measure I offer to my family, who continually inspire me and challenge me to live up to their examples. I dedicate this book to my mother, Melva Brooks Jimerson, and to the memory of my father, Reverend Norman C. "Jim" Jimerson. They taught me the importance of living fully, dedicating oneself to the needs of others, and seeking a world of freedom, equality, peace, and justice. My brothers and sisters, Ann, Paul, Sue, and Mark, have shared both wonderful and difficult experiences, and have offered me numerous examples of generosity and selflessness, both in their personal and professional lives. My daughters, Laura and Beth, are the joys of my life, and it has been an honor and privilege to see them grow into such fine young women. At this writing, Laura is serving her second Peace Corps assignment, this time in Liberia, and Beth is teaching English in Italy. Joyce has more than kept her promise that if I married her my life would never be boring. Her passion for everything she does—from gardening, rain barrels, and worm bins to travel, yoga, research, and family get-togethers—provides a constant reminder of the joys life can offer. Now she is starting a vital education project, Carbon Masters^{TM}, to encourage activism on behalf of the global challenges of climate change and environmental responsibility.

My gratitude to all these people! Of course, none of them is responsible for any wrong-headed ideas, erroneous statements, and other mistakes contained in this book. Those are mine alone. For anything useful herein I owe a debt of thanks to my colleagues, friends, and family.

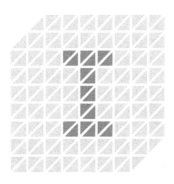

INTRODUCTION:
Embracing the Power of Archives

In my dream I am entering a temple. Its ornate façade and tall spires give me hope. I will find enlightenment here. I push open the massive door and enter. The door clangs shut behind me. I am in a dimly lit room with high windows that prevent the sunlight from reaching me. Despite the heat outside it is cool here. A security guard approaches. The temple has become a prison.

The guard tells me to surrender my pens and put my briefcase in a locker. I sit at a table, filling out forms to prove my identity. Guards and security cameras watch me constantly to prevent escape or theft. I realize that I am hungry. A young woman hands me a menu. The prison is now a restaurant.

"What do you want?" the waitress asks. The menu she hands me does not list food items, only the names of food creators—General Mills; Vlasic Foods International; Kraft Foods; Hormel. "May I suggest a Cajun specialty?" She pulls down a menu for Touch of the Bayou, Inc. It lists a series of categories, including the Bayou Magic brand. "Bring me some Bayou Magic, please," I politely request.

Soon a cart arrives laden with several boxes. My food must be inside. I open one box at a time—correspondence, reports, and financial ledgers. In the last box are recipes. Gumbo. Crawfish étouffée. Jambalaya. No food, only the promise of food.

The waitress recommends Gumbo. She brings me a box filled with okra, cayenne peppers, onions, garlic, tomatoes, and other primary sources of nutrition. After all this, I still have to cook my own meal.

IMAGES OF ARCHIVES

Changing images of the archives, as sites of power. The temple reflects the power of authority and veneration. The prison wields the power of control. The restaurant holds the power of interpretation and mediation. These represent the trinity of archival functions: selection, preservation, and access. Archives are places of knowledge, memory, nourishment, and power. Archives at once protect and preserve records; legitimize and sanctify certain documents while negating and destroying others; and provide access to selected sources while controlling the researchers and conditions under which they may examine the archival record. As Dutch archivist Eric Ketelaar has stated, archives often resemble, both architecturally and procedurally, temples and prisons.[1] These are two seemingly opposite sites of power. Archives embody these contradictions, and more.

Historians and others who depend on archives for information and knowledge increasingly recognize the important role of archivists. Their imagery echoes the concepts of archives as sacred spaces, institutions of control, and sources of nourishment. Historians, legal researchers, and others have long recognized that they would "lose public trust" or legal judgments if they did not explain "with clear reference to the historical archive, just how and why they reached their conclusions and present an argument for preferring their interpretation to that of their opponents."[2] Until recently, although researchers regarded the primary documents housed in archives critically and with healthy skepticism, to most readers "the archive itself remained essentially unproblematic, imagined as a fundamentally unbiased universe of potential histories."[3] Scholars now question who creates these archives and for what purposes. The intermediary power of the archivist increasingly emerges in public discussion. This "archival turn" in historical discourse acknowledges the necessity of "engaging with the limits and possibilities of the archive as a site of knowledge production, an arbiter of truth, and a mechanism for shaping narratives of history."[4] Employing the image of archives as temples, historian Antoinette Burton writes, "the archive (as a trope, but also as an ideological and material resource) has acquired a new kind of sacral character in a variety of contemporary domains. This sacralization occurs as more and more people seek and help to create access to a more democratic vision of the archive: that is, as different kinds of archival subjects and archive users proliferate, with their own archive stories to tell."[5] Burton also echoes the image of archives as restaurants or sources of nourishment, stating that "all archival sources are at once primary and secondary sources: neither raw nor fully cooked, . . . but richly textured as both narrative and meta-narrative, as both archive and history-in-the-making."[6] Such imagery depicts the broad range of meaning conveyed by and through archives.

Rather than hide from their power in the realm of history, memory, and the past, I hope that archivists will embrace the power of archives and use it for the good of mankind. Before looking at the responses to this challenge of using archival power, we need to understand some of its manifestations. There are three essential aspects of the power of archives, reflected in these metaphors:

- the temple: the archivist's authority and power to shape social (collective) memory;
- the prison: the archivist's responsibility and control over preservation and security of records;
- the restaurant: the archivist's role as interpreter and mediator between records and users.

THE TEMPLE

In the archival temple, records of human activity achieve authority and immortality (or at least its semblance). "In the ancient world and in medieval times, the treasury in temples and churches contained both the treasures and the records, safely stored and hidden from the strangers' gaze," Eric Ketelaar observes.[7] Even the architecture of many archives buildings deliberately embodies imagery of temples and shrines. "In approaching such an archive, one sees a large and impressive building, usually with a broad staircase, at the top of which are heavy metal doors which open on to an impressive atrium," observe Richard Harvey Brown and Beth Davis-Brown. "Beyond its functional purpose it reminds you that you are entering a sanctum, a domain of being that is larger than yourself."[8] Many modern French archival structures have been compared to the nation's famous cathedrals. This is particularly true of national archives, such as the Archivo General de la Nacion of El Salvador and the original National Archives building of the United States, located on the national mall next to prominent national museums and close to federal office complexes. While laying the cornerstone on February 20, 1933, President Herbert Hoover proclaimed, "This temple of history will appropriately be one of the most beautiful buildings in America, an expression of the American soul. It will be one of the most durable, an expression of the American character."[9] Such architectural statements convey the significance and value of archives and assign to them a sacral character. "Temples and churches convey by their architecture the idea of surveillance and power," Ketelaar states. "Whatever their architecture, archives serve symbolically as temples shielding an idol from the gaze of the uninitiated, guarding treasures as a monopoly for the priesthood, and exercising surveillance over those who are admitted."[10]

Documents, photographs, electronic records, and other materials placed in such temples acquire special significance. The very acts of selection and preservation set some records apart from others and give them heightened validity. They represent evidence, information, truth, and social memory. As Canadian archivist Arthur Doughty proclaimed in 1924, "Of all national assets, archives are the most precious. They are the gift of one generation to another and the extent of our care of them marks the extent of our civilization."[11] As one example of embodying this concept architecturally, the Gatineau Preservation Centre of the National Archives of Canada, opened in June 1997, is a modernist "symbolic treasury, the 'storehouse of the nation's memory,'" according to Lilly Koltun. "The very presence of a collection in Gatineau would imply a rigorous (or omnisciently 'divine'?) selection process justifying inclusion in such a costly treasure house."[12] Simply being deemed worthy of preservation in the archives provides validity and significance to documents of all forms. The archivist's decisions about such things convey power over knowledge. "Archivists need to realize that appraisal is part of a larger process of building public memory and a process of connecting to other societal events related to the past," Richard Cox argues. Cox quotes Michel-Rolph Trouillot, who states in *Silencing the Past* that the "making of archives involves a number of selective operations: selection of producers, selection of evidence, selection of themes, selection of procedures—which means, at best the differential ranking and, at worst, the exclusion of some producers, some evidence, some themes, some procedures." Trouillot continues, "History does not belong only to its narrators, professional or amateur. While some of us debate what history is or was, others take it in their own hands."[13] This is a call to action for archivists.

In the archival temple, archivists make value-laden decisions with momentous implications for the knowledge that the future will have of the past. A few precious relics gain recognition as "rare or sacred like Dead Sea Scrolls or Shakespeare first folios," treasured for "their talismanic worth as tangible witnesses to some personal event or personality," as historian David Lowenthal explains. "According primacy to 'the fetish of the document,' the archive is revamped from information center to reliquary shrine."[14] Archivists make vital decisions about which documents will be saved for future generations and which will be excluded or destroyed. "The appraiser's values, quality of work, perspectives, interaction with the creators and owners of records, engagement with the policy he or she is implementing, and so on all become markings in the appraisal and determine what becomes the archival record," South African archivist Verne Harris explains. "The appraiser is a co-creator of the archival record."[15]

Archivists have long recognized that they are somehow in the "memory business," but they have not always understood their role or the extent of their job description. The idea that archivists play a part in shaping public memory, Richard Cox suggests, should affect "the identification of what records should reside within the archives or be designated as archival in value." He sees archives as "a symbolic way station on the road to a collective memory."[16] What we preserve in archives represents a complex array of social values. As Elisabeth Kaplan argues in an essay on archives and the construction of identity, "We are what we collect, we collect what we are."[17] By preserving some records and not others, archivists affect society's collective understanding of its past, including what will be forgotten.

Archives, however, do not constitute the past itself, nor our collective memory of the past. René Magritte reminded us of this distinction with his famous painting of a curved pipe, under which he wrote "Ceci n'est pas une pipe." In fact it is not a pipe, only a painted representation of a pipe. We should not confuse archives—or history—with memory. "History is the enemy of memory," historian Richard White cautioned, after researching his mother's stories of growing up in Ireland. "When left alone with memories, historians treat them as detectives treat their sources: they compare them, interrogate them, and match them one against the other."[18] Archival sources proved many of White's mother's memories to be false.

In the blockbuster novel *Harry Potter and the Half-Blood Prince*, Professor Dumbledore promises to help the young wizard learn the secrets of his past by accompanying him into the Pensieve, a magical device into which people's thoughts and memories can be downloaded—to be retrieved or explored later. As they set out Dumbledore warns Harry, "I told you everything I know. From this point forth, we shall be leaving the firm foundation of fact and journeying together through the murky marshes of memory into thickets of wildest guesswork."[19] Archivists, of course, recognize that what Hogwarts School needs is a good archives.

Archives help us clarify the "murky marshes of memory" and substitute documentation for guesswork. What archives provide is the record of an agreement made at a certain time, by one or more persons, about individual actions, events, and stories. Archives do not testify to the accuracy or truth of these accounts, as Luciana Duranti argues in her study of diplomatics, but rather to the accuracy of how and when the account was created.[20] Collectively, these records of the past provide a corrective for human memory, a surrogate that remains unchanged while memory constantly shifts and refocuses its vision of the past. Although the documents and images in archival records do not visibly change, the postmodernists remind us that our understanding and interpretation of them do constantly shift and refocus.

THE PRISON

The second site of archives power is the archival prison. From security doors to lockers for researchers' belongings, from closed stacks to reading room surveillance cameras, archives often resemble prisons or fortresses. If the most common architectural metaphor and model of archival facilities is the temple or shrine, a secondary metaphor emphasizes security and protection. In the 1960s the state of Washington constructed its first (and still functioning) archives building as a three-story facility, mainly underground. The state archivist secured funding for the facility—this was at the height of the cold war—by convincing the legislature that it could serve double duty as a bomb shelter for state workers in the nearby Capitol. The building constructed in the 1980s for the Departmental Archives of Guadeloupe offers another example. "In a curious architectural gesture, the new building was built partly surrounded by a moat and a wall, so that it looks not a little like a fortress," according to Laurent Dubois.[21] The records are imprisoned (for their own security, of course), but so are the researchers, who must consult records in closely guarded chambers under vigilant surveillance. For a visual icon recall the researcher in "Citizen Kane," who consults the family records in the Thatcher Library, a barren high-ceilinged room as intimidating as any dungeon. Thirty years ago, while I was conducting my doctoral dissertation research, the Library of Congress Manuscripts Division actually had an armed guard, pistol in his holster, perched on a platform overlooking the research room.

Eric Ketelaar compares the archival reading room to Jeremy Bentham's panopticon, "a prison where the inmates were kept under constant surveillance (pan-optical) by guards in a central control tower."[22] Bentham's panopticon "instilled in the prisoners the self-consciousness of knowing that they were constantly being watched and guarded." This concept became the iconic central image of Orwell's *Nineteen Eighty-Four*. "Big Brother is watching you, not by keeping his eyes continually fixed on you necessarily but primarily by making and ever checking your file," Ketelaar observes.[23] Both in their design and operation, archival reference rooms echo Bentham's goal of panopticism, ensuring security and control.[24] This "panoptical archive" extends even to the physical ordering of records and "the knowledge-power of the finding aids, as representation of what the public may not see openly, but may expect to find behind the closed doors of the prison-like repository." The noble arguments for preservation and secrecy, Ketelaar suggests, are "to a large extent rationalizations of appropriation and power."[25] In entering the archives, researchers undergo a variety of "policing measures," such as signing a register, displaying identification documents, reading research rules, leaving their bags and personal belongings outside the reading room, maintaining silence, and undergoing constant surveillance. The user of archives becomes an "'inmate' of the search room."[26]

Novelist Martha Cooley's fictional archivist declares that his job is to safeguard written accounts of human experience. "As an archivist I have power over other people. I control access to materials they desire," he declares. "Of course this power has limits," he concedes. "I can't arbitrarily bar from the library someone who is entitled to use it, nor can I prevent materials from entering the collection simply because I don't like their authors or content." He concludes, "A good archivist serves the reader best by maintaining, throughout the search, a balance between empathy and distance."[27] Control equals power. "The surveillance and discipline are ingrained in the archivists' professional distrust of anyone other than the archivist using the archives," Ketelaar concludes. "The rituals, surveillance, and discipline serve to maintain the power of the archives and the archivist."[28] Preservation, security, and administration of access all represent aspects of the archivist's control.

In exercising this power, archivists imprison not only their boxes of records and their researchers, but also the meanings of the archival records and identities of their creators. The archivist wields a power of interpretation over the records in her custody—a term usually reserved for those arrested by the police—and thus controls and shapes the meaning of these imprisoned sources.

THE RESTAURANT

The archivist's power of interpretation appears most strongly in the image of archives as a restaurant, where those hungry for truth or knowledge seek nourishment. Archival power governs the research process, from the finding aids that may at first appear to be strange and exotic menus of choices difficult for the first-time customer to interpret, to the one-on-one consultation by which archivists mediate between user and document. Just look at archival menus! They reduce the complex life story of a person to a "Bioghist" element, and the complexities of thousands of documents to a "Scopecontent" note.[29] As interpreters of the menu, archivists mediate between customers and records. Explaining this concept, philosopher Jacques Derrida declares, "The first archivist institutes the archive as it should be, that is to say, not only in exhibiting the document but in establishing it. He reads it, interprets it, classes it."[30] The affirmation of truth, Derrida argues, "bases its authority . . . on the precedence of an archive . . . as it is interpreted by the archivist."[31] The archivist may not claim omniscience, but this role of mediation approaches an unstated, implicit claim to omnipotence over the archive. This mediation separates the reader from direct access to the record, which archivists argue must be placed in context, arranged, and explained before it can be approached and used. The researcher remains in the dining room, as a consumer of information, while the most important work of the restaurant takes place out of sight in the kitchen. The reference archivist serves researchers much as the waitress serves restaurant customers. Meanwhile, the archival kitchen staff—head chef, sous-chef, cooks, and dishwashers—decide what will be on the menu, and prepare records for use (selection, acquisition, arrangement, description), and keep everything neat and sanitary (preservation, security). These vital processes mainly take place out of public sight.

Many historians and other users of archives do not recognize—or they contest—this notion of the archivist's influence. Speaking to a University of Michigan seminar, Carolyn Steedman argued that unlike human memory—which actively processes, suppresses, and distorts traces of past experience—material placed in archives "just sits there until it is read and used and narrativized." She argues, "the archive is thus quite benign. The historian, the user, the social rememberer give the archive's 'stuff' its meaning."[32] Steedman and some other historians discuss "the archive" as an essentially unmanaged institution, as though the archivists were absent or invisible. However, Patrick Geary concludes that medieval archivists largely determined what aspects of the past could be accessed and, to a significant degree, what the past would be: "Archivists, one might well argue, are not preservers of their documents: they are their authors, engaged in work as creative, and subjective, as that of those who originally penned individual texts or those modern historians who pretend to tell the past to the present."[33] There are no innocent encounters with archives. All who touch them leave fingerprints, altering and shaping the meaning of the documents. As many archivists now recognize, according to Francis Blouin and William Rosenberg, "we are currently moving into a very active age of archival intervention, one that can be described as beyond postcustodial, in which the processes of selection, access, and even description are increasingly structured by particular cultural values, social biases, and political inclinations."[34]

As Canadian archivists Terry Cook and Joan Schwartz point out, the archivist plays a carefully scripted role in this research drama, since "the practice of archives is the ritualized implementation of theory, the acting out of the script that archivists have set for themselves."[35] Typically archivists do not even recognize that they are playing a specifically designed role in a performance through which the researcher and the archivist interact. Cook and Schwartz contend that the archivist plays a critical part "as mediator and interpreter, as an important shaper of the documentary record of the past that will be passed to the future. The archivist is an actor, not a guardian; a performer, not a custodian." They conclude, "The archival performance should not only be consciously acknowledged, but enthusiastically celebrated."[36] It is this theatrical role that endows the archivist with authority and power.

The roles played by archivists follow three major discourses, according to Verne Harris. The first presents archivists as "workers with the record," following a self-explanatory script drawn from western positivism, as formulated by Dutch archivists S. Muller, J. A. Feith, and R. Fruin in the 1890s.[37] The second stream of discourse posits archivists as "keepers of the record," which is "something to be defined against rationally determined frames and measures." Harris presents this concept as "flowing out of the Enlightenment, its core energies those of a vigorous modernism." The influence of British archivist Hilary Jenkinson, author of the first English language manual of archival practice in 1922, is most strongly evident in this discourse. The third role for archivists, coming out of postmodernist conceptualizations, presents archivists as "narrators of the record," which is "something always in the process of being made." Harris identifies Canadian archivist Hugh Taylor as the progenitor of this stream of archival discourse. Although most archivists do not fit clearly within a single one of these streams or their sub-currents, Harris clearly prefers the perspective offered by the postmodernist discourse. "Of all the streams, it is the one most open to 'the other,' the voices and the knowledges marginalized by a Western-dominated global mainstream," he concludes.[38] Each of these roles offers archivists a measure of authority, control, and power.

In the archival restaurant, the waitress welcomes the customer, interprets the menu, suggests an entrée or dessert, and collects the money before the customer exits. She offers a menu of choices that permit the customer to select the appropriate or desired foods. She explains (interprets) both the menu and the types of food offered. She keeps and preserves, she ensures safety, she provides a comfortable dining experience. She offers advice (narrates the record), but often only when requested. It is a service role, but it comes with a measure of power and requires a reassuring smile if one wants a generous tip.

ARCHIVISTS' RESPONSIBILITIES

Just as diners in a restaurant may have only a superficial understanding of what takes place behind the scenes (in the kitchen and the manager's office) before their meals can be served, so do archival researchers often remain uninformed about the actual work that archivists perform. Before examining the role of archivists in society, therefore, it is important to review the role of archivists within the archives. The basic functions of archivists are usually described as identifying, preserving, organizing, and providing access to manuscripts and archival records. These can be explained under the headings of deciding what to preserve, organizing and controlling materials, and providing reference and access services for users.

It is important to recognize that within common responsibilities, functions, and services, archivists manage a broad variety of types of archival facilities. Archival repositories are operated by colleges and universities, governments (at national, state, county, and municipal levels), businesses and corporations, labor unions, religious organizations, historical societies (both public and private, at national, state, and local levels), libraries (public, private, academic, and corporate), museums, and special interest groups (such as ethnic communities, gays and lesbians, science and technology groups, etc.). These broad categories only suggest the rich variety and combinations of factors that characterize archival institutions. Archival records include public and private sources; textual, visual, sound, and electronic formats; accessible and restricted materials; and other categories of documentation. Likewise, archival users include administrative staff of these institutions, legal researchers, genealogists, local history buffs, academic scholars, high school and college students, citizens seeking to document their rights and interests, and numerous other identifiable categories of people for whom archives contain useful information or documentation. Throughout this study, emphasis will be on commonalities rather than distinctions among these various constituencies of archivists and users. However, most of the concepts and arguments presented apply, to one degree or another, to all archival repositories, materials, and users.

For the benefit of those less familiar with archival theory and practice, we begin by outlining some of the key responsibilities of archivists and how these concepts have developed, particularly during recent decades. We will refer to these archival functions throughout this study, and will return at the end to consider them in the context of recent debates over the role of archivists in modern society.

DECIDING WHAT TO PRESERVE

One of the critical functions of archives is to determine which records are necessary to fulfill legal, administrative, and cultural requirements for documenting organizations and individuals. Given the nature of modern societies and the voluminous records they produce, archives cannot save everything that might conceivably interest future researchers. The selection of some records for archival preservation necessarily means that other records will not be preserved, and the documentation of certain aspects of society means that others will not be documented.[39]

Until the 1970s the prevalent assumption was that deciding what archival records or manuscripts to collect was a straightforward process of evaluating the repository's needs and interests—such as those of potential researchers, donors, and other constituents—and searching for available materials. Archival acquisition grew naturally out of the institution's mission, purpose, and goals. As a repository determined its research constituencies, it could define the source materials appropriate for its needs and objectives.[40] In recent decades archivists have more and more often taken an active part in seeking broader documentation, based on efforts to represent all aspects of society and its peoples.

In institutional archives, the decision of what records constitute the archives grows out of an organized and systematic records management program. Often working closely with archivists, records managers evaluate the legal, fiscal, and administrative requirements for record-keeping, to ensure that adequate documentation is being created and preserved and that records are not kept longer than required by either external criteria (e.g., federal or state regulations, legal requirements, or auditing needs) or internal needs (e.g., administrative review and oversight, decision-making processes, or quality control). Once these requirements have been met, the records can and should be destroyed.[41] This both ensures economy and efficiency of recordkeep-ing, and protects the organization from unwarranted information disclosure. Records that have satisfied legal, fiscal, and administrative requirements may also be reviewed to determine whether historical documentation needs might warrant ongoing preservation.

In a manuscripts repository, the collecting policy supports the institution's mandate, and can be modified to meet changing demands and needs. Factors influencing acquisition and preservation decisions include: the institution's mission and goals; collecting policy criteria such as geographic scope, time period, record formats, donor categories (e.g., labor unions, business companies, or literary authors), and subjects; donor relations; legal and financial considerations, such as copyright and available repository resources.[42]

Whether working in institutional archives or manuscript collecting repositories, archivists must consciously decide what to collect and preserve. Archival appraisal requires a determination of the significance of records, not their monetary value. Such decisions require careful deliberation, since the decision not to save unique documents is irrevocable. As Maynard Brichford wrote in 1977: "Appraisal is the area of the greatest professional challenge to the archivist. In an existential context, the archivist bears responsibility for deciding which aspects of society and which specific activities shall be documented in the records retained for future use. Research may be paralyzed either by unwitting destruction or by preserving too much."[43] Archivists have thus declared that their first responsibility is the "selection of records of enduring value." All other archival activities depend on the "ability to select wisely."[44]

Although almost any scrap or fragment of manuscripts from past centuries might provide missing clues to the past, the vast records created and saved since the early twentieth century make it essential for archivists to be selective about what to preserve. Otherwise the proliferation of modern records would quickly overwhelm modern archives and manuscript repositories.[45] In the United States appraisal concepts developed in response to the National Archives' need to contend with the voluminous records created by government agencies during the New Deal and World War II. Similar problems arose in business firms, universities, and other organizations.

Because of its central importance in archival management, appraisal has become a highly contested area of archival theory. English archivist Sir Hilary Jenkinson argued in 1922 that archivists should avoid imposing their bias on the records by encouraging records administrators to discard unneeded records before transfer to the archives.[46] However, while avoiding archivist-imposed values, this approach permits the records creator—the person with the greatest self-interest in shaping the documentary legacy—to choose which records will be preserved.[47] In modern institutions the archivist is often the one person positioned to consider the overall interests and needs of the organization in terms of documentation, accountability, legal requirements, and historical purposes.

Appraisal is also vital for collecting repositories. Although some user groups, such as historians, may want the repository to save everything, archivists must evaluate whether specific records contribute to the repository's collecting policy objectives. Typical criteria include: the significance of the organization or individual that created the records; the importance of subjects represented in the records and the quality of documentation; consideration of duplication, uniqueness, format, scarcity, and record linkage; the value of records in meeting information needs and interests of the repository's research clientele; and the value of the records compared to the costs of preservation, including staff time and facilities required.

For institutional archives these considerations may be moot if maintenance of the records is required for legal, accountability, documentation, administrative, or fiscal purposes. However, these criteria apply both to private manuscripts and institutional archives when evaluating historical or informational needs. Archival appraisal provides a means for making decisions in a systematic and thoughtful manner.

ORGANIZING AND CONTROLLING RECORDS

B ecause modern organizations—and even many individuals in today's society—engage in extensive networks of activities and functions, archival records have become voluminous, challenging the powers of intellectual and physical control over them. The principle of provenance—based on the concept that the true significance of information contained in archives is best realized by understanding the context of activities and functions within which the records were originally created—stipulates that records originating in one office, agency, or individual must be grouped together and not intermingled with those created by any other office or individual.[48]

The principle of provenance provides a logical and coherent framework for organizing archives and manuscripts, based on their origins. It protects the integrity of archival sources by ensuring that the purposes for which they were created are identified and retained. It also suggests that one solution to the dilemma of managing voluminous modern records is to retain the filing arrangement established by the records creator, thereby preserving evidence of the office's functions and activities.[49]

Arrangement is often described as the process of bringing order out of chaos. When manuscripts and archives arrive at a repository jumbled into boxes or crates, archivists create a simple, logical, and usable arrangement based on knowledge of the organization and its records, and an understanding of research needs and likely uses for the records. Throughout the arrangement process archivists keep two goals in mind: protecting the integrity and identity of the records, and making them accessible for research.

Based on extensive experience in managing complex and voluminous groups of materials, archivists have developed distinctive procedures for informing all potential users about the nature of their collections. Archival description focuses on groups of materials rather than discrete items. It would require countless years of staff-time to item-catalog most modern manuscript collections.

The essential elements of description include: identifying the records creator, record types, time span, and origin/function of the records; indicating available finding aids for intellectual access; describing physical format, condition, and quantity of records; explaining physical or use restrictions; providing information about origins and context of records creation; and describing archival actions and control methods (e.g., appraisal, processing, and preservation). These descriptive elements provide the essential information necessary for intellectual and physical control of archives and manuscripts.

Archivists employ a variety of descriptive tools to provide access to their holdings. Internal access tools facilitate administrative and research use and external tools meet the needs of outreach and distant access. These archival finding aids include: accession documents to record receipt or transfer of materials; indexes and catalogs to provide access by names, subjects, record types, etc.; repository guides; subject or specialized guides; national guides; and databases.[50] Archival inventories and registers are the most important tools for archival description. Prepared for each manuscript collection or archival record group, they provide information about the creator of the records, descriptions of the records series, and other data needed to locate, access, and use the materials. These basic descriptive elements enable the user—whether a visiting researcher or a staff member—to identify, locate, and access archives and manuscripts.

The four purposes of archival descriptive standards, as summarized by the International Council on Archives, are:

1. to ensure the creation of consistent, appropriate, and self explanatory descriptions;
2. to facilitate the retrieval and exchange of information about archival material;
3. to enable the sharing of authority data; and
4. to make possible the integration of descriptions from different locations into a unified information system.[51]

Archivists generally follow several fundamental principles governing archival description. The principle of provenance (*respect des fonds*) is the basis of archival arrangement and description. Description follows and reflects arrangement of archival records. It is based on the principles of multilevel description, from the general to the specific. In addition, archival description must accommodate all media and records. Despite some historical distinctions between institutional and private archives, the principles of archival description apply equally to records created by corporate bodies and by individuals or families. Fundamental to the concept of provenance is the belief that the creators of archival materials, as well as the materials themselves, must be described. Efforts to establish international standards and methods for describing archives have met only partial success, but archival description is continually being refined and adapted by archivists and manuscript curators to meet the needs of a wide variety of archives users and researchers.

REFERENCE, ACCESS, AND USE

The purpose of selecting, acquiring, and preserving manuscripts and archives is to make them available for use. Intellectual and physical accessibility are vital components of managing these important information resources. Each repository that manages archives or manuscripts needs to identify its user clienteles, develop outreach methods for informing users and potential users, provide intellectual and physical access, establish and administer access policies, and provide on-site and/or remote reference services.

Reference use of manuscripts and archives almost always requires mediation by the reference staff.[52] For security reasons physical access to stacks is limited to the staff, and intellectual access requires interaction between patrons and staff. Many users of manuscripts and archives need assistance in defining their queries, identifying possible sources of information, and understanding the nature of archival documentation. Good finding aids are essential, but the personal knowledge of the reference assistant is crucial for successful reference interactions involving complex or unusual requests.

Archives and manuscript repositories, whether large independent institutions or small units within a library or museum department, need to identify and understand their user clientele in order to provide effective service. A generation ago many assumed that the principal clientele for archives and manuscripts was scholars, particularly historians. With growing interest in genealogy and local history, and greater recognition of the possible uses of archival materials for legal, investigative, administrative, and other types of research, archivists now recognize that they serve a broad array of clienteles.

Users need to have both intellectual and physical access to manuscripts and archives. Each of these access types requires repository policies and procedures, both to assist users and to protect the rights of donors and third parties who might be affected by disclosure of sensitive information. Archivists provide intellectual access to information about the repository's holdings (e.g., finding aids, bibliographic databases, and web access); information from holdings (particularly for remote user access or in-house administrative queries); information about records creators; and referrals to sources outside the repository.

Intellectual access makes reference use of archives and manuscripts possible, but users also require physical access. Archivists must balance access goals with the need for security and preservation measures to protect fragile or unique materials. Concerns for personal privacy and the rights of third parties sometimes require limiting both physical and intellectual access to certain records. Security can never completely prevent theft, loss, or damage to archival materials, but it is essential as a deterrent. A delicate balance must be achieved, however, between security and preservation concerns, and user-friendly service.[53] It is essential that users not be intimidated by strict access rules.

One of the frustrations and challenges for archivists is that many people who could benefit from using such collections do not even know that these repositories have the types of information they seek. Other potential users think that archival research will be too time consuming, that archives are not open to them, or that the process is daunting.[54] It is often necessary to create an active outreach program to overcome such misunderstandings and to inform potential users about the benefits of using manuscripts and archives. As Elsie Freeman Finch states, "Use is our reason for being. And, if archives are properly explained and made readily accessible, they will be used and likely be funded."[55] Thus, outreach becomes essential both for the benefit of potential users and also for the success of archives and manuscript repositories. To meet these needs, some repositories have undertaken user studies, examining the concerns of both current and potential users. Using techniques adapted from librarians, archivists have developed models for user studies[56] and have conducted such studies in specific institutional settings.[57] However, there has been no broad national study of manuscripts and archives users.

Thousands of archives and manuscript repositories around the world have used the Internet to provide access to information about their holdings, programs, and services to researchers who would otherwise have difficulty locating such information.[58] Although some repositories are experimenting with placing images of manuscripts and archives on websites for research use, the volume of modern manuscript and archival collections makes it impractical for most records series to be made entirely available. Websites thus generally display only carefully selected documents, which may lose their archival context, and the mediated nature of the sites makes most of them comparable to an online exhibition rather than a fully contextualized archival or manuscript collection. In future years the possibility of making entire manuscript collections or archival records series available online holds intriguing possibilities. In the

near future, however, the technical difficulties of doing so, and the
intellectual limitations of self-service online research, pose daunting
obstacles.

THE ROLE OF ARCHIVISTS IN SOCIETY

Despite this broad range of responsibilities, archivists often
think of themselves as neutral and passive, lacking power.
Negative stereotypes of archivists in fiction, films, and news
media convey an image of knowledgeable but ineffective toilers
in dark, mysterious basements.[59] For archivists, as former editor
of the *American Archivist* Philip Eppard states, "the anxiety over our
professional image reflects our uncertain status as an emerging
profession," which the public often does not understand. "When
the obsession with image becomes more problematic, however, is
when it results in whining, like Rodney Dangerfield, that we never
get any respect," Eppard warns.[60] But in an information-based
society, knowledge provides a means to power. "Knowledge does
not equal power, as the cliché would have it, but power cannot be
exercised without it," Verne Harris asserts. "Information is essential
to efficient and thereby effective democracy."[61] In modern society,
archivists have more than their share of this knowledge-power.
What archivists need to do, as Richard Cox argues, is transfer some
of the power contained in the records to the records professionals
and their repositories.[62] The archivist's role of interpretation, both
in creating finding aids to guide users of records and in providing
reference services, conveys stories of the human condition. "Telling
stories of our pasts is a quintessentially human activity," Verne
Harris declares. "Story is crucial to our construction of meaning
and is carried by our dream of the impossible. Without story we are
without soul."[63] These stories are primal and hence powerful, both
for individuals and within society's public sphere.

Historians increasingly recognize this "archontic power" of archives.
Bringing the past to life offers insights into the human condition,
allows us to extrapolate from our own small range of experience to
a broader horizon of past lives stretching back to the beginning of
recorded history. "To enter that place where the past lives, where
ink on parchment can be made to speak, still remains the social
historian's dream, of bringing to life those who do not for the
main part exist, not even between the lines of state papers and legal
documents, who are not really present, not even in the records of
Revolutionary bodies and factions," Carolyn Steedman explains.
"The Archives is this kind of place, that is to do with longing and
appropriation. It is to do with wanting things that are put together,

collected, collated, named in lists and indices; a place where a whole world, a social order, may be imagined by the recurrence of a name in a register, through a scrap of paper, or some other little piece of flotsam."[64] Steedman regards the archive as "a place of dreams . . . of making the dead walk and talk."[65] Such dreams, of course, remain beyond our reach—impossible, unattainable. Yet this quest, this hope, gives rise to historical imagining and lures readers back to the archives time and again. Many endure a hunger that never abates.

This study addresses the role of archivists, both in their institutional settings and within the wider society they serve. It places the archivist in a contemporary context, no longer regarded as the neutral guardian of historical source materials—the "raw materials" of history, as the traditional industrial manufacturing metaphor depicted archival records—but as active agents in the process of shaping our knowledge of the past. Archivists engage in selecting which materials will be preserved for future use, documenting some aspects of society and neglecting others, constructing memory, protecting evidence for accountability, interpreting these resources and thereby shaping how researchers and other users will regard them, and ensuring legal, administrative, financial, and cultural benefits for society. In doing so, they also provide the foundation for strengthening—or weakening—democratic principles, including the rights of citizens, the accountability of public leaders, the representation of social diversity in the historical record, and the promotion of social justice.

In recent years scholars in many disciplines have examined the memory of society and its relationship to national identity, power relationships, collective psychology, and history. Although many historians have probed these issues, few have examined in detail the relationship between memory and documents. Even such prominent writers as David Lowenthal and Michael Kammen have paid scant attention to archives and recordkeeping.[66] Yet implicit in their works—and evidenced by their footnotes—historians rely on documents and on the integrity of records preserved in archives for much of their contemporaneous sources of information about the past. As historian Stephen Haycox states, " . . . neither historians nor attorneys put much faith in unaided human memory. For reliability, memory has to be corroborated by documentary evidence. The documents may not be 'true,' but unlike memory, they stay the same unless they've been altered . . ."[67] Given this reliance on documents and archives, the historical process by which they are compiled and preserved deserves careful scrutiny.

Recent discourses regarding the concept of social memory have begun to address "the archive," as a conceptual locus of documentation, evidence, and primary sources. Scholars have challenged positivist assumptions about objective, neutral, and impartial archives providing unimpeachable evidence of the past. The archive has become a focal point for analysis and contestation, not simply a hallowed shrine of Truth. Yet most scholars still discuss "the archive" as though such repositories somehow operate as disembodied institutions, with no human intervention or control. Their analyses of archival sources rarely acknowledge the role or agency of the archivist, who manages the repository and makes decisions affecting the sources acquired, preserved, and organized before the user can gain access to this evidence.

Archivists who have joined this discourse about the archive have already begun to suggest that these new conceptual lenses—including deconstruction and postmodernism—for viewing archives and the role of archivists can refocus the work of archivists. At least in some situations, archivists can address societal concerns for open government, accountability, diversity, and social justice. This volume seeks to extend this discussion, to consider some of the conceptual and theoretical bases for these claims, and to propose new ways to think about the role of archivists and the application of archival ethics to the search for social justice and professional responsibility.

The starting point for this discussion is recognition that archives are—and always have been—sites of important power relationships within society. The role of the archivist in such settings necessarily assumes a significant degree of power and influence over the documentary record of society. Because I believe that archivists need to take an active role in responding to the concerns of society and be advocates for the interests of all people, chapter titles embody action verbs to reflect the central activities of archivists. As a background for understanding these broad conceptual issues, chapter 1, "Weaving the Life of Our Ancestors," provides historical context for contemporary developments, by briefly tracing the development of recordkeeping and archives from the ancient world through the nineteenth century. Chapter 2, "Documenting American Society," focuses a historical lens on the slow emergence of historical societies, manuscript collections, and institutional archives in the United States, emphasizing the (usually limited) role of archivists in American society.

The third chapter, "Resisting Political Power," examines the significance of archival documentation as a counterweight to entrenched political power, beginning with a consideration of the political implications of memory, truth, and documentation. It opens with a John Ross poem, "Against Amnesia," which shows the efforts of ruling classes to cover up their abuses of power and the seamier sides of national history. Many of these issues can be seen most powerfully through the eyes of George Orwell, still an important visionary regarding the dangers of political power when combined with control over information, documents, and memory of the past. Other writers, such as Czech novelist Milan Kundera, echo Orwell's concerns regarding political power and archival documentation. Analysis of the contested field of social (collective) memory provides the focus of the fourth chapter, "Constructing Memory," emphasizing the distinctions between archival documentation, individual human memory, collective memory, and historical interpretations. Although frequently cited as "the memory of society," this metaphor for archival records does not stand up to critical analysis. Archives are both more and less than memory, perhaps an antidote to fallible human cognition and remembrance— although even that analogy begins to crumble when we consider the malleable and ever-changing nature of archival documentation.

If the purpose and benefits of archives do not equate to memory, other archivists have argued that a more important contribution comes from their use for institutional accountability, open government, diversity, and social justice. Recent conferences and writings provide examples of these and other societal benefits provided by archival sources, either directly or potentially. Although archivists have advocated many of these causes for nearly four decades, much of the recent discourse arises from, or has been shaped by, the experience of South African archivists in the final years of the apartheid regime and the early years of majority rule and by the emerging democracies of former colonial states. Chapter 5, "Serving the Public Good," explores these concepts and argues that archivists can play an important role in contributing to such positive social goals, by creating archives of the people, by the people, and for the people. These initiatives raise serious questions regarding archival ethics and professional responsibility, as the conclusion argues. Some scholars contend, however, that it is possible to engage political issues and to play an active role in shaping a multicultural and inclusive archival record without sacrificing professional standards, objectivity, and individual responsibility. As archivist David Wallace observes, "There is a sense that justice is a professional ethic and a moral mission."[68]

Chapter 6, "Responding to the Call of Justice," examines how these ideas would affect both the daily work of individual archivists within their repositories, and the archival profession's engagement in public advocacy. Archivists in the United States have been struggling to define their role in society—and their identity as members of a profession—for the past century. Are they historians with a specialized purpose focused on preserving historical documents? Are they a subset of librarians, concerned with making archival information available for users? Are they documentation assistants to administrators or legal staff? Are they protectors of evidence—or guardians of culture? Listening to these debates, one remembers the story of the blind men trying to identify an elephant. Each effort to define archives and the role of archivists is at least partially correct, but only by recognizing the commonalities among the various parts of the archival elephant can we understand the true purposes of archives and archivists. Common bonds unite the archival profession, even though separate groups define their own purposes and roles in different and (at times) seemingly contradictory terms. As individuals, archivists are as diverse as their repositories and employers—governments, corporations, universities, historical societies, libraries, religious institutions, Native American tribes, not-for-profit organizations, and others—yet they share some common professional commitments and responsibilities. Archivists must exercise caution to avoid letting their differences divide them, and to rally around shared purposes in serving the broad and diverse needs of society. In doing so, their work should be informed by a sense of social responsibility and a commitment to personal morality and professional ethics. Although individual archivists may differ in their interpretation of these purposes, their shared values and concern for documenting human experience provide essential contributions to society. These debates over the societal roles of archivists affect all citizens either directly or, more commonly, indirectly.

The conclusion, "Rethinking Archival Ethics," returns to more conceptual issues related to professional ethics and the responsibility of archivists to engage in public debates over such concerns as accountability, diversity, and social justice. The concept of professional ethics challenges archivists to address these issues directly, and to consider the potential benefits of defining their professional values within an ethical context that accepts the inevitably political implications of archival endeavors. These are issues that the archival profession has begun to address. They are also concerns that should engage all users of archives, both researchers examining archival documents and the larger public who are indirectly affected by what does or does not occur in society's archives.

Throughout this work, my emphasis is on *why* archivists perform their professional responsibilities in particular ways. What are the historical antecedents of modern archives and archivists? Why is it important to remember the past, and to have accurate records of human activity? Why should archivists engage in public debates or respond to public policy concerns? How can archivists, when they choose to do so, respond to the challenges of working for a more just and diverse society? Why should archivists—and those who rely upon archival documentation—care about new perspectives on social and professional ethics? Archivists often seem most comfortable developing technical procedures for organizing records, preparing finding aids to guide researchers, and preserving and managing everything from paper documents to photographic, film, and electronic records. Gaining expertise in these techniques provides valuable tools to meet professional responsibilities and provide services to the users of archives. Yet too much emphasis on *how* to fulfill their duties can obscure *why* archivists complete these tasks. It is important to step back occasionally and remember the ultimate purposes that archivists fulfill, the societal needs they satisfy, and the contributions they make to their fellow citizens and to posterity. Thinking through these matters clearly and deliberately enables archivists to perform their necessary and proper roles in society. My hope is that this volume will help to remind archivists of these broader horizons, and will enable non-archivists to understand the perspectives and contributions of archivists to society.

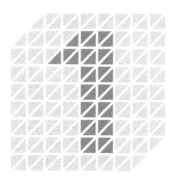

Weaving the Life of
Our Ancestors

*To be ignorant
of what occurred before
you were born
is to remain always a child.*

*For what is the worth
of human life,
unless it is woven into
the life of our ancestors
by the records of history?*

– Cicero[1]

*If you know your history,
then you would know where you're coming from.*

– Bob Marley[2]

The "information revolution" taking place in today's society transforms how data is created, stored, transmitted, and preserved for future reference. The speed of information transmittal makes possible a global community of shared economic, cultural, and social interactions. Media experts and technology pundits repeatedly declare that this transformation of information systems is "unprecedented" in human history. However, if we look back to earlier eras of changing information infrastructure, we can see precedents for today's changes in the previous introductions of industrial technology, the printing press, paper, parchment, the Greek alphabet, clay tablets, cuneiform scripts, and structured language itself. In order to understand the role of archives and archivists in contemporary society, we must step back to see how human societies since ancient times have used a variety of technologies for recording and preserving information. As both the Roman orator Cicero and the Jamaican reggae singer Bob Marley recognized, we cannot understand the present unless we know the past.

There are many precedents for the current information age, and understanding how people developed and responded to these previous eras of change can help us to understand our own times more clearly. "The introduction of writing systems into previously oral cultures was more of a revolution in human affairs than the spread of cheap and available computer technology," James O'Toole argues, "and it seems obvious that understanding such earlier revolutions might help us get through our own."[3] In the long sweep of human life on earth, writing defines the separation between "prehistoric" and "historic" eras. The capability of capturing and preserving memory in durable form distinguishes preliterate societies from those we now consider "civilized."[4] Concerning prehistoric existence we know only what we can infer from very limited physical relics, such as Iron Age weapons, cooking implements, and human skeletons.

Throughout history people have sought means of communicating effectively with each other, and of preserving archival records of their own activities. Our earliest glimpses of how our human ancestors actually lived derive from an era when they began to paint images of their lives and experiences on cave walls and protected rock formations. Such early forms of recording human events eventually evolved into increasingly sophisticated methods of creating and preserving records. For millennia such written records served to supplement an oral culture of transmitting critical information, most likely beginning with accumulated knowledge necessary for survival in a dangerous and hostile environment and extending to an era of sophisticated thought, reflection, and philosophy about the human experience. As writing became a useful technology of communication, written records could be accumulated and preserved in proto-archives to ensure their durability, authenticity, and reliability. The important role of "remembrancers" in oral cultures anticipated the responsibilities of ancient recordkeepers in literate cultures and of archivists in modern societies.

CREATING AND KEEPING RECORDS

Written records mark the beginning of civilization in ancient Mesopotamia, where the Sumerians developed this "key feature of civilization"[5] shortly before 3000 BCE, using inscribed clay tablets to document transactions between individuals and with their rulers. Societies that do not employ writing, as westerners understand the term, use a variety of means to enhance personal memory. In the Inca empire knotted cords of different colors and lengths represented numbers, chronology, and perhaps even the names and qualities of past rulers.[6] Ancient Mayan writing employed glyphs to represent calendrical designations, names, or even phonetic symbols. The Aztecs created books using deerskin or native paper made from agave fibers.[7] Oral cultures typically employ remembrancers to preserve and transmit information through formulaic phrases or mnemonic devices. Other forms of memory objects include the totem poles of the Pacific Northwest natives, Pictish stones of ancient Scotland, and the modern urn bearers of Buganda, who "have to process before the king at the new moon identifying by name the umbilical cords of his ancestors."[8] When oral traditions cease to be transmitted continuously they are lost to posterity, whereas written inscriptions or documents can be ignored for centuries yet still decoded and understood when rediscovered. These are some advantages of creating and preserving written records.

Writing fulfills the human need to preserve memory of agreements, transactions, and experience. As a technology of artificial memory, writing transmits information across distance and time. People create written records in order to ensure that events, decisions, and actions can be recalled to mind in the future, or to send information over distances too great (or inconvenient) for direct personal delivery. Such records include fundamental social contracts, such as the Magna Carta or Declaration of Independence, as well as more personal notations for future reference. Ancient scribes of Assyria, for example, often added notations on small memorandums "written down so as not to forget."[9] Nearly three millennia later, in *Through the Looking Glass,* Lewis Carroll echoed this human need for written surrogates of memory:

> "The horror of that moment," the King went on, "I shall never, NEVER forget!"

> "You will, though," the Queen said, "if you don't make a memorandum of it."

Alice looked on with great interest as the King took an enormous memorandum-book out of his pocket, and began writing.[10]

This desire to create documents in order to avoid forgetting important information amounts to an archival imperative. In literate cultures, written records replace reliance on human memory and separate the storage of information from individual consciousness. This depersonalizes people's access to such information by placing data in stable media subject to verification. Such relatively inflexible storage media provide benefits but also disadvantages. Those of us in western cultures have become so accustomed to rely on written sources that we can hardly see the benefits of oral societies, with their rich traditions and cultures. We define writing as synonymous with civilization, culture, and progress, and disdain cultures that do not use technologies of writing to codify and preserve their heritage. Although this study focuses on western culture, it is important to bear in mind that societies in other parts of the world echoed some of these developments, but often diverged, particularly in respect to the persistence of oral communication and traditions.

To understand the modern archival imperative, we must seek its origins in the ancient purposes for which human beings have entrusted their memory, culture, and social agreements to written records. Records serve as surrogates for speech. The term "record" comes from combining the Latin words *cor* ("heart") and *dare* ("to give"), emphasizing that a record gives information back to the heart and mind after the passing of time.[11] By developing systems of signs and symbols to represent spoken words and numerical concepts, people found a method to store information in a fixed form, so that it could be retrieved and used with accuracy and precision. Writing could transcend the limitations of human memory to store large quantities of information for long periods of time and to transmit it over great distances. The "speaker" and the "listener" no longer had to be in each other's presence. The external storage of information improved upon the capacity, reliability, accuracy, and longevity of oral transmission of knowledge.

Even with sophisticated techniques of human "remembrancers," such as using poetic and formulaic language to assist an individual's memory, oral societies must rely upon the personal abilities of individuals to store, retrieve, and reproduce valuable information. The frailty and fallibility of human memory demonstrate the advantages of external information storage media. In the famous statement of Horace, *"verba volent, littera scripta manet*—'words are fleeting, written letters remain.'"[12] Recording information provides a mechanism for checking or correcting human memory, an external and seemingly more reliable information storage system, and a socially accepted form for ensuring accuracy and resolving disputes. It also enables us to learn from past experience and to transmit our own thoughts to future generations. As western societies became increasingly complex, it became necessary to organize and preserve written records in an orderly fashion. This gradually led to creation of both formal institutional archives and private collections of manuscripts and documents.

The importance of archives and the role of archivists in society can only be understood in historical context, beginning with the earliest known forms of records creation and preservation. This historical perspective will enable us to understand the contemporary manifestations of archives, their function as surrogates for human memory, the role of archivists in shaping this documentary heritage, and the means by which archives and archivists contribute benefits to all members of society.

ARCHIVES IN THE ANCIENT WORLD

The oldest surviving archival records originate from the ancient Near East. For several millennia archival recordkeeping systems developed in Mesopotamia before spreading to Egypt, Mycenae, and the Persian empire.[13] Archeological discoveries of ancient clay tablets in the Near East first enabled us to understand ancient civilizations, beginning in the mid-nineteenth century. These earliest known examples of writing provide glimpses into the lives of ancestors previously known only through myth and legend. Although often disturbed from their natural state by nonscientific excavations and treasure-seeking scavenging, some clay tablet sites remain intact enough to suggest that these ancient records accumulated both in libraries and as archival holdings. Under the Third Dynasty of Ur (ca. 2100 BCE), both Sumer and Akkad developed "archival systematics" to manage clay tablets. According to Assyriologist Nikolaus Schneider, these clay tablet archives included documents and records stored for future use in "special archival premises." These economic texts (no "library works" were included) were stored according to a subject arrangement in specially designed clay containers, with attached clay bulls that identified the container, the types of documents included, and the size of the document collection.[14] Scholars of the ancient world define archives both as "a collection of stored documents" and as "a physical space within a public space (palace or temple complex, public archive) or within a private building" in which such documents were maintained. There were no "public" archives in the modern sense, however, since ancient archives belonged to the kings, priests, or other political authorities who administered the state.[15] Archives existed in order to provide access to documents. It took many years of trial and error to develop effective methods for creating, preserving, and using records, but by the third millennium BCE recordkeepers had created "a professional system of documentation."[16]

Clay tablets provided the primary form of recordkeeping in the civilized Western world for nearly three thousand years. The clay tablet region eventually extended from the Euphrates-Tigris basin to the Hittite Empire, Phoenicia, and the Aegean cultures of Knossos, Pylos, Mycenae, and Thebes. According to Ernst Posner, "For more than half the time mankind has communicated in writing, most of the writing has been on clay, and this record output far exceeded that of all of Europe during the Middle Ages."[17] As early as the third millennium BCE, for example, a temple at Nippur (in modern day southeastern Iraq) established archive rooms filled with clay tablets.[18] The archives at Mari on the Euphrates River contained twenty thousand tablets of Assyrian rulers (1813-1781 BCE) and their successors. After the Babylonian conquest of Mari, Hammurapi's archivists surveyed and reclassified these tablets, perhaps seeking to glean intelligence about Mari's connections with the Hittites and Egyptians. Babylonia established a large archives headed by a director of archives, who supervised a "house of rolls where the treasures were laid up."[19] In 1980 archeologists discovered remains of the royal palace of Ebla in Syria, including a main archives room filled with two thousand clay tablets that had apparently been stored on wooden shelves. Most of these tablets were administrative records relating to distribution of textiles and metals by palace authorities, while others recorded animal breeding, agricultural production, and lists of professions and other information.[20] In Seleucid Mesopotamia, different types of archives existed. Most common were royal archives serving the king or palace, temple archives, and private archives of family enterprises. In addition, at Tell 'Umar a public city archive, accessible to an entire community of citizens who wished to preserve their documents, existed in "a building expressly built and equipped for the preservation of documents," according to Antonio Invernizzi.[21] This facility did not belong to a private or religious institution but served a communal purpose.

About 90 percent of surviving clay tablets constitute records of economic transactions. Sumerians meticulously recorded the buying and selling of sheep and merchandise and sale and leasing of land and other property.[22] Writing itself seems to have arisen as "a primitive form of bookkeeping," necessary for everything from routine inventories of crops and property to complicated interactions between government and subjects.[23] Among the early business archives are those of Assyrian merchants trading in faraway Cappadocia, who frequently designated an archives room in their houses, and even established a joint repository for safeguarding financial records.[24] Some archival collections remained intact over long periods, such as the records of the Egibi banking family of Babylon, which document six generations from 690 to 480 BCE.[25] Governmental systems often adopted the administrative and recordkeeping practices developed by the private commercial sector. The requirement to create written records of every stage of transactions sometimes led to bureaucratic paralysis, even in such ancient cultures as that of Assyria.[26] In the Neo-Babylonian period (beginning in the late sixth century BCE) private individuals wrote and kept archival documents, mainly as evidence of property ownership or to prove that an obligation either existed or had been discharged. The reliance on clay tablets as evidence in court demonstrates that recordkeeping was routine and commonplace among the Neo-Babylonian urban propertied class.[27] Such records thus served essential societal purposes in keeping order and resolving disputes.

The cuneiform writing system for recording information began in the fourth millennium BCE, when palace administrators in the city of Ebla (ancient Tell Mardikh) began using styli to inscribe clay tablets.[28] In ancient cultures clay provided the most abundant resource for creating convenient writing surfaces. Malleable while wet, it could be inscribed easily and when sun-dried became durable, making alterations difficult and detectable. Once baked—either deliberately to ensure longevity, or accidentally as a result of fire damage—clay tablets became "as indestructible as stone."[29] In addition to clay, wax-covered tablets made of wood or ivory provided a more convenient surface for quickly recording transactions and accounts, and could be re-used by smoothing out the surface.[30] These clay tablet and cuneiform societies also created documents written on papyri and parchment,[31] although these fragile media seldom survived. The cuneiform writing system provided an efficient and adaptable method for inscribing information on clay or wax. It quickly spread throughout Mesopotamia and beyond. Ironically, as new technologies developed for creating records, they became more ephemeral. When papyrus and other perishable technologies for writing replaced clay tablets and cuneiform script, "textual evidence was virtually extinguished"[32] insofar as modern survivals are concerned.

In ancient societies still primarily dependent on oral transmission of information, the scribes who recorded transactions on clay and wax tablets required special education in the difficult art of writing. Before being entrusted with supervision of large accumulations of archival records, scribes learned to write in schools associated with temples, thereby achieving the training necessary for the important position of ensuring accuracy and reliability in society's essential governmental and economic interactions. In Mesopotamia scribes belonged to the upper strata of society, and were highly respected. Recruited among the sons of governors, ambassadors, temple administrators, tax officials, military officers, and other social leaders, these scribes and archivists received enough training that they seemed to "shine brightly like the sun" in their exalted positions. These scribes created and preserved the intellectual and artistic coherence that formed the backbone of civilization.[33] Even monarchs claimed exalted status based on their accomplishments as scribes. King Ashurbanipal, who ruled Assyria from 668 to 627 BCE, boasted of his intellectual achievements "in the scribal art," and declared, "the signs of writing, as many as have been devised, I wrote on tablets, I arranged [the tablets] in series, I collated [them], and for my royal contemplation and recital I placed them in my palace."[34] Those scribes given responsibility to maintain formal archives achieved even higher status among the intellectual leaders of ancient society. Whether admitted into the executive leadership or remaining in custodial functions, these proto-archivists provided essential services for public administration and the early development of bureaucratic systems of order and control, based on accurate, reliable, and usable records.

As ancestors of modern archivists, Mesopotamian scribes developed methods for organizing, classifying, locating, and preserving the essential records of society. They arranged clay tablet documents according to subject matter for accessibility and ease of retrieval, and developed systems for storing tablets in purpose-built clay receptacles kept in secure storerooms to ensure preservation of valuable information. Scribes used labeling mechanisms to identify the documents kept in each records container and to quantify the number of tablets. In order to authenticate written documents, scribes of the Seleucid period used a stamp or seal.[35] Archivists of the ancient world could provide some level of accountability for business processes of commerce and government, and developed strategies for retention and disposal of records.[36] Scribes even recognized—perhaps through bitter experience—the need to take preservation precautions to ensure that clay tablets would not become brittle and crumble in the hot Mesopotamian climate. For example, the Eanna temple in Uruk equipped its storage room with an ingenious "air-conditioning" system, featuring a grooved floor through which water could flow and evaporate to ensure proper humidity for records preservation.[37] Although it would be anachronistic to compare such techniques directly to modern archival practices, taken together they illustrate the value that Mesopotamians placed on their clay tablet archives and the innovations they devised to organize, preserve, and use these early records.

Under the Pharaohs, Egypt expanded the use of records throughout its extensive bureaucracy, making record consciousness integral in the daily lives of its people. However, because they relied on perishable materials such as papyrus, leather, and wooden writing boards, Posner observes, "only an infinitesimal part of the country's record production has been preserved."[38] Egyptian art frequently represents scribes with their record chests, papyrus rolls, and writing boards always attentive to recording, counting, measuring, and documenting the administration of the country and the exchange of goods and services that formed a central part of daily life.[39] The very functioning of the Egyptian economy and government relied on creating, preserving, and using both land records and tax rolls to maintain its economic life, which depended on harnessing the waters of the Nile to maintain an agrarian society in the north African desert. Therefore, as Hermann Kees observes, every measure to regulate ownership and use of precious arable real estate had to be conducted "on the basis of the royal archives and the documents it preserves in its capacity as a land office."[40] The fragile lifeline of the Nile valley depended on accurate recordkeeping. "It is no accident that among all sedentary people the pioneers of hydraulic agriculture and statecraft were the first to develop rational systems of counting and writing," Karl Wittfogel concludes. "The masters of hydraulic society were great builders because they were great organizers; and they were great organizers because they were great record keepers."[41] This link between organizational sophistication and recordkeeping occurs throughout the history of civilization. Management, control, and efficiency depend upon coordination and organization of resources, which requires careful documentation, systems for exchanging complex data and information, reliance on planning, and reference to precedents in making decisions.

The insistence on careful recordkeeping for economic purposes carried over into government administration and daily life. Two of the important government offices were named the House of Counting the Cattle and the House of Measuring the Grain, and the army scribe ranked among the top officers. Every detail of administration had to be put in writing, and numerous documents carried annotations such as "to be copied" or "stays in the archives." As one writer instructed his recipient, "Preserve my letter so that in the future you can use it as evidence!"[42] All Egyptian judicial procedures had to be made in writing, requiring extensive archival procedures for organizing and maintaining legal records. The supreme court's archival office apparently held custody of written laws, since papyrus or leather rolls, on which laws were recorded, appear in illustrations of court proceedings.[43]

Beginning with the reign of Cheops in the Fourth Dynasty (ca. 2627-2513 BCE), the office of vizier became critical in a highly centralized government. The vizier supervised all departments but the military, and also served as president of the supreme court, director of all works of the king, and director of the royal writings. This included oversight responsibilities for archival holdings, such as the House of the Royal Writings, the House of the Sealed Writings, and the House of the Writings or Archives.[44] Extensive systems of archival repositories and registers supported the smooth functioning of government at all levels. However, one litigant proved that his mother's right to her fields had been violated when the pertinent registers were tampered with, by eliminating her name. He won the case. This shows that although the Egyptian bureaucracy made significant provisions to preserve records they did not always safeguard the records' integrity.[45] Similar concerns have plagued archives ever since. The difficulties of preserving physical documentation, of protecting the integrity and ensuring the authenticity of records, and of ensuring efficient access to information remain troubling, particularly when financial and administrative support for the archives cannot be guaranteed at sufficient levels.

The difficulty of preserving written records over long periods of time can be seen in the disappearance of the great library at Alexandria. Conceived as a repository for all written knowledge of the ancient world, this library symbolized Egyptian scholarship, which built upon earlier Greek examples. The library contained hundreds of thousands of papyrus scrolls and served as a center of Hellenistic scholarship, not merely a place to collect and store written sources. This led to a text-centered academic culture, founded on the idea that knowledge is a valuable resource or commodity that the regime could accumulate and use to bolster its power.[46] Recent scholarship largely disproves the commonly accepted account that this famous library succumbed to fire, either as a deliberate destruction or by accident. Rather than burning up, the great library at Alexandria gradually decayed as a result of neglect rather than destruction.[47] Without rulers and societal leaders committed to protecting the library at Alexandria, its collections gradually disappeared or succumbed to neglect. As Alexandrians lost the ability to read ancient Greek and other languages, the library became less useful. Over time they exerted fewer efforts to protect fragile papyrus from fluctuations in moisture and aridity, insects and vermin, and occasional small fires.[48] The lesson for us today is that lack of concern and funding presents a greater danger to libraries and archives than deliberate destruction. Unless such repositories of knowledge provide tangible benefits and useful resources, they will not receive adequate attention and protection.

THE CLASSICAL AGE: GREECE

Following these early Near Eastern efforts to develop practical methods of creating and managing documentary evidence, the Classical Age of Greece and Rome brought institutions and systems that more closely resemble modern archival practices. In Greece the ancient reliance on a "memory man," who served as a mental recorder of business transactions carried out in his presence, transformed into an archival function after the use of writing became common. The secretary of city government assumed custody of formal documents for which he signed as witness, in addition to the official records of the city. Over time the validity of transactions became dependent on registering them in public records. As Theophrastus (ca. 372-287 BCE) explained, "registration tells whether a piece of property is free and unencumbered and the legitimate property of the seller."[49] As such methods gained increasing validity within the Greek city-states, the Greek language gave the Western world the internationally accepted terms for designating official records, the institutions in which they are maintained, and the individuals entrusted with their management. Although several names were used for documentary repositories, the designation *archeion,* used by twenty city-states, proved most enduring.[50] This term derives from *arche,* which means foundation, origin, power, and authority. Depending on context, *archeion* could mean "government palace, general administrator, office of the magistrate, records office, original records, repository for original record, [or] authority."[51] Greek archives thus conveyed power and authority, supporting the ruling classes.

Greek civilization developed after the emergence of the Greek alphabet in the eighth century BCE. This new alphabet replaced earlier pictographic systems for recording speech, such as cuneiform, providing a more flexible and complex mechanism for transmitting information and ideas. Scholars of literacy regard this as a fundamental restructuring of human thinking. Information could be written down on an external medium that could be retrieved and used whenever needed, allowing people to expand their mental functions beyond the need to remember complex systems of information.[52] In the Graeco-Roman world, William Harris identified more than forty different uses of writing and recording information. In addition to common legal, economic, and administrative purposes, writing could be used to label things, display political slogans, commemorate the dead, petition authorities, curse someone, dedicate objects to the gods, and even compile collections of information.[53]

Despite these advantages, writing never fully replaced oral traditions of remembrance in Greek culture. Literacy and orality continued to coexist, serving distinct purposes, in a continually shifting relationship. Socrates expressed a common concern that writing weakened personal memory and could not be trusted to convey information accurately. He argued that only speech could lead to truth, since oral transmission of ideas enabled one to consult the reputation of the speaker and to interrogate him concerning his utterances. Written words could only repeat the same information over and over, without further elaboration. Writing could not be trusted because it remained detached from the character, honor, and actions of an individual speaker.[54] Scholars debate the relative balance between these two methods for transmitting information in Greek society. The majority of Greek citizens seldom had reason to pay attention to the written word, according to Rosalind Thomas, and Greece remained "an oral society in which the written word took second place to the spoken."[55] However, James Sickinger insists that written documents played an important part in the civic life of fifth-century Athens. Despite the persistence of oral traditions, Greek citizens also created, used, and preserved written records concerning their public business.[56] As in modern society, Greek citizens often depended on documents and archival records even when they were not conscious of this fact. This remains a common experience in our own contemporary society. Systems of recording and using information often seem transparent, receding into the background as daily life moves forward. Only in times of crisis or emergency—such as losing a purse or wallet with its numerous forms of documentation and identification—do we recognize the importance of secure storage of such data.

Archives played a vital role in Greek public life, indispensable to the democratic system of government. In depicting the model state Aristotle attested to the importance of archival functions:

> The fifth office deals with the registration of private contracts and court decisions; indictments have also to be deposited with it, and preliminary proceedings begun before it. In a number of states this office (like that of the city superintendent) is divided into departments, though a single officer (or board of officers) remains in general control of the whole. The holders of the office go by the name of public recorders, masters, plain recorders, or other similar titles.[57]

This office held important authority in the city-state government, ensuring proper care for both official records and private transactions recorded in order to gain recognition as valid agreements. Responsibility for recordkeeping belonged to the position of secretary-archivist, who was chosen by lot. "He has supreme powers over public records, keeps the texts of the decrees, keeps transcripts of all other business and sits in the meetings of the Council," Aristotle explained. Previously this position, known as secretary of the presidency, had been elected "by show of hands," he stated, and "the most illustrious and trustworthy citizens" were selected for this important office. "In fact, his name is inscribed on pillars at the head of the texts of alliances and of decrees granting to aliens citizenship or the status of guest of honor."[58] Aristotle thus recognized the importance of maintaining accurate and reliable documents in the archives, and of ensuring that only "illustrious and trustworthy" citizens held this position of responsibility. He was clearly displeased that this official was now chosen by lot rather than by election.

Greek archives originated from the need to preserve information in a durable format and a secure location. For public or governmental activities the process of creating archival documentation occurred in six stages, according to John K. Davies. First came a decision reached by some part of the polity, whether king, council, or the people. Next came the need to establish a record of that decision. Initially this was entrusted to memory, through the office-holders known as remembrancers, charged with remembering judicial and political decisions. The third stage transferred the record to writing, either because the memorization system broke down or due to an increase in the quantity of information that had to be retained. This required creating an official position of scribe to write down and remember both secular and divine affairs of the city. The fourth step established a permanent or semi-permanent form for the record, with a distinction made between temporary and indefinite retention of the information. Fifth came a public display of the record so that citizens could learn what had been decided, what actions had been taken, or other important information. Finally, provision might be made to ensure that useful documents would survive long enough to make a scholarly or longer-lasting record of public affairs. Those records not deemed to have long-term value would be discarded after serving their immediate purpose. For example, potsherds inscribed with the names of politicians whom citizens wished to exile—called *ostraca,* from which we derive the term *ostracism*—would be dumped en masse into a well after being counted.[59] Documents and records which required ongoing preservation had to be kept in a secure location.

In Athens archival records were preserved in the Metroon, established at the end of the fifth century BCE as a storage facility for state documents.[60] The Metroon took its name from the Mother of the Gods, signifying its importance in Athenian life. Centrally located in the Agora, the Metroon provided secure storage for public records until replaced by a Hellenistic structure in which the Metroon likely occupied two rooms. Citizens relied on these records as evidence both for personal and public purposes. For example, in a 343 BCE speech criticizing Aeschines, Demosthenes referred to a document that "is in your public records in the Metroon."[61] Written records supported the administration of government by consolidating information needed to make decisions and by enabling officials to keep track of complex political and administrative responsibilities. Such records also ensured accurate representation of the laws and their enforcement, provided a measure of impartiality in cases of dispute, ensured precise and stable descriptions and measurements for property lines, and enabled officials to communicate effectively over long distances with allies and enemies.[62] Athenian government rested in part on the principle of accountability of public officials. Financial documents recorded on wooden tablets and rolls of papyrus provided a basis for audits and other checks on the honesty of public officials. They thus became powerful tools to ensure accountability.[63]

The Metroon's physical proximity to other central governmental buildings demonstrates its symbolic significance. The archival holdings of the facility included laws and decrees of the General Assembly; minutes of Council and Assembly meetings; records relating to foreign relations, budgetary, and financial matters; records of public trials (including that of Socrates); state contracts with individuals; inventories of the temples and the guaranteed measures and weights kept in the Tholos; and other public records. At the request of orator Lycurgus, the Metroon also preserved official copies of the dramas of Aeschylus, Sophocles, and Euripedes.[64] Because the city archives also accepted documents verifying the completion of business transactions, this strengthened their importance as repositories of official records, according to Posner.[65] The Athenians understood the value of archives as evidence and, therefore, the necessity of protecting the integrity of records. In the Metroon records achieved sanctity necessary to ensure their authenticity, and the law prohibited bringing false documents under its aegis. In 330 BCE Lycurgus dramatically conveyed the vital importance of archival integrity. "Come now, gentlemen, if anyone went into the Metroon and erased a single law, and then alleged in defense that this law meant nothing to the city, would you not have him put to death?" he exhorted his audience. "I believe you would have been justified in doing so, if you wanted to protect the other laws."[66] This oratorical flourish linked the archival repository to the protection of democratic governance. Violation of one would compromise the other. Archival records served as arsenals of authority and law in Greece, but also as repositories of civil rights and democracy.[67] Although defacing archival records no longer ranks as a capital offense, this declaration by Lycurgus reveals the importance of secure archival evidence for social and political stability in a democratic society.

The documents that Lycurgus extolled and defended suffered erasure of a different sort through the effacement of time and climate. Instead of the clay tablets most commonly used in the Near East, the Greeks used papyrus, wooden boards, and other perishable materials for most of their documents. Virtually all of these records have disappeared.[68] However, the Greeks inscribed copies of some important public records on stone pillars (*stelae*) or walls, in order to honor prominent individuals or to bring public attention to significant events, activities, or announcements. Commemorative inscriptions on marble celebrated heroes and ensured that their noble deeds would not be forgotten.[69] In Priene an "archive wall" six meters high in the temple of Athene Polias displayed "every document which confirmed the status of the city from its formal refoundation by Alexander," including royal letters of Alexander, boundary arbitrations, and other proofs of the city's property and privileges.[70] The numerous stelae that survive provide abbreviated versions of many original archival records, including honorary decrees, treaties, financial records, and inventories of sacred objects. Unfortunately, the original documents created on wood and papyrus have been lost to the ravages of time and decomposition. Thus, although we gain some glimpses into public affairs from these more permanent stone inscriptions, the full contents of Greek archives can be determined only by contemporary descriptions and our own inferences.[71]

It is clear, however, that the Greeks highly valued written records for public accountability, evidence, and remembrance. The rights of citizens depended on access to such records, whether in public inscriptions or in archival repositories, where members of the polity had access to consult the public record. The Agora served as a proper location for public display of certain documents, and the archeion provided a temple or sanctuary in which archival records could be protected and examined. In the Greek city-states, the extent to which public documents and archives served the people's needs reflected the degree to which democracy had advanced. Athens provided a model for both archival practice and democracy, followed by Argos, Miletos, Thebes, and the Achaian and Aitolian Leagues. On the other hand, the much smaller quantities of public documents found in Sparta, Corinth, and Rhodes reflect their oligarchic political regimes.[72] From these examples in ancient Greece, we can see the importance of documents, public records, and archives in democratic societies. In addition to reflecting a greater flowering of creative and linguistic expression, such records also demonstrate the expectation of democratic citizens that they will have the means to hold public officials and leaders accountable for their decisions and actions. Records also served essential administrative functions. So important were these documents that Alexander the Great carried his most important records on his campaigns. When a fire in Eumenes' tent destroyed these records, Alexander ordered his satraps and military commanders to send copies of their own documents to him in order to restore his lost archives. Official documentation thus served a critical role in administering Alexander's empire.[73]

THE CLASSICAL AGE: ROME

As in so many aspects of culture and public affairs, the Romans built upon Greek foundations in recordkeeping and archives. Many of the documentary practices in Rome echoed those of Greece. Reliance on papyrus and tablets made of wood and wax prevents us from directly examining Rome's archival records, although scattered remnants survive. For example, in Pompeii wax tablets of the archives of C. Sulpicius Cynnamus, who owned grain storage facilities and loaned money to producers, were preserved because they were immersed in swampy tidelands.[74] For most Roman recordkeeping practices we must rely on secondary sources of information, which reveal the importance of records for administration of both the Roman Republic and the later Empire. Perhaps the greatest archival achievement of the Roman Republic occurred with the creation of an impressive central records facility, the Tabularium, in 79 BCE. "For the first time in the history of mankind, a monumental and fire resistive structure for housing the state's archives was erected," Posner declares.[75] By absorbing the records of numerous government offices and agencies, the Tabularium became a central archives for the Republic, providing records services to both magistrates and individual citizens. Without a civil service system of government workers, Rome could not provide the continuous and systematic care needed for full protection and management of archival records, but the Tabularium served important administrative purposes.[76]

The Tabularium grew out of administrative needs of the Aerarium, the state treasury. Located near the Temple of Saturn on the Forum, the Aerarium served both as a treasury house for public funds and precious metals and as a repository for documents. Public archives developed slowly in Rome, since magistrates maintained records of their official business in their private *tablina* (house archives or tablet rooms). As a division of the treasury, the Tabularium became a quasi-central archives gathering together agency archives, although it did not gain control over all archival records of the government.[77]

Little is known about the methods used to store records in the archival structure, although its construction of durable stone and brick indicates the importance placed on establishing a fireproof hall of records.[78] Responsibility for the Tabularium rested with elected quaestors, young career officials who served only one year. These inexperienced officials relied upon subordinate public servants (*apparitores*), who served practically for life, including a highly regarded cadre of scribes. One of the most distinguished of these scribes was Horace, who used his inheritance to buy a position as quaestorial scribe in 41 BCE. Long regarded as an emeritus scribe by his former colleagues, the famous poet might be considered a distinguished ancestor of the archival profession. Although the scribes performed what we might regard as highly skilled secretarial duties, the more lowly copyists were called *librarius,* from which our term *librarian* stems.[79] However, neither of these bureaucratic servants occupied what we would regard as skilled professional positions in the Roman archives.

The holdings of the Tabularium could be examined for research purposes, but only by permission from the *sex primi,* chief among the quaestorial scribes. Permission to use and make copies of records (termed *potestas inspiciendi describendique*) would be granted to some applicants—such as Cato the Younger, who prepared a summary of public revenue and expenditures—but not to others. For example, one person identified as "L. Alenus" was sued in court for forging a permit to copy official records. Cicero considered public life and scholarship inseparable. When searching Rome's history for edifying stories or political ammunition, he frequently requested information from the senatorial archives. Despite efforts to coordinate recordkeeping in the Tabularium, security problems prevented assurance of the authenticity and reliability of archival documents. As Cicero complained, "We have no custody of the laws and therefore they are whatever the *apparitores* want them to be; we have to ask the copyists for them, but we have no memory confided to the public records."[80] This allegation indicates not only lapses in the completeness of archival holdings, but also problems with security and access. Researchers apparently had to rely on lowly copyists for service, rather than the higher-ranking scribes or secretaries of the state archives.

Following the collapse of the Republic, Imperial Rome experienced a metamorphosis that deeply affected recordkeeping practices. First came an increasing centralization of administrative, judicial, and legislative authority under the emperor. With this concentration of power came a vast bureaucratic system of civil servants and governmental machinery necessary to control a vast empire. This civil service produced enormous quantities of official records, challenging the archival capabilities of the Roman Empire.[81] The expanding bureaucracy and the resultant information explosion (to use a modern phrase) might have been expected to enhance the importance of archivists and archival repositories. However, as the imperial government under Diocletian became "a migratory body" moving from place to place, the records became decentralized once again. Each government agency kept its own records and the central Tabularium lost its prominence. With the locus of power shifting from the Capitoline Hill, where the Tabularium was located, to the Palatine Hill, home of the emperors, the idea of a central archives serving all government offices declined.[82]

The emperor assumed control over both the power and the mechanisms of government, including the important state offices and their records. The Tabularium continued to function as a senatorial archives until the middle of the third century CE, but as the Senate declined in power and importance so did its archival repository. The records kept by the emperors on the Palatine became the new archives of the imperial government, known as the *tabularium Caesaris* (emperor's records office), even though administered separately by the various departments. Some of these records repositories occupied offices on the Palatine, while others were scattered in departments in the city. So badly did the Tabularium decline in its effectiveness as an archival repository that in 16 CE Emperor Tiberius had to appoint three curators to locate missing records and repair damaged documents. Thirty years later this charge had still not been fulfilled.[83]

During the imperial era one significant change in the technology of recordkeeping provided a more convenient and flexible medium for writing. Following the conquest of Egypt, papyrus replaced wooden tablets as the most common writing surface. Although deficient for long-term preservation of information, papyrus was cheap, efficient, and effective for the unprecedented demands placed on the Empire's governmental recordkeeping system. Communication on a scale required to coordinate the vast network of administrative and military outposts of Imperial Rome could not have been carried out using only the bulky and inflexible wood tablets of earlier times. Many Roman officials no doubt shared the views—if not the flowery rhetoric—of Flavius Magnus Aurelius Cassiodorus (ca. 490-580s), a Roman high official in the Ostrogothic Kingdom, who rhapsodized about the benefits of this new medium:

> Then was papyrus invented, and therewith was eloquence made possible. Papyrus, so smooth and continuous, the snowy entrails of a green herb; papyrus which can be spread out to such a vast extent, and yet be folded up into so little space; papyrus, on whose white expanse the black characters look beautiful; papyrus which keep the sweet harvest of the mind and restores it to the reader whenever he chooses to consult it; papyrus which is the faithful witness of all human actions, eloquent of the past, a sworn foe of oblivion.[84]

This poetic praise combines an appreciation for the physical and tangible aspects of the newer technology of writing with many of its functional capabilities, in phrases redolent of later paeans to the advantages of such new technologies as the printing press, microfilm, photography, and digital imaging. Papyrus was flexible and compact, taking up less space than wood tablets or stone stelae. It carried with it the human desire for accurate and convenient remembrance. As with the later development of photography, papyrus seemed to be "the faithful witness of all human actions." Above all, it counteracted the oblivion of lost information and offered eloquent reminders of the past. Cassiodorus concluded that monasteries should be designed specifically to preserve manuscripts of antiquity. He set out to collect systematically the great works of ancient eras and trained his monks to copy and correct them.[85]

The advantages of written records for accuracy and accountability could also be turned to more sinister purposes. As Rome extended its rule over the known civilized world, its bureaucratic and recordkeeping systems kept pace. Imperial archives in the capital city required counterparts in the provincial centers. Each province thus established a *tabularium Caesaris,* both for financial administration of the empire's domains, such as collecting taxes, and as an archival agency to preserve census lists and other vital records. According to Dio Cassius, Caligula used the census archives of Gaul to identify prominent landowners so that he could put them to death and "inherit" their property.[86] Roman cities of all sizes established archival repositories. For example, excavations at the city of Herculaneum, buried by the same eruption of Mount Vesuvius that destroyed Pompeii in 79 CE, revealed blackened fragments of scrolls held in a room in the Villa of the Papyri.[87]

During the persecution of Christians by the emperors, on the other hand, provincial archives provided documentation of the courage and unshaken faith of the martyrs. After being sanctioned by Emperor Constantine, the Christian church developed its own organizational structure and administrative procedures, including the creation and preservation of records. These church archives could be accessed when needed, as St. Augustine demonstrated during the Donatist controversy, when he stated, "The necessary documents I have obtained either from the ecclesiastical or the public archives (*gesta*)."[88] In other cases problems arose with recordkeeping. Rome's archives remained disorganized and inadequate in numerous respects. For example, despite regulations permitting creation of documents to protect people's rights,

Justinian denounced those who drew up documents only for financial gain, and complained, "as there are no archives in which these documents can be deposited, they are lost; and no monuments of former times are ever found in the possession of those who receive them, . . . or where any are found, they are not worthy of consideration or have been defaced to such an extent that they can no longer be deciphered." The emperor therefore charged the prefects to ensure that in the provinces "a public building be provided in each city in which the defenders can store their records conveniently, and to elect somebody in the province who will have custody of them, so that they will remain uncorrupted and can be quickly found by those who require them."[89] There is no evidence whether this decree effected the desired result. During many centuries to follow, however, similar problems and needs continued to arise. Effective support and methods of establishing, maintaining, and accessing archival records remained elusive.

Following the decline of Rome, the connection between the state and the individual fell apart. Throughout western Europe the idea of creating and maintaining records ceased to be a broad administrative responsibility of central government and concern for recordkeeping became a responsibility only of ecclesiastical and local authorities.[90] Writing became a temporary expedient for personal communication. With little demand for official decrees and speeches, very little was written as a permanent record of society.[91] For several centuries, leadership in creating and preserving records passed to the Moslem world, which developed a sophisticated system of records and communications retained in archival institutions. Islam preserved the heritage of books and writing. Because Allah had instructed Mohammed and his followers to copy the Quran, Muslims became enthusiastically literate. Calligraphers and illustrators created beautiful written works, and great libraries and manuscript repositories flourished throughout the realm of Islam.[92] The Islamic scholarly tradition synthesized religion and law, as well as oral tradition and written texts, elaborating through speech what remained latent and only partially expressed in writing. Concern for reliable and documented texts led Islamic manuscript copyists to incorporate a list of prior transcribers and commentators, creating a "golden chain" of authentic documents.[93] Religious and sacred texts provided one impetus for Islamic scholarship, but the needs of public governance and administration also fostered a culture of manuscript preparation. The Fatimid dynasty (968-1171 CE) in Egypt, for example, developed a manual for the state chancery that established a position of archivist and detailed how he should keep records and what types of access methods—what a modern archivist would call finding aids—should be developed. As Ernst Posner declares, "At a time when in Europe documents on parchment were still drafted and laboriously penned by ecclesiastics, the Moslem governments had well-organized chanceries and knew how to control the masses of records these chanceries produced with the help of archivists."[94] When the Fatimids later conquered Sicily, they took their sophisticated methods of creating, organizing, and preserving records with them. The Normans subsequently learned the administrative techniques of recordkeeping in Sicily and carried these methods into western Europe.[95] This transference brought concern for archival documentation and preservation back to Europe.

LITERACY AND ARCHIVES IN CAROLINGIAN EUROPE

The benefits of creating written records for economic, political, and social purposes eventually led to the triumph of literacy over orality for human communication and transmission of information. This transformation, begun in the Ancient Near East, did not achieve its culmination in the West until the Renaissance. For nearly a millennium—from the fall of Rome until this "rebirth" of culture and knowledge—Europeans contended with the slow technological evolution by which writing largely supplanted oral transmission of information, economic exchanges, and legal rights and obligations. Compared to our contemporary technological revolution, from paper to electronic recordkeeping, this shift from one information paradigm to a new one seems remarkably slow—an evolution, not a revolution. What took them so long to see the benefits of written records? The process appears slow and at times indecisive. Yet in its implications for a vast reconceptualization of human means of communication, the revolutionary nature of this transformation becomes apparent.

As written records became increasingly necessary for society's stability, so also did the need for secure repositories to preserve and ensure access to such documents. These records repositories form another historical precedent for modern archives. The gradual revolution that made western societies dependent upon written records and archives occurred in myriad local settings in response to specific and pragmatic needs. Although trade and commerce linking towns and cities to distant markets and political centers eventually led to common practices and shared methods of recordkeeping, the variations of local needs deserve attention. For present purposes, we will focus on three critical points along a much more complex line of historical development: the Carolingian era, England after the Norman conquest, and the Italian states during and after the Renaissance.

Although many people long believed that literacy and reliance on the written word survived through the early Middle Ages only through the activities of the Christian clerical elite, recent scholarship shows clearly that secular systems of government and social institutions also contributed to the preservation of literacy. Oral traditions and transactions remained important, but European states in the early Middle Ages cannot be considered purely oral societies, untouched by knowledge of writing and formal records. An "orality" mindset characterized the Carolingians and their contemporaries, but both their Christian religion—a religion of the book—and their government and legal practices depended on the written word. As Rosamond McKitterick declares, "The written word became a fundamental element of Carolingian culture, and Frankish society in the Carolingian period was transformed into one largely dependent on the written word for its religion, law, government and learning." For the Franks literacy and recordkeeping became essential for the proper functioning of society and provided the keys to faith, knowledge, and power.[96] Dissemination and preservation of information required uniformity and consistency. Memory was not sufficient. In both religious and secular realms, the Carolingians depended on the written word for communication, administration, and recordkeeping.[97]

Until the late fifth century, Frankish society remained pre-literate. Beginning in the late Merovingian period, however, the combination of the Christian church's promotion of a "religion of the book" and the demands of secular law and administration led to an increasing integration of writing into society. As McKitterick observes, "the process of expansion, political assertion and social integration in sub-Roman and Merovingian Gaul meant that legal norms gradually ceased to reside in the memory of each man in the community, but instead were recorded in writing and preserved, and thus given a new character."[98] The extensive use of documents for legal transactions in classical Roman law provided a model to which the Carolingians later returned. Although early medieval legal practice depended largely on oral forms, documentary evidence provided the best kind of proof. The Burgundian laws, adopted in the late fifth century or early sixth century, emphasized the use of writing and required documentary evidence for a legal transaction to be valid. Other laws required gifts to the church to be confirmed by means of a charter, attested to by at least six witnesses.[99] This combination of oral tradition (witnesses) with written documentation indicates the transition stage to a legal system more dependent on writing than oral testimony.

Charters became the most widely recognized form of legal records in the medieval era, both because they bridged the gaps between orality and literacy and between church and state, and because their forgery and falsification ultimately required systems for authentication and verification of documents. In the early Middle Ages, charters confirmed legal transactions regarding property. "The reality of a transfer of land might involve cutting a piece of turf and handing it from one party to the other before witnesses," Hugh Taylor explains. "The charter subsequently prepared was simply a memorandum."[100] As time passed the charter itself became the best evidence of such an agreement, or even constituted the transaction itself. Written on single sheets, charters documented "gifts or sales of land or moveable property, the manumission of slaves, the grant of land . . . in exchange for a rent or services . . . or exchanges of property." Most surviving charters relate to a single monastery or cathedral church, because these institutions were more likely than private individuals to preserve their archives.[101] The archival record of the Carolingian era thus creates a strong ecclesiastical bias in documentation, largely because such institutions had greater resources for long-term preservation of records.

Although initially created to establish proof of property ownership, charters gradually came to constitute the legal transaction itself. Writing and signing a charter served as a ritual transaction with symbolic importance in legal business. As charters became synonymous with property ownership, the temptation to forge documents became irresistible. Some of the boldest forgeries of the Middle Ages took place in the Carolingian period. "The power of the written word could be exploited to deceive as well as to prove," McKitterick observes. Yet despite these fraudulent efforts to alter documents, all parties to a transaction seem to have possessed records or had access to them in a safe archive.[102] Churches and monasteries recognized the value of archives both as a secure storage area from which documents could be accessed and used and as a symbolic verification of the authenticity of charters and other important legal and financial records. These archives thus secured the power and prestige of established institutions and confirmed their legal rights to property and their authority over the local population.

The church played an important role in fostering the spread of literacy in the Carolingian era, largely because the Frankish people already had developed some literate practices. The church preserved Roman methods of recordkeeping, which became critical to a more general adoption of written modes by other sectors of society. Monasteries, such as St. Gall near Lake Constance, may not have been the principal record makers in society, but served as the primary keepers of records.[103] They thus provided an important archival function, ensuring the preservation and accessibility of vital documentary sources for the local communities. Monasteries promoted use of written documents and trained scribes who contributed to literacy in the community. The monastery thus played a role in conducting public business. McKitterick refutes the traditional view of a literate clergy and monks set apart from an illiterate population. The communities she studied reflect many degrees of literacy, with the monastery and local priests forming part of a literate society. This does not mean that a majority of the population could read or write, but rather that there was widespread involvement in literacy by the Franks. Monasteries did not introduce written methods to the population. Literacy and written records already existed.[104] The church participated in a complex and nuanced social network of literacy and provided services such as creating and archiving documents. It clearly contributed to the spread of literacy, although it was not a solitary beacon of knowledge shining in a dark age.

Carolingian scholars developed libraries of books in order to promote education and learning. They thereby consolidated much of the intellectual and cultural heritage of classical antiquity with that of the early Christian church and provided a foundation for subsequent scholarship in western Europe.[105] These libraries also demonstrated the close link between secular uses of literacy and religious purposes. The inventories of property required by Carolingian rulers provided a model for compiling library catalogs.[106] Monasteries such as St. Gall established important libraries, active scriptoriums, and schools. Within local communities they thus emphasized the connection between learning as a means of understanding the word of God and the secular uses of literacy in everyday life.[107] These library catalogs represent a systematic organization of knowledge that "effectively defined the intellectual framework within which literate skills were to be exercised" by the laity as well as by ecclesiastical scholars.[108] Carolingian scholars extolled the virtues of the written word. Alcuin concluded his poem on scribes with the opinion, "it is better to write books than to dig

vines / One fills the belly but the other serves the soul." Hraban
Maur likewise praised the holiness of scribal labors:

> As God's kingly law rules in absolute majesty over the wide world
> it is an exceedingly holy task to copy the law of God. . . .
> No work sees the light which hoary old age
> does not destroy or wicked time overturn:
> only letters are immortal and ward off death
> only letters in books bring the past to life.[109]

The Christian church, which embodied a religion of the book,
conferred high status on the written word and thus encouraged the
development of a literate population. Even among the nobility,
however, such learning emphasized "pragmatic literacy" sufficient
to function effectively in administration and daily economic and
legal transactions. Nobles rarely became scholars, but they learned
enough to read laws and royal legislation and to use charters in
conducting their own business. The growing prominence of
written records in the conduct of such daily affairs led to creation
of an educated class of administrators and officials who pursued
administrative careers and judicial business, in addition to the
need for literacy in church affairs.[110] Apart from churches and
monasteries, archives developed only occasionally as repositories for
charters and documents of local and state government during the
Carolingian era. Yet the importance of preserving both ecclesiastical
and secular documents ensured a continuation of at least some of
the archival practices of the classical age and antiquity.

In Carolingian society education and literacy provided a path
for social advancement as well as for religious devotion. Frankish
society adopted the Roman assumptions and administrative methods
concerning the important role of written records for secular life
and legal systems. Legal transactions of the Carolingian royal
administration depended upon written law and charters. The written
word became central to the daily functioning of society, both as a
tool and as a resource, guide, and inspiration for people at many
levels of the social hierarchy.[111] This broadening of literacy did
not mark a "triumph" of the written word over oral traditions and
cultural practices based on speaking and direct communication. Nor
was there a flowering of archival repositories in which significant
documents could be consulted for historical investigation. The
collections of documents that might be considered as "proto-
archives" of the Carolingian era served to entrench the powers and
privileges of the ruling classes and (what was often the same thing)

the clergy. Yet there was a growing recognition of the power of documentary evidence, particularly in settling legal, economic, and even theological disputes. During the Carolingian period archives did not achieve the same level of importance as during the Greek or Roman classical ages, but the concept of archival documentation did survive on the local level. The archives of monasteries, cathedrals, and castles provided links between people and documented their legal, economic, and social interactions.

ENGLAND UNDER THE NORMANS

These social and cultural webs of documentation deepened and broadened during the High Middle Ages. Written records became essential in conducting daily affairs of communities and individuals, and deliberate preservation of records in archival repositories assumed greater significance. The expansion of records creation and preservation in England during the period following the Norman Conquest of 1066, as M. T. Clanchy argues, illustrates notable progress in the transition "from memory to written record" as a basis for social interactions. Although charters and other documents existed prior to this era, apart from the king's court and larger monasteries, when local communities sought knowledge of the past they looked first not to books but to the oral wisdom of elders and remembrancers. Remembered truth remained local, simple, and personal. Since authority could be traced back only within the memory of living persons, it remained flexible and up to date. Within two centuries, however, only written documents could be regarded as trustworthy legal evidence. This movement from memorizing information to writing things down and keeping records exerted an impact on individual intellects and on society as profound as the later shift from script to printing.[112]

Faced with this technological change from oral testimony to written documentation, people grappled with the relationship between the spoken and written word. As John of Salisbury observed, "Fundamentally letters are shapes indicating voices. Hence they represent things which they bring to mind through the windows of the eyes. Frequently they speak voicelessly the utterances of the absent." Writing often emulated oral communication. Documents had to be read publicly to have the same validity as direct testimony. Charters and other documents of this transition period therefore addressed "all those seeing and hearing these letters, in the future as in the present," or "all who shall hear and see this charter." Such records could thus address future witnesses as well as contemporaries. As the Winchcombe Abbey cartulary declares, "when the voice has perished with the man, writing still enlightens posterity."[113] Despite such advantages, written records could only gain acceptance after a long testing period in which they served largely as symbolic confirmations of oral testimony. This reluctance to accept written evidence can be seen in a controversy of 1101 CE in which envoys from the pope contested the meaning of his written and verbal messages to King Henry I. One side argued that credence should be given to documents attested by the pope's seal rather than to "the uncertainty of mere words." The other disputants preferred to rely on the word of three bishops sent by the king rather than on "the skins of wethers [i.e., sheepskin] blackened with ink and weighted with a little lump of lead."[114] The latter argument reflects the common principle that oral witness deserved more credibility than written evidence. Not until the late thirteenth or early fourteenth century would the balance shift to written records.

The increasing production and retention of records during the two and a half centuries from the Norman Conquest to the death of Edward I resulted in widening literacy among the English people.[115] The ready availability of documents and their increasing necessity in daily life spurred this increase in literacy, rather than the other way around. Reading extended to a broad public only on the basis of pragmatic need, not from a desire for scholarship or cultivation[116] —a development that McKitterick had also observed in the Carolingian period. The impetus for creating records, however, began with the kings, noblemen, and clergy. Following the Conquest, English monks and nobles sought to justify their traditional practices to the new rulers. In the 1090s Eadmer of Canterbury lamented the lack of a documentary heritage. This monk observed "men of the present age anxiously trying to find out about the actions of their predecessors . . . yet they cannot for all their pains succeed in doing as they would wish because the elusive scarcity of documents [*scriptorum inopia fugax*] has buried them in oblivion."[117] It is unclear whether this shortage of records resulted from a lack of document-keeping precedents or from Norman dispersal of Old English documents and archives.

The need for literacy gradually spread from the upper to the middle and even lower classes of society. Symbolic of the growing importance of written culture are two classic documents, the Domesday Book and the Magna Carta, which represent the centrality of written legal systems for government in Norman England. As recent anthropological studies have shown, literacy itself is a "technology of the intellect," which depends upon each specific society's systems to acquire its potential qualities.[118] Governance in England following the Norman Conquest developed as a product of distrust rather than social progress. William the Conqueror established his control over the Anglo-Saxons in part by requiring a detailed census of property known as the Domesday Book. This extensive document established William's power over a humiliated people and ensured the rights and privileges of the conquerors.[119] Because the inventories of Domesday were not updated and maintained accurately, it performed primarily a symbolic rather than a practical function. Although the Domesday survey provided the king's government not only with a powerful tome but also an archive of writings for later reference, this archive was not carefully preserved and it disappeared without leaving a trace.[120] The great volume remained as a symbol of royal power, but only much later did England establish regularly accumulated archives.

If the Domesday Book showed the king's distrust of his subjects, the Magna Carta illustrated the complementary side of the people's distrust of their rulers. In 1215 the Magna Carta established English precedent for putting legislation into writing. Yet to take effect it had to be distributed and read aloud to the people of local communities, literally as a proclamation. Despite yearly proclamations of the terms of this agreement between the crown and the populace, not until about 1300 did Englishmen place as much significance on seeing the document as on hearing its terms read aloud. Despite the importance of the Magna Carta for English law, it was not officially enrolled in the royal archives during this period.[121] The king's government needed archives in local communities as well as a central repository. Cathedrals and monasteries, under the king's protection, protected his valuables—including documents—both in Anglo-Saxon England and after the Norman Conquest. For example, the knights of Wiltshire deposited one copy of Magna Carta for safekeeping at Lacock Abbey. The royal archives, however, had no permanent home, but depended on the reliability of archivists to ensure their protection, as an *arche* of documents, kept in portable chests. Not until 1320 did the White Chapel in the Tower of London become established as a central archive under the king's direct control.[122] This concern for royal archives reflected the growing importance of governmental functions and the emergence of bureaucracy.

In the century following the Norman Conquest, the number of documents created by the royal government increased more than ten times, and this progression expanded geometrically during the thirteenth century. The use of written records extended to nearly all spheres of government, both centrally and at the local level. This expanded government activity required the creation of a bureaucracy in order to manage affairs, and the bureaucracy itself led to increased literacy.[123] Literacy had immediate practical purposes for laymen. To deal with governmental demands and to protect their own interests, both economic and political, people needed the ability to read and understand documents and to create them as well. With its remarkably centralized monarchy, the government became the principal producer of documents in English society.[124] By 1285 legal statutes required every significant town in England to appoint a clerk to document debts (in duplicate) and to write bills of obligation authenticated by a royal seal. Only sealed documents provided an enforceable contract between civil parties.[125] Written records had by then clearly replaced human memory as a basis for evidence of property rights and other public interests.

This ascendancy of the bureaucracy ensured that literacy would spread to the masses, at least insofar as people had to use written records and know something about them. Even if they could not read or write Latin, French, or English—the three commonly used languages—Englishmen (and more rarely, women) needed to be familiar with written forms of documentation. Literacy only became truly common in the late Middle Ages, when writing began to record a substantial aspect of common people's own heritage in their vernacular language. This was a complex social phenomenon involving the clergy, laity, and public officials, not simply a matter of schools and education.[126] The educated clergy led the way in creating and using written documents and fostering literacy, followed by government officials and bureaucrats. By 1200 CE, royal officials such as sheriffs and judges clearly required knowledge of Latin in order to perform official duties demanding use of written documents. A century later knowledge of Latin extended to manorial and village officials, including stewards, bailiffs, beadles, and reeves. The landed gentry and bourgeois merchants likewise needed to be able to create, use, and preserve records relating to their financial and social obligations. Even lesser merchants depended on book learning and book keeping once they established offices and stores in place of traveling with their wares.[127] The demands of business and government control created what seemed at the time an explosion of recordkeeping requirements. Knights responsible for county business, and even peasants acting as manorial reeves, had to be able to read warrants presented to them and to keep records themselves.[128] The use of charters as titles to property worked its way down the social hierarchy. By the death of King Edward I in 1307, even serfs used charters to convey property to each other. Their rights and responsibilities began to be recorded in manorial rolls.[129] Although written records could thus serve to give voice to the poor and dependent in society, they could also be used as tools of control and oppression. The complex interplay of social forces affecting knights, merchants, serfs, and lords lies beyond the scope of this account. It is worth considering, however, that the initial impetus for creating and using documents often serves the needs of those with the power, wealth, and learning necessary to develop complicated social systems of governance and control. As Clanchy observes in more modern societies, literacy enforces conformity on disadvantaged or dissident groups, and "provides models for oppression as much as for enlightenment."[130] Such patterns can be seen throughout human history, including the Middle Ages.

When a true account of events did not fulfill the needs of monastic orders, the clergy, or other leaders in medieval society, a skillfully forged document or charter might suffice. The problem of forgery cited by McKitterick during the Carolingian era persisted through the High Middle Ages in England and elsewhere. Information could be lost or distorted if not preserved accurately. "With the loss of books," Orderic Vitalis warned, "the deeds of the ancients pass into oblivion . . . with the changing world, as hail or snow melt in the waters of a swift river swept away by the current never to return." Such losses or alterations could disrupt proper social and economic relationships by altering evidence of prior events. "Since memory is frail," a twelfth-century writer declared, " . . . it is necessary that things which are said or done be reinforced by the evidence of letters, so that neither length of time nor the ingenuity of posterity can obscure the notice of past events." In the thirteenth century a lawyer stated more prosaically, "Gifts are sometimes made in writings, that is in charters, for perpetual remembrance, because the life of man is but brief and in order that the gift may be more easily proved."[131] The danger of imperfect memory of the past became especially problematic when people deliberately falsified documents.

Because they gained credence as reliable testimony of the past, documents carried great power. Charters could determine the fortunes, both literally and metaphorically, of monasteries, churches, and families. Monks such as Gervase of Canterbury recognized the importance of recording events worthy of memory, but monastic writers sought to use records to convey to posterity a consciously selected and carefully crafted version of events. Because monks recognized the power of such documents, they deliberately controlled both what was recorded and which records were kept and which destroyed. Anselm refused to send copies of his letters to another Canterbury monk, who sought to collect them, "because I do not think it useful for them to be preserved." When documents supporting the property rights of a monastic house did not exist, the pious monks considered it justified to fulfill God's purposes by creating an appropriate charter. What seems a flagrant act of forgery to our modern minds appeared natural and legitimate to God's servants seeking to meet their divine obligations. This ambivalent approach would allow posterity to know the past, but did not allow records to accumulate naturally nor to speak for themselves. The truth could not be left to chance.[132] Only by controlling the written record could medieval monks ensure that their perspectives and interests would be protected. Truth came from prayerful understanding of God's will rather than from passive acceptance of human accounts of the past.

The temptation to forge charters became particularly irresistible in the century after the Norman Conquest. Numerous monasteries created charters and other documents to convince the new rulers of their ancient privileges and dignities. Some of these forged charters contained accurate information, based on reliable oral traditions or authentic documents from an earlier time. Forgers sought to produce a form of record that would be acceptable in a court of law.[133] An authentic charter might thus be deemed false because it appeared in different form than those currently used, whereas a forged document would be accepted in court because it met contemporary expectations. Such distinctions certainly lessened the ethical scruples over creating a new (and improved) charter.

When conflicts arose between contradictory charters or between documents and personal memory, some means of verification had to be developed. Signatures and wax seals provided one measure of authentication, but even they could be forged. A notary also offered some protection against forgery, since he could verify documents presented to him. The notary would state his name and legal authority, write the document in his own hand (or add a notation to its authenticity), and add his name and personal signum, drawn with a pen. The notary could also be questioned if a dispute arose during his lifetime. The notary's attestation did not necessarily prove that the facts asserted in a document were true in themselves, but that they were true in the eyes of the law.[134]

Another means of certifying the authenticity of documents was to deposit them in an archives—a safe repository for preservation and protection from damage or alteration. To a modern historian the value of such a repository seems obvious. Medieval rulers did not immediately recognize the need or usefulness of archives.[135] The triumph of written documents over oral tradition had not been completed and access to piles of documents seemed daunting at best. Although Henry II had personally insisted in 1164 that a copy of important documents should be placed "in the royal archives," it was only in 1195, under the authority of Archbishop of Canterbury Hubert Walter, that records were first deliberately created in order to be kept for archival purposes.[136] The French royal archives also originated in the same decade, as the value of preserving documents for future consultation became apparent. Authentic documents could be retained in archives, with copies transcribed onto rolls and indexed in registers, for later reference.

Beginning with the English royal Chancery and Exchequer, establishing archives soon spread to provincial centers.[137] Hubert Walter led the effort to require all offices of the royal government to emulate the Exchequer's practice of keeping records and creating documents, thereby laying the foundations of an accumulating archival memory. The assumption that memory could extend back only as far as the earliest time that could be recalled by the oldest living persons gave way to documentary evidence, which could persist as long as the media on which it was recorded remained stable. Preserving records over long periods of time had always been a central purpose of archives. By the beginning of the fourteenth century the need for ready access to such information became apparent. An effort to bring together the archives of one government office, in 1302, declared its goal, "so that we can be advised of things at all times that we want, and these books and rolls are to remain in the Wardrobe in perpetual remembrance." Despite registers and other methods of indexing, the goal of convenient access remained elusive through the medieval era as the vast information resources of government archives proved difficult to consult without later archival improvements in access systems. The goal of making royal archives accessible did improve somewhat as a result of Bishop Stapledon's survey of the records in 1320. His report outlined problems with records being moved about repeatedly, being mislaid, and otherwise poorly managed. Although it produced few immediate changes, Stapledon's commission marked the Crown's formal recognition that its administrative documents should be kept for posterity, and that they could serve useful purposes for the king's successors.[138]

In this process of establishing governmental archives, the purposes and uses of records had been transformed during the Middle Ages. Created at first in monasteries as part of religious worship and to provide spiritual guidance for posterity, by the twelfth century formal written documents became part of the daily business of the royal government. Accumulated in archival repositories as a trove of written precedents, documents became "a treasure like the crown jewels," Clanchy declares. In 1300 Edward I ordered an extensive search of these royal records seeking precedents for his actions. However, despite the subsequent historical importance of such records, at the time they proved only temporarily valuable for the purpose of governance. The authority of Edward, as with other monarchs, rested more on armies and castles than on his archives.[139] Part of the reason for this was the lack of systematic organization of Edward's records, which lay in chests scattered in numerous locations without listings of their contents. Effective consultation remained impossible until archival systems for access could be devised. Yet an important milestone had been reached. By the early fourteenth century archives had become an important part of English government and a valuable repository of information and treasured artifacts.[140]

Near the end of the Middle Ages official archives became consolidated in many parts of Europe, as monarchs established permanent residences and expanded their administrative responsibilities. Primitive forms of archival repositories emerged as a result of the need for accurate information and control over complex realms. The Anjou archives in Naples, for example, prepared an inventory of records and regulations for their management as early as 1284. Pierre d'Etampes cataloged the chests and registers of the French Trésor des Chartes in 1318, and chanceries and governmental offices throughout Europe began to pay increasing attention to preserving archival materials.[141] Royal archives most often legitimized and perpetuated the rule of kings, the privileges of noblemen, the authority of the clergy, the wealth of merchants, and the subjugation of the landless poor. The seeds of change had begun to take root, as documents now recorded both obligations and rights of the common people, but it would be several more centuries before archives could be considered a protection against oppression rather than a tool for control by the ruling classes.

THE RENAISSANCE AND EARLY MODERN EUROPE

During the Italian Renaissance that followed the Middle Ages, humanist scholars claimed to have rescued Europe from a millennium of medieval barbarism by giving the continent a rebirth of knowledge and enlightenment. The humanists fostered a popular belief in progress and a concept that the past was dark, distant, and alien to a modern sensibility. Seeking to distance themselves from their ancestors, they labeled the past a "Dark Age" of superstition, ignorance, and illiteracy. In these efforts, as Michael Clanchy argues, "the Renaissance humanists' programme of studies was deliberately elitist and backward-looking," as they sought to dominate cultural life rather than bring literacy to the masses.[142] Yet the Italian city-states of the late Middle Ages and Renaissance also witnessed a continuing development of concepts of public recordkeeping and archives.

The emergence of bureaucracy, which Clanchy traces in England, also affected the rest of western Europe. The rise of long-distance commerce and trade, combined with the information needs of nation states, greatly expanded the role of recordkeeping and documentation. The first European university, founded in Bologna in 1158, provided a course of study in "notarial art" that taught students how to create legally and administratively useful documents, keep registries of records, and organize documents to facilitate retrieval. Luciana Duranti, an Italian-educated archivist, argues that "record-makers were on their way to becoming the first identifiable profession in the Western world, as the scribes had been in the ancient Near East."[143] Objective, consistent, and usable documents established clear communication networks essential to organized society. This created a seemingly overwhelming flood of paperwork. As a fourteenth-century Italian merchant complained, "we spend half our time reading letters or answering them."[144] The need to manage financial and administrative operations similarly imposed upon the growing cadre of municipal clerks and government officials. In fifteenth-century Florence, however, the concept of public records, like the development of public libraries, did not imply open access to the masses. The Medici family established libraries to ritualize their power, and recordkeeping likewise strengthened the authority of the church, the nobility, and influential mercantile families in the Italian states. The accumulation and control of knowledge and information provided a new basis for their power.[145]

By the mid-1300s the republican city-states of northern
Italy developed state bureaucracies to rationalize government
administration, including institutional recordkeeping. In an era
of protracted warfare and nearly constant civil unrest, the Italian
city-states could not have stabilized their power without effective
recordkeeping. The capability of the state to regulate commerce,
control land rights, collect taxes, and administer justice depended
on the creation, organization, preservation, and use of accurate
records. Cities such as Ferrara appointed chancellors and secretaries
to create and maintain documents regarding feudal estates and
local landowners. By the mid-fifteenth century the bewildering
complexity of local government led to "a virtual 'explosion' of
record creating under the management and control of professional
bureaucrats" employed by the prince's household, according to
archivist-historian Richard Brown. This led to massive expansion
of administrative records and increasingly sophisticated methods of
recordkeeping.[146] The corrupt and despotic government of Ferrara
strengthened its control over the population, in part, through
ritualized ceremonies of records destruction. The prince and his
servants conducted public events in which debts were forgiven or
pardons granted for minor offenses. Debtors or those convicted
of crimes could petition the rulers for mercy, creating "pardon
tales" to justify their requests. Forgiveness required the erasure of
written evidence of the offense. Destruction of documents such as
tax bills and other symbols of economic oppression—either carefully
staged as public acts of forgiveness or managed as "outbreaks" of
popular violence—enabled the rulers of Ferrara to demonstrate
their magnanimity or to blame the economic woes of the city-state
on noble families or external forces. Between 1450 and 1505 the
chronicles of Ferrara document at least fifteen instances of public
ceremonies featuring large-scale records destruction, through which
the rulers offered rituals of public amnesty.[147]

The economic plight and resentment of the poor could not always
be so easily ameliorated or placated. Buffeted by flood, famine,
and the plague, Ferrara lost one-third of its population in the
late fourteenth century. The ruling Este family imposed harsh
measures, including repeated tax increases, on the people in order
to maintain their lavish lifestyle and ill-advised military expeditions.
When official actions could not quell popular unrest, the citizens of
Ferrara formed a mob to storm the Palazzo della Ragione on 3 May
1385. Entering the Hall of Justice, the mob dragged the secretary
of the chancellery from his bed to the piazza, where they skewered
his head on a pike for public display and burned his body parts on

a pyre fueled by financial documents looted from the chancellery. Symbolically, the citizens thus executed the official responsible for keeping records of income taxes and other obligations, destroying the documents of their oppression in their own ritual of cleansing the public record.[148] This mob action thus mirrors, in grotesque caricature, the ceremonial destructions of records sponsored by the Este princes. It also indicates the people's recognition of the close connections between economic and political control and the documentary records that supported the rulers' power.

The lynching of the recordkeeper of Ferrara demonstrates the understanding, by the powerless classes in society, that creating and preserving records solidifies the state's authority. Charters, statutes, tax lists, and other forms of documentation enabled the ruling classes to maintain control over the masses. They presented tangible symbols of power. "Besides serving basic administrative and legal purposes, and providing the means to generate additional revenue for a cash-starved political regime, the production, management, and destruction of records by the Estensi bureaucracy were also used for the purposes of social control and public demonstration of authority," Richard Brown reports. In both subtle and overt ways the citizens of Renaissance Ferrara became "ensnared in a 'web of chancellery' spun from records."[149] Those engaged in recordkeeping practices, including interpretation of documentary sources, all contributed to the writing and preservation of historical memory. In medieval and early modern Europe, little distinction was made among the occupations of remembrancer, chronicler, annalist, historian, editor, librarian, or archivist. Working with both governmental and personal papers, they all sought to shape and interpret the past for their own purposes. As in monasteries seeking to secure their own rights and privileges through documentation— including forgeries when necessary—the Italian chancellery actively shaped the public record. In collusion with a corrupt civil service, the governmental offices of Ferrara manipulated documentary sources to produce their own version of "public truth," often quite different than what had actually occurred in the past.[150] It was the best "public memory" that distortion, forgery, and deceit could buy.

As we see throughout the medieval era—in the Carolingian Empire, post-conquest England, and the Italian city-states—the problem of forgery plagued recordkeeping practices. Charters and other forms of documentation validated claims to property, wealth, and status. With so much at stake, it may be little surprise that the temptation to cheat so often overcame even the most pious of monks and prelates, let alone princes and noblemen. Even when justified as restoring the intended purposes of divine will, such forgeries clearly violated legal and moral principles. As humanist scholars of the Renaissance sought to untangle the competing claims of medieval charters and documents, they began to apply sophisticated historical analysis to these records. In the fourteenth century, Italian scholar Francesco Petrarca proved that the privileges granted to Austria by Caesar Augustus and Nero in the first century were forged, and a century later Lorenzo Valla proved that the donation supposedly made by Constantine to Pope Silvester was a forgery.[151] Other scholars developed these techniques into one of the archival sciences, known as diplomatics. Diplomatics "is the discipline which studies the genesis, forms, and transmission of archival documents, and their relationship with the facts represented in them and with their creator, in order to identify, evaluate, and communicate their true nature."[152] Following these early Italian humanists, scholars in other countries refined the techniques of textual criticism. This culminated in 1681 with publication of *De Re Diplomatic Libri VI,* by Dom Jean Mabillon, Benedictine of the Congregation of Sait-Maur in France.

Meanwhile, in Siena the process of governmental recordkeeping combined concern for financial and administrative needs with an unusual artistic sensibility. In 1257 the Office of the Biccherna, charged with managing all revenues and expenses of the city, initiated the practice of commissioning panel paintings from the best artists of the region to serve as covers for Siena's public ledgers. As the central financial office of the Sienese government, the Biccherna represented the full power and authority of the state. The value placed on its semiannual collections of financial records can be seen in the beautifully detailed paintings in which these *biccherne* volumes were encased. The earliest extant *biccherna* cover (1258) portrays the city bursar, Ugo di San Galgano, preparing the account books at his desk. Later illustrations showed the bursar surrounded by his books, sacks filled with coins, storage chests, and his family shield. A painted cover from 1340 depicts the bursar interacting with a client.[153] These painted covers also served as indexes to the volumes, with detailed Latin and Italian inscriptions indicating the contents and purpose of each ledger.

As Siena's influence expanded, the biccherne illustrations shifted from routine business transactions to allegories of religious and political life in the city-state. A panel from 1467 represents the Virgin protecting the city during an earthquake, while citizens seek protection in tents outside the city walls.[154] Another contrasts the financial condition of the city in times of peace and war, illustrating the importance of social stability and, by implication, the beneficial effects of sound financial management and recordkeeping. Over one hundred biccherne covers, on wood tablets, have been preserved and are now on display in the rooms of the Archivio de Stato in Siena, with the original ledger volumes—from which the covers have been removed—lining high banks of shelves. It makes an impressive display of the importance that the Sienese rulers placed in their financial and administrative records, and of the veneration held for these historic documents even today.[155]

Although archives often prohibited access to all but the officials of state, things were beginning to change as citizens gained some measure of influence in the political process. In Venice the recordkeepers had to be illiterate so that they could not read the documents they protected, and not even the doge could enter the archives unaccompanied. Archives literally guarded "secrets of state."[156] However, the free commune of Padua illustrates the importance that some societies began to place on archives to safeguard the rights of citizens. Shortly after Padua's domination by Ezzelino da Romano (1237-1256), when municipal liberties were repressed, the restoration of commune institutions and legal regulations included specific rules governing archival management. These archival regulations, adopted in 1263, required preservation of the *statuti* (municipal constitutions or laws), with separate copies kept in four locations including the archives. In 1265 the Padua municipal constitution added a requirement for keeping records locked in a "strongwardrobe" in order to ensure the authenticity and security of the records. This recognition of the legal importance of records led to further safeguards in 1275. In order to protect collective rights of the people, five citizens chosen from local judges and notaries would staff the archives. These procedures ensured that citizens would have access to records in order to protect their rights.[157]

Despite repeated upheavals—such as domination of the city by Venice, beginning in 1405, and a 1420 fire that destroyed many of Padua's archival records—the city continued to recognize the need to preserve archival records. By the second half of the eighteenth century, historical researchers began to seek archival records and to analyze both public and private documentary evidence. By the time of the Risorgimento, which led to the nineteenth-century unification of Italy, research in archival sources became more intense as part of "a civil mission aimed at restoring national identity," as one historian reports.[158] The historical development of Padua's archives thus represents several critical themes in archival history: the importance of archives for legal and administrative needs, their significance to protect citizens' rights, their susceptibility to loss or neglect, their value for cultural and historical research, and their usefulness in creating or confirming national or group identities. There was no straightforward march of progress in archival management, in Padua or elsewhere, but these concepts had been identified as part of the significance of archives for citizens of a free society.

Not only did archival management proceed along many separate lines of development, but there was also no common European pattern of progress. Each country established its own recordkeeping methods, based on distinct governmental and bureaucratic systems. For example, in Flanders the town hall kept private contracts between citizens, and public archival repositories in Hungary were called *loci credibiles,* or places which gave legal credibility to documents located within. In the sixteenth century the Archivo de Simancas in Spain created a prefiguration of the modern national archives model.[159] By the seventeenth century, western Europeans had become dependent upon documents and records. Archives organized and preserved this growing abundance of records, serving an essential function in early modern society. In 1632 Baldassare Bonifacio of Treviso, Republic of Venice, prepared a fervent testimonial to the importance of archives and records. As bishop of Capo d'Istria and a doctor of theology and law, Bonifacio stated that if deprived of records, "we should all be compelled to grope in the dark, to feel our way with our hands." He advocated creating and preserving records, because "there is nothing more useful for instructing and teaching men, nothing more necessary for clearing up and illustrating obscure matters, nothing more necessary for conserving patrimonies and thrones, all things public and private, than a well-constituted store of . . . documents and records—as much better than navy yards, as much more efficacious than munition factories, as it is finer to win by reason rather than by violence, by right rather than by wrong." Because documents were so important, archives had been established "by public funds, through the generosity of princes," under supervision of highly skilled men. "Indeed, care over the archives was given only to great and learned men," Bonifacio continued. Because order was "something divine" and "the soul of archives," he advocated preparation of indices, syllabi, and "lists and catalogues in alphabetical order" so that "whatsoever will be needed we will have before our eyes immediately."[160] Bonifacio's treatise thus explained some of the concepts of caring for documents that archivists would later embrace, although his methods and criteria for organizing materials would require conceptual modifications for later needs. This was at least a step in the direction of careful consideration for the needs of archival order and accessibility.

One of the crucial technological changes marking the end of the medieval era and the transition to modern society came with Johann Gutenberg's introduction of movable type. Using movable type, the printing press provided a far superior product. Books and other printed documents could now be created with much greater quality, accuracy, reliability, quantity, and speed than ever before. The seemingly instantaneous print explosion, in retrospect, mirrors the late twentieth-century information revolution in rapidity, extent, and social impact. In the forty-plus years from Gutenberg's first printed Bible until the end of the fifteenth century more than 20 million printed volumes were produced in Europe. By the end of the following century that number had reached nearly 200 million. The book was the first mass-produced commodity of the modern industrial era.[161] This signaled a technological transformation in producing and preserving documentation, although the printed word emerged mainly as a public information system rather than a personal or organizational means of recordkeeping.

Mechanical reproduction of information thus divided the forms of documents into one mode directed toward a mass audience and another mode that remained grounded in personal interactions and organizational transactions. Print opened avenues for public participation in learning and the social life of information. As Benedict Anderson observes, "If manuscript knowledge was scarce and arcane lore, print knowledge lived by reproducibility and dissemination."[162] Mass movements, including the Protestant Reformation and the rise of nationalism, required the rapid and widespread dissemination of ideas and information. As these changes swept through Europe during the Renaissance and early modern eras, reliance on manuscripts and limited-circulation documents remained prominent in the daily functions of government, business, private organizations, and individuals. It is the latter stream that we will follow in examining the transformations that continued to occur with documents and archives, even as the print revolution transformed public affairs at a different level.

Although print culture ultimately usurped the place of manuscript culture, this technological shift provoked resistance, skepticism, and reluctant acquiescence. As with the earlier transformation from orality to writing—and the later shift from print to electronic technology—many people mistrusted the new innovation. During the Renaissance and Reformation, a Republic of Letters emerged, by which an international community of learned men (and women) communicated ideas and innovations through handwritten letters, which bound together the leading intellects of western societies. Letter writing took the place of face-to-face conversation, producing both intimacy and immediacy across great distances. Scholars trusted personal letters from individuals whose reputations inspired confidence. Printed books could ensure the fixity and reliability of texts, but could also circulate and magnify errors. They could not always be trusted. Whenever possible scholars sought to verify printed texts by reference to more familiar manuscript sources.[163] Unpublished documents thus served two very different purposes. One use provided formal records of government, business, religion, and other societal institutions. The other contributed to the formulation and transmission of culture, knowledge, and learning. Through the Renaissance and early modern eras in Europe, manuscript sources thus played an important, if not always publicly acknowledged, role in maintaining social order and preserving culture. Royal archives buttressed the support of kings and ruling dynasties, which soon encountered challenges to their authority and power from popular democratic movements for social and political reform. In Ming China, scholars had begun to employ ancient texts as a basis for demanding reform of an imperial government that theoretically held absolute power. European intellectual leaders, by contrast, had abandoned politics and the struggle for governmental power in favor of a scholarly quest for "objective" truth and knowledge.[164] The demand for social reform, in France and other European states, would come from the masses rather than the educated classes.

THE FRENCH REVOLUTION AND DEMOCRATIC ARCHIVES

As in so many aspects of modern society, the French Revolution dramatically realigned many of the attitudes, habits, and practices of western Europeans toward documents and archives. The localized and primitive archival depositories of royal dynasties, monasteries, and business offices had gradually expanded in scope and purpose during the eighteenth century. For example, centralized archival depositories arose in the House of Savoy in Turin, and in St. Petersburg (1720), Warsaw (1765), Venice (1770), and Florence (1778).[165] Within a decade following its unification in 1705, Hanover erected a special building to store records from various regions of the country. Despite such efforts to centralize and administer archives, in the late eighteenth century decentralization remained "the characteristic trait of archives administration," according to Ernst Posner. For example, in 1749 Austria transferred archival materials from the House of Habsburg to its Hausarchiv, Hofarchiv, and Staatsarchiv.[166] In 1770 there were 405 depositories of archives in Paris, and 5,700 in France, including 1,780 seigneurial seats and 1,700 monasteries.[167] Archives remained largely the responsibility of each administrative unit of government or of small private organizations, such as landed estates, local church parishes, monasteries, guilds, and business firms.

The concept of archives prior to the French Revolution referred almost exclusively to documents providing legal or economic privileges to the state, the church, the nobility, or the merchant class. Although the Enlightenment elevated to public consciousness such concepts as individual rights, self-governance, and intellectual exploration, archival documents remained largely monuments to the past. Even the *Encyclopédie* of Diderot and d'Alembert—one of the crowning literary achievements of the century—emphasized the importance of archives not as sources of information and ideas but as protectors of legal and economic interests of the elites: "Archives is the term used for those old titles or charters which contain the rights, pretensions, privileges, and prerogatives of a house, a town, or a kingdom." It defined a title as "any act which establishes some right," and charters as "very old titles, as from the 10th, 11th, 12th and 13th century, or at least anterior to the 15th century."[168] Such records underpinned the governance and legal structure of society. As archival historian Judith Panitch observes, "The power of archival records, then, could be vast, for upon them rested the entire legal, political, and economic legitimacy of the monarch and nobility."[169] Little wonder then that official state archives remained closely guarded in the possession of the sovereign, or that access to archives of all types remained highly secretive.

The French Revolution overturned this understanding of archives and their purposes. Under the banner of democratic rights and the slogan "liberty, equality, fraternity," the revolutionary leaders redefined archives as a bulwark of citizens' rights rather than a bastion of privileges for the elites. The Revolution fundamentally changed the relationship between citizens and archives in three essential ways, according to Ernst Posner. First, it established the administrative structure for a national public archives, thereby overcoming the decentralized nature of archival repositories. Founded in 1789, the Archives Nationales truly became a national archives after 1794, when it gained authority over scattered agency and provincial depositories. Second, the state acknowledged its responsibility to protect the documentary heritage of the past, and recognized that written documents deserved preservation for their historical value as well as their legal and economic importance. The Bureau du Triage des Titres, established in 1796 and headed by the archivist of the republic, ensured preservation of historically important documents of the past. The third essential change in archives policy brought by the French Revolution recognized the principle that all citizens should enjoy access to archival records in order to ensure their rights and freedom. As the 1794 decree stated, "Every citizen is entitled to ask in every depository . . . for the production of the documents it contains."[170] This regulation arose not from a concern for scholarly research, but from a desire to protect the legal and property interests of citizens. These three concepts reinforce each other. Effective access to archives depends on recognition of their ongoing value. Centralization makes management of records more efficient and enhances ready accessibility by reducing the number of locations where records could be found. By establishing these foundational principles of archives, the French Revolution ushered in the modern era of archival management. Archives would no longer remain the exclusive prerogative of monarchs, priests, and nobles. From this point onward, in western society, archives became essential elements of a free, democratic society and its citizens.

As with other social and political upheavals unleashed by the French Revolution, this paradigm shift in archival identity brought with it some violent clashes. At the outset, many revolutionaries regarded archives as hated symbols of feudal oppression, both by the state and the church. Spontaneous hostility toward documents, which served the rulers at the expense of the people, erupted during the Gran' Peur, the rural insurrection following the fall of the Bastille—another symbol of oppression—in the summer of 1789. Philippe Sagnac wrote in 1898 that during this outburst of revolutionary fury, the peasant "took his own Bastille, invaded the châteaux, ran straight to the seigneurial archives, held at last in his hands the charters, monuments of his own servitude, and delivered them to the fire."[171] Newly liberated, peasants defaced or destroyed symbols of oppression—churches, statues, coats of arms, ornate carriages, and feudal documents—in acts of retribution designed to prevent a return to previous forms of subjugation.

The Revolution's leaders likewise seized this means of obliterating the past and preparing for a new age of liberty and equality. Laws passed between 1789 and 1793 appropriated the property of the monarchy, clergy, nobles, and émigrés, including the written records that granted land and privileges to them. In 1792 the Legislative Assembly proclaimed that documents of the nobility and knights, stored in the Augustine Convent, should be burned in the Place Vendôme. Condorcet, the rationalist mathematician who was one of the few Enlightenment *philosophes* still active in public affairs, praised such bonfires. "It is today that, in the capital, Reason burns, at the foot of the statue of Louis XIV, 600 folio volumes attesting to the vanity of this class whose titles will at last disappear in smoke."[172] As in Ferrara three hundred years earlier, government officials often incorporated the destruction of records into patriotic festivals and public celebrations. Paper and parchment documents also proved valuable in manufacturing artillery munitions or for recycling to make paper.[173] Eliminating feudal records thus served practical as well as symbolic purposes, although the catharsis of destroying documents proved most satisfying.

The revolutionaries' motives for destroying documents partially echo those of the first emperor to unite the warring states of China. In 221 BCE the Qin ("Chin") emperor sought to eliminate rival political philosophies by ordering a general burning of books. The legalist scholar Li Si advised the emperor that this would eliminate private learning, and scholars would no longer be able to trust their own teachings instead of the emperor's decrees. "Your servant suggests that all books in the bureau of history, save the records of Qin, be burned," Li Si wrote. Punishment should be severe: "Those who use the past to criticize the present should be put to death together with their relatives."[174] In both revolutionary France and Qin dynasty China, control over written records offered the promise of political power and subordination of rival ideologies. The Chinese had sought to eliminate knowledge of alternative political philosophies. The French hoped to erase the vestiges of oppression and royal power.

Ceremonial bonfires did not result in widespread despoliation of France's documentary heritage, however. Records with practical uses in confirming land titles could be incorporated into the new regime for the benefit of those who took over confiscated lands and other property. More significantly, the Revolution's leaders acted quickly to ensure the preservation of important documents in a newly created national archives. Only two weeks after the fall of the Bastille, the Assembly established its own legislative repository to preserve "all original documents relating to the operation of the Assembly," and appointed an archivist, to be elected from the Assembly members by majority vote. On September 12, 1790, the recently established Archives Nationales gained official status as "the repository of all the acts which establish the Constitution of the Kingdom, its laws, and its division into departments." The archivist would be appointed for a term of six years and the Archives would be open to the public three days a week, from 9 AM to 2 PM and 5 PM to 9 PM. For the first time, this law established the public's right to consult documents in the archives.[175] Although it would be many years before public access to archives became common practice, the movement had begun toward a more democratic and egalitarian purpose for archival recordkeeping. The connection between the public interest and archives was beginning to gain acceptance in western society.

The French Revolution also linked public archives to the emerging concept of national identity. During the nineteenth century this contributed to the growth of nationalism in western European states. Although archival documents played an important administrative and legal role in previous regimes, including the monarchies and city-states of Europe, the French and American revolutions marked the first self-conscious use of documentary sources in establishing new nation states based on popular participation in shaping national consciousness. "The creation of new repositories helped the Revolution to affirm its own identity, while the triage and reclassification of old records guaranteed that a particular interpretation of the past would be imposed upon succeeding generations," Panitch states. She concludes that the new Archives Nationales thus became one of the symbols around which "the notion of 'the nation' could in part crystallize and take hold in the collective consciousness," and that it became central for the regime's political and psychological legitimacy. "The archives afforded a sacred space in modern society, designated to represent the nation's origins, its past, and its identity."[176] Rather than simply providing legal and administrative services to the rulers and elites, French archives now existed, at least in part, as a means of protecting the rights and interests of citizens. Archives also symbolized national identity, history, and culture. Founding the new French Republic required establishing a national archives in order to reinvent the nation's identity.

NATIONAL IDENTITY AND ARCHIVAL THEORY

As European monarchies and dynasties began to lose popular legitimacy in the wake of the revolutions in France, North America, and Haiti, the quest for national identity spawned the rise of nationalism, liberalism, and—by the mid-nineteenth century—liberal revolutions and efforts to form new political states based on "national" characteristics. Justifications for these new nations and for redefined national loyalties in existing states led to a renewed search for historical roots and antecedents. Historical analysis intersected with the emergence of scientific research in a marriage necessary to justify the historians' increasingly lofty claims to authority and legitimacy. It was no longer satisfactory to regale an audience with heroic tales of moral virtue. Historians had to justify the very creation and existence of new nations, based on ancient ethnographic, cultural, and historical affinities of the peoples of geographic territories as broad and diverse as Germany, Italy, and Russia. Seeking a scientific research model, historians seized upon the extant archival sources found in government offices, churches, monasteries, guild halls, seigneurial estates, and numerous other locations. Archival research gave legitimacy to historical depictions of national identity, which provided justification for the formation and definition of new or redefined nations.

Prior to the French Revolution, most European countries denied scholars access to governmental archives. When they did gain approval to conduct archival research, it was granted as a favor—often because the scholar had connections or friends in high places—not as a right of access. The French Revolution established the right of public and scholarly access to the archives, and these archival concepts spread to other European states when Napoleon's troops established French administrative structures in occupied territories.[177] Throughout the nineteenth century historians set their sails to the prevailing winds of liberalism, nationalism, and romanticism as they found new purposes for their craft. Resistance to Napoleon's conquest of European territories stirred resistance among peoples who began to see their common identities as a historical heritage, leading to popular nationalistic movements. The Revolution's celebration of *liberté, egalité et fraternité* fostered concepts of public rights and liberties, spreading an interest in personal and group identity and a demand for public participation in governance. The Romantic movement that emerged with these other currents of change began to glorify the past, including works of art, monuments, and literature. Publishing documentary sources that recounted the history of the country and writing new "national" histories connected these intellectual and cultural movements to the people's archival heritage of documentary evidence.[178] As scholars entered the archives to conduct historical research, the character and purpose of governmental archives gradually shifted from legal and administrative use by government officials and bureaucrats to a dual use by intellectuals interested in exploring the historical roots and cultural heritage of the nation and its people.

Historians bolstered their reputation for accuracy and trustworthiness by developing a methodological approach called "scientific" history. By appropriating the growing legitimacy of scientific method, they hoped to enjoy the public's trust as purveyors of stories of the past. They rejected oral testimony and personal memory as reliable sources of information, and turned instead to written documents, which seemed less susceptible to distortion and alteration. History would become "scientific" by adopting a coldly objective approach to investigation of the past, rejecting the warm, personal, and subjective realm of memory and oral transmission.[179] The positivist historians of the nineteenth century believed that their only responsibility was to identify and locate objective facts. Truth consisted of compiling unambiguously true statements about events, impartially and without intervention by the historian. This "fetishism of facts" arose from an assumption that Truth was timeless, unchanging, and universal. The professed goal was a scientific dedication to the protocols of objectivity.[180] Most prominent among these historians was the German Leopold von Ranke. "Ranke piously believed that divine providence would take care of the meaning of history if he took care of the facts," E. H. Carr observed a century later. "This was the age of innocence, and historians walked in the Garden of Eden . . . naked and unashamed before the god of history."[181] Ranke's devotion to manuscript sources bordered on the erotic. "Yesterday, I had a sweet, magnificent fling with the object of my love, a beautiful Italian," he wrote concerning one cache of Venetian documents, "and I hope that we produce a beautiful Roman-German prodigy"—a work of scholarship.[182] As Ranke and his disciples searched for the "facts" of history, they found seemingly limitless sources of treasure available in archives, attics, and public offices. Documents created at or soon after the events they recorded afforded seemingly untainted evidence of historical facts. In the famous formulation of Charles V. Langlois and Charles Seignobos, the fundamental creed of the historian became, "No documents, no history."[183] The mutual dependence of archivist and historian arose from this conception of historical evidence. Archives no longer served only the bureaucrat and administrator, but also Clio, the muse of history.

The discipline of history emerged, adopted a scientific (or more accurately, pseudo-scientific) methodology, and formed professional organizations at the same time as the European nation-states united and extended their power over smaller political entities. The newly professionalized discipline of history provided an ideological support for the state in Germany, France, and England, as well as in the United States.[184] Formulating a historical past solidified nationalism and confirmed the nation's exercise of power. "Professional history and the modern nation state grew up in partnership . . . because creating a national history would help form national citizens, thus affirming the nation as the primary form of solidarity," according to historian Jeremy Black. Particularly in the newly emerging public schools, history provided the vision of a united people with a national destiny. Historians thus defined and contained human experience within national borders and emphasized the common heritage of the peoples within new state boundaries.[185] Archives created by national governments formed the richest sources for such historical investigations. As a result, the management of archives emerged as a profession amidst the same intellectual and political forces that shaped the historical profession.

In the generation following the French Revolution, archivists began to develop a coherent theory of archival management, based on the bureaucratic needs of the emerging national state and its administrators. During the Second Empire, France joined the growing movement to exploit state records in writing national histories. Adopting a policy that defined the archives as a depository of documents serving the public interest, archivists created inventories to guide scholars to archival resources, with classification systems to organize massive quantities of papers into discrete and accessible groupings.[186] Instead of organizing archival records according to pre-determined classification schemes based on subject matter or content, French archivists developed the central concept of *respect des fonds*, in which all records originating from an administrative authority, corporation, or family would be brought together in a *fonds* based on their origins and functions. First articulated by Natalis de Wailly in 1841, in a French archives circular, this principle became the basis for the Prussian concept of *provenienzprinzip* and still stands as a founding concept for modern archival arrangement.[187] The emergence of archival theory—distinct from bureaucratic, historical, or library approaches to documents—marked the beginnings of a nascent new profession of archivists.

Archivists struggled to define their professional identity. They served both the growing bureaucratic needs of government and private organizations and the emerging needs of the historians and scholars who relied on archival sources for their research. Prior to 1830, the French archives had been open only to government bureaucrats. Permitting historical research marked a change in policy, but one that remained cautious in allowing access only to trusted researchers.[188] Liberated from the secretive nature of the Old Regime, in which archives served only lawyers, government officials, and interests of the crown, nineteenth-century archives promised to serve the public interest. Léon de Laborde, director general of the Imperial Archives of France (1857-1868), declared that by opening the "arcane, impenetrable Archives" to public access, the "light of history" could again shine from its proper source. Laborde shared his generation's faith that the Archives represented a single, self-evident Truth. However, opening the Archives to public scrutiny could also assist those who challenged the Empire's interpretation of history and thus even its political legitimacy. Archives became central to the political disputes over national identity, the legitimacy of the Empire's rule, and the rights of citizens. By serving the public and providing access to the archives, the archivist became part of the nation-building process. He stood at the nexus between citizen and state and negotiated between the requests of citizens and the needs of government. The role of the archivist became problematic, because he had to mediate between complex and often competing interests of state and citizen, public interest and private rights, history and administration, and politics and scholarship.[189] Archivists thus assumed significant authority and power—albeit often only tacitly acknowledged or even explicitly denied—and appointments to such positions became highly valued prizes.

The archives also served as an arbiter of truth. "History will search the Archives for its documents," declared Prince Napoleon-Charles-Joseph-Paul Bonaparte, who had been appointed in 1863 by his cousin Louis Napoleon to publish the *Correspondence* of Napoleon Bonaparte.[190] Rather than examining the archives in an impartial search for truth, historians typically sought to confirm their conclusions with evidence found in the records. The prince thus recognized the link between political authority—the legitimacy of the Bonapartes' rule—and the archives, which served as much as an administrative apparatus as a historical patrimony.[191] Self-interest would lead the rulers to keep the archives secret or at least to monitor their use carefully. Disputes over access to the Imperial Archives revealed that they served not only as a storehouse of national memory, but as a symbol of conflict over such memory. Despite rhetoric about accessibility to the public and service to the nation, the French archives established internal policies that protected the secrets of government.[192] Even with a tradition of public access, the archives succumbed to political pressure to suppress or even subvert the truth, in the interest of the state and its leaders. Certainly there was more public accessibility than under the Old Regime, but the democratic and egalitarian ideals of the Revolution did not fulfill their promise in the century following the creation of the Archives Nationales.

By the end of the nineteenth century, the French model for modern archives had spread throughout most of western Europe. Napoleon Bonaparte's troops had brought French administrative systems in their wake, as the French Empire ruled both conquered nations and their local communities. By the 1850s most European countries had adopted or modified French archival practices regarding transfer of government records to archival repositories, appraisal of these records' importance, organizing and describing them, and opening records to public research.[193] When the French retreated from the Netherlands in 1813, for example, the country did not return to its former federal political system, but remained a unitary state retaining French bureaucratic systems. As Dutch archivist Peter J. Horsman observes, the recordkeeping system established in Amsterdam by the French survived well into the twentieth century, although smaller towns such as Dordrecht largely escaped French influences on local administration and recordkeeping. In Dordrecht, traditional recordkeeping systems, which closely followed the local government procedures for decision-making, continued through most of the nineteenth century despite changes in administrative structure and composition of the town's political bodies. By the end of the century, however, recordkeeping adapted to the shift of government administration to the bureaucratic system based on civil service. The French influence on Dutch local recordkeeping remained, but was largely indirect, such as requirements that local communities report regularly to the national government and the increasing importance of bureaucratic systems and the civil service.[194]

Even more significant than the French influence on Dutch administration and recordkeeping was the impact of French archival theory. Throughout the nineteenth century Dutch archivists began to adopt archival practices from German and French manuals on diplomatics, from Tuscan writers on archival practice, and from

English concepts of custody of records. The French concept of *respect des fonds* shifted archivists' focus from chronology and subject matter to circumstances of creation of records and the context of recordkeeping practices. By 1891, Dutch archivists had become aware of their common interests and established the world's first professional association for archivists. The new association founded a professional journal in 1892, and in 1898 a commission of three Dutch archivists published the first modern-era manual of archival practice.[195] This *Manual for the Arrangement and Description of Archives,* by S. Muller, J. A. Feith, and R. Fruin, became the world's most influential guide to archival practice. In codifying the central archival principles of provenance and original order, and establishing standard terminology for archival concepts, the *Manual* represented the culmination of several centuries of European archival development.[196] Widely translated, it established a theoretical basis for organizing, managing, and protecting the integrity of archival records. The Dutch manual directly influenced the first English language text on modern archival administration, Hilary Jenkinson's *A Manual of Archive Administration,* published in 1922.[197] Virtually all European and North American writing about archival theory owes a debt to Muller, Feith, and Fruin.

With the combination of a professional society dedicated to their needs and a manual of best practices, archivists had finally achieved their own identity as a professional group separate from historians, librarians, and administrators. This professionalization marked the emergence of archivists as self-conscious participants in the management of information resources, both for legal and administrative purposes, and for cultural significance. Archivists had achieved a recognized role in society, albeit one that continued to be contested and shaped throughout the twentieth century. Nowhere did these complex interrelationships of legal documents, administrative records, historical manuscripts, and archival practice more clearly reveal the push and pull of archives and society than in the United States. The interplay of archives as sites of power, truth, memory, and social values emerges more fully in examining the historical development of American archives, to which we now turn our attention.

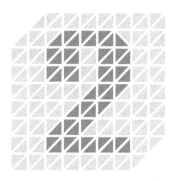

Documenting
American Society

Two young French aristocrats landed in Newport, Rhode Island in the spring of 1831, ostensibly to study the American prison system as a basis for reforms in France. Yet their personal agendas led to an analysis of the young Republic that forever altered the way the world viewed Americans and their society. For nine months they traversed the United States, from New England to the frontier regions of Michigan and Wisconsin, as far south as New Orleans, ending in New York. In addition to their commissioned report on American prisons, published in 1833 as *On the Penitentiary System in the United States and Its Application to France,* each author used his travel experiences in America for a personal project. Gustave de Beaumont wrote a fictionalized exposé of the evils of American slavery, entitled *Marie; or, Slavery in the United States: A Novel of Jacksonian America.*[1] As his companion later noted, Beaumont included in the novel, by way of authenticating his exposé of the cruelties of slavery, "a very large number of very precious and entirely unknown legislative and historical documents."[2] Yet it is Beaumont's companion whose writings would create an unforgettable depiction and interpretation of the United States. Alexis de Tocqueville published *De La Démocratie en Amerique,* translated into English as *Democracy in America,* in two volumes, in 1835 and 1840.

Tocqueville's analysis has shaped virtually all subsequent discussions of the nature of American government, society, and national character. As the book's most recent translators declare, "*Democracy in America* is at once the best book ever written on democracy and the best book ever written on America."[3] Tocqueville's work is too well known to require detailed explanation here. He examined American society and dissected both the benefits and dangers of democracy. As a French aristocrat, he was both fascinated and appalled by features of the American political landscape, such as freedom, social equality, town government, individualism, voluntary associations, latent racial conflict, and the dangers of a "tyranny of the majority." His interpretation of these and other social and political features of the United States has been almost continually debated, analyzed, and cited for more than 170 years.

What has not received much attention has been Tocqueville's underlying concern for evidence, documents, and archives. In 1956, T. R. Schellenberg quoted Tocqueville's observation that in America, "no one cares for what occurred before his time . . . no archives are formed; and no documents are brought together when it would be easy to do so. Where they exist, little store is set upon them."[4] Although this passage suggests that Tocqueville disparaged Americans' lack of concern for archives, a closer reading indicates his conclusion that documents and records played an important role in establishing and maintaining American democracy. "Without ever speaking of 'accountability' (this was still a new word in English in Tocqueville's lifetime, and there was no precise French equivalent), *Democracy in America* recognized that records might serve that crucial purpose in a free society," James O'Toole concludes.[5] Documentary evidence enabled citizens to force public officials to answer for their actions, and easy access to information provided a counterweight to privilege and power.

Tocqueville recognized that American government rested on written documents. The Mayflower Compact, the first formal political agreement among the colonists, was so important to the development of American democracy that Tocqueville reproduced its full text in *Democracy in America.* "Democracy such as antiquity had not dared to dream of sprang full-grown and fully armed from the midst of the old feudal society," he declared.[6] Tocqueville also recognized the importance of colonial charters, although he saw even greater significance in the legislation and legal codes adopted by citizens of the colonies. Such laws established the basis of democratic government—"intervention of the people in public affairs, free voting of taxes, responsibility of the agents of power, individual freedom and judgment by jury"—which began at the township level and percolated upward through colonial governance.[7] From this colonial reliance on written laws, charters, and political covenants, after the Revolution the Americans quickly established written state constitutions, which Tocqueville frequently cited, and a national Constitution, to which he devoted substantial attention.

At the local level, in particular, Tocqueville noted the importance of written records and recordkeeping procedures. Although not a specific focus of his inquiry, his reliance on such documents and his discussion of the political functions they supported provide useful insights to the important—if seldom acknowledged—role of public records in American society. In the township—"that fertile seed of free institutions"[8]—making and maintaining records contributed to orderly political and social relations, a pattern established by the original settlers. Tocqueville reported that "townships had public registers in which the result of general deliberations, deaths, marriages, [and] the birth of citizens were inscribed," and that "court clerks were assigned for the keeping of these registers."[9] Clerks derived income from such duties, and were paid a set fee for various types of document creation, but they could also be fined for neglect of this duty.[10] The pervasive role of records in local government carried over into state, territorial, and national life. For example, colleges needed charters in order to operate and public oversight took place through required reports. In the court system, forms established for recordkeeping protected individual citizens and the public from "lapses in democracy" and provided a "brake that moderates and arrests" human passions.[11] Public records formed but one part of a widespread system of information that freely circulated through society. Tocqueville particularly noted the importance of the printing press, newspapers, and the postal system—which could as easily "deposit enlightenment on the doorstep of the poor man's hut as at the portal of the palace"—for disseminating the information necessary for a literate public to engage in public affairs.[12] Creating and using written records thus formed a routine of daily life, so commonplace as to go unnoticed as busy men and women performed their normal functions and roles in society.

If American citizens relied on written records for their social re-lationships, Tocqueville himself also depended on documentary evidence for his research. The most accessible sources of original documents were published editions, such as *Historical Collections, Consisting of State Papers and Other Authentic Documents,* by Ebenezer Hazard.[13] In examining the colonial origins of town governments, political systems, and social customs, he frequently consulted and cited the *Collections of the Massachusetts Historical Society,* which "contains a host of very precious documents" relating to New England history. "One finds in it unedited correspondence and authentic pieces that were buried in provincial archives," Tocqueville reported.[14] When published sources did not answer his inquiries, appropriate government authorities gave him permission to consult local and state archives, to which he frequently refers.[15] Tocqueville carefully sought the most reliable evidence in such archival sources. As he explained, "When a point could be established with the aid of written documents, I took care to recur to original texts and to the most authentic and esteemed works."[16] In this respect he followed a scholarly practice that was beginning to achieve dominance on the continent: consulting archival sources and seeking the most authentic original records available. When Tocqueville commented on American documents and recordkeeping practices, he spoke both as an observer and as a researcher dependent upon such authentic and trustworthy source materials.

His reliance on reliable documents made Tocqueville all the more concerned about Americans' casual regard for their own archival sources. Despite a tradition of reliance on written records, including such foundational documents as the Mayflower Compact and the Constitution, Americans seemed to have little concern for their own history or for archival preservation. Rapid changes in public leadership resulted in "oral and traditional" forms of administration, which often left few traces, since what little was written "flies off at the least wind, like the leaves of Sibyl, and disappears without returning," he lamented. "The only historical monuments of the United States are newspapers," he reported, but if one issue is missing, "the chain of time is almost broken: present and past are no longer joined." Tocqueville warned, "I do not doubt that in fifty years it will be more difficult to gather authentic documents on the details of the social existence of Americans of our day than on the administration of the French in the Middle Ages." This led him to conclude, "No one worries about what has been done before him. No method is adopted; no collection is composed; no documents are gathered, even if it would be easy to do it."[17]

As in so many fields of observation, Tocqueville thus hit upon the central inconsistency of Americans' relationship with their documentary heritage. The American people have always had an ambivalent relationship to their history and to archives. Founded in part on the notion of escape from the shackles of European traditions and with the vision of being a "city on the hill" for a utopian new world, the United States has often been future-oriented and indifferent to the past. As Tocqueville recognized, despite a high literacy rate that led the early settlers to rely upon written documents for their political and social organization—to an extent unprecedented in European history—Americans seemed so eager to push forward the frontiers of the future that they gave little heed to earlier times. So intent were they on breaking the shackles of the past and forging new social and political systems that they neglected, or actively sought to cast off, all reminders of the past.

Despite these conflicting tendencies, George Bancroft, the most prominent American historian of the nineteenth century, observed in 1838—only three years after Tocqueville published the first volume of *Democracy in America*—that New Englanders "have always been a documentary people."[18] Since the founding of the colonies Americans have relied on documents and records to define their social and political relations, to proclaim and defend their liberties, and to record their deeds for posterity. Examining the social history of documents and archives in America reveals the powerful subcurrents of our dependence on documents as sources of information, history, power, freedom, rights, and memory.

COLONIAL AND REVOLUTIONARY ROOTS

The early development of archival consciousness in the United States illustrates the power of documents and their importance both in establishing national identity and securing the authority of the ruling elite. Knowledge conveyed power. Documents that validated the ruling class and celebrated past heroes sanctioned their privileges. Although occasionally regarded in a legal sense, more often documentary evidence conveyed historical legitimacy to political and cultural narratives of the nation's founding and development.[19]

Documents in America initially played important roles in both religion and governance. The journals carefully kept by Pilgrim leaders John Winthrop and William Bradford recorded the progress of the new religious community. Throughout the colonial era interest in documenting regional history was strongest in New England, largely because of religious motives.[20] This concern for preserving the memory of societal events focused on the cultural and historical value of records and documents. This formed one of the two central benefits of archival sources.

Colonial Americans also recognized the value of documentary records in protecting civil and political rights. As Tocqueville implicitly recognized, from the Mayflower Compact to colonial charters
to the Declaration of Independence and the Constitution, American law and the people's rights depended on written documents.[21]
In Connecticut the defense of the royal charter of 1662 required
secrecy and cunning. To prevent its capture and surrender, the
charter was—according to legend—hidden in an oak tree, which later
gained fame as the "Charter Oak," still the most prominent symbol of Connecticut's history.[22] The emphasis on public policy, the
rights of citizens, and the authority of the ruling classes validated the
concept of public records, serving a societal purpose with legal and
administrative significance. Political power in the new world had to
be defined and conferred through documentary sources.

The decision to separate the colonies from English control
thus naturally assumed the form of a written Declaration of
Independence, a document that not only announced the creation
of a new sovereign state, but also informed all other nations of
the causes of such separation. This document also was necessary to
inform the colonists of the decision of their chosen representatives
and to enlist their allegiance and support of the revolutionary cause.
In the Declaration, when listing King George III's "injuries and
usurpations," the fourth item listed was: "He has called together
legislative bodies at places unusual, uncomfortable, and distant
from the depository of their public Records, for the sole purpose
of fatiguing them into compliance with his measures."[23] The
significance of this complaint is its implicit recognition that public
records provided essential evidence for governance and self-rule
in a democratic state. Printing and distribution of copies of the
Declaration took place immediately. A year later, however, Congress
ordered "an authenticated copy of the Declaration of Independency,
with the names of the members of Congress subscribing the same, be
sent to each of the United States, and that they be desired to have the
same put on record."[24] This formal receipt of the document would
confirm the actions of the collective states and commit each of them
to the ongoing war against England. The continued veneration of
the original Declaration of Independence, now enshrined in the
National Archives rotunda, demonstrates the power of this original
document, not only for the actions it set in motion but also as a
symbol of American independence and liberty. It has become the
most important document of the nation, but it also represents the

power and significance of many other documents that have helped to fulfill and to record the promises made by its adoption.

One of the compelling arguments for adoption of the new Constitution in 1787-1788 was the power of such a document to codify and limit governmental power, at the same time that it strengthened the authority of the central government. American Federalists placed their confidence in this new document, which was specific in enumerating government powers, while remaining broad and vague enough for interpretation and future amendment. Even at its inception, however, the Constitution could not gain ratification without being amended by the Bill of Rights. Veneration for the Constitution has been the leitmotif of American politics since its adoption, and this important document takes its place, literally, beside the Declaration of Independence in the rotunda of the National Archives, located (significantly) on Constitution Avenue in the nation's capital. [25]

In an emerging nation governed by the rule of law, it was essential that accurate records be kept of the public's business. The democratic age demanded no less. The significance of public records led the new Congress, soon after adoption of the Constitution, to approve "An act to provide for the safe-keeping of the acts, records, and seal of the United States . . ." in September 1789. This act required the secretary of Congress to publish every "law, order, and vote" in at least three newspapers, and to send printed copies to each senator, representative, and state governor. In addition, "he shall carefully preserve the originals, and shall cause the same to be recorded in books to be provided for the purpose." [26] Publication of congressional actions would inform the public directly, and indirectly through their representatives, of the government's actions. It would also hold those leaders accountable to the people. The citizens were assumed to enjoy what would later become known as "the public's right to know" what the government was doing. Written records would be one important means of protecting these rights. Duplication of copies would serve both to disseminate information widely and to ensure preservation of important records. These are responsibilities now assumed by many governmental or institutional archivists. Other archivists and manuscript curators select and preserve documents with historical or cultural significance, including personal papers, historical materials, and private documents.

Documents represent both tangible evidence of the past and proof of actions and events. Above all they convey seemingly irrefutable facts. This positivist assertion of objective truth, by nineteenth-century Americans, provided the underlying support for accepting documents as historical evidence.[27] The necessity of citing authorities only gradually gained acceptance. One Revolutionary general asked historian Jeremy Belknap not to quote from his letters. "It cannot be important to the world to know when or where you collected them," he wrote. "The only important question is are they facts."[28] This argument—that a presumed objective truth would not require proof and authorities—was slowly giving way to the requirement for historical documentation.[29]

HISTORICAL REPOSITORIES

Two distinct approaches to preserving documents for researchers began to emerge by the time of the Revolution. In 1774 Ebenezer Hazard began to collect American documentary sources for publication, and Jeremy Belknap requested Harvard College to establish a repository for documents relating to the revolutionary crisis for use by future historians. These two approaches—publication or repository—represent what would become separate traditions in American documentary preservation. Hazard and Belknap thus framed the debate concerning historical research, preservation of documents, and accessibility of sources.

The creation of archival repositories in the United States arose from the needs and initiatives of historians, particularly those seeking access to reliable primary sources relating to the founding of the nation and its colonial and Revolutionary past. Without venerable traditions, common ancestry, religious uniformity, and other forms of social cohesion common in European states, Americans sought to create a common history based on written records of the Revolution and its antecedents. Self-consciously they began to construct a national identity in place of a patriotic folk culture.[30] Beginning as early as 1774 Reverend Jeremy Belknap proposed establishing a repository for historical documents relating to the emerging new nation and its origins. Without access to a research library in the 1770s, Belknap diligently searched public offices and "the garrets and rat-holes of old houses,"[31] to glean information. He declared, "I am willing even to scrape a dunghill, if I may find a jewel at the bottom."[32] To avoid this necessity, he sought to create a secure facility to preserve and protect historical gems.

Belknap's plans came to fruition in 1791 when he led a group of Boston's social and political elite—clergymen, lawyers, physicians, judges, politicians, and even a librarian and a historian—in found-

ing the Massachusetts Historical Society, the country's first repository for collecting and preserving historical artifacts and manuscripts.
By documenting the deeds of national heroes, archival repositories
played a patriotic role in defining national identity and in strengthening the power of ruling elites. Belknap promised an active role for
the new historical society in Boston: "We intend to be an *active*, not
a *passive*, literary body; not to lie waiting, like a bed of oysters, for
the tide (of communication) to flow in upon us, but to *seek* and *find*,
to *preserve* and *communicate* literary intelligence, especially in
the historical way."[33]

The Massachusetts Historical Society spurred other states and
regions to establish historical societies, with uneven success.
Prior to the Civil War in 1861, Americans created more than one
hundred historical societies—from national organizations, such
as the American Antiquarian Society, to local groups, such as the
Louisa County (Iowa) Pioneer Settlers' Association—although
only a few achieved either fiscal or administrative stability.[34] These
were, of course, creatures of the elite educated class of society,
not repositories intended to document the working classes, new
immigrants, women, slaves or free blacks, or Indians (except as
curiosities of peoples on the verge of extinction—which most white
Americans accepted without lament). Much of the early leadership
in collecting and preserving historical documents came from the
northeastern states, which enjoyed the highest concentrations of
population, education, and intellectual achievement. However,
there were important historical initiatives under way by the 1830s in
several southern states, including indexing public records, founding
historical societies, and copying documents relating to state history
in foreign archives. The sporadic nature of such initiatives prevented
southern states from establishing lasting programs or institutions to
preserve historical records.

Developments in antebellum Virginia, the largest and most
prosperous southern state, illustrate the high aspirations, good
intentions, and disappointing results of historical initiatives in
the South. The state that had been the first colony to establish a
permanent English settlement in the New World and that gave
the Union such prominent leaders as Washington, Jefferson,
Madison, Monroe, and John Marshall, came late to the concept
of institutional efforts to preserve its history. Not until December
1831 did Virginians get around to establishing a historical society,
and even then the effort met only partial and temporary success.
Virginia was beginning to see its power decline in the national

arena. The "Virginia dynasty" of presidents ended with the election of John Quincy Adams in 1824, shortly after Virginia had slipped to second rank in population. The Panic of 1819 had sent the state into economic decline, and the Nat Turner rebellion in 1831 inflamed growing fears of slave insurrection. Tensions between whites in eastern and western parts of the state erupted during the Constitutional Convention in 1829, showing that the Tidewater planters would not maintain their authority forever. By 1831 Virginia's political leaders were debating a proposal for gradual emancipation, which if passed would have overturned both the economic and social systems of the state.[35] The state clearly was headed for ongoing crises, diminishing its proud heritage as the national leader in government and culture.

One response to these crises was to celebrate the state's proud heritage, in hopes that the memory of the founding fathers and Revolutionary heroes would revive the spirits and the fortunes of Virginia. Following a newspaper announcement of plans for a new historical society, a group of prominent political and social leaders met to form the Virginia Historical Society in December 1831. The founders of this society—including the governor, members of the legislature, a former congressman, prominent attorneys, and newspaper editors—represented the political power brokers and social elite.[36] This was not a voluntary association for commoners.

The historical societies formed in each state listed their topics for documentation, which focused on the white male leadership of society, its "eminent and remarkable Persons," and their political, military, religious, and economic affairs. Women, racial and ethnic minorities, and the working classes did not appear.[37] It was an accepted right of the powerful to control the nation's history. Documents provided evidence of past accomplishments and guaranteed the social privileges of the ruling class. Archival repositories thus confirmed and sanctioned the power of the social and intellectual elite.

HISTORICAL EDITING AND DOCUMANIA

In early America the difficulty of creating a fireproof and secure repository led many to argue for publication as the best means of documentary preservation. Borrowing a phrase from Jeremy Belknap, Thomas Jefferson wrote: "Time and accident are committing daily havoc on the originals deposited in our public offices; . . . but let us save what remains; not by vaults and locks, which fence them from the public eye and use in consigning them to the waste of time, but by such a multiplication of Copies as shall place them beyond the reach of accident."[38] Historical editing and publication of documents not only ensured the preservation of information, but also made such sources readily available to multiple users. In many respects such publishing efforts have served as extensions of archival practice, in effect bringing the records to the people, but they have also seemed to offer a competing alternative to creating secure repositories.

The first American historical editor, Ebenezer Hazard, began collecting an enormous cache of "American State Papers," with the goal of "saving from oblivion many important papers," which would prevent later historians from, "groping in the dark, and perplexing themselves in the labyrinths of error."[39] He published *Historical Collections: Consisting of State Papers and Other Authentic Documents* in two volumes in 1792 and 1794. Hazard declared that the sources he compiled "will, of themselves, form the best history that can be published, as they will furnish facts free from the glosses of commentators."[40] In this respect, at least, edited documentary publications duplicate the purpose of archival repositories. Both methods provide authentic and reliable evidence. Hazard's son Samuel followed his father's example, publishing the *Pennsylvania Archives* in twelve volumes (1852).[41]

During the antebellum era this concern for preserving and publishing historical documents of the colonial and Revolutionary eras led to what historian David Van Tassel called "documania."[42] This passion for documents reflected, primarily, a patriotic and nationalistic fervor for reliable accounts of the Founding Fathers. But American readers also seemed to understand the value of getting as close as possible to the minds and hearts of their national heroes. They implicitly believed, as one historian stated, that these accounts had been "drawn from Documents which cannot err."[43] As historian Jared Sparks declared, "Tradition can never be trusted when it conflicts in any degree with written records."[44] Authentic documents seemed to promise direct, authentic evidence, in much the same way as the emerging technology of photography. Both served as an aide-mémoire, a device of memory. As one contemporary declared—in a commentary on photography that could also apply to documents— " . . . by the wondrous science, we are now enabled to preserve and hand down to future generations the truth-telling portraits of our statesmen, our heroes, our philosophers, our poets, and our friends." Another observer stated that photography every day "enriches the archives of history with some precious document."[45]

Written documents also connected people to heroes of the past. The American reading public eagerly devoured documentary chronicles of the new country's origins. Multivolume editions of the papers of national heroes such as George Washington and Benjamin Franklin became run-away best sellers in a young nation searching for its place in history. Foremost among these historical editors were Jared Sparks and Peter Force.

Jared Sparks, the first American appointed as a professor of history, edited and published numerous multivolume documentary editions of the correspondence and writings of Washington, Franklin, and other Revolutionary heroes, beginning in the 1830s. With the Revolution beginning to fade into the past, Americans became obsessed with accounts of national heroes, making history the most remunerative literary genre of the Jacksonian era.[46] One historian wrote to another that "we could both make handsome fortunes in a few years, as well as a reputation that would last as long as our national history. The publishers seemed ready to jump at any thing I would write."[47] As an historical editor, Sparks became a best-selling author with his compilations of documents of the Founding Fathers. He corresponded freely with the leading figures of his day, from President John Quincy Adams and the Marquis de Lafayette to prominent historians such as George Bancroft, Francis Parkman, and Lyman Draper. Sparks collected, copied, and published original documents to ensure historical accuracy. As he explained: "my object is to verify and illustrate historical facts."[48] Archival documents also served nationalistic purposes. As Sparks wrote to General Lafayette, his goal was "recording for the use of posterity the deeds of our heroes and patriots."[49] In 1828 Sparks wrote to Lafayette, who helped him secure access to the French Archives, "The manuscript letters & other papers . . . will contribute to fill out many defective parts of American history, to solve doubts and correct errors." Sparks added this self-serving boast: "Next in importance to the performing of great acts for a nation's liberties, is a faithful record of these acts, as an example for posterity to admire and imitate. Human events are transient, but history is immortal."[50] This was a bold assertion to make to one of the great heroes of the Revolutionary War. As Sparks asserted, the historian, using archival sources, helped to shape national identity.

Another prominent nineteenth-century documentary editor was Peter Force. A Washington, DC printer and politician, Force edited and published nine volumes of American Revolution era documents under the title *American Archives*, from 1837 to 1853.

Force and his partner, Matthew St. Clair Clarke, obtained contracts
for this ambitious project from Congress, signed by Secretary of
State Daniel Webster, and had to respond to complaints that the
publication cost too much.[51] Force declared that he had searched
widely for "any authentic papers that relate to the public affairs of
the country," in order to compile "a collection of materials for an
authentic history of the United States from the settlement of the
Colonies, to the year, 1789."[52] Such efforts to collect and preserve
historical documents prevented the irreplaceable loss of essential
information, which Force believed to be part of a broad movement
"throughout the considered world to gather to preserve and to
scrutinize all the materials which can rescue the history of the past
from the obscurity in which time has enveloped them."[53] In his
appeals for congressional funding, Force emphasized the urgency
of acting quickly to prevent further loss of documents. "Time and
accident have already abstracted many materials for [authentic
history of the nation], of cardinal importance, and the work of
destruction is rapidly progressing."[54] The condition of historical
documentation required immediate intervention. As Force
undertook his daunting project of collecting all available sources
on early American history, Jared Sparks offered to "facilitate your
operations" by sharing his notes and information about American
state archives.[55] Both Sparks and Force believed that, without
secure archival repositories capable of protecting unique original
documents, the safest alternative was publication. By multiplying
the copies, as Jefferson and Belknap had both declared, such losses
could be minimized.

Force and Sparks also agreed on the national interests that such
documentary publication served. "A complete collection of the
materials for a history of this country would not only be a proud
monument to the memory of our ancestors whose deeds they
commemorate and whose opinions they embody, but would serve
as an invaluable guide to us and to our posterity," Force argued.
The lessons of America's history, he declared, included "purity
of principle, . . . respect for lawful authority, . . . opposition
to tyranny, . . . [and] vigilance in detesting . . . despotism."[56]
Publication of archival documents thereby served a patriotic
purpose. Unlike Jared Sparks, who thought nothing of improving
Washington's grammatical lapses, Force presented documents
verbatim and attempted to include every document pertaining to
his subject.[57] However, his diligence and passion for including all
documents—even those previously published elsewhere—led some
in Congress to charge Force with padding his publication in order

to enhance his profits. Force countered that the documentary record required full context, accuracy, and completeness.[58] In Force's defense, Robert Walsh, editor of the *American Quarterly Review*, predicted that Force's *American Archives* project would "place history upon an immovable basis," and make it "a record of facts, beyond cavil or doubt—a simple relation of what actually occurred, clothed in the plain and noble garb of truth."[59] This confidence that truth was objective and discoverable reflects the positivist approach to history. All one had to do to establish past events conclusively was find the pertinent facts, which would speak for themselves without elaboration.

The persistence of Sparks and Force in tracking down important historical documents inspired another avid collector, Lyman Draper. Draper followed the lead of others in seeking to document Revolutionary era heroes, but he focused not on the Atlantic coast leaders of Massachusetts and Virginia, but on those of the trans-Appalachian interior—pioneers and military leaders such as George Rogers Clark and General Joseph Martin. Draper charmed the elderly pioneers and their widows and acquired thousands of original documents for his extensive research and publication plans (few of which he ever completed). In traversing the country for months at a time, Draper reported in a printed circular designed to solicit still more sources, "I have amassed a large amount of most precious material—some 5000 foolscap pages of notes of the recollections of warrior-Pioneers, either written by themselves, or taken down from their own lips; and well nigh 2000 pages more of original manuscript journals, memorandum books, and old letters written by nearly all the leading border heroes of the West." Seeking absolute accuracy in every detail of his extensive research, Draper never could seem to stop collecting information. "These numerous and valuable manuscripts throw much new light upon Western history, and correct many errors which have crept into the published works extant."[60] When he could not pry loose the manuscripts themselves he secured permission to hand copy documents. He also conducted what must be considered some of the first American oral history interviews, taking copious notes on frontier battles, settlements, and pioneer heroes.

After nearly twenty years as an itinerant researcher and collector, Draper found employment at the new state historical society of Wisconsin, where he attempted to fill in contemporary history by interviewing Civil War recruits and encouraging them to record their own experiences for posterity. Draper's extensive collections eventually found a home at the Wisconsin Historical Society, where they remain the premier research collection for the early midwestern pioneers.[61]

While Sparks acquired copies of European archival records in order to compile documentary editions of source materials, several states—including New York, Massachusetts, North Carolina, and Georgia—also sent researchers to gather materials relating to their colonial origins from European archives.[62] Prominent historians of the era also conducted private research and copying initiatives in Europe. George Bancroft, Francis Parkman, and William Prescott hired copyists to transcribe British, French, German, and Spanish archives. Bancroft explained this passion for documentary evidence to Richard H. Dana: "We historians, like you lawyers, are obliged to demand of every anecdote a passport duly countersigned, authenticated, & cross-question every witness."[63] Francis Parkman declared that his books involved "a prodigious amount of mousing in libraries and archives," including repeated visits to England and the Continent in quest of materials. "The manuscripts copied entire for the work now exceed 70 large volumes, besides masses of notes and what extracts taken from the original documents," he reported in 1887. Parkman wrote to Bancroft that the "manuscripts preserved in the Bibliothèque Imperiale" were "a fountain of authority" for his research on the British and French conflict over North American territory.[64] These diligent quests for manuscript sources in the archives of European capitals anticipated the archival research efforts of later historians.

The gentleman historians of the mid-nineteenth century viewed history as a literary craft designed to instill moral lessons. Bancroft deliberately fashioned a historical account that would instill patriotic pride in American readers. He did so in part by ignoring past conflicts, omitting unsavory elements, and dismissing as unimportant the experiences and perspectives of women, servants, slaves, Indians, immigrants, and the working classes.[65] As Victorian era moralists, both Bancroft and Parkman concluded that the white, Protestant, New England perspective should determine how Americans understood their historical past. Bancroft celebrated the unprecedented progress of American liberty and the imperialist triumph of Manifest Destiny, while Parkman portrayed a perceived racial superiority of Anglo-Saxon peoples in conquering the French, Spanish, and Indians with whom they struggled for control of North America.[66] In their view the role of the historian was as moralist, patriot, and apologist for the dominant white, male, Anglo-Saxon, Protestant ruling class of the United States. Neutrality and impartiality had no place in their historical chronicles. Archival records and historical manuscripts provided the basis for a frankly and unapologetically partisan account of the American past. Celebration excluded dissident voices. Ethnic minorities, recent immigrants, women, and the poor remained on the margins of society.

PUBLIC ARCHIVES AND PROFESSIONAL HISTORY

The modest efforts of private historical societies in collecting and publishing historical documents did preserve some important archival sources, but with little public or governmental support. Although several states and some federal agencies identified and protected their archival records, the first governmental archival agency in the United States was not established until 1901. Meanwhile, most of the official governmental records of the nation and the states languished in conditions that could at best be termed benign neglect. Jared Sparks conducted the first archival survey in 1826, visiting southern states to locate their colonial and state records. He compiled information about these state "archives" and found that most governmental offices did little to protect or preserve their early records. After examining "all the historical materials in the public offices of the old states," Sparks told former President James Madison in 1827 that "they are meagre beyond what any one could have conceived."[67] Peter Force and Matthew St. Clair Clarke echoed Sparks in the preface to *American Archives*, stating, "we have personally examined the public records in each of the thirteen original states [and] . . . have found these in many instances in a lamentable state of deterioration, confusion and decay." They added that many documents and public proceedings had been irretrievably lost, but that their efforts had rescued many documents "of inestimable value from the very jaws of destitution."[68]

Sparks also pioneered research for documents relating to early American history in European archives, including those in London and Paris, which he deemed "a treasure of historical facts."[69] In his dealings with French archivists, Sparks reported on the power and influence they had in controlling access to the records.[70] French concepts of public access emphasized the citizen's right to information, but did not always extend to historical research, particularly by foreigners.

Sparks, Bancroft, Parkman, and other patrician historians of the mid-nineteenth century established a commitment to basing historical interpretation on archival documents. Their sweeping historical narratives, infused with patriotic and nationalist fervor, gradually gave way to the scientific historians of the emerging historical profession by the 1880s. As German methods of scientific history reached American shores in the mid-nineteenth century, the demand for primary sources grew even stronger. The American Historical Association (AHA), founded in 1884, provided an organizational base for professional historians as they gradually replaced the "well-to-do cultivated amateurs" who had long dominated historical writing.[71] The AHA was part of a broad social movement to create professional standards and intellectual enhancements in the social sciences. This also reflected a middle class effort to master or guide the fast-moving currents of industrial, urban, and ethnic change in America.[72]

The members of the American Historical Association intensified the concern for documentary research previously expressed by gentleman historians such as Bancroft, Parkman, and other amateurs. This new scientific history was based on concepts developed in the German universities. Herbert Baxter Adams, in particular, brought the theories of Leopold von Ranke and other German professors to the New World. Following in Ranke's footsteps, Adams proclaimed that his own historical writing was "based entirely on original records."[73] So influential was Ranke that AHA members selected him as the first honorary member of the young professional society. Writing to tell Ranke of this honor, AHA President George Bancroft addressed him as "My venerable master and dear and most highly honored friend," and called Ranke "the greatest living historian."[74]

Historians embraced the fashionable concepts of scientific method and applied them to studying the human past. Secular, standardized, and objective analysis would replace explanations of history based on divine will and intervention, sweeping narratives, personal opinion, and partiality. Historians taught their students "how to distinguish fact from legend by the rigorous examination of documents" based on "research in archives and original sources."[75] Scientific history emphasized careful analysis of facts, gathered from reliable sources, with an assumption that such investigation would reveal the "Truth" of the past. Like the civil service reformers of the same era, historians established impersonal standards, subjecting passion and caprice to objective law.[76] Following the positivist model, these scientific historians believed that careful collection of documents, patient examination and comparison of sources, and the accumulation of facts would reveal laws of historical development.

They assumed that such rigorous methods would lead any researcher examining the same documentary sources to a single version of the truth.[77]

Despite their claims to objectivity, detachment, and neutrality, the scientific historians perpetuated the consensus view of history established by Bancroft, Parkman, and their contemporaries. Most of the new History PhDs came from the same elite social caste—northeastern, Protestant, ethnic British, well educated, and affluent. "History has always been . . . the most aristocratic of all literary pursuits, because it obliges the historian to be rich as well as educated," Henry Adams observed.[78] Historians publicly espoused the creed expressed by Harvard historian Albert Bushnell Hart in 1910: "genuinely scientific history, which shall remorselessly examine the sources, . . . critically balance evidence, . . . [and] dispassionately and moderately set forth results."[79] However, they continued to present a consensus interpretation which excluded women, blacks, workers, Indians, immigrants, and others who did not belong to their own social elite. What the devotees of Ranke did not recognize was that his public renunciation of moral judgment did not represent disinterested neutrality, but a deeply conservative political outlook. Far from a neutral reporter, Ranke sought to establish the central principle that the course of history revealed God's divine intervention in human affairs.[80]

The scientific historians focused much of their attention on the political and economic aspects of the past. As they sought documentary sources, they quickly recognized that there were no public archives worthy of the name, either at the state or federal level. Public records lacked careful management, organization, or preservation. Soon after its founding, the AHA turned its attention to the lack of documentary sources. Its Historical Manuscripts Commission, founded in 1895, began by searching for and compiling lists of private manuscript sources scattered around the country. The commission soon turned its focus to publishing selected documents in order to make them widely available. Recognizing the need for archival repositories to preserve original public records, the AHA established its Public Archives Commission in 1899, beginning a long campaign to establish public archives in the states and for the federal government.[81]

These two AHA commissions represented separate traditions in American archival history. On one hand the Historical Manuscripts Commission emphasized the Hazard-Sparks-Force tradition of historical editing and publication as a means to preserve documentary sources and make them widely available to the reading public, whereas the Public Archives Commission emphasized the creation of secure archival repositories to protect original documents for research and administrative use. However, within the latter emphasis on repositories, dual traditions existed, according to archivist Richard Berner. One line of historical development centered on historical societies and libraries concerned with establishing research collections for historians (the historical manuscripts tradition), and a second line focused on the growing interest in governmental records for administrative and legal purposes (the public archives tradition). In the historical manuscripts camp Berner included both historical society leaders, such as Jeremy Belknap and Lyman Draper, and documentary editors, such as Jared Sparks and Peter Force. The public archives movement gained little momentum until the very end of the nineteenth century, when scientific history coalesced in the AHA as a professional society.[82]

Despite the extensive nineteenth-century initiatives to collect historical manuscripts, no state created a formal archives until 1901, with establishment of the Alabama Department of Archives and History. This marked a critical milestone for the public archives movement. The leading figure in securing approval for the first state archives was Thomas M. Owen, a young politician and lawyer whose interest in Alabama's history had led him to accumulate a personal collection of published and unpublished materials concerning his native state. Beginning in 1897, Owen "single-handedly revitalized" the Alabama Historical Society, in order to collect and preserve the state's historical resources. Owen's principal motivation was to defend and justify Alabama's historical legacy. In the post-Civil War era—when Jim Crow segregation laws and the United States Supreme Court's ruling of *Plessy v. Ferguson* had recently strengthened white supremacy in the South—Owen sought to celebrate his state's reputation.[83] Owen used this private organization to lobby for an official state archives. The United Sons of Confederate Veterans, led by Owen as "Commander-in-Chief," petitioned for the archives as a means of assuring availability of Confederate muster rolls and rosters to establish pension claims and membership in veterans' groups.[84] Both cultural and political motivations thus lurked behind the creation of the first state archives. They would serve a decidedly partisan purpose.

The legislation establishing the Alabama Department of Archives and History in 1901 gave it a broad mandate to preserve all historical resources and to promote knowledge and research in state history.[85] Owen secured the position of director of the new archival agency. Although "primarily motivated by cultural-educational concerns that were strongly tinged with Lost Cause nostalgia," Owen came to recognize that the core mission of the new archives should be care and preservation of the records of state and local government.[86] As he stated in a report to the AHA in 1905, a state archival agency had one "exclusive duty"—a responsibility of "first and supreme importance"—"the care and custody of official archives."[87] In addition to this official responsibility, Owen vowed that a state archivist "must keep in touch with the people" and must daily "demonstrate the usefulness of the Department and its work."[88] Largely as a result of Owen's dedication to proving the value of archives to the people and to state government, a 1918 report on Alabama's social problems by the Russell Sage Foundation—which relied on information from the state archives—declared that Owen's department was "one of the most important agencies in state government."[89] An archival agency begun as an effort to justify Alabama's historical legacy thus became an integral part of the administration of official state business. Archives could serve both a historical role and a public administration function.

One year after Alabama established the first state archives, neighboring Mississippi followed its lead in creating the nation's second state archives. As in Alabama, Mississippians began by reviving their state historical society. Members of the former antebellum power structure sought to preserve historical records to justify the role of their state and its favorite son, Jefferson Davis, during the secession and Civil War era. Institutions of public memory would memorialize the Lost Cause and celebrate the heritage of Mississippi.[90] As a circular letter written to support creating a state archives declared, "there is nothing wrong with our history, but in the writing of it," and creating an archival repository would "provide the most effective means for the correction of this defect."[91] The version of history envisioned by the prominent citizens supporting the archives legislation would serve their own interests in white supremacy. These were the Bourbons who had overthrown Reconstruction, denied black suffrage, and enacted the Jim Crow regime of racial oppression. The first director of the Mississippi Department of Archives and History, following its establishment in 1902, was Dunbar Rowland, an attorney and avocational historian with a planter background. Rowland had published fiery articles about the rise and fall of Negro rule in Mississippi during Reconstruction, the nobility of the antebellum planter class, the benevolence of slavery, and the political heroes of the state.[92] He could be counted on to shape the archival programs of the state along similar ideological lines.

As state archivist of Mississippi from 1902 until his death in 1937, Dunbar Rowland became an active member of the Public Archives Commission, a leader in national archival activities, and an early convert to the European theories of archival management. He gained support to hire copyists to transcribe European archival records relating to the history of Mississippi, along lines established generations earlier by Jared Sparks and others interested in archives. In 1910 he was one of four representatives of the AHA Conference of Archivists who attended the International Congress of Archives in Brussels, where he presented a paper on the desirability of centralized government archives. He toured European archives and adopted such practices as those enunciated in the 1898 Dutch manual by Muller, Feith, and Fruin. As a vigorous supporter of creating a national archives, in 1934 Rowland lobbied intensely but unsuccessfully to become the first archivist of the United States.[93]

Despite these impressive credentials as one of the leading archivists of his generation, Rowland used his influence in Mississippi to shape an archival program dedicated to the perspectives and goals of the white supremacist elite of the state. In his public speeches he "painted a chivalrous picture of antebellum planter society and a lurid portrait of carpetbagger Reconstruction," and "advocated that the inferior black race be segregated from the white race." Of the original nine members of the archives department's board of trustees, whose selection Rowland significantly influenced, at least two were Confederate veterans, three were sons of veterans, one a legislator who helped to overthrow northern control during Reconstruction, and two had participated in the convention that denied black suffrage. Throughout Rowland's tenure, the board continued to represent such connections to prominent families and white supremacy convictions. He also assigned priority in archival collecting and services to records of Confederate history and veterans' affairs. "If there is one duty of this Department which should stand before all others it is that sacred duty to preserve the record of the Confederate soldiers of Mississippi who gave up everything for country and made forever heroic the time in which they lived," he wrote in 1903 in his second annual report as archives director.[94] This was not a private expression of opinion, but a prominent public declaration in his official capacity as state archivist.

So closely did Rowland wrap himself in the Confederate mantle of nostalgia that his obituary in the *Mississippi Valley Historical Review,* a prominent regional journal, noted that he was "author of the national law that opened the Confederate archives in the Department of War." As Rowland himself declared in 1910, ". . . while the activities of the Department embrace the care and custody of the State records since provincial days, and the records of every period are carefully preserved, no period has received more especial attention than that of the Civil War."[95] Despite recommendations from the Mississippi Historical Commission that the archives should cover all aspects of life in Mississippi—including "The Negro in Mississippi as Slave and Citizen" —Rowland concentrated his attention almost exclusively on a few topics of personal interest. For example, although the commission recommended collecting "War Records" for all conflicts, including the Indian wars, Rowland devoted the series solely to Confederate records. As Patricia Galloway concludes, in analyzing his career as state archivist, the most serious accusations that could be made against Rowland are "that he failed to obtain collections that were representative of all the people of Mississippi while they were still available to collect"; "that he looked determinedly backward to a romanticized Lost Cause of the Confederacy"; and that he failed to provide "assistance to African-American scholars," including those from state-funded colleges.[96] What Rowland's career reveals, above all, is the direct and powerful influence that a single archivist in a position of authority can wield over the records that enter the archives, those topics that remain ignored, and which researchers receive the highest level of professional service and which do not. Despite Dunbar Rowland's public embrace of European archival principles, he failed to live up to his responsibilities to the entire populace of his state.

By the 1920s a new generation of archivists entered public service, determined to follow the high standards of professional practice being imported from Europe. Foremost among these was the first state archivist of Illinois, Margaret C. Norton, who served in that capacity from 1922 until her retirement in 1957. Although trained in both history and library science, Norton argued that archivists needed to establish their own identity as a profession, separate from these "parent" disciplines. Despite their close association with history, archives also served important administrative and legal needs within government. In a 1929 conference paper, "The Archives Department as an Administrative Unit in Government," she argued that the popular misconception of archives as nothing more than historical documents blocked progress for the profession, and that "the greatest handicap . . . to getting adequate support for archives work is the belief that archives work is just another function of the state historical society." From these premises, Norton concluded that, "The archivist should be a public official whose first interest is business efficiency, and only secondarily should be interested in history."[97] Following the lead of American historian Waldo Leland and British archivist Sir Hilary Jenkinson, Norton argued that archives should be considered principally as legal and administrative records and only secondarily as historical manuscripts. By emphasizing the legal and administrative value of archives, the profession could move closer to centers of political influence and power. Although Norton disclaimed any connection to the Progressive movement, her commitment to governmental solutions to archival needs reflects the spirit of Progressivism.[98] Her influence eventually led to a widening gap between the practices of government archivists and private manuscripts curators. However, Norton emphasized these differences largely from a pragmatic need to gain funding and support for the Illinois State Archives, as an agency distinct from the State Historical Society.[99]

Despite her pragmatic reasons for emphasizing the legal and administrative—rather than historical—significance of archives, Norton strongly believed in "the necessity for accurate documentation," both for governmental efficiency and for the rights of citizens. "It is important to everyone that the records upon which he may wish to base his claim of citizenship, his parentage, his rights to old age pensions and his real estate—but to name a few items—should be preserved," she declared in 1939. Few people cared for history, except for antiquarian purposes, she continued, but everyone "does or should care for archives as legal records."[100] Norton articulated an alternative identity for archivists, free from the confining embrace of historians, who regarded archival records as mere sources of historical research. Norton recognized that they also provided essential evidence for legal and administrative purposes of government (and implicitly for other institutions), and for documenting and protecting the rights of all citizens.

Norton absorbed and then adapted European archival theory to meet American circumstances and needs. Although inspired by the American archival pioneers Waldo Leland and J. Franklin Jameson, Norton stated that the greatest influence on her thinking was English archivist Sir Hilary Jenkinson. She stated, "Hilary Jenkinson's Manual of Archives was my Bible."[101] However, Norton observed that, unlike her own struggles to establish the Illinois State Archives' authority, European archivists secured control of records with little objection from government officials. She attributed this to "the European monarchical idea that archives are the personal property of the sovereign, who may make any disposition of them by law which the central government sees fit; as opposed to the democratic idea that all records are public records and belong to the community which created them, not to the central government."[102] Norton worked diligently, both in Illinois and in national conferences of archivists, to establish a distinctive American approach to archives. By the end of her career, the concept that archives served essential legal and administrative purposes had become "a generally accepted tenet of archivists in the United States."[103] Norton herself did recognize that archives also served a historical purpose, but she regarded this as secondary to the legal benefits, which she thought more likely to secure funding and support from government officials and the public. Once people recognized how essential archival records were to guaranteeing their rights to property ownership, economic security, political freedom, and family heritage, they would ensure protection and funding for archives. This recognition, Norton realized, must begin at the grass roots and gradually percolate upward into the national public consciousness. This is one reason that public archives developed earlier at the state and local level than within the federal government.

ESTABLISHING A NATIONAL ARCHIVES

Despite the nationalist rhetoric that emerged in the post-Revolutionary generation and flowered during the northern states' defense of the Union in the Civil War, Americans continued to perceive their society largely from a local perspective. Until late in the nineteenth century most Americans lived in small towns or rural communities, constituting "a nation of loosely connected islands" rather than a truly unified nation.[104] The principal responsibilities of the federal government, once the crisis of war and Reconstruction abated, returned to gathering income and appropriating funds. Few Americans expected the government to address social ills, which in the emerging cities became the purview of urban bosses and corrupt political machines.[105] Responding to problems of political corruption, industrial "robber barons," urban blight, rapid immigration, and poverty, reformers such as the Populists, Farmers Alliance, and Progressive Party sought governmental solutions to the challenges of American life. From the Interstate Commerce Commission, established in 1887 to regulate the powerful railroads, to the Pure Food and Drug Act of 1906, the expectation that government could serve the public's interests began to take hold. Progressive reformers, in particular, sought administrative efficiency, bureaucratic order, and scientific control over these problems.[106] They made these issues matters of public policy.

The drive to establish state and municipal archives arose, in part, from this same impulse. As Americans' political horizons lifted from the local and state level to the national arena, so too did their concern for the records of the federal government. Prior to 1906, the sporadic demands for protection of federal records garnered little sustained interest. In 1810 a congressional committee appointed to examine the condition of the "ancient public records and archives of the United States" reported that these early records were "in a state of great disorder and exposure; and in a situation neither safe nor convenient nor honorable to the nation."[107] This led to construction of fireproof rooms for storing records of the state, war, and navy departments, but not to any permanent repository for federal records. For the next century, interest in protecting government records rose after each fire or other disaster causing loss or destruction of important files. The two most dramatic such disasters were a 1910 fire in Albany, which destroyed an "incalculably valuable" body of New York State records dating back to its colonial era, and a 1921 fire in the Commerce Building in Washington, which destroyed the "priceless" original census records of 1890 and damaged census records from several other decades.[108] Such disasters highlighted the danger of unprotected records, and served as examples of the need for both state and federal archives.

Once the first state archives had been established, historians renewed their efforts to secure a national archives for federal records. Shortly after its founding, the American Historical Association first turned its attention to the need for government support of research and archives. In 1895 the AHA created its first standing committee, the Historical Manuscripts Commission, which began publishing personal papers and manuscripts relating to American history. The AHA's Public Archives Commission, established in 1899 to investigate and report on the archives and public records of the state and federal governments, focused on preserving and organizing archival materials and published inventories of state archives.[109] One of the principal leaders in creating these two commissions was John Franklin Jameson, the first recipient of a PhD in History from Johns Hopkins University. As chair of the Historical Manuscripts Commission and editor of the *American Historical Review,* Jameson pointed out that the United States government displayed less concern for the publication of historical documents or the preservation of unpublished records than even the smaller countries of western Europe.[110] He argued that providing primary sources for research was essential "as prerequisite to further progress" for the historical profession.[111] Under Jameson's leadership, the AHA began a long and often frustrating campaign to establish a national archives.

After his appointment as director of the Carnegie Institution of Washington's Department of Historical Research in 1905, Jameson focused his attention on locating, describing, and publishing archival sources. To achieve his grand dreams Jameson needed a resourceful, diplomatic, and meticulous partner. He found the ideal person in Waldo G. Leland, who—at Jameson's recommendation— left Harvard after earning a master's degree in 1903 to assist Claude H. Van Tyne in compiling the *Guide to the Archives of the Government of the United States in Washington,* the first historical publication funded by the Carnegie Institution.[112] Leland's experience in compiling this inventory convinced him that essential records of the federal government would be lost to neglect or disaster without creation of a national archives.

As Jameson's assistant and collaborator for twenty-two years at the Carnegie Institution, Leland gained extensive knowledge of archival issues both in the United States and in Europe. He also served much of this time as Secretary of the AHA. From 1907 to 1914, and from 1922 to 1927, Leland coordinated the Carnegie Institution's research on sources for American history in European archives, from his office in Paris. His principal work was compiling the *Guide to Materials for American History in the Libraries and Archives of Paris.*[113] Leland patiently answered reference requests from scholars and guided novices through the research process for French archives. Although based in Paris he traveled extensively in Europe conducting archival surveys.[114]

Immersed in the archives of Europe as a researcher and bibliographer, Leland naturally established friendships with European archivists and learned their methods and precepts. As he studied archival theory he recognized its value to American practitioners, and undertook "an effort to apply European know-how in the United States."[115] Leland's extensive contacts with European archivists gradually led him to understand and endorse their principles and techniques. He attended international archives congresses and brought the concepts of provenance and original order, among others, to the attention of American archivists.

In a 1912 article Leland articulated the importance of developing a national archives for the United States. "The care which the nation devotes to the preservation of the monuments of its past may serve as a true measure of the degree of civilization it has achieved," Leland proclaimed. "The chief monument of the history of a nation is its archives, the preservation of which is recognized in all civilized countries as a natural and proper function of government."[116] Leland recognized the essential dualism of archives: that they serve both administrative and legal needs, as well as cultural and scholarly purposes. As he stated in a 1949 presentation to the American Historical Association, "The ultimate purpose of the preservation and efficient administration of the public records goes far beyond the improvement of administrative processes and the facilitation of the public business." Archives "make it possible for our present generation to have enduring and dependable knowledge of their past." Leland argued that although archivists must understand technical and administrative processes, "it is in the high ideals and purposes of scholarship and in its concern for the public good that the archivist must find his motives and seek his inspiration."[117] Archivists could thereby ensure both the rights of citizens and the "public good" as well as the needs of intellectual investigation and scholarship. These dual objectives provided the incentives for establishing a national archives. In securing congressional support for this enterprise, however, the need to protect the interests of the federal government had to be emphasized.

The effort to establish a national archives had begun with the first congressional act for protecting federal records, signed by President James Madison in 1810. Despite sporadic efforts to establish either a hall of records (to provide secure storage for governmental documents) or a federal archives (for more systematic management of agency records), advocates achieved little progress prior to J. Franklin Jameson's arrival in Washington, DC in 1906. For twenty years he provided the intellectual leadership, political skills, and driving energy behind the effort to create a national archives. The AHA and its Public Archives Commission strongly supported this campaign. In 1910 the AHA petitioned Congress to erect in Washington "a national archive depository, where the records of the Government may be concentrated, properly cared for, and preserved."[118] An AHA committee led by Jameson provided the rationale for such action: government papers were scattered in a hundred storage facilities; access to these records remained difficult; storage facilities were unsuitable for protecting documents; many records "declared to be useless" for current administration and therefore destroyed might have significant historical value; records destroyed by fire caused millions of dollars in lost claims; and the only remedy for such problems would be "a national archive commensurate with the greatness of the country and the importance of its history."[119] An editorial on "Our National Archives" in the *Nation* supported this proposed legislation, citing the lack of accessibility to governmental records, such as those in the War Department, which allowed no one to examine its records. "They are kept in greater secrecy than surrounds the archives of any European country," the *Nation* complained.[120] Despite such appeals to democratic values and national pride, Congress failed to approve the proposed national archives.

In building support for the archives plans, Jameson drafted bills and courted influential congressmen and senators. Even with backing by political leaders, however, repeated attempts to secure archival legislation passed one house but not the other. Controversy arose over the responsibilities and authority of the archival agency, over various proposed sites for an archives building, and over construction costs, among other objections. For two decades Jameson continued to press for the archives, proving to be "not only a tireless but also an ingenious lobbyist," as colleagues observed.[121] Jameson vigorously pursued the patriotic societies, including the Daughters of the American Revolution, securing their support for the archives project. During the First World War the *Military Historian and Economist* issued a lead editorial of six pages, examining problems with federal recordkeeping, indiscriminate disposal of records under wartime conditions, and the need for an archives facility. The editorial lamented that the United States "lagged behind every civilized people in the matter of housing our national records." Even though the nation had more museums, more local records repositories, and more local historians than any other country, its national records "are still wholly neglected" and "in many cases arbitrarily destroyed" merely for immediate convenience of government workers.[122] Support from such allies ultimately provided the vital political leverage needed to secure legislation for a national archives.

President Coolidge proved to be a strong supporter of archives legislation, although funding bills continued to die in committee or without support from both houses of Congress. Finally, in July 1926 an appropriations bill that included, among many other priorities, funding to construct "an extensible archives building" and acquisition of an appropriate site, passed both the House and

Senate. President Coolidge signed the bill, culminating a lengthy campaign to create a national archives.[123] The secret to success ultimately came from active support and lobbying by the American Legion. Following the First World War, Jameson had convinced American Legion leaders to support an archives facility in order to ensure protection of veterans' records, pension files, and related essential evidence. As the leading historian of the National Archives campaign concluded, "even after the AHA did start moving on the problem, by enlisting the efforts of hereditary societies and state and local historical societies, all the vocal support generated for the archival cause had a minimal influence on Congress." Without a grass-roots constituency to exert voter pressure, the professional historians lacked political clout. Even the local historical societies and patriotic organizations lacked sufficient influence to gain congressional support. The American Legion, however, could mobilize thousands of votes in each congressional district, placing it "in a position to compel a congressman to think twice about failing to support the archival demand."[124] All of the high-minded arguments, patriotic rhetoric, and appeals to citizens' rights marshaled by Jameson and his colleagues ultimately exerted far less influence than the voting power of the American Legion.

It took nearly seven years from the legislation to approve funding until the cornerstone-laying ceremony for the National Archives building. On February 20, 1933, President Herbert Hoover presided over the ceremony. "The building which is rising here will house the name and records of every patriot who bore arms for our country," he declared, in language that reflected the American Legion's support for the archives. Hoover also declared that the archives would protect "the most sacred documents of our history, the originals of the Declaration of Independence and of the Constitution of the United States," as well as "the romance of our history" and national life. "This temple of our history will . . . be one of the most beautiful buildings in America," he boasted, a symbol of the country's greatness and enduring strength.[125] The National Archives Act, approved in June 1934 by President Franklin D. Roosevelt, legally established the new federal agency. After a contested campaign among historians seeking to lead the new archives, Roosevelt appointed Professor R. D. W. Connor of the University of North Carolina as the first archivist of the United States. With completion of construction, the monumental National Archives building, located on the National Mall between Constitution and Pennsylvania avenues, finally could be occupied in November 1935.[126] The United States now had both a repository

for the essential records of American governance and public life
and a symbol of the critical importance of archives for the nation
and its people. The next step would be to determine the roles and
responsibilities of the archivists who would define the nation's
historical record and thereby shape an important part of its legal and
cultural heritage.

FORMING AN ARCHIVAL PROFESSION

The American archival profession grew out of the historical
profession. Three critical developments in the mid-1930s
shaped this new profession: the founding of the National
Archives in 1934; the surveys of public records and privately held
manuscripts by the Works Progress Administration, beginning in
1935; and the organization of the Society of American Archivists,
established in 1936.[127] The latter development deserves special
consideration, since it was principally led and sustained by archivists
themselves. The Society of American Archivists emerged as an
independent professional association from foundations laid by the
AHA's Historical Manuscripts Commission and Public Archives
Commission. The PAC established the Conference of Archivists
in 1909 as a forum to discuss archival concerns. In addition to
supporting legislation to establish state and municipal archives and
leading the movement for a national archives, the Public Archives
Commission also sponsored valuable surveys to inventory state
and local archives, and published regular reports in the American
Historical Association's *Annual Report.* Led by professional historians
on behalf of all historians seeking research sources, these inventories
and reports emphasized locating and preserving historical
documents more than organizing or administering archives.[128]

As the complexities of managing archival records gradually became
clear, archivists began to seek their own professional connections.
By 1912 Waldo Leland recognized that historians would not provide
sufficient support to meet the nation's neglected archival needs.
Their research agendas required archival source materials, but
they demonstrated little interest or concern for the managerial
and technical requirements of archival repositories. Writing in the
American Historical Review in 1912, Leland declared that he was "strongly
tempted to conclude that those who should be the best friends of
archives have but the slightest appreciation of their worth."[129] New
York State historian Victor Hugo Paltsits, a long-standing member
of the Public Archives Commission, echoed Leland, declaring:
"using archives or manuscripts is one thing, administering them
is quite another matter. The latter is an unknown quantity to the

general run of academic scholars."[130] The poor public image of the historical profession, in any case, would provide little support for archivists.

Even many of the historians most active in promoting archives seemed to have little understanding or respect for the role of archivists. Jameson himself denigrated his own role, stating that his professional calling was to prepare the ground for more accomplished scholars by developing archives and documentary publications. In self-deprecating language, Jameson wrote in 1908 that his occupation was "with the mere foundations of the historical edifice."[131] At other times he likened his work with archives and documentary editing to "long confinement at hard labor in the subterranean caverns of history," calling for "the patient steadiness of the plough-horse rather than for the wings of Pegasus."[132] Writing to acclaimed historian Henry Adams, Jameson declared, "I struggle on, making bricks without much idea of how the architects will use them, but believing that the best architect that ever was cannot get along without bricks, and therefore trying to make good ones."[133] Although this shows Jameson's personal modesty, the statement presents "an almost tangible image of steady, cumulative progress"[134] and an optimistic confidence that almost anyone could thus contribute to the historical edifice. Such sentiments perpetuated the unfortunate concept that archivists serve as menial "handmaidens" to historians. In fact, however, Jameson did recognize that those who labored in archival and documentary fields required important skills and qualities of mind and disposition.

Faced with problems concerning their public image and perceived role, many archivists by the 1930s recognized the need for a separate organization, apart from historians or librarians, to address their own concerns. Having been active in the AHA's Public Archives Commission and the Conference of Archivists, Margaret C. Norton became one of the leaders in founding a professional society for archivists. The strongest reason for an independent organization, she argued, was "because there is somewhat of a conflict of interest between what historians want and archivists need."[135] Norton contended that town clerks and other public officials provided stronger support for archives and archival interests than did historians. Only by separating from the AHA could archivists address their most pressing concerns and gain their own professional identity.

The starting point had to be development of a body of professional principles and methods to guide archival practice. Waldo Leland's speeches and writings had first articulated archival theory for an American audience. He urged the PAC to sponsor a meeting to "enable those who actually have charge of public records" to discuss technical problems connected with the administration of archives.[136] At the first Conference of Archivists, held in New York City on December 30, 1909, Leland presented a paper on "American Archival Problems," in which he endorsed the principle of provenance adopted by French, German, and Dutch archives. "The archives should be classified according to their origin; they should reflect the processes by which they came into existence," Leland declared. "Nothing is more disastrous than the application of modern library methods of classification to a body of archives."[137] In this presentation Leland began the infusion of European archival theory into the United States.[138]

Although it would take more than two decades for European concepts to gain widespread acceptance in the United States, Waldo Leland had prepared the way for development of an American archival profession.[139] European archival principles provided the framework for establishing American archives and the methodology required for archival records to serve needs broader than those of historians. Despite their reliance on European archives for theory, principles, and even building designs, both Leland and Jameson recognized that such concepts would have to be modified to fit American circumstances.[140] As T. R. Schellenberg observed, "With the establishment of the National Archives in 1934 the principles of Leland and others, which represented to a large extent views derived from European practices, were applied for the first time to a voluminous mass of modern records."[141] First translated into English in 1940, the Dutch manual on archival methodology at last became accessible to American archivists.[142]

With the founding of the National Archives in 1934, archivists finally had a flagship institutional base and the necessary sense of identity to create their own professional association. At the AHA convention of 1936, ninety-six men and twenty-nine women from twenty-three states, plus Canada and Cuba, met to form the Society of American Archivists (SAA). The new association adopted a constitution, which declared: "The objects of The Society of American Archivists shall be to promote sound principles of archival economy and to facilitate cooperation among archivists and archival agencies."[143] With this new organization, the American archival profession had achieved an identity separate from both the historical discipline, from which it had developed, and from the library profession, to which it was often linked both by common interests in information resources and by administrative organizational structures—since many manuscript and archives repositories existed within library systems.

For several decades the archival profession sought to define its role. Some continued to argue that archivists were simply "independent scholars" who provided research materials for historians. Others argued that archivists were a special class of librarians, applying technical standards for organizing, preserving, and describing unpublished materials and providing reference access. Still others saw archives as extensions of the legal department, ensuring compliance with documentation and accountability requirements. In some corporations archivists seemed valuable mainly in providing interesting historical images or quaint reminders of the past that could help in advertising, public relations, or sales.

The Society of American Archivists grew slowly, seeking to define its role on behalf of a new occupational group that had to create its own sense of identity and gain public acceptance as a socially significant profession. As a means of garnering public recognition and support, in 1942 SAA named President Franklin D. Roosevelt its first honorary member. Roosevelt thanked SAA President R. D. W. Connor—who also served as archivist of the United States—and expressed his "lifetime interest in the building up of archives throughout the nation." Following the Second World War, SAA supported establishment of the International Council on Archives (ICA) and an archives for the newly formed United Nations.[144]

During the 1960s, as social and political firestorms of change swept the United States, the archival profession slowly and cautiously began to respond. The turmoil of the civil rights movement, the Vietnam War, college free speech campaigns, and liberation movements—for women, Latinos, Native Americans, gays and lesbians, among other groups—affected the historical and library professions before it touched archivists. Historians called for new approaches and perspectives to studying the past, resulting in demands for archival sources for underrepresented social groups. This new cohort of young historians committed themselves "to listen to the voices that had been silenced by elite indifference" and to create "powerful identities for those people on the bottom who had so long been ignored."[145] As children of immigrants, laborers, and minority groups entered the historical profession, they radicalized the definition of historical scholarship. Howard Zinn, for example, declared that his experiences growing up in New York tenements, working in shipyards, serving in the military during World War II, and participating in civil rights demonstrations, "made me lose all desire for 'objectivity,' whether in living my life, or writing history." However, he vowed to maintain professional standards, scrupulous honesty, and avoid ideologically motivated history. Zinn turned to writing "people's history" in order to add information and perspectives that had been left out of most earlier works.

In a 1971 essay, "On Being a Socialist and a Historian," Eugene Genovese declared, "In fact what we stand for is the realization that all historical writing is unavoidably political intervention."[146] One challenge of presenting the perspectives of ordinary people would be to locate sufficient documentation to tell their stories.

As these new social historians of the 1960s sought to uncover the lives of those who had lived and worked in tenement houses, shop floors, sod houses, slave quarters, and barrios, they found new information resources in previously ignored corporate personnel files, local government records of births, marriages, and deaths, probate records, land titles, tax assessments, slave sales, and other "forgotten" sources. New questions about the past required fresh research, and social historians discovered that archives vaults, public records offices, and private account books contained valuable documents that no one previously had thought worthy of attention.[147] From such sources they began writing histories of the many peoples who had been marginalized and ignored by earlier researchers.

Howard Zinn and Sam Bass Warner brought this radical view of history to the annual meeting of the Society of American Archivists in 1971. Zinn challenged his audience with the argument that the archivist's "supposed neutrality" was "a fake." As he contended, "the existence, preservation, and availability of archives, documents, records in our society are very much determined by the distribution of wealth and power" and archival collections were "biased towards the important and powerful people of the society, tending to ignore the impotent and obscure."[148] Using Progressive era reformer Lincoln Steffens' phrase "The Shame of the Cities" as his title, Warner argued that in respect to urban studies, historians and archivists had "made themselves comfortable with the classic concerns of famous politicians, leading families, reformers, and the patronage of high culture to the neglect of the essential issues that determine everyday life in American cities." Current sources underrepresented the experience of ordinary people, Warner continued. "If archivists are to escape being the prisoner of their record sources they must become aggressive collectors of current as well as past material," and "we must seek the records and papers of the Panthers, Post Office strikers, welfare mothers, anti-school-busing pickets, and so forth."[149] Radical historians thus challenged archivists to re-examine their assumptions and policies, which reinforced the status quo of elite power relationships, and to engage actively in balancing the documentary record with the voices of marginalized groups.

A small but influential cadre of archivists heeded the call to social activism and sought to define their own profession's perspective. Writing in the *American Archivist* in 1975, former SAA President F. Gerald Ham complained that "archival holdings too often reflected narrow research interests rather than the broad spectrum of human experience." Ham argued that the archivist should "fill in the gaps" by becoming "a historical reporter for his own time," using such techniques as creating oral history, generating a photographic record of otherwise undocumented topics, and collecting survey data on contemporary events. In order to meet the challenges of the future, "the archivist must realize that he can no longer abdicate his role in this demanding intellectual process of documenting culture," and that archivists could not remain "passive, uninformed, with a limited view of what constitutes the archival record."[150] Other archivists, including Patrick Quinn and Archie Motley, followed Ham in supporting a more activist approach to archival endeavors.

Archivists also began to demand a more open and democratic leadership within SAA. In 1971 a group of socially concerned members formed ACT, an informal group of "activist archivists" to seek changes in SAA's internal operations and to encourage the association to take positions on political and social issues.[151] "Activist archivists are those archivists who persistently seek to address major social concerns of the archival profession and the public it serves and to improve their own work places, their professional organizations, and the archival profession in general," Motley later declared. He advocated for public ownership of the president's papers, the equal rights amendment, a nuclear freeze resolution, and efforts to eliminate the sexist "old boy" system within SAA, and insisted that these issues "are very proper subjects for consideration by members of a professional organization."[152] The social and political ferment of the 1960s had penetrated the often conservative realms of the archival profession, and a growing number of archivists challenged the old order and called for social action on behalf of archival service to the public interest.

These demands to make the archival profession more responsive to social changes and public policy concerns coincided with significant demographic changes beginning to affect the profession. Rapid expansion of American colleges and universities under the GI Bill in the post-World War II era led, by the 1960s, to increased funding for academic and research pursuits. Institutions of higher learning established manuscript collections and archival programs, seemingly as a symbol of their intellectual ambitions, in order to promote research for both students and faculty. As the dominant leadership of federal and state archivists within SAA began to dwindle, archivists in new repositories—mainly academic, but also new business and religious archives—gained greater influence. By 1970, one-third of SAA members worked for colleges and universities, while only 13.5 percent came from state archives. By 1971, SAA reached a milestone of one thousand members.[153] These new members sought new programs and services from SAA, and began to agitate for a stronger representation of social conscience issues within the profession.

In response to such concerns, SAA President Philip Mason appointed the Committee for the 1970's, which issued its final report in 1972. The committee recommended increasing SAA's effectiveness by hiring an executive director rather than relying on unpaid volunteers; conducting contested elections with dual nominees for positions; opening up committee membership to more members; expanding the publications and education programs of SAA; developing guidelines and standards for professional practice; and creating more opportunities for younger and newer members to participate. The committee also addressed concerns for "social relevance," suggesting that "SAA should be actively committed to the social goals of racial justice, equal employment, and reasonable access to research materials. . . . To this end, the SAA has a moral obligation to take official positions on those contemporary public issues, however controversial, which affect the archival profession."[154] Soon after this, SAA established a Committee on the Status of Women, promoted recruitment of minorities into the profession, and endorsed a comprehensive resolution to end discrimination within the organization on the basis of "race, color, religion, national origin, sex, marital status, age, life style, or political affiliation."[155]

In 1974 SAA fulfilled another recommendation of the Committee for the 1970's by hiring Ann Morgan Campbell as its first paid executive director, with an office in Chicago. The archival profession, represented by its national professional association, thus grappled with the social upheavals of the time by accepting the responsibility to engage actively in those public policy debates that affected either archival records or those responsible for their management and care. SAA would continue to voice concerns— not always consistently, but at least occasionally—regarding such socio-political issues as the equal rights amendment, nuclear proliferation, public funding for archives and records programs, and access to public records. For example, at the 1978 business meeting SAA members passed a resolution supporting ratification of the equal rights amendment and voted to ban all future meetings of the Society from states that had not passed the amendment. "Archival advocacy had transformed archivists from being haphazard in their focus on pertinent archival legislation in the 1960s to being publicly forceful defenders of citizens' rights inside and outside the purview of the archival domain," observes one historian of the archival profession.[156] Archivists began to assert themselves both within the profession and in relationships with allied professions. They also sought to define and clarify their role in society at large.

SEEKING AN IDENTITY FOR ARCHIVISTS

Many of the important developments in the field since the early 1980s either derived from or eventually contributed to archivists' quest for professional identity and recognition. At times this effort stirred passionate debates over the nature of American archives, the role of archivists in society, the relationship between archives and other professions, and the education necessary for archivists, among other topics.[157]

In order to take advantage of outreach opportunities to assist researchers, archivists recognized that they needed to investigate their research constituencies, rather than operate under possibly false assumptions about who did or could make use of archival sources. Lawrence Dowler outlined a research agenda related to the availability and use of records, suggesting that archivists need to answer such questions as: "What do users use, how do they use it, what do they do with what they use, and how do they find their way to the archives in the first place? Who, in fact, are archival users?"[158] Conducting user studies of the type suggested would require systematic research rather than relying on impressionistic or anecdotal evidence. This type of formal research was exactly what some American archivists had recently begun to advocate as a means of enhancing archival practice and strengthening its basis in archival theory.

The initial resistance of American archivists to archival theory had deep roots in American history. Since the founding of the colonies, many Americans have believed in their own exceptionalism and the irrelevance of European approaches to solving American problems. The Revolution severed ties with a monarchical and hierarchical Europe, where rulers and nobility enjoyed rights and privileges that offended the American quest for democracy and egalitarianism. The distrust of external authority heightened the individualism that has largely defined the American character. Americans think of themselves as practical, innovative, and resourceful people who can solve their own problems. This American pragmatism, which sometimes appears as a strain of anti-intellectualism, has strengthened the egalitarian disdain for overarching theory. According to J. Rogers Hollingsworth, "most Americans of the eighteenth and nineteenth centuries placed a premium on such non-intellectual tendencies as rough and ready habits, rapid decisions, and quick seizure of opportunities. Experience was preferred to speculation, pragmatism to idealism, the inventor to the pure scientist."[159] These national characteristics led many twentieth-century American archivists to believe that they must solve problems unique to their times and their society, and to adopt European practices selectively.

This is precisely the approach that Harold Pinkett—the first African American elected to SAA Council—applauded in a 1981 article. Pinkett began by quoting Max Lerner: "In the European sense Americans have had little 'grand theory,' whether of the state, the economy, the society, the culture, Nature, or God." Pinkett observed, "American theory has evolved essentially from European archival principles adapted to deal with unique characteristics of American record-making and record-keeping practices, from concepts of the democratization of the use of archival materials, and from innovative thinking about archival interest in the management of current and semi-current records."[160] Thus, Pinkett accepted the pragmatic nature of American archival practice as a culturally influenced phenomenon. To be American is to be practical, not theoretical. It also means seeking individualistic solutions rather than accepting collectivistic standards.

This apparent conflict between theory and practicality, and between individualism and collectivism, has led some American archivists to a crisis of professional identity. They see archivists in Europe and Canada enjoying a clearer sense of professional purpose, a greater unity of agreed upon principles and methods, and a stronger recognition and respect from the public. The United States remains a relatively young nation, and Americans continue to focus attention on the future and to regard the past with suspicion or disdain. Part of this comes from the Revolutionary War heritage, in which a new democratic nation shed its ties to a European past in order to forge a new egalitarian identity committed to a better future for mankind. When they have paid attention to their own history, Americans have often filtered it through patriotic or nostalgic lenses, or have imagined conspiracies and dark secrets. Examples of these tendencies abound, from Disneyland's Main Street USA to Oliver Stone's film *JFK*. Such popular culture approaches to history run diametrically opposed to the realm of archives, which values evidence, authenticity, and historical objectivity.[161]

The search for professional identity has led American archivists to develop external initiatives to increase public awareness of archival resources and services, partly in order to obtain increased funding and higher salaries. Within the profession there have been initiatives to improve standards of archival practice. Whether explicitly or implicitly, these efforts have often been closely related to underlying goals of increasing professionalism and gaining public recognition. This process of professionalization can be understood by examining its three broad manifestations: developing internal standards for professional recognition; enhancing the public image of archives and archivists; and strengthening the research and theoretical foundations of the profession.

By the late 1970s American archivists had identified three potential internal standards by which archivists and their institutions could be judged worthy of professional status. These standards could measure the professionalism of archival education programs (guidelines for graduate education), of individual archivists (certification), and of archival repositories (institutional evaluation). Although some archivists supported only one or two of these methods, those who advocated all three believed that in combination they would provide a strong basis for defining minimum standards for professionalization of archivists and archival institutions. However, there was no common agreement on these proposed methods for setting professional standards, not even universal acceptance that any such efforts were needed or practicable. Such disagreements led to heated discussions that still continue within the American archival profession, even though two of the three internal standards have been adopted.

While efforts to establish internal professional standards for archivists were under way, American archivists had also begun a more systematic approach to planning for the profession. In 1982 SAA established a Task Force on Goals and Priorities, which published its recommendations, under the title *Planning for the Archival Profession*, in 1986. Seeking to promote consensus on archival goals and objectives, the task force sought to clarify the professional identity of American archivists. The first step was to define a mission for the entire profession: "To ensure the identification, preservation, and use of records of enduring value." The task force's report identified broad goal statements for this three-fold mission, with fifteen objectives and dozens of activities needed to achieve these goals and objectives. The report also listed priorities for action. One of the basic assumptions outlined in *Planning for the Archival Profession* was that archives needed greater public support. "Present conditions, which are inadequate to ensure the identification and preservation of archival records, will not improve unless there is greater support for archival activity from outside the archival community," the report stated.[162] The necessity of public support for archival programs and collections led SAA to undertake a year-long examination of the role of archives and archivists in American society.

ARCHIVES AND SOCIETY INITIATIVE

Concerned with their professional identity, archivists had begun efforts to enhance their public image and recognition as members of a profession that provides significant benefits to society. The problems seemed daunting. Frustrated by years of neglect, by inadequate funding and institutional support, and by popular stereotypes of archivists as dusty inhabitants of underground caverns, archivists asked how these images could be changed. Waldo G. Leland had noted in 1917 that historical scholarship was regarded as "a harmless, though amiable pursuit, but one of little 'practical' use," and "the student of history as a person who, having too few red corpuscles in his blood, is content to bury his head in the dust of the past, oblivious to the interests and exigencies of the present."[163] Archivists now faced a similar image problem. A series of archival needs assessment grants in two dozen states had revealed troubling problems with funding and awareness of archives. As William Joyce concluded after reviewing the state reports regarding historical manuscripts repositories: "Lack of public understanding and regard leads to underfunding of historical records repositories and underutilization of their holdings."[164] The situation was no better in state archives, as Alabama state archivist Ed Bridges concluded:

"The assessment reports show little evidence that we have clearly defined the products of our work or have convincingly demonstrated their value to our states." Bridges compared the funding problems of state archives to the "cycle of poverty" found in many developing countries.[165]

Changing the stereotypes seemed essential to gain greater visibility and support for their important work. In 1984 SAA President David Gracy announced formation of a Task Force on Archives and Society, which would examine these concerns and suggest remedies. The task force charge included drafting a statement on "the importance of archives to and in society," and proposing "ways and means that we—as individuals, as professionals in our societies, and as employees of our institutions—can use to raise public awareness, appreciation, understanding, and support of archival work." As Gracy declared, "The archival service to society—the obtaining, preserving, and making available of the permanently valuable records and papers of our institutions and our people—has fallen to its saddest condition since modern archival institutions took root in this country fifty years ago with the founding of our National Archives."[166]

One of the major initiatives of the Task Force on Archives and Society was to commission a survey of resource allocators, those administrators who controlled the budgets of archival repositories, to determine their attitudes toward archives and archivists. This study, conducted by Sidney Levy and Albert G. Robles, concluded that resource allocators viewed archives as useful and important, but also saw archivists as quiet, benign, and powerless: "Archivists are perceived as quiet [and] professional, carrying out an admired but comparatively subterranean activity." Archivists would not be likely to demand additional resources and support, and thus could not compete successfully with programs that seemed more essential to an institution's existence and success. As Levy and Robles concluded in their report, *The Image of Archivists,* archivists faced significant obstacles both in securing the necessary funding to maintain and expand their programs and in gaining public recognition as a dynamic and significant profession. Part of the problem was that, "Archivists' professional identity is unclear." To overcome this, Levy and Robles recommended, "archivists need to define more coherent identity objectives, and communicate greater freshness and distinctiveness in imagery by their training, programs, self-assertion, publicity, advertising, and relevance to modern life." The problem was not just how to project a more positive image, but how to reach agreement on exactly what image the profession wished to send forth. In order to improve their status, archivists would have to become unabashed promoters of archives. "Archivists need to translate their importance into more power," Levy and Robles advised. "That requires more self-assertion, more concerted action, being less sympathetic to or understanding of the resource allocators' budget problems."[167] A recent study of popular literature confirmed that these stereotypes and images of archivists persist in the public imagination.[168] The public image of archives and archivists thus suggests stagnation and irrelevance.

The Task Force on Archives and Society suggested steps to overcome these unflattering stereotypes. The starting point would be self-assessment. Archivists re-evaluated how they looked at themselves as professionals. They could enhance their prestige by building on the profession's perceived virtues and by using archival knowledge and skills to gain a competitive edge. Archivists would need to communicate their needs more effectively to resource allocators. In addition archival outreach suggested opportunities to present a more positive image of the profession both to researchers and to other constituencies.[169] By presenting archives as important repositories of essential evidence for institutions and of research materials for a wide range of potential users, archivists sought to overcome the negative images. Public visibility required outreach and advocacy.

In 1987 David Gracy summarized the difficulties facing archivists in changing public perceptions, but offered glimpses of how it could be accomplished. "The society in which we live and which we serve is uncertain of the need for, value of, and use of archives," Gracy reported. He cited several authors who presented negative metaphors to describe archives: archives are trash, and archivists find value in documents and papers that others discard; archives are things people don't care about; and archives are "words and doodles" in "the ultimate attic."[170] These writers thought they were complimenting archivists, yet their disdain clearly showed. By contrast, Gracy cited a journalist's report on the National Archives: "To read original documents from the Archives is to bring to life the drums and gunfire of a thousand battles, the laughter and exaltation of a million immigrants." This recognition of the personal connection to the past that archives offer illustrates one value of archives. Yet archives also provide broad cultural benefits. César Gutiérrez Muñoz, former chief of Peru's national archives, "set a bold example," Gracy stated, in his 1987 Christmas card. "Without a before, now did not exist and even less tomorrow.

The archives, whose groups [of records] document the various aspects of the passing of humanity, give meaning to this inescapable continuity," Gutiérrez Muñoz declared. "Consequently, their preservation, organization, and use is a thing of transcendent importance, or said in other words, something of life or death." On the envelope of the Christmas card was a stamped message: "Care of the documentary patrimony of the nation is the obligation of all Peruvians."[171] Clearly, Gracy thought this should become a motto for all archivists. Only by taking such bold and positive positions could archivists hope to overcome apathy, neglect, or—perhaps worst—well-intentioned pats on the back, thanking them for being such selfless servants of the past.

CHALLENGES OF THE DIGITAL AGE

Perhaps the most challenging negative image faced by archivists in recent decades is that they represent a fossilized remnant of ancient scribal practices irrelevant in the "modern" technological age. The ubiquity of computer technology and its offspring—from laptop computers to hand-held scanners, text messaging, Web 2.0, blogs, wikis, social tagging, Flickr, and iPhones—seemingly relegates archives to a technological dead-end street. Bypassing traditionally credentialed gatekeepers of cultural knowledge, these seemingly more democratic technologies actually make the quest for reliable and authentic knowledge more difficult. Reliance on new forms of communication often obscures the fact that knowledge has always involved connecting people more than simply collecting bits of information.[172] According to numerous reports, the information revolution created by rapid technological change is as profound and pervasive as the development of writing, the invention of movable type and printing, or the industrial revolution.[173] Dramatic new innovations have created widespread reliance on information technology and digital records. These technological challenges affect archivists around the globe, but they pose special difficulties for American archivists, who already face public indifference from a population desperate to rush forward into the future without a glance over the shoulder.

Perhaps ironically, considering their cachet as barometers of modern technology, computers owe their origins to ancient technologies for counting, accounting, and communicating. By the nineteenth century character codes enabled the telegraph to transmit messages almost instantly over great distances. For the first time in human history, information could be transmitted faster than the speed of human travel.[174] In the early twentieth

century, teleprinters—such as AT&T's teletype, developed in
the 1920s—eliminated the need for human translation of coded
messages. However, the first modern digital computers emerged
in the 1940s, with the ENIAC computer, designed during the
Second World War to calculate artillery firing tables. As researchers
developed increasingly sophisticated computers, the output media
for both programs and data shifted from punched cards to magnetic
tape and paper.[175] In a groundbreaking 1945 essay, Vannevar Bush
envisioned a mechanized private filing system, which he called a
"memex." Prefiguring desktop computers and electronic filing
systems, the memex would be "a device in which an individual stores
his books, records, and communications, and which is mechanized
so that it may be consulted with exceeding speed and flexibility. It is
an enlarged intimate supplement to his memory."[176] This definition
of the memex could apply equally to later computers and to archival
repositories. Both provide a form of memory and access to such
stored information.

The basic architecture of digital documents emerged by the late
1960s, when digitally encoded text could be stored on external
media such as computer discs, tapes, and cards. Exchanging data
between computers, unless physically linked to a mainframe
network, remained difficult if not impossible until development of
Arpanet—a forerunner of the Internet—in the 1960s.[177] These and
other technological breakthroughs barely registered on archivists'
radar screens until the 1960s, and even then only a few considered
the development of computer systems relevant to archival practice.

Meanwhile, changes occurred incrementally in recordkeeping
practices, first in scientific and academic research and then in
business and government. At first these new computer systems
seemed esoteric and alien, things best left to technicians and
engineers. Analog metaphors and practices persisted. Computer
printouts, rather than computer tapes or other electronic media,
seemed to be "the record" needed for documentation purposes—if
such needs were even considered. For many years the mindset
persisted, sometimes still actively in certain institutions, that the
proper means for maintaining records of electronic systems is to
print the data in paper form rather than to preserve data in digital
form. Computer tapes, for example, might be kept as a backup, but
not as the proper evidence or record of transactions.[178]

One important archival institution did recognize, at least in part,
the significance of these technological changes for archival practice.
The National Archives—known as the National Archives and Records

Service (NARS) from a 1950 reorganization, which placed it under the General Services Administration until 1985, when it gained independence from GSA—responded to the surge of federal data processing technology by claiming that "machine-readable data was already covered by the legal definition of record," and thus fell within the purview of the Archives. Meyer Fishbein, former director of military archives at NARS, stated that by 1964 he was convinced that data tapes constituted official government records and that federal agencies were creating machine-readable records having permanent value. Fishbein recognized that these new records would enlarge the user base for the National Archives, particularly among policy makers dependent on the new computer systems. By 1968 NARS created a data archives staff, which developed into a Machine-Readable Archives Branch in 1974. Unfortunately, the resources available for NARS's electronic records initiatives dwarfed in comparison to the challenges of rapidly evolving technology. Even short-term preservation of magnetic tapes required vast expenditures, and access to such data required agencies to operate their own expensive equipment. The National Archives assumed that mainframe computers, operating with magnetic tape, would produce records in the form of flat file databases. On all three points, the direction taken by information technology confounded NARS's expectations.[179] This result largely prevented the archival profession from responding effectively to the emerging digital age, and limited its ability to help shape the recordkeeping systems of the late twentieth century.

As the electronic future took shape, archivists—like other professionals whose responsibilities it would transform—tried to guess which new developments would become standards for further expansion and which would be dead ends. One critical concern for archivists was whether electronic recordkeeping would transform and overturn their traditional methods and concepts or merely require some adjustments to keep up with new developments. This is still an openly contested issue, so it is little surprise that archivists in the 1970s and 1980s could not achieve consensus. However, as Thomas Hickerson declared in his SAA presidential address in 2000, if archivists could demonstrate leadership regarding how to manage electronic records they would "be recognized as a source of much-needed expertise and reliability in an area of increasingly critical importance to the functioning of contemporary society."[180] There has long been a tension between archivists' hope that they could untangle the complex challenges posed by electronic records and their recognition that computer systems designers rarely considered archival concerns.

The first step in addressing digital challenges requires determining how electronic records have altered the recordkeeping landscape. Some experts argue that fundamental changes have occurred in how records are created, maintained, and used. In his 2006 SAA presidential address, Richard Pearce-Moses observed that familiar formats have been transformed in the digital environment. Correspondence, diaries, typescripts, and reports have been replaced, respectively, by e-mail, blogs, word processing files, and web pages. He concluded, "The advent of technology has fundamentally changed the nature of records and recordkeeping."[181] One prediction made a generation ago has not occurred. The idea of a completely paperless office has proven to be a myth. Although the volume of electronic information has increased exponentially in recent decades, the quantity of paper-based information and communications continues to grow, albeit at a slower rate. Paper remains important because it makes information readily accessible, manipulable, and flexible. Paper also gives information "a persistent presence."[182] One of the significant changes brought by digital formats is that text and physical format "have been pulled apart," so that the stability of documents must be established and maintained virtually rather than tangibly.[183] "Digital materials have undergone a kind of schizophrenic split," David Levy observes, separating the digital representation of documents from their perceptible forms. Without proper care, digital media degrade and become inaccessible after a few years. Efforts to "guarantee fixity and permanence" are just beginning to show results.[184] Another prominent difference is the instability of digital documents, which have been created on hardware and software platforms that are volatile and quickly become obsolete.[185] The digital objects of contemporary society are "the incunabula of a not-too-distant tomorrow . . . the refuse of our restless and inconsolable appetite for change and immortality," according to a recent history of libraries.[186]

Research projects to develop methods and standards for ensuring reliability and accountability in electronic recordkeeping, vast by archival standards though not in relation to other technology programs, have pulled apart the principles and concepts of archival theory in order to find workable solutions. These remain in developmental stages, despite some valuable progress.[187] Meanwhile, as digital technologies infiltrate every corner of the globe, their effect is to destabilize institutions and practices that depend on the stability that documents are supposed to provide.[188] New technologies sometimes produce widespread impacts. For example, as John Seely Brown and Paul Duguid point out, the photocopier did not just replace carbon paper, it "transformed the way people used documents to organize work—as the Web is doing once again."[189] Such transformations affect both those using the new documentary forms in their daily work and the archivists who must ensure the longevity of records having ongoing value for legal, administrative, accountability, or historical purposes.

As early as 1979, a conference on archival management of machine-readable records concluded that traditional archival theory could be "applied satisfactorily" to organizing and accessing computer-generated records, but that traditional practices required adjustments.[190] "The traditional archival principles—evidential and informational values, provenance, levels of arrangement and description—continue to undergird archival practice," Trudy Huskamp Peterson, a prominent National Archives leader, confirmed a decade later. "That practice will continue to grow and change, but the principles will endure."[191] However, other archivists saw the technological shift to electronic records as an opportunity to "reinvent archives." The growing gap between archivists' social responsibility—"ensuring adequate documentation of our society"—and the meager resources available to accomplish this task led David Bearman and Margaret Hedstrom, among others, to seek alternatives to traditional archival practice. Using the "reinventing government" initiative proposed by David Osborne and Ted Gaebler as a model, Bearman and Hedstrom proposed cost-saving approaches such as "steering" policy rather than "rowing"; moving from expensive custodial programs to decentralized management of electronic records; adopting enterprising and customer-driven approaches to service delivery; and focusing on guiding organizational behavior rather than administering physical material.[192] These proposals, if adopted by archivists, would replicate some of the concepts of e-government, which delivers government information and services online through the Internet, radically altering both services provided and customer expectations.[193]

Few radical changes have thus far occurred in archival praxis. Almost a decade into the twenty-first century, archives are still beginning the process of adapting to the digital age. Many archival concepts remain valid. The technology shift from paper to electronic records has altered how we create archives, how we use them, and how we think about archives. Yet archives have always been products of technology. "The Web is infinitely more flexible than the clay tablet," observes historian of technology Steven Lubar, "but similar in its recording of the structures of power."[194] Recordkeeping has always depended upon technology, from clay tablets and parchment to paper and photographic film, from wax seals and codices to filing cabinets and digital video discs. Each new form of technology solved some problems of the old technology and created some new ones. As John Seely Brown and Paul Duguid observe, new technologies typically "augment or enhance existing tools and practices rather than replace them."[195] In efforts to ease the transition from old to new systems, digital technologies adopt conventions and terminology from their analog predecessors. The World Wide Web, for example, mimics books and paper documents, borrowing from the older technology terms such as web pages, bookmarks, indexes, and tables of contents.[196]

Many core concepts of archival practice continue to be useful in managing digital resources. "The introduction of electronic records does not appear to have changed in fundamental ways the underlying meaning of 'recordness,' at least not yet," states information management expert Richard Barry, even though dramatic changes in record making technologies will change how organizations conduct their recordkeeping.[197] As Brown and Duguid argue, "Documents not only serve to make information but also to warrant it—to give it validity." They serve a social role of attesting to reliability. "More intriguing, perhaps, documents also help structure society, enabling social groups to form, develop, and maintain a sense of shared identity," they conclude.[198] These characteristics remain unchanged whatever the medium of record. With electronic information, the essential archival functions of ensuring trustworthiness, reliability, and accountability through recordkeeping can be documented using metadata, according to Minnesota state archivist Robert Horton.[199]

Archivists have begun, with mixed success, to join the national debate over the future of digital information and recordkeeping. Research projects relating to electronic records and digital archives, such as the international InterPARES project and those conducted at the University of Pittsburgh, Indiana University, and elsewhere, have provided a clearer theoretical base for future planning. In addition to these academic projects, several state archives have established electronic records programs at operational levels, and the National Archives and Records Administration has launched a major Electronic Records Archives project to improve recordkeeping throughout the federal government.[200] Archivists have also begun to turn their attention to born-digital records, digital curation, and digital archives. These challenges require increasingly sophisticated understanding of information and communications technologies.[201] Archivists are experimenting with developing separate facilities devoted to digital records, such as the Washington State Digital Archives.[202] Such innovations bring archives into direct interaction with computer systems designers, information technologists, and other technical experts.

Archivists will be left behind by rapid technological change unless they demand that their voices be heard and their professional perspectives considered by those planning the digital future. "The time has come for archivists to reassert their interests and expertise with the documentary aspects and issues associated with preserving and accessing the human record," Anne Gilliland-Swetland declared in 1995. Archivists should assume a leadership role in cooperative programs with colleagues in related disciplines, such as computing, communications, organizational theory, library and information science, and records management.[203] The challenges facing archivists are significant. "Today we live in an Amazoogle world, where people expect comprehensive information, accessible 24/7, offering immediate gratification, and customized to the consumer," reports Richard Pearce-Moses.[204] Archivists need to watch the horizon for important trends and changes, to embrace technology, to find creative and practical approaches to new technologies, and to plan and evaluate methods to meet patrons' needs. Core archival principles remain appropriate, Pearce-Moses argues. How archivists perform their responsibilities will change to meet the demands of the digital age, but what they do and why they do it will remain the same.[205] Archivists can bring to these discussions their expertise based on centuries of archival development, the growing awareness and understanding of society's need for reliable evidence and documentation, and techniques developed out of necessity and refined by practice and experimentation. The history of archives in American society thus shows the continuing quest for professional identity and for a means of explaining the value of archival principles, resources, and services to the wider society.

ARCHIVES IN CONTEMPORARY SOCIETY

The technology of making records has changed dramatically over the past three millennia, but the essential human impulse to record information remains largely constant. Whether entrusting information to clay tablets, carved stone, papyrus, parchment, paper, photographic emulsions, sound recordings, computer hard drives, or electronic impulses, people have sought reliable methods for preserving, transmitting, and using recorded knowledge. People create records for a variety of reasons. Some records serve a personal need to ensure our memory of events, people, or ideas. From shopping lists to vacation photographs, from "to do" lists to personal diaries (including blogs and Facebook pages), we create documents so that we can consult them later at our convenience.[206] In examining the ancient archives of the "great river cultures of the Nile and of the Euphrates and Tigris," Ernst Posner identified six basic types of records, which have remained constant since then in western governmental, religious, and economic institutions. These include: formal laws of the land; records created as evidence of administrative action; financial and accounting records; documentation of land ownership and taxation; records facilitating control over persons for military service, labor, or personal taxes; and "notarial" records of state agencies to protect private business transactions between individuals.[207] Similar types of records—and recordkeeping—can be found throughout history, from the "royal skins" of Persian kings, to registers of the popes, to chancery rolls of English kings, to computer databases of the American Internal Revenue Service.

Among the earliest known motives for creating records are economic needs to confirm financial and property transactions. From personal IOUs to bills, receipts, investment reports, and tax returns, economic records remain prominent among personal papers. Modern organizations could not survive without sophisticated recordkeeping systems to track financial and administrative activities. Another significant motive for creating records comes from legal matters. Governments create vast quantities of records in order to ensure order and control through the governance process. Such legal records can protect citizens' rights in a democracy, but they can also control and manipulate people (for example, secret police files in totalitarian states and surveillance records in both authoritarian and democratic nations). Many records serve utilitarian or functional purposes. Examples include architectural drawings and blueprints, scientific data, maps, and navigation charts.[208]

Some personal records are intended only for our private use, while others are created to communicate directly with others, either specific individuals or a wider audience, such as Internet users. Many records are socially created, intended for purposes such as the activities of organizations. The process of creating records confirms the social linkages among people and the records themselves may serve to create or sustain both formal and imagined communities.[209] Beyond these utilitarian purposes, many people create records for symbolic purposes. Family bibles with genealogical notations, Christmas and birthday cards, and school diplomas remind us of events, family members, friends, or pleasant experiences. We create and save them for their sentimental appeal, as reminders of days past, not for any functional usefulness. They aid our memory, they represent important aspects of our lives, and they contribute to our sense of identity, both individually and collectively as members of a family, a community, or a nation.

The vast majority of documents and records serve a temporary usefulness, after which they are destroyed, either deliberately or through neglect. Personal IOUs, for example, can be destroyed after the temporary loan is repaid. Bills, receipts, and many other financial documents are no longer needed after the financial transaction has been completed or audited. Records necessary for tax returns or government regulatory oversight must be retained for a specified time period, after which they can be destroyed. Corporations often dispose of business records once their legal requirements have been met, in order to avoid unwanted future liabilities. On a personal level, romantic souvenirs and letters might be discarded after a relationship ends. The impulse to destroy often equals the desire to preserve documents and records.

Nonetheless, there are important legal, financial, administrative, personal, and historical reasons to save some records longer than others. We preserve records because they contain information or associations that we might need in the future. Protecting legal rights and requirements necessitates careful attention to laws and regulations governing recordkeeping. Financial interests impel both organizations and individuals to retain documentation of their economic concerns. Efficient and effective administration of organizations, from the corner grocery to global corporations, demands adequate documentation of operations, planning, decision-making, and other functions. Individuals seek to retain documents important to their personal lives or those with sentimental value. People who lose their homes to fire or floods often express the greatest regret over losing irreplaceable family photographs, scrapbooks, diaries, and memorabilia. Such relics enable us to recollect the past and to maintain collective or personal associations valuable either for organizational or individual purposes. Documentation of our own experiences also offers some reassurance that our lives have purpose and meaning beyond the present day, that those who come after us might remember what we have done. As an Egyptian scribe wrote four thousand years ago, "A man has perished and his body has become earth. All his relatives have crumbled to dust. It is writing that makes him remembered."[210]

Such concern for potential immortality can be a powerful motivation, but it rarely affects the human process of recording information. Above all, records are a method by which people communicate. They serve a social purpose as "intentional substitutes for speech," according to James O'Toole and Richard Cox:

> Records are ways of addressing other people in different times and places, even the other people we ourselves become with the passage of time. Archival records are preserved, therefore, not for their own sake or to satisfy some mystical need to save evidences of earlier times. Rather, records are preserved to be used, and their useful life does not end as they enter the archives.[211]

The archives in which we preserve records of human activity thus represent "fundamental aspects of human life and society," those essential qualities that define us as individuals, as groups, and as human beings. "Because of this intimate connection with the processes of life that produce them, archives and manuscripts are alive with human nature in all its diversity," O'Toole and Cox declare. "Understanding archives and manuscripts opens the door to understanding ourselves, and that remains one of the enduring challenges and joys of archives work."[212] Archivists thus contribute to social and cultural heritage, as well as legal and administrative benefits for organizations, government agencies, and all citizens.

Several important themes emerge from this review of the historical role of archives and archivists in American society. For the most part, recordkeeping has served the interests of those in positions of power, from political and governmental leaders to corporate and institutional executives, and from academic and intellectual arbiters of culture to technology experts who establish information systems. Documents have significance as "unchanging" conveyors of facts and evidence, although we now recognize the selectivity and cultural biases that shape what we have regarded as "historical" as well as the mediation of archivists.

Archives were initially established both for patriotic motives (including veneration of Revolutionary heroes) and to validate and enshrine the social and political elite's concept of the past. This power-knowledge connection remains strong but is often overlooked or denied. To most citizens it remains invisible. As concern for the past emerged after the American Revolution, two competing but complementary modes of preserving historical documents provided options to meet separate needs. Protecting rare or unique materials and making them widely available for distribution motivated historical editors to publish documentary sources. Concern for preserving original records led others to focus on establishing archival repositories, which ensured the survival of irreplaceable documents and made them available under supervised and managed oversight at given locations.

Despite nationalistic appeals for distinctly American solutions to documentary and archival needs, American archives have never operated independently of concern for European sources. Even Jeremy Belknap, founder of the first historical society in the United States, recognized that America's early history was locked up in the British State Papers Office and other European archives. Historians and archivists from Jared Sparks and Francis Parkman to Waldo Leland have surveyed and copied European documents for use in American historical research. By the twentieth century Leland and Ernst Posner brought European archival concepts to the United States, although it took two generations before these principles and practices gained widespread acceptance.

Throughout these developments leading to a small but important archival profession, archivists often denied or failed to recognize their own impact on the ecology of recordkeeping in American society. The powerful roles of archivists as mediators and gatekeepers—even when they have tried to hide behind cloaks of neutrality or invisibility—belie the Jenkinsonian ideal of the disinterested, impartial, and virtually passive archivist, transparently "making available" the archival sources required by researchers. By recognizing these powerful historical traditions and the hidden pressures to serve the powerful groups in society, archivists may emerge from this with a better understanding of what they do, and why. This examination of the historical uses of documents, of the development of archives, and of the role of the archivist may help them to understand their own place in history. Archival records can provide a corrective to popular myths and collective memory. In the same way, accounts of the development of the archival profession may provide a more accurate assessment of their role in contemporary society.

The following chapters examine these conceptualizations of archives and the role(s) of archivists in society. One of the enduring beliefs regarding archives is that they enshrine "the truth" in unchanging forms that provide accurate evidence from the past. As stated publicly—and attested by their footnotes—historians, legal researchers, and other investigators rely on the integrity of records preserved in archives for much of their contemporaneous sources of information about the past. Neither historians nor attorneys trust unaided human memory, which requires documentary evidence for corroboration.[213] Given this reliance on documents and archives, the process by which they are compiled and preserved deserves careful scrutiny. Documents and archives have been used repeatedly to consolidate the power and authority of the state and of other powerful groups in society. Thus, the emphasis on records as agents of truth needs to be examined within a political context. The power conferred by knowledge makes records creation and preservation a significant locus for political influence in society. Archives thus need to be evaluated as centers of power.

Following this we will consider the concept of archives as repositories of memory. This widely used metaphor for archives requires careful exploration to see the nuanced meanings that memory holds in social relationships, and how archival sources and the interventions of archivists shape or construct such meanings. If archives sometimes provide a corrective or standard against which memory can be evaluated, they may also afford social benefits in relationship to public accountability, open government, documentation of diversity and multivocality in society, and perhaps even social justice. After exploring these issues, we will conclude with consideration of the ethical implications of an activist or interventionist approach to archival endeavors. Part of this discussion arises from the recognition of archives as sites of power, of archivists as mediators and power brokers, and of the necessity to respond to this enhanced awareness of the authority and influence that archivists can wield in contemporary society.

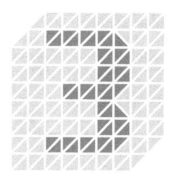

Resisting
Political Power

In Uruguay now, in Chile,
it is official,
there is no memory,
you are not allowed to remember
the bad times, they are over,
and the rememberers
have been ordered
by the Commission of Oblivion
to forget. . . .

In my own country
amnesia is the norm,
the schools teach us
to unremember from birth,
the slave taking, the risings up,
the songs of resistance,
the first May first,
our martyrs from Haymarket
to Attica to the redwoods of California
ripped whole from our hearts,
erased from official memory,
when we die
there will be no trace.

Here too in these green hills
in the free territories of Ovantic and Polho,
they will try and make us forget
the mass graves,
the babies ripped from the wombs,
the wounded families and towns,
the languages they speak,
they will shrug and say it never happened,
it is written nowhere,
no pasa nada aqui, señor, . . .
but . . .
the Indians will never let go,
never abandon the memory of their dead,
never leave the past behind
because the past will never go away,
it is like a boomerang,
it will always return,
it is always present,
it is always future,
it is the most fundamental human right,
memory,
what belongs to us.

– John Ross, "Against Amnesia" [1]

In some societies people who present historical interpretations that contradict the ruling power's orthodoxy can be jailed, or even made to "disappear." Remembering unpleasant truths is illegal. Thus, memory becomes a political act, charged with social meaning. Historians and archivists work in a public arena, which is unavoidably political. Every choice we make—about what documents and evidence to save, what to include in our research, and how to frame the questions for our interpretations of the past—reflects our own personal and collective perspectives on the world. This is as true of the historical past as it is of the political present. As John Ross warns in "Against Amnesia," those who dispute the past "will shrug and say it never happened, it is written nowhere."

This is why it is essential for societies to preserve documentation of the past—to prevent collective amnesia, to ensure an accurate record of events that will serve as a corrective to false memories or oblivion. This is why archives are so important—not only to historians, but to all citizens concerned about truth, accountability, and social justice. By maintaining accurate records of the past, archives establish their

significance for society. This endows archives—and the archivists who
manage them—with a measure of political power.

ARCHIVES AND POLITICAL POWER

In the densely packed introductory note to *Archive Fever,* Jacques
Derrida discusses three images inherent in the concept of
archives. Tracing the origin of the word "archive" to its Greek
roots, he finds in it "the *physical, historical,* or *ontological* sense" of
"the originary, the first, the principal, the primitive, in short to
the commencement." The Greek *arkheion* was "initially a house, a
domicile, an address, the residence of the superior magistrates,
the *archons,* those who commanded." Derrida introduces the
prison/protection/control image. "The archons are first of all the
documents' guardians," he states. "Entrusted to such archons, these
documents in effect speak the law: they recall the law and call on
or impose the law. . . . It is thus, in this *domiciliation,* in this house
arrest, that archives take place." Derrida acknowledges the reverence/
authority/privilege of the archival temple. Documents are "kept
and classified under the title of archive by virtue of a privileged
topology" and they inhabit "this place of election where law and
singularity intersect in *privilege*" and "authority." He also recognizes
the archive's power of classification/interpretation/mediation, which
we have associated with the role of the waitress providing a menu of
choices. "The archontic power, which also gathers the functions of
unification, of identification, of classification, must be paired with
what we will call the power of consignation," which includes both
"the act of assigning residence or of entrusting so as to put into
reserve (to consign, to deposit)" and the "act of consigning through
gathering together signs."[2]

From this consideration of the essential meanings of archives,
Derrida examines the "politics of the archive," its unavoidable
influence on society. "There is no political power without control of
the archive, if not of memory. Effective democratization can always
be measured by this essential criterion: the participation in and
the access to the archive, its constitution, and its interpretation."[3]
Derrida thereby unites the prevalent images of archives with the
political power they convey and embody. Archives are truly sites
of power. Their very essence, purpose, and structure produce
important consequences for society.

Archives are significant for the same reasons that documents
themselves are important for both individuals and collective
social groups. As information scientist David Levy explains, social

institutions—including law and government, commerce and administration, science, religion, education and the arts—rely on "the stabilizing power of documents" to achieve their objectives. Human culture depends on the ability to establish information resources that are durable, unchanging, and repeatable. Documents extend the human consciousness. They are "bits of the material world—clay, stone, animal skin, plant fiber, sand—that we've imbued with the ability to speak."[4] Part of our attachment to documents is their stability, which provides "meaning, direction, and reassurance in the face of life's uncertainties." Documents thus address "the great existential questions of human life." What makes them special is that we create them in our own image, so that through documents we leave behind something of ourselves and thereby achieve some possibility of immortality. Writers seek to preserve their own words and ideas in a (somewhat) permanent medium so that future readers can remember them. This is also an important motivation for those who keep personal journals or save old love letters. "But I would go one step further and suggest that all our documents have a sacred quality about them, that all of them are religious in nature," Levy adds. "They are concrete manifestations of our longing to be more powerful, more connected, more in-the-know. And in this sense they are religious . . . because they arise from the same deep, existential source as do our religious traditions."[5]

These impulses can be seen not only in personal letters and diaries, but also in public records and bureaucratic documents. "We may not be able to predict the future, but in looking at documents we can perhaps see something at least as important: ourselves," Levy concludes. "For to look at our written forms is to see something of our striving for meaning and order, as well as the mechanism by which we continually create meaning and order."[6] When gathered together as records of lasting importance, the documents preserved in archives thus convey essential meanings about people's lives, hopes, and aspirations, as well as the complex networks of agreements and connections that link humanity together in societal systems. This gives archives, and those who select and manage them, primal powers in society.

THE ILLUSION OF NEUTRALITY

However much they protest their impartiality and neutrality, archivists cannot avoid leaving their own imprint on these powerful sources of knowledge and identity. Since the emergence of "scientific history" in the nineteenth century, historians have relied on archives and other primary sources to create and buttress their interpretations of the past. The seminar, introduced in the 1830s by German history professor Leopold von Ranke, taught the techniques of reading and dissecting historical documents. Students exploited newly opened state and church archives as places where truth might be found through rigorous comparison of document after document.[7] These archives would provide a scientific laboratory for historical investigation. "The records themselves were viewed as value-free vessels reflecting the acts and facts that caused them to be created," Terry Cook explains. "Archivists kept the records, in the words of one early theorist, 'without prejudice or afterthought' and were thus viewed—indeed, extolled—as impartial, neutral, objective custodians."[8] English archivist Hilary Jenkinson stated the archivist's ideal of impartiality, neutrality, and passivity in 1922:

> The Archivist's career is one of service. He exists in order to make other people's work possible. . . . His Creed, the Sanctity of Evidence; his Task, the Conservation of every scrap of Evidence attaching to the Documents committed to his charge; his aim to provide, without prejudice or after-thought, for all who wish to know the Means of Knowledge. . . . The good Archivist is perhaps the most selfless devotee of Truth the modern world produces.[9]

As Elisabeth Kaplan points out, Jenkinson's appeal to nineteenth-century canons of positivism—even after exposure to the twentieth-century thinking of Einstein and Freud—seems in retrospect "a stunningly reactionary statement."[10] Yet nearly a century later this is still the ideal held up to archivists by many of their colleagues. Even in recent years archivists often described themselves, proudly, as "the handmaidens of historians," Terry Cook observes. "In retrospect, that phrase is astonishing for its servility and its gender connotations."[11] In China, archivist Du Mei observes, "Since archival work has long been regarded as secret, political, and rote, archivists used to be characterized by traits such as 'modest and unassuming' and 'sedate and obeying.'"[12] Even if archivists were to accept the possibility of such neutrality and passivity, do they really want to be obsequious Uriah Heeps, handmaidens to history? They certainly should have more self-respect than this. If they pride themselves in their humility they may end up like the man given a small medal for being the most humble person in town. He had it taken away when he was seen wearing the medal in public.

The postmodernist perspective only recently seeped into the American archival discourse, but it has already influenced archivists' perspectives on the traditional core values of archives. As one scholar explains, "Postmodernism calls into question Enlightenment values such as rationality, truth, and progress, arguing that these merely serve to secure the monolithic structure of modern . . . society by concealing or excluding any forces that might challenge its cultural dominance."[13] Amid the postmodernist debate over meaning and influence, South African archivist Verne Harris argues, "the notion of public archivists as impartial custodians has been swept off the stage by the view of archivists as active shapers of social memory and documents of society."[14] Although archivists may "naively imagine that we can stand outside the exercise of power," Harris states, as recordmakers they are "from the beginning and always, political players" and "active participants in the dynamics of power relations."[15] Archivists "cannot be merely custodians and brokers," Harris argues, since "any attempt to be impartial, to stand above the power-plays, constitutes a choice, whether conscious or not, to replicate if not to reinforce prevailing relations of power."[16] The archivist's role unavoidably engages in politics. According to Terry Cook, postmodern archivists have challenged five central principles of the traditional archival profession:

1. Archivists are neutral, impartial custodians of 'Truth,' managing records according to universal, value-free theories.
2. Archives as documents and as institutions are disinterested by-products of actions and administrations.
3. The origin or provenance of records must be found in or assigned to a single office rather than situated in the complex processes and multiple discourses of creation.
4. The order and language imposed on records through archival arrangement and description are value-free re-creations of some prior reality.
5. Archives are (or should be) the passively inherited, natural or organic metanarrative of the state.[17]

From the postmodern perspective, archives establish and reinforce power relationships in society. "Creating archives produces power. So too does using archives," insists Steven Lubar, historian of technology at the Smithsonian Institution. "We must think of archives as active, not passive, as sites of power, not as recorders of power. Archives don't simply *record* the work of culture; they *do* the work of culture."[18] Archives play an important role in shaping society and influencing political, economic, and cultural institutions and processes.

As Harris, Cook, and others argue, archives cannot remain neutral or passive. This realization occurred before the postmodernists arrived, but they have reinforced awareness of the problem. In 1970 Howard Zinn, the radical historian, told an audience of archivists that the archivist's "supposed neutrality" was "a fake." "The archivist, even more than the historian and the political scientist, tends to be scrupulous about his neutrality, and to see his job as a technical job, free from the nasty world of political interest: a job of collecting, sorting, preserving, making available, the records of the society," Zinn declared. However, he continued, "the existence, preservation, and availability of archives, documents, records in our society are very much determined by the distribution of wealth and power." Zinn added that archival collections were "biased towards the important and powerful people of the society, tending to ignore the impotent and obscure."[19] Such bias derives from the basic assumptions of archival practice. It is not conscious or deliberate. It is endemic.

The anthropologist Claude Lévi-Strauss clearly linked written documents to economic and political power. "The only phenomena [sic] which, always and in all parts of the world, seems to be linked with the appearance of writing . . . is the establishment of hierarchical societies, consisting of masters and slaves, and where one part of the population is made to work for the other part," he stated in 1961. In early societies writing "was connected first and foremost with power: it was used for inventories, catalogues, censuses, laws and instructions . . . to keep check on material possessions or on human beings."[20] Since the era of ancient Sumeria, archives have consolidated economic and political power. "There is no need to return to the Greek city state, nor to the *archon* and his house cluttered up with municipal documents, in order to know that the modern European public archive came into being in order to solidify and memorialise first monarchical, and then state power," Carolyn Steedman points out.[21] According to Jennifer Milligan, "the Archives nationales is a central institution for the production of histories of France, but it is above all an institution with a history . . . that is deeply implicated in the politics of the nation-state as well as the production of scholarship and the promotion of national memory and identity."[22] In fact, Milligan concludes, the Archives "stands at the nexus of state and citizen, public interest and private rights, and . . . between history and administration and politics and scholarship." By the 1860s French leaders "came to understand the power of the Archives as the arbiter of historical truth."[23] Archives, libraries, and museums have never been neutral. Throughout western history they have served the interests of the state and its elites. As library historian Matthew Battles declares, libraries have always been "a battleground for contesting ideologies." Ruling classes have used them to support their own power, and "regardless of the library's alleged political neutrality, its transparency, its seeming lack of roots, it contains the buried and often contradictory impulses of the princes, philanthropists, and academicians who are its authors."[24] The same is true for museums and archives, indeed for any institutions responsible for the cultural heritage of societies.

Archival partisanship exists in both monarchial and democratic societies. Even the founding of the United States National Archives in 1934 legitimized democratic institutions and ideas of popular power. These power relationships in archives affect private as well as public repositories. As Patrick Quinn wrote more than thirty years ago, "Many traditional notions of what types of primary source materials should be collected and from what sectors of the population source materials should be solicited encouraged an elitist approach to writing history, an approach that in effect ignored the history of blacks and other minorities, women, working people and the poor."[25] Since the authority and legitimizing influence of archives typically serve those in power, Quinn appealed for active engagement to balance state power by giving voice to the common people.

In its most useful application to archival theory, postmodernism extends our understanding of the power relationships that exist in archives. As Terry Cook and Joan Schwartz have pointed out, "the records emerging from the creation process are anything but natural, organic, innocent residues of disinterested administrative transactions. Rather they are value-laden instruments of power."[26] Elisabeth Kaplan found that although both anthropologists and archivists claim to be "disinterested selectors," both serve as "intermediaries between a subject and its later interpreters, a function/role that is one of interpretation itself." Kaplan concluded that, "This power over the evidence of representation, and the power over access to it, endows us with some measure of power over history, memory, and the past."[27] The power of archives carries with it a significant measure of responsibility. If the adage that power corrupts is true, archivists must be on their guard.

Recognizing this power that archivists wield in the universe of knowledge, some have been tempted to seek pseudo-scientific methods of distancing themselves from their decisions. They want to believe in their neutrality. When exposed with their hands on the controls, they may wish to echo the Wizard of Oz, who told Dorothy and her friends, "Pay no attention to the man behind the curtain!"

Derrida places authority at the center of the power of archives. The archive "is not only the place for stocking and for conserving an archival content *of the past* which would exist in any case," he declares, but "the technical structure of the *archiving* archive also determines the structure of the *archivable* content even in its very coming into existence and in its relationship to the future. The archivization produces as much as it records the event."[28] This power of creation—this effect of causation—reflects a force associated with temples and worship. Derrida locates this force within his central concept of "archive fever" (*mal d'archive*), which embodies both origins and a nearly religious passion. "The *trouble d'archive* stems from a *mal d'archive*. We are *en mal d'archive*: in need of archives," he insists. "It is to burn with a passion. It is never to rest, interminably, from searching for the archive right where it slips away. . . . It is to have a compulsive, repetitive, and nostalgic desire for the archive, an irrepressible desire to return to the origin, a homesickness, a nostalgia for the return to the most archaic place of absolute commencement."[29] This concern for the past—this burning, feverish passion—produces the human desire for archives, for a recording that enables us to know our own origins. In its essence this resembles a religious quest for meaning, for the secrets of life. It also suggests a search for meaning beyond the grave. "The archive has neither status nor power without an architectural dimension," according to South African historian Achille Mbembe. Yet he sees in the physical spaces of archives an "austerity that gives the place something of the nature of a temple and a cemetery: a religious space because a set of rituals is constantly taking place there, . . . and a cemetery in the sense that fragments of lives and pieces of time are interred there, their shadows and footprints inscribed on paper and preserved like so many relics."[30] A cemetery is at once a site for remembrance but also a site of consignment and concealment. Archives thus represent both a compulsion to remember and a desire to forget, to preserve traces of some events and persons of the past and to exclude—to bury, to destroy—others.

This control by archivists reflects the power of the political state in controlling archival resources. Historian Jeff Sahadeo encountered the power of the Uzbekistan government to control access to the archives. "The archive constitutes a source of power in Uzbekistan. It is at the nexus of a number of different and overlapping clashes: between the West, Russia and the former Soviet Union, and the local; between state elites and society; between the Uzbek government and its neighbors; and, above all, between past, present, and future."[31] Such control provides archives with political power. "The Uzbek regime's use of archives to create national myths and legitimize existing power structures finds parallels across the globe, particularly . . . in states seeking to come to terms with the legacy of European imperialism," Sahadeo concludes.[32] Peter Fritzsche connects this archival power to institutions of social control. He contends that "the archive is widely recognized as one of an array of disciplinary institutions such as hospitals, prisons, and asylums that manage the technologies of power that are indispensable to the maintenance of social collectives and the enforcement of social norms."[33] Following the collapse of the Soviet Union in 1991, archivists in Russia gained much greater influence, as a new national identity had to be formed. Constructing the past became a serious political activity not merely an academic exercise. "In the 1990s, the politics surrounding the fate of the Soviet-era archives centered around the age-old question of who would control access to the past," Abby Smith reports, echoing George Orwell's dictum that whoever controls the past controls the future. "Archivists and archival administrators suddenly became more important and, in some sense, more powerful than historians."[34]

The imprisoning power of archives captures and enforces the authority of those holding sway over society. Knowledge workers—such as curators, archivists, or librarians—gain authority as "the orthodox representatives of knowledge and memory" over those who lack such formal sanction. This boundary between institutional and freelance representatives shows the power that is structured in "the official knowledge discourse of the archive."[35] Archival control also extends to the processes of arrangement and description. Derrida argues, "that there could be no archiving without titles (hence without names and without the archontic principle of legitimization, without laws, without criteria of classification and of hierarchization, without order and without order, in the double sense of the word)."[36] This control enforces archivists' rules in structuring how researchers approach the records. "In naming, we bring order to chaos. We tame the wilderness, place everything in boxes, whether standard physical containers or standardized intellectual ones," Wendy Duff and Verne Harris observe. "In the realm of descriptive standardization, using big boxes such as fonds or series, or small boxes such as dates of creation or acquisition, we bring order to wild realities."[37]

The authority that archivists exercise within their domain partakes in political power, since access to information and knowledge conveys such power. Yet it is a power often unrecognized by most members of society, who do not see or understand the role archivists play in the contested realms of power distribution and control. Although public controversies, such as the fight for control of Richard Nixon's White House tape recordings, occasionally bring documentary sources to the forefront, archivists seldom share the spotlight. However, archival records often provide a means for holding public leaders accountable and for documenting significant societal events. Control over records documenting the past often provides power over current and future events. Records may define the intersection of history, memory, and political power. Without accurate records it is difficult to determine what actually occurred in the past.

To explore the implications of these concerns regarding recordkeeping and political power, we turn to two prominent twentieth-century novelists, George Orwell and Milan Kundera. Their writings blur the lines between political reporting and fiction, but both recognized the significant consequences of a world in which political power could be gained or consolidated through control of written records and personal memories.

ORWELL ON POLITICS AND HISTORY

The nightmare world for those concerned about history, memory, and recordkeeping is perhaps best represented in the writings of George Orwell. In his totalitarian dystopias and in his essays, Orwell warned against powerful rulers who controlled their subjects, in part, by hiding or distorting the truth through destruction or alteration of records. The only means for preserving accurate accounts of the past, Orwell argued, was through reliable records and human memory. Although he never directly addressed the nature of archives per se, his writings about the necessity for authentic written records clearly embed Orwell in the realm of archives. His perspective and his commitment coincide with subsequent efforts to demonstrate the centrality of archives to modern society and the dangers of a world without access to reliable information about the past and present.

George Orwell was the pen name of Eric Blair, born into what he called "the lower-upper-middle class"[38] in Bengal in 1903 and educated at Eton. In his youth, Orwell later recalled, "I knew that I had a facility with words and a power of facing unpleasant facts."[39] During his service with the Indian Imperial Police in Burma, Orwell developed distaste for imperialism and racism. "In order to hate imperialism you have got to be part of it," he observed. In his police service he was "part of the actual machinery of despotism," and "it is not possible to be part of such a system without recognizing it as an unjustifiable tyranny."[40] In one of his early novels, *Burmese Days* (1934), the central character states that the Indian Empire is a despotism, benevolent perhaps, but "still a despotism with theft as its final object."[41] White supremacy formed the core of British rule in Burma. When a native doctor is proposed for admittance to the Club, one character denounces the "little nigger-boy" as part of "a set of damn black swine who've been slaves since the beginning of history."[42] Such denunciations of imperialism and racism lead Christopher Hitchens to call Orwell "one of the founders of the discipline of post-colonialism" and a literary forerunner of "the historic transition of Britain . . . to a multicultural and multi-ethnic" society.[43]

After returning to England, Orwell wrote a series of novels and social commentaries examining economic and political problems in Europe. In *Down and Out in Paris and London* (1933) Orwell tackled the problems of poverty and class divisions. To understand the situation of the poor he deliberately lived among them in the slums of Europe's most cosmopolitan capitals. He observed, "It is this fear of a supposedly dangerous mob that makes nearly all intelligent people conservative in their opinions." However, he concluded, "The mass of the rich and the poor are differentiated by their incomes and nothing else, and the average millionaire is only the average dishwasher dressed in a new suit. Change places, and handy dandy, which is the justice, which is the thief?"[44]

Orwell investigated working class life in *The Road to Wigan Pier* (1937), once again immersing himself among the lower classes to understand their lives and attitudes. To escape from imperialism and "every form of man's dominion over man" he submerged himself "right down among the oppressed, to be one of them and on their side against their tyrants."[45] He denounced the three modern evils of industrialism, nationalism, and imperialism as contributing to poverty and intolerance. In English mining towns he found offense in "not only the dirt, the smells and the vile food, but the feeling of stagnant meaningless decay" where people creep "like blackbeetles, in an endless muddle of slovened jobs and mean grievances."[46] Industrialism created unhealthy ways of living. "A belching chimney or a stinking slum is repulsive chiefly because it implies warped lives and ailing children," he charged.[47] In a theme he continued in later essays, Orwell denounced "all nationalistic distinctions—all claims to be better than somebody else" because of appearance or dialect as "entirely spurious."[48]

The answer to these problems, he argued, was socialism. "We have got to fight for justice and liberty, and Socialism does mean justice and liberty when the nonsense is stripped off it. It is only the essentials that are worth remembering," he declared.[49] As Hitler, Mussolini, and Franco wielded control in Europe, taking the continent to the verge of war, Orwell warned "there is no certainty that Fascism will ever be overthrown" unless socialist doctrine is quickly diffused. "For Socialism is the only real enemy that Fascism has to face. The capitalist-imperialist governments, even though they are about to be plundered, will not fight with any conviction against Fascism as such."[50] His concern for economic and social justice and his support for socialism as the antidote to fascism led Orwell to volunteer with the anti-Franco loyalist forces in Spain. This experience transformed him into a committed political writer. It also showed him the importance of reliable documents and records in establishing truth in a world turned mad.

Orwell developed a coherent argument about the importance of history, records, and memory in a series of essays and books written between 1938 and 1949, in the midst of the world's greatest crises—totalitarian ideologies, global warfare, and atomic weapons. After joining the anti-fascist struggle during the Spanish Civil War, Orwell turned from writing novels to political journalism. He worked for two years in the British Broadcasting Corporation, which later served as the model for the "Ministry of Truth" in his novel *Nineteen Eighty-Four*. Orwell's "everyday experience of propaganda" in the BBC also inspired the concept of doublethink and much of his description of Big Brother's thought control.[51] During the Second World War he wrote numerous political essays and contributed regularly to the *Tribune*, which he described as "a sociopolitical weekly which represents, generally speaking, the left wing of the Labour Party."[52] His ideas on historical truth coalesced around three critical challenges: the struggle between propaganda and truth; the need to verify facts through accurate records; and the necessity of personal memory as a bulwark against lies and state-imposed public amnesia. Even before writing his two most famous novels, Orwell explored the danger that totalitarian leaders would entrench their power by distorting historical knowledge through control of written records and human memory. (By "written records" we should now include all forms of recording, whether textual, visual, sound, or electronic.) Authentic records—the very stuff of archives—provide one of the strongest bulwarks against totalitarianism.

Orwell's interest in history, records, and evidence grew out of his personal experiences as a volunteer fighting against Franco during the Spanish Civil War. In his 1938 memoir of the war, *Homage to Catalonia,* Orwell stated that, although his personal perspective was limited to a narrow eyewitness view, he saw and heard "quite enough to contradict many of the lies that have been circulated." From this he concluded that nine-tenths of what had been written about the fighting in Barcelona was untruthful: "Nearly all the newspaper accounts published at the time were manufactured by journalists at a distance, and were not only inaccurate in their facts but intentionally misleading."[53] Most of the reporting from Spain amounted to little more than propaganda for one side or the other. Orwell concluded, "It will never be possible to get a completely accurate and unbiased account of the Barcelona fighting, because the necessary records do not exist. Future historians will have nothing to go upon except a mass of accusations and party propaganda."[54] In Orwell's experience, personal memory could expose the falsity of collective memory and historical accounts of events that he had witnessed. However, without records (archival memory) the necessary corroboration could not exist. Orwell could not have anticipated that with the fall of the Soviet Union, forty years after his death, "newly available documents from the Soviet Military Archive in Moscow" would reveal the secret plotting behind the attempted communist coup in Barcelona in 1937.[55] Although it took decades for this information to surface, this does indicate the significance of archives in correcting falsehoods and disclosing the truth. As Christopher Hitchens observes, "Catalonia has freed itself from the fascism against which Orwell fought, and to which it never submitted. . . . Perhaps most important, however, it has rescued its history and its records from years of falsification and denial." In tribute to Orwell, in 1998 Barcelona's socialist mayor dedicated "a rather plebeian square" as "Placa George Orwell."[56] This tribute came too late for Orwell to appreciate. The fact that archival records ultimately disproved Orwell's pessimistic view that the truth about the Barcelona fighting would never be known shows the importance of creating and preserving archival documentation. Orwell clearly would have rejoiced over being proved wrong, even though it took decades for the truth to emerge.

In two essays about the Spanish Civil War, Orwell explained his commitment to historical truth, based on accurate records. "During the Spanish Civil War I found myself feeling very strongly that a true history of this war never would or could be written. Accurate figures, objective accounts of what was happening, simply did not exist," Orwell wrote in 1944. ". . . And if Franco or anyone at all resembling him remains in power, the history of the war will consist quite largely of 'facts' which millions of people now living know to be lies."[57] Even if he were overthrown, Orwell asked in 1943, "What kind of records will Franco have left behind him? Suppose even that the records kept on the Government side are recoverable—even so, how is a true history of the war to be written?" Almost any account was bound to be partisan and unreliable even regarding minor events. In Spain Orwell saw newspaper reports that contradicted known facts: "I saw, in fact, history being written not in terms of what happened but of what ought to have happened according to various 'party lines.'" Some kind of history would be written, Orwell predicted, "and after those who actually remember the war are dead, it will be universally accepted. So for all practical purposes the lie will have become truth."[58] This clearly presages an important theme that he developed further in his 1949 novel, *Nineteen Eighty-Four*.

The lies about past events of the Spanish Civil War led Orwell to warn against "a nightmare world in which the Leader, or some ruling clique, controls not only the future but the past."[59] He recognized the deep-seated impulse to use history—or at least "lessons" learned from historical analogy—as a means of securing political power. As John Lewis Gaddis contends, "The search for a past with which to attempt to control the future is inseparable from human nature: it's what we mean when we say we learn from experience."[60] After seeing the assaults on "objective truth" by Franco and Hitler, Orwell concluded that the interpretation of "the present war" that "finally gets into the history books will be decided not by evidential methods but on the battlefield." Perhaps no historical account could ever be entirely accurate or objective, but Orwell still believed that facts and truth should be sought and recorded. "In the last analysis our only claim to victory is that if we win the war we shall tell less lies about it than our adversaries. The really frightening thing about totalitarianism is not that it commits atrocities but that it attacks the concept of objective truth: it claims to control the past as well as the future."[61] Joyce Appleby offers a more reassuring assessment of the power of documentary evidence to overcome the distortions that Orwell feared if Franco and Hitler emerged victorious. "Imagine a willful forgetting of the Holocaust had the Nazis won World War II," Appleby declared in her 1997 American Historical Association presidential address. "Eventually someone would have picked up the trail of clues or stumbled over the contradictions in the documents created by the victors."[62] Truth would emerge from the archives.

In his essays Orwell clearly explained the importance of truth as a protection against tyranny and dictatorship. In a totalitarian state propaganda replaces honest reporting about current and past events. The starting point for such abuses of power, Orwell claimed, was nationalism, which he identified as "the habit of identifying oneself with a single nation or other unit, placing it beyond good and evil and recognising no other duty than that of advancing its interests." Unlike patriotism, nationalism "is inseparable from the desire for power," he argued. A committed nationalist believes that the past can be altered. "Much of the propagandist writing of our time amounts to plain forgery. Material facts are suppressed, dates altered, quotations removed from their context and doctored so as to change their meaning," Orwell contended. "The primary aim of propaganda is, of course, to influence contemporary opinion, but those who rewrite history do probably believe with part of their minds that . . . their own version was what happened in the sight of God, and that one is justified in rearranging the records accordingly." Distortions of the truth could create genuine doubt about enormously significant events. "Indifference to objective truth is encouraged by the sealing-off of one part of the world from another, which makes it harder and harder to discover what is actually happening."[63] This would allow unscrupulous leaders to mislead and gain control over the populace.

The web of lies produced by such rulers obscures the truth and even challenges the very concept of objective truth. "Totalitarianism demands, in fact, the continuous alteration of the past, and in the long run probably demands a disbelief in the very existence of objective truth," Orwell stated in a later essay. "The organized lying practiced by totalitarian states is not, as is sometimes claimed, a temporary expedient of the same nature as military deception. It is something integral to totalitarianism, something that would still continue even if concentration camps and secret police forces had ceased to be necessary." Orwell recognized that human beings could not avoid errors in telling the truth, but "What is really at issue is the right to report contemporary events truthfully, or as truthfully as is consistent with the ignorance, bias and self-deception from which every observer necessarily suffers."[64] The problem in the mid-twentieth century was the willful distortion of truth by unscrupulous leaders, both in totalitarian dictatorships and even within the English political system.

ORWELL ON MEMORY AND RECORDS

Orwell repeatedly lamented the fragmentary record of the past and the resulting gaps in our knowledge of historical events. His experiences in the Spanish and world wars, however, caused him to recognize that, "History is written by the winners."[65] This affected his view of all historical accounts: "When I think of antiquity, the detail that frightens me is that those hundreds of millions of slaves on whose backs civilization rested generation after generation have left behind them no record whatever."[66] These silences of the archives, the absence of records, deeply troubled Orwell.

When faced with the difficult task of distinguishing truth from lies, Orwell concluded, the first recourse is through authentic records. Without reliable records, he warned, "One has no way of verifying the facts, one is not even fully certain that they have happened, and one is always presented with totally different interpretations from different sources." The problem was identifying which of the competing allegations were true and which false. "Probably the truth is discoverable, but the facts will be so dishonestly set forth in almost any newspaper that the ordinary reader can be forgiven either for swallowing lies or failing to form an opinion," Orwell stated. "The general uncertainty as to what is really happening makes it easier to cling to lunatic beliefs. Since nothing is ever quite proved or disproved, the most unmistakable fact can be impudently denied."[67] First-hand accounts, accurate newspaper reporting, official records, and personal papers could establish claims to veracity. Such records formed the best antidote to lies and propaganda, as Orwell had recognized from his Spanish Civil War experience. In writing about history and records Orwell expressed a positivist confidence in objective "Truth" and in human ability to separate truth from lies, based in part on written evidence. A generation later, most western intellectuals understand truth to be contingent rather than absolute. The truth of any version of the past is always contested. This does not mean that Orwell was wrong, or that each account of the past can be equally true, but it suggests that one must read Orwell as a product of his times.

The significance of written records—whether in textual, visual, sound, or electronic media—rests on cultural assumptions that give validation to particular kinds of evidence. "As traditional memory fades, we feel obliged religiously to accumulate the testimonies, documents, images, and visible signs of what was, as if this ever-proliferating dossier should be called on as evidence in some tribunal of history," writes Pierre Nora. "In former times, only great families, the Church, and the state kept records; today memories are recorded and memoirs written not only by minor actors in history but by their spouses and doctors."[68] Any records deemed appropriate to retain in archives thereby acquire even greater value and meaning. As Michel Foucault argues in "The Historical *a Priori* and the Archive," language itself affords authenticity to archived documents and we covet the written word as a direct connection to past reality.[69] Those records preserved in archives achieve significance, Francis Blouin and William Rosenberg explain, in part from "the notion that archival documentation embodies particular kinds of truth: ones that can be referenced and hence 'verified,' ones that are at least partly, in other words, created by the real and symbolic capital of archival institutions themselves."[70] Even without the imprimatur of archival custody, records that can be authenticated provide a basis for constructing truth claims about the past. They offer a corrective to false statements, lies, and propaganda. Citizens can rely on such documents to achieve accurate knowledge and to counter the power of unscrupulous leaders and demagogues.

However, to control popular thought totalitarian leaders can either destroy or falsify records. This danger became central to the plot of *Nineteen Eighty-Four*. In a 1944 essay on the popularity of crime stories, Orwell depicted one gangster story as "a day dream appropriate to a totalitarian age . . . in which such things as mass bombings of civilians, the use of hostages, torture to obtain confessions, secret prisons, execution without trial, floggings with rubber truncheons, drownings in cesspools, systematic falsification of records and statistics, treachery, bribery and quislingism are normal and morally neutral, even admirable when they are done in a large and bold way."[71] This reads in retrospect as a check-list for writing his later novel *Nineteen Eighty-Four*. Remarkably, in the middle of a list of weapons of torture and murder, Orwell includes "systematic falsification of records and statistics" as one method of wielding totalitarian power. "From the totalitarian point of view history is something to be created rather than learned," Orwell wrote in "The Prevention of Literature" in 1945. "A totalitarian state is in effect a theocracy, and its ruling caste, in order to keep its position, has to be thought of as infallible. But since, in practice, no one is infallible, it is frequently necessary to rearrange past events in order to show that this or that mistake was not made, or that this or that imaginary triumph actually happened."[72] Such concerns prefigured fictional portrayals in his two post-war novels. However, the danger that significant public records can be destroyed exists even in democratic societies. Government agencies often create a culture of secrecy by limiting access to public records. As one researcher discovered, when he sought to locate records of 1970s farm work in Great Britain, a government official told him that the file had been archived. "When I asked where the archive was kept, I was told that 'archived' meant 'destroyed,'" he reported.[73]

Once corrupt leaders destroy or alter all available written records, only the memory of eyewitnesses can re-establish a truthful account of events. "It is pointed out that all historical records are biased and inaccurate, or on the other hand, that modern physics has proven that what seems to us the real world is an illusion, so that to believe in the evidence of one's senses is simply vulgar philistinism," Orwell declared. "A totalitarian society which succeeded in perpetuating itself would probably set up a schizophrenic system of thought, in which the laws of common sense held good in everyday life and in certain exact sciences, but could be disregarded by the politician, the historian, and the sociologist."[74] This assault on the veracity of human memory undermined the dignity and challenged the intelligence of the population. In *Nineteen Eighty-Four* Orwell would demonstrate the crushing effects of such attacks on human memory.

Personal memory is fallible and can be challenged or undermined. Totalitarian leaders can exploit this weakness to strengthen their control over the population. In an essay in which he tried to recall his childhood memories, Orwell observed, "In general, one's memories of any period must necessarily weaken as one moves away from it. One is constantly learning new facts, and old ones have to drop out to make way for them."[75] The malleability of memory rendered it less reliable than written records. These dangers led Orwell to conclude that by controlling both human memory and written records unscrupulous leaders can control the past and turn history to their own purposes. "The organized lying practiced by totalitarian states is not, as is sometimes claimed, a temporary expedient of the same nature as military deception," he warned. "It is something integral to totalitarianism, something that would still continue even if concentration camps and secret police forces had ceased to be necessary."[76] This was the ultimate nightmare for modern society. It haunted Orwell and prompted him to commit his writing career to counter this potential for future catastrophe.

ANIMAL FARM AND THE POLITICS OF MEMORY

Orwell's essays warning of such dangers reached a limited readership. By turning to fiction he gained a worldwide audience, portraying the dangers of totalitarianism in vivid imagery. Central to the themes of *Animal Farm* and *Nineteen Eighty-Four* are the concerns outlined above regarding history, memory, and records. Although it would be a stretch to claim that these are novels about archives (Orwell never used the word), in both works the importance of records is critical in securing the ruling elite's control over public thought. Without the ability to refer to authentic documents it becomes impossible to contradict political orthodoxy.

In *Animal Farm* Orwell created a "fairy story" revealing the tendency toward totalitarianism among barnyard animals who escape the tyranny of their human masters only to suffer oppression from their own kind. Central to the development of this allegory is the concept of a written document—a rudimentary constitution—designed to protect the rights of the animals. However, the ruling pigs alter the written rules to suit their needs. They cover up this falsification of the record by challenging the other animals' memory of the past. When the animals claim that they had all agreed on a resolution never to engage in trade with humans, spokes-pig Squealer claims that such a resolution "had never been passed, or even suggested." Squealer asks shrewdly, "'Are you certain that this is not something you have dreamed, comrades? Have you any record of such a resolution? Is it written down anywhere?' And since it was certainly true that nothing of the kind existed in writing, the animals were satisfied that they had been mistaken."[77] Without written evidence, memory could not be verified.

As their selfish interests change, the domineering pigs furtively alter the painted sign listing the Seven Commandments governing Animal Farm by adding words or phrases that change the meaning of these social rules. When the pigs decide to move into the farmhouse and sleep in the beds, for example, they amend the commandment "No animal shall sleep in a bed" by adding the words "*with sheets.*" The faithful horse Clover "had not remembered that the Fourth Commandment mentioned sheets; but as it was [written] there on the wall, it must have done so."[78] After the pigs kill several dissident animals, they add another amendment. "'No animal shall kill any other animal *without cause.*' Somehow or other, the last two words had slipped out of the animals' memory. But they saw now that the Commandment had not been violated . . ."[79] Each time a written rule is altered, the animals question their own memory, rather than doubt the validity of the documents.

When falsifying existing records is not enough, the pigs create or "discover" new documents to solidify their absolute power. In order to discredit the rebellious pig Snowball, Squealer tells the animals that Snowball was a secret agent of farmer Jones. "It has all been proved by documents which he left behind him and which we have only just discovered," Squealer claims. When the noble horse Boxer argues that Snowball had been a hero of the Battle of the Cowshed, Squealer replies, "That was our mistake, comrade. For we know now—it is written down in the secret documents that we have found—that in reality he was trying to lure us to our doom." As Squealer depicts Snowball's treasonous actions, the animals edit their own memories of the event. "Now when Squealer described the scene so graphically, it seemed to the animals that they did remember it."[80] Later, Squealer falsely tells the animals that Snowball himself had spread the "lie" that he had been given a medal for heroism, when he had actually been censured for cowardice. "Once again some of the animals heard this with a certain bewilderment, but Squealer was soon able to convince them that their memories had been at fault."[81] Memory could thus be altered by powerful lies and vivid descriptions as well as by falsified documents. Repeated often enough, and without contradictory documentary evidence, such lies become truth.

The pigs use their mastery of writing to solidify their power and authority. Squealer tells the animals that the pigs "had to expend enormous labours every day upon mysterious things called 'files,' 'reports,' 'minutes,' and 'memoranda.' These were large sheets of paper which had to be closely covered with writing, and as soon as they were so covered, they were burnt in the furnace."[82] (This is what a records manager would call a very short-term retention schedule.) For the pigs of *Animal Farm,* it is simply a way to use written records to mystify and dominate the proletarian animals. Without recourse to their own records, the animals lack both personal and collective memory of the past:

> Sometimes the older ones among them racked their dim memories and tried to determine whether in the early days of the Rebellion, when Jones's expulsion was still recent, things had been better or worse than now. They could not remember. There was nothing with which they could compare their present lives: they had nothing to go upon except Squealer's lists of figures, which invariably demonstrated that everything was getting better and better.[83]

Animal Farm depicts a totalitarian society in which the rulers consolidate their power through control of both memory and records. With no verifiable records of the past, the animals' memory can be altered or crushed by the domineering pigs. Orwell thus found a fictional setting to illustrate his growing alarm for a society in which absolute power could be wielded not with a gun but with a pen. Without records, without archives, there could be no authentic and reliable evidence of the past.

NINETEEN EIGHTY-FOUR AND THE DESTRUCTION OF MEMORY

Orwell brought these concerns to full realization in his final novel, *Nineteen Eighty-Four*. In portraying a bleak totalitarian dystopia, he demonstrated the ability of the rulers to control their subjects through constant surveillance, thought control, and manipulation of language. Central to this power was the Party's control over written records and human memory:

> The mutability of the past is the central tenet of Ingsoc. Past events, it is argued, have no objective existence, but survive only in written records and in human memories. The past is whatever the records and the memories agree upon. And since the Party is in full control of all records, and in equally full control of the minds of its members, it follows that the past is whatever the Party chooses to make it.[84]

Orwell clearly distinguished memory from records. They are alternative means of understanding and representing the past. Yet it is clear that written records—the very stuff of archives—hold primacy in this system of thought control.

The Party gains control over records both by destroying and by altering them. Winston Smith, the ill-fated hero of *Nineteen Eighty-Four,* works in the Records Department of Oceania, where he daily must go back into the archives of government reports, newspapers, books, and party speeches to alter the historical record in accordance with changing needs of those in power. To show the leader's infallibility, Smith and his fellow records specialists would "rewrite a paragraph of Big Brother's speech in such a way as to make him predict the thing that had actually happened." Once a revised version of the record has been substituted, the obsolete records of the past are quickly discarded down the "memory hole"—Newspeak for a chute that leads to an enormous central incinerator.[85] Winston reflects on this revision of the past, when the Party controls all written records. "The past, he reflected, had not merely been altered, it had been actually destroyed. For how could you establish even the most obvious fact when there existed no record outside your own memory?"[86] Winston felt this loss personally. He held few memories from "the dim period of his early childhood." Remembering anything proved extremely difficult. "Beyond the late Fifties everything faded," he lamented. "You remembered huge events which had quite probably not happened, you remembered the details of incidents without being able to recapture their atmosphere, and there were long blank periods to which you could assign nothing."[87] As Orwell recognizes, memory relies on corroborating evidence, on records that provide tangible links to the past.

These concerns emerged in public life clearly during the cold war. In an October 1945 essay entitled "You and the Atom Bomb," Orwell anticipated the central scenario of *Nineteen Eighty-Four*. "We may be heading not for general breakdown but for an epoch as horribly stable as the slave empires of antiquity," he warned, beset by "the kind of world-view, the kind of beliefs, and the social structure that would probably prevail in a State which was at once unconquerable and in a permanent state of 'cold war' with its neighbours."[88] Both sides sought to control knowledge of the past, through "a continual reprocessing of approved views of the past (or amnesia about the past) and the accretion of new dimensions of myth," E. P. Thompson writes. Using a virtual "memory hole" approach to records, Thompson states, these "'anti-historians' actively involved in the destruction of evidence include not only government 'weeders'—bureaucrats who cleanse the archives of potentially harmful material before releasing them to readers—but also officers in charge."[89] Destroying records alters the past. Memory can expose the lies of the rulers, but without documentary evidence memory cannot be proven correct.

Dissenters can be eliminated without a trace when there are no records to expose such acts. "People simply disappeared, always during the night. Your name was removed from the registers, every record of everything you had ever done was wiped out, your one-time existence was denied and then forgotten."[90] Total control over records gave the Party absolute power over knowledge of everything outside one's personal experience. "If the Party could thrust its hand into the past and say of this or that event, it never happened—that, surely, was more terrifying than mere torture and death," Orwell warned. ". . . And if all others accepted the lie which the Party imposed—if all records told the same tale—then the lie passed into history and became truth. 'Who controls the past' ran the Party slogan, 'controls the future: who controls the present controls the past.'"[91] The power over history thus shapes the political power of the ruling elite, and this power over historical reality comes from control of written records—from archives.

It is significant that Winston Smith works in the Records Department, which plays a central role in solidifying the Party's power. Documentary evidence lies at the heart of Orwell's depiction of totalitarianism. "Day by day and almost minute by minute the past was brought up to date," he explains. "In this way every prediction made by the Party could be shown by documentary evidence to have been correct; nor was any item of news, or any expression of opinion, which conflicted with the needs of the moment, ever allowed to remain on record. All history was a palimpsest, scraped clean and reinscribed exactly as often as was necessary."[92] This falsification of records requires extensive archival institutions, perverting the proper role of archives. "There were the vast repositories where the corrected documents were stored, and the hidden furnaces where the original copies were destroyed," Orwell explains.[93] The Records Department is only a single branch of the Ministry of Truth, which is responsible for a broad array of information and entertainment, all serving the Party's propaganda goals.

As Winston Smith and other rewriters of the past prepare different versions of these fake documents, "some master brain in the Inner Party would select this version or that, would re-edit it and set in motion the complex processes of cross-referencing that would be required, and then the chosen lie would pass into the permanent records and become truth."[94] In addition to written records, virtually all information sources have to be manipulated by the Party. "Every record has been destroyed or falsified, every book has been rewritten, every picture has been repainted, every statue and street and building has been renamed, every date has been altered," Winston explains to Julia, his co-conspirator and secret lover. "I know, of course, that the past is falsified, but . . . [t]he only evidence is inside my own mind, and I don't know with certainty that any other human being shares my memories."[95] In this situation personal memory requires confirmation from external records or from some form of collective or social memory. Only when memory and records corroborate each other can one discover the truth of the past.

Under the apartheid regime in South Africa the struggle over public records and social memory echoed Orwell's warnings.

Public archives became first the supports for apartheid control and later a means of reconstructing the truth of the nation's past. "In imposing apartheid ideology, the state sought to destroy all oppositional memory through censorship, confiscation, banning, incarceration, assassination, and a range of other oppressive tools," archivist Verne Harris recounts. "This was the context within which public archivists practiced under apartheid—struggle informed not only their institutional and social environments, it permeated the fabric of their daily professional work. Impartiality was patently a pipe dream."[96] Regardless of the personal intentions of individual archivists, as part of the state bureacracy the public archives services became tools of the apartheid regime. The government's disregard for accountability and transparency resulted in "numerous cases of unauthorized destruction of public records by government offices" in a "systematic endeavor to secure a selective amnesia as the apartheid system crumbled."[97] "Between 1990 and 1994, the state engaged in large-scale sanitization of its memory resources designed to keep certain information out of the hands of a future democratic government," reports Verne Harris.[98] Hilda Bernstein describes South Africa's history as one of "torn and missing pages," and Harris asserts, "Any nation that has an incomplete understanding of its past rests on shaky foundations, and . . . government must be made accountable, especially in the light of the historically repressive role of the South African state."[99] This experience echoes both Orwell's memory holes and the forced forgetting of which John Ross warns in "Against Amnesia."

Efforts to control the past through restricting access or destroying records characterize totalitarian and closed political regimes. "Terror works on ignorance, on the ungraspable nature and undefined scope of the arbitrary power of the oppressor," historian Jeremy Black explains. "The authoritarian state needs to locate its opponents, to understand and control dissidence, but does not wish to be understood, other than as a comprehensive force. The end of communist rule transformed the situation." Thus, in the Baltic States and former Soviet Union, "As part of reconstruction, previously blank periods in national records could now be studied," and the "archives of Communist states and parties were opened for examination." The end of communist rule also "enabled scholars in former Eastern-bloc countries to gain access to Western literature and archival sources."[100] This opening of archives to public scrutiny provides opportunities to correct past injustices and to hold perpetrators of injustice to public accountability. As Orwell implicitly recognized, archives thus emerged as central to the efforts to resist, to overcome, and eventually to understand and remember the oppression of totalitarian dictatorships.

In *Nineteen Eighty-Four* memory takes several forms—personal memories of one's own experiences, collective memories shared by all members of society, memories grounded in historical interpretation of the past, and archival memory embedded in documents, statues, monuments, and even an antique glass paperweight. Early in the story Winston reflects on the impermanence of personal memory. "When there were no external records that you could refer to, even the outline of your own life lost its sharpness," he laments.[101] Later, he despairs of enlisting the proles in resistance against the Party because they cannot remember their own lives before the Revolution. He tries to query one elderly prole, but concludes, "The old man's memory was nothing but a rubbish heap of details. One could question him all day without getting any real information." Soon no one would be able to compare his or her life before the Party's takeover to the present; hence no one could identify the lies being told about the past. "They were like the ant, which can see small objects but not large ones," Smith despairs. "And when memory failed and written records were falsified—when that happened, the claim of the Party to have improved the conditions of human life had got to be accepted, because there did not exist, and never again could exist, any standard against which it could be tested."[102] Remaining human—retaining his personal identity and mental coherence—creates for Smith a duty to preserve the truth of the past. This same human impulse arose among the victims of the Holocaust, particularly those who survived to bear witness to its horrors. Even amid the deprivations and looming near-certainty of death, prisoners carved small enclaves of freedom. "Every memory became a protest; every smile was a call to resist; every human act turned into a struggle against the torturer's philosophy," Elie Wiesel reports.[103] As Orwell recognized, the last recourse of victims may be their memory, their determination not to forget the acts of their oppressors.

Fighting against historical amnesia becomes essential in a society that seeks to deny the past. Quoting Pierre Nora's monumental *Les lieux de mémoire,* Nancy Wood states, "Under the impact of the waning fortunes of 'environments of memory' in the modern world, individual memories acquire ever-greater significance as the guarantors of social continuity, instilling an 'obligation to remember' that assumes the 'power of an internal coercion.'"[104] Such forms of memory thus carry significance for social stability, as Orwell recognized, and as protection against totalitarianism and political repression. The call for preservation of human memory echoes most clearly in efforts to preserve the memory of the Holocaust, lest such atrocities be repeated. In their examination of war and remembrance in the twentieth century, Jay Winter and Emmanuel Sivan argue that "experience is intrinsically social" and that remembrance is "a process, dependent upon groups of people who act over time"—a "collective enterprise through which *homo agens* creates and maintains." Although recognizing that "state agency and manipulation" have been well documented, Winter and Sivan counter Orwell's pessimism about the possibility of overcoming such efforts at control. "Even in totalitarian situations," they argue, "state agency does not control individual or group memory completely."[105] The bleak world of *Nineteen Eighty-Four* reveals the consequences if such state power over memory and the past become absolute.

In his own effort to preserve memory as a corrective to state-enforced amnesia, Winston Smith encounters two objects—a newspaper photograph and a glass paperweight—that provide tangible links to the past. His hope of disproving the Party's lies rests on these seemingly inconsequential objects. In 1973, in his daily work routine, he had unrolled a wad of documents that included a half-torn newspaper page dated ten years earlier. This scrap of paper included a photograph of three men, later executed for conspiracy, at a Party function in New York. This evidence proved that they had not been in Eurasia on that date, as their subsequent confessions claimed, thus proving that their confessions were lies. Smith had never believed that these people had actually committed the crimes of which they were accused, "But this was concrete evidence: it was a fragment of the abolished past, like a fossil bone which turns up in the wrong stratum and destroys a geological theory."[106] Fearful of being caught with such evidence, Smith had "dropped the photograph into the memory hole, along with some other waste papers." Eleven years later, he reflects that now he probably would have tried to keep the photograph. "It was curious that the fact of having held it in his fingers seemed to him to make a difference even now, when the photograph itself, as well as the event it recorded, was only memory," he thought. "Was the Party's hold on the past less strong, he wondered, because a piece of evidence which existed no longer had once existed?"[107]

By now, however, such facts would have little significance, apart from the evidence that the Party's "truth" consisted of lies. Smith can understand "the immediate advantages of falsifying the past," but the "ultimate purpose was mysterious." Big Brother's fierce visage could almost convince one to deny the evidence of the senses. "Not merely the validity of experience, but the very existence of external reality was tacitly denied by their philosophy," Smith concludes.[108] Memory can carry forward knowledge of the past and fills gaps in the written record. Yet to sustain memory over time one needs some form of reliable evidence. "Memory is an image of the past constructed by a subjectivity in the present," as historian Allan Megill states. "It has long been clear that, without independent corroboration, memory cannot serve as a reliable marker of the historical past."[109] Orwell clearly recognizes this necessary linkage between memory and documentation through tangible traces of the past.

Smith's photographic evidence reappears after his capture, during an interrogation by O'Brien. "You believed that you had seen unmistakable documentary evidence proving that their confessions were false," O'Brien taunts Smith, showing him another copy of this same photograph. "It exists!" Winston cries. "No," says O'Brien, before dropping it into a nearby memory hole. "Dust. It does not exist. It never existed." "But it did exist! It exists in memory. I remember it. You remember it," Smith cries out. "I do not remember it," says O'Brien.[110] This is doublethink. It is an effective means of denying the past.

The second memory trace, tangible evidence of the past, is an antique glass paperweight with a piece of coral embedded in it, which Smith finds at a "prole" neighborhood junk shop. He buys it simply because it is old. "I don't think it was ever put to any use. That's what I like about it," he tells Julia. "It's a little chunk of history that they've forgotten to alter. It's a message from a hundred years ago, if one knew how to read it."[111] In a room upstairs from the junk shop, Smith sees a small bookcase that contains only rubbish. "The hunting-down and destruction of books had been done with the same thoroughness in the prole quarters as everywhere else," Smith reflects. "It was very unlikely that there existed anywhere in Oceania a copy of a book printed earlier than 1960."[112] Lacking written records, Smith buys and hides the glass paperweight as a reminder of the past. He thereby enacts a common human response to antique objects. "The aesthesis of history amounts to an aesthetic orientation toward objects that are left over from the past, or that appear as if they are left over from the past," Allan Megill observes. People focus on "the sensual aspect of the objects being contemplated."[113] Archivists frequently see this response, or experience it themselves, toward old manuscripts or documents from earlier eras. Such relics connect us to the past, show that we are not alone in the relentless onrush of time, and provide a sensual and esthetic pleasure.

For Winston Smith such pleasures come at great cost. During a raid on the secret room where he meets Julia for illegal sexual liaisons, they are both arrested and imprisoned for re-education. One of the Party policemen ("solid men in black uniforms, with iron-shod boots . . . and truncheons") deliberately shatters the glass paperweight on the hearthstone, exposing the fragment of coral. "How small, thought Winston, how small it always was!"[114] This forms a perfect metaphor for human memory and for evidence of the past. Without protection memory and records cannot survive intact; they cannot convey the past to future generations.

This control of both records and memory is essential to the Party's ongoing power. In his efforts to undermine the Party's control, Winston imagines the possibility of a resistance movement, "small groups of people banding themselves together, and gradually growing, and even leaving a few records behind, so that the next generation can carry on where we have left off."[115] Records could link together these rebel bands, who could verify each other's memories of the past. The futility of such hope becomes apparent at the end, when Party loyalist O'Brien interrogates the captured Winston Smith:

> O'Brien smiled faintly. . . . "Does the past exist concretely, in space? Is there somewhere or other a place, a world of solid objects, where the past is still happening?"
>
> "No."
>
> "Then where does the past exist, if at all?"
>
> "In records. It is written down."
>
> "In records. And —?"
>
> "In the mind. In human memories."
>
> "In memory. Very well, then. We, the Party, control all records, and we control all memories. Then we control the past, do we not? . . . I tell you, Winston, that reality is not external. Reality exists in the human mind, and nowhere else. Not in the individual mind, which can make mistakes, and in any case soon perishes; only in the mind of the Party, which is collective and immortal. Whatever the Party holds to be the truth is truth."[116]

Once all documents have been falsified or destroyed, the only hopes for salvation are the human memory and the will to resist the Party's mind control. "It will be seen that the control of the past depends above all on the training of memory," Orwell explains. "To make sure that all written records agree with the orthodoxy of the moment is merely a mechanical act. But it is also necessary to remember that events happened in the desired manner. And if it is necessary to rearrange one's memories or to tamper with written records, then it is necessary to forget that one has done so."[117] This completes the cycle, perfects the lie. It fills the archives with doctored records, and the human mind with false memories. As Winston recognizes, "History has stopped. Nothing exists except an endless present in which the Party is always right."[118] In the end, of course, Winston Smith succumbs to the mind control of the Party and comes to love Big Brother. Yet Orwell did not think the future hopeless for mankind. As he stated in a letter to Francis Henson, he set the story in Britain "in order to emphasize that the English-speaking races are not innately better than anyone else and that totalitarianism, if not fought against, could triumph anywhere."[119] The possibility of—the necessity for—resistance to tyranny gave Orwell some optimism about the future. *Nineteen Eighty-Four* was not a hopeless lament, but a cry for action, a call to unseat the forces of totalitarianism wherever they might arise.

POLITICS AND LITERATURE

The nightmare world of *Nineteen Eighty-Four* carries a clear political message, a warning against totalitarianism. Orwell intended this to apply both to fascism and to communism, and even to English socialism (Ingsoc in the novel's abbreviated form). When criticized for being a political writer, Orwell countered that "every writer, especially every novelist, has a 'message,' whether he admits it or not, and the minutest details of his work are influenced by it. All art is propaganda."[120] He insisted that every work of literature was "an attempt to influence the viewpoint of one's contemporaries by recording experience," at least to some degree. "There is no such thing as a genuinely non-political literature, and least of all in an age like our own, when fears, hatreds, and loyalties of a directly political kind are near to the surface of everyone's consciousness."[121]

In an era of war, fascism, concentration camps, and atomic bombs, Orwell argued, these are "what we daily think about, and therefore to a great extent what we write about." Politics invade literature, in large measure because writers develop "an awareness of the enormous injustice and misery of the world, and a guilt-stricken feeling that one ought to be doing something about it, which makes a purely æsthetic attitude towards life impossible." Therefore, "no thinking person can or does genuinely keep out of politics, in an age like the present one."[122] In writing about the Barcelona fighting, for example, Orwell stated that "no one can be completely objective" on such a momentous issue. "One is practically obliged to take sides," he argued, and he warned the reader of his "bias" and his possible mistakes. "Still, I have done my best to be honest," he pledged.[123]

In an essay explaining "Why I Write," Orwell acknowledged the impact of the Spanish Civil War on his literary career. "Every line of serious work that I have written since 1936 has been written, directly or indirectly, against totalitarianism and for democratic socialism, as I understand it." If a writer is forced to consider political issues, Orwell admonished, "the more one is conscious of one's political bias, the more chance one has of acting politically without sacrificing one's esthetic and intellectual integrity."[124] This ideal of maintaining honesty and integrity, of acknowledging one's own interpretive framework, provides the writer's best protection against lies and propaganda. This is true for historians, novelists, and all writers.

The very language used by writers conveys political messages and subtexts. Orwell's brilliant essay "Politics and the English Language," written in 1946, argues that "the decline of a language must ultimately have political and economic causes." Concerned about the dishonest writing of the era, Orwell contends that "the slovenliness of our language makes it easier for us to have foolish thoughts," but argues that this process can—and must—be reversed, since "to think clearly is a necessary first step towards political regeneration."[125] He details the common use of stale metaphors, verbal false limbs, passive voice, pretentious diction, vague and meaningless words, intentional deception, and ready-made phrases, as symptoms of a writer who is not particularly interested in what he is saying. "A scrupulous writer, in every sentence that he writes, will ask himself at least four questions, thus: What am I trying to say? What words will express it? What image or idiom will make it clearer? Is this image fresh enough to have an effect?" Orwell adds, "And he will probably ask himself two more: Could I put it more shortly? Have I said anything that is unavoidably ugly?"[126] Political writing often seeks to diminish rather than expand thinking, in favor of conformity. This is the essential characteristic of Newspeak.

In *Nineteen Eighty-Four* Orwell demonstrates the dangers of allowing language to deteriorate to the point that people could not express coherent ideas. Winston Smith learns this from Syme, one of many people working on the revised Newspeak dictionary. "Don't you see that the whole aim of Newspeak is to narrow the range of thought? In the end we shall make thought-crime literally impossible, because there will be no words in which to express it," Syme tells Winston. "The Revolution will be complete when the language is perfect."[127] Orwell explains this in detail in an appendix, "The Principles of Newspeak." Oceania needed a new official language. "The purpose of Newspeak was not only to provide a medium of expression for the world-view and mental habits proper to the devotees of Ingsoc, but to make all other modes of thought impossible. . . . This was done partly by the invention of new words, but chiefly by eliminating undesirable words and by stripping such words as remained of unorthodox meanings."[128] Words such as *honor, justice, morality, democracy,* and *science* have been eliminated, and each edition of the Newspeak dictionary contains fewer words than the previous. Such reductions benefit the Party, "since the smaller the area of choice, the smaller the temptation to take thought."[129] Party loyalty "demands a continuous alteration of the past, made possible by the system of thought . . . known in Newspeak as doublethink."[130] The ability to hold "two contradictory beliefs in one's mind simultaneously" and accept both of them forms the essential act of the Party, "to use conscious deception while retaining the firmness of purpose that goes with complete honesty."[131] Thus, the Party faithful accept the slogans, "WAR IS PEACE. FREEDOM IS SLAVERY. IGNORANCE IS STRENGTH."[132] Newspeak and doublethink extend the Party's control over thought, which the destruction of accurate records had begun. Without reliable memory, authentic records, or effective modes of language, no one can challenge the autocratic rulers of Oceania. Control over both language and records leaves memory powerless.

Any use of language to convey ideas or influence another's thinking becomes political. Overtly political writing is particularly dangerous, Orwell argues. "In our time, political speech and writing are largely the defense of the indefensible," Orwell claims. "Thus political language has to consist largely of euphemism, question-begging and sheer cloudy vagueness." Such language, he contends, "is designed to make lies sound truthful and murder respectable, and to give an appearance of solidity to pure wind. Once cannot change this all in a moment, but one can at least change one's own habits." As a writer, Orwell recognizes that "if thought corrupts language, language can also corrupt thought." To express any ideas in writing constitutes a political act. "In our age there is no such thing as 'keeping out of politics.' All issues are political issues, and politics itself is a mass of lies, evasions, folly, hatred and schizophrenia. When the general atmosphere is bad, language must suffer."[133] There can be no neutrality in such circumstances. Each writer—each citizen—must take sides. Thus writing is essentially political. The same is true for those responsible for written records, in all formats, and for shaping institutions of social memory. Historians and archivists cannot avoid taking actions that are fundamentally political. In fact, nearly every decision they make, nearly every word they speak or write, enters the political fray. If their actions do not challenge the status quo, they will reinforce it.

ORWELL IN THE ARCHIVES

If it is true that the victors write history, as Orwell declares, it follows that they often employ archives to institutionalize their power. This has been true throughout human history. Despots, kings, religious leaders, and presidents have legitimized their authority through documents, both symbolic and real. From Greek and Roman archives preserving records of governmental power, to medieval charters, to the American Constitution, such documents have strengthened the power of the rulers. Yet the rights of subjects have also been protected by resort to documents, from the Magna Carta to the American Bill of Rights and the French Declaration of the Rights of Man.

In archives, from ancient to modern times, the preponderance of records has documented the activities and interests of the more powerful groups in society. Education, literacy, and access to power have reinforced the entrenched interests of the elite classes. Representation in archives has privileged the stories of these groups, since it is their voices that are most often recorded and thus most frequently heard in historical accounts. Examples abound of societies in which the powerful have ruled by controlling and manipulating information and records. As Noam Chomsky argues, "elites depend on sophisticated information systems, media control, surveillance" and related measures to maintain their positions.[134] Echoing the implicit objective of Orwell's Ministry of Truth, Jacques Derrida explicitly links political power to the archives: "There is no political power without control of the archive, if not of memory."[135]

Even in democratic societies, public officials often seek to control public discourse by manipulating access to information, as former Society of American Archivists president Tim Ericson stated: "Nothing has been able to slow the growth of secrecy in government.

Many suspect it serves the interests of politics, malfeasance, misdeeds, and potential embarrassment more than our national security."[136] Government secrecy is the enemy of truth, and the beginning of amnesia. Thus, as we look at the relationships among political power, memory, history, and archives, we should keep in mind that these are vital concerns. At times the nature of our social and political systems—including our personal and collective liberties—may be at stake.

As George Orwell reminded us, the very act of remembering can be a powerful political statement. What we remember, and how we form and preserve our memories, defines us as individuals, as members of various social groups, and as a society. Confronted by demands for sanitizing the past—for a collective drink of the fatal kool-aid of amnesia—we can join Winston Smith in resistance. Faced with the overpowering totalitarian control of the Party, Smith places his hope in history. When members of a clandestine resistance group offer a toast, the leader asks, "What shall it be this time? . . . To the death of Big Brother? To humanity? To the future?" "To the past," Winston suggests. "The past is more important," his comrade agrees.[137] For Orwell, memory—both personal and collective—provided the only antidote to totalitarianism. The political act of defiance required both personal memory and the corroborating evidence of authentic and reliable records. Orwell found his answer to the dangers of political repression in the archives.

MILAN KUNDERA ON TRUTH, MEMORY, AND OPPRESSION

Orwell's warnings about totalitarianism, oppression, and the police state have found numerous echoes in world literature. Writers who have battled directly against repressive regimes could hardly avoid calling forth similar images and stories of brave people resisting the power of the state. Few have done so more effectively than Czech writer Milan Kundera. The themes Orwell expounded regarding the struggle for truth, power, memory, and identity play out clearly against the background of the Soviet Union's oppression of Czechoslovakia during the cold war era, as Kundera depicted it in his novels and essays. For Kundera, however, the public arena of politics forms the background and context in which to explore personal stories of love, honor, betrayal, death, identity, and existence. In his novels and essays, Kundera demonstrates how, in the slogan popularized by 1960s protestors, the personal truly is the political.

Born in Brno, Czechoslovakia in 1929, Kundera represents the generation that came of age following the Second World War. Starting his career as a poet, he published three volumes of poetry between 1953 and 1964, before turning to the novel as his primary medium. In 1967 his first novel, *The Joke*, established Kundera as an important dissident voice during the reform movement leading up to the 1968 Prague Spring. This short-lived democratic movement ended with Soviet tanks rumbling through the streets of Czechoslovakia's capital. In the aftermath, Kundera and other non-communist writers lost their jobs and had their books removed from libraries and bookstores. Initially prevented from traveling to the West, Kundera eventually found sanctuary and a teaching job in France in 1975. Following his exile, he published the novels *Life Is Elsewhere* and *The Farewell Party*, before completing *The Book of Laughter and Forgetting* in 1979. In 1984 he published his best-known novel, *The Unbearable Lightness of Being*, adapted as a movie in 1988. His later novels include *Immortality* (1990), and *Ignorance* (2000), among others. Although his focus rests upon fictional characters and their struggles to make sense of existential questions, Kundera both explicitly and implicitly addresses the central political issues of his era. In doing so, he provides insights into the intersection and collision of truth, memory, and political power.

As George Orwell recognized, any writer who pays attention to what is happening in the contemporary world must address fundamental questions of truth, power, and morality. It is impossible to ignore the past or to blot it entirely from one's purview. Even those who seek to forget the past because of its suffering or its seeming irrelevance to current problems will fondly recall personal incidents from their own pasts. In the literary study *Atrocity and Amnesia: The Political Novel Since 1945*, Robert Boyers states, "One is involved in time, like it or not, and can no more succeed in escaping the past than in launching oneself directly into the future of one's dreams."[138] As writers confront the past—including the recent past of world-wide warfare, the Holocaust, Soviet gulags, and totalitarian oppression—they engage political realities. As Franz Fanon argues, politics is the collective assertion of the will to power.[139] This is the context in which both Orwell and, a generation later, Kundera wrote about resisting political power. For Orwell, fascism provided the reference point for a political orientation shaped by the Spanish Civil War, the Second World War, and the cold war. Kundera addressed the post-war dominance of Soviet power in Eastern Europe, particularly his home country, Czechoslovakia. Although neither writer explicitly focused on archives, their examinations of the meanings of truth, memory, and freedom indicate how documents and archives contribute to the struggle against political power.

In two interviews conducted with American novelist Philip Roth during his first visits to London and the United States, Kundera directly addressed the political situation in Czechoslovakia. "In the course of a mere half-century, it experienced democracy, fascism, revolution, Stalinist terror, as well as the disintegration of Stalinism, German and Russian occupation, mass deportations, the death of the West in its own land," Kundera stated. "It is thus sinking under the weight of history, and looks at the world with immense skepticism."[140] Soviet control over Czechoslovakia had dismantled Czech literature, by proscribing 200 Czech writers ("including the dead Franz Kafka") and dismissing 145 Czech historians from their posts. History was rewritten and monuments demolished. "A nation which loses awareness of its past gradually loses its self," Kundera warned. "Politics unmasks the metaphysics of private life, private life unmasks the metaphysics of politics." Thus, he told Roth, "what terrifies us about death is not the loss of the future but the loss of the past. Forgetting is a form of death ever present within life . . . . But forgetting is also the great problem of politics."[141] In the same way that Winston Smith offered a hopeful toast "To the past," Kundera also declared that remembering the past provides the greatest bulwark against totalitarianism.

For Kundera, however, resistance to oppression arises from questioning rather than from pronouncing answers. "What Orwell tells us could have been said just as well (or even much better) in an essay or pamphlet," Kundera argues. As we have seen, Orwell in fact started by publishing essays before determining that fiction would reach a wider audience. Kundera correctly suggests, however, that Orwell approached his novels as a vehicle for expounding solutions to world problems. "The world of one single Truth and the relative, ambiguous world of the novel are molded of entirely different substances," Kundera states. "Totalitarian Truth excludes relativity, doubt, questioning; it can never accommodate what I would call the spirit of the novel." In the novel, he declares, "a dogmatic thought turns hypothetical."[142] Kundera told Roth that he remained wary of the words *pessimism* and *optimism*. "A novel does not assert anything; a novel searches and poses questions," he declared. "The stupidity of people comes from having an answer for everything. The wisdom of the novel comes from having a question for everything." The novelist shows us how to understand the world as a question.

"The totalitarian world, whether founded on Marx, Islam, or anything else, is a world of answers rather than questions."[143] It is this spirit of openness and exploration that characterizes not only the best novelists but also the best citizens. In an oppressive society, questioning authority—as Orwell also recognized—holds the key to human survival and the persistence of humanism. People living in democratic societies, however, also require this spirit of questioning.

In his first novel, *The Joke,* Kundera presents a series of love stories—often tales of obsession, told by a handful of characters whose lives intersect—against the backdrop of Czech postwar politics. The spirit of the book, as Kundera later declared, "was diametrically opposed to the official ideology" of Soviet-controlled Czechoslovakia.[144] The central character, Ludvik Jahn, runs afoul of party leaders when he sends an intentionally ironic and iconoclastic postcard to a young woman who had spurned his entreaties and headed to a communist youth camp for the summer. She writes to him, "chock full of earnest enthusiasm" for the calisthenics, discussion, songs, and "healthy atmosphere" at the camp. Ludvik states, "So I bought a postcard and (to hurt, shock, and confuse her) wrote: Optimism is the opium of the people! A healthy atmosphere stinks of stupidity! Long live Trotsky! Ludvik."[145] Intended as a joke, the three-sentence postcard unintentionally becomes documentary evidence of his disregard for party loyalty and his rebellious spirit. Denounced even by his university friends in a public inquisitional hearing, Ludvik ends up in a military prison working in the mines. According to his interrogators, "a man either was a revolutionary, in which case he completely merged with the movement into one collective entity, or he wasn't, . . . and therefore suffered constant guilt." Ludvik gradually accepts the fact that his words, even though intended as a joke, nonetheless mark a transgression against the Party, and "torrents of tortured self-criticism started whirling through my head."[146]

Kundera counterposes Ludvik with another character, Helena, who represents the faithful party *apparatchik.* "People call me a hard-liner, a fanatic, a dogmatist, a Party bloodhound," Helena declares, " . . . but they'll never make me ashamed of loving the Party and sacrificing all my spare time to it. What else do I have to live for?" In phrases reminiscent of the party faithful in *Nineteen Eighty-Four,* Helena gushes, "the Party is almost like a living being, I can tell it all my most intimate thoughts."[147] Even Ludvik describes how he felt dazzled upon joining the Communist Party, which offered "the feeling (real or apparent) of standing near the wheel of history." Young party leaders practically ran the universities single-handedly, since there were few Communists on the faculty. This was not exactly the "intoxication of power" but a milder feeling: "we let history bewitch us; we were drunk with the thought of jumping on its back and feeling it beneath us, and if, more often than not, the result was an ugly lust for power," an illusion remained that all men "would no longer stand outside history, no longer cringe under its heel, but direct and create it."[148] This sense of power and control, although illusory, proved irresistible to many young men and women under the Soviet regime—as it had throughout human history, when people sensed their ability to gain influence and control over others.

Themes of remembering and forgetting, past and present, truth and mystery infuse *The Joke*. Obsessed with Lucie, a young woman whom he fails to seduce, Ludvik later recognizes that "having become part of the irrevocable past (something that lives in the past, but is dead to the present), she gradually lost all corporeality, physicality in my mind and turned into a kind of legend or myth, inscribed on parchment and laid in a metal casket." The imagery of parchment and metal casket calls to mind the documentary evidence of the past enshrined in archives and libraries. For Ludvik, his personal experience "takes the form of a rebus whose message must be deciphered," because "the stories we live in life comprise the mythology of our lives and in that mythology lies the key to truth and mystery."[149] Lucie also becomes an obsession for Ludvik's nemesis Kostka. "I watched her smile," Kostka says while watching Lucie working in the field. "Until then her soul had been in eternal flight from both past and future. She had been afraid of everything. Past and future were treacherous maelstroms. She clung desperately to the leaky lifeboat of the present, a precarious refuge at best."[150] In this metaphor, Kundera illustrates the challenge facing all humans in reconciling past, present, and future.

In efforts to establish stable connections to the past, people often turn to tradition, folklore, and cultural heritage. One of the main themes in *The Joke* centers on a local Moravian village's annual celebration of a tradition believed to originate from a legend about Hungarian King Matthias fleeing from Bohemia in defeat. "The Ride of the Kings was said to be a reminder of that historic event, but all it took was a brief perusal of source documents to show that the tradition of the Ride antedates by far the misadventures of the Hungarian king," Ludvik relates. He thereby shows the usefulness of archival documents in separating truth from legend. Yet the legend persists. It serves the cultural needs of people who long ago forgot its origins or what it signified. No one knows what it means, Ludvik states, but the reenactments convey meaning, "just as Egyptian hieroglyphs are most beautiful to people who cannot read them."[151] People today lack the patience to listen to such traditions. "At some point far in the past a group of people had something important to say," he muses. "By now history is nothing more than the thin thread of what is remembered stretched out over the ocean of what has been forgotten," Ludvik concludes, " . . . and the consequences will be dire: man will lose all insight into himself, and his history—unfathomable, inscrutable—will shrink into a handful of senseless schematic signs." Then he realizes, "most people willingly deceive themselves with a doubly false faith; they believe in eternal memory (of men, things, deeds, people) and in rectification (of deeds, errors, sins, injustice)." Both beliefs are shams: "All rectification (both vengeance and forgiveness) will be taken over by oblivion. No one will rectify wrongs; all wrongs will be forgotten."[152] Kundera stated in a preface added years after the initial publication that the Ride of the Kings forms "a frame of forgetting." Nostalgia provides the strongest link binding us to a life eaten away by forgetting. "If a man loses the paradise of the future, he still has the paradise of the past, paradise lost," he declares.[153] Yet nostalgia is a poor substitute for truth. Accurate history depends on evidence, on a clear understanding of meaning and purpose. In this novel, at least, Kundera does not recognize the possibility of documentary evidence—preserved in archives, libraries, and museums—as a means of preventing oblivion and forgetfulness. Archival evidence provides one available tool not only for preserving heritage, but also for redressing wrongs and holding oppressive rulers to account before the gaze of public opinion.

In *Immortality* (1990), Kundera explores the human desire to leave a mark on the pages of history. This is also a common motivation for individuals considering placing their personal papers or organizational records in an archival repository, where future generations can learn of their achievements. The flip side of this shows through in a surveillance society, such as Orwell's Oceania, where Big Brother watches over all citizens. Cameras, telescreens, and documentary records provide the means of surveillance in *Nineteen Eighty-Four*. In *Immortality* a young woman dies during a completely minor operation because of "a carelessly administered anesthetic." In response a consumer-protection organization proposes that in the future "all operations should be filmed and the films permanently filed." This leads Agnes to imagine a scenario reminiscent of Big Brother's panoptical presence: "in the end one single stare will be instituted that will not leave us for a moment, will follow us in the street, in the woods, at the doctor's, on the operating table, in bed; pictures of our life, down to the last detail, will be filed away to be used at any time, in court proceedings or in the interest of public curiosity." Agnes remembers that as a child her mother told her, "God sees you," in order to keep her from lying or biting her nails. She had imagined God always watching her. Now cameras seemed to be everywhere, capturing images of injured plane crash victims, celebrities, even the Queen of England's sister on a nude beach. "God's eye has been replaced by a camera. The eye of one has been replaced by the eyes of all," Agnes thinks.[154] When these video cameras feed images into computer systems for long-term storage, the archival systems need to sort out those with long-term value from more transitory information.

Public opinion polls likewise contribute to this sense of popular voyeurism, a constant process of creating or defining truth in modern democratic societies. In polling everyone has a voice, and equal influence over the public's perception of reality. "Public opinion polls are a parliament in permanent session, whose function is to create truth, the most democratic truth that has ever existed," Kundera declares. This results in powerful imagery ("imagologues") shaping the "parliament of truth" according to popular criteria divorced from historical causation. "Ideologies fought with one another, and each of them was capable of filling a whole epoch with its thinking," as Agnes's husband Paul concludes: "ideology belonged to history, while the reign of imagology begins where history ends."[155] These two forces thus take modern society into what we might now call a "reality show" paradigm. Ubiquitous cameras constantly watch people as they perform daily activities, increasingly self-conscious that they are being watched and therefore self-consciously play-acting for the camera. When instant television polls ask viewers to text their answers to a computer-linked telephone system, the illusion of participatory democracy replaces real human interaction. Even in supermarket checkout counters, frequent shopper "discount" cards enable the merchandizing conglomerates to track highly personal and individual data. This can be used for benign purposes, but its ultimate purpose is to expand marketing opportunities within increasingly specific consumer niches. Such surveillance, Orwell and Kundera warn, can also feed the needs of governmental powers both in totalitarian and democratic societies.

Immortality presents several additional ideas for consideration in regard to memory, truth, and political power. Kundera depicts Europeans as longing for a lost history. "World history, with its revolutions, utopias, hopes, and despair, had vanished from Europe, leaving only nostalgia behind," he states. This leads both Agnes's daughter Bettina and her sister Laura to seek some new form of immortality. Bettina wishes to say, "I refuse to die with this day and its cares, I wish to transcend myself, to be a part of history, because history is eternal memory." Laura's aspiration to immortality is more modest, but she wants "to transcend herself and the unhappy moment in which she lives to do 'something' to make everyone who has known her remember her."[156] These are the two personal sides of immortality for Kundera. The first seeks to be known to future generations whom one has never met. The latter, to achieve a smaller measure of immortality by continuing to live in the memories of people one has known. In the first aspect, archives and documentary records—books, memoirs, letters, diaries, account books, photographs, even entries in census records or personnel department databases—contribute to the immortality of people otherwise unknown to future generations. This is one reason that some people become self-conscious about the image they will bequeath to posterity.

Numerous instances exist of children or close friends carefully selecting, editing, shaping the documentary record left behind by a loved one. Kundera recounts the story of Bettina Brentano, a young woman who carried on a long flirtation—and correspondence—with the immortal German literary figure Johann Wolfgang von Goethe. Seeking to gain her own immortality by association with the famous author, after Goethe's death Bettina spent three years correcting, rewriting, and adding to the letters she had exchanged with him. She was disappointed in rereading her own compositions, which did not seem suitably elevated or detailed. Even worse, she found Goethe's letters to her too brief, too reserved, even impertinent. Editing for publication, she changed his phrase "my dear friend" to "my dear heart," and added sentences suggesting that Goethe regarded her as his inspiring Muse. Unless extended by a tradition of oral culture, personal memory lasts a much shorter time, confined to the lives of individual people. "Nobody questioned the authenticity of the correspondence until 1920, when the original letters were discovered and published," Kundera explains. He surmises that Bettina did not burn the original letters, which later revealed her false claims to intimacy with the great Goethe, because burning such intimate documents would be like admitting to yourself that you could die tomorrow. One puts off such destruction until one day it is too late. "Man reckons with immortality, and forgets to reckon with death," Kundera concludes.[157] The personal valuation of documents, whether sentimental or intellectual, makes them too dear to cast away. This may also delay an individual's decision to donate such materials to an archival repository, which is why many institutions encourage potential donors to include provisions in their wills to ensure their papers will reach the archives.

In his recent work, Kundera returns to the theme of memory, linking it directly to archives. In his novel *Ignorance*, he devotes one chapter to these concerns. Memory cannot be understood without considering a mathematical approach, Kundera posits, since "the memory retains no more than a millionth, a hundred-millionth, in short an utterly infinitesimal bit of the lived life." This affects the very essence of mankind. "If someone could retain in his memory everything he had experienced, if he could at any time call up any fragment of his past, he would be nothing like human beings: neither his loves nor his friendships nor his angers nor his capacity to forgive or avenge would resemble ours," he states. "We will never cease our critique of those persons who distort the past, rewrite it, falsify it, who exaggerate the importance of one event and fail to mention some other," yet we must not avoid the obvious fact that reality cannot be reconstructed. "Even the most voluminous archives cannot help." The old diary kept by Josef, the central character of the novel, is "an archival document that preserves notes by the authentic witness to a certain past; the notes speak of events that their author has no reason to repudiate but that his memory cannot confirm, either."[158] Thus, the archival record attests to facts, experiences, ideas, and opinions that cannot be corroborated by personal recollection. In such cases, one must assume either that the written account is correct or that it was falsely recorded at an earlier time.

Josef cannot remember an incident described in his diary. He cannot claim that his record of the event is identical with what he had actually experienced: "he knew that it was only the plausible plastered over the forgotten." Memory remains partial, incomplete. Two people meeting after many years may think they are linked by common experiences from the past, Kundera observes, yet their memories may not correspond: "each of them retains two or three small scenes from the past, but each has his own; their recollections are not similar; they don't intersect." For example, Irina remembers every detail of a long-ago meeting with Josef at the airport, but

Josef remembers nothing. Even when two people live in the same apartment and love each other, "by tacit and unconscious consent they leave vast areas of their life unremembered, and they talk time and time again about the same few events out of which they weave a joint narrative that, like a breeze in the boughs, murmurs above their heads and reminds them constantly that they have lived together."[159] Diaries and old love letters might fill these gaps, providing archival evidence of prior events, shared experiences, passionate feelings, or personal opinions. Yet few spouses create such documents, unless separated for extended periods of days or weeks. With the omnipresent e-mail, written messages may become more common but less permanent, less substantial, dependent on rapidly changing technology.

When his wife dies, Josef gradually loses the clear and intense memories of her smiles, her funny comments, the experiences they had shared. "After his wife's death Josef noticed that without daily conversations, the murmur of their past life grew faint," Kundera observes. "And there lies the horror: the past we remember is devoid of time. Impossible to reexperience a love the way we reread a book or resee a film. Dead, Josef's wife has no dimension at all, either material or temporal."[160] Because their life together resided in a system of oral communication ("daily conversations"), memory could not hold fast to the details of daily experience. Kundera contrasts this ability to revisit experience with the fixity of books and films. The same is true for archival documents, official records, personal love notes, and a myriad of forms by which people keep track of their lives and leave footprints on the ever-shifting sands of time. Archival sources may not be created for the purpose of immortality, but they do convey human experience over time and distance, allowing us to verify accounts of the past, to confirm (or disprove) memory, and to provide a sense of continuity both for individuals and for society itself.

The archival impulse to document and preserve carries a potential danger for the individual. As memory becomes enshrined in repositories, we become distanced from our own pasts, our own experiences. The torture of trying to retrieve forgotten moments of his wife's existence drives Josef to despair. Every successful recall of a shared experience merely reveals "the immensity of the void around that moment," the infinitesimal fraction of the past that he could resurrect. "Then one day he forbade himself that painful ramble through the corridors of the past, and stopped his vain efforts to bring her back as she had been," Kundera recounts. "He even thought that by his fixation on her bygone existence, he was traitorously relegating her to a museum of vanished objects and excluding her from his present life." Josef and his wife had never destroyed their private correspondence or their daily appointment books, but "it never occurred to them to reread them."[161] Remarkably, even when documentation of the past existed, they did not use it to remember or relive their life together. After his wife's death, Josef may have found such personal archives too painful, too evocative. Yet this failure to recognize the potential value of archival sources may stand as a metaphor for the general neglect of archives by society at large. Even when such records could meet pressing immediate needs, they often are overlooked, ignored, or unrecognized. On both a personal level and a societal scale, such neglect leaves us impoverished and uninformed.

For Kundera such concerns about photographs, documents, and the archival imperative remain secondary to his main project, understanding and representing human experience. These archival issues constitute part of the historical background in which his characters confront each other and the harsh realities of modern life. In *The Art of the Novel,* his most significant work of nonfiction, Kundera defines the novel as "The great prose form in which an author thoroughly explores, by means of experimental selves (characters), some themes of existence."[162] In an address given upon accepting the Jerusalem award for international literature, Kundera distinguishes between the writer and the novelist. "The novelist is one who, according to Flaubert, seeks to disappear behind his work," he states. "To disappear behind his work, that is, to renounce the role of public figure."[163] Kundera increasingly found this difficult. During the Soviet era in Czechoslovakia, and even after it ended, the Western world regarded him as the exiled spokesman for the Czech people. Yet Kundera continued to resist this public role, and to argue that he was not a journalist, historian, or political figure. "If the writer considers a historical situation a fresh and revealing possibility of the human world, he will want to describe it as it is," he stated in an interview with Christian Salmon. "Still, fidelity to historical reality is a secondary matter as regards the value of the novel. The novelist is neither historian nor prophet: he is an explorer of existence."[164] However, Kundera also recognized that the novelist needed to take a public stance at times. In his address in Jerusalem, he declared that European culture faced threats from within and without "over what is most precious about it—its respect for the individual, for his original thought, and for his right to an inviolable private life." Faced with such threats, he stated his belief

that the "precious essence of the European spirit is being held safe as
in a treasure chest inside the history of the novel, the wisdom of the
novel."[165] This image of a treasure chest could also signify one of the
central purposes of archives. The protection of culture and heritage,
even human spirituality—those in the Jerusalem audience could
not help but think of the Torah and the Ark of the Covenant in the
metaphor of a "treasure chest"—motivates not only the novelist, but
also the librarian, the museum curator, and the archivist. This is
not their only purpose or meaning, but it is one of the fundamental
contributions made by archivists and their repositories, their
"treasure chests."

When Kundera addresses the historical reality underlying his novels,
he speaks directly to the politics and power relations of Europe,
particularly his native Czechoslovakia and his adopted France. In *The
Art of the Novel* he writes at length about history and historiography.
He begins by distinguishing between the novel that examines "the
historical dimension of human existence" and the novel that is "the
illustration of a historical situation, the description of a society
at a given moment, a novelized historiography." The latter type
violates the novel's purpose, its *raison d'être*. In his novels, he declares,
"I behave toward history like the stage designer who constructs an
abstract set out of the few items indispensable to the action." As
a novelist, he keeps historical situations in the background, used
only to "create a revelatory existential situation" for his characters.
"Historiography writes the history of society, not of man," he insists.
"That is why the historical events my novels talk about are often
forgotten by historiography."[166] In making this distinction, however,
Kundera fails to recognize the recent trends in historiography to
examine life from the bottom up, to uncover precisely the forgotten
events and situations he prizes. Bound by rules of evidence,
authenticity, and documentation, historians enjoy less freedom
for the imagination, but many have begun to explore the human
condition, the individuals previously unseen in the broad brush
strokes of societal history.

Asked whether it is important to know the history of Czechoslovakia
to understand his novels, he answers, "No. Whatever needs to
be known of it the novel itself tells." Yet he acknowledges that to
understand any novel one must understand the broad historical
context of European history. "I can understand *Don Quixote* without
knowing the history of Spain. I cannot understand it without some
idea, however general, of Europe's historical experience—of its
age of chivalry, for instance, of courtly love, of the shift from the

Middle Ages to the Modern Era."[167] Historical reality thus forms the backdrop for fiction, for the exploration of essential themes of human nature, existence, and interaction. Although Kundera regards such context as the backdrop for the personal stories of individual characters, one cannot fully understand these characters' actions or motivations without knowing the historical context in which they live. Furthermore, Kundera's explication of his characters enriches the reader's understanding of that historical context. Seeing his characters respond to the events of the Prague Spring, for example, helps one to grasp both the political implications and the personal impact of the Soviet tanks and the cowardly acquiescence of Alexander Dubcek. Both novelist and historian enrich our understanding of the human experience. Both contribute thus to a political response, to our knowledge of how people respond to and are affected by historical events, political decisions, and human actions. Documenting these processes informs the professional responsibilities of librarians, museum curators, and archivists.

THE UNBEARABLE LIGHTNESS OF HISTORY

In Kundera's best-known novel, *The Unbearable Lightness of Being*, one of the prominent themes is the feeling of continuity or "heaviness" associated with memory, and the contrasting sense of "lightness" created by forgetting. This concept connects the individual to political events in many of his works. Weighed down by responsibilities, people have long admired the mythic Atlas, who literally carried the weight of the world on his shoulders. In *The Unbearable Lightness of Being* Kundera focuses on human relationships—love, eroticism, loyalty, infidelity, betrayal, and friendship—but still reveals some of his concepts of history, archives, and memory. According to literary critic Robert Boyles, *Unbearable Lightness* is not a political novel, but uses the politics of the cold war as a background against which the characters enact their fates.[168] This may be a matter of definition, however, since it is impossible to separate the personal stories of Kundera's characters from their political context. The impact of Soviet invasion and occupation forms a theme second in prominence only to sexual conquest and erotic encounters. Didactic exposition of the events of 1968 and their aftermath figures prominently in the novel. In addition, several references to archives reveal the links connecting political power, oppression, recordkeeping, and resistance.

The central story of *Unbearable Lightness* is the relationship between Tomas and Tereza, linked to stories of their circle of friends and acquaintances. These stories emerge amidst the upheavals of the

Prague Spring of 1968, "that dizzying liberalization of Communism which ended with the Russian invasion,"[169] which disrupted the lives of Czech people at all levels. In the humiliation of Dubcek by the Soviets, Tereza sees the weakness of those who resist totalitarian power. Summoned to Moscow after the tanks rolled through Prague's streets, Dubcek faced possible execution before being sent back to resume his role as head of state. "He returned, humiliated to address his humiliated nation," Kundera reports. "He was so humiliated he could not even speak." Long pauses, when Dubcek seemed unable to breathe or speak, showed Tereza and others the depth of his humiliation and weakness. At the time, most Czechs hated Dubcek and felt offended by his weakness. "Those pauses contained all the horror that had befallen their country," Kundera states. In thinking back, after seeking asylum in Switzerland, Tereza found Dubcek's speech a rallying point for resistance. "She realized that she belonged among the weak, and that she had to be faithful to them precisely because they were weak and gasped for breath in the middle of sentences."[170] Tereza thus casts her lot with the oppressed people of her native land, taking pride in the weakness that nonetheless led them to resist the power of Soviet tanks, secret police, surveillance, and intimidation.

Another character in the story, Sabina, emigrates to France, where she witnesses demonstrations against Soviet imperialism on the anniversary of the Russian invasion of her country. She finds herself unable to join the protests. As she wants to tell her French friends, but can't, she sees that "behind Communism, Fascism, behind all occupations and invasions lurks a more basic, pervasive evil and that the image of that evil was a parade of people marching by with raised fists and shouting identical syllables in unison."[171] Even worse than the exertion of naked political and military power, Sabina thinks, is the conformity and mass hysteria of mindlessly supporting any ideological cause. As she recognizes, "the people who struggle against what we call totalitarian regimes cannot function with queries and doubts. They, too, need certainties and simple truths to make the multitudes understand, to provoke collective tears."[172] This surrender of individuality to the groupthink mentality of the mob frightens and troubles Sabina. It offers an important reminder of the necessity for clear thinking and analysis in responding to political power struggles.

The power of the Soviet regime encompassed many of the forms that Orwell had detected in European fascism: destruction of incriminating evidence, surveillance, interrogation, and punishment for dissenters. The invasion of Czechoslovakia, however, provided tangible evidence of Soviet oppression:

All previous crimes of the Russian empire had been committed under the cover of a discreet shadow. The deportation of a million Lithuanians, the murder of hundreds of thousands of Poles, the liquidation of the Crimean Tatars remain in our memory, but no photographic documentation exists; sooner or later they will therefore be proclaimed as fabrications. Not so the 1968 invasion of Czechoslovakia, of which both stills and motion pictures are stored in archives throughout the world.

Czech photographers and cameramen were acutely aware that they were the ones who could best do the only thing left to do: preserve the face of violence for the distant future.[173]

Tereza joins the ranks of photographers, roaming the streets to photograph Russian soldiers and officers in compromising positions, showing the harsh face of oppression. Many of her photographs turn up in the western press. "They were pictures of tanks, of threatening fists, of houses destroyed, of corpses covered with bloodstained red-white-and-blue Czech flags," and images of "young girls in unbelievably short skirts provoking the miserable sexually famished Russian soldiers by kissing random passersby before their eyes."[174] As Kundera explains, the Russian invasion was both a tragedy and a carnival filled with a curious euphoria.

Significantly, in this description Kundera shows how archival evidence can provide a means of resisting political power by documenting acts of oppression and violations of human rights. The surveillance mechanisms themselves—which Orwell envisioned in the menacing visage of Big Brother and the ubiquitous telescreens—often provide incriminating documentation once the totalitarian regime loses power. In the aftermath of the Prague Spring and Russian invasion, Tereza's husband Tomas loses his position as a respected surgeon due to a seemingly innocuous article he had written about the political situation. During an unsuccessful attempt by members of a dissident group to enlist him in signing a petition against the Soviet regime, someone jokes about the chances that the police are listening to their conversation through surveillance microphones. He declares that he has nothing to hide, but adds, "And think of what a boon it will be to Czech historians of the future. The complete recorded lives of the Czech intelligentsia on file in the police archives!"[175] Not only would such archival documents provide valuable information about the thoughts of dissidents, but they would also preserve evidence of suppression, atrocities, and abuses of power. This could eventually undermine the totalitarian regime, or at least expose its excesses for the eyes and ears of posterity.

In the immediate future, of course, this documentation could fulfill its original purpose. Soviet authorities could uncover secret plots, obtain unintended confessions of complicity, or simply embarrass opponents. When Tomas seeks to explain why he refuses to sign the petition against the Russians, he realizes the dangers of being overheard. "He had more to say, but suddenly he remembered that the place might be bugged," Kundera writes. "He had not the slightest ambition to be quoted by historians of centuries to come. He was simply afraid of being quoted by the police." Tomas does not want to provide fodder for the communist propaganda mills, because "he knew that anything anyone in the country said could be broadcast over the radio at any time. He held his tongue."[176] Likewise, Tereza recognizes that her passion for photographing the Russian tanks could be turned against the very people she thought she was supporting. "How naïve they had been, thinking they were risking their lives for their country when in fact they were helping the Russian police," she thinks.[177] In the same way that Winston Smith realizes that his acts of resistance had come to nothing in the face of overwhelming political power, Tomas and Tereza recognize the seeming futility of their gestures of defiance. However, as both Orwell and Kundera intimate, the act of defiance itself can be meaningful. When combined with documentary evidence, whether preserved by individuals or in archival repositories, such resistance can resonate for future generations.

In *The Unbearable Lightness of Being,* Kundera also shows the value to individuals of personal letters, photographs, official records, and documents. When Tereza claims that she must return to Czechoslovakia from Switzerland because her mother's cancer has worsened, Tomas suspects this is not the real reason for the trip. He exposes the lie by telephoning her mother's local hospital and asking for information from her medical file. "Meticulous records of the incidence of cancer were kept throughout the country," so he had no trouble finding out that she had never been suspected of having the disease, nor had she consulted a doctor in the past year.[178] In another scene, Sabina's lover Franz muses on the proliferation of cultural information in societies where people no longer have to work with their hands. Students need to come up with dissertation topics, for example, so the outpouring of written information grows continuously. "Sheets of paper covered with words pile up in archives sadder than cemeteries, because no one ever visits them, not even on All Souls' Day," he declares. "Culture is perishing in overproduction, in an avalanche of words, in the madness of quantity."[179] The modern information society thus extends not only to business transactions, government regulation, and other forms of archival documentation, but even to the production of literary and cultural works. For an archivist, the evocation of "archives sadder than cemeteries" harkens to the difficulty of gaining public recognition of and interest in the vast resources of information available for consultation. Although Franz may think that "no one ever visits" archival repositories, Tomas recognizes the availability and usefulness of such records, even while they are still in active files in such institutions as hospitals.

Despite his declaration about the overproduction of cultural information, Franz comes to recognize the personal value and importance of even simple forms of documentary evidence. When Sabina leaves him, he regrets never asking for any of her paintings or drawings, or even a snapshot of her. "As a result, she disappeared from his life without a trace. There was not a scrap of tangible evidence to show that he had spent the most wonderful year of his life with her."[180] By refocusing from the broad cultural problem of excessive documentation, Kundera shows the personal necessity that all people feel for "tangible evidence," which is the basis of archival resources and one important purpose served, for the broader population, by archival repositories.

As a testament to the necessity of resisting totalitarian regimes, *Unbearable Lightness* celebrates the power of individual will and the importance of acts of conscience. Amid numerous sexual conquests, Tomas becomes obsessed with the secret and unknown features of the women he seduces, both physical and emotional characteristics. "What is unique about the 'I' hides itself in what is unimaginable about a person," he thinks. "The individual 'I' is what differs from the common stock, that is, what cannot be guessed at or calculated, what must be unveiled, uncovered, conquered."[181] Although framed in the context of eroticism, Tomas's declaration likewise serves as a testimonial to the significance of individual lives in a political context. Just as Orwell celebrates the importance of individuality through the character Winston Smith, so too does Kundera pronounce the centrality of individual identity and the value of each person, even when his characters may not seem entirely sympathetic or praiseworthy. Kundera prizes the individual willing to stand up against oppression and to display personal courage. When Franz joins a demonstration of doctors, intellectuals, and celebrities marching to the volatile border of Cambodia to offer medical assistance to war victims, his actions call to mind the Czech intellectual who organized a petition to liberate political prisoners. "His true goal was not to free the prisoners; it was to show that people without fear still exist," Kundera states.[182] This bravery in the face of oppression echoes Winston Smith's resistance to the power of Big Brother and the Party in Oceania. This is also the determination, the will to resist, that John Ross celebrates in "Against Amnesia."

Kundera also shares Orwell's view that history provides an essential lens through which to view human events and political struggles. After refusing to sign the petition to free political prisoners, Tomas agonizes over his decision. He wonders whether he made the right choice. Would the petition become a justification for a "new wave of persecution" by the rulers? "Is it better to shout and thereby hasten the end, or to keep silent and gain thereby a slower death?" Tomas concludes that since human life occurs only once, with no second, third, or fourth life in which to compare decisions and determine the best course of action, "we cannot determine which of our decisions are good and which bad" in given situations. "History is similar to individual lives in this respect," Kundera reflects. "The history of the Czechs will not be repeated, nor will the history of Europe. The history of the Czechs and of Europe is a pair of sketches from the pen of mankind's fateful inexperience. History is as light as individual human life, unbearably light, light as a feather, as dust swirling into the air, as whatever will no longer exist tomorrow."[183] Although people can be weighed down—burdened and imprisoned—by history, by the accumulated detritus of the past, history can also seem ephemeral and insubstantial in the face of oppression and naked power. The obligation to resist such power may prove more weighty, more burdensome, than an individual person can bear. But it is this call to conscience, to resistance in the face of overwhelming odds, that both Kundera and Orwell consider essential. Memory, evidence, and documentation provide tools for exposing the corruptions of totalitarian regimes, for preventing collective amnesia, and for resisting political power.

LAUGHTER, FORGETTING, AND POLITICS

Kundera's *The Book of Laughter and Forgetting*, published in 1979, provides his most extensive commentary on these issues of memory, documents, and the personal impact of political power. Although focused on personal stories, it draws more extensively than his other works on public events. "The basic event of the book is the story of totalitarianism, which deprives people of memory and thus retools them into a nation of children," Kundera told Philip Roth. "All totalitarianisms do this. And perhaps our entire technical age does this, with its cult of the future, its cult of youth and childhood, its indifference to the past and mistrust of thought."[184] The political framework of the novel is the intimate relationship between cultural disorder and political corruption. By presenting these issues in a starkly political context—from the onset of communist control over Czechoslovakia in 1948 to the repression of the Prague Spring and the democratic resistance twenty years later—Kundera directly addresses the political struggle to remember.[185]

The novel opens with a historical account reminiscent of Winston Smith's lost photograph, which proved that the Party had lied. A famous photograph of Czech leaders celebrating the February 1948 communist takeover in Prague had to be doctored later after one of the party leaders was charged with treason and hanged. "The propaganda section immediately airbrushed him out of history and, obviously, out of the photographs as well," Kundera reports. This brief opening scene leads directly into a passage that historians and archivists have often quoted: "It is 1971 and Mirek says that the struggle of man against power is the struggle of memory against forgetting."[186] Mirek has been keeping a diary, preserving his correspondence, and taking notes at meetings in which Soviet oppression was discussed. When his friends call him careless (meaning reckless for his disregard of reprisals), Mirek responds that trying to hide one's beliefs marks "the beginning of the end." Yet he soon decides to secrete these incriminating papers in a safe place.[187] Like Winston Smith, Mirek recognizes the dangers of documentary evidence and its potential threat to those in power. Also like Smith, Mirek experiences a police raid, during which they seize "letters from Mirek's friends, documents from the early days of the Russian occupation, analyses of the political situation, minutes of meetings, and a few books."[188] Mirek himself is not led off to torture and brainwashing, but the seizure of his documents illuminates their potential power for subversion, for the struggle against forgetting. Kundera acknowledged that this story echoed "Orwell's famous theme: the forgetting that a totalitarian regime imposes." Yet Kundera insisted that the originality of Mirek's story derives from a central fact of human experience: "Before it becomes a political issue, the will to forget is an existential one: man has always harbored the desire to rewrite his own biography, to change the past, to wipe out tracks, both his own and others'. The will to forget is very different from a simple temptation to deceive."[189]

Kundera recognizes that the rapid succession of modern calamities and injustices creates a sense of amnesia in cold war society. A bloody massacre in Bangladesh "quickly covered over the memory of the Russian invasion of Czechoslovakia," the assassination of Allende in Chile "drowned out the groans in Bangladesh," and so on, until "ultimately everyone lets everything be forgotten."[190] The sheer frequency of such horrific events becomes swallowed by the banality of everyday life. This mirrors Orwell's Oceania, which remained in a constant state of war in order to numb people to the tragedies surrounding them. Kundera repeats Orwell's argument that political power requires control over memory. After describing the Soviet army's incursion into Bohemia on August 21, 1968, to suppress the popular expression of freedom known as the Prague Spring, he declares that this "stain on the nation's fair history" had to be nullified. "As a result, no one in Czechoslovakia commemorates the 21st of August, and the names of the people who rose up against their own youth are carefully erased from the nation's memory, like a mistake from a homework assignment."[191] Truth and memory are casualties of totalitarianism, because they threaten the party's power and control. Reminders of the past—personal letters, unaltered photographs, official records—contain the seeds of resistance, the potential to undermine an oppressive regime.

As in *Nineteen Eighty-Four,* Kundera portrays the power of personal memory and privately held documentation of the past. Mirek attempts to regain possession of love letters he had sent to a former girlfriend. He cannot remember what he had been like when he was younger, and he wants to return to this personal correspondence "to find the secret of his youth, his beginnings, his point of departure."[192] His personal identity has become entwined with the documentary evidence of the past, just as social classes and nations find their sense of identity through and in written records. Yet Mirek also wants to obliterate the painful memories of his past love. He wants to destroy the love letters, to cast them into the equivalent of the Ministry of Truth's memory holes. "He airbrushed her out of the picture in the same way the Party propaganda section airbrushed Clementis from the balcony where Gottwald gave his historic speech. Mirek is as much a rewriter of history as the Communist Party, all political parties, all nations, all men," Kundera declares. "The only reason people want to be masters of the future is to change the past. They are fighting for access to the laboratories where photographs are retouched and biographies and histories rewritten."[193] The compulsion to alter the past, which Orwell saw as a means to political power, appears to Kundera as the purpose for which people seek such power. The goal is to cleanse our minds, eliminate painful memories, and remake our own—and society's—image as we want it to be. Perhaps this is the difference between personal and political concerns for control of memory. As individuals our focus is on the emotional content and self-identity afforded by memory, and the documentation that preserves it and brings it to life. Political entities seeking power within society use the control of the past, as Orwell argues, to control the present and the future.

Another character in *The Book of Laughter and Forgetting*, Tamina, notices with desperation that her memory of her late husband is "growing paler and paler" with the passage of time. All that she has left to remember him is his passport picture. When they had begun dating, she recalls, he had asked her to keep a diary to document both their lives. "He was ten years older than she was and had some idea of how poor the human memory can be," Kundera explains. Tamina had argued that acknowledging that such experiences could ever be forgotten would make a mockery of their love. Now she regrets that the diary she did keep contains only fragmentary entries and many blank pages. Tamina attempts to fill in the gaps in her diaries. She tries to bring back memories as reference points to "provide a basic framework for the past as she recreated it."[194] Personal memory—as well as organizational memory—requires documentary confirmation, written (or visual) evidence, or some tangible inscription.

Unfortunately for Tamina, who now lives in a small village in western Europe, her diaries remain at her mother's apartment in Czechoslovakia. Correspondence seeking the return of the diaries would have to go through the secret police and Tamina "could not resign herself to the idea of police officials sticking their noses into her private life." Her late husband had been on the Czech blacklists, and Tamina realizes that "police files are our only claim to immortality." At the same time, she understands that her western neighbors could never understand why private letters and diaries might be confiscated, so she tells them that she is concerned about her "political documents."[195] In a repressive state, the personal indeed becomes political. Even old love letters are subject to inspection, suppression, and censorship. Receiving them can be an act of political subversion, just as Winston Smith's glass paperweight symbolized his independent thinking and secret opposition to authority. As Tamina realizes, "what gave her written memories value, meaning, was that they were meant for her alone." The diaries helped to define her identity. That was why she so desperately sought to regain them, "before the image of the past they contained was destroyed."[196]

These personal diaries symbolize the power of written records to embody both personal memory and the individual's assertion of identity in the face of political repression. Such documents thus carry the capacity to resist power. Although Tamina cannot tell her western friends that the documents she wants to retrieve from Czechoslovakia are personal diaries rather than political documents, her friend Hugo grasps the underlying message concerning political power. "I have come to realize that the problem of power is the same everywhere, in your country and ours, East and West," he tells Tamina. "We must be careful not to replace one type of power with another; we must reject the very principle of power and reject it everywhere."[197] Kundera, like Orwell, thereby connects the personal concerns of his characters to the political repression of the police states in which they live. Truth and memory, an accurate representation of the national past and of personal lives, depend on documentary sources. Without explicitly linking this realization to the existence of archives, Kundera attests to the power that such repositories can exert. In fact, if Kundera had discussed archives he would most likely have regarded them as tools of state oppression rather than sources of liberation and truth. Under the Soviet system, as in all political regimes, archives have more often been part of the state's mechanisms of power.

Kundera returns to the opening scene of communist leaders speaking to the crowds in Prague in 1948, reporting that Franz Kafka had attended school in the building from whose balcony they later spoke. He reflects on Kafka's writings about time, memory, and identity. "Prague in his novels is a city without memory. It has even forgotten its name. Nobody there remembers anything," Kundera writes. "No song is capable of uniting the city's present with its past by recalling the moment of its birth." The street on which Tamina was born had been renamed after each political upheaval, Kundera writes, as successive regimes sought to "lobotomize" it. The monuments of the past were ghosts, demolished in turn by the Czech Reformation, the Austrian Counterreformation, the Czechoslovak Republic, and the communists. Where statues of Stalin had been torn down, Lenin statues had sprouted up "like weeds on the ruins, like melancholy flowers of forgetting."[198]

This seemingly wistful metaphor soon gives way to darker images. In the following sentence, starting a new chapter section, Kundera begins, "If Franz Kafka was the prophet of a world without memory, Gustav Husak is its creator." The seventh president of Czechoslovakia, Husak was known as "the president of forgetting." He presided over the worst massacre of culture and thought since 1621. Among other assaults, he dismissed some hundred and forty-five Czech historians from universities and research institutes, including Kundera's friend Milan Hubl. "'The first step in liquidating a people,' said Hubl, 'is to erase its memory. Destroy its books, its culture, its history. Then have somebody write new books, manufacture a new culture, invent a new history. Before long the nation will begin to forget what it is and what it was.'"[199] This pronouncement could have come directly from Big Brother's manual for thought control. It reiterates the Ministry of Truth's reasons for constantly rewriting all records and accounts of the past.

Both George Orwell and Milan Kundera thus connected the concept of personal memory with political dissidence, portrayed the importance of documents to corroborate and preserve memory, and warned against the power wielded by regimes that control memory and representations of the past. These concerns have broad political implications, but they also provide a mechanism for examining the construction of memory and the roles played by archives and archivists. Often referred to as "houses of memory," or the "collective memory" of society, archives clearly engage in the process of remembering and recalling the past. The direct equation of archives and memory breaks down upon further inspection, as the next chapter explains, but the complex interactions of memory, documents, and institutions concerned with history deserve careful examination.

EMBRACING SOCIAL RESPONSIBILITY

One challenge for archivists is to embrace the power of archives and use it to make society more knowledgeable, more tolerant, more diverse, and more just. The first step is to abandon the pretense of neutrality. As Allan Spear, a professor of history and Minnesota state senator, told a Society of American Archivists audience in 1983, "The concepts of neutrality and objectivity are impossible to achieve and, more often than not, smoke screens to hide what are really political decisions in support of the status quo. Inaction can have political consequences as far reaching as action."[200] The performance of archivists, their use of power, needs to be opened to debate and to accountability. As

Terry Cook and Joan Schwartz argue, "Power recognized becomes power that can be questioned, made accountable, and opened to transparent dialogue and enriched understanding."[201] Once archivists acknowledge their professional and personal viewpoints, they can avoid using this power indiscriminately or, even worse, accidentally.

Archivists have already made many thought-provoking suggestions on how to acknowledge and use the power of archives. Eric Ketelaar urges archivists to open their decision-making to public scrutiny: "In a democracy, the debate about selection and access should be a public debate, subject to verification and control by the public."[202] Paraphrasing Abraham Lincoln, Ketelaar calls archivists to ensure "Archives of the people, by the people, for the people."[203]

Archivists' focus on the technical side of their duties sometimes obscures their social and cultural responsibilities. Shirley Spragge warned in 1994 of an emerging "abdication crisis of archivists' cultural responsibility." Too much emphasis on recordkeeping systems, accountability, and evidence, John Dirks adds, creates concern that "what could be termed as 'the right brain' of the archival mission—our cultural role in preserving heritage, and social memory—has been unfairly neglected, sidelined, and even de-valued." In addition to holding accountable those leaders in politics, business, academics, and other fields whose records they manage, archivists themselves, Dirks reminds us, "will be held accountable by tomorrow's users, who depend on our making well formulated, professional decisions that can stand the test of time. Indeed archivists are vital players, not passive observers, of the relationship between history, memory, and accountability."[204] Power carries responsibility. It also raises the stakes of what archivists do and how they perform their roles.

Hilary Jenkinson set an unattainable ideal of the archivist as one who served researchers but never engaged in interpretation of the records. However, as Tom Nesmith asserts, "an act of interpretation is always at the heart of the management and use of documents." The archivist's role in society is "the assessment and protection of the integrity of the record as evidence." Nesmith adds, "Thus the utility, reliability, and authenticity of archival records are directly related to the ability of the archivist to interpret or contextualize records as fully as possible, rather than based simply on observing and guarding those attributes of records."[205] Like the records they manage, archivists must be authentic, reliable, and trustworthy. Their professional responsibilities are vital and profound.

In their role as creators of the documentary record, archivists help to ensure accountability and documentation, and to provide a means to verify or correct personal and collective memory through documentation. Accountability lies at the heart of Orwell's fear of Big Brother's control over public memory. As Milan Kundera warned in the face of Soviet attempts to obliterate memories and compel the silence of the Czechoslovakian people, "the struggle of man against power is the struggle of memory against forgetting."[206] American geographer Kenneth Foote observes, "For archivists, the idea of archives as memory is more than a metaphor. The documents and artifacts they collect are important resources for extending the spatial and temporal range of human communication."[207] Archives provide essential benefits for society. "The care which the nation devotes to the preservation of the monuments of its past may serve as a true measure of the degree of civilization it has achieved," historian Waldo G. Leland declared in 1912. "The chief monument of the history of a nation is its archives, the preservation of which is recognized in all civilized countries as a natural and proper function of government."[208] Archives not only hold public leaders accountable, they also enable all citizens to know the past.

Archivists therefore become responsible to all citizens in a democratic society. They play an important function that often goes unnoticed. Archives document society and protect the rights of citizens. A generation ago Gerald Ham challenged archivists to "provide the future with a representative record of human experience in our time," and to "hold up a mirror for mankind" so they could help people "understand the world they live in."[209] Although archivists may be less sanguine now than then about their ability to do so, this is still a noble calling. At its heart, Ham's challenge is to represent all of society in the archives, to give voice to the poor, the impotent, and the obscure. Archivists, both individually and collectively, must commit themselves to ensuring that their records document the lives and experiences of all groups in society, not just the political, economic, social, and intellectual elite. In 1971 Howard Zinn urged archivists to "take the trouble to compile a whole new world of documentary material, about the lives, desires, needs, of ordinary people." This would help ensure "that the condition, the grievances, the will of the under classes become a force in the nation."[210]

In responding to this challenge, archivists have made great strides. There are more archives devoted to—or at least concerned with—documenting women, racial and ethnic groups, laborers, the poor, gays and lesbians, and other marginalized peoples. Archivists can still do more. They should aspire to improve on their past successes. In addition to ensuring documentation of these marginalized groups, archivists also need to document the Christian right, the conservative "silent majority," and extremist groups on both ends of the political spectrum, from the Ku Klux Klan and militia groups to anarchists and eco-terrorists.

Paying attention to the need for accountability and documentation serves the cause of human rights and social justice. "Archives not only aid in holding today's organizations legally and fiscally accountable to society, they also hold yesterday's leaders and institutions accountable, both in terms of morality and effectiveness," John Dirks claims. The availability of archives is essential to serve "a society's need for the prevalence of justice, and the preservation of rights, and values."[211] Archival records have been used to rehabilitate people wrongly convicted of crimes under totalitarian regimes, and to obtain restitution from their former oppressors.[212]

Archivists must strive, as Duff and Harris urge, "to investigate the aspects of records that are not being described, and the voices that are not being heard." However, they remind archivists to be careful not to inject their own biases and assumptions in giving voice to the marginalized groups in society. "It is imperative that we not romanticize 'otherness,'" they insist.[213] There is an inherent tension in documenting groups that have traditionally been neglected or marginalized. Who owns their history? The controversy over Native American graves and artifacts illustrates a problem of ownership that affects other groups in society. One reason that African Americans, ethnic groups, gays and lesbians, and others have created their own repositories is to retain control over their own documentation, over its presentation and interpretation, and over the very terms of access. Among Native Americans, for example, there are some rituals and traditions that only specified families within a tribe are entitled to know. The archival concept of open and equal access must be modified to respect such cultural traditions.[214] Jeannette Bastian describes the loss of cultural memory suffered by the people of the Virgin Islands when the governmental records of Dutch and American colonial rulers were removed to those respective nations. Too narrow a definition of provenance led to a loss of control over the people's archives, history, and memory.[215]

Archivist Joel Wurl recounts an incident that vividly illustrates the power of archives to represent and protect the history and collective memory of a community. During the riots in Los Angeles following the Rodney King verdict, looters and arsonists approached the Southern California Library for Social Studies and Research, a major repository depicting contemporary social justice movements and underrepresented communities. "Standing guard, Building Manager Chester Murray responded by telling them the library contained the history of African Americans, Latinos, and working class people and persuaded them to leave it alone. Many of the surrounding buildings were damaged or destroyed, but not the library."[216] Archivists should strive to be as effective as Chester Murray in explaining the importance of archives and their social and political value.

As archivists and the many constituencies that use archives, either directly or indirectly, confront the power relationships at work within archives, they must consider the context in which such powerful social forces operate. The historical origins and development of archives demonstrate the potential influence of archives and archivists in the construction of memory, in accountability and public interest concerns, and in using this power of archives to achieve socially responsible goals while ensuring professional integrity. Archives must serve all sectors of society. By embracing the power of archives, archivists can fulfill their proper role in society, to ensure archives of the people, by the people, and for the people. In doing so, archivists can help those struggling to resist political power.

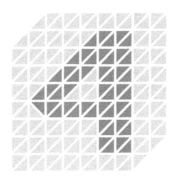

Constructing
Memory

To remember is to create links between past and present, between past and
future. To remember is to affirm man's faith in humanity and
to convey meaning on our fleeting endeavors. The aim of memory is
to restore its dignity to justice.

— Elie Wiesel[1]

For Holocaust survivors such as Elie Wiesel, memory of past atrocities holds the key to preventing their repetition. As the generation of survivors passes from the scene, written records and other forms of documentation must take the place of personal memory. The connections among history, memory, and written records outlined by George Orwell anticipated historians' recent discourse on collective (social) memory. For more than two decades historians have examined the concept of memory and its implications for professionals who study the past. Historians have also begun to recognize that archives are not simply locations to examine authentic and reliable records of the past, but are also active agents in shaping what we know of human history. The historians' discourse, however, often posits "the archive" as an uninhabited landscape awaiting discovery (and implicitly, conquest) by intrepid explorers. The role of archivists in this interplay of history, truth, memory, and evidence requires examination. As collectors, guardians, appraisers, and interpreters of the archival record, archivists actively shape society's knowledge of the past.

Memory disrupts the continuity of time. As we think about
the past, those events "re-called" to mind become part of our
present experience and shape our concept of the future. Billy
Pilgrim, the central figure of Kurt Vonnegut's *Slaughterhouse-Five,*
survives the firebombing of Dresden as a prisoner of war during
the Second World War, but years later, after being kidnapped by
aliens from Tralfamadore, he gains an understanding of the inter-
connectedness of his memory of the past, his life in the present, and
his hopes for the future. The Tralfamadorians "had many wonderful
things to teach Earthlings, especially about time," Billy Pilgrim
states. "All moments, past, present, and future, always have existed,
always will exist. The Tralfamadorians can look at all the different
moments just the way we look at a stretch of the Rocky Mountains,
for instance. They can see how permanent all the moments are, and
they can look at any moment that interests them. It is just an illusion
we have here on Earth that one moment follows another one,
like beads on a string, and that once a moment is gone it is gone
forever."[2] In such a universe, memory and experience form a single
perception of reality. The past lives on, as does the future.

Even with this nonlinear conception of time, Tralfamadorians
convey ideas through written sources. Billy reports that
Tralfamadorian books consist of "brief clumps of symbols separated
by stars." Each of these clumps of symbols is "a brief, urgent
message" describing a scene or a situation. "We Tralfamadorians
read them all at once, not one after the other," a voice tells him.
The books have no beginning, middle, or end, but "when seen
all at once, they produce an image of life that is beautiful and
surprising and deep." The Tralfamadorian concludes, "What we
love in our books are the depths of many marvelous moments seen
all at one time."[3] Vonnegut weaves the story of Billy Pilgrim from
his memories of the horror of war, the disappointments of the
present, and the fantasies of his abduction by the Tralfamadorians.
Appropriately named, Pilgrim becomes a time traveler, continually
immersed in these various dimensions of time. Vonnegut thus
echoes William Faulkner's character, Gavin Stevens, who states, "The
past is never dead. It's not even past."[4] For those who remember
them, prior events, people, and experiences become living
reminders of the past. As John Ross states in his poem "Against
Amnesia," "the past will never go away / . . . it is always present, / it is
always future."[5] Both for individuals and for society, the past forms
a vital component of the present. Billy Pilgrim and Gavin Stevens
share this insight.

Time and memory shape who we are, both individually and collectively. As we attempt to remember the past and to preserve our connections to earlier times, we seek mnemonic devices of recall or means of recording and fixing the past to (relatively) unchanging structures. These may include anything from official records of national and international political significance to personal mementoes significant only to a single individual, as in the Classics IV song, "Traces":

> Faded photographs, covered now with lines and creases
> Tickets torn in half, memories in bits and pieces . . .
> Ribbons from her hair, souvenirs of days together
> The ring she used to wear, pages from an old love letter
> Traces of love, long ago, that didn't work out right . . . [6]

For those seeking to understand and recreate the past, tangible evidence and documentation provide the necessary sources of reliable information. However, anyone seeking to extract meaning from documents or *aides-de-mémoire* such as "tickets torn in half," ribbons, or love letters must understand the context in which records were created—by whom, when, with what authority, and for what purpose. With written records, understanding these factors constitutes one of the most important functions performed by archivists. In selecting which records to preserve, providing information about their context, and assisting users in interpreting them, archivists play an active role in constructing memory for all members of society.

HISTORY VS. MEMORY

In common parlance we often equate history with memory and assume that both provide avenues to accurate recreations of the past. The stories we tell about our own lives and about our collective existence in social groupings seem to be based on solid facts and irreducible truths. Somehow, we think, if we can discover enough facts we can construct an accurate depiction of the past. As recent scholarship in the field of social memory reveals, this is a naïve and superficial way of thinking about memory. Memory, history, and evidence interact and conflict in complex and fascinating ways.

When researching his own family history, Richard White found that many of his mother's stories about her early life in Ireland and her immigration to the United States altered chronologies and forged connections and relationships that clashed with documentary evidence. "I once thought of my mother's stories as history. I thought memory was history," White declares. But after becoming a historian he realized that "only careless historians confuse memory and history. History is the enemy of memory. The two stalk each other across the fields of the past, claiming the same terrain."[7] From this personal exploration of his family's stories White fashions a nuanced understanding of the relationships among memory, identity, history, and archives. At the heart of his mother's personal memories were stories by which she created her own identity. "History can interrogate these stories; it can complicate them, but it cannot kill them," White argues. "Beneath these personal stories simmers an ongoing contest over what America is and means and who gets to define it."[8] Thus personal memory has a public significance. The personal is political.

As he explored his mother's memories and compared them to external evidence, White found, "They seem a record of what happened, but memory is the shifting record of the sense we make of things." Above all, we alter our stories, dropping some details and adding others. As we change, our stories change. "Memory is a living thing vulnerable to this dead past until memory itself dies with its creator," White concludes. "We can record memories, but then they are fixed on the page, pinned like insects in a collection, bodies of what was alive."[9] Above all, what we remember is closely linked to what we forget, whether consciously or not. As he heard his mother's stories change over time, White saw that her memory did not always correspond to external evidence. Some scenes she recounted could not have occurred at the time nor with the persons she remembered being there. "We edit our memories. We choose to forget," White states.[10] As he explored his mother's early life, at times he found her resisting his probing, particularly regarding his father. "She wants to protect his memory, her memory," White observes. "When she is silent, she wants those things about which she refuses to speak to remain as quiet as the tomb. That is the ultimate power of stories. They take on themselves the decision about what will be remembered and what will be told."[11]

Acting as a historian, Richard White examines his mother's stories and seeks to corroborate them with any available evidence he can find at her Irish birthplace, in newspapers, in family photographs and documents, and in public archives. In doing so he discovers the clashes between memory and documentation, between stories and history. "History values what is forgotten, hidden, what was recorded at the time in stone or on parchment or paper or on the land itself," he writes.[12] "The irony is that only history can recall a world once held in memory," White muses upon finding that accounts of personal experiences during his mother's childhood have been preserved by the Department of Irish Folklore at University College in Dublin. "The stories remain frozen, taken out of memory and deposited in history."[13] Bringing his mother to the archives, he watches as she opens a copybook in which her own cousin had recorded her experiences in 1936. Six decades later his mother combines these family accounts with her own personal memories. "Now there are two sets of stories rejoined after more than sixty years: one has lived in memory, the other has survived in the archives," White states. "Only in this archive in Dublin can we recover many of the stories she heard as a child in Ballylongford."[14] Documentary evidence thus supplements, confirms, and contradicts various aspects of his mother's memories, which she had kept alive through decades of retelling and reshaping her own stories. In this depiction of one historian's quest to uncover the truth behind family tales we see the divergence of personal memory from historical memory, and the usefulness of archival memory as a fixed form of reference. This provides a useful starting point for our exploration of the role of archivists in constructing memory.

THINKING ABOUT MEMORY

In the spring of 1998 a new sign over the entrance to the Central State Archive of the Republic of Uzbekistan reminded visitors and researchers of the importance of archives. "Without the past there is no future," declared the message painted on a whitewashed wooden board.[15] As George Orwell recognized, our knowledge of the past depends on a combination of memory and written records. The Uzbekistan Archive announced its own important role in preserving the past for the future. In examining the social purpose of archives, however, we must also consider their engagement in the politics and poetics of human memory. Archives are not the sole guardians of society's memory, nor are they exclusively caught up in preserving memory. Similarly, although history shares memory's claim to represent the past, they are two different but interrelated processes. This story is much more complex than we have yet acknowledged.

As Richard White discovers, history often functions as the enemy of memory. They make competing claims on our intellect, our emotions, and our loyalties. French sociologist Maurice Halbwachs recognizes "the ultimate opposition between memory and history."[16] Memory appeals to us because it confirms continuities between past and present, making the past seem once again alive in our imaginations. By contrast, Halbwachs regards the purpose of history as reconstructing the past from a critical distance, thereby emphasizing the separation between past and present. As Patrick Hutton explains, Halbwachs "believed that the historian's first task is to keep memory honest, to remedy its distortions of the past by comparing its suspect claims to those based on documented historical evidence."[17] Writing emerged in early societies partly as an expansion of human ability to remember important information. "The utilization of a spoken and then a written language is a powerful extension of the storage capacity of our memory, which can thereby move beyond the limits of our bodies and locate itself either in others or in libraries," explains Henri Atlan. "That means that before being spoken or written, a certain language exists in our memory as a form of information storage."[18] The human need for accurate remembrance over time thus led to the creation of records, ultimately placed in secure repositories for safekeeping. In this way, archives first emerged as a result of the same impulse for remembering that later gave rise to the study of history. In order to understand history as well as archives we must understand the meaning of memory.

Memory is an elusive concept. In a societal context it exists on four separate but sometimes intersecting planes: personal memory, collective (or social) memory, historical memory, and archival memory. These four types of memory interact in complex and sometimes baffling ways to enable us to understand the past and to draw lessons from it. However, each type of memory is distinct and offers us a valuable means of examining the past.

PERSONAL MEMORY

❝ I can't make new memories. Everything fades, nothing sticks," Leonard Shelby tells an acquaintance. "By the time we finish this conversation I won't remember how it started, and the next time I see you I won't know that I've ever met you before."[19] In Christopher Nolan's film "Memento" (2001) Leonard's memory problem provides the structure and narrative theme for a provocative exploration of the problem of memory loss. "I have no short-term memory," Leonard explains. "I know who I am and all about myself, but since my injury I can't make any new memories."

Without memory life would be a jumble of unsorted impressions and experiences. We would be unable to remember and build upon prior experiences. "Memento" provides a disturbingly clear understanding of what it is like to live without short-term memory. The film follows former insurance investigator Leonard Shelby in his quest for vengeance after his house is broken into, his wife is raped and murdered, and he is assaulted. As a result of his injuries, Leonard suffers from a rare brain disorder (anterograde amnesia), which prevents him from forming new short-term memories.[20] The film mirrors Leonard's perception of the world, presenting each scene in reverse order, so that the viewer struggles to frame the action in a context that is always incomplete.

Leonard carries a Polaroid camera and a pen with him at all times to allow him to capture images so he can recognize people he meets and places he visits, including the cheap motel where he now lives. His life is a constant search for clues to the identity of his wife's killer. As he gathers facts, he has at best a ten-minute window of memory in which to focus and write things down. In addition to his pocketful of Polaroids, Leonard inscribes the "facts" regarding the killer in tattoos on his arms and legs, and (in reverse so he can read them in the motel mirror) across his chest and torso. As Leonard explains his elaborate system of tattoos and annotated photos, "I'm disciplined and organized. I use habit and routine to make my life possible." He thus literally inscribes his body as a crude archival repository for the information necessary to allow him to function without short-term memory.

In his quest for justice and revenge, Leonard encounters several shady people who seek to turn his memory deficit to their own advantage. The character Natalie mockingly taunts him, "Must be tough living life according to a few scraps of paper. Mix up your laundry list and your grocery list, you'll be eating your underwear. But I guess that's why you got those freaky tattoos."

"Lenny, you can't trust a man's life to your little notes and pictures," warns Teddy, who claims to be a policeman who had investigated his wife's murder. "You don't remember what you've discovered or how. Your notes might be unreliable." Leonard replies:

> Memory's unreliable. Memory's not perfect. It's not even that good. Ask the police, eyewitness testimony is unreliable. The cops don't catch a killer by sitting around remembering stuff. They collect facts, make notes, draw conclusions. Facts, not memories: that's how you investigate. I know, it's what I used to do. Memory can change the shape of a room or the color of a car. It's an interpretation, not a record. Memories can be changed or distorted and they're irrelevant if you have the facts.

For Leonard Shelby, the only remedy for memory loss becomes
a careful routine of documenting his actions and newly acquired
information by creating notes, photographs, and tattooed messages.
His experience depicts the importance of personal memory as
well as the necessity to supplement, confirm, or replace memory
with external documentary evidence. The solution differs from
that offered by George Orwell, but the problems addressed in
"Memento" echo Orwell's belief in the necessity to corroborate
personal memory with written records.

Cognitive psychologists distinguish three primary levels of personal
long-term memory: *episodic, semantic,* and *procedural.*[21] Episodic memory
encompasses recollection of direct personal experience (real or
imagined), based on voluntary or involuntary recall of episodes or
states of mind in one's own life. It is essentially autobiographical.
Semantic memory recalls information about the world in which
one lives, including second-hand information learned from
parents, friends, teachers, books, media, and other sources. This
type of memory might be termed indirect, vicarious, or virtual
memory, although historian Harry Ritter considers this to be "bogus
memory, confabulation, or pseudomemory."[22] Semantic memory
incorporates what Alison Landsberg terms "prosthetic memory"—
individual memory that incorporates external experiences, such as
public ceremonies, cinema, and mass media as "a more personal,
deeply felt memory of a past event through which he or she did not
live."[23] The third type of long-term memory is procedural memory,
which ingrains habits or skills that enable us "to replicate tasks
and behavior patterns automatically, without consciously trying to
remember—riding a bicycle, driving an automobile, etc."[24] Most
experiences leave memory traces, recorded in our episodic memory
system, which encodes events or experiences. Such memories differ
in their accessibility for recognition or recall, and in their density,
or weight, according to Jay Winter and Emmanuel Sivan. They
argue that emotionally charged experiences or those with clear
autobiographical importance—such as combat experience—enhance
the density of memory, and thus its impact and strength.[25]

In examining personal memory our focus is on episodic memory,
although semantic memory becomes important in understanding
collective (social) memory. The importance of episodic memory can
be seen in patients suffering from amnesia. Oliver Sacks, professor
of clinical neurology and clinical psychiatry at Columbia University,
recounts the case of Clive Wearing, an eminent English musician
and musicologist, struck by a brain infection affecting the parts

of his brain concerned with memory. "To imagine the future was no more possible for Clive than to remember the past—both were engulfed by the onslaught of amnesia," Sacks reports.[26] Unable to preserve new memories, Clive also suffers retrograde amnesia, deleting nearly his entire past. Each time he blinks his eyes, he awakes to an entirely new and confounding world.

Clive can converse about some past events, such as the bombing of London during the Second World War, but this appears to be an expression of semantic rather than episodic memory.[27] His illness cost Clive some loss of semantic memory, but not as catastrophically as his episodic memory. "Yet semantic memory of this sort, even if completely intact, is not of much use in the absence of explicit, episodic memory," Sacks reports. As Lawrence Weiskrantz explains, "The amnesiac patient can think about material in the immediate present. . . . He can also think about items in his semantic memory, his general knowledge. . . . But thinking for successful everyday adaptation requires not only factual knowledge, but the ability to recall it on the right occasion, to relate it to other occasions, indeed the ability to reminisce."[28] Therefore semantic memory is useless without episodic memory. Despite suffering from "the most severe amnesia ever recorded," Clive's musical powers and memory have been nearly perfectly preserved, Sacks observes. This demonstrates that "two very different sorts of memory" can exist independently, "a conscious memory of events (episodic memory) and an unconscious memory for procedures—and that such procedural memory is unimpaired by amnesia."[29]

Clive Wearing's amnesia illustrates "the fact that, unlike episodic memory, procedural memory can remain largely intact even in the face of extensive damage to the hippocampi and medial temporal-lobe structures," where episodic or explicit memory develops. "Episodic memory depends on the perception of particular and often unique events," Sacks explains, "and one's memories of such events, like one's original perceptions of them, are not only highly individual (colored by one's interests, concerns, and values) but prone to be revised or recategorized every time they are recalled."[30] Clive's continuing ability to sing, play, and conduct music may indicate that "remembering music is not, in the usual sense, remembering at all," Sacks concludes. "Remembering music, listening to it, or playing it, is wholly in the present." As Victor Zuckerkandl, a philosopher of music, states, "The hearing of a melody . . . should fill the consciousness entirely, . . . nothing should be remembered, nothing except it or beside it be present in consciousness. . . . Every melody declares to us that the past can be there without being remembered, the future without being foreknown."[31] Billy Pilgrim and the Tralfamadorians would certainly understand this nonlinear, overlapping aspect of past, present, and future. Memory remains fluid, continually revised and adapted to new realities and new needs.

In our personal lives we constantly create, edit, reinforce, test, and recount our own memories of events. Memory exists in all human societies and among many animal species. As Jack Goody observes, "in all societies individuals hold a large quantity of information in their genetic heritage, in their long-term memory, and temporarily, in their active memory."[32] The memory of participants in historic events provides testimony that can be used to test and either corroborate or correct our knowledge of the past. Eyewitness experiences clarify our historical understanding of the past and bring it to the level of feelings, motives, and the direct and tangible ways that events affect people. For many of us it is this knowledge of how historic events shape the lives of individuals that makes history come alive.

Yet personal memory changes with time. Memory develops from numerous cognitive sensations rather than as fully formed stories of experience. Historian David Thelen reports, "biologists now support the recent subjectivist thrust in psychology that envisions each memory as an active and new construction made from many tiny associations, not a passive process of storing and retrieving full-blown objective representations of past experience."[33] Memory thus emerges as a product of thought and associations, not as an objective entity. As we form stories of our own lives we continually reshape them to give new meaning and interpretations. Sigmund Freud believed that the human psyche preserves the entire record of an individual's memory in the unconscious, but that the conscious mind can only glimpse part of these truths. He wrote that childhood memories "are not fixed at the moment of being experienced and afterwards repeated, but are only elicited at a later age when childhood is already past; in the process, they are altered and falsified, and are put into the service of later trends."[34] As we reconstruct our life histories, therefore, we are only able to create fictionalized accounts.[35] "It is not surprising for persons to recall a past which is simply consistent with their present views," psychiatrist Walter Memminger observes. "Remembering is a reconstruction using bits of past experience to describe a present state."[36] Memminger quotes Elizabeth Loftus: "Truth and reality, when seen through the filter of our memories, are not objective facts, but subjective, interpretive realities. We interpret the past, correcting ourselves, adding bits and pieces, deleting uncomplimentary or disturbing recollections, sweeping, dusting, tidying things up."[37] Forgetting—as well as remembering—is a natural impulse, part of what makes us human.

Personal memories permit the continual reinterpretation of the past in relationship to our present identities, but they are unreliable as guides to what actually happened. As Israel Rosenfeld states, "Memories are not fixed but are constantly evolving generalizations—recreations—of the past, which give us a sense of continuity, a sense of being, with a past, a present, and a future."[38] Memory is fluid and can be molded and recast to meet our psychic needs, to redefine our personal identity, or to explain our connection to the past. It can be a fascinating and rewarding means of uncovering a hidden past, but it must be approached and used cautiously. As archivist Brien Brothman states, memory blurs the perceptual line between past and present. "In memory, all knowledge, which includes what we habitually call knowledge of the past, gains in immediacy and is embraced as absolutely relevant."[39] Memory is thus distinct from—and at times antithetical to—history:

> Memory is not a place; it is a process. It is a process of knowledge construction in anticipation of performance. Nor is memory about the past. Memory involves diminishing "the pastness of the past" and shaping existing informational material to present purposes. In the framework of memory, "the past" is simply a term of convenience, one that encompasses certain categories of information available for use by contemporary individuals, organizations, and society.[40]

As Richard White observes, it is the fluidity of memory and its application to personal or social needs that separate memory from history. Personal memory is more closely related to collective (social) memory than to the document- or evidence-based reconstruction of the past.

The fluidity and instability of personal memory led our ancestors to develop writing as one means of stabilizing information over time. Despite doubts expressed by Socrates and other ancient thinkers, written records gradually replaced orality as a method of preserving accurate remembrance of the past. For example, in 1174 Guy, Count of Nevers, granted the inhabitants of Tonnerre a charter, in which he claimed, "The use of letters was discovered and invented for the preservation of the memory of things. What we wish to retain and learn by heart, we cause to be written down, so that what we cannot keep perpetually in our weak and fragile memories may be preserved in writing and by means of letters that last forever."[41] André Leroi-Gourhan links this belief in the stability of written records to the computer age of machine-based communications. Arguing that computer memory endures longer than personal memory, he adds that, "human memory is particularly unstable and malleable (a criticism that has become traditional in modern psychology, with reference to judicial testimony, for instance), whereas the memory of machines is respected for its great stability, which is comparable to the memory represented in books, but combined with a previously unheard-of ease of recall."[42] Such critical views of personal memory, coupled with claims for the superiority of written records, prompted the first efforts to establish archival repositories as a means of perpetuating human memory. Another means of extending the power of individual memory exists, however, in the concept of collective memory, or social memory, as it is often called.

COLLECTIVE MEMORY

In recent decades historians have constructed theories of social memory emerging from shared experience of the past. The concept of collective memory posits that collections of individuals, such as members of an ethnic group or citizens of a nation, share some common perceptions of the past. This does not mean that all members of the group "remember" past events in the same way, but that there is enough overlap in personal memories to warrant depiction of common perceptions. Such group memories often shape collective identities. "Properly speaking, a collective memory is what arises when a number of people experience the same set of historical events," historian Allan Megill explains. "These people can then be said to have a 'collective' memory of those events, not in the sense of a memory that exists supra-individually—for there is no such thing as memory apart from individuals—but in the sense that each person has, within his or her own mind and within her own reports, an image, or gestalt, of an experience that other people also underwent."[43]

Other theorists suggest a broader definition of collective memory, encompassing both shared experiences and those that have become imbedded in tradition or cultural practices. "Collective memory is an elaborate network of social mores, values, and ideals that marks out the dimensions of our imaginations according to the attitudes of the social groups to which we relate," Patrick Hutton argues.[44] Maurice Halbwachs compares collective memory to sea waves breaking on a rocky shore. As the tide of living memory recedes, what remains of the sea's presence are only "miniature lakes nestled amid the rocky formations." The rocks, as places of memory, shape and contain our recollections, which reveal only a diminished presence of the full tide of memories.[45]

In *History and Memory* Jacques Le Goff states that the "quest for collective memory . . . constitutes a major change in historical vision," one expressed less in texts than in the spoken word, images, rituals, and festivals. It arises from the public at large, "which is obsessed by the fear of losing its memory in a kind of collective amnesia—a fear that is awkwardly expressed in the taste for the fashions of earlier times, and shamelessly exploited by nostalgia-merchants; memory has thus become a best-seller in a consumer society."[46] Collective memory therefore embodies aspects of group identity, cultural heritage, and nostalgia for a vanished, or disappearing, past.

The most ambitious attempt to explore the concept of collective memory has been Pierre Nora's seven-volume study, *Les Lieux de Mémoire*, published between 1984 and 1992. Nora sought to examine the history of France through a study of its most salient memories—to present "une histoire de France par la mémoire"—by identifying sites of memory ("lieux de mémoire") that have achieved enduring or emotive symbolic significance for the French people.[47] Nora interprets the pervasiveness of contemporary discussions of social memory as a symptom of the decline of memory in daily life. "We speak so much of memory because there is so little of it left."[48] The sites of memory that Nora explores represent impoverished substitutes for the environments of memory ("milieux de mémoire") that provided earlier generations a direct connection to the past. Nora argues that premodern societies live within memory, whereas modern societies place memory at arm's length, emphasizing discontinuities between past and present. Modern societies thus become "historical" societies.[49] David Lowenthal depicts the same distancing of the past, arguing that for modern societies "the past is a foreign country."[50]

Collective memory contributes to shaping the self-identity of social units, from small interest groups to communities and nations. It embraces stories about the group's past. By enshrining certain events and experiences as part of a common history it embodies values, rituals, and directions for future actions. "Public memory, which contains a slowly shifting configuration of traditions, is ideologically important because it shapes a nation's ethos and sense of identity," according to Michael Kammen. "That explains, at least in part, why memory is always selective and is so often contested."[51] Although valued for its applicability to current events, collective memory needs to be examined to determine its validity, authenticity, and reliability. It is changeable and constantly subject to reinterpretation to suit current needs. Like most human constructs, it can serve both positive and life-affirming purposes and also parochial and destructive ends, depending on how it is used. The nature of collective memory, however, is to simplify human experience and to select only certain aspects for retention while ignoring more complex and perhaps disturbing elements of the past.[52] Examining the historical writings, monuments, and physical representations of the past created by a society provides a clear signal of what groups wield political and social power. After studying American historic sites, James W. Loewen concluded, "When only one segment of society—usually the white elite—controls public memory, distorted history is the result."[53] Political influence trumps historical investigation. Social memory selects only those elements of the past that confirm the dominant beliefs of those in power.

As Pierre Nora's *Les Lieux de Mémoire* suggests, collective memory emerges most clearly in efforts to understand or to shape national or group identity. Michael Roth states, "In modernity memory is the key to personal and collective identity . . . the core of the psychological self."[54] Jeremy Black finds examples throughout the world of countries that consciously shape national identity by constructing collective memory and history. Upon its founding in 1948 the new nation of Israel began creating a narrative of historical antecedents to establish its legitimacy. In a "deliberate identification with the biblical past," Hebrew became the official language of the state.[55] Indonesia, Ethiopia, Iran, China, and other nations have undertaken similar efforts, although the resulting national memories often become "seriously ahistorical," Black argues, sacrificing accuracy to achieve political and cultural needs.[56]

The late twentieth-century "truth/justice" trials of "alleged perpetrators of state-sponsored brutality," according to Allan Megill, sought to achieve "the shaping of a new collective identity through the forming of collective memory." Such efforts cannot simultaneously discover historical truth while achieving a predetermined political goal. They thus reveal "that history and memory are sharply different, as manifested above all in the radically different histories that different people or groups 'remember.'" Such efforts to strengthen group identity by creating collective memory are dangerous, he argues, because "truth and justice (or whatever stand-ins for truth and justice remain to us) require at least the ghost of History if they are to have any claim on people at all."[57] Megill contends that appeals to collective memory actually reveal an absence or weakness of group identity and cohesion. "An identity that solidly exists has little need for an explicit, thematized appeal to memory," he reasons. "In other words, an appeal to memory—that is, an appeal to what is subjective and personal—is likely to arise only when objectively existing supports are felt to be inadequate." The uncertainty of identity in the modern age "undermines the arrogance of both history and memory: on the one hand, the arrogance of definitiveness; on the other, the arrogance of authenticity."[58] Thus, history loses its claim to accuracy and completeness and memory surrenders its supposed emotional immediacy.

Social memory all too often is based on myth or simplistic stereotypes, rather than on thoughtful analysis and evaluation of the historical record. Collective memory in most societies tends to become celebratory, seeking to enshrine the heroic aspects of shared cultural history and to gloss over the seamier aspects of the past. In contemporary America the term *heritage* is often applied to these efforts to shape collective memory as a celebration of national history or of the history of ethnic groups or other segments of the population. Heritage often serves as "a euphemism for selective memory," according to Michael Kammen, or as "an antidote to historical actuality" passing as "sugar-coated history." Nostalgia selects the "good" aspects of the past as defined by the arbiters of mainstream culture, and represses the unpleasant. "Heritage is comprised of those aspects of history that we cherish and affirm," Kammen argues. "As an alternative to history, heritage accentuates the positive but sifts away what is problematic."[59]

Many people conflate memory and history, and confuse the feel-good emphasis on heritage with the reality of the past. Kammen clearly distinguishes between collective memory and historical memory:

> Nostalgia, with its wistful memories, is essentially history without guilt. Heritage is something that suffuses us with pride rather than shame. Although written history can never be complete, memory must inevitably be less so. History and memory are not merely fractured. They are frequently at odds.[60]

In the public consciousness, efforts to achieve group cohesion often require distortions of social memory. This "normative desire for political stability," Kammen warns, "is achieved at a price: a tendency to depoliticize the civic past by distorting the nation's memories of it—all in the name of national unity, stability, and state-building."[61] One result is that collective memory can easily succumb to nostalgia or a feel-good consensus about the past.

Collective memory thus carries the danger of distorting the past in order to buttress the power of the ruling classes at the expense of the poor, the uneducated, and the marginalized groups in society. Nancy Wood argues, "memory's inherent intransigence" can exert a benign nostalgic hold on social communities, but in a "more lethal form" locks them into a compulsion to repeat past antagonisms.[62] As Gary Nash found in studying the forging of public memory in Philadelphia, this very process arouses fierce passions and demonstrates who wields power in society. Nash found that "the shaping of Philadelphia's past was a partisan activity, involving a certain silencing of the city's history," and that "remembering the past in heroic, almost providential, terms was an exercise in stabilizing society and legitimating order, authority, and status."[63] Once the "official" or agreed-upon version of the past is accepted, consensus brings stability.

Despite these claims for the power of collective memory, many commentators lament that there seems to be so little of it. In many countries, including Great Britain and the United States, there often seems to be little public interest in the past, little sense of social memory. "There is no country in which memories are notoriously shorter," Geoffrey Elton writes regarding Great Britain, ". . . nowhere else does the present regard itself as less committed by what happened in history." Elton thus challenges the presumed supremacy of the United States in the category of historical amnesia, or disregard for the past. "We have no collective memory, none. If it happened more than six hours ago it is gone," American journalist Meg Greenfield charges in an essay titled "Chronic Political Amnesia." "What this says to me is that we just don't know how to think about the past—and so we try not to. . . . There is neither memory nor history nor whole people nor even any sense of time."[64] Such laments for Americans' low level of historical consciousness and awareness of the past have become common-place in recent years. There seems to be little public interest in objective truth about the past, nor in remembering it accurately without blinking at its unpleasant aspects.

Alison Landsberg looks to the mass media—often blamed for limiting the public's historical consciousness and for distorting the past—as a possible corrective to this loss of collective memory. Landsberg states that in the twentieth century, "new technologies like the cinema, along with the emergence of a commodified culture, transformed memory by making possible an unprecedented circulation of images and narratives about the past." Mass media thus affords an alternative type of collective memory. "This new form of memory, which I call *prosthetic memory*, emerges at the interface between a person and a historical narrative about the past, at an experiential site such as a movie theater or museum." The prosthesis metaphor suggests that the newly acquired "memory" becomes part of the individual's identity, as she or he "takes on a more personal, deeply felt memory of a past event through which he or she did not live."[65]

Landsberg argues that these prosthetic memories provide a means of producing "empathy and social responsibility as well as political alliances that transcend race, class, and gender." One study of cinema viewers indicates that what people see on the screen "might affect them so significantly that the image would actually become part of their own archive of experience." Such experiences could be "powerful enough to shape or construct identity," Landsberg concludes. She extends the concept to include culturally mediated experiences such as commemorations, pageants, museum exhibits, and other methods of inducing an emotional or visceral contact with the past. Visitors to the Charles H. Wright Museum of African American History or the United States Holocaust Memorial Museum, for example, may obtain a (false) sense of witnessing the actual historical events depicted, thereby gaining empathy for victims of past injustice. From this personal connection to history, Landsberg hopes that "the acquisition of prosthetic memories . . . might well serve as the ground on which to construct new political alliances, based not on blood, family or heredity but on collective social responsibility."[66] Although this result seems unlikely, it does suggest the benefits of engaging people in a visceral experience of the past in order to enhance empathy and awareness of others' perceptions and needs.

The concept of collective memory provides a convenient metaphor for self-consciousness among a group of people in society. However, ultimately the metaphor enjoys only limited validity. A societal group, no matter the number of members, cannot truly "remember" or "experience" anything apart from individual consciousness. "Collective memory has no existence independent of the individual, and in consequence, 'collective memory' has a *shelf-*

life, after which individuals cease to share and express it," Winter and Sivan conclude.[67] Likewise, Jacques Le Goff argues that collective memory is "essentially mythic, deformed, and anachronistic"— and that history "must illuminate memory and help it rectify its errors."[68] Writing in the journal *History and Memory,* Noa Gedi and Yigal Elam dissect the concept of collective memory and dispute its existence. "Collective memory is actually a fabricated version of that same personal memory adjusted to what the individual mind considers, rightly or not, as suitable in a social environment," they contend. "'Collective memory' is but a misleading new name for the old familiar 'myth' which can be identified, in its turn, with 'collective' or 'social' stereotypes. Indeed, collective memory is but a myth."[69] Amos Funkenstein observes that consciousness and memory reside only in individuals. "Just as a nation cannot eat or dance, it cannot speak or remember," he points out. "Remembering is a mental act, and therefore absolutely and completely personal."[70] However, Funkenstein offers a nuanced conception of memory. While acknowledging that "only individuals are capable of remembering," he suggests that the concept of collective memory reminds us that all acts of remembering take place in a social context and discourse.[71]

Memory, whether personal or collective, selects and shapes fragments of the past into a story or image that helps us understand the present. It remains personal, emotional, fluid, dynamic, and evocative. Rather than precisely reflecting what actually occurred in the past, memory reveals how we choose to interpret and understand the times in which we live.[72]

HISTORICAL MEMORY

Of all the experiences and memories that mark human consciousness, the historian can know only those that "have been enshrined in material form."[73] The study of history employs evidence such as artifacts, archival documents, and personal testimony as a counterbalance to personal and collective memory. Historical memory arises through the interpretation of the past based on evidence and analysis. One purpose of history is to test our collective memory against the contemporary evidence of past events and personalities. Historians seek to achieve objectivity in their interpretations—or at least the appearance of objectivity. Dependent upon evidence to support their conclusions, they nevertheless also select and interpret evidence to achieve desired effects. Yet their reliance on documentation and evidence distinguishes historians from politicians, poets, and others who shape collective memory.

"The claims that memory makes are only possibly true. In its demand for proof, history stands in sharp opposition to memory," Allan Megill argues. "History reminds memory of the need for evidence coming from eyewitnesses (*autopsy*) and from material remains."[74] The historian always asks "what evidence supports each claim that she makes," Megill states, and this "imposes an intellectual discipline that encourages precision."[75] History demands accuracy and corroborating sources. "Document-based historical practice . . . nurtures a deep respect for the autonomy and integrity of the past," according to archivist Brien Brothman. "The past is comprised of surviving physical artifacts, of independent objects available for critical, scientific inspection and analysis."[76] These archival documents stand as surrogates of memory and as sources for historical inquiry.

In constructing historical memory, historians rely mainly on primary sources created at the time when the events that they describe took place or soon thereafter. Such sources include original documents, archival records, newspapers, government reports and documents, personal testimony by eyewitnesses, oral history interviews, and material culture artifacts. Historical memory is thus built upon a foundation of archival memory (documents) and personal memory (eyewitness accounts and oral history). These sources are cross-examined, compared, and tested to determine their accuracy and reliability. Rules of evidence and authenticity require the historian to use only sources that can be trusted. Contradictory evidence must be weighed and evaluated, not ignored or dismissed without examination. The resulting interpretation would thus be granted a measure of legitimacy, but only if the historian's explanation of the past is logical, well documented, and convincing. Herodotus compiled his histories with the explicit goal of "preserving from decay the remembrance of what men have done."[77] His successor Thucydides thought that the historian had to correct such memories, including his own, by checking various accounts against each other. He incorporated into his historical writing knowledge gained "from eye-witnesses whose reports I have checked with as much thoroughness as possible."[78] As Jacques Le Goff more recently stated, "History must illuminate memory and help it rectify its errors."[79]

In addition to corroborating facts based on evidence, history weaves the threads of past experience into an explanatory narrative. Historians always interpret the past. Leopold von Ranke initiated the nineteenth-century scientific history movement with an influential denial that the historian played any role in judging the past or "instructing the present for the benefit of future ages," and an avowal that his purpose was "only to say what actually happened."[80] Despite such claims of neutrality, any attempt to select, organize, and convey past events represents an act of interpretation, a judging of what to include, what to omit, and how to explain the past. Historical memory therefore constitutes an interpretation or explanation of the past based on evidence. As Allan Megill writes, "In an experiential sense, 'historical memory' denotes the experience of people who actually went through the historical events under discussion. More accurately, historical memory denotes the recovery and conversion into narrative of that experience."[81] Although some historians cling to Ranke's objectivist belief in the historian's ability to recapture past events without intervention or interpretation, most now accept that their own experiences and perspectives influence their depictions of prior times and personalities.

Some go further. Despite historians' efforts to present objective accounts of the past, Patrick Hutton suggests, "What is called history is no more than the official memory a society chooses to honor." Historical memory "places events of past and present within invented chronologies," Hutton argues, and it therefore represents not so much an accurate rendering of the past but an account based on "reconstructive interpretation."[82] This new perspective on historical "truth" emphasizes its subjectivity. "History is interpretation, and as such it is subject to exactly those same societal biases that are supposedly the weakness of 'memory,'" according to archivist Mark Greene.[83] Historians continually "rewrite" the past because they always interpret it through their contemporaneous perspectives. These, in turn, reflect society's collective memory.

ARCHIVAL MEMORY

The mobility and rapid change of the wired global community challenge the capacity of human memory, both individually and collectively, to retain accurate information about even the recent past. Responding to these social upheavals, French historian Pierre Nora asserts that "modern memory is, above all, archival. It relies entirely on the materiality of the trace, the immediacy of the recording, the visibility of the image."[84] In evaluating the reliability of archival records, Allan Megill distinguishes between historical traces and historical sources. "A trace is anything remaining from the past that was not made with the intention of revealing the past to us, but simply emerged as part of normal life," he explains. "A source, on the other hand, is anything that was intended by its creator to stand as an account of events." Sources rely more heavily on memory than do traces. Because accidental traces of the past do not bear the marks of deliberate action, he adds, such "inadvertent evidence is a far more solid foundation for historical knowledge than is the evidence that people in the past have intended to stand as evidence." Historical traces "are insulated from people's conscious or unconscious wishes to remember and testify in a particular way," he concludes. "Memory lacks this kind of objectivity."[85] Archives preserve both historical sources and the more ephemeral traces of the past. They thereby perpetuate aspects of human memory recorded in a variety of tangible sources, from textual records to photographs, sound recordings, and electronic media.

Because memory is fragile and malleable people create surrogates that can attach memory to unchanging forms. Artifacts, documents, even geographical places present information about the past in fixed media that do not change with new circumstances of time or place. Human societies often regard time as a "dimension of life that ultimately can be submitted to cultural control," according to Anthony Aveni. "The material embodiment of time evident in the book, the codex, the carved door lintel, the ceremonial stela, as well as the grandfather clock—all have the effect of making past and future concrete and official."[86] Since the era of Hammurabi's Code and Moses's stone tablets, we have attempted to codify memory and ensure its authenticity and reliability. As Jacques Le Goff argues, writing provides two methods of preserving collective memory. Commemoration or celebration of landmark events can be recorded through inscriptions on monuments such as runes, steles, obelisks, and other epigraphic structures. "These 'stone archives' added to the function of archives proper the character of an insistent publicity, wagering on the ostentation and durability of this lapidary and marmoreal memory," Le Goff states. Secondly, written documents preserve memory through support structures, which have developed from "experiments with bone, cloth, skin, cinders and letters of clay or wax in Mesopotamia, birchbark in ancient Russia, palm leaves as in India, or tortoise shells as in China, and finally with papyrus, parchment, and paper." Such documents serve two principal functions, according to Le Goff: "the first is information storage, which allows communication across time and space and provides men with a means of marking, memorizing, and registering"; the other purpose, "while ensuring the passage from the auditory to the visual domain," enables people "to examine in a different way, to rearrange, to rectify phrases and even isolated words."[87] Thus, documents embody reminders of the past, which can be used and interpreted in numerous different ways.

Such documents are not memory itself, but surrogates for memory. They attach memory to fixed objects in order to perpetuate it over time and distance. "Archives, computer banks, and written texts are in some ways substitutes for memory but they are not memory, and the processes of information retrieval associated with them are not the same as recognizing the past through memory," historian Harry Ritter argues. "A record is not a memory; feelings, images, and ideas are not embedded in resources; memory is something that happens, not an artifact; one type of record is not automatically as good as any other."[88] Ritter correctly distinguishes archival records from personal memory. However, as a means of preserving knowledge of the past, archival records perform one function of memory. They enable human beings to remember previous times with greater or lesser degrees of accuracy. As Ritter argues, some records do this better than others. The most useful records are those that can be checked, evaluated, and verified as authentic and reliable conveyors of accurate information. The value of such records lies in what they tell us about the past. As Maurice Mandelbaum states, the writings of historians "refer to past occurrences whose existence is only known through inferences drawn from surviving documents; but it is not to those documents themselves, but to what they indicate concerning the past, that the historians' statements actually refer."[89] Documents convey information and instruct us about previous events, personalities, or ideas. An important distinction between documents and monuments emerges from the Latin roots of these terms. "Monument" derives from *monere* (to "make remember"), while "document" comes from *docere* (to teach or instruct). "Though both monument and text locate and preserve the past through visual practices (seeing, reading), words have an explicit pedagogical function which is only implied by the veneration or celebration of commemorative imagery," explains Matt Matsuda. "Monuments guard the past, but words instruct the present and teach the future."[90] Archival documents thus perform an active function of instruction and teaching. They are not passive or inert objects for commemoration.

From the human need for accurate evidence of interactions—from legal agreements to financial transactions to cultural representations—emerges the concept of archives as institutions of social memory. Canadian archivist Jean-Pierre Wallot sets the goal for archivists of "building a living memory for the history of our present." By creating "houses of memory," archivists can provide "keys to the collective memory" that will enable the world's citizens to open doors to personal and societal connections with the past and their own roots.[91] As repositories managed by those actively engaged in preserving documents in multiple formats, archives represent a distinct form of human memory. "Unlike verbal and nonverbal action, which is ephemeral and disappears as it occurs, the physical durability of objects, artifacts, and documents allows them to be passed from person to person and from place to place over long periods of time," observes geographer Kenneth Foote. Thus, "archives can be seen as a valuable means of extending the temporal and spatial range of human communication."[92] Such records provide both evidence of formal, official transactions and general information about the past—the "traces" described by Nora and Megill.

Archival records are the byproducts of human activity. At their most transparent they appear to be unselfconscious creations intended not to interpret or investigate a particular topic but to complete a normal and often routine transaction. In modern archival theory, such records derive reliability and authenticity as evidence due to this assumption that they result from activity itself, and not from deliberate efforts to influence thought. However, recent scholarship suggests that this assumption crumbles upon close inspection. "History in its traditional form undertook to 'memorize' the monuments of the past, to transform them into documents and to make these traces speak, although they are not often verbal, or silently express something other than what they say," according to Michel Foucault, but "in our time history is what transforms documents into monuments, and in the place where one used to decipher the traces left by men, where one tried to recognize the image of what they had been, it now deploys a mass of elements that it tries to isolate, group, make pertinent, to put into relationships, and to constitute as wholes."[93] Archival records appear no longer as impartial or neutral carriers of facts. The archival record is complex, problematic. It represents power relationships in society, both in the events, persons, and ideas memorialized in the documents themselves and in the process of how they are selected for preservation and validation within archival repositories.

The records protected in archives gain significance from their legal, administrative, financial, and intellectual usefulness. They often document formal transactions between two or more people—sometimes, as in the British Magna Carta or the Constitution of the

United States, affecting entire nationalities or populations. Archival records may carry important legal significance, provide evidence of administrative or financial transactions, or demonstrate valuable creative or intellectual contributions. At times their significance may be only symbolic or ceremonial, such as a college diploma or a family vacation photograph.[94] In contrast to European traditions, in China the written documents that constitute history "do not have a memory function . . . but rather a ritual, sacred, magical function" as a method of communicating with the gods, as Jacques Le Goff recounts. "The document is not intended to serve as a proof, but to be a magic object, a talisman."[95] In the western tradition, written records serve first as legal, administrative, and financial evidence. In addition, many archival documents provide essential sources for historical investigations of the past. Since at least the mid-nineteenth century, the basis of modern historians' methodology is the creed formulated by Charles V. Langlois and Charles Seignobos: "No documents, no history."[96]

Archival documents do not constitute history, nor do they constitute memory. By conveying markers for past events, however, they make it possible for contemporary and future historians—for all people, for all purposes—to access, use, and interpret information about previous times. On close inspection, though, the metaphor of archives as memory breaks down.[97] As Carolyn Steedman argues, "an Archive is not very much like human memory, and is not at all like the unconscious mind." Archives do accumulate texts, documents, and data, which are organized and classified so that they can be retrieved at later times. "The Archive is made from selected and consciously chosen documentation from the past and also from the mad fragmentations that no one intended to preserve and that just ended up there," she states. "And nothing happens to this stuff, in the Archive," Steedman contends. "It is indexed, and catalogued, and some of it is not indexed and catalogued, and some of it is lost. But as stuff, it just sits there until it is read, and used, and narrativised."[98] In portraying archival documents as passive, awaiting the researcher's magic touch to spring to life and reveal their hidden truths, Steedman displays a historian's narrow perspective, placing herself at the critical juncture between "mute" records and public disclosure by the scholar. In fact, the archivist also plays an important role in selecting, shaping, presenting, and interpreting the archival record. Archivists mediate between user and record. Even when they strive for neutrality, their daily imprint on the archival record is inescapable.

Equating archives and memory leads to serious conceptual difficulties and false metaphors. Documents and records serve as surrogates for memory traces, but they are not the same as human memory itself. "The most common strategy for justifying the analogical leap from individual memories to Memory—social, cultural, collective, public, or whatever—is to identify memory as a collection of practices or material artifacts," argues Kerwin Lee Klein. The most common tropes presented as "memory" are archives and public monuments. "Ideally, the memory will be a dramatically imperfect piece of material culture, and such fragments are best if imbued with pathos," Klein asserts, as "readers confront the abject object: photographs are torn, mementos faded, toys broken." Discussion of memory leads to false generalizations, as authors "move freely from memories as individual psychic events to memories as a shared group consciousness to memories as a collection of material artifacts," with little distinction among these separate concepts. "The new 'materialization' of memory thus grounds the elevation of memory to the status of a historical agent," Klein concludes, "and we enter a new age in which archives remember and statues forget."[99]

Although such anthropomorphic metaphors prove misleading, archival records and documents can convey emotional and intellectual links to people and events of previous eras. Symbolically, documents such as the Declaration of Independence and the Constitution represent American freedom and self-government— concepts that help define our national identity and that remind us of the struggles to achieve these goals. The story of Connecticut's Charter Oak, for example, reveals the common belief that possession of a single document (the colonial charter) by itself protected the rights of colonists. To prevent its capture and the resulting loss of their political rights, colonists hid the charter in an oak tree, still the most prominent symbol of Connecticut's history.[100] Personal letters, such as those written by soldiers during the Civil War, or by women pioneers on the Great Plains, or by unemployed workers during the Great Depression, provide vivid reminders of the hardships endured by our ancestors. Such documents also reveal the complexity and variety of human experience, the emotional impact of public events on individuals, and the importance of knowing the past in order to understand the present. However, records and documents can be altered or destroyed to serve political or cultural goals, as George Orwell recognized. The task of the archivist is to select, preserve, and ensure access to records that are authentic, reliable, trustworthy, and verifiable. This results in a usable and essential form of archival memory, even when taking into account the archivist's mediation.

ARCHIVES AS CONSTRUCTED MEMORY

Archives have traditionally been regarded as neutral and unbiased repositories for authentic records of human activity against which the researcher can evaluate other more subjective sources of information. Because they are created, for the most part, contemporaneously with the events that they record, archival documents have been viewed as unbiased witnesses to historical events.[101] Recent writings by postmodernists challenge such confident assumptions about archival records. According to one explanation of its complex concepts, "Postmodernism calls into question enlightenment values such as rationality, truth, and progress, arguing that these merely serve to secure the monolithic structure of modern . . . society by concealing or excluding any forces that might challenge its cultural dominance."[102]

Texts and documents, according to this view, are never exactly what they purport to be. They are constructed to reflect particular perspectives and to seize the power to interpret human society, past and present. Dutch archivist Eric Ketelaar declares that although this postmodern view of archives threatens traditional archival values such as "authenticity, originality, and uniqueness," it also acknowledges "the archive's power: the archives as 'repository of meanings,' the multilayered, multifaceted meanings hidden in archivalization and archiving, which can be deconstructed and reconstructed, then interpreted and used by scholars, over and over again."[103] Power relations play out daily in archives, according to Richard Harvey Brown and Beth Davis-Brown, since "archives are the manufacturers of memory and not merely the guardians of it." The creation of collective memory in archives involves "struggles behind the scenery (and outside the theatre)" in establishing reality and truth. "As with most forms of modern social control, the power of archivists and curators is embedded in technical-rational processes that are ostensibly non-political," they argue. However, these technical decisions "do help shape the collective national public memory" and contribute to formation of group identity. "In this basic sense, archives, libraries and museums are political," Brown and Davis-Brown conclude. "And to the extent that these political/discursive functions are unrecognized, the technical-rational decisions and practices of archivists are ideological."[104] Archivists thus play an important role in the contested nature of national identity, collective consciousness, and the construction of memory.

This power places archivists near the center of debates over history, memory, and meaning. South African archivist Verne Harris, who has witnessed vast social changes in his own country, thus states that the archive "is not a quiet retreat for professionals and scholars and craftspersons. It is a crucible of human experience. A battleground for meaning and significance. A babel of stories. A place and a space of complex and ever-shifting power plays."[105] Because archives confer significance and authority on the documents they house, this power can shape the perspectives that we have on individuals and social groups. Far from being a neutral repository for recorded memory, archives (and archivists) actively mediate and shape the archival record.

In states undergoing rapid transition from colonial or authoritarian control to democratic systems, these political implications of archives feature prominently in public discourse. This can be seen clearly in modern China. "A political way of thinking, as an ideological heritage, has deeply embedded itself and greatly influenced the construction of archival reality and culture," observes Chinese archivist Du Mei. "At present, in addition to being wary of archives of power, we should also be on the alert concerning the power of archivists," she cautions. "When enjoying our legal privilege, archivists commonly lack the necessary awareness of how this privilege can be abused and become autocratic." Researchers depend on archivists, who thus participate in writing history and creating memory. "Up until now, archivists have not consciously examined how and to what extent they should mediate the original records," Du Mei asserts. "They are not even aware it constitutes an issue or problem."[106] For archivists in all cultures, such awareness must precede responses to the potential power that they frequently wield in mediating the past and shaping the future.

As historians during the last four decades turned their attention toward issues of power, underrepresented minority groups, gender, race, and related concerns, they discovered that these topics "are not so easily studied through existing documentation," according to Francis X. Blouin. "The underrepresented, the disfranchised, the conquered, and the suppressed did not create documents or, if they did, sadly, those documents are not represented in the archives." Power thus may have "corrupted the archive as a repository for social memory."[107] Since archives are institutions that require funding, authorization, and legitimacy, it is no wonder that they traditionally have reflected the dominant culture and privileged the voices and stories of the powerful.

Not surprisingly, then, one means of securing a claim to this power—to having one's voice heard—would be to secure a place in the archives. Failing that, the disfranchised could create their own archives. American Jews took the latter approach when they founded the American Jewish Historical Society in 1892, at the height of a wave of anti-Semitism and nativism. "The historical society would serve as a sanctioned, authoritative base which would enable the collection of archives, carefully selected for their content," Elisabeth Kaplan states.[108]

This same impulse guided African Americans in creating archival repositories to document and celebrate their history and culture. It represents an assertion of racial pride and an effort to secure the power that comes from being able to tell the group's collective story of tragedy, suffering, achievement, and success. As Canadian archivist Terry Cook observes, there is "a growing awareness of other voices, other stories, other narratives, other realities—other than those that traditionally have filled school readers, history books, museums, public monuments, popular media, and archives."[109] These voices confer power. Archives provide a forum to recognize and legitimize the role of disfranchised groups in society.

Closely related to the concept of power is that of identity. Art, literature, museums, libraries, and archives all help to create a sense of identity for marginalized groups, when they are able to participate in these forms of cultural and symbolic recognition. Archives can tie people to each other. Australian archivist Adrian Cunningham reminds us that archives provide "that sense of connecting with the wonderful depth and richness of human experience in all its complexity and contrariness by preserving and providing access to its documentary residue; the sense that somehow the souls of human beings now departed can yet resonate through the written artefacts of their lives."[110] In tracing the origins of the American Jewish Historical Society, Elisabeth Kaplan shows that archives can perform a critical role in constructing history and historical identity, as a marginalized group seeks "to establish and present to the larger culture a cohesive identity." As Kaplan discovers, archives are not sites of objective historical truth. "The archival record doesn't just happen; it is created by individuals and organizations, and used, in turn, to support their values and missions, all of which comprises a process that is certainly not politically and culturally neutral." Archives thus become "major players in the business of identity construction and identity politics."[111]

The postmodernist perspective inextricably links documents and texts to the purposes for which they are constructed and to the nature of their interpretation and use. "Everything in records is shaped, presented, represented, re-presented, symbolized, signified, constructed by the writer, the computer programmer, the photographer, the cartographer, for a purpose," Terry Cook asserts. "No text is an innocent by-product of administrative or personal action, but rather a constructed product."[112] This process extends to the creation of archives, and to the formation of social memory itself. "The making of memory involves the active construction of present knowledge out of continually evolving informational materials together with the elaboration on data relationships collected in the past," Brien Brothman contends.[113] Memory thus represents active thought and deliberate action, not a passive accumulation. The rock of memory is not sedimentary but volcanic, molten, or metamorphic.

The decision to create a record, or to preserve it, or to place it in an archival repository becomes an act of memory construction. Archivists consciously decide to shape the archival record, even when they do not realize they are doing so. Some of these decision-making processes are subconscious; others are embedded in routine decisions based on professional criteria that are culturally influenced. The very designation of the archives as a "permanent" repository for valuable documents derives from an assumption that we can create an unchanging expression of the past for future generations. For example, the mission statement of the National Archives of Canada enshrines the concept of memory: "To preserve the collective memory of the nation and of the Government of Canada and to contribute to the protection of rights and the enhancement of a sense of national identity." As National Archivist Ian Wilson acknowledges, "The archival holdings in this sense are not inert." Researchers must interact with the holdings, searching for and recognizing pattern, context, significance, and value in forming their interpretations. "Only through this dynamic interaction do the holdings fulfill their potential, being transformed from information to meaningful memory," Wilson asserts. "The role of the archives becomes to reunite the public with the evidence of their past, making the archives a vital link in creating the social memory."[114] Archivists thereby assume an important role in society, one much larger than that of custodian or caretaker for the inert relics of the past.

The political and social ferment of the 1960s led some historians and archivists to argue that archivists should actively intervene to ensure documentation of underrepresented social groups in American archives, which had generally reflected the powerful groups in society. In 1970 Howard Zinn charged that the archival record was biased toward the rich and powerful elements of society—government, business, and the military—while the poor and impotent remained hidden in archival obscurity. Zinn urged archivists "to compile a whole new world of documentary material about the lives, desires and needs of ordinary people."[115]

This challenge to the archival profession not only led to some important new initiatives in documenting minority groups in archives, but also opened a debate over the "neutrality" and "objectivity" of archival acquisition. Certainly a strong argument can be made in favor of actively redressing the underrepresented groups in society through active "affirmative action" by both public and private archives. One danger to avoid, as Kaplan points out in respect to Jewish archives, is that by narrowly defining the boundaries of archival acquisition archivists may run the risk of driving wedges between the ethnic or "minority" groups whom they seek to document.[116]

In order to counter such bias archivists need to recognize and acknowledge that they are not neutral, passive servants of Clio—or any other muse—but active agents in shaping social memory. Canadian archivist Tom Nesmith explains that "contrary to the conventional idea that archivists simply receive and house vast quantities of records, which merely reflect society, they actually co-create and shape the knowledge in records, and thus help form society's memory."[117] The "central archival professional myth" of neutrality obscures the reality that archivists hold "enormous power and discretion over societal memory, deeply masked behind a public image of denial and self-effacement," Nesmith argues. "Some of what makes a record meaningful is inscribed in it by those who literally made it, but most of what makes a record intelligible lies outside its physical borders in its context of interpretation," he declares. "Archivists, who do much to shape this context, therefore share in authoring the record."[118] Not only do archivists select the records that will be acquired and preserved, they also create finding aids that describe them and provide controlled access to vast quantities of materials. How they perform these archival functions will shape the accessibility of these materials for all future research. "Since few researchers can simply plunge into the vast amounts of archives and just start reading without this guidance, the archives and the recorded reality researchers actually see (for better or worse) are largely the ones constructed for them by archivists," Nesmith asserts.[119]

This power carries with it significant responsibilities. As Francis Blouin admonishes archivists, they must become more aware of their role as "mediators between records creators and records repositories, between archives and users, between conceptions of the past and extant documentation."[120] This understanding may lead to more self-awareness and hence more transparent processes of archival acquisition, appraisal, description, and access. These archival functions take place amid a political reality in which documentation of the past shapes our knowledge and understanding of historical events.

FORGETTING THE FUTURE

In all of these concerns for memory creation, archivists and those who use archives should also become more conscious of the obverse of memory—forgetfulness. Each act of remembering entails an act of forgetting. They are inextricably linked, both for individuals and for groups of people. "Every society defines itself by what it chooses to remember and what it chooses to forget," asserts Lesley Richmond. "If the means to remember does not exist, in the form of archives, reliable authentic knowledge of that subject matter will not exist."[121] Memory construction is a political act. For it is in the interstices of documentation that important perspectives and voices have often been lost. Sometimes this is deliberate, as in Orwell's *Nineteen Eighty-Four* or John Ross's poem "Against Amnesia." Ruling powers seek control by effacing memory. As James O'Toole recounts, records may be honored as objects of veneration or, by contrast, feared and despised as objects of loathing. "During the French Revolution, for instance, crowds sometimes directed their fury against collections of records because those documents seemed to embody the systems of oppression from which they sought liberation," O'Toole explains. Destroying records might offer immediate benefits "by removing specific evidence of debt or obligations of service," but the enthusiasm behind ritualized destruction of documents "bespeaks a more visceral antagonism" toward such symbols of oppression.[122] O'Toole also cites the "partisan destruction of offending works of theology and service books" during the Reformation and "the smashing of Confucian texts during the Cultural Revolution in China in the late 1960s" as further examples of such deliberate obliteration of written records. [123]

At other times the loss or destruction of records is not a conscious decision but the seemingly inadvertent result of choices and assumptions that people make. For archivists, deciding to acquire one set of documents often precludes obtaining others. Limited time and resources require archivists to be selective in what they collect and preserve. As Verne Harris concedes, archivists "offer researchers a sliver of a sliver of a sliver"—a mere fragment of the recorded experiences or collective memory of a nation.[124] In determining what records to preserve for posterity, Terry Cook observes, archivists engage in "remembering the future."[125] Yet since only a miniscule percentage of all records produced in modern society will survive the processes of loss, neglect, archival selection, and appraisal, one could argue that archivists engage principally in destroying documentation. It may be more honest to state that archivists daily engage in forgetting the future. Those aspects of the past that are not remembered limit what the future will know, and diminish its memory-knowledge.

Recording memory in tangible form—archival memory—presumes the loss of memory concerning those things that are not recorded. As literacy first began to exert its influence over the ancient Greeks, Socrates warned his young friend Phaedrus of the dangers of writing. Socrates said that when Theuth, the inventor of letters, boasted that his invention "will make the Egyptians wiser and give them better memories," Thamuz replied:

> This discovery will create forgetfulness in the learners' souls, because they will not use their memories, they will trust to the external written characters, and not remember of themselves. You have found a specific not for memory but for reminding. You give your disciples not truth, but the appearance of wisdom; they will be hearers of many things without in fact learning them; will appear to be omniscient and will generally know nothing; they will be hard to be with, seeming to be wise when they are not.[126]

Writing thus weakens memory by causing those who rely on recorded information to diminish their personal powers of remembering.

Socrates' warning reminds us that memory and amnesia are inextricably entwined in our relationship to the past. Julius Caesar echoed Socrates' concern that written records would diminish men's capacity for memory. In his *Gallic Wars* (VI, 14), Caesar reported that although they used the Greek alphabet to record public and private accounts, the Druids believed their religion forbade writing down certain important verses and stories. "They seem to me to have established this custom for two reasons," Caesar concluded, "because they do not wish to divulge their doctrine, or to see their pupils neglect their memory by relying on writing, for it almost always happens that making use of texts has as its result decreased zeal for learning by heart and a diminution of memory."[127] From ancient to early modern times, written records contested oral tradition and memory for supremacy in meeting the human need to remember the past. Archives thus often have joined history in opposing memory, or in replacing it.

Concern for recorded memory extends both to public institutions and to the personal realm. As stated in the previous chapter, in *The Book of Laughter and Forgetting* Czech novelist Milan Kundera states that one of the founders of communist Czechoslovakia, was "airbrushed" out of history after he was charged with treason and hanged. This leads one character to declare "that the struggle of man against power is the struggle of memory against forgetting."[128] Kundera addresses this concern in terms of national political purposes for effacing or altering collective memory, but Patricia Hampl extends this to the importance of each individual recording her or his account of events. "Memoir must be written because each of us must have a created version of the past," she explains. "Created: that is, real, tangible, made of the stuff of a life lived in place and in history." Despite the inevitable subjectivity of such personal memoirs, Hampl states "in the act of remembering, the personal environment expands, resonates beyond itself, beyond its 'subject,' into the endless and tragic recollection that is history." This leads her to conclude, "There may be no more pressing intellectual need in our culture than for people to become sophisticated about the function of memory. The political implications of the loss of memory are obvious. The authority of memory is a personal confirmation of selfhood."[129] The role of memoir in capturing personal perspectives on the past mirrors that of archives in preserving the written accounts of individuals, organizations, and society as a whole.

Archivists daily make decisions about what aspects of the past and present will be recorded and preserved for future use. Yet this active choice of remembering arises within a social context bounded by present realities. Allan Megill asserts that evidence never speaks for itself, but must be understood and explained in context. Although we talk of remembering the past, he argues, we cannot actually do so. "It is the present that we remember: that is, we 'remember' what remains living within our situations now," Megill contends. "We think the past: that is, we construct it or reconstruct it on the basis of certain critical procedures. The relevant motto is: 'Remember the present, think the past.'"[130] Archives emerge amid "the problem of boundedness, the shifting definitions of pertinent evidence,"

Peter Fritzsche asserts. "The archive was not simply constituted as a powerful way to contain the past but developed in relationship to a past that was regarded as fragmented, distant, and otherwise difficult to hold onto." The impulse to preserve arises from the fear of amnesia. "The history of the archive is the recognition of loss," Fritzsche contends. "For archives to collect the past, the past has to come to mind as something imperiled and distinctive."[131] Consciousness of the past only arises when it appears distant, cut off from the times in which people live. Since "the past is a foreign country," as David Lowenthal declares, we need archives, libraries, museums, and monuments to remind us of its relevance to our own era.[132] Thus, as Megill argues, we think about the past in order to remember the present.

Acting on behalf of society—or at least its representatives in the form of officials and administrators who authorize the creation and maintenance of archives—archivists perform daily rituals of remembering and forgetting. As Brien Brothman observes, "Remembering and forgetting are two sides of the same coin of information selection, which forms useful institutional memory."[133] Verne Harris portrays this process in poetic terms. "What we remember we keep in the light; what we forget is consigned to darkness. To remember is to archive. To archive is to preserve memory. In this conceptual framework the archive is a beacon of light, a place—or idea, or psychic space, or societal space—of and for sight," Harris declares. Yet every act of memory carries the weight of consigning some other aspect of human experience to oblivion. "There is no remembering without forgetting. There is no remembering that cannot become forgetting," Harris concedes. "Forgetting can be a way of remembering. They open out of each other, light becoming darkness, darkness becoming light." Decisions about memory and loss require artistic sensibility as well as legal and administrative expertise, Harris seems to say. "The dance of imagination, moving effortlessly through both conscious and unconscious spaces, shapes what is remembered and what is forgotten, and how the trace is configured," he writes. "And each time the trace is revisited, this dance is busy with its work of shaping and reshaping."[134] The archivist thus performs a choreographed process of opening and closing doors, of including some information—records, evidence, memory—in the archives and excluding others.

In the highly charged political atmosphere of South Africa under apartheid—and since the end of that oppressive regime—Harris has seen the powerful human drive to remember the past as well as the inevitably linked impulse to forget. Working closely with the Truth and Reconciliation Commission (TRC) between 1996 and 2001, he "was seduced by the TRC's dominant metanarrative: that its mission was to promote reconciliation through . . . an exercise in remembering, a quintessentially archival exercise."[135] During a visit to South Africa in 1998, however, Jacques Derrida challenged this reassuring view. A successful archives, "even if you really succeed in gathering everything you need in reference to the past, and that you interpret it in a way which is totally satisfactory . . . produces memory, but produces forgetting at the same time," Derrida cautioned his audience of academics and archivists. "And when we write, when we archive, when we trace, when we leave a trace behind us . . . the trace is at the same time the memory, the archive, and the erasure, the repression, the forgetting of what it is supposed to keep safe. That's why, for all these reasons, the work of the archivist is not simply a work of memory. It is a work of mourning. And a work of mourning . . . is a work of memory but also the best way just to forget the other," Derrida contended. "When I handwrite something on a piece of paper, I put it in my pocket or in a safe, it's just in order to forget it, to know that I can find it again while in the meantime having forgotten it," he continued. "So, suppose that one day South Africa would have accomplished a perfect, full archive of its whole history . . . everyone . . . would be eager to put this in such a safe that everyone could just forget it."[136] Derrida thus dared suggest that the purpose of the TRC might be to forget the past by separating it from daily experience and thereby making it safe. In doing so he clearly echoed Socrates' warnings about writing and forgetfulness.

Memory embodies amnesia. Each act of remembrance entails the forgetting of something else. "Archiving, traditionally understood as an act of remembering, is at profound levels a simple act of forgetting," as Harris recognized after Derrida's visit.[137] "The ultimate test of the TRC as archive is the extent to which it becomes a space for the play of remembering, forgetting, and imagining," he concluded.[138] Writing an op-ed piece for the *Natal Witness* in 2002, he publicly challenged the comforting view that the TRC had ensured ongoing public memory of apartheid abuses. He suggested that, "for the state the TRC is no more than a tool for providing a nod at remembering in the interests of a profounder forgetting," and that "while the state says it is dealing with the past, in fact it is intent on getting back to business as usual as quickly as possible."[139] The South African archives, likewise, provide a means both for remembering and forgetting past events, including apartheid-era atrocities and oppression.

In *Archive Fever: A Freudian Interpretation,* Jacques Derrida expressly links Freud's concept of the death drive to the destruction of archival records. Freud used the terms *death drive, aggression drive,* and *destruction drive* as if they were synonymous. This "three-named drive" is mute, and "since it always operates in silence, it never leaves any archives of its own," Derrida explains. "It works *to destroy the archive: on the condition of effacing* but also *with a view to effacing* its own 'proper' traces." The death drive "will always have been archive-destroying," he asserts. This destruction "not only incites forgetfulness, amnesia, the annihilation of memory . . . but also commands the radical effacement, in truth the eradication, of . . . the archive," Derrida contends. *"There is no archive without a place of consignation, without a technique of repetition, and without a certain exteriority."*[140] Archives cannot preserve records, cannot separate and select those worthy of safeguarding, without excluding other sources, other voices. The death drive threatens every archival desire. It is *"le mal d'archive,* 'archive fever,'" Derrida declares. Moreover, "its silent vocation is to burn the archive and to incite amnesia, thus refuting the economic principle of the archive, aiming to ruin the archive as accumulation and capitalization of memory on some substrate and in an exterior place."[141] The desire to forget clashes with the desire to remember, yet both exist simultaneously, inextricably linked in the human mind and in societal institutions.

This close connection between memory and amnesia suggests a yin/yang relationship, in which neither concept or action can be understood apart from its apparent opposite. Memory and forgetting are inseparable. As Allan Megill suggests, with reference to Nietzsche, "every remembering is also a mode of forgetting and every forgetting a mode of remembering."[142] There are, of course, some advantages to forgetting certain aspects of the past, and we should recognize and understand this mutuality of conflicting desires. What we need, suggests Nancy Wood, is "a new balance of forces between the obligation to remember and the 'capacity to forget,' a capacity that ensures a society's ability to extricate itself from memory's incapacitating grip."[143] As recent South African history demonstrates, both individually and collectively, people must be able to maintain a balance between remembering and forgetting, particularly in the face of a painful and disruptive past. Public memory "shapes a nation's ethos and sense of identity," which explains, at least partially, "why memory is always selective and is so often contested," according to Michael Kammen. "Memory is more likely to be activated by contestation, and amnesia is more likely to be induced by the desire for reconciliation."[144] Although writing about American culture, Kammen's observation proves accurate also in respect to the TRC in South Africa.

Some aspects of our history are so controversial or painful that society seeks to efface them from memory. Societies have deliberately destroyed buildings associated with Nazi power in Berlin, the site of the Salem witches' executions, and the former home of serial murderer John Gacy. Although "the cultural effacement of memory" is "alien to prevailing archival values," geographer Kenneth Foote contends, archivists must be aware of the social pressures to exclude certain aspects of historical memory from the archives.[145] One example of this desire to cleanse archives of painful racial memories is the controversy that erupted when Central Michigan University accepted documents from a local Ku Klux Klan chapter for preservation in its archives. Some people in the local community viewed this archival acquisition as tacit endorsement of the Klan and its heritage of racial intolerance. They denounced the archivists and university officials as "just a bunch of bigots."[146] The public furor that arose over this decision reflects the struggle to define the past and the impulse that many people sometimes feel to control or limit the perspectives and voices represented in archives.

At times the effacement of memory provides positive benefits for individuals and society. African American novelist Ralph Ellison reminds us that "not all of American history is recorded" and that "Americans can be notoriously selective in the exercise of historical memory." Rather than lament this erasure of the past, however, Ellison states that it prevents Americans from losing heart in the face of vast discrepancies between their democratic ideals and social reality. "Perhaps this is why we possess two basic versions of American history," Ellison suggests, "one which is neatly written and as neatly stylized as ancient myth, and the other unwritten and chaotic and full of contradictions, changes of pace, and surprises as life itself."[147] Individuals also may seek to escape their past, either to hide their mistakes or to protect their privacy. Wrongly convicted criminals, or those who have completed their jail terms, may have their records expunged, the slate wiped clean. In a provocative essay on "the right to social oblivion," Danish archivist Inge Bundsgaard argues, "it is a question of the right of the individual to be forgotten through the protection of privacy versus the right of society to its social, cultural, and historical memory as contained in the archival records."[148] Once again, forgetting becomes part of healing, part of society's negotiated truce with its painful past.

Efforts to efface the past occur in virtually all historically oriented societies. The vast destruction of books and other cultural sources during the Maoist Cultural Revolution is well known. Similarly, in 1981 Sinhalese nationalists burned the Tamil library of Jaffna in Sri Lanka, destroying "one of South Asia's greatest repositories of culture and history," containing thousands of manuscripts, palm leaf scrolls, and books.[149] During the conflict in Bosnia–Herzegovina in the early 1990s, "Serbian forces besieging Sarajevo purposefully destroyed or damaged several carefully chosen institutions of collective memory," including the Olympic Museum, the Oriental Institute, and the National and University Library, according to historian Robert Donia. The warfare destroyed artifacts, documents, provincial government records, and Ottoman-era manuscripts. "In both the Serbian- and Croatian-controlled sections of Bosnia there has been wholesale destruction of the reminders of Ottoman rule and the Islamic faith," Donia reports. The burning of Sarajevo's library "has become a global emblem of the 'memoricide' practiced by the nationalist extremists," he concludes.[150] The term "memoricide" aptly captures the essence of such attempts to efface all traces of a society's past. The destruction of hundreds of libraries, museums, and architectural treasures in Croatia, Bosnia, Herzegovina, and Kosovo constituted a deliberately political act of erasing memory. According to librarian and scholar András Riedlmayer, "libraries, archives, museums and cultural institutions have been targeted for destruction, in an attempt to eliminate the material evidence—books, documents and works of art—that could remind future generations that people of different ethnic and religious traditions once shared a common heritage."[151]

In times of war and armed conflict, records may be destroyed either deliberately, through neglect, or incidentally. The American invasion of Iraq in March 2003 unleashed violent looting of cultural treasures. Widespread destruction of artifacts and documents in the Iraq Museum in Baghdad, only a few days after American forces invaded the city, attracted international condemnation, but this was only the most visible symbol. "Vast amounts of irreparable damage have been done—it is hard to overestimate it—by a variety of agencies, from local inhabitants to armed forces, through neglect, ignorance, or willful destruction," reports University of Cambridge scholar Eleanor Robson. "Almost all the major academic libraries have been torched and pillaged. Nearly every archeological site in the southern desert has been systematically plundered."[152] In October 2004, Dr. Saad Eskander, director-general of the Iraq National Library and Archives, reported that in Baghdad "most cultural

institutions were looted and burnt" in mid-April 2003, including
the National Library and Archives. "It was a national disaster beyond
imagination," he lamented.[153] American forces did little to prevent
such looting and destruction of cultural property, including archives
and ancient manuscripts. Instead of protecting cultural sites, they
were deployed to protect the Ministry of Oil.[154]

Such indifference to the loss of irreplaceable cultural materials
suggests, at best, a lack of understanding of the importance of
cultural heritage to the people of Iraq, and at worst, a negligence
deliberately designed to diminish their national patrimony.
According to Jeff Spurr, Islamic and Middle East specialist at
Harvard's Fine Arts Library, the message conveyed by American
forces on the ground seemed to be, "we do not care enough to see
that your administrative, educational, and cultural institutions are
protected."[155] In August 2007 the Society of American Archivists
protested the decision to place American troops in or near Iraqi
archives and cultural institutions. "Such acts endanger documents
and other materials that are essential to the cultural patrimony of
Iraq's citizens," SAA Council declared.[156] The motives attributed
to the looters themselves range from "deliberate destruction of
records that might now prove damning"[157] to the former regime,
to "[e]ndemic unemployment and poverty [that] necessitated
archaeological theft for economic survival."[158] In addition, there
may have been "extremists with political, religious, and other
agendas; hooligans caught up in the rush of a society's unraveling;
and ordinary Iraqis intent on removing any perceived symbol of
Saddam's rule," Verne Harris suggests. "There might even have
been *agents provocateurs,* deployed by who knows what forces," he adds.
"What is clear though is that in Baghdad there wasn't a sufficient
groundswell of appreciation for archival treasures, of a sense of
public ownership in them, to prevent the destruction."[159] American
soldiers and civilians joined the looting, taking home souvenirs
from one of Saddam Hussein's palaces while Iraqis were looting
other sites.[160]

Less dramatic, but more common, are attempts to sanitize the
archival record in order to promote the interests of one segment
of society, usually the ruling class. Examples of this can be found,
among many others, in China under the Qing dynasty (1644-1912)
and in modern China. Although Qing archivists demonstrated a
"laudable willingness to save almost everything," even when much
of the governmental record remained locked in secrecy, Beatrice
Bartlett observes, "neither official nor unofficial memories can be

preserved in all their fullness of detail." For example, "Few private and unpublished family or business papers from Qing times are today available for consultation." For government archivists, "the primary aim of archival preservation would have been, of course, to protect the regime and allow no antigovernment views to circulate widely, even if inscribed in government documents." Secondly, "The emperor had to be portrayed in the best possible light." A third concern "would have been to preserve the face of officials, provided that such did not conflict with the first or second aim." As Bartlett observes, "The archival supervisors' aims, if carried out, guaranteed a view of the government as all-powerful, effective, and orderly."[161]

Above all, Qing archivists deliberately limited the quality of the archival record by "restricting the kind of information collected in the first place," by such methods as manipulating confessions of wrongdoing—a technique perpetuated in Stalin's Soviet Union and Orwell's *Nineteen Eighty-Four*. "Much information we might like to have is forever lost, and the information that survives in the archives has to be interpreted in the light of the suspicion that some of it may have been noted to clear officials of blame rather than to determine facts," Bartlett concludes. The disappearance of potentially embarrassing archival records "strongly suggests the use of that special archival oubliette—an archivist's purposeful destruction of a set of documents." Thus, Qing archivists served the ruling powers, "protecting the imperial face" at the expense of historical knowledge and truth.[162]

Even today in modern China, according to archivist Du Mei, "Our perception of society tends to focus on what is positive and visible and neglect that which is negative and invisible." Archivists "tend to follow the politics of the present order," she observes. "That is, we do our job within the priorities and directions of the dominant forces of society."[163] In their daily work archivists contribute to the goals of their institutions—government, business, academic, historical, and religious structures. By doing so they perpetuate the status quo of power relationships in society. Unless archivists respond to a higher calling to professional responsibility and social conscience, such relationships—consciously or unconsciously—will persist.

The control exerted over public memory and archives by ruling elites produces gaps in the historical record. Some voices are silent, others absent from the written record. This fact troubled George Orwell, who recognized that no records exist for the vast numbers of slaves who labored to create ancient monuments.[164] Writing about more recent slave societies, Laurent Dubois echoes Orwell. Dubois observes, "the French Caribbean has seen a rich discussion about both the possibilities and the limits of the archives left by slavery and emancipation." Lacking full documentation of slave life in the Caribbean, historians have conceded to novelists the authority to convey this hidden past. Several recent novels focusing on Caribbean slavery have incorporated archival documents as a literary form. "These novels interestingly confront a broader problem faced by all those who seek to write the history of slavery and, more particularly, the stories of the slaves themselves—the absences and silences in the archives," Dubois asserts. "Some novelists have argued that traditional historical work, because of its dependence on archives written by white masters and colonial officials, can never tell the true story of the Caribbean, while historians have sometimes criticized the ahistorical and mythological approaches of novelists."[165] Colonial archives exclude those lacking political and social influence. Thus, "archives are not only about what they contain within their walls," Adele Perry asserts. "They are also about absence, although the absences in the colonial archive are not neutral, voluntary, or strictly literal. They are . . . silences borne of and perpetuated by violence and radical inequality."[166] In the silences and absences of the archives we see the playing out of social, political, and intellectual power. Whose history will be preserved? Whose memory? Whose records? Whose stories?

OPENING ARCHIVES TO THE FUTURE

Predispositions and cultural biases have skewed archival holdings in favor of the rich and powerful in society. Disfranchised and marginalized groups often have found themselves excluded from the hallowed halls of historical memory because archival documentation was unavailable or deemed unimportant. However, efforts in recent decades to solicit and acquire archival materials documenting ethnic communities, labor and working classes, women, African Americans, and civil rights have achieved significant progress in balancing the historical record and rescuing these forgotten voices. Because meaning is something that is always constructed and not inherent in documents, the postmodernists argue, archivists need to think clearly about how to determine which manuscripts and records should be collected and preserved. In making such decisions archivists should seek to minimize (or at least recognize) personal and institutional biases and to ensure adequate documentation of all aspects of society.

Knowledge of the past opens the door to the future. One cannot exist without the other. As Elie Wiesel observes, "The opposite of the past is not the future but the absence of the future; the opposite of the future is not the past but the absence of the past. The loss of one is equivalent to the sacrifice of the other."[167] The silences in the archives require careful attention. We must listen attentively, search diligently, and imagine what is absent. To hear the lost voices among the archival records we must read "against their grain." Just as historians in the 1960s began to write history "from the bottom up" in order to disclose the lives of the working classes, women, and minorities, anthropologist Ann Laura Stoler contends that engagement with colonial archives requires "a reading of 'upper class sources upside down' that would reveal the language of rule and the biases inherent in statist perceptions." This helps to counter the power of ruling classes to control historical memory. As Stoler argues, "colonial documents were rhetorical sleights of hand that erased the facts of subjugation, reclassified petty crime as political subversion, or simply effaced the colonized."[168] As Carolyn Steedman states, "historians read for what is *not there*: the silences and the absences of the documents always speak to us." Steedman points to Jules Michelet, a nineteenth-century French historian, "who first formulated the proper subject of history: all the numberless unnoticed *miserabiles personae*, who had lived and died, as mute in the grave as they had been in life."[169] These are the silences and absences with which historians contend. As archivists consider their role in society, one valuable service that they could provide would be to open their archives to these silent voices, to seek and preserve traces of this forgotten past.

The stakes are high. Memory and records, as Orwell vividly demonstrated, perpetuate the power of the ruling classes. Yet they also carry the secret to overturning such authority. Giving voice to the marginalized masses, providing an opportunity for others to hear a choir of diverse songs and stories, affords alternate conceptions of society and new openings to the future. The struggle for power continues. "To make themselves the master of memory and forgetfulness is one of the great preoccupations of the classes, groups, and individuals who have dominated and continue to dominate historical societies [i.e., those with an active conception of the past]," Jacques Le Goff states.[170] When political and spiritual leaders "engage in memory distortion or 'practice' historical amnesia, we must recognize that members of the public at large are often likely to believe and internalize the rationalizations they receive," Michael Kammen warns. This leads to "egregious instances of memory distortion whose sole or primary purpose is to legitimize a regime, empower a rising social class, or else reduce (or even eliminate) the stigma of war crimes or inhumane atrocities."[171]

Archivists concerned with the forgotten voices of marginalized groups need to be aware of how decisions are made concerning what to acquire and preserve in archives. These choices reflect the roles played by records creators, archivists, records managers, and users—all of which take place within the changing contexts of society. According to Verne Harris, the archival record, "far from being an innocent byproduct of activity, a reflection of reality, . . . is a construction of realities expressing dominant relations of power. It privileges certain voices and cultures, while marginalizing or excluding others."[172] Citing Michel Foucault, Peter Fritzsche states that "the archive is widely recognized as one of an array of disciplinary institutions such as hospitals, prisons, and asylums that manage the technologies of power that are indispensable to the maintenance of social collectives and the enforcement of social norms." From this Foucauldian perspective, the archive "defines and establishes categories by which documents and other materials are stored and can be retrieved." In order to reinforce the viability of the nation-state, which government archives—and even many nongovernmental archives—serve, "the archive must exclude evidence from the margins that would jeopardize the continuous instantiation of a common past."[173] Archives thus enact a ritual of secrecy, but the archive is primarily "the result of the exercise of a specific power and authority, which involves placing certain documents in an archive at the same time as others are discarded," argues South African historian Achille Mbembe. "The archive is, therefore, not a piece of data, but a status."[174] Even in the most comprehensive archives, there are often missing pieces and neglected sources of information. "What has been excluded from the record determines its meaning as much as what was included. They are both part of the provenance," explains Dutch archivist Eric Ketelaar.[175] Archivists must recognize this and provide the best service possible given such limitations. By acknowledging and overcoming the tendencies toward privileging the records of powerful groups in society, archivists can provide a more balanced perspective on the past. This will enable future generations to examine and evaluate the activities and contributions of all voices in our culture. Archives thus serve an important role in identifying and preserving the documentation from which we fashion our historical memory.

The critical point for archivists in assessing their impact in co-creating or co-authoring the archival record lies in the appraisal function. Archival appraisal is "[t]he process of determining the length of time records should be retained, based on legal requirements and on their current and potential usefulness."[176] Beyond determining the legal requirements for retaining records, appraisal becomes highly subjective, dependent on the archivist's personal perspective, institutional requirements, and anticipated needs of researchers and other potential users. "Appraisal is the area of the greatest professional challenge to the archivist," University of Illinois archivist Maynard Brichford wrote in 1977. "In an existential context, the archivist bears responsibility for deciding which aspects of society and which specific activities shall be documented in the records retained for future use. Research may be paralyzed either by unwitting destruction or by preserving too much."[177] Given the vast output of documents and information since the mid-nineteenth century, archivists can only preserve a small fragment of the available records of modern society. "The truth is, archivists select a few records for inclusion in the archives and consign the vast majority of documents to the dumpster," Frank Boles writes in a recent Society of American Archivists manual.[178] Archivists estimate that they preserve only about one to five percent of all documents created in today's information-rich society.

Archivists thus perform, often behind their professional curtains, a vitally important function of determining what sources of information society will be able to access in the future. "Appraisal imposes a heavy social responsibility on archivists," Terry Cook asserts. "As they appraise records, they are doing nothing less than shaping the future of our documentary heritage. They are determining what the future will know about its past, which is often our present." Switching to first person, he continues, "As a profession, we archivists . . . are literally creating archives. We are deciding what is remembered and what is forgotten, who in society is visible and who remains invisible, who has a voice and who does not." Society's memory is at stake. "Appraisal is thus central to the archival endeavour—indeed, it is the *only* archival endeavour, a continuing activity without end, the heart of archives."[179] As part of their appraisal procedures, Cook argues, archivists should "ask who and what they are excluding from archival memorialization, and why, and then build appraisal strategies, methodologies, and criteria to correct the situation." In appraising records, archivists should seek to avoid cultural biases and assumptions: "Appraisal would attend as carefully to the marginalized and even silenced voices as it now does to the powerful voices found in official institutional records."[180] Similar concerns about the archivist's role apply not only to appraisal, but to all archival functions and decisions—from selecting which records to solicit and acquire, to preserving, arranging, classifying, describing, publicizing, and providing access and reference services for these records.

A RESPONSIBILITY FOR TOMORROW

Returning to the starting point of the archivist's construction of memory, we can see more clearly how memory disrupts the linear progression of time. As Billy Pilgrim learns from the Tralfamadorians, we live constantly at the intersection of past, present, and future. Archivists traditionally claim that they preserve the past for the future. Although their gaze often lingers longer over the prior events documented in the archival record, there would be no purpose—no reason, no professional calling—to protect traces and sources of the past without an even greater imperative to serve the needs of the future. The International Council on Archives adopts the image of the Roman god Janus as its symbol. The double-faced Janus looks both to the past and to the future, as archivists always must do. However, the weight of the archivist's responsibility surely lies more with the future than with the past. It is the promise of future usefulness that justifies the archival enterprise.

Unlike the historian, whose attention fixes on understanding and explaining the past, the archivist focuses on the needs of the future. "A historian as such never looks to the future, which in the end does not concern him," Derrida asserts.[181] Whenever historians attempt to predict the future or to anticipate how the past will affect the subsequent outcome of contemporary issues, they generally fail miserably. Their praxis, expertise, and theory enable them to understand and interpret the past but not the future. Archivists do not predict the future either, but their focus is—or should be—on future needs for archival information and evidence and on the concerns of posterity. "Archiving is not about history looking backward, but about storing and securing for the future," Eric Ketelaar observes. "Archiving—all the activities from creation and management to the use of records and archives—has always been directed towards transmitting human activity and experience through time and, secondly, through space."[182]

The archivist's fixation on the future forms a central part of Jacques Derrida's argument in *Archive Fever*. The desire or fever for archives, he declares, arises from "their opening on the future, their dependency with respect to what will come, in short, all that ties knowledge and memory to the promise."[183] Archives speak to the future more than to the past. "As much as and more than a thing of the past, before such a thing, the archive should *call into question* the coming of the future," Derrida insists.[184] The archive thus carries "the irrepressible . . . force and authority of this transgenerational memory," without which there "would no longer be any essential history of culture, there would no longer be any question of memory and of archive, . . . and one would no longer even understand how an ancestor can speak within us," he asserts. Therefore, "the question of the archive is not, we repeat, a question of the past . . . It is a question of the future, . . . of a responsibility for tomorrow."[185] Archivists preserve records in service to the future, not the past. It is this responsibility that Derrida identifies as the significant role for archivists in society, fulfilling both an obligation to remember and a duty to posterity.

Derrida thus understands the essential purpose of archives more clearly than those who consider the archives to be only relics of the past, dusty traces preserved only for legal, administrative, antiquarian, nostalgic, or historical uses. Such purposes are important, particularly in meeting the immediate needs for archival functions within institutional settings. Yet the wider cultural and social value of archives lies in their relationship to the future. As Derrida states, the interpretation of the archive—whether by administrators, historians, archivists, or other users of the archival record—can "only illuminate, read, establish its object, namely a given inheritance, by inscribing itself into it, that is to say by opening it and by enriching it enough to have a rightful place in it." The archive gains its authority by "incorporating the knowledge deployed in reference to it," by expanding its field of vision and understanding. "The archivist produces more archive, and that is why the archive is never closed. It opens out of the future," Derrida repeats. One may be tempted to associate the archive with "repetition of the past," but "it is the future that is at issue here, and the archive is an irreducible experience of the future."[186] Derrida thus explicitly separates the historian, who seeks to understand and interpret the past, from the archivist, who addresses needs and concerns of the future.

The recognition of the archivist's responsibility to posterity is not new, but the emphasis on a perspective oriented more to the future uses of archives than to the records of the past opens new vistas. In recent years, American archivists in particular have begun to focus on understanding and responding to the needs of a multiplicity of users of archival records.[187] At its core, this emphasis speaks to the future. It privileges the usability of archives over simple estimates of their value in documenting the past. "The archive, all archives, feed our yearning for this coming," declares Sello Hatang, director of the South African History Archive. "It is not, in the end, about the past. It is about the future." He adds, in the Setswana language, thoughts translated as, "If you do not listen to the teaching of the elders you will be impoverished. You will end up eating the shit of your peers. The teaching and the wisdom of the elders, as with the archive, are not for the past. They are for the present and, most importantly, they are for the future."[188] Archival memory takes account of the past, but its orientation is to the present and future uses of such knowledge. The perspectives and needs of today and tomorrow provide the rationale for all archival functions. Far from being lost in the past, archivists constantly anticipate and prepare for the future. As they do so, archivists construct memory and reconstruct it to meet the ever-changing needs of society.

This consideration of how archives, and the archivists who manage them, contribute to society is the next major issue to which we turn our attention in the following chapter. Archives have traditionally, since ancient times, reinforced the power of the politically, economically, socially, and intellectually powerful members of society. Yet they also document the lives of common people, those overlooked by earlier generations of historians or ignored by monarchs and political leaders. Concern for these marginalized peoples leads increasing numbers of archivists to engage in political actions in order to correct previous neglect or exclusion. Archives can thus serve society not merely as a storehouse of past experience, but as an active agent in today's struggles for open government, accountability, diversity, and social justice.

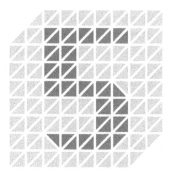

Serving the
Public Good

*One of our challenges as we build and extend democracy is the need to
ensure that our youth know where we come from, what we have done to
break the shackles of oppression, and how we have pursued the journey to
freedom and dignity for all. . . . This is what archives are about.*

- Nelson Mandela

Archivists have only recently begun to re-examine
their assumptions about the influence of archives and
recordkeeping in modern society. In the "information age,"
knowledge is power. This power gives those who determine what
records will be preserved for future generations a significant degree
of influence. In addition to protecting the rights and interests
of all citizens, archives preserve vital aspects of cultural heritage.
These dual responsibilities give archivists great potential power,
not only over questions of recordkeeping in today's society but for
future generations. They should use their power for the benefit
of all members of society. By adopting a social conscience for the
profession, they can commit themselves to active engagement in the
public arena. Archivists can use the power of archives to promote
accountability, open government, diversity, and social justice. In
doing so it is essential to distinguish objectivity from neutrality.
Advocacy and activism can address social issues without abandoning
professional standards of fairness, honesty, detachment, and

transparency. These are goals and values that all citizens can and should embrace. By advocating such measures and providing one means of achieving these results, archivists can offer an essential public service. In doing so they can earn the respect and support of citizens concerned about regaining control over public policy and governance. This may not be enough to guarantee full public awareness of archives, but it would provide an essential prerequisite for public recognition and support for archival programs, both public and private, that offer benefits to all people in society. Many of these social benefits can be seen in the transition from apartheid to freedom in South Africa.

NELSON MANDELA IN THE ARCHIVES

At the ceremony launching the Centre of Memory and Commemoration Project on September 21, 2004, Nelson Mandela stated, "In our view the work of archives in the South Africa of today is potentially one of the most critical contributions to restoration and reconciliation. All of us have a powerful moral obligation to the many voices and stories either marginalised or suppressed during the apartheid era."[1] Symbolically, the first documents acquired by the Centre of Memory consisted of two notebooks written by Mandela during his lengthy imprisonment on Robben Island. Donald Card, a former security policeman, had confiscated the notebooks when they were sent to him for censorship review. After secretly preserving the two notebooks for many years, Card presented them to Mandela during this public ceremony—their first meeting in thirty years, since Card had given evidence against Mandela during the Rivonia Trial.

Mandela framed the interpretation of this donation as an act of reconciliation. The two notebooks are "more than just the working documents of a prisoner," he declared. "They represent the hope that we can recover memories and stories suppressed by the apartheid regime." The quest to locate other documents relating to the apartheid era and the movement that overthrew this oppressive regime, Mandela added, "is part of our unfinished business of dealing with the past and ensuring that restoration takes place. Mr. Card is to be commended for his contribution to restoration and reconciliation."[2]

However, if archival records can symbolize healing and reconciliation, they also can support and perpetuate oppression. "Under the apartheid regime it was a common practice for the authorities to take documents from those they regarded as enemies,"

Mandela reminded the audience. "Sometimes they used these documents as evidence in court cases. Sometimes they used them in various forms of intimidation. Sometimes they simply destroyed them." Documents became tools of control. They could be used to prosecute those who opposed the apartheid regime. "For all of us who were part of the struggles for justice and freedom in this country, committing information to paper was a very risky business. We had to be careful about how we did this, and careful about what we kept and where we kept it," Mandela recounted. "This reality in itself was a form of intimidation. And one of the results is that today there are relatively few archives documenting the thinking and the inner processes of the liberation movements."[3] South African authorities succeeded, in some measure, in silencing their opponents. The archival record presented only the approved voices of the ruling powers.

The new Nelson Mandela Centre of Memory and Dialogue seeks to overcome this silence in the official archives, to revive and preserve the voices marginalized during the colonial and apartheid eras. "We want [the Centre] to be part of what we have called the processes of restoration and reconciliation," Mandela declared. "It is our hope that from these small beginnings it will grow into a vibrant public resource offering a range of services to South Africans and visitors from all parts of the world. We want it to work closely with the many other institutions that make up the South African archival system. And, most importantly, we want it to dedicate itself to the recovery of memories and stories suppressed by power. That is the call of justice: the call that must be the project's most important shaping influence."[4]

The archival record can thus foster the work of reconciliation, healing, and social justice. The first step in this process is to remember the past in order to overcome oppression and to hold former leaders accountable for their actions. "The history of our country is characterised by too much forgetting. A forgetting which served the powerful and dispossessed the weak," Nelson Mandela warns. "One of our challenges as we build and extend democracy is the need to ensure that our youth know where we come from, what we have done to break the shackles of oppression, and how we have pursued the journey to freedom and dignity for all. . . . At the same time, for those of us who are older and have lived through the transition from apartheid to democracy, the processes of remembering offer us healing and a means of respecting the many comrades who made it possible." Mandela concludes, "This is what archives are about. This is what we want the Centre of Memory Project to be about."[5]

Nelson Mandela's concern for history and truth arose during his youth and strengthened through his imprisonment. As son of a Thembu chief, he observed the tribal leaders—"wise men who retained the knowledge of tribal history and custom in their heads"— conducting tribal governance democratically, allowing all men to voice their opinions as equal citizens.[6] Mandela began to understand the importance of his people's history. From Chief Joyi he learned the history of the Bantu-speaking peoples and discovered that "the real history of our country was not to be found in standard British textbooks, which claimed South Africa began with the landing of Jan Van Riebeeck at the Cape of Good Hope in 1652." The Nationalist Party, which gained political power in South Africa in 1948, entrenched the Eurocentric concepts of national history through the apartheid system, which "represented the codification of all the laws and regulations that had kept Africans in an inferior position to whites for centuries," Mandela explained in his autobiography, *Long Walk to Freedom.*[7] History was one of many casualties of apartheid. "Part of the legacy of colonialism is the dominance of the history, language, culture and religion of the colonial powers," Mandela explained in a 1999 speech. "We know many details of European royalty but how many of us can tell the story of Hintsa or Tuan Guru to our children? . . . Few of us know how we came to be the nation we are."[8] African identity requires knowledge of history.

Announcing that he was "prepared to die" for a "democratic and free society in which all persons live together in harmony and with equal opportunities,"[9] Nelson Mandela began serving a life sentence for opposition to the apartheid regime in 1964. Throughout his twenty-seven years of incarceration he observed how documents and records served the power of the state and how they could be used against the system that sought to restrict his freedom. Prison authorities "carefully recorded, duplicated and filed every piece of paper relating to Mandela," including "results of medical tests, correspondence with family and friends, formal complaints against prison conditions and early negotiations with his captors."[10] Revealing both the web of surveillance and the extent of paranoia concerning this prominent prisoner, these records inadvertently depict the power he wielded even from his prison cell. The National Archives in Pretoria maintains "76 brown archival boxes" containing Mandela's official prison record from 1964 to 1990. In counterpoint to this official record, as spokesperson for a group of thirty anti-apartheid prisoners, Mandela "was himself an avid documenter, deeply conscious of the role, and the power, of the record. As a result, his files are filled with accounts of the prisoners' engagement with the authorities over nearly three decades." The result is a rich record of both Mandela's captivity and the birth of democracy in South Africa. "Ironically, the doggedness of the regime in recording Mandela's every word and every move ensured an extraordinarily rich record of his years in captivity," according to the Nelson Mandela Foundation.[11]

Despite this extensive documentation, Mandela's official prison record has been depleted. Items confiscated from him during arrests and raids remain unaccounted for, as well as documents from the files of both the Security Police and National Intelligence. Part of this loss undoubtedly came during the "systematic destruction of state records between 1990 and 1994," including forty-four tons of documents from the National Intelligence Service destroyed in three months of 1993 alone. Even before this purging, few of the letters Mandela wrote from prison ever reached their intended destinations. In the two notebooks later donated to the Mandela archives by Donald Card he "meticulously tracked receipt of his letters and documented which of the letters he had written were never received." He could thus write in August 1970 that his children had received none of the letters that he had written to them in the previous fifteen months. "Letters from me hardly ever reach destination and those addressed to me fare no better," he complained to Senator Douglas Lukhele, in Swaziland.[12] Mandela resorted to clandestine methods to smuggle out of prison an account of his experiences that formed the basis of his subsequent autobiography, using the power of words and documents to oppose a political regime that sought to suppress all public knowledge of his condition. Further testimony to the importance of documents can be found in the letters Mandela frequently addressed to South African leaders P. W. Botha and F. W. de Klerk, which eventually led to open negotiations concerning his release and the easing of apartheid sanctions.[13]

For Mandela documents serve a personal as well as political purpose. During his imprisonment arsonists burned down his home, destroying "invaluable family records, photographs, and keepsakes," Mandela reports. "I had always thought that someday when I left prison I would be able to recapture the past when looking over those pictures and letters, and now they were gone. Prison had robbed me of my freedom but not my memories, and now I felt some enemies of the struggle had tried to rob me of even those." When finally released from prison in 1990, however, Mandela reports that he filled more than a dozen crates with possessions, "mainly books and papers."[14] Documentation of his experiences could also be seen in his face and physique, observers noted, after decades without having seen the celebrated prisoner. "The archive of the prison experience was inscribed in his person, etched in his body, profoundly shaping his consciousness and embedded in his consciousness," according to a later account.[15] Those seeking documentation of Mandela's prison life could thus examine not only the written, visual, and sound records, but also his physical presence and appearance.

After gaining his freedom, Mandela soon assumed leadership of the African National Congress and within four years was elected president of a democratic South Africa. Under his leadership the nation formed a Truth and Reconciliation Commission (TRC) to investigate abuses under the apartheid regime and seek to heal the wounds of a bitterly divided people. In commissioning the TRC in February 1996, Mandela emphasized the importance of historical understanding. "All South Africans face the challenge of coming to terms with the past in ways which will enable us to face the future as a united nation at peace with itself," he proclaimed.[16] Speaking in 1997 at a Heritage Day ceremony on Robben Island, site of his imprisonment, Mandela insisted, "With democracy we have the opportunity to ensure that our institutions reflect history in a way that respects the heritage of all our citizens." Part of the process of national rebirth, he declared in 1999, would be "the recovery of the silenced histories of our different communities," through museums, schools, and other cultural institutions. In 1996 Mandela rededicated a historical monument that sought to reconceptualize South African history in light of the post-apartheid inclusion of diverse voices. "There are monuments which open the past to scrutiny, recalling it in order to illuminate it and transform it into part of our living and changing society, and merging the tradition from which they emerged with the rich diversity of South Africa's cultures," he stated. "Such monuments, if they are successful, are a beacon for the future of all our people as much as a memory of the past."[17] These statements reflect the abiding interest of Nelson Mandela in history, commemoration, and documentation. Archives play a critical role in documenting and remembering the past, in reconciliation and rebuilding in today's South Africa, and in creating a better future for all members of a diverse and progressive democratic society.

RECORDS FOR OPPRESSION AND FOR LIBERATION

As this story about Nelson Mandela demonstrates, archives express and hold numerous oppositions: memory and forgetting, suffering and hope, power and accountability, confinement and liberation, oppression and justice, conformity and diversity, silence and vocality. Archives can serve the interests of entrenched power, but they can also empower the marginalized groups in society. Since ancient times archives have been used to bolster the prestige and influence of the powerful elites in societies. Archivists have a moral professional responsibility to balance the support given to the status quo by giving equal voice to those groups that too often have been marginalized and silenced. We can see many precedents for this professional imperative. Examples of the use of records and archives to redress social wrongs and support the causes of justice and community consciousness among marginalized groups are growing more numerous. Archivists can become active agents for change, in accordance with their existing professional principles, by taking active steps to counter the biases of previous archival practices.

The need for accurate documentation of oppression and abuses of political and social control arises in part from the power of memory as a means of securing justice. The South African Truth and Reconciliation Commission followed the lessons learned from survivors of the Holocaust. "We remember Auschwitz and all that it symbolizes because we believe that, in spite of the past and its horrors, the world is worthy of salvation; and salvation, like redemption, can be found only in memory," Elie Wiesel attests. "Memory and hatred are incompatible, for hatred distorts memory. The reverse is true: memory may serve as a powerful remedy against hatred." For Wiesel and many other Holocaust survivors, remembering the past provides the only hope for a better future. As Wiesel insists, "Justice without memory is an incomplete justice, false and unjust. To forget would be an absolute injustice in the same way that Auschwitz was the absolute crime. To forget would be the enemy's final triumph."[18] This spirit of resisting oppression through memory and documentation echoes Orwell's insistence on these means of preserving one's humanity in the face of totalitarianism. Even when such political power is less absolute than in Orwell's Oceania or Hitler's German Reich, memory and documentation remain powerful antidotes to the control of ruling classes and unscrupulous leaders.

Historical examples abound of societies in which the powerful ruled by controlling and manipulating information and records. From ancient times to the present, disquieting use has been made of archival records to establish, document, and perpetuate the influence of power elites. Noam Chomsky observes that "elites depend on sophisticated information systems, media control, surveillance" and related measures to maintain their positions.[19] The Third Reich provides one of many useful examples of this power of documentation. In order to establish a racially pure society, the Nazis "required not only the mobilization of existing records for political ends but the creation of new records that would recognize the biological categories the Nazis held to be so consequential," Peter Fritzsche observes. As Josef Franz Knöpfler, director of the Bavarian archival administration, stated in 1936, "There is no practice of racial politics without the mobilization of source documents, which indicate the origin and development of a race and people. . . . There is no racial politics without archives, without archivists."[20] This pronouncement prefigures Jacques Derrida's claim, "There is no political power without control of the archive, if not of memory."[21] Although the influence of written records and archives usually supports political and cultural control by elites in society, there is increasing evidence that marginalized and oppressed peoples can seize a measure of power through effective use of written records. "Records, then, may be instruments of power, but paradoxically, the same records can also become instruments of empowerment and liberation, salvation and freedom," Dutch archivist Eric Ketelaar asserts. "The Nazis' obsession with recording and listing also made them receptive to the liberating effect of lists, as everyone knows who has seen Schindler's List," he adds. "The detailed record-keeping system of the Nazis still forms an excellent source for restitution and repatriation."[22]

In addition to the widely recognized proficiency of Nazi recordkeeping, modern examples of the impact of records to support oppression include the use of official records to bolster the apartheid regime in South Africa,[23] and documentation of the Cambodian genocide under Pol Pot. As Australian archivist Chris Hurley observes, "Historically, tyrants have more regard for good recordkeeping than democrats. Totalitarians are notoriously good recordkeepers."[24] Such records become instruments of control, essential to the effective use of power. When the Khmer Rouge were evacuating Phnom Penh ahead of the Vietnamese in January 1979, they gave orders to the prison chief to destroy all of the records of the secret prison, of which the outside world knew nothing. However, according to Ben Kiernan of the Yale University Genocide Studies Program, "he preferred to kill the last surviving prisoners instead, in the couple of hours of time that he had before the Vietnamese arrived at the prison. When they did get there, they found 100,000 pages of archives of the prison—execution schedules, daily record of torture of prisoners and their forced confessions." Kiernan adds that the "archives of the Khmer Rouge prison system across the country, showing high-level involvement and the implication of the top leaders of the Khmer Rouge in the crimes that were committed" made it impossible for them to deny their genocidal crimes.[25] This is but one example of how archival records can overcome efforts to deny the past.

Even in democratic societies, public officials often seek to control public discourse by manipulating access to information. Government secrecy is the enemy of truth, accountability, and social justice. "The relationship between the archive and the state," as South African historian Achille Mbembe observes, " . . . rests on a paradox. On the one hand, there is no state without archives—without its archives. On the other hand, the very existence of the archive constitutes a constant threat to the state." This power of archives arises from "the archive's ability to serve as proof of a suspect fragment of life or piece of time."[26] It is thus little surprise that rulers and social elites often seek to control and limit the extent of archival influence in order to dominate and shape the public record of events.

Despite these unpleasant truths—or more accurately, because of them—there is reason to be optimistic that archivists can become agents of change in the interests of accountability, social justice, and diversity. If we do not seize this opportunity, in the words of archivist Gerald Ham a generation ago, " . . . then I do not know what it is we are doing that is all that important."[27] Promising evidence of archivists' role in supporting the cause of justice comes from recent events in which archives and records have contributed to the public interest in four ways:

1. by holding political and social leaders accountable for their actions,
2. by resisting political pressure in order to support open government,
3. by redressing social injustices, and
4. by documenting underrepresented social groups and fostering ethnic and community identities.

This evidence comes from many sources, but in particular from five recent volumes of essays: *Archives and the Public Good: Accountability and Records in Modern Society,* edited by Richard Cox and David Wallace;

Political Pressure and the Archival Record, edited by Margaret Procter, Michael Cook, and Caroline Williams; *Refiguring the Archive,* edited by Carolyn Hamilton, Verne Harris, Jane Taylor, Michael Pickover, Graeme Reid, and Razia Saleh; *Archives, Documentation and Institutions of Social Memory: Essays from the Sawyer Seminar,* edited by Francis X. Blouin, Jr. and William G. Rosenberg; and *Archives and Justice: A South African Perspective,* by Verne Harris.[28] These accounts help us to understand how records and archives can be used as resources to counter injustice and abuses of power, and to develop a strategy for using the power of archives.

ACCOUNTABILITY

In a democratic society public officials serve the interests of the people and their actions are subject to public scrutiny. Even in the private sector, corporate officers, academic leaders, and the heads of not-for-profit organizations—such as hospitals, foundations, and fraternal and charitable organizations—can be held accountable for their actions. Although this principle is often observed in the breach, it provides one of the essential safeguards for the public interest.

Documents and records provide the best means for ensuring such accountability. As Canadian archivist John McDonald states, "Without records, there can be no demonstration of accountability. Without evidence of accountability, society cannot trust in its public institutions."[29] Proper recordkeeping is necessary, but not sufficient, to ensure accountability, as Australian archivist Chris Hurley contends. During one public crisis over accountability, the auditor-general of the Commonwealth of Australia commented, "poor recordkeeping attracts corruption like flies to a carcass."[30] To be effective as a tool for providing accountability, Hurley concludes, recordkeeping must be based on sound ethical purposes for maintaining records. Officials must specify requirements for documenting activities, monitor performance, and enforce recordkeeping requirements.[31]

Thus, archives and archivists become key players in the often-contentious process of political, corporate, and academic power relationships. By maintaining accurate, reliable, and authentic records, archivists serve the public's interest in accountability. When "judiciously appraised, acquired, described, and made available," archival records allow "citizens to seek justice in righting past wrongs, from aboriginal displacements to war crimes, from medical neglect to ethnic discrimination," as Terry Cook asserts. Archivists also provide "the underpinning of just governments, through transparency, accountability, and freedom of information, indeed, underpinning democracy itself, all resting on the creation of reliable records and their sensitive appraisal and controlled destruction."[32] Governmental regulation of private sector organizations—from corporations to charities—requires accurate recordkeeping for effectiveness. Documents and archival records have played an important part in many recent events in which public and private leaders, and the agencies and organizations they manage, have been held accountable. Some of these stories represent triumphs of democratic oversight; others suggest the limitations imposed on such efforts to ensure accountability. Yet each features the central importance of records, archives, and archivists.

The Watergate crisis in the mid-1970s focused public attention on the importance of records in discovering political crimes and holding public figures accountable for their actions. Only with the "smoking gun" of the secret tape recordings of Oval Office conversations could the true story of the Nixon administration's obstruction of justice be proven. This led directly to the House of Representatives' impeachment proceedings and the president's resignation. In response to Nixon's abuses of power, Congress passed the Presidential Records and Materials Act (1974) and other legislation to establish the principle of public ownership and access to presidential records. Control over presidential records surfaced again with the PROFS case, which revealed an attempt by the officials of the George H. W. Bush administration to destroy computer tapes, including electronic mail (on the PROFS software system) containing explosive revelations of illegal activities of the Reagan-Bush administrations regarding the Iran-Contra affair; investigations of Panama's leader Manuel Noriega; and billions of dollars loaned to Iraq before the first Gulf War. "What the Nixon and the PROFS case[s] demonstrate is that the archival community, and indeed all its allied professions, must be ever vigilant in helping to ensure that American citizens have all the requisite information to make informed decisions regarding the activities of their government," Bruce Montgomery concludes. "Archivists have always played an important, albeit obscure, role in the enterprise of promoting the public's right to know. But this role is also contingent on the need to speak out on issues of vital historical concern."[33] The importance of Nixon's presidential papers can be seen in the protracted legal struggle to control their disposition and accessibility. This struggle lasted long after Nixon's death.

In the 1980s, the Iran-Contra scandal itself showed that, although Oliver North and other Reagan administration officials destroyed documents relating to their illegal activities, some records (including e-mail backup tapes) remained to prove their guilt. The Tower Commission, which investigated the Iran-Contra charges, concluded that the "whole matter was handled too informally, without adequate written records of what had been considered, discussed, and decided." According to the Tower Commission Report, adequate records of decisions would be "essential for conducting a periodic review of a policy or initiative, and to learn from the past." Not only did North and National Security Advisor John Poindexter destroy critical records of illegal activities, they also engaged in "creating a false history of events" to cover up their actions.[34]

Despite their zealous efforts to destroy and alter records, North and Poindexter overlooked crucial backup tapes, which allowed investigators to recover e-mails that provided a "first-hand contemporaneous account of events." Independent counsel Lawrence Walsh concluded that the central participants in this scandal "were reluctant to provide truthful information unless they were confronted with difficult-to-refute documentary evidence." As David Wallace concludes, "aggressive oversight and power to seize the documentary record provides one of the few means by which democratic accountability can be secured in a national security context." Since government officials could not be trusted to tell the truth, Wallace adds, "only by having the power to seize and have unimpeded access to the documentary record will investigations have any hope of yielding an accurate accounting of events."[35] Records thus provide an essential measure of accountability. Even with extensive efforts to alter and destroy such records, the Iran-Contra conspirators could not escape such evidence. To ensure accountability it is critical to establish clear recordkeeping requirements, to protect important records from destruction, and to understand and value proper recordkeeping practices.

In Australia, the Heiner affair of the 1990s demonstrated the possibility of co-opting the records managers and archivists to cover up governmental misdeeds under the guise of records disposition. To prevent public airing of charges of physical and sexual abuse in Queensland's institutions for teenagers and children, government leaders ordered the destruction of all records of the investigation led by Noel Heiner. As a group of seven distinguished legal practitioners later charged, the Queensland Cabinet in March 1990 destroyed the Heiner Inquiry documents "to prevent their use as evidence in anticipated judicial proceeding, made worse because the Queensland Government knew the evidence concerned abuse of children in a State youth detention centre, including the alleged unresolved pack rape of an indigenous female child by other male inmates."[36] Although this violated the fundamental principle of administration of justice by preservation of evidence, as well as the Australian Libraries and Archives Act of 1988, the cabinet pressured the state archivist into carrying out this destruction of records. This incident became a public media sensation largely because Kevin Lindeberg, a union employee assisting a union member involved in the case Heiner had been investigating, blew the whistle on this illegal destruction of records. Lindeberg revealed a widespread systematic cover-up of the child abuse. The Heiner affair gained notoriety as "shreddergate," one of more than a dozen prominent records-shredding scandals of the twentieth century.[37]

During a hearing in 1995 government officials argued that the sole business of a state archivist was to determine the "historical" value/status of a document, while its "legal" value/status rested elsewhere.[38] However, as archivist Chris Hurley argues, "Of more significance is the role of an independent archives authority in preventing the untoward destruction of evidence of government corruption and wrong-doing by establishing a regime of records management that supports the public interest in government accountability." The "value added" by archives, Hurley concludes, is "that agencies must submit their records practices to external scrutiny. This provides additional safeguard for the public interest in records retention (to ensure that governments cannot 'cover up') and a safeguard too for individual citizens in conflict with government."[39] In such situations, archivists cannot avoid political engagement. According to Hurley, archivists respond to public concerns in a societal context, from which professional values derive. "It is because we live in a democracy, therefore, not because we are archivists, that our professional standards and practices support democratic values," he asserts.[40] Archivists always act within a context that is, either explicitly or implicitly, political.

The Heiner affair continues to echo with political repercussions. In August 2008 Kevin Lindeberg testified before the Tasmanian Joint Select Committee on Ethical Conduct about his firing as a result of blowing the whistle on the Heiner scandal. Despite allegations of involvement in the Heiner cover-up, in September 2008 Quentin Bryce was appointed governor-general. Both

Lindeberg and journalist Piers Ackerman continue to lead in calling for further investigations into charges against Bryce and others involved in the Heiner scandal.[41] "The Heiner affair will now likely be thrust into the middle of our national debate as to whether or not we should become a republic," Lindeberg argues, because key national figures currently holding high office in the political landscape have been implicated in the affair due to their handling of it at an earlier time in its evolution. At the epicenter of this scandal rests the illegal shredding of public documents, "an act of improper recordkeeping." In testimony before a Select Tasmanian Parliamentary Committee in November 2008, Lindeberg quoted the Roman satirist Juvenal: "Who shall watch the watchers themselves?" He charged that efforts to unravel the Heiner affair created "Orwellian overtones" because the "so-called integrity tribunals" had either intimidated elected officials or subverted the process of oversight and accountability for improper prima facie partisan purposes.[42] This Australian scandal highlights significant concerns for archivists and anyone concerned about accountability and political abuses of power. According to one American expert, the Heiner affair "exemplifies one of the boldest and most egregious examples of a breach of 'the rule of law' at the highest level of state government," and reveals "that there was not only an illegal destruction of records on false premises but a generation-long cover-up—a potentially separate criminal offense." Central to this cover-up is "the extraordinary manner in which the records were appraised and disposed of within 24 hours," separately rather than as part of an established records management disposition schedule.[43]

The Heiner affair showed both the power of records to document abuses and—as in the Iran-Contra scandal—the incentive that government leaders sometimes have to destroy public records. For an archivist or records manager to comply with improper requests to approve document destruction is a clear violation of professional ethics. The SAA Code of Ethics states: "Archivists strive to promote open and equitable access to their services and the records in their care without discrimination or preferential treatment, and in accordance with legal requirements, cultural sensitivities, and institutional policies."[44] However, the fact that government leaders felt the need to obtain such archival authorization demonstrates that archivists have power to protect the public interest, when they uphold their obligations.

The Enron/Arthur Andersen scandal, exposed in 2001,
demonstrated that the legal system can, at times, intervene to ensure
that records cannot be destroyed or altered without consequences.
As concerns mounted about Enron's financial future, auditors at
Arthur Andersen received a memo directing them to destroy all
but routine auditing records relating to Enron. As *Time* magazine
reported in January 2002:

> Any deliberate destruction of documents subject to subpoena is illegal.
> In Arthur Andersen's dealings with the documents related to Enron,
> "the mind-set seemed to be, If not required to keep it, then get rid of
> it," says Ken Johnson, spokesman for the House Energy and Commerce
> Committee . . . . "Anyone who destroyed records out of stupidity
> should be fired," said committee chairman Billy Tauzin, a Louisiana
> Republican. "Anyone who destroyed records to try to circumvent our
> investigation should be prosecuted."[45]

This scandal is a cautionary tale of corporate power run amok and of
the dangers of improper management of records. Yet it also shows
that with regulation, such as the Sarbanes-Oxley Act passed as a
result of such abuses, it is possible to assert professional standards of
records management and archives.[46]

Recent political developments in the United States, resulting from
the terrorist attacks of September 11, 2001 and the invasion of Iraq
in March 2003, highlight the importance of holding public officials
accountable for their actions. Archivist William L. Joyce, who served
during the 1990s on the Assassination Records Review Board that
declassified thousands of documents relating to the assassination
of President John F. Kennedy, reports that recent government
efforts to shield public records from scrutiny raise serious concerns.
Developments such as "passage of the PATRIOT Act shortly after
9/11, the removal of large quantities of government information
from government documents and Web sites, and the emergence of
a new, extralegal category of government information—sensitive
security information—demonstrate that the government has in fact
become less open, less accountable, and less susceptible to rational
deliberation as a vehicle for change," Joyce concludes. "The need
for persistent vigilance in protecting the public's right to know
and the importance of holding government officials accountable
have never been more urgent."[47] Ian Wilson, national archivist of
Canada, places the obligation for preserving records that ensure
accountability on the shoulders of archivists. "Our fundamental
professional responsibility is to apply clear and defensible appraisal

criteria to the official record, ensuring the protection of citizens' rights whether or not they ever think of contacting the archives," Wilson vows. "We preserve the integrity of the archival record—the authoritative information in its context of origin as evidence—and provide it, when that is all that is needed with our professional warranty as to its degree of authenticity."[48] Archival records thus provide the necessary means of documenting the actions of public leaders and protecting the rights of all citizens. Such protection depends on the ability to access these records in order to ensure accountability.

OPEN GOVERNMENT

Democracy rests on an informed citizenry. The public's right to know what its political, corporate, and academic leaders are doing must be held sacrosanct. Although personal privacy and national security concerns must be acknowledged and protected, in most instances the need for open access to information prevails. There can be no accountability without documentation, but documentation itself is effective only when people can access reliable records. In examining access policies for State Department records, Anne Van Camp states, "One hallmark of a society's openness is the degree of public access to the archives and records of its government."[49] As Jacques Derrida asserts, "Effective democratization can always be measured by this essential criterion: the participation in and access to the archive, its constitution, and its interpretation."[50] Writing in 2004, Verne Harris, Sello Hatang, and Peter Liberman reported that twenty-six countries had "adopted new laws promoting access to information in the last decade alone," and that "South Africa's 1996 constitution is the only one in the world that enshrines access to information as a fundamental right."[51] This concern for public access to documents and records places added responsibility on archivists to ensure the preservation of essential records that protect the public's interests in corporate and political accountability and in open government.

The necessity of professional archival control over records becomes especially clear when considering the importance of public access to governmental records. The French Revolution established the principle of public control of records to prevent governmental abuses and to protect the rights of citizens.[52] Concern for public access to records, essential for trust and accountability, stems from the long history of government leaders' efforts to use the interpretation of the past to secure their power. In his essay "Why Do Ruling Classes Fear History?" historical sociologist Harvey

Kaye quotes J. H. Plumb, who wrote that from ancient to recent times, "The past was constantly involved in the present, and all that enshrined the past—monuments, inscriptions, records—were essential weapons in government, in securing the authority, not only of the king, but also of those whose power he symbolized and sanctified." Kaye also notes that Soviet leader Nikita Khrushchev recognized the power of historical knowledge, when he stated, "Historians are dangerous people, capable of turning everything topsy-turvy. They have to be watched."[53] Given this Soviet suspicion of history, it may seem surprising that the former communist countries have opened their cold war archives more quickly than western nations. "Whereas the archives have been opened in Berlin and Moscow, American and other Western secrets about state and corporate crimes committed under license of the Cold War are only beginning to seep out," Kaye wrote in 1994. He cited a former U.S. official's estimate that "possibly, one-third of American history is classified." This control over information affects both totalitarian and democratic governments. Kaye argued that ruling classes fear history because they recognize "that history has been, and remains, a process of struggle for freedom and for justice."[54] Historical understanding, particularly when embedded in the records of social institutions and individuals, makes both history and archives dangerous to those seeking to maintain their political power.

This is one reason that kings, tyrants, and even democratically elected government officials almost always seek to control the people's knowledge of their actions and to limit access to governmental records. In the United States, for example, efforts to enforce government secrecy began with the founding of the nation. "Our curtain of secrecy has been a long time in the making, and some of its threads date back to the very founding of our country," states Timothy Ericson. "The situation today has resulted, in part, because of the historically indifferent attitude Americans have had toward issues related to records since the early days of the republic."[55] The Continental Congress established the precedent of secret government committees in 1775, in order to protect those providing arms to the Continental army. The modern era of classification of government information began in 1940, as Americans debated whether to enter the Second World War, when President Franklin D. Roosevelt signed Executive Order 8381, giving "civilian government employees the authority to classify information," and creating three levels of classification—*Secret, Confidential,* and *Restricted.*[56] Although most tendencies have been to increase rather than limit government secrecy, occasional legislation such as the 1966 Freedom of Information Act (FOIA), have articulated the public's right of access to information about government actions, particularly relating to individual rights. During the FOIA debates Congressman Donald Rumsfeld stated, "[P]ublic records, which are evidence of official government action, are public property, and there . . . should be a positive obligation to disclose this information upon request."[57] Ironically, Rumsfeld would later become secretary of defense in one of the most secretive administrations in modern American history.

The George W. Bush administration was not the first democratic government to limit public access to information and records of its activities, although its policies drastically reduced such access. In 2001, Bruce Shapiro of the *Nation* magazine denounced the administration's policies as "information lockdown." He cited the Justice Department's refusal to release the names of individuals jailed as suspected terrorists; Attorney General John Ashcroft's memorandum authorizing federal agencies to deny Freedom of Information Act requests; and the removal of certain information from agency websites, on the claim of national security.[58] In 2004 a *Washington Post* reporter characterized this government mania for secrecy as a "substantial surge in the urge to submerge," and noted that executive agencies had "discovered more than 14 million new secrets last year"—a "25 percent increase over the previous year."[59] Even before the terrorist attacks of September 11, 2001, government secrecy had increased substantially, with "an astounding 133,043,903 decisions to classify information" in the decade prior to 2004, according to Ericson.[60] This led Oregon senator Ron Wyden to declare, "[F]ederal, state, and local governments are shutting down access to public records in what some experts say is the most expansive assault on open government in the nation's history."[61] The report *Government Secrecy: Decisions Without Democracy 2007* documents how executive power had dramatically expanded while executive accountability diminished. "Increased secrecy is just one of the ways that the Bush Administration has made the government less accountable," Ralph G. Neas, president of People For the American Way Foundation, stated in July 2007. "At a time when technology should make it easier than ever to promote openness in government, George W. Bush and Dick Cheney have taken unprecedented steps to cloak themselves in secrecy."[62] Patrice McDermott, director of OpenTheGovernment.org, added, "The current [Bush] administration has increasingly refused to be held accountable to the public, including through the oversight responsibilities of Congress. These practices lead to the circumscription of democracy and our representative government; neither the public nor Congress can make informed decisions in these circumstances."[63]

As archivist Thomas Connors observed, "This push toward ever greater control of information access is seen by many as a threat to the democratic political process and to open government."[64] One of the most dangerous recent limitations on open government was Executive Order 13233, issued by President George W. Bush on November 1, 2001, which removed power to grant access to presidential records from the archivist of the United States and claimed such power for the executive office of the president. "How can a democratic people have confidence in elected officials who hide the record of their actions from public view?" SAA president Steve Hensen asked in response to this executive order. "Access to the vital historical records of this nation should not be governed by executive will; this is exactly the situation that the existing law was created to prevent."[65] Less than two years later, another executive order strengthened the executive branch's authority to restrict access to information from foreign governments, under the guise of national security. "The new executive order also makes it easier for the government to classify information for longer periods of time and easier for departments and agencies to exempt their records from automatic declassification," Ericson reports.[66] Such control over access to public records prevents citizens from knowing exactly what their elected officials and government workers are doing. It strikes at the heart of democratic government—citizen oversight and the sovereignty of the people, whose interests should be greater than the secrecy concerns of public officials.

Significantly, one of the first official actions taken by Bush's successor, President Barack Obama, revoked Executive Order 13233. Issued on January 21, 2009, Obama's Executive Order 13489 restored the requirement that only the incumbent president, not former presidents or their heirs, could claim executive privilege in blocking access to presidential records. The new policy also restored the function of the archivist of the United States as independent arbiter of access to presidential records, and stated clearly that the law also applied to records of the vice president, a matter disputed by former Vice President Dick Cheney. According to the watchdog group National Coalition for History, "President Obama firmly committed his administration to a new policy of transparency by symbolically issuing the executive order on his first full day in office."[67] The new president also reinforced his commitment to open government and accountability by reversing the Bush administration's resistance to Freedom of Information compliance. On January 21, 2009 the White House issued a press release announcing that all federal agencies would henceforth "adopt a presumption in favor of disclosure, in order to renew their commitment to the principles embodied in FOIA, and to usher in a new era of open Government." The statement clearly articulated the importance of accountability, both in the interest of the government and of all citizens: "A democracy requires accountability, and accountability requires transparency. As Justice Louis Brandeis wrote, 'sunlight is said to be the best of disinfectants.'"[68] These two decisions, both issued on President Obama's first day in office, signal a reversal of federal policy and a renewed commitment to open government. However, the temptation to exercise power can be difficult to resist. While applauding President Obama's policies, American citizens must remain vigilant to protect their rights and interests. "The community of scholars is celebrating this victory, but even more so this decision is a win for the very concept of restoring government accountability at a time when so much trust in government had been lost," as Mark Rozell and Mitchel Sollenberger state. "It is a good start, but, in time, the new president's principles will be tested and there will be temptations to close down access to what has commenced as an open administration."[69]

In all democratic societies, "the need of the citizenry to have access to the information that allows it to judge how the democratic process is working remains constant," Thomas Connors observes. "As archivists, as members of the larger information profession, and as citizens of democratic societies, we have a definite stake in working to restore and expand open access to government information as a means of protecting our fragile democracies."[70] Having been entrusted with responsibility for keeping records, archivists have not only an interest but also an obligation to ensure open access for the greater public good. Thus, the new commitment to open government by the Obama administration received praise from archivists, as well as others interested in citizens' rights. In a letter to President Obama, Society of American Archivists President Frank Boles wrote on January 22, 2009, "to thank you for your actions yesterday that—in important ways—helped to restore transparency and openness to the government of the United States."[71] Despite this positive step by the Obama administration, however, archivists need to remain vigilant on behalf of the public's interest in open government and access to public records.

Problems of government secrecy and the dangers of political influence on recordkeeping have ancient origins. "Written texts entrenched theocratic tyranny over vast reaches of monotheistic time and space," according to David Lowenthal. "Most archives originated as instruments of landowners' and lawgivers' control. . . . Archives confirmed and certified rights to land, labor, rents, and produce. Entry to archives was confined to princely, priestly, and scribal elites."[72] Following the French Revolution, the principle of public access to records increasingly gained recognition. "The guarantee of access, raised as a check against the secret workings of government, was designed to give the citizen power vis-à-vis government," Jennifer Milligan explains.[73] In nineteenth-century France, the Archives became "more than a mere repository of governmental knowledge; it was an active articulation of the relationship of nation and state." Documents "served an essential, legitimizing function for the state," Milligan states, since the government needed to prove that its actions were not capricious. "The Archives' integrity was a moral imperative for the state that would govern justly in the name of the public it claimed to represent." Any government that would remove documents from the Archives or tamper with archival evidence "would be acting against its people and thus would render itself illegitimate," as one French official argued. "Sovereignty required the inviolability of the Archives," Milligan concludes. "This put the director of the Archives and his staff in a precarious position: the archivist was both guardian of the state's business and a watchdog against the improper exercise of its power."[74] This dilemma remains important for twenty-first-century archivists, although often unacknowledged.

In numerous countries throughout the world, archivists and others entrusted with public records have resisted political pressure in order to maintain open access to records. They have thereby sought to preserve an accurate account of past events, to counteract the natural secretiveness of governments, and to protect the public interest. This has made the archives—particularly governmental archives—contested grounds for political power. As Verne Harris argues, "the archive *is* politics"— it is not "political," it is in its very nature politics itself. Harris explains:

> The structural pull in all our recordmaking is towards the replication of existing relations of power, with the attendant exclusions, "privilegings," and marginalisations. We cannot avoid complicity. But we can work against the pull; and for me it is a moral imperative to do so.[75]

Harris calls for archivists to enter the power struggle on the side of social justice. He argues that creators of records (including archivists) cannot be impartial or insulate themselves from politics. "Impartiality is a chimera turning recordmakers into the pawns of those who have power," he argues. "Any attempt to be impartial constitutes a choice, whether conscious or not, to replicate if not to reinforce prevailing relations of power." If archivists do not enter the power contests on behalf of democracy, Harris concludes, "then they turn their backs on higher callings and condemn themselves to being merely bureaucrats and functionaries."[76] This call to action would place archivists clearly on the side of democracy, truth, and justice. It does not require archivists to assume a partisan position, but it does require them to acknowledge that their profession is inherently and unavoidably engaged in political power struggles to define the nature of society.

Without a commitment to archival protection, governmental powers have often sought to destroy or falsify the historical record, as George Orwell warned. At the end of the Second World War "the Japanese authorities destroyed almost all important records relating to wartime administration, both in inland and overseas territories," according to University of Tokyo professor Masahito Ando.[77] This lack of records makes it possible for some Japanese politicians and scholars "to deny or distort the facts of Japan's war crimes." Exposing such destruction of archives, Ando concludes, "is fighting against the distortion of history."[78] Destruction or confiscation of records by an enemy state could impair a nation's cultural and political heritage. As the 1954 Hague Convention for the Protection of Cultural Property in the Event of Armed Conflict concluded, such protected property should include "manuscripts . . . and important collections of books or archives" and buildings such as "depositories of archives."[79]

Control over records has often led to political tensions and conflict. The widespread capture of German records during the Second World War provided "a priceless source for operational intelligence while the war lasted" and "crucial evidence for the trial of major war criminals" after Germany's surrender, according to historian Astrid Eckert.[80] Such archives also possessed significant political power. By the "beginning of the Cold War, both sides of the Iron Curtain had already realized that historical research and archival access were an 'inexpensive resource in the battle of the political systems,'" Eckert concludes. "They were simply deemed too important to be left to historians and archivists alone."[81] Political concerns for records carried over into the post-reunification period. In October 1998, when Gerhard Schröder replaced Helmut Kohl as chancellor of Germany, his staff "discovered the loss of a remarkable amount of records, particularly the deletion of several gigabytes of electronic information in the Bundeskanzler- amt (the Chancellor's Office)," which led the mass media to refer to this as "Bundeslöschtage, or days in which federal information is destroyed."[82] The struggle to protect the archival record from partisan control and misuse assumes international significance.

In Russia archivists fulfill a function of "crucial importance" in protecting the record of Russian history, according to historian Ziva Galili, since "it is the preservation of documentation that ensures the potential for questioning even the most established, dominant, and pervasive narratives." A project to document the Menshevik party during the revolution of 1917 shows that "an archival record can survive the vagaries of politics and ideology to reemerge and challenge a dominant historical narrative," Galili asserts. "Preserving the integrity of the archival record was of paramount importance precisely because of the highly contested and ideological nature of Russian political history." By enabling citizens to question or challenge the ruling party's interpretation of the past, archives make possible "a multiplicity of histories, written from a variety of vantage points, each based on the relevant archival record," Galili concludes.[83] Such counternarratives form the basis of political participation as societies emerge from oppressive or colonial regimes to more open and democratic systems.

Another noteworthy example of the essential nexus between democratic rule and access to public records comes from the Republic of Korea. Korea's tradition of regarding rulers' records as important materials goes back at least to the fourteenth century. *The Annals of the Dynasty of Chosun,* filling 2,077 volumes, chronicles daily events spanning nearly five centuries (1392-1863) and the reigns of twenty-five Chosun kings. As "the longest continuous historical record in the world," according to archivist Kyong Rae Lee, it documents final decisions of policymakers, as well as "the procedure of policymaking and the atmosphere of cabinet conferences" when such decisions were made. The "dark tunnel of undemocratic and repressive military politics" during the twentieth century, beginning with Japanese colonization in 1910, undermined this archival tradition. Passage of the Korean Public Records Management Act in 1999 finally regulated systematic management and public access to presidential records, "thereby re-establishing the ancient Korean tradition of preserving rulers' records intact, and even improving

upon this tradition by allowing public access to them," Lee declares.
As in South Africa and other repressive societies, South Korea
experienced political scandals linked to "the secretive control and
destruction of public documents."[84] Such scandals led a large group
of Korean historians, scholars, and teachers to declare that "'a
participatory government should achieve the reform of management
of public records and disclosure of information' throughout the
country," Lee states. "These scholars warned that 'there is neither
democracy nor history in a nation if the records of the state's
affairs are not managed precisely and thoroughly.'" Lee regards
these developments as hopeful signs, even though South Korea's
recent record of archival management and access still falls short of
international democratic standards. "The modern development of
presidential records in the Republic of Korea demonstrates a close
relationship with political democracy. . . . The health of the Korean
archival system is keenly sensitive to the level of Korean society's
political maturity," Lee concludes. President Roh's "drive for
archival reform, as in the disclosure of the minutes of state council
meetings, exemplifies one move toward political reform that seeks
to expunge the legacy of long-lasting authoritarianism from the
public sphere. Hence, even if it has not been wholly decisive, the
democratic maturity of Korea has certainly been a catalytic factor in
accelerating the future trajectory of the archives toward systematic
organization and open and free access."[85] Archives can thus play
a vital role in ensuring and fostering the open inquiry and access
to information that are critical to democratic governments. The
lessons of archival reform amidst political upheaval and oppression
provide further signs of hope for progress in many nations around
the globe.

SOCIAL JUSTICE

Accountability and open government provide essential
prerequisites for political and social justice. Archivists
concerned about their role in society can provide a
valuable foundation for social justice initiatives by fulfilling their
professional responsibility to document all aspects of society, all
segments of the populace. Jacques Derrida states that justice is
central to the mission and purpose of archives. "I have, for my
part, . . . tried to situate justice, the justice which exceeds but also
requires the law, in the direction of the act of memory, of resistance
to forgetting," he vows. He quotes Yosef Yerushalmi's query, "Is
it possible that the antonym of 'forgetting' is not 'remembering'
but *justice*?" Accepting the implied affirmation of the question,

Derrida extends the argument, equating memory with justice. To serve justice, such memory must be inclusive. "Because if it is just to remember the future and the injunction to remember, namely the archontic injunction to guard and to gather the archive, it is no less just to remember the others," Derrida concludes.[86] Archives therefore need to represent all voices in society. As Terry Cook suggests, archivists can extend "the notion of 'justice' into the opening, hospitable welcoming of 'story' into archives, the telling and retellings of stories by archivists and by multiple users, multiple ways of seeing and knowing being invited in, rather than excluded from, the archives." This call for justice is central to "conceptions of the archive of memory and forgetting, of our role as mediators of past, present, and future," Cook states.[87] The power that archivists wield—in constructing memory, in selecting which aspects of society will be documented and preserved, and in interpreting the record for subsequent users—carries social obligations. For Derrida, Harris, Cook, and others, this responsibility requires attention to the call for justice in society.

The quest for social justice connects with archivists' work most dramatically in South Africa, which has undergone a long and difficult transition from the oppressive apartheid regime to democracy. We may never know the full extent of injustices committed under the previous regime, due to the state's extensive attempts to efface knowledge of its brutality from public memory. Following the end of apartheid, the South African Truth and Reconciliation Commission reported, "The tragedy is that the former government deliberately and systematically destroyed a huge body of state records and documentation in an attempt to remove incriminating evidence and thereby sanitise the history of oppressive rule."[88] As in George Orwell's *Nineteen Eighty-Four,* control over records enabled the government to shape its own version of public memory. "Under apartheid, the terrain of social memory, as with all social space, was a site of struggle," according to Verne Harris. "In the crudest sense it was a struggle of remembering against forgetting, of oppositional memory fighting a life-and-death struggle against a systematic forgetting engineered by the state." To maintain its power, the apartheid government "generated huge information resources, which it secreted jealously from public view. It routinely destroyed public records in order to keep certain processes secret."[89] Control over records formed part of a broader exercise of state power. "In imposing apartheid ideology, the state sought to destroy all oppositional memory through censorship, confiscation, banning, incarceration, assassination, and a range of other oppressive tools," Harris reports.[90]

Archives supported the South African regime. Frustrated in her efforts during the apartheid era to examine the history of the 1976 Soweto uprising, historian Helena Pohlandt-McCormick concluded "that the South African state archives, charged with minding the documentary records of the nation, had instead engaged in their systematic destruction during the apartheid years." She found numerous files in the archives "filled only with a small slip of paper upon which are written the ominous words: '*Vernietig*/Destroyed.'" The archival record had been sanitized. "In the repressive, authoritarian context of apartheid South Africa, official or publicly sanctioned memories and histories were shaped around silences and lies," Pohlandt-McCormick asserts. "Archivists carefully controlled access to the records that remained in the archives according to strict rules and pro-government biases."[91] According to Verne Harris, a white archivist who worked in the archives while secretly supporting opponents of apartheid, "apartheid's memory institutions . . . legitimized apartheid rule by their silences and their narratives of power," and "official secrets were protected by the Protection of Information Act and numerous other pieces of interlinking legislation." Under apartheid, "the state recordmaking system faithfully reproduced oppressive relations of power," privileging white cultures and voices while marginalizing or excluding others.[92]

Despite vigorous efforts to control public knowledge and memory, however, archival traces remain. Like the newspaper photograph and the antique glass paperweight that Orwell's Winston Smith prized as evidence of the past, South African documents and personal memories provide a counternarrative exposing the harsh realities of apartheid rule. As Pohlandt-McCormick observes, "old letters, pamphlets, and speeches from the time of 'the trouble' . . . combined with interviews and other voices that come to us more indirectly through recordings, transcriptions of testimony, recorded statements, and affidavits, allow us, through their rich diversity and their indisputable authenticity, to see something of a past consciousness that has so often been seized and claimed for narratives that were not the participants' own." Such sources provide a sense of the complexity and intricate levels of historical meaning. "Accounts of the experiences of ordinary people create a historical picture that may not be neat or straightforwardly argued but that is a little closer to the multiple realities of historical experience," she states.[93] Harris suggests that the lessons archivists should learn include "the necessity for transparency and accountability in government"; "the public right of access to information, particularly that held by the state"; the need for clear archival selection procedures, "choosing what to remember and what to forget"; and "the need for a democratic state to take appropriate measures to prevent the sanitizing of official memory resources."[94] Harris's account of archives under apartheid demonstrates how recordkeeping can contribute to reinforcing the power of the ruling elite and perpetuating the status quo. It highlights the essential nature of proper recordkeeping to protect citizens' rights and to secure social justice.

Although archives can serve to reinforce oppressive political regimes, they can also provide the antidote for poisonous efforts to subvert people's rights and interests. The power of archivists to shape the public consciousness reveals itself most clearly in South Africa. As the Truth and Reconciliation Commission (TRC) revealed, institutional memory resides in countless documentary records, under the purview of archives. The TRC itself relied on "access [to] documents relevant to the human rights violations it was investigating, documents . . . which would have a significant impact on its findings," Pohlandt-McCormick states. "The work of the TRC made clear that institutions such as archives play an important role in preserving the documentary record of human memory."[95] Under the apartheid regime, state archives supported oppression and injustice, but subsequently the archives provided security for records documenting previous abuses. Institutions such as archives are "only as good or bad as the people who run them," Pohlandt-McCormick concludes. "Danger comes, even now, when controls put in place to protect people or evidence are suddenly used to control access to information and to restrict knowledge."[96] The power of archives thus becomes a force for justice or injustice, remembering or forgetting, truth or falsehood, depending on who controls it and how they use it. Archivists therefore play a crucial role in society's institutional systems and cultural representations.

In the 1980s, the South African History Archives (SAHA) deliberately sought to counter "the dominant narratives of the Apartheid regime." In his presentation at the July 2003 Liverpool conference on "Political Pressure and the Archival Record," Verne Harris argued that SAHA's "most important accounting is to the call of justice." The question Harris addressed was, "Why 'archives for justice' rather than 'archives for truth,' 'archives for memory,' or 'archives for accountability'?" His experience in South Africa convinced him that "the call of justice is the most important of all." Since elites "use 'the archive' as an instrument of power," it is a moral imperative to counter such control and the abuses it can create.[97] Harris has been a leading figure in efforts to overturn

South Africa's apartheid-era culture of political secrecy and control of records, and to replace it with a more transparent and open archival process. The Truth and Reconciliation Commission used records and archives to uncover past abuses under the old regime, although access to such records remains hotly contested. For example, recent changes in archival policy have brought "the National Archives more tightly under the control of the bureaucracy," and access policy to the records of the Truth and Reconciliation Commission has still not been finalized. Valuable records in the Transkei archives have been exposed to improper storage, showing "a reckless disregard for the preservation of a priceless and irreplaceable resource."[98] Despite these obstacles, the efforts of South African archivists provide a documentary basis for efforts to secure a greater degree of social justice in their troubled nation.

South Africa is one of many countries that established truth commissions in recent years to overcome secrecy and expose past social injustices. Nearly two dozen truth commissions have been established, most in South and Central America and Africa, as temporary bodies set up to investigate abuses of former repressive regimes when countries transition to more democratic rule. As Trudy Peterson concludes after studying twenty such truth commissions:

> Oppressive regimes try to impose selective amnesia on society. The purpose of a truth commission is to break through that wall of silence and restore knowledge of the hitherto hidden hands in history. Destroying the records ensures that only those things that made their way into the report will be remembered officially, and thereby opens the way for persons opposed to the commission to win yet again. Saving the records ensures that amnesia does not prevail.[99]

Archival preservation of truth commission records protects the rights of individual victims to know the truth. "The right to know is also a collective right, drawing upon history to prevent violations from recurring in the future," according to distinguished legal scholar Louis Joinet in a report to the United Nations Commission on Human Rights. "Its corollary is a 'duty to remember,' which the State must assume, in order to guard against the perversions of history that go under the names of revisionism or negationism; the knowledge of the oppression it has lived through is part of a people's national heritage and as such must be preserved."[100] Placed in national archives or other safe repositories, such records provide a bulwark for social justice and a means to redress past abuses.

One of the most highly publicized international efforts to use records and archives to redress past injustices has been the campaign to restore Holocaust-era assets to the families of Nazi victims. "The Nazi era witnessed the direct and indirect theft of well over $150 billion of assets of victims of Nazi persecution," according to Greg Bradsher.[101] In seeking to uncover the extent of such misappropriation, researchers relied extensively on records held by the United States National Archives and Records Administration. John W. Carlin, then archivist of the United States, declared, "Everyone should understand the role of the records in establishing and legitimizing identities and liberties."[102] As a 1998 *U.S. News and World Report* article declared, archival institutions "have become drivers of world events. Their contents have forced apologies from governments, opened long-dormant bank accounts, unlocked the secrets of art museums, and compelled corporations to defend their reputations."[103] The Vilnius Forum on Looted Cultural Property adopted a declaration that, in part, recognized the need "to ensure that archives remain open and accessible and operate in as transparent a manner as possible." As Bradsher concludes, archives have served "as important resources in the search for truth and justice, and as Stuart Eizenstat frequently says, turning history into justice."[104] The Holocaust assets project thus demonstrates the value of archives in the quest for justice.

Another example of success in using archival records to redress past injustices is the exposure of the Tuskegee syphilis study. Lasting from 1932 to 1972, this study by the United States Public Health Service allowed 399 African American men to suffer and die from syphilis without receiving treatment. This unethical study has been called the "longest non-therapeutic experiment on human beings in medical history."[105] The original records of this study provide the evidence necessary to hold the U.S. government accountable for its actions. Discussing this case, Tywanna Whorley insists:

> For records that reveal illegal and improper governmental actions, archivists must not hesitate in exposing the existence of such records. As Kent Haworth states, "The . . . purpose of the archivist is to hold in trust for society the evidence of the truth, the evidence of justice and injustice in the society our archives document."[106]

However, as Whorley charges, the National Archives and Records Administration refused to make these records openly accessible, despite public demand for government accountability, due to an "archival policy on restricting archival records that contain personal information without reconciling the right to know versus the right to privacy."[107] Despite continuing controversy over releasing these records, their existence offers at least some assurance of the power of records to secure a measure of social justice for those who have suffered from government mistreatment.

The quest for social justice also engages archivists in countries with less tradition of democratic governance. In Uzbekistan, for example, the post-Soviet regime "has sought to limit the examination of archival documents, to avoid in particular the exposure of links between the former Communist Party and the current government, both led by the same figure, Islam Karimov." According to Jeff Sahadeo, "Uzbek leaders, meanwhile, are shaping the past to secure their own political futures." This has included narrowing access to historical documents, censorship, and funding cuts that "have strangled libraries and archives," he reports. However, there are signs that Uzbekistan's history is opening to more liberating uses of documentation. The new Victims of Repression Memorial Museum, opened in 2002 by President Karimov, uses archival sources to document earlier periods of repression. "Archival documents and photographs illustrated tsarist repression of multiple Central Asian deaths in the 1930s," Sahadeo states. "Most prominently, documents exposed the scope of Stalinist campaigns that resulted in hundreds of thousands of Central Asian deaths in the 1930s." Karimov himself, after touring the museum, decried the suffering and humiliation of the former colonialist regime, vowing, "'The people respect their history and ancestors at all times. This is one of the main factors in a people's self-recognition.'"[108] Despite such rhetoric, Karimov has continued to crack down on political opposition and to remove records from public scrutiny. "The archive constitutes a source of power and authority in Uzbekistan," Sahadeo contends. "As the Soviet experience showed, use of the archives to produce 'official' histories for an authoritarian state can produce counternarratives, albeit subtle, that may provoke eventual challenges to the regime's legitimacy."[109] However, the power of the current regime in Uzbekistan has prevented such developments in recent years. Social justice remains elusive, even though the promise of using archival records to support people's rights provides a glimmer of hope for Uzbek historians and critics of the ruling party.

These are but a few of numerous recent instances in which records and archives have contributed to social justice by holding accountable those responsible for abuses of trust and power. By preserving records that can provide evidence of injustice, archivists can contribute positively to attempts to overcome past uses of archives and records by elites to secure power. Such benefits can also be seen in Sierra Leone, where records management improvements have been targeted to support the "Poverty Reduction Strategy" and national recovery from a ten-year civil war. In 2003, President Kabbah declared, "The poor storage and retrieval of information slows down work of the public service and impacts negatively on policy formulation, planning and financial control. The improvement of record keeping is absolutely essential for moving the reform process forward."[110] Archival protection of records thus serves the vital need to ensure social justice and protect citizens' rights. By holding public leaders accountable to the people, by documenting the rights of citizens and the lives and voices of marginalized groups, by ensuring public access to essential records, and by providing a secure repository for reliable and authentic records, archivists and the archives they preserve contribute to the public interest. Archives for all become archives for justice.

DIVERSITY AND IDENTITY

The United States population, like that of many other nations throughout the world, comprises numerous racial, ethnic, social, and cultural groups. Many of these have been neglected or under-documented by traditional archival practices. Awareness of such oversights and biases is the first step in correcting the problem. Archivists have already made significant contributions to a more representative and just society by creating racial, ethnic, and community-based repositories, and by ensuring adequate documentation of their perspectives in university, historical, government, and business repositories. As Elisabeth Kaplan has shown, such repositories play important roles both in promoting a more diverse society and in fostering community identity among groups often marginalized by more powerful elites.[111] An oft-voiced professional credo that is not always followed states that the archival "record must reflect full diversity and complexity, not an edited compendium that celebrates a specific world view or a single group."[112] In the 1960s, a number of archivists responded to the challenge raised by social activists and expanded documentation of underrepresented social groups.[113] Among the most encouraging developments of the past forty years, from the perspective of social diversity, is the number of archival repositories dedicated to documentation of women, African Americans, ethnic groups, gay and lesbian communities, laborers, and other marginalized communities. Although public and academic repositories actively collect their records, many of these groups have seized the initiative to document their own lives and tell their own stories.

The "new social history" of the 1960s led to expansion of source materials for underrepresented groups in American society. "Literally an embarrassment of riches, documentation of the lives of women, workers, farmers, enslaved persons, and Native Americans flushed out a disquieting connection between history and national identity," according to historian Joyce Appleby.[114] When the disenfranchised find themselves excluded from existing repositories, they sometimes create their own archives.[115] Women, ethnic and racial groups, religious communities, laborers, and other marginalized communities have established archival repositories to document and celebrate their histories and cultures. Other repositories, which have a broader collecting and documentation mandate, incorporate diversity goals into their program priorities. These voices confer power. Archives provide a forum to recognize and legitimize the role of disenfranchised groups in society.

Although comprising slightly over half of the human population, women have never achieved parity in the archival record. Their stories, perspectives, and activities seldom receive adequate attention from male-dominated political, academic, intellectual, and social institutions and discourses. As feminist scholar Gerda Lerner demonstrates, the first documents and archives and the subsequent formation of collective memory emerged amid social systems that were remorselessly and intentionally patriarchal. Although women have always played central roles in building civilization, and "have also shared with men in preserving collective memory," Lerner states, "Until the most recent past, . . . historians have been men, and what they have recorded is what men have done and experienced and found significant."[116] Although a majority of the population, women had thus become marginalized as historical persons. "History gives meaning to human life and connects each life to immortality," Lerner contends. "In preserving the collective past and reinterpreting it to the present, human beings define their potential and explore the limits of their possibilities." The advent of writing extended the division between men and women. "From the days of the Babylonian king-lists forward, the record of the past has been written by men and interpreted by men and has primarily focused on the deeds, actions, and intentions of males," Lerner asserts. Women continued to participate in and maintain oral tradition and cultic functions, but their importance declined in literate societies ruled by patriarchy.[117] From the ancient world until the late twentieth century, archival procedures based in this political and social milieu delegitimized women and their stories.[118] Men held political power—they controlled the present and therefore the past and future, in Orwell's formulation—and they denied women a role in the broad sweep of historical narratives.

In the 1960s and 1970s, a new generation of scholars, including women, began to seek out the stories of women's lives and to accord them agency in social history. They created a new discipline of women's history, which required both new methods of reading archival records and an increasing demand for identification and preservation of archival sources necessary to document women's lives and perspectives. One of the American pioneers of women's history was Eleanor Flexner, whose *Century of Struggle: The Woman's Rights Movement in the United States* (1959) "paved the way for a new approach to women's history that was rich, analytical, and archivally based."[119] Flexner lamented that despite the volume of sources for women's history, "in the form of letters, journals, organizational records, newspapers and other publications, relatively little use has been made of it" by historians. "There are unfortunately large gaps in the sources available," she pointed out, because documents and records had been "dissipated and lost." This reflected "not only the low worth put on it by historians and sociologists, but a general attitude of the relative unimportance of women and their activities." However, Flexner applauded the "growing number of women's archives" such as those at Radcliffe and Smith College.[120] These specialized repositories encouraged later development of women's archives and those devoted to other neglected groups in society. As Lerner observed in the 1980s, two decades of women's history scholarship disproved the fallacy that women have no history, "by unearthing an unending list of sources and uncovering and interpreting the hidden history of women."[121] The Women's History Sources Survey, funded by the National Endowment for the Humanities in the late 1970s, identified primary sources depicting the roles of women in American society in more than three thousand repositories, demonstrating that archival records could be used effectively to examine women's history. This project published *Women's History Sources: A Guide to Archives and Manuscript Collections in the United States,* edited by Andrea Hinding, which further stimulated archival acquisition of women's sources. [122]

Seeking sources for women's history also sometimes requires creative research methods. "Looking for—and finding—women as witnesses in court proceedings, to cite just one example, historians of women interrogated primary documents creatively in order that women's pasts might become visible," feminist historian Laura Mayhall states. "Despite this productive shift in perspective, however, the archive itself remained essentially unproblematic, imagined as a fundamentally unbiased universe of potential histories."[123] In Great Britain following the First World War, the Suffragette Fellowship sought to redress this deficiency by creating an archive of suffrage pamphlets, contemporary records and documents, and information sources created deliberately to document women's activities. Focusing on suffragettes who had faced imprisonment, this feminist organization distributed questionnaires seeking information about the experiences and imprisonment of militant protestors. By 1936 the organization asserted that "the Fellowship endeavors to correct all false or damaging stories which may be circulated, not only about the militant movement, but of the women who took part in the militant campaign. In this way, the Fellowship hopes to hand down to posterity a true and accurate account of the Militant Movement and its leaders."[124] This deliberate effort to document women's actions thus assumed a political purpose of defining the movement's identity and countering external images of suffragette leaders. The Fellowship thereby created its own archive, separate from those of patriarchal institutions, and, as Mayhall recounts, "the archive itself is both a physical collection of objects and the material through which political agendas are performed."[125] Unwilling to entrust their history—the memory traces and sources of their lives, actions, and thoughts—to male-dominated archival repositories, women created their own archives.

Some of the groups often marginalized by mainstream society leave no formal records, or at least no conventional written documents, to tell their stories. Jeannette Bastian shows that even among a people whose history was never recorded—the natives of the Virgin Islands—a creative approach to archival documentation can provide a communal history and identity. "Throughout the 250-year colonization of the islands, the Danish colonial bureaucracy kept meticulous records and when the Danes left the islands [in 1917], they took most of these records with them and deposited them in the Danish National Archives in Copenhagen," Bastian explains. The National Archives of the United States claimed similar records when the islands fell under American control. "Except for property records and some court records, the only records found in the Virgin Islands today are contemporary ones dating from the mid-twentieth century,"[126] Bastian reports. The problem for colonial peoples is not that their history under foreign control has been forgotten, but that it "was never recorded, therefore not remembered [officially]," Bastian observes. "Archives can provide the key to that quest if the searcher recognizes that records have both a text and a subtext, that records are both evidence and action, and that behind the record lies the trace." As one Virgin Islander argues, "it's our story and we should have access to it, when we need to have access to it to even write our story or even just to understand, to have a complete picture . . . otherwise anyone could tell you anything they want."[127] These various efforts to expand archival documentation beyond the elitist focus on the "great white males" of previous generations promise a more representative depiction of society and of human history.

Archivists' practice of identifying, selecting, and managing records according to the provenance of their creation automatically privileges the colonial rulers and their bureaucracy over the perspectives of native peoples. The latter often base their culture on oral tradition and oral sources of recording and remembering essential information rather than written records. In Australia, for another example, government regulations required "careful record keeping by governors and other officials charged with reporting their actions in detail to the British colonial authorities." This resulted in copious archives from the white perspective, but little recordkeeping reflecting the actions and viewpoints of the aboriginal population, according to historian Ann Curthoys. In addition to routine records of governance, royal commissions, select committees, and even missionaries created extensive documentation. "Yet if the bureaucracy of colonialism led to plentiful record creation, there were also alternative tendencies leading to considerable record destruction or abandonment," Curthoys notes, and "records could easily vanish."[128] Whether from deliberate efforts to efface the history of indigenous peoples or from simple indifference to their culture, colonial records privileged and reinforced the supremacy of the imperialists and occupiers of these lands.

Researchers using colonial records must thus read them "against the grain," seeking to hear the silent voices and to infer the missing stories from the few scraps of documents pertaining to indigenous peoples. "Students of the colonial 'mine' the content of government commissions and reports but rarely attend to their peculiar form," reports anthropologist Ann Stoler. Examining how documents are made and used enables one to recognize "archives not as sites of knowledge retrieval but as sites of knowledge production," actively shaping our understanding of the past. This requires "a more sustained engagement with those archives as cultural artifacts of fact production, of taxonomies in the making, and of disparate notions of what made up colonial authority."[129] Using such archives requires careful consideration of reliability and trustworthiness of the records, based on fundamental questions such as "what political forces, social cues, and moral virtues produce qualified knowledges [sic] that in turn disqualify others," Stoler cautions. "Colonial archives were both sites of the imaginary and institutions that fashioned histories as they concealed, revealed, and reproduced the power of the state."[130] Although particularly evident in such colonial contexts, these are concerns affecting all archives, even the most seemingly unbiased and transparent. The mediating role of the archivist cannot be ignored. "Archival conventions might designate who were reliable 'sources,' what constituted 'enough' evidence, and what could be inserted in the absence of information," Stoler observes. "As Ian Hacking says of social categories, archives produced as much as they recorded the realities they ostensibly only described. They told moral stories, they created precedent in the pursuit of evidence, and not least they created carefully tended histories."[131] However, historians also must read the archive "along the grain," in order to understand how records were created, used, interpreted, and exploited. Bureaucratic documentation might provide an illusion of order and control. In the Netherlands Indies, for example, "epistemic uncertainties repeatedly unsettled the imperial conceit that all was in order, because papers classified people, because directives were properly acknowledged, and because colonial civil servants were schooled to assure that records were prepared, circulated, securely stored, and sometimes rendered to ash."[132] Colonial records thus need to be understood in context, given the assumptions and constraints of administrators and petty officials of the colonial power.

Another difficulty in using colonial records—or those of indigenous populations—is that many people outside the bounds of western culture rely principally on oral traditions that produce very little tangible documentary evidence. "The past of the new African nation [Senegal] is recorded in the old colonial archive," observes Frederick Cooper. This obvious colonial perspective poses the added difficulty that "the categories and units of analysis that shape the colonial archive also shape other forms of historical preservation and memory," Cooper states. "African historians, since the 1960s, have trumpeted that oral tradition is the antidote to the Eurocentrism of the written record—popular memory set against elite documents."[133] The Eurocentric point of view against which Cooper contends can be seen in architectural historian Sir Banister Fletcher's 1950 dismissal of non-western buildings as insignificant, because they were "non-historical," and in historian Hugh Trevor-Roper's disdainful claim in 1965 that there was no African history worth teaching, because, "The history of the world, for the last five centuries, . . . has been European history."[134] Only literate western-influenced cultures deserve consideration for study, according to such arguments. Orality thus continues to challenge literacy, as it has since ancient Greece.

In creating archival repositories, societies with persistent oral traditions need to accommodate the diverse voices of oral cultures. A 1991 legal dispute over Indian (First Nations) land claims in Canada's British Columbia province juxtaposed the indigenous people's oral tradition against the dominant European-influenced legal system. The Gitksan and Wet-suwet-en peoples claimed ownership of lands in northern British Columbia, but there were no written treaties to rely upon in resolving the dispute. In *Delgamuukw v. British Columbia,* the province's chief justice Allan McEachern argued that their claims were impossible to verify without adequate documentary evidence. "The most significant document in the oral archive of the Gitksan is the *adwaak,* the verbal records of a house and its history," according to historian Adele Perry.[135] McEachern ruled that he was "unable to accept . . . oral histories as reliable bases for detailed history," unless these indigenous sources of recordkeeping could be corroborated by written documents from repositories steeped in western sources of knowledge. The justice's decision stated, "Generally speaking I accept just about everything they [the white historians] put before me because they were largely collectors of archival, historical documents. In most cases they provided much useful information with minimal editorial comment."[136] He thereby negated nearly a century of historical theory that recognized the agency of historians in imagining and interpreting the past, even when seemingly presenting only "factual" evidence. "In 1991 history thus found itself firmly positioned in its nineteenth-century place, as a positivist discipline rooted in the archive and a muse to the nation and the state and the practical keeper of empire," Perry declares. The 1991 court judgment thus perpetuated the nineteenth-century "ontological link between orality and savagery on the one hand and literacy and civilization on the other," by which "the absence of written records was used to validate European claim to the so-called new world and to consign Indigenous people to what Anne McClintock memorably dubs 'anachronistic space,'" Perry concludes.[137]

Beyond its ignorance of modern historical practice, this ruling more significantly negated the validity of an entire indigenous culture based on clearly defined concepts of oral tradition and personal rights. "Demanding that an indigenous people prove their very existence in evidentiary terms that they lack," Perry argues, establishes " . . . the incessant yet unanswerable demand that Aboriginal peoples demonstrate 'tradition.' The result is that Indigenous people and their claims against settler societies are forever and necessarily found insufficient, impartial, and inauthentic."[138] As Shauna McRanor concludes, "Much of the disfranchisement of aboriginal people that has occurred is due, in part, to the Eurocentric idea of the superiority of static objectified records over dynamic oral testimony as proof for establishing 'fact' or attaining absolute notions of 'truth.'"[139] McEachern's decision chronicled the actions of European men serving the needs of a western nation-state, while denying the perspective of the native peoples of Canada. Only western written sources could be considered authentic and reliable. "The human past that is not recorded in this archive is deemed unknown and unknowable, while the archive's inconsistency, polyvocality, and partiality slips below the radar," Perry asserts.[140] Justice McEachern thus ignored recent scholarship in both the discipline of history and the field of archives.

The McEachern decision demonstrates that the struggle between indigenous oral traditions and the dominant culture's reliance on written records persists even in contemporary political struggles. "Superficially, *Delgamuukw v. British Columbia* indicates the unmitigated triumph of history and archives in the service of empire," Perry states. "Likewise what we might call the 'voice of history'—the putatively dispassionate cataloguing of the documented activities of European men acting on behalf of nation-states—lives on in McEachern's decision." However, in 1997 the Supreme Court of Canada reversed McEachern's judgment on appeal, arguing that he had not paid sufficient attention to the indigenous oral archive. This both overturned the 1991 ruling and opened the door for future cases involving indigenous peoples to be argued using oral evidence. It thus marks "the significant recognition of oral history as admissible evidence in land-claims cases throughout Canada." Although this represents a very different context than the South African Truth and Reconciliation Commission report, Perry asserts, "both remind us how the colonial archives can alternately and sometimes simultaneously work to defend or challenge the states that create and sustain them."[141] Even the archival records of the dominant culture can sometimes protect the rights and interests of oppressed or marginalized peoples. Recognition of the validity and importance of indigenous sources of information and human memory, such as oral traditions and testimony, provides another opening of the archive to the needs of a diverse and heterogeneous population. If archives are to serve the needs of all people and groups in society, such recognition is critical to the goal of diversity.

In the United States, concern for diversity encompasses women, racial and ethnic minorities, gays and lesbians, and other marginalized communities. Rather than examine each of these groups in detail, we can demonstrate the progress of archival representation of diversity by looking at how archivists have responded to concerns for documenting, for example, the lives and perspectives of African Americans. The development of an archival presence shows both an assertion of racial pride and an effort to secure the power that comes from being able to tell the group's collective story of tragedy, suffering, achievement, and success. As early as 1914, several universities and libraries established research collections focusing on the African American experience in the United States. These include the Schomburg Center for Research in Black Culture[142] at the New York Public Library, the Moorland-Spingarn Research Center[143] at Howard University, and the Amistad Research Center[144] at Tulane University. "These are notable beginnings by Negroes in the preservation of the evidence of their accomplishments," Harold T. Pinkett wrote in 1944. However, "Much more can and needs to be done. To begin with, the nature and value of existing collections should be more widely publicized with a view toward stimulating more interest in documentary materials."[145]

In addition to repositories established to document the broad range of African American and minority history, several focus specifically on the modern civil rights movement itself. These deliberate efforts to preserve the perspective of the movement or to memorialize civil rights leaders take an openly partisan or celebratory approach to the subject. Some of them are housed within civil rights museums or in research institutions with a special interest in civil rights. Examples include the King Center in Atlanta,[146] the Birmingham Civil Rights Institute,[147] and the Civil Rights in Mississippi Digital Archive at the University of Southern Mississippi.[148] These institutions actively seek to shape the public discourse on civil rights and sometimes even attempt to advocate a particular interpretive vision of the movement. Such efforts may blur the line between scholarship and political partisanship.

Closely related to the concept of power is that of identity. The King Center in Atlanta deliberately seeks to shape the public memory of one of the leaders of the civil rights movement. According to its mission statement, "Established in 1968 by Mrs. Coretta Scott King, the King Center is the living memorial and institutional guardian of Dr. Martin Luther King, Jr.'s legacy."[149] The King Library and Archives shares the center's purposes: "The King Library and Archives' mission is to promote the appropriate application of archival principles in the preservation, processing, and description of materials relevant to the life and work of Dr. Martin Luther King, Jr. and the modern civil rights movement."[150] In addition to the papers of Dr. King, the Library and Archives maintains the records of many civil rights organizations and the personal papers of other civil rights activists. This confers legitimacy on them as part of the movement's legacy.

Many civil rights archives focus on the formal records created by organizations engaged in civil rights activities—such as the National Association for the Advancement of Colored People, the Southern Christian Leadership Conference, and the Student Nonviolent Coordinating Committee—and on the personal papers of nationally recognized figures such as King, Rev. Ralph Abernathy, and Rev. Fred Shuttlesworth. Historical studies of the movement depict these organizations and leaders most often, both because of their recognized prominence in civil rights and because records of their activities are readily available.

There remains a need to understand and document the experiences of ordinary people, those who seldom receive public attention. Howard Zinn challenged archivists a generation ago to compile documentation of "the lives, desires, and needs of ordinary people."[151] Since then, significant progress has been made, but much more remains to be done. In documenting diversity in our society, notable achievements in preserving records of prominent organizations and papers of individual leaders have been made. But archival repositories still need to turn their attention to collecting and preserving the records of ordinary people. These forgotten voices continue to represent an under-documented texture in our social fabric. "The voices and experiences of the weak, the underprivileged, the disadvantaged, the marginalized will either be in the margins of the record, or simply absent," warns Verne Harris. "In every society, the dominant cultures will dominate the record."[152] The challenge for archivists is to overcome this inherent slanting of the archival record, this privileging of documentation, this exclusion of marginalized voices, in order to present an archival record that represents all peoples, all perspectives, all voices of our diverse societies.

THE CALL OF JUSTICE

Archives provide a basis for empowering all citizens in a democratic society. They preserve documentation that serves as an authentic record of human activity, which can corroborate or invalidate appeals to precedent and heritage. Archives thus serve as one means of holding accountable public leaders in all sectors of social interaction. If archivists—and those who provide support and authority for their work—accept the challenges and opportunities afforded by the power of records (including textual, visual, sound, and electronic media), the archival record can support the goals of democracy, open government, social justice, and diversity. Archives can meet the needs of all members of society.

The Centre of Memory that bears his name embodies Nelson Mandela's understanding that freedom is not given to one, but is created. "The Centre is premised on a commitment to documenting stories, disseminating information, and contributing to continuing struggles for justice," according to its chief executive, John Samuel. It promotes the idea of archives for social justice through a variety of programs, including comic books designed to reach young people who might resist a formal or didactic approach to the story of South Africa's past and present. In responding to Mandela's call to justice, Samuel concludes, "Action, if it is to be true to the legacy it claims to represent, must flow from and be shaped by memory."[153] The archival imperative thus provides the basis for understanding the past and for seeking democracy and social justice.

"In the life of any individual, family, community or society, memory is of fundamental importance. It is the fabric of identity," Nelson Mandela writes. "At the heart of every oppressive tool developed by the apartheid regime was a determination to control, distort, weaken, even erase people's memories." This attack on memory could be felt in the bodies of those separated from loved ones, locked away from their homes. "The struggle against apartheid can be typified as the pitting of remembering against forgetting," Mandela continues. "It was in our determination to remember our ancestors, our stories, our values and our dreams that we found comradeship." The mandate of the Nelson Mandela Centre of Memory and Dialogue focuses on locating, documenting, and facilitating public access to "the many archives that contain traces of my life and those who have lived it with me," Mandela explains. "Anyone who has explored the world of archives will know that it is a treasure house, one that is full of surprises, crossing paths, dead ends, painful reminders and unanswered questions. Very often, the memories contained in archives diverge from the memories people carry with them," he acknowledges. "That is its challenge. And its fascination. . . . Engagement with archives offers both joy and pain."[154]

Archival records thus represent the nexus of memory and forgetting, of power and accountability, of oppression and justice. As both yin and yang, they can serve opposite callings, depending on who wields their power over past, present, and future. Fifteen years after the apartheid regime ended the ban of the African National Congress and other liberation movements and released Nelson Mandela from prison, he opened an exhibition of photographs and documents from his years at Robben Island by stating, "All of us tend to associate archives and museums with a remembering of the past. But that is only part of their work. If justice is their most important shaping influence, then they are also about making the future." South Africa had made significant progress in fifteen years, Mandela added, "But let us not forget that much still remains to be done. The shackles of our apartheid past have not been broken entirely. At the same time, new global realities pose huge obstacles to bringing justice to all."[155]

The continuing work of the Nelson Mandela Centre of Memory represents a commitment to the future, part of the call to justice and reconciliation. It is a commitment open to all archivists and to anyone who supports the goal of opening the archival record to all voices, all experiences, and all people. This model and the goals it represents can be emulated in any political or cultural context. Society can and must embrace archives for all.

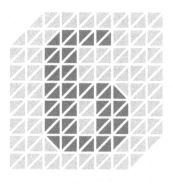

Responding to the Call of Justice

The newspaper editor needed one more community interest story for the next day's paper. Noticing an e-mail message announcing "American Archives Month," he sent seven interns and junior reporters to find out what archives are and what purpose they serve. Each went to a different archives in the city, but when they met to discuss their findings, arguments broke out at once.

The reporter who visited the City Archives declared, "Archives exist only to protect the legal rights of citizens and administrative needs of government." Another reporter returned from the County Historical Society, convinced that archives create the "collective memory" of the local community, celebrating the role of prominent citizens. "You are both wrong," argued the intern who had spoken to the City College archivist: "Archives provide research materials for educational purposes."

"Anyone in the city can use the Public Library Archives to find genealogical information," said another. "No way! The public can't use archives, because they serve only the institution that pays for them," said the reporter from the City Manufacturing Company Archives. The intern who had interviewed the archivist at First Church of the City declared that archives connect people to spiritual values and beliefs. "No," insisted the reporter who had visited the County Tribal Archives Center, "the chief value of the archives is to create a sense of community heritage and identity."

"Enough!" cried the exasperated editor. "If you knuckleheads don't know what archives are like, I'm going with a story about the City Zoo's new baby elephant."

As archivists debate their professional identity, it often seems that they mistake one part of the profession for the whole. Like the elephant of the ancient Buddhist fable, the archival profession seems to consist of diverse and seemingly contradictory parts. Rather than define the profession in narrow terms, it is time to understand its commonalities and collective identity. It is pointless to insist that the archival elephant resembles only a rope or a tree—an institutional archives or a manuscripts repository. In one of Walt Kelly's Pogo cartoons, Porky states, "Ever'body got their own way of lookin' at *anything* . . . Din't you ever hear the story of the blind men an' the elephant? . . . Each one was partly right." To this the great philosopher Pogo responds, "Yeah . . . an' each was mostly wrong."[1]

Archivists in the United States have been struggling to define their role in society—and their identity as members of a profession—for the past century. Are they some type of historians, or a subset of librarians? Do they assist administrators, or protect legal evidence, or guard cultural heritage? Each effort to define archives and the role of archivists is at least partially correct, but only by recognizing the common characteristics among the various parts of the archival elephant can archivists understand their true purpose. Common bonds unite the archival profession, even though separate groups define their own purposes and roles in different and (at times) seemingly contradictory terms. Archivists must not let their differences divide them, as they serve the broad and diverse needs of society. In doing so, their work should be informed by a sense of social responsibility and a commitment to personal morality and professional ethics.

A DIVERSITY OF ARCHIVES AND ARCHIVISTS

Archivists constitute a diverse profession, representing many types of institutions and a variety of functions and specific specialties. The earliest of ancient archivists served the needs of government and rulers of the state. During the early and High Middle Ages, religious archivists became prominent, and by the late Middle Ages recordkeeping in capitalist businesses gained economic and social significance. By the Renaissance and particularly the Enlightenment, historical research interests fueled the growth of archival repositories, museums, libraries, and other cultural institutions. The growing prominence of universities led to research centers based in libraries and manuscript repositories. In the United States the first archivists worked with personal and family papers, and occasional organizational and governmental documents, in historical societies and libraries. By the twentieth century, state archives and eventually the National Archives renewed the prominence of governmental archives. Many of the founders of professional associations, such as the Society of American Archivists, came from these new government repositories. With the rapid growth of colleges and universities following the Second World War, academic archives proliferated. By the 1980s college and university archivists made up the largest institutional affiliation category in the American archival profession. In 2004 they comprised 36 percent of SAA membership, followed by archivists in government agencies at 31.6 percent.[2]

These various types of archival institutions have specialized interests and needs, even though they share many common concerns. This variety can be seen in the organizational structure of SAA groups. SAA recognized these differences by creating separate "sections" and roundtables (a less formal designation within SAA for smaller interest groups) based on institution type, archival functions, and specialties. Currently the SAA sections defined by type of institution include: government records, college and university archives, business archives, religious collections, manuscript repositories, and museum archives. Archivists from institutions with numerically smaller representation have formed roundtables, including: labor archives, local government records, performing arts, and science, technology, and healthcare. Sections based on archival functions include: acquisitions and appraisal; description; reference, access, and outreach; and preservation. Function-based roundtables include: management, educators, security, and records management. There are also sections grouped around interests in records formats, including electronic records, visual materials, and oral history. Roundtables based on record formats include architectural records, congressional papers, recorded sound, and metadata and digital objects. In addition the smaller roundtables include groups based on subject interests, such as archival history, international archival affairs, issues and advocacy, and privacy and confidentiality. Organizationally, SAA represents diversity through a standing Committee on Diversity and roundtables for: archivists and archives of color, Latin American and Caribbean cultural heritage, lesbian and gay archives, Native American archives, women archivists, and women's collections.

These numerous groupings within the professional association enable archivists with common interests and needs to meet together during the SAA annual conferences and to establish online newsletters and listserve discussion groups. However, the potential fault lines separating archivists with distinct specialties have already led to splintering. In the 1950s records managers formed their own professional society, now known by the acronym ARMA International. By the 1980s, many government archivists concluded that their interests were not adequately met by SAA, which was increasingly dominated by academic archivists. They formed the National Association of Government Archives and Records Administrators (NAGARA). Some governmental archivists maintain membership in both NAGARA and SAA, although they often have to choose between the two groups' annual meetings. Since the early 1970s, regional, state, and metropolitan archival associations have also flourished, meeting the needs of archivists in specific geographical areas.

This splintering of archival professional societies often results from matters of cost, convenience, and proximity, as well as specialized interests and needs. Particularly as regulatory considerations and technical changes increase, specialization becomes important. However, archivists in all types of institutions, performing any (or all) archival functions, focused on any (or all) records formats or subject specialties all share common principles, techniques, knowledge, expertise, and values. The issues discussed in this volume can apply—perhaps in varying degrees—to any archivist concerned about documentation, evidence, and public service. In seeking common ground, in affirming their shared values and goals, archivists should not lose sight of their diversity. It is that diversity—that breadth of experience, perspective, and background—that gives the archival profession much of the strength it needs to serve society.

One of the most powerful objections to the new ethical imperatives, outlined in this volume, is that employers and resource allocators for many archival programs would not allow archivists the latitude to make such changes. Clearly, these initiatives will be easier to undertake for archivists in academic or private collecting repositories, who can more readily adapt collecting policies and goals to reflect a more inclusive approach to documenting society. Government regulations, institutional policies, attorneys, and corporate accountants limit the options for many archivists. Organizational needs and interests may trump professional activism. However, even in institutional archives some changes could be effected. Ensuring the protection of records required for legal accountability should be both a goal and a policy for all institutional archives and records programs. Institutional archivists could also consider retention and appraisal policies to ensure that records and documentation are preserved for all people affected by institutional activities, including workers, clients, and consumers as well as executives and stockholders. Finding aids can be prepared with consideration given to all potential future users, and careful consideration can be given to terminology used and assumptions made in how records and records creators are described. Such changes would not require major alterations to the mission or policies of an institutional archives, nor would it be necessary to endanger institutional support or funding for archives and records management.

The nature of the archivist's role in meeting these expectations varies somewhat according to the type of institution the archivist serves. Questions of acquisition and donor relations differ significantly between governmental archives and private archives, such as business or religious archives. Rules regarding access to archival records likewise vary dramatically between public and private archives. In the former there are usually stringent regulations providing open access to most public records, except when over-ridden by privacy or confidentiality concerns. Secrecy is antithetical to a democratic society and its governmental records. In private archives, there are few if any such requirements. Although it is desirable to make records open for public use so as to enhance our understanding of contributions made by private organizations to society's history, private archives do not have a legal obligation to do so. When public funds are used to support activities or recordkeeping of private groups, however, access requirements may apply.

PUBLIC INSTITUTIONS AND PRIVATE ARCHIVES

Before articulating the implications of the call of justice and the potential demands of a new concept of archival ethics, it is necessary to address the objection that many archivists will not be able to accept these new perspectives. That is true. Some archivists will be constrained by institutional policies, by their reluctance to endanger their job security, by time constraints in the face of new initiatives, or by their own ideological or personal opposition to such concepts. There should be no stigma or criticism for archivists who do not accept these recommendations as personal or professional goals. By the same measure of tolerance, archivists who do embrace these concepts should be accepted as practitioners of a shared professional identity.

Briefly examining two types of private archives, religious and business, will help us see some of these concerns, and to identify

how both religious and business archivists might choose to accept
this call of justice and a new archival ethics. The perspective of tribal
archivists is presented in the conclusion.

Religious archives in the United States document a wide variety
of religious traditions and institutions, including Protestant,
Catholic, evangelical, Jewish, Muslim, Buddhist, Baha'i, and
others. Within these religious groupings there are at least four
types of religious archives: denominational archives also collecting
local records; denominational archives focused on national level
administrative records; state or diocesan archives with no national-
level archives; and local circuit or parish-level archives.[3] What
makes religious archives different from others derives from the
nature of religious organizations and their perspectives on society.
In many religious archives there is constant reference to external
beliefs, ideologies, and values—the essence of religious faith. The
religious archivist must define her or his role in relation to the
organization's beliefs, either by subscribing to them or by making a
"separate peace" with them. These religious beliefs and experiences
may be "very intangible, often fleeting, and perhaps in the end
undocumentable."[4] Although many religious archives prefer to
hire members of their own faith community, this is generally not a
requirement. A majority of religious archivists probably do accept
the faith of their employing body, but many do not.

Religious archivists may struggle with the competing demands of
religious faith and their professional principles as archivists. James
M. O'Toole, former archivist of the Roman Catholic Archdiocese of
Boston, poses the question, "Where do the archives' final loyalties
lie: with the beliefs of the religious group or with the canons of
professional practice?"[5] Although in daily work these conflicts rarely
arise, there is always a possibility that such choices will need to be
made. Those who subscribe to the religious faith of the employing
organization may find it more difficult than others to stand up for
professional principles in the rare instances when such conflicts
might occur. However, religious archivists daily function within an
environment permeated by value systems, concepts of ethics, and
adherence to a "higher law" to guide daily activities. Unless there
is conflict between the values represented in the archival call of
justice and their religious value system, it might be less difficult for
religious archivists than for secular archivists to accept and adhere
to such ethical objectives. It is worth remembering that although
religious archives typically focus on the institutional records of the
religious body, such records have significant value for many other

types of research. Religious archives contain valuable information concerning secular issues such as women's history, genealogy, social history, politics, education, business, and ethnic history.[6] Archivists of religious collections thus should make every possible effort to provide access to researchers interested in these topics.

Nowhere are the potential barriers to accepting the societal responsibilities of the call of justice more difficult for archivists than for those employed in private sector institutional archives. Business archivists, in particular, often face difficulties in justifying the benefits of their programs to administrators concerned about financial stability and the interests of their customers, shareholders, and managers. It would be presumptuous for anyone not directly engaged in the field of corporate archives to create a rigid model for ethical practice or to suggest requirements for adopting the broader conceptions of archival ethics presented in this volume. Corporate archivists often work within organizational constraints and competing demands, perhaps more so than any other group within the archival profession. However, because business enterprises constitute a vital component of society, the records of their activities and services comprise an essential resource for understanding social issues, from consumer demands to the economic and societal impacts of production, employment, inventions, research, marketing, and cultural iconography, to name a few examples. "Business enterprise has long exerted influence on culture, values and social organisation," as business archives expert Lesley Richmond observes. "Can society in the twentieth and twenty-first centuries be understood without an understanding of business?" Business archives comprise essential resources for understanding the history and development of a region, a nation, or a community. Historians and other users "have turned to business archives for their source material for labour, social, design, transport, architectural, technical, regional, local, urban and agricultural history," Richmond states.[7]

Corporate records possess primary importance and value for the organizations that create and maintain them, but they also form part of the societal heritage of the broader communities within which the corporations operate. Just as corporations must maintain personnel and regulatory records to protect the rights and interests of employees, consumers, shareholders, and the public, so should they maintain and provide access to documentation affecting their communities. Of course, sensitive records of corporate decision-making, product development, and financial interests should be protected. Similar protections already cover personnel and confidential records. Beyond these considerations, however, citizens of the communities and nations affected by corporations should expect some level of access to historical records pertaining to societal concerns. Similar expectations apply to other private sector repositories, including religious and tribal archives. However, in some instances religious archives may enjoy some latitude based on the principle of separation of church (or synagogue or mosque) and state. Tribal archives gain some added control over access to their materials because they often represent sovereign or semi-sovereign entities within society, and because of the need to protect cultural and religious practices.

Despite the significance of corporate records, "little legislation exists in any country in the world that secures a public responsibility for business archives," Richmond reports.[8] Some countries protect business archives as part of the cultural heritage of the nation, but most corporate records are classified as private records, with little public influence or control. With increased emphasis on regulation, accountability, and responsibility, the nature of corporate recordkeeping has changed significantly in recent years. The dramatic impact of digital records emphasizes the need to include business archives as part of the broad documentation of society and to plan strategies for protecting and preserving digital business records. "Global multinational companies have more power and influence than many small nations and they have the ability to affect and shape the archival heritage of many nations," Richmond argues. "One solution is the concept of world business collections, on the same model as world heritage sites, defined either in terms of their contribution to the world of business or in terms of their international consumer base."[9] Legislation to ensure archival preservation of private records, in both public and private repositories, would guarantee citizens of a country access to their national heritage. This may be a distant goal, but it recognizes the vital societal interests inherent in documentation regarding important aspects of cultural heritage, as well as the individual interests of employees, consumers, stockholders, and citizens.

In the United States, business archives typically follow different concepts of access and public service than do public archives and most private archives. In this respect, they often resemble tribal archives or religious archives, with carefully delineated priorities for access and service. In a joint paper presented at the Japan-U.S. Archives Seminar in May 2007, Becky Haglund Tousey of Kraft

Foods Archives and Elizabeth W. Adkins of Ford Motor Company Archives outlined the access philosophies of American corporate archives. It is imperative for corporate archivists to demonstrate their value to the business. "They must directly link their mission, services and policies—particularly access policy—to helping the company meet its business goals," Tousey and Adkins report. The "open and equal access" policies of not-for-profit and publicly funded archives do not apply in most corporate settings. "This access ethic represents a key difference between these repositories and corporate archives," they conclude, because corporate archives must focus on "meeting the needs of internal clients or customers rather than those of external researchers."[10] Although this appears to close corporate archives to the public, two-thirds of U.S. corporate archives "have allowed outside researchers to physically review their records" for research purposes.[11] Yet Tousey and Adkins also acknowledge that corporate archivists "act as gatekeepers to records of ongoing business value to our companies," including protecting both privacy rights of individuals within the company and the institution's reputation. "We must take into consideration the intent of a researcher when we make a decision about whether to permit access to certain records," they state, and outside research requests are therefore "handled on a case-by-case basis."[12]

However, Ford and several other corporate archives provided essential access to corporate records for investigators examining American companies' "possible connections between their German subsidiaries and Nazi-era atrocities," as well as public policy questions regarding companies that might have had historical connections to the American slave trade, either directly or by supplying services that supported slavery.[13] These actions demonstrate commendable voluntary cooperation in historical investigations with significant societal implications. "Corporate archives exist to serve two purposes—first and foremost, the good of the business, and second, the public good through the corporate records," Tousey and Adkins declare. "And, if we serve our institutions and our people with professionalism and integrity, chances are the public good will also be well served."[14] Corporate archivists thus remain committed primarily to the interests of their employing institutions. This can raise ethical concerns in the rare instances when the public good conflicts with corporate priorities.

The difficulty of addressing ethical concerns in corporate archives can be seen in the recent controversy known in the American archival profession as "Raisingate" or "The Raisins of Wrath." The cover of the Fall/Winter 2003 issue of the *American Archivist* featured a bright red reproduction of a political poster from the California farm workers' protest against Sun Maid raisin company. Although the poster illustrated Susan Tschabrun's essay on the powerful messages conveyed by political posters, eight corporate archivists wrote to the editor to protest the journal's "inappropriate" and "inflammatory" cover, which they argued "communicates a strong antibusiness message" that could "undermine the professional credibility of SAA members who work in business settings."[15] University of Wyoming archivist Mark Greene also protested that the "Sun Mad" cover illustration was "an attack ad against corporations" that placed "sensationalism and circulation above all other priorities."[16] These letters provoked Richard Cox to wonder, "Is the mission of a corporate archives only to make the organization look good or to serve a public relations purpose?" Referring to "recent corporate scandals," Cox questioned "how the individual functioning as an archivist or records manager can work in the corporate environment in any realistic way, adhering to any sense of professional ethics or mission."[17] This, in turn, prompted the president and president-elect of SAA to respond. "As members of a professional society we should respect each other's perspectives, even when—especially when—they differ from our own," they stated. "We should be especially careful to avoid even the appearance of questioning the ethics of an entire segment of our members." They concluded by calling on all archivists "to unite in the goal of documenting society in all its many aspects, and to respect the diverse perspectives and needs of our colleagues in all types of archives."[18]

This incident unfortunately widened the perceived gap between corporate archivists and those working in the public sector or not-for-profit organizations. Some business archivists had long thought that SAA did not fully address their needs and that public sector archivists disdained those whose employers required different approaches to access, appraisal, and description of archival materials. As one business archivist explained, corporate archives differ from public archives in numerous ways: processing, client interactions, budgeting, resources, user bases, hiring and promotion practices, organization structures, access policies, and even skills sought in an archivist.[19] These concerns led Bruce Bruemmer, corporate archives director for Cargill, Inc., to complain that the *American Archivist* had never before "used such a negative depiction" of any sector of the archives profession as in the "Sun Mad" cover. This convinced him that many public sector archivists questioned the contribution of corporate archives to the greater good of society. "Rather than shills and spokespeople, corporate archivists are on the front line documenting the record of the nation," Bruemmer argues. "Yes, much of this record is not available to the public, but as a profession associated with the events of the past, one would think that archivists could take a long-term view." Corporate archivists struggle daily to demonstrate that their existence does not put the company at risk. "Archivists argue that evidence is a two-edge sword; while records can harbor a smoking gun they can also be used in defending the corporation."[20] The transparency with which Ford Motor Company addressed allegations of corporate ties to Nazi Germany, as an independent counsel declared, was a "credible example of a company accepting and implementing the code of 'corporate social responsibility' regarding a most delicate issue."[21] Bruemmer argues that the very existence of corporate archives demonstrates such corporate social responsibility, "going beyond mere compliance and taking calculated risk in a society generally suspicious of big business." The tensions between accountability, responsibility, service to one's employer, and service to the public good will eventually confront archivists in every type of repository.[22]

In a paper originally presented at the 2006 annual meeting of the Society of American Archivists, business ethicist Andrew V. Abela links the "Sun Mad" dispute to uncertainties in the field of ethics. "If being a corporate archivist poses any kind of ethical problem, this is not due to corporate ownership, but to problems with the field of ethics itself," Abela argues. As Abela points out, the SAA Code of Ethics for Archivists lists nine principles, but "when tensions arise between different principles, it is hard to determine which one should take priority."[23] This poses a dilemma: professional codes of ethics can only suggest how to think about ethical choices; they cannot easily resolve such problems. "Because of the lack of consensus within Western society, at least since Nietzsche, on fundamental issues about the meaning of life and definitions of good and evil, it should not be surprising that so many ethical problems appear to arise," Abela states. He outlines a broad range of ethical theories, including ethical egoism, deontology, utilitarianism, justice, virtue, feminist ethics, and ethical relativism. He then posits that the notion of "good" in relation to the role of archivists in society can help us define the meaning of being a "good" archivist. "If we understand the role of the archivist in society, then the 'good' archivist conforms to this role," Abela states. "From here we can work through ethical issues that arise." Another useful concept comes from stakeholder theory, which "advocates considering the perspective of every stakeholder in the community." For archivists, this would include donors, archives owners, subjects of archives, and the public. Archivists themselves should also be considered stakeholders. In addition, "A corporation, by creating and maintaining a corporate archives, arguably provides some benefit to society, not just to itself."[24] The current archival Code of Ethics thus respects the right of the institution to establish its own policies on access and to protect its privacy.

Archivists in every type of institutional setting—government, business, academics, religious, tribal, historical, and not-for-profit archives—need to confront both the traditional ethical concerns of the profession and the new ethical concerns relating to social justice, accountability, and public responsibility. Even within archival settings that allow only limited flexibility and acceptance of responsibility for the public interest, there are options available to contribute—perhaps in a limited range of personal choice—to these social justice imperatives. Those able and willing to participate fully in archival activism should be accepted as conscientious and ethical archivists. The same is necessarily true for those archivists who, for whatever reasons of personal or institutional consideration, can act upon only a few—or even none—of these recommendations. The archival profession needs to acknowledge that there is a broad range of acceptable ethical choices, and to welcome and support those who act upon their own personal system of values and morality. This does not mean that there are no criteria for measuring and evaluating ethical conduct. It simply recognizes that archivists can legitimately exercise a range of ethical options in carrying out their important professional and societal responsibilities.

OBJECTIVITY IS NOT NEUTRALITY

Archivists who choose to respond to the cause of social justice can do so in their professional roles in selecting records for preservation, ensuring evidence and accountability, and opening the archives to diverse perspectives and multiple voices. This process begins with a commitment to accurate, reliable, authentic, and broadly conceived documentation of institutions, societal groups, and individuals. This activist approach also requires careful consideration of archivists' external relations with recordmakers, donors, researchers, and employers. Public advocacy is essential for the archival profession's survival. It is also the most direct means by which archivists can contribute to the public interest. Archivists need to be willing to take a public stand at times, or a nonpublic position in certain situations when publicity could be counter-productive. In addition, archivists should re-examine their own professional assumptions, methods, and practices in light of the desired outcomes of justice and diversity. There is no easy solution for the long-standing problems of social injustice, discrimination, and unchecked political power.

If archivists are to avoid perpetuating the dangers of situations in which political rulers manipulate records to control history and prevent access to accurate information, they have their work cut out for them. They can contribute to this effort if they recognize that their role in society has significant implications and a high degree of power. As Verne Harris argues, "the archive is politics." Archivists cannot escape by hiding behind a veil of innocence, neutrality, and impartiality. "I would insist that even as we impress upon our students the imperative and value of objectivity and its limits, we must reject the spurious equation of objectivity with neutrality," historical sociologist Harvey Kaye admonishes his fellow teachers, "and encourage students to apply their newly acquired scholarly skills, knowledge, and insights both to analyzing and to speaking out on public issues."[25] Archivists should heed this call to activism. It is essential to seize the power of archives, and to use it to hold institutional and governmental leaders accountable. All aspects of society should be documented, not simply those where power has traditionally resided. As Terry Cook argues, "The justification for archives has shifted from being grounded in concepts of the nation state and its scholarly elites (primarily historians) to broader socio-cultural justifications grounded in public policies of accountability, freedom of information, and wider public/citizen use."[26] The call to justice demands a socially responsible re-conception of archival ethics. Building upon ideas recently introduced in the archival literature, we can propose a few suggestions for archivists in responding to these monumental challenges. For now these recommendations are necessarily broad and aspirational. Once archivists accept such strategic goals, their next steps will be to fill in the details and action plans.

Before entering this discussion, however, it is necessary to distinguish between the often-conflated terms *neutrality* and *objectivity*. We often speak of neutrality and objectivity as synonymous, or as two sides of the same relationship between individuals and the expression of values and perspectives toward contested issues. In an extensive critique of the development of the American historical profession, Peter Novick contends that the "ideal of 'objectivity' . . . has been the key term in defining progress in historical scholarship:

moving ever closer to the objective truth about the past." Novick
states, "The objective historian's role is that of a neutral, or
disinterested, judge; it must never degenerate into that of advocate
or, even worse, propagandist." In adhering to this ideal, historians
must display "judicial qualities of balance and evenhandedness,"
avoid "partisanship or bias," and "purge themselves of external
loyalties" [i.e., outside the profession].[27] Novick contends that
the "myth of objectivity" has led historians to avoid controversy
within the discipline and has blocked them from taking positions
on social and political issues. "'Objectivity' has been one of the
central sacred terms of professional historians, like 'health' for
physicians, or 'valor' for the profession of arms," he asserts.
Similarly, lawyers invoke "justice" and journalists pledge fealty to
"a free press in a free society."[28] Historians of the late nineteenth
century thus embraced the model of scientific method, which Novick
characterizes as "rigidly factual and empirical, shunning hypothesis,"
and as "scrupulously neutral" on matters of meaning and purpose.[29]
Because this concept of objectivity both sets an impossible goal
and also precludes historians from advocating social or political
causes, Novick rejects the ideal as "not just essentially contested, but
essentially confused."[30] Only by denying the validity of objectivity
can Novick justify historians' engagement in public policy debates.

In a highly critical review of Novick's book, Thomas Haskell argues
that the central fallacy that Novick and others perpetuate is to conflate
objectivity with neutrality. Haskell defends the validity of the concept
of objectivity, while attempting to rid it of "unwanted connotations"
such as neutrality, selflessness, and passivity. "Objectivity is not
something entirely distinct from detachment, fairness, and honesty,
but is the product of extending and elaborating these priceless and
fundamentally ascetic virtues," Haskell contends.[31] Historians (and
others) can be objective without forsaking engagement in discussions
of values, politics, or social policy. "The demand is for detachment
and fairness, not disengagement from life," he argues. The historian's
"primary commitment" to truth does not prohibit political advocacy,
Haskell states, but it does "set intellectually responsible limits to it,"
so that one cannot claim "the privilege of lying or obscuring the truth
for good causes."[32] Although rejecting the idea of neutrality, Haskell
endorses professional objectivity, based on evidence, logic, fairness,
and honesty.

Professional standards, including objectivity, need not prevent
us from addressing moral, ethical, or political issues. A common
fallacy is to equate objectivity with neutrality.[33] One can maintain

professional standards even while advocating a cause or defending a moral or ideological perspective. Active engagement with the ideas and arguments of opposing perspectives becomes critical to the concept of objectivity. In fact, critical detachment enables us "to channel our intellectual passions in such a way as to ensure collision with rival perspectives." Addressing the arguments of one's opponents clarifies one's own thinking—"faithful to the complexity and fragility of historical interpretation"—and establishes a more powerful argument, which Haskell deems "the highest fruit of the kind of thinking I would call objective."[34] This ideal of objectivity, he argues, derives from a conviction that we all share, at least tacitly, that in choosing between conflicting interpretations, one account will prove superior to others as a representation of the way things are or were.[35]

Haskell states, "there is widespread recognition within the [historical] profession that political commitment need not detract from the writing of history—not even from its objectivity—as long as honesty, detachment, and intelligence are at work." Sustaining intellectual and professional principles—such as "respect for logical coherence, fidelity to evidence, detachment, candor, honesty, and the like"—must accompany any advocacy for moral or political values. As Haskell warns, "When the members of the scholarly community become unwilling to put intellectual values ahead of political ones, they erase the only possible boundary between politically committed scholarship and propaganda and thereby rob the community of its principal justification for existence."[36] These criteria provide a context within which professional debate can occur.

Historian Allan Megill extends Haskell's argument that objectivity does not equate neutrality, arguing that objectivity does not mean "balance"—another term with which it often is confused. The Fox News Channel slogan "Fair and Balanced" implies that one should remain neutral between different perspectives on public issues. This fallacy leads some secondary school systems to give equal time in biology classes to evolutionary and anti-evolutionary interpretations. Such understandings of "balance" imply that objectivity emerges when all points of view are recognized and heard, as though "no particular account of reality can count as objective." As Megill observes, this peculiar concept of objectivity "says nothing about the stupidity (or not) of the different competing perspectives." Balancing "one stupid ideological position and another stupid ideological position does not equate to 'objectivity'" any more than a "balance" in schools teaching both scientific evolution and religious creationism. Megill further insists that objectivity is not neutrality because "some measure of commitment is necessary if we are to 'see' the historical object at all," and that "angularity of perspective can bring out aspects of historical reality that would remain obscure from more 'moderate,' 'middle of the road' points of view," as implied by the "neutrality" of a "balanced view" of things.[37] What historians offer is a critical perspective on the past, on the present, and on our present use of the past, revealing "fissures and contradictions" within these perspectives. Above all, historians should offer a model of high epistemological standards through their treatment of evidence and their arguments to support their own claims and interpretations.[38]

What unites both the historical discipline and the archival profession remains their underlying commitment to objectivity. As Megill explains, objectivity is best understood as a set of divergent but interconnected senses of objectivity:

> There is a disciplinary objectivity, amounting to consensus among subgroups of historians; there is a dialectical objectivity, involving a sensitivity on the part of historians to the peculiarities of the historical objects that they describe, explain, and interpret; there is a procedural objectivity that is primarily methodological in character; and there is, above it all, the unrealizable ideal of absolute objectivity, the world as it would be seen by a single omniscient divinity.[39]

Although arguing that the last category is unattainable, Megill concludes that these four "conceptual types" of objectivity cannot resolve the problem of objectivity addressed by Novick. However, by paying attention to different aspects of what objectivity means, historians can think more clearly about the challenge of historical description, analysis, interpretation, and justification.[40] These separate aspects of objectivity also provide a basis for archivists to consider their own assumptions, theories, and methodologies. Ultimately, the quest for objectivity requires attention to complexity, nuance, multiple perspectives, and the implications of how honestly and fairly members of a profession face their responsibilities and serve all members of society.

When the future of human society is at stake, neutrality is an abdication of responsibility. Amid the chaos following the Second World War—which infused fascism, concentration camps, and atomic bombs into the public consciousness—Orwell argued that writers could not ignore politics. The daily news aroused "an awareness of the enormous injustice and misery of the world, and a guilt-stricken

feeling that one ought to be doing something about it, which makes
a purely æsthetic attitude towards life impossible."[41] Therefore,
no thinking person can ignore political issues. All public activities
exist within a political context. In the aftermath of the Holocaust,
Elie Wiesel argues, no one has the right to abstain. "When the life
or death—or simply the well-being—of a community is at stake,
neutrality is criminal, for it aids and abets the oppressor and not his
victim."[42] The stakes do not need to be so high as in a world war or
genocide for neutrality to become untenable. As Howard Zinn states,
"You can't be neutral on a moving train."[43] Anyone concerned about
the political and social conditions in society should seek to change
the situation and create a better future. For archivists, this may
mean recognizing the impossibility of neutrality while accepting the
responsibility of professional objectivity. This seeming contradiction
involves applying appropriate standards of archival principles
while seeking to overcome many centuries in which archives have
strengthened the rulers and marginalized the powerless classes.

ACCEPTING PROFESSIONAL RESPONSIBILITIES

By recognizing the distinction between objectivity and
neutrality, it is possible for a historian—or archivist, or
librarian—to engage in moral or political advocacy without
sacrificing his or her professional standards. The call to an ethics
of social justice invites archivists to consider the political context
in which they carry out their daily functions. Some archivists will
be unable or unwilling to accept this challenge. It demands both
an acceptance of personal responsibility for their professional
actions and a willingness to undertake roles that are not rewarded
by—and may be contrary to the wishes of—their employers. In
1977 Patrick M. Quinn urged archivists to respond to the "swirl
of social forces" surrounding them, such as civil rights, women's
liberation, and anti-war protest. "Our job is to interpret,
understand, and anticipate those forces so that we might have some
control over them," Quinn argued. However, he saw that this
would take a significant conceptual leap for many of his colleagues.
"Not looking beyond the confine of his archives, the archivist is
concerned primarily with the day to day requirements of the job," he
observed, and thus archivists "have necessarily found it difficult to
conceptualize the historical and societal framework of their role."[44]
For those who choose such a path, acknowledgment of the archivist's
inevitable imprint on the archive affords the opportunity to engage
these professional actions deliberately and mindfully.

The political and social ferment of the 1960s led some historians

and archivists to argue that archivists should actively intervene
to ensure documentation of underrepresented social groups in
American archives, which generally reflected the powerful groups
in society.[45] This challenge to the profession not only led to some
important new initiatives in documenting minority groups in
archives, but also opened a debate over the "neutrality" of archival
acquisition. Once considered a routine and impartial process,
defining an institutional collecting policy for manuscripts and
archives has recently been challenged by calls for archivists to
recognize that the decision to collect some manuscripts and not
others is freighted with cultural value systems that privilege certain
groups in society over others. Decisions about acquisition of archives
and manuscripts have significant implications for documentation of
modern society, yet critics charge that archival selection often occurs
without conceptual thinking about purpose and methods.[46]

The following sections outline some of the questions that archivists
should bear in mind as they consider the implications of this moral
and ethical call of justice. Some archivists will be unable or unwilling
to engage directly in some—or perhaps all—of these challenges, due
to personal values or institutional constraints. In some cases redefining archival praxis may place some at risk or entail added burdens that
they are not able to assume. This is not intended as a test of professional identity or a means of separating "ethical" archivists from
"unethical" archivists. Rather it is a call to personal conscience and
an assertion that it is permissible for members of the archival profession to redefine their relationship to social and political systems of
power, influence, and activism. The hope is that considering such
matters openly and mindfully will engage archivists in deeper thinking
about *why* they do things in particular ways. This discussion will take
archivists, for a time, away from the *what* and *how* of professional praxis
in order to envision the ultimate purposes and societal benefits of
the archival enterprise. From a consideration of how these concerns
might affect various aspects of archivists' professional responsibilities,
this discussion will consider how new voices and perspectives can be
incorporated more fully into archival praxis, what role archivists can
play in public policy and advocacy, and how this affects both public institution archivists and those in the private sector. The starting
point for this discussion encompasses traditional archival responsibilities and functions as these new ethical perspectives might affect them.

In carrying out their daily responsibilities, archivists can thus
respond to the moral and ethical implications of their involvement
in societal systems of power and privilege. Recognition of the

historical context in which archives have always functioned, from the earliest forms of written records to the dominant presence of digital and Internet communications, reveals the ongoing influence and control exercised by some members of every society over the majority of the populace. As participants in this process—whether or not willingly and consciously—archivists have opportunities to push against these forces of power and control, to assert a vigorous and active engagement in societal power relations, and to ensure a more nearly complete and accurate documentary record of human experience.

Many archivists remain constrained by external forces, including their employers, resource allocators, donors, researchers, and cultural expectations. Institutional archivists often define their primary responsibilities in relation to the needs of the organizations they serve, with little flexibility to influence major policy decisions shaped by legal and administrative requirements. However, even in such circumstances those archivists who choose to respond to ethical callings may find some opportunities to do so, without risking their livelihood, support, and resources.

Concern for ethical responses to archival endeavors will lead some archivists to consider how they can incorporate into their individual and collective responsibilities such social concerns as representative documentation, accountability, openness in government and other institutions, diversity, and social justice. These issues have already been examined in preceding chapters, but the following discussion will consider some ways in which archivists can directly address these concerns. In this section we will therefore suggest how archivists can welcome and include documentation of subaltern classes and indigenous populations, accept oral testimony to supplement western concepts of *record* and *evidence,* and thereby create and preserve an archival record more truly representative of the rich diversity and multi-vocality that exist within every society.

Some of these suggestions challenge fundamental assumptions not only of the archival profession but also of the western tradition within which that profession has developed. As the archival profession considers such new conceptions of its societal role, some archivists will embrace the full range of these suggestions, some will reject these expanded notions of professional responsibility, and others will accept some but not all of these approaches. The hope is that these ideas will generate active consideration and discussion concerning *why* archivists perform their duties, within a social-political context, not that archivists will establish yet another set of criteria to separate one group from another. It should be acceptable for archivists to engage in any range of activities suggested by these recommendations—all, some, or none—without being denigrated as less than equal members of a profession that serves the diverse needs and interests of society. Some of the implications for archivists concerned about responding to the call of justice can be seen in the following discussion of internal archival policies and procedures. Later sections explore how this could affect public advocacy efforts by archivists.

WELCOMING STRANGERS INTO THE ARCHIVES

As George Orwell recognized, the historical record is never complete. People in the lower ranks of society seldom appear in accounts of the past. We have little if any knowledge of the slaves who built the Egyptian pyramids, the serfs of medieval society, or the illiterate peoples in lands colonized by European conquerors.[47] Not only does western society emphasize the perspectives of peoples who create written or visual documentation of their activities and ideas, but it privileges accounts created by those with greater political, economic, intellectual (defined by western standards of education), and cultural influence. Despite significant documentation of many aspects of the past, as David Wallace observes, "almost all of human history is permanently irretrievable," resulting both in the loss of knowledge about "the voices of the majority of humanity" and in the elevation of celebratory and triumphal perspectives to be enshrined as "the past."[48] It would be impossible to create and preserve documentation of every individual, of every community, simply because the resources to do so are inadequate. Some voices will almost inevitably be lost, like animal and plant species becoming extinct. The challenge for archivists is to make the documentary record more complete than it has been, not to make it absolutely complete and flawless. This requires sensitivity to the silences in the archives, to the people pushed aside from the historical stage, to the voices missing from the human chorus of the past and present. This will give voice to the forgotten and marginalized members of society.

Archival principles and functions developed largely in the context of nineteenth-century bureaucratic states. The principle of provenance, for example, reflects assumptions about organizational structures and hierarchies that privilege those in power and those with a recognized collectivity. After examining the loss of community archives in the Virgin Islands, Jeannette Bastian suggests that archivists should expand their understanding of provenance—the context of records creation—to include not just the individuals and elites empowered to create written records, but the entire community or society in which they operate.[49] Because meaning is something that is always constructed and not inherent in documents, archivists need to think clearly about how they determine which manuscripts and records should be collected and preserved. Bastian confirms the arguments of Hugh Taylor and Terry Cook that a broader concept of provenance is needed in some contexts. Taylor argued in 1970 that archivists should focus more on why and how people have created documentation, rather than on their subject content. This would extend their understanding of the provenance of documentation deeply into the societal origins of human communication.[50] As Bastian discovered in the Virgin Islands, "records become 'witnesses' to a silent society, a community that is the subject of the records rather than their maker but one that is no less involved in their creation." To ensure that "the voiceless population is not the silent witness but a full partner in the record-creating process," Bastian argues, "all layers of society are participants in the record-making process, and the entire community becomes the larger provenance of the records."[51] Likewise, Adele Perry contends that "the absences in the colonial archive are not neutral, voluntary, or strictly literal"; they are "silences borne of and perpetuated by violence and radical inequality."[52]

Concern for the "voiceless populations" in society should lead archivists to adjust their procedures for all basic archival functions. In selection and appraisal archivists need to be conscious of the potential bias in their traditional methods. Archival choices have long been shaped by the constraints of power relations and sources of funding. "Silences are inherent in history because any single event, however defined, enters history with *some* of its constituting parts missing," Haitian historian Michel-Rolph Trouillot observes. "*Some* thing is always left out, while another one is recorded."[53] The silences in archives "can be used to reveal the differential power of various groups of agents in producing history," from the making of sources, to the making of archives, and ultimately to the making of history. He contends that "the physical traces of the past, once turned into sources, privilege some events over others."[54] In examining the founding of the Mississippi State Archives under Dunbar Rowland, for example, Patricia Galloway concluded that there is "nearly always an inherent tension between what historians and archivists would like to collect and preserve and what economic and political constraints allow them to collect and preserve."[55]

To counter these biases archivists should seek opportunities to preserve records of those often overlooked by their collecting strategies and recognize the broader concept of provenance for an entire community (including those groups often marginalized or silenced in archival collecting policies and appraisal guidelines). For example, even within institutional archives archivists could also recognize the historical value of records documenting workers, community relations, and other aspects of corporate or organizational activities beyond the legal, fiscal, and administrative requirements.

The archival silences in colonial societies echo in indigenous communities around the world. Recent studies of Aboriginal communities in Australia, for example, attest to the necessity of some form of recordkeeping for proof of identity in securing individual rights, establishing community identity, reclaiming histories, holding governments accountable, and ultimately for healing. "Because of the impact of past government policies on Indigenous communities, archives can sometimes be the only place of recorded information about language and cultural practices," according to an article written by Aboriginal archivists.[56] They recommend hiring more indigenous people to work in archives and making archives accessible and open to those traditionally excluded, whether by policy, custom, or simply unfamiliarity. Australia's Aboriginal people in 1995 adopted the *Aboriginal and Torres Strait Islander Protocols for Libraries, Archives and Information Services,* which advocates delivering library and archival products and services in a respectful and culturally appropriate manner and working towards the return of cultural material to the communities to which they belong. In 1998-1999, a special training program resulted in hiring the first Aboriginal archivist with professional qualifications and creation of a permanent position of Aboriginal liaison in the New South Wales State Records office.[57] In the United States a similar process is currently under consideration. Using the *Aboriginal and Torres Strait Islander Protocols* as a model, a document entitled *Protocols for Native American Archival Materials* serves as a statement of principles for responding to concerns of Native Americans seeking control over their documentary heritage.[58]

Archivists responding to the call of justice, for the delineation of a new concept of professional ethics and responsibility, need to consider the issues raised by the Australian and American *Protocols* for Aboriginal, Native American, and other indigenous records. However, concern for the rights of less powerful societal groups should not obscure the troubling questions arising from outside professionals intruding in these communities, nor the potential for over-compensation. The role of historians, anthropologists, and archivists must be clearly defined. "Do such voicings constrain or nourish the powerful?" ask Gerald Sider and Gavin Smith. "Does the fact of powerlessness imbue voice with some special authenticity *sui generis*?"[59] They argue, "power must be understood as engendering chaos and havoc—conceptual, cultural, and social-relational—as much as it does order . . . and that people must struggle against both."[60] Professional observers who participate in these documentary processes must also remain alert to the dangers of overly romanticizing "the other," and thereby either further alienating and drawing cultural boundaries around them, or uncritically privileging their voices as more authentic or valuable than those of other societal groups.

SELECTING AND APPRAISING RECORDS

In recent years an increasing number of archivists have responded to studies of social memory and of postmodernism by recognizing that their role in selection and acquisition does shape the documentary record. According to Francis X. Blouin, Jr., archivists are "mediators between records creators and records repositories, between archives and users, between conceptions of the past and extant documentation."[61] Decisions that archivists make in acquisition reflect their personal interests and values, and in turn shape the record of the past that will survive for future research.[62] Because designating a document as archival endows it with elevated status, archivists must make such decisions deliberately, as Tom Nesmith argues, "as visible, active, agents in the construction of this history and the societal knowledge it shapes."[63] Records in institutional archives are important as evidence, but they are also important as societal documentation.[64]

One of the most creative responses to these concerns has been the concept of documentation strategy, first proposed in the mid-1980s. In response to the call for active engagement in collecting underrepresented sources, documentation strategy challenged archivists to move beyond their institutional walls and to examine sources from many institutions for documenting broad aspects of society. Documentation strategies acknowledged the need for activism in order to "assure the documentation of an ongoing issue, activity, or geographic area," in the midst of an increasingly complicated modern society.[65] This approach encouraged inter-institutional cooperation and consideration of all formats of information and documentation, including print and artifact sources, and provided a planning mechanism for systematic analysis and selection of documents.[66] Although sometimes criticized as unworkable, the concept of documentation strategies provided an instructive challenge to archivists weighing decisions about records selection and documentation of society. At the very least it encouraged archivists to consider archival records as simply one part of the larger universe of information.[67]

In making such decisions regarding archival selection and appraisal, archivists run the risk of intruding their own concepts of history and society into the archival record. However, this is an inevitable consequence of archival agency. As Eric Ketelaar explains, in making any appraisal or selection decision, "we alter [the records'] context and meaning, we infuse new meaning into the record, to what is left of the series and the fonds, archivists add new narratives to the archives and its constituent parts."[68] Remaining neutral or invisible is impossible for archivists engaged in selection, appraisal, arrangement, description, and reference services. "Archivists inevitably will inject their personal values into all such activities," Terry Cook asserts, "and thus will need to examine very consciously their choices in the archive-creating and memory-formation processes, and they will need to leave very clear records explaining their choices to posterity."[69]

Archival appraisal typically reflects power relations established by state agencies, business corporations, religious establishments, academic institutions, and other power brokers. "In the records we preserve, too often the voices of the governed, especially the underclasses, are either filtered through the voices of bureaucrats or are absent," Verne Harris argues.[70] "The appraiser's values, quality of work, perspectives, interaction with the records creating agency, engagement with the policy s(he) is implementing, and so on, all shape and are reflected in the appraisal," according to Harris. "The appraiser is not simply identifying records with archival value; s(he) is creating archival value."[71] The archivist making appraisal decisions quite literally determines what evidence and information future generations will be able to see. In this sense, the archivist shapes documentation for the future as much as the original creator of the records. The archivist thereby becomes co-creator of the archival record.[72]

The question is not whether the archivist imposes her or his personal interpretation, but whether the action is taken consciously and documented openly. When Norway's "war children" (born during World War II to Norwegian mothers and German soldiers) sought compensation for years of suffering and discrimination, Norwegian archivists recognized that archival evidence to support their claims was "very often defective and unreliable." One option advocated by archivist Gudmund Valderhaug was for archivists "to engage in the processes of recordmaking in order to secure sufficient documentation and thus minimize the risk of future impairment to people's access to justice." When records reflect "the dominant social and cultural values" and reproduce existing power relations, archivists need to find alternative means to document overlooked aspects of society.[73] It may no longer be enough to select and acquire records that have already been created. Archivists may need to consider going beyond their custodial role and to fill in the gaps, to ensure that documentation is created where it is missing, and to address the needs of those outside the societal power structures.

LISTENING FOR ORAL TESTIMONY

Fundamental to offering hospitality toward "the stranger" is recognition that modern western concepts of documentation and "record-ness" need to acknowledge other forms of evidence and knowledge. Archivists concerned about the voices of marginalized peoples must pay particular attention to oral testimony, and may need to supplement the written archival record through oral history. These are two separate but related means of recognizing the value of oral transmission of information and culture. The first recognizes the primacy of oral tradition in some cultures. The second seeks to fill gaps in the written record of literate cultures. Both approaches open the archives to new voices, new traditions, and new forms of information and evidence.

The historical interplay between literacy and orality, outlined briefly in chapter I, shows that written documents did not enjoy primacy in early societies. Not until the Renaissance did western Europe fully embrace writing for legal purposes. In many indigenous communities writing is still not trusted, or at least not given preference over oral communications and other forms of testimony about the past—about community history, culture, and identity. "For African societies, oral tradition, oral history and written records constitute a unified mode of historical consciousness," according to a modern Nigerian educator. A University of Ibadan archivist explains that for nonliterate Africans their oral traditions constitute their archives, preserving the values and ideals of the society.[74] In the Virgin Islands, Jeannette Bastian observes, the "written communications of the colonizer and the oral traditions of thousands of enslaved Africans brought to the colony" existed side by side for centuries; both are vital to understanding the colonial past.[75] Wherever found in oral cultures, these oral testimonies are "complex cultural products," which interweave private, individual, and public memories and experiences in "cultural representations of the past and of the present," states historian Dora Schwarzstein.[76] Such societies cannot be understood without the archival record embodied in oral testimony. Not only does oral evidence fill in gaps in the written record; in some cases it is the only available form of cultural information.

In his seminal work, *Oral Tradition as History,* Jan Vansina has traced the characteristics of oral traditions and their use as historical evidence. Drawing most of his evidence from modern central African cultures, Vansina argues that orality offers valuable evidence that must be approached differently than written sources. In oral societies people believe that memories "can be faithful repositories which contain the sum total of past human experience" and thus help them understand present conditions. "Whether memory changes or not, culture is reproduced by remembrance put into words and deeds. The mind through memory carries culture from generation to generation," he concludes.[77] Because oral traditions exist only in memory, it is important to remember—as we have seen in chapter 4—that "memory is not an inert storage system like a tape recorder or computer. Remembering is an activity, a re-creation of what once was."[78] In order to provide authentic evidence, oral transmission requires a close link between the living tradition and its performance or expression. In evaluating oral information as evidence, the historian must ask, "what is the relationship of the text to a particular performance of the tradition involved and what is the relationship of that performance to the tradition as a whole?" It is the performance, the telling of a story, that must be evaluated for authenticity, originality, authorship, and place and time of composition.[79] Vansina recognizes that reliance on memory causes anachronisms in oral tradition, which may reorder stories by placing accounts of a later period with those of earlier times or vice versa. (This is also what Richard White discovered in exploring his mother's stories of her childhood in Ireland.) The lack of chronology in most oral traditions marks one of its most severe limitations.[80] However, a significant contribution of oral tradition is its ability to reveal culture and human experience of otherwise undocumented peoples. "In oral and part-oral societies, oral tradition gives intimate accounts of populations, or layers of population, that are otherwise apprehended only from outside points of view, Vansina explains.

"Without oral traditions we would know very little about the past of large parts of the world, and we would not know them from the inside."[81] Particularly in the African cultures Vansina has studied, these insights form essential evidence of human history.

In Kenya, Zimbabwe, and other nations, national archival institutions have worked closely with research programs "to ensure that information related to marginalized groupings was captured and preserved," according to Ndiyoi Mutiti. "Biases in the official records prevalent in the colonial era have not been totally addressed," he warns, partly because "the social and cultural norms of these people are still being recorded by 'third parties' that only cover their specific areas of concern."[82] Aboriginal archivist Loris Williams observes that government files provide some information about indigenous peoples, but "to gain the full picture an oral history project needs to be undertaken to gain knowledge of Indigenous people's personal experiences."[83] Horacio Roque Ramirez declares, "For marginalized communities constantly involved in struggles for visibility, political identity, and space—the business of 'cultural citizenship'—*testimonios* about their existence are critical acts of documentation."[84] Gathering unrecorded stories and perspectives affords one of the few resources for bringing to light experiences not recorded in dominant societal narratives. Archivists who engage in gathering oral sources participate in "giving voice to the voiceless," Verne Harris declares. The African National Congress's Archives Subcommittee, for example, recommended oral documentation programs "as part of a programme of democratization and empowerment of the voiceless."[85] Beyond simply filling in gaps, such oral history initiatives articulate political goals, serving the public interest and empowering the underprivileged, those often excluded from archival documentation.

Participating in oral history projects takes the archivist into a different relationship to the archival record. No longer a custodian of documentation created by others, the archivist accepts personal—and professional—responsibility for ensuring adequate documentation of subjects, events, and people that might otherwise remain unrecorded. American archivist James Fogerty states that the more he used oral history to fill in gaps in documentation of business and the corporate world, the more he "began to see the archivist as activist—a professional whose mission might include active participation in the creation of documentation."[86] Regarding "the archive" as the collective repository of cultural information and evidence of human activity and ideas opens up new vistas on the role of the archivist. Listening for oral testimony, particularly in societies that do not rely on written forms of documentation, broadens our awareness of archival traces. In addition to bureaucratic (written) records—such as property records, drivers' licenses, letters, diaries, account books—oral records essential to community documentation "could include folktales, parades, commemorations and performances." A Virgin Islands folklorist points out that, even though many folktales are written down, nuances in the physical movements of a storyteller's performance "make the story come alive."[87] Surely such rich sources of human knowledge and experience constitute part of the archive. "Are the tracings in people's memories—shared in collective contexts, conveyed and performed by storytellers—not already archive?" asks South African archivist Sello Hatang. "An archive without archive? Do we not trouble the boundaries between memory and archive?"[88] Part of the archivist's response to the knock of the stranger is to open the archives to a new visitor. An ethical praxis also calls for the archivist to listen to the stranger's voice, to accept oral testimony as part of the archive. More than that it asks the archivist to hear the silences of the archive and to respond by actively seeking to find or create documentation that includes as much as possible of the community's experience, as many people as society's archives can accommodate.

ENSURING DIVERSITY IN THE ARCHIVAL RECORD

Welcoming the stranger into the archives, searching for the stories of indigenous and subaltern classes, and listening to oral testimony all contribute to a more diverse and representative archival record. Archivists who embrace this call to activism on behalf of such goals seek to locate, identify, and preserve documentation of society's rich diversity. Although attention to diversity in the archival record surfaced much earlier in some repositories, by 1970 increasing numbers of archivists responded to the calls for inclusiveness issued by Howard Zinn, Sam Bass Warner, Gerald Ham, Patrick Quinn, and others. In 1972 the Society of American Archivists (SAA) Committee for the 1970's resolved to guard against "elitism in manuscript collecting," and to commit the professional association to broader "social goals of racial justice, equal employment and reasonable access to research materials."[89]

A diverse and representative archival record can only be sustained over time by a diverse profession of archivists. Therefore, the report of the Committee for the 1970's also urged SAA to make its own governing council more representative of diverse interests within the profession and urged creation of a standing committee to press for the rights and advancement of minority groups in the profession.[90] One immediate response by SAA resulted in establishing a Committee on the Status of Women and a Women's Caucus.[91] By 1978 archivists joined together with historical society and museum professionals to form a joint SAA/AASLH/AAM Committee on Opportunities for Minorities.[92] SAA also created a Task Force on Minorities, replaced in 1987 by SAA's Minorities Roundtable, which soon changed its name to Third World Archivists Roundtable. In 1994 this group adopted its current name, Archivists and Archives of Color Roundtable. In two decades the roundtable has slowly moved the professional society forward on issues of racial and ethnic diversity. In addition a Task Force on Diversity secured a renewed commitment to diversity by the SAA Council, which issued this resolution in June 1999:

> The Society of American Archivists is committed to integrating diversity concerns and perspectives into all aspects of its activities and into the fabric of the profession as a whole. SAA is also committed to the goal of a Society membership that reflects the broad diversity of American society. SAA believes that these commitments are essential to the effective pursuit of the archival mission "to ensure the identification, preservation, and use of the nation's historical record."[93]

In May 2003 SAA established a Committee on Diversity, charged with ensuring that SAA's services, activities, and policies "support the goal of a more diverse SAA and professional archival community" and with serving "as the organization's 'conscience' in monitoring, evaluating, advocating, and reporting on matters pertaining to the diversity of archival practitioners and documentation."[94] Committee recommendations have already resulted in significant changes to SAA annual meetings, committee composition, and other organizational functions. When the SAA Council initiated a new strategic planning effort to identify and analyze a "radar screen" of challenges or threats to the profession— potentially disruptive forces that could have significant negative impact on the profession if not addressed adequately—diversity emerged as one of the three highest priorities for action. As the Council's strategic issues statement explained, "The relevance of archives to society and the completeness of the documentary record hinge in part on the profession's success in ensuring that its members and the holdings that they manage reflect the diversity of society as a whole."[95] This statement thus closely links the diversity of professional membership to diversity in the archival record. Success in one area should contribute to success in the other, but failure to achieve either goal would likewise contribute to failure of the second goal.

Archivists can celebrate their own diversity and commit themselves to building an archival profession that truly and accurately reflects the diversity within society—in their membership, archival programs, and professional activities. One significant symbol of the archival profession's commitment to diversity is Elizabeth W. Adkins's focus on diversity in her 2007 SAA presidential address. "Archivists, along with librarians and museum professionals, share responsibility for ensuring that the holdings of our cultural institutions reflect the diversity of our society and for making sure that the services we offer take diversity into consideration," Adkins declared. She then quoted Lonnie Bunch, who stated in 2002, when he served as president of the Chicago Historical Society, "[W]ithout fully embracing the challenges of diversity, [cultural] institutions cannot be the glue that helps to bind a city or a nation together."[96] Adkins provided an overview of SAA diversity efforts, including ongoing commitments to outreach, education, scholarships, new member development, mentoring, and public awareness. "Addressing diversity is not easy. It's hard work," Adkins concluded. "But the journey cannot stop; we must keep moving forward—not just with words, but with action."[97] Adkins focused on membership diversity within the archival profession, but her arguments apply equally to ensuring diversity in the archival record.

As shown in the previous chapter, archivists have made significant progress toward the goal of broader documentation of minority groups and marginalized populations in societies around the globe. Yet much work remains to be done. Archivists working in collecting repositories—which have broad mandates to document communities, regions, or specific subject areas—have greater flexibility in responding to the challenges of documenting diversity in society. Yet institutional archivists can also respond, by ensuring that their criteria for documentation do not exclude women, racial and ethnic minorities, laborers, gays and lesbians, or other societal groups often ignored in traditional archival practices. Due to centuries of neglect and obscurity, such marginalized groups may need a form of "affirmative action" in archival acquisition, preservation, and documentation programs. Institutional archivists will not be expected to overturn their legitimate emphasis on the needs of the parent organization—whether government, business, academic, or another type of institution—but there is room to broaden the perspective, to open up the criteria for archival selection, to review appraisal criteria, and to ensure that diversity becomes a deliberate consideration in writing finding aids, providing reference service, and conducting outreach initiatives.

As archivists respond to the challenges of addressing diversity, they should remember that their actions are only part of a broader commitment to diversity by cultural institutions, which is necessary for societal progress. Archivists are not the only ones responsible for cultural heritage. They are certainly one of the smaller constituencies and, ultimately, represent only a small portion of the documentary riches required for a more diverse historical record of society. Archives are, above all, institutions of exclusion, as Margaret Hedstrom reminds us. Despite idealistic pleas for inclusion, for filling documentary silences, and for responding to the marginalized, archives routinely and inevitably practice exclusion. Even the most comprehensive archival repositories or cooperative programs can preserve only a small portion of the documentation created by human beings—a sliver of a sliver of a sliver, as Verne Harris states.[98] The challenging questions for archivists are: What should be kept out of the archives? What will be ignored when it does not get in the door? Archives cannot stop being selective, cannot accept every form of documentation created in society. If archives are by necessity institutions of exclusion, Hedstrom asks, "How does one practice exclusion ethically?"[99] Archives serve to exclude some documentation and to legitimate others. The challenge is to make such choices openly, deliberately, and mindfully—listening for the marginalized voices, opening the door to the stranger whose concerns enable us to understand the diversity of society. This is part of the new ethical challenge for archivists.

IMPROVING ARCHIVAL DESCRIPTION SYSTEMS

The type of impact archivists have on the meaning of archival records is nothing new. It is the power of interpretation, traditionally viewed as the preserve of historians and other researchers. As Michael Kammen argues in his study of the role of tradition in American history, people like to think of the past as immutable, based on truth and facts; however, "societies reconstruct their pasts rather than faithfully record them, and that they do so with the needs of contemporary culture clearly in mind—manipulating the past in order to mold the present."[100] As they engage with the archival record, both within governmental, business, academic, and other institutional archives and in manuscript collecting repositories, archivists also manipulate the past, either deliberately or, far more often, subconsciously. Tom

Nesmith observes that in both description and reference, archivists "significantly shape what counts as meaningful context." This considerable power "can clearly influence readings by users of archives."[101] For example, in conducting research on Indian women who cohabited with or married European men between 1760 and 1840, Durba Ghosh found that in India, "documents that spoke directly to my topic were difficult to find," and that in Britain, "ways of cataloging and listing the archive's contents" made her success unlikely since "most of the documents are ordered by and collected under categories like revenue, judicial, foreign, political—all matters that likely barely touched these women's lives."[102] Even basic practices based on provenance and original order can thus reflect hidden assumptions that skew archivists' approaches to the past, to the record.

A central underlying purpose of archival finding aids is control. Archivists conscious of their motivation to fix and stabilize information about records can acknowledge the impact that this process exerts on the ability of future researchers to understand and access evidence and information. The human urge to classify and control information originated among our primitive ancestors. In recent times it emerged in the nineteenth-century search for efficiency and bureaucratic control, exemplified by the development of corporate and governmental recordkeeping systems[103]; the classification grids of census takers, mapmakers, and museum curators[104]; and the creation of library classification systems such as Melvil Dewey's decimal system for organizing all human knowledge.[105] This power to control information carries with it responsibility for archivists to be accountable for how they manage records. Preparing standardized finding aids documents the archivist's "account" of this responsibility, showing how she/he carries out part of this obligation by providing a means of access for researchers.[106] Another aspect of the archivist's responsibility is ensuring the authenticity of archival records. Archivists must be able to prove that their records are what they claim to be (their identity) and that they have not been altered or corrupted (their integrity). "Archivists explain the records—and the additions or changes to them over time—to demonstrate to all interested persons that we have protected their authenticity," Heather MacNeil states.[107] The ethical archivist thus takes responsibility for the power of control by accepting accountability for the accessibility and authenticity of records.

Archival description is inherently subjective. Archivists must constantly choose what facts are important and which are not as they create a narrative that will "guide" (note the implications of this archival terminology) researchers to the records. Finding aids are not merely "neutral tools for facilitating research," MacNeil argues, but "cultural texts, historically situated in time and place," which "shape what they include and exclude, what they emphasize and what they ignore."[108] Wendy Duff and Verne Harris warn, "what we choose to stress and what we choose to ignore is always and unavoidably subjective, and the value judgments that archivists make affect in turn how researchers find, perceive, and use records." They conclude, "Description is always story telling—intertwining facts with narratives, observation with interpretation."[109] Archivists wield substantial power in these processes, and they must use it to achieve positive outcomes.

The solution to this problem is not to attempt to restore the lost innocence of archivists' neutrality, but to recognize their unavoidable influence on the process and to make their actions as transparent as possible. Archivists seeking a more inclusive and ethical approach can begin by acknowledging the hidden assumptions behind traditional practices. The form and content of archival finding aids have changed over time, following new research interests, societal conventions, and professional standards.[110] Despite efforts to portray archival description standards as "uncontested statements of the best practice and thinking," Tom Nesmith argues, they are in fact "changeable, forged in hard choices and compromises" that reflect cultural and political perspectives.[111] The modernist classification imperatives of the nineteenth century sought to universalize knowledge and prescribe norms for investigation and research. In 1901, for example, the Library of Congress codified common practice in cataloging to create standardized subject headings. As Nancy Bartlett reports, "The Library of Congress subject headings and the Anglo-American cataloging rules favored the English language, the Christian faith, the academic canon, and the American worldview."[112] Such standardized approaches to describing information require continual revision and updates, as terminology and cultural values change. Subjects that do not fit neatly into preconceived categories can be easily overlooked or ignored. Being aware of such constraints and limitations marks the first step to overcome them. Ethical practice requires vigilance and mindfulness. Although they do not always have the power or authority to overcome institutional or political barriers to action, archivists cannot—and should not—continue to pretend to be passive observers and handmaidens to history.

In preparing finding aids archivists should be alert for subtle shadings of bias and privilege in how they refer to social groups and individuals. This is what Verne Harris identifies as "the politics of archival description."[113] A "BiogHist Note" that refers only to a records creator's professional career and not to his or her family and social relations may reflect the documented aspects of the person's life but not the context in which such actions took place. Subtle shadings of language—adjectives, adverbs, dependent clauses—can reflect archivists' own assumptions and biases. They may look with dismay at a previous generation's depiction of gays and lesbians with terms such as "social deviant" or worse; but what are their own cultural blinders? In a revealing analysis of archival finding aids produced between the 1930s and the present, Rainbow Koehl has found telling examples of value-laden terms being used with little apparent awareness of the cultural meanings and interpretations they embody. The finding aid for a state Department of Civil Defense, for example, indicated that the files contained information about national security, civil defense activities, and "fringe" areas such as antinuclear protests, unidentified flying objects, and other topics. Using a term such as *fringe* to marginalize certain topics is a political act. The same finding aid states that the records reflect activities associated with the "Cold War, Korean conflict, Berlin Crisis, Cuban Crisis, Vietnam War, [and] the civil disturbances of the 1960s and 1970s." As Koehl points out, "To call one event a war and another conflict is quite different. . . . When the archivist uses the phrase 'civil disturbances' it also minimizes the protests that occurred across the nation against the Vietnam War as well as the protests of the civil rights movement."[114] In other finding aids Koehl finds references to Mexican "bandits," a "Spanish-American War Hero," and similar value-laden terms. Koehl explains, "Single words carry much more than their denotations: they also carry connotations that are usually heavily culturally bound."[115] Archivists need to examine their own professional assumptions and procedures, to avoid perpetuating status quo power relations.

One ethical response to these challenges is to recognize that "the creation of finding aids, and with it the promise or potential of access, is inherently a political act," as Elizabeth Yakel argues. "Archival representation processes are neither objective nor transparent. As such, archivists need to be more conscious of the activities that structure the creation of representations, their social construction, as well as their appropriate uses."[116] Conducting research in archives in Uzbekistan, Jeff Sahadeo observed, "Soviet-era published guides, still the first documents handed to patrons,

worked, just as did published archival material, to promote a
particular vision of politics and society." These guides excluded
significant portions of the archive's holdings and firmly divided
pre- and post-1917 records into "historical" and "revolutionary"
sections, thereby deterring "any efforts to locate continuities
across regimes."[117] Archivists rarely impose such heavy-handed
interventions in describing their research materials, but there are
always gaps between the available evidence and what can be included
in finding aids. Archival representation of records is necessarily
selective and incomplete. It is impossible to convey full information
about all records, but making the process transparent to the user is
essential. Archivists should avoid "creating a misleading impression
of completeness" and should "signal to users the gaps in our
knowledge," Heather MacNeil states.[118] The ethical archivist tells the
user when information is fragmentary, and clearly distinguishes what
the archivist does not know from what she does know. Full disclosure
avoids misrepresentation.

Providing such information requires modifying traditional
processing methods and descriptive systems. Informed by the
postmodern imperative for openness and accountability, several
archivists have proposed new techniques for conveying information
about archival materials. Michelle Light and Tom Hyry suggest two
supplements to finding aids. Information about the actions taken by
archivists in selecting and organizing records can be incorporated in
a colophon, which "may self-consciously alert the researcher about
the subjective and mediating role of the processor in appraising,
arranging, and describing a set of records." While a colophon
describes the archivist's involvement in creating the finding aid, users
of the records could add their own commentaries, explanations,
and interpretations through an option of annotating the finding
aid itself. As Light and Hyry suggest, "annotations to finding aids
would allow multiple voices to express different perspectives and
readings of a collection after processing is complete."[119] Another
option, suggested by Tom Nesmith, would add "as a general
overlay to any descriptive system, a series of essays on the approach
taken to description by the system/archives and the nature of the
contextual information found in it." Written by archivists, these
essays could describe the history of the repository itself, the societal
and institutional contexts that have shaped it, the appraisal criteria
applied to a given group of records, or any other information that
would help researchers understand the archives and the records being
consulted.[120] Such additional information—annotations, colophons,
and essays—could be conveyed most effectively through web-based

access, such as hypertext links to the finding aids. For archivists who are often over-burdened with processing backlogs and other duties, these added obligations may seem excessive. However, an ethical approach to archival description should incorporate at least some of these suggestions, such as the acknowledgment of the archivist's role of mediator between researchers and records.

PROVIDING INCLUSIVE REFERENCE AND ACCESS

Archives create potential societal value through the process of identifying and preserving documentation, but unless records are accessible and used for evidence, accountability, or research there is no true benefit to society. Reference and access services provide the essential link between records and people. However, potential users may not even know of the existence of such documents unless information about the archival resources can be provided through public programs and outreach. The ethically conscious archivist acknowledges this responsibility to publicize archival resources and services, and to provide open and equal opportunities to all members of society who could benefit from the archives. During 1993 Senate hearings regarding access to the papers of former Supreme Court Justice Thurgood Marshall, SAA President Anne Kenney testified, "A primary goal of an archivist is to provide fair, equitable, and timely access to materials for researchers," adding that "in relations with their donors and researchers, archivists embrace a position that supports making historical papers accessible with all due speed."[121] While respecting legitimate privacy and confidentiality rights of individuals, archivists support public access to information.

Archivists serve many constituencies and sometimes need to mediate conflicting interests among records creators, donors, researchers, and their own institutions. Some decisions are easy. Legal rights such as copyright and open access to public records must be respected. However, other conflicts within the archives must be resolved by consideration of professional ethics. Such choices may be unclear or difficult, requiring tact, diplomacy, and balancing contradictory interests to gain a satisfactory result. Even when archivists agree on the need for equal and open access, applying the concept in complex cases is difficult. As Elena Danielson of the Hoover Institution discovered, there is often a "remarkable lack of consensus" on such decisions.[122]

Archivists must balance the sometimes-conflicting rights of donors, records creators, researchers, and "third parties" affected by archival disclosure.[123] Privacy rights of third parties, in particular, should be protected. Archivists must secure clear legal authority to administer materials donated or transferred to the archives or manuscript repository, whether from an individual or corporate donor. They must also adhere to the wishes of donors regarding access or restrictions on access to materials. Finally, they must provide access to materials not subject to restrictions on an equal, open, and fair basis. Except in rare cases, it is unacceptable to allow access by one category of users (e.g., academic scholars) but deny it to others (e.g., journalists or genealogists).[124] Archivists should avoid the elitist notion that certain researcher groups, such as academic scholars, should be afforded special access privileges.

In reference and access services archivists must permit the freest possible use of their records, not limiting access to "serious researchers" or "scholars." Professional archivists have, for the most part, abandoned past practices that sometimes discriminated between favored and less welcome constituencies, but there are some instances in which reference practices do not meet this professional standard. In South Africa, "lack of public access to the archive . . . remains a persistent and especially troubling matter," according to a 2007 report to the Minister of Arts and Culture. "The culture of locking up materials in the archive persists even in the wake of the TRC [Truth and Reconciliation Commission], which so forcefully made the case for an open and accessible archive as fundamental for social justice."[125] Access to archival records provides one of many necessary safeguards for securing social justice, particularly in countries that have experienced extremes of oppression. This is also true in more open and democratic states.

All governments, indeed all institutions wielding power over groups of individuals, entrench their authority through control of information. Governmental officials and bureaucrats commonly establish codes of concealment—whether by blanket policies covering all information sources or by selective application of "state secrets" designations for particular types of records—to regulate what information the people can examine. In the Dutch Indies, "State secrets named and produced privileged knowledge and reminded readers of what was important to know, what kinds of knowledge were coveted, inaccessible and what kind was not," according to Ann Laura Stoler. "State secrets make up a basic feature of the archive, the raison d'être of state institutions charged with producing foundational fictions of concealment and access embodied in content as well as form."[126] Similar examples can be found in nearly all colonial, monarchical, and totalitarian regimes. But state secrets also conceal political manipulation and raise the potential for falsehoods and distortions of the truth in democratic societies, including the United States.[127] As George Orwell warned in *Animal Farm* and *Nineteen Eighty-Four,* control of information and documentation provides an essential condition for oppression and state control of society.

Just as archivists insert their own values into the creation of finding aids and indexes, usually without even realizing it, so too do they intrude into the reference process. Archivists decide which subjects are of prime importance, Rainbow Koehl contends:

> Researchers, of course, may peruse the records themselves and come to their own conclusions. However, when archives compile summaries and index terms for researchers it invites the researchers to be lazy in their work and rely wholly on the information provided for them without questioning its omniscience and exploring the documents on their own. Again, the danger is that rarely do they appear to realize that they are passively relinquishing the power to interpret history to archivists.[128]

One example of this was the experience of a graduate student conducting archival research in 1975. He found that a prominent historian had used a quotation from a plantation mistress, found in the finding aid for her diary and other papers, stating that southern women hated slavery because bondage reminded them of their dependence on husbands. In reading the entire diary, covering more than thirty years, the graduate student found that this was the only comment that even remotely suggested such an opinion. The prominent historian erred by reading the finding aid and not the entire diary. Even worse, this quotation became the basis for an inaccurate interpretation in a widely read book. Clearly this was an instance of laziness on the part of the historian, but it also cautions archivists that highlighting some information privileges one perspective of the past, which can distort the meaning of archival records.

The ethically conscious archivist ensures fair and equitable services to all researchers. In this heightened awareness of the call of justice, Tom Nesmith argues for a broader conception of traditional reference service. "Reference is not so much about helping people to retrieve records and knowledge that already exist, or are frozen in time, but about assisting users to create them anew, by guiding users to records with contextual descriptions about how records were created (including the archival contribution to their creation) and in learning from researchers their contribution to understanding this contextuality."[129] Contextual information, when provided in finding aids, provides a better understanding of how and why records are created, preserved, and organized by archivists.

Public programs and outreach promote archival research and highlight the information and services offered by the archives. Responding to the ethical imperative for archivists, Tom Nesmith suggests extending outreach into new venues of social policy and practice. As he argues, public programming should "no longer be only about informing society about the existence of archival records and their possible uses, but also about explaining how recording and archiving actions help make our sense of reality or truth, and about the social and political power of archiving processes."[130] In doing so, archivists must not overstate their case by claiming to have "the truth" in the records. It is enough to declare that archives contribute to what we, as a society, need to know.

The traditional approach to archival practice often denies any responsibility to exert added effort to reach those who do not already understand or use archives. However, archivists open to the call of justice seek to expand their research and user constituencies by identifying and connecting to groups who do not even know that they could benefit from archival resources and services. One exemplary demonstration of this surfaces in the response of Norwegian archivists to the quest by Norway's "war children" to secure compensation for their suffering. The children born to Norwegian mothers and German fathers during World War II had been kidnapped and taken to Germany to be raised as "pure" Aryans. Separated from their motherland, when they did return to Norway they faced discrimination as living proof of their own mothers' treason in consorting with enemy soldiers. By the 1990s the Norwegian government acknowledged the suffering of the "war children" and provided a compensation plan based on documentation that individuals could produce to support claims of discrimination and personal harm ("grave suffering, loss, or damage" in governmental language). As archivist Gudmund Valderhaug concludes, reliance on public records proved defective and inadequate for most claims, due to selective recording and underreporting of discrimination in the archival documentation. Seeking to secure justice for these "war children" claimants, Valderhaug and his colleagues exceeded their professional obligations and undertook a time-consuming effort to develop expertise on administrative procedures relating to post-war childcare policies. Valderhaug argues that such "extra service" became both necessary and defensible because the inherent skewing of the archival records would have precluded legitimate claims for compensation by the victims of state policy. The social dynamics of recordmaking and recordkeeping either failed to document injustices or misidentified abuses through inaccurate or misleading terminology. Valderhaug concludes that archivists must go beyond their prescribed duties if they choose to serve justice. It is not enough to provide equal access to the archives. Archivists must also ensure that all potential users have an equal right to benefit from the archives, and even to participate in the creation of archival documentation. Archivists have to take sides, particularly when someone stands in front of the reference desk seeking information to secure justice. In addition to access services, Valderhaug advocates public involvement in defining the records worthy of archival preservation, particularly for formerly marginalized groups such as the "war children."[131]

The archival ethics of justice may require providing "unequal services" to individuals who do not know how to conduct archival research or to read sources against the grain to uncover the truth, particularly when victims seek to redress past injustices. "Equal rights to archival information can't be reduced to equal rights to access, but it must also include equal right to benefit from the archive," Valderhaug states.[132] This may require additional efforts by the archivist. "The emergence of real justice will be dependent on society's willingness to show hospitality to the victimised, the marginalised, 'the other,' and in this effort the archives may have a special mission," Valderhaug declares, echoing Jacques Derrida: "To invite 'the other' in, to give them the opportunity to record their own (his)stories, to archive these stories and make them available for use; thus giving the silenced voices the possibility to add [to] and rectify the archival heritages."[133] The power of archivists to secure justice for such people can prove decisive for their future lives. This power is present in archival appraisal, arrangement and description of records, access, and outreach. Valderhaug attests, "The archivist's power can give people back their histories."[134] In this act the archivist offers justice to those outside the dominant power structures in society.

The call of justice also brings a responsibility to broaden the public impact of archives by bringing new and often overlooked constituencies to the archival exhibit galleries, lecture halls, and reading rooms. South African literature professor Bhekizizwe Peterson calls on archivists to "devise more creative encounters between archival material and different sites and communities," including nontraditional users of archives.[135] Exhibits, workshops, community celebrations, and public events provide opportunities for outreach and for making archives accessible and useful to all sectors of society. This opening up of the archives enables the archivist concerned about social justice to reach and serve both those who have been marginalized and the traditional users of archives. By taking the archives to the people, Verne Harris contends, public archives can be "transformed from a domain of the elite into a community resource."[136] Archives thus become accessible and valuable to all members of society.

EMBRACING NEW TECHNOLOGIES

One inescapable feature of modern society is its reliance on digital technology. From massive computer networks—controlling communications, manufacturing, transportation, and other super-scale applications—to miniature computer chips in everything from household appliances and wristwatches to children's toys, daily life in western societies depends on electronics. Even in developing countries, technology plays an increasing role, although few of the poorest people will ever touch or use a computer. Some social observers hail the digital age as a revolutionary milestone in human progress. Others lament its apparent depersonalization of social interactions and its potential for curtailing personal freedom and privacy. Both sides make valid arguments, which must be considered in determining how best to exploit the benefits of new technologies while avoiding their worst dangers. Before considering how new technologies can contribute to a more open and democratic approach to archival documentation and access, these concepts need some context.

The digital age permeates the archival profession and its dual commitment to preserving the electronic records and digital archives that are essential for institutional and cultural needs, and to using digital applications for archival functions such as creating finding aids, providing reference services, and promoting outreach and accessibility. In looking at these new technologies, it is essential to recognize that electronic records and computer applications are simply a new generation of tools with which people order, manage, and document their interactions and their ideas. Technology alters how we communicate and how we work, but it does not fundamentally alter the basic needs and reasons we do so. From ancient times to the present, people have required some form of recording and documenting their lives and thoughts.

There has always been a basic human need to remember legal, financial, operational, and historical transactions and events. Computers—like the cuneiform tablets, papyrus scrolls, illuminated manuscripts, printed books, and other forms of recordkeeping of the past—affect how people interact but not why they do so. Most of the fundamental issues examined in this volume apply equally well to electronic and digital media as to paper-based textual records, photographs, moving images, sound recordings, and other formats of documentation.

In considering how archivists can respond to the challenges of memory, accountability, diversity, and social justice, however, electronic recordkeeping and new technological applications pose new challenges but also provide tools to meet these challenges. It is not possible here to provide a detailed examination of the complex issues of electronic records, Internet access, and Web 2.0 applications. But in thinking about how archivists can address these concerns, a few preliminary thoughts about the digital revolution should indicate the benefits of embracing new technologies to meet archival challenges.

Electronic records have increased exponentially in recent decades, while the quantity of textual records continues to grow steadily as well. Archivists have conducted several important research projects to explore the implications of the new media, focusing on functional requirements for electronic recordkeeping, ensuring authenticity of electronic records, preservation challenges of records needed much longer than the projected life-span of computer hardware and software, and methods to ensure accessibility and security for such records. In addition to sessions at national and regional professional meetings, archivists and records managers have addressed electronic records issues at separate annual conferences, such as the Electronic College and University Records (ECURE) Conference, organized by Arizona State University, the Managing Electronic Records Conference, sponsored by Cohasset Associates, and the Electronic Discovery and Records Retention Conference. Important research projects have explored a variety of concerns regarding electronic records. To cite one example among many, the Indiana University Electronic Records Project, directed by Phil Bantin, explored functional requirements for maintaining electronic records. This project found that data and information systems did not meet some significant needs for reliable recordkeeping systems. In order to ensure long-term preservation of fully functional records, metadata specifications would need to be built into systems at the

design stage. To meet these needs, archivists should participate
in planning and design of recordkeeping systems throughout the
"life cycle" of records. To do so, they will need to obtain new skills
in order to communicate effectively with information technology
(IT) experts.[137] The future of electronic recordkeeping is too
important to leave solely in the hands of technical specialists. For
many purposes this might suffice. But when records are needed
for long periods of time as evidence or historical documentation,
archivists and records managers need to contribute their
knowledge of authenticity, reliability, and context. Records are
not simply aggregates of data or information, but a form of legal,
administrative, financial, and historical evidence that requires
archival expertise.

Managing electronic records as evidence and documentation
demands knowledge of legal requirements, administrative functions,
and historical context. Digital archives, such as the Washington
State Digital Archives and the Electronic Records Archives being
developed by the National Archives and Records Administration,
offer one means of addressing these concerns. However, when IT
experts direct such operations, without the expertise of records
managers and archivists in designing systems and protocols, the
results can be less than satisfactory. In the field of information
management, digital archiving is one aspect of a broader concept
of digital curation, which the Digital Curation Centre in Glasgow,
Scotland defines as "maintaining and adding value to a trusted
body of digital information for current and future use."[138] Digital
curation encompasses separate specialties in digital preservation,
digital librarianship, digital archiving, and data management. Just
as archives differ from libraries and museums, so do digital archives
differ from digital libraries and museums. According to Australian
archivist Adrian Cunningham, "Digital archiving requires active
archival intervention across the entire records continuum."[139]
Archivists need to join IT specialists, records managers, and other
professionals in designing recordkeeping systems, implementing
their active use in offices and agencies, and ensuring their long-
term preservation and accessibility.

In order to enhance access to their collections, archivists have used
the Internet extensively. More than five thousand archival websites,
including nearly three thousand in the United States and Canada
alone, provide information ranging from a brief brochure-style
introduction to the repository to elaborate multilayered descriptions
of archival records and digital reproductions of photographs, maps,

and documents. Archival websites promote access and use of archival sources. Some archivists have begun to digitize portions of their holdings for display on their websites.[140] The more extensive sites begin to approach the vision of a repository of information available 24-7 for users around the globe. Despite these signs of progress toward greater access, however, "web pages are nonetheless a very powerful form of mediation and gatekeeping," according to archival educator Helen Tibbo.[141] For many researchers the website may replace the physical archives as the repository of information they will access. This means that content made accessible on a website is privileged over the vast majority of archival records. Finding aids and digitized documents require context and reference guidance, which are difficult to provide on websites. Archival sources need to be understood in relation to other documentation, not as isolated bits of information.

The web has already transformed how many researchers locate and use information. Frequent users of the web sometimes assume that all the information they need is available on the web. If it cannot be located online and accessed quickly, it is unlikely to be incorporated into research projects. "The web has become the ubiquitous starting point for discovering all types of information and conducting a wide array of research," according to Richard Szary. Web users "expect a level of access and service that repositories are not, and never have been, expected to provide."[142] Archivists have already seen changes in public expectations regarding access to sources and services, as researchers demand ready access to archival information, available at any time and any place.[143] As a 2004 library research report discovered, "users want granular pieces of information and data, at the moment of need, in the right format. . . . The mantra will be: 'Everything, everywhere, when I want it, the way I want it.'"[144] Such expectations become increasingly difficult to meet, particularly for archivists already swamped with documents and short on time and resources.

In recent years numerous web-based services have expanded the original concepts and applications available through the Internet. This second generation of Internet services, known collectively as Web 2.0, enables users to interact, collaborate, and share control over information resources in unprecedented ways. Perhaps the best known of these applications—thanks to news and entertainment media coverage—are blogs (short for weblog, a public online journal or bulletin board); Wikipedia, the online encyclopedia in which anyone with access to the web can post or edit information; and

YouTube, which allows any user to link video clips and moving images to the website.[145] According to one of its early pioneers, Tim O'Reilly, Web 2.0 applications take advantage of the Internet as a platform linking all connected devices. These multiple applications are capable of "delivering software as a continually-updated service that gets better the more people use it, consuming and remixing data from multiple sources, including individual users, while providing their own data and services in a form that allows remixing by others, creating network effects through an 'architecture of participation,'" O'Reilly declared in 2005, as Web 2.0 began to develop.[146] The critical concept of Web 2.0 applications is to expand social connections directly, with minimal mediation by external experts or gatekeepers. At heart it is a democratically inspired approach to Internet use. The key concepts underlying these applications, according to Dutch-Canadian archival entrepreneur Peter Van Garderen, are usability, openness, and community. By openness he means open architecture, open standards, open content, and open source (nonproprietary) software. The concept of community emphasizes people connecting to each other, taking responsibility and ownership of web services, technology, and content.[147] One ultimate goal is thus to establish an independent media-savvy network of people seeking common means of direct communication and unmediated access to information.

Beyond such lofty rhetoric, the best way to understand Web 2.0 is by seeing its applications. Individually, they express various aspects of these democratic and community-based purposes; collectively they present an alternate route to achieve many of the goals that libraries, museums, archives, and other information professions have long sought to reach. Archivists in many repositories have extended their use of websites to encompass a wide range of Web 2.0 applications, which leads some observers to anticipate "Archives 2.0" (a term already in use) as a network of social media tools. These relatively new technologies include:

- institutional blogs to highlight archival repositories, ranging from Yale University's Beinecke Library to the Sandusky, Ohio Library Archives Research Center;

- personal blogs by archivists, focusing on everything from professional technical issues to opinions about historical or archival topics;

▶ Flickr, which includes the Library of Congress's posting of over three thousand images from its photographic collections;[148]

▶ podcasts, such as the University of South Florida's informational program about what to expect on a first research visit and the National Archives and Records Administration's posting of historical sound recordings from presidential libraries;

▶ tagging, commenting, and sharing applications, offering archival users the opportunity to comment on collections, add data to the online catalog, or assist other users with research suggestions;

▶ wikis, enabling users to present stories, photographs, or anecdotes related to archival collections;

▶ YouTube postings highlighting sound and moving image resources for presenting information about the archives or its holdings;

▶ microblogging, such as "Twitter," which presents information rapidly for dissemination;

▶ Facebook and MySpace profiles, encouraging users and potential users to join as friends of the archives; and

▶ Mash-ups or combinations, using more than one of these applications to achieve multiple access points for information.[149]

As this list indicates, there are many Web 2.0 applications available for archivists and others to employ. These constitute numerous varieties of "social media tools" designed to foster user engagement.[150] As one recent study concludes, archivists need to "embrace technology in order to remain vital and essential to current and future users in the digital era," and the archives should "give the *greatest possible access* to their materials, thus conveying a greater sense of worth and vitality to the community it serves."[151]

In 2005 students and faculty in the University of Michigan School of Information formed a research group to explore possibilities for "next generation" finding aids. The group conducted an experiment in an ambitious effort to apply a combination of social media tools to create an interactive finding aid for the Bentley Historical Library's Polar Bear Expedition Collections. The functionalities selected for the finding aid project included: bookmarks, enabling users to save links to individual items; comments, for supplying information about sources or discussing concerns with other users; link paths to previously used web pages; browsing categories, to provide new access points; enhanced searching capabilities within the finding aid; and optional user profiles, by which website visitors can engage in direct interactions with each other. These tools allow users to customize finding aid sites to their own needs and interests and to interact with archival staff or other users during their research visits to the site. The project's central goal was to demonstrate a more transparent, user-centered, and need-based approach to archival finding aids. Researchers who did use these enhanced features reported being very satisfied with their experience. Unfortunately, the overall result was very limited use of some of these new features, perhaps because researchers did not know how to exploit new methods of access and research.[152] Despite limited success, the project does illustrate how creative approaches to archival access can enhance future research.

As these examples suggest, the central thrust of using Web 2.0 for archival purposes focuses on enhanced access, particularly for researchers who have not previously used archival collections. Reliance on websites for research access makes archives available to a "generation of users, with fundamentally different perspectives on the past, who will approach archives through computer interfaces, rather than visiting physical archives and interacting with tangible documents"[153] This alters the role of archivists in the reference process, and creates challenges for providing context and guidance in using virtual archives rather than tangible sources. Elizabeth Yakel observes that archivists who employ interactive access tools "have ceded some control over those core archival functions to their visitors and are reimagining the ways in which researchers can interact with the archival record and with fellow travelers in the virtual archives."[154] This partial surrender of power is not easy for many archivists, but it offers some hope for improved accessibility and use of archives by people from all walks of life, including those who have seldom used traditional archives in the past. In order to use archival sources effectively, however, researchers need to understand archival systems, principles, practices, and institutions—what Yakel calls "archival intelligence."[155] In "Archives of the People, by the People, for the People," Max Evans introduces the concept of "commons-based peer-production" as a means for archival institutions to manage their burgeoning collections in an era of limited resources, budget cuts, and changing expectations. By encouraging user participation in contributing to archival finding aids and interactive research, archivists might gain enhanced levels of access—such as item-level descriptive information about collections—without spending staff time or other resources.[156] This may reflect wishful thinking on behalf of archivists, but the interactive nature of social media tools does foster a closer partnership between archivist and researcher, and among researchers themselves.

Archivists are using such methods both to reach the "millennial" generation for whom these applications are daily parts of their social and communal lives, and also to cast a wider net to bring in researchers, casual visitors, and people who might not have heard about archives from more traditional sources of information. The new technologies employing Web 2.0 applications and related methods require archivists to modify some of their long-held assumptions about archival sources, reference services, and research strategies. In proposing "An Archivist's 2.0 Manifesto," Kate Theimer adapts a librarian's proposed guidelines for incorporating new technologies. Among the pledges Theimer asks archivists to make, several recognize this changing landscape of information access and incorporate a more inclusive, open, and shared approach to reference services:

> I will recognize that the universe of information culture is changing fast and that archives need to respond positively to these changes to provide resources and services that users need and want. . . .

> I will avoid requiring users to see things in archivists' terms but rather will shape services to reflect users' preferences and expectations.

> I will be willing to go where users are, both online and in physical spaces, to practice my profession.

> I will create open websites that allow users to join with archivists to contribute content in order to enhance their learning experience and provide assistance to their peers.[157]

The reorientation in archival thinking and practice proposed by those who embrace these new technologies prepares the way for a more inclusive and democratic approach to archival systems. Because Web 2.0 offers new ways for people to interact and to share information, it "provides many opportunities for increasing the diversity of the users of archives and exposing and empowering societal diversity." This promotes a culture that is "open, connective, creative, participatory, and non-hierarchical" and allows people who had been marginalized by traditional approaches to archives, libraries, and museums to participate actively and contribute to the creation, preservation, and use of community memory and history.[158] This is an important part of the appeal of these new technologies for those concerned about the role of archives and archivists in achieving democratic goals of inclusiveness, diversity, and community.

While archivists may want to accept and promote such technological tools, it is important to note that they may bear a steep price tag, that they may promise more than they can deliver, and that there remain many people unable to use these tools because they cannot afford access or cannot learn the necessary techniques. Sometimes the hype is greater than the benefits. Technology critic Andrew Keen reports meeting someone working on a software project who enthused, "It's MySpace meets YouTube meets Wikipedia meets Google. On steroids." Keen replied that he was working on a polemic about the destructive impact of the digital revolution on our culture, economy, and values. "It's ignorance meets egoism meets bad taste meets mob rule," he declared. "On steroids."[159] Keen's resulting polemic, *The Cult of the Amateur: How Today's Internet Is Killing Our Culture,* laments politicians using YouTube to trash their opponents and media companies using the same web service to broadcast "reviews" of their own products. "The irony of a 'democratized' media is that some content producers have more power than others," he warns. "In theory, Web 2.0 gives amateurs a voice. But in reality it's often those with the loudest, most convincing message, and the most money to spread it, who are being heard."[160] Without gatekeepers, there is no one to filter public messages or protect consumers.

Similar concerns are heard about Wikipedia, which many college and university professors will not accept as a valid source of information for student papers, and about other unmediated sources. Yet such concerns have always cropped up with traditional information sources, including materials housed in libraries, museums, and archives. The powerful leaders of society have always controlled access to learning and knowledge. What makes Keen's critique especially troubling is his account of CIA "spy-blogging" and the prevalence of secret monitoring of individuals through aerial photographs, surveillance cameras, and other methods. This represents "the collective implosion of our privacy rights," he charges. His concerns echo themes introduced in earlier chapters of this book. "In this digital panopticon, teachers watch the kids, college administrators watch the students, and peers watch peers," Keen declares. Orwell's *Nineteen Eighty-Four* depicted a top-down surveillance society, and "the Web 2.0 is the democratization of that Orwellian nightmare; instead of a single all-seeing, all-knowing Orwellian leader, now anyone can be Big Brother. All you need is an Internet connection."[161]

Another concern being raised about the rush to apply new technologies is that their steep price tag sometimes leads archival institutions to rely on corporate partnerships for support. "These partnerships usually come with strings attached, and these strings do not always benefit the users," according to Kate Theimer. For example, the National Archives and Records Administration has established partnerships "that restrict public access to the digitized materials."[162] Although the results may be beneficial, archivists and other researchers need to recognize the potential pitfalls and avoid compromising their values in exchange for financial rewards.

Dire predictions of technology run amok have permeated one strand of social criticism for two centuries. During the early disruptions of the Industrial Revolution, for example, English Luddites destroyed the machinery that threatened to eliminate their jobs, threaten their livelihood, and disrupt traditional society. Internet critics such as Andrew Keen may overstate the dangers of new technologies, such as Web 2.0, but their message needs to be heard and considered. Technology can disturb social relations and some of the capabilities of new surveillance monitoring and other threats to privacy need to be kept under control in order to protect individuals and social groups who could be targeted. However, in the applications thus far employed by archivists to enhance their services and empower archival users, such dangers seem relatively distant. With a wary eye on the horizon, archivists can embrace these new technologies as part of a reorientation toward a user-centered approach to archival practice.

PUBLIC ADVOCACY

These internal policy and procedural changes will improve archival services and make them more inclusive and open. Yet archivists must also engage the public on behalf of documentation through advocacy. Archivists concerned about their role in society should recognize the essential nature of their collective responsibility to ensure the preservation of evidence for accountability, individual rights, and social justice. Public advocacy provides a vital means of asserting archival influence.[163] As Harvey Kaye declares, "following the horrors of the past several generations, the persons who should be accorded the greatest recognition are those who, taking up the task of bearing witness to the exterminations, the massacres, the tortures, direct our thoughts to the past and to the imperatives of remembrance, realizing that the final victories of the murderers and the torturers would be the suppression, deliberate or otherwise, of the knowledge of their criminal acts." Kaye cites the Memory Prize, first awarded by the France-Libertes Foundation in 1989, as a promising recognition of the importance of this human need: "Intended to recognize those who labor to secure our collective memory and to prevent the falsification of the historical record, the idea for the prize arose out of the growing awareness that 'the expression, transmission, and preservation of Human Memory is the most effective means of struggling against the recurrence of barbarism.'"[164] Given the nature and significance of this award, archivists should aspire to see members of their own profession recognized by receiving such an honor. Short of this, there are important steps that archivists can take to support a more just and equitable society, by performing their professional responsibilities.

When confronted by external pressures (from administrators, donors, constituents, or others) to alter recordkeeping systems or archival practices, archivists and records managers must stand firm. They must protect the integrity of records and of the recordkeeping systems that hold organizations and individuals accountable. This adherence to professional principles applies equally in public and private institutions, although protections for those who resist such pressures will vary from one setting to another. As in the case of South African archives under apartheid (and after the end of apartheid), archivists must defend the public's right of access to the most accurate records possible, despite political pressure.[165] The Heiner affair in Australia also illustrates the importance of refusing to succumb to political pressure to change our recordkeeping procedures. As these and other examples indicate, resisting political pressure can entail personal risk. Although such situations are rare, these are risks that members of a profession should be willing to consider.

For archivists advocacy takes many forms and provides a variety of benefits. In different situations it can encompass outreach, public relations, political lobbying, relations with other professionals, or efforts to ensure better understanding of the profession's concerns. In the context of archival institutions the archival advocate may be a small repository's "lone arranger," the head of a larger archival agency, or a public relations or media liaison. For broader professional concerns the advocate may represent a local, state, regional, or national archival association. Each of these advocates can play an important role in archival advocacy. However, in responding to public policy concerns, professional archival associations, at the national, regional, and local levels, should accept an important advocacy role on behalf of the profession. As William Maher declared in 1997, advocacy defines the archival profession and reinforces its mission as "service to society at large."[166]

In a democratic society, archival concerns for public records provide an essential safeguard against government secrecy, control,

and unbridled power. Open access to government records is
the hallmark of democratic government. It is vital to protect the
rights and privileges of each citizen. As professionals charged with
ensuring adequate documentation of actions by government and
other organizations, archivists recognize the necessity of holding
our leaders accountable. Our democratic institutions depend on
accurate records and public access to such information.[167] As the
Nation stated in an April 15, 2004 editorial entitled "The Haunted
Archives": "The national archivist is crucial in a democratic society:
He preserves our history and makes government records available
to the public. He should also serve as an advocate for greater
openness."[168] The National Archives and Records Administration
(NARA) plays a vital role related to public records at the federal
level. State and municipal archives provide essential recordkeeping
and accessibility services at the local level, but institutional archives
for religious bodies, colleges and universities, corporations, and
other repositories share these responsibilities within their own
spheres of influence.

Both individually and collectively, archivists must speak out in
defense of archival values, including open access to public records,
standards of accountability and authenticity, and protection
of the rights of all citizens. Tim Ericson chides archivists for a
"lackadaisical attitude" toward government secrecy. "Collectively
we have acquiesced uncritically to those who call for patriotism,
national security, loyalty, [etc.]," he charges. "Archivists should be
acquiescent no more! We should instead begin to be aggressive as
professionals and as citizens to fight this unprecedented tilt toward
secrecy."[169] The natural tendency of those controlling political
power is to limit access to information and records. The George
W. Bush administration took this to unprecedented extremes in its
efforts to hide records from the public. The rationales presented
by administration officials to withhold records from public scrutiny
eerily echoed the Nixon administration's arguments during
the Watergate scandal more than thirty years earlier. At the very
beginning of the Bush presidency, White House chief of staff Andy
Card quietly issued a directive "to wall off records and information
previously in the public domain," according to former Nixon
counsel John W. Dean. The Bush administration's secrecy and
duplicity led Dean to call its abuses "worse than Watergate."[170] Such
policies threatened the public interest. The freedom that Americans
claim to represent depends on an informed citizenry.

Because governmental archivists mediate between citizens and the records of government agencies, they should become advocates for open access—with due consideration for proper privacy and confidentiality protections when warranted—in order to protect the public interest. As a professional group, archivists should demand the elimination of policies that cloak our public servants' actions in secrecy.[171] For this reason archivists should celebrate the early signs from President Barack Obama that his administration will "adopt a presumption in favor of disclosure" regarding Freedom of Information requests, in order "to usher in a new era of open Government."[172] In addition to reasserting the importance of freedom of information, President Obama quickly revoked President George W. Bush's Executive Order 13233, thereby reasserting the limitations on presidential power to prevent public access to presidential records. As SAA President Frank Boles states, these actions "helped to restore transparency and openness to the government of the United States."[173]

Records are powerful tools. Most political figures attempt to restrict or limit access to their papers and to governmental records, fearing the consequences of public disclosure. Events in recent decades have shown the power of archival records. For example, the political careers of Ferdinand Marcos of the Philippines and Kurt Waldheim of Austria disintegrated when records of their actions during World War II came to public attention.[174] Likewise, Richard Nixon's secret White House tapes provided proof of his illegal actions and forced his resignation as president. The potential impact of records disclosure is one reason that the Bush administration went to extreme lengths, unprecedented since Watergate, to close governmental records from public scrutiny and to do "the public's business out of the public eye," as a December 2003 investigative report concluded.[175] "George W. Bush has a fetish for secrecy," the late historian Hugh Davis Graham observed, and his executive order marked a victory for government secrecy "so total that it would make Nixon jealous in his grave."[176] Such excessive secrecy creates ethical dilemmas for archivists, who are responsible for maintaining and providing access to records. Archivists concerned about their professional responsibilities to society will strive to create and preserve accurate records and to ensure public access to the information essential to hold leaders accountable.

The willingness of American archivists in recent years to speak out in defense of open government and access to records is another positive sign, amid the appalling abuses of power represented by the George W. Bush administration's efforts to shut down such access. The Society of American Archivists (SAA) has taken public positions opposing government secrecy, and it entered several lawsuits seeking to ensure open access to public records. In 2005, SAA joined numerous other organizations as a member of OpenTheGovernment.org, a watchdog for unjustified secrecy and limited access to information about public officials and their actions. "The American way of life demands that government operate in the open to be responsive to the public, to foster trust and confidence in government, and to encourage public participation in civic and government institutions," the organization's statement of values declares. "The public's right to know promotes equal and equitable access to government, encourages integrity in official conduct, and prevents undisclosed and undue influence from special interests."[177] This principle is a vital part of the American archival profession's mission. Open access to information—particularly regarding government actions—is essential for effective democracy and citizens' rights.

In addition to advocacy on behalf of the archival profession and its own concerns—such as funding for the grant agency National Historical Publications and Records Commission, and supporting the right of "Unabomber" Ted Kaczynski to place his papers at a public university repository—SAA has taken action on several important recent public policy issues:

▶ In November 2001 SAA President Steve Hensen expressed "grave concern" with President Bush's Executive Order 13233, which unilaterally overturned important post-Watergate provisions of the 1978 Presidential Records Act, giving the president control over access to presidential records. Hensen charged that this executive order "potentially threatens to undermine one of the very foundations of our nation"—"free and open access to information."[178] "How can a democratic people have confidence in elected officials who hide the records of their action from public view?" Hensen asked in an op-ed editorial in the *Washington Post*. As he argued, "the president's papers are not in fact the president's [personal] papers, but rather the records of the people's presidency."[179]

▶ In the wake of terrorist attacks against New York and Washington, DC, in September 2001, the Bush administration pushed through Congress the USA PATRIOT Act of 2001, which provided vastly increased surveillance procedures for suspected terrorists, leading some analysts to compare its impact to Orwell's Big Brother.[180] Among other provisions, section 215 of the act enabled federal investigators to examine library and archives records concerning researchers. After delays in responding to this invasion of archival interests, SAA finally adopted a public position opposing selected provisions of the PATRIOT Act when it came up for renewal in July 2004. This belated response insisted that archivists believe in protection of "the civil liberties that Americans cherish," and that "Archivists believe that democracy thrives when public officials can be held accountable for their actions."[181]

⏺ SAA took a bolder stance regarding the National Energy Policy Development Group, which held a secret meeting in January 2001, chaired by Vice President Dick Cheney, to establish federal policies on energy. After several advocacy groups sued the task force to disclose whether industry representatives participated in these policy discussions, SAA joined the lawsuit on the basis of public disclosure of government records. "Cheney's adamant refusal to provide information on who advised the group was about presidential power pure and simple," archivist Thomas Connors observed.[182] In May 2005 the U.S. Court of Appeals supported Cheney and blocked access to information about participants in this secret policy meeting.

These three examples indicate the importance of vigilance regarding government secrecy and access to public records. As former president Harry S. Truman declared many years ago, "Secrecy and a free, democratic government don't mix."[183] Archivists assume a professional responsibility to ensure access to public records. Legitimate personal privacy and confidentiality considerations place some limitations on what—and when—information can be released to the public, but in the United States the presumption favors accessibility. These concerns extend to recent efforts to slow declassification of government records, to block release of CIA tape recordings regarding interrogation of suspected terrorists, and unauthorized deletion of White House e-mails, among many other threats to public access to information.[184] Both individually and collectively, archivists have an obligation to oppose such threats to public access to records and efforts to employ government secrecy to preclude holding public leaders accountable. These concerns also extend to private sector leaders, who should be accountable to shareholders, consumers, and taxpayers. Archivists should not assume responsibilities as roving public watchdogs, but when concerns arise regarding documentation, recordkeeping, and accountability, these become legitimate professional responsibilities.

United as a profession, archivists can build stronger alliances with those who share many of their goals and values: librarians, records managers, historians, museum curators, historical editors, oral historians, but also consumer advocates, legal investigators, government officials, religious leaders, and public citizens, who depend on accurate and reliable records and on the cultural information they may contain. With these stronger alliances archivists can become more effective as vocal advocates on behalf of the public interest in records and archives. By forming alliances and partnerships with numerous organizations and groups committed to protecting the public's rights, SAA can continue to play a vital leadership role in bringing archival concerns to public attention and in advocating for better funding and increased attention to the requirements of recordkeeping and documentation in a democratic society.

Public advocacy provides one of the most important societal contributions that professional organizations can make. The health of the archival profession itself also depends on public awareness and concern for archival issues. "To the extent that the public understands that archives exist to be used for reasons that affect their lives, property, civic well-being, and political influence, the public will be disposed to support and encourage archives," Elsie Freeman Finch wrote in the introduction to *Advocating Archives: An Introduction to Public Relations for Archivists.* Finch argued, "if archives are properly explained and made reasonably accessible, they will be used and likely be funded."[185] Advocacy thus serves both the public good of society and the professional interests of archivists themselves.

MACHO HEROES

One example of an archivist asserting professional responsibility in the face of powerful political resistance brought media attention to the role of archivists in the federal government. Beginning in 2003, Vice President Dick Cheney claimed his office did not have to comply with the presidential order that established government-wide procedures to ensure federal agency compliance with requirements for protecting classified information. In June and August 2006, J. William Leonard, director of the Information Security Oversight Office within the National Archives, contested the vice president's claim that his office was not an executive branch agency subject to these regulations. When the vice president did not respond to Leonard's letters, he referred the matter to the attorney general, who also failed to respond. However, the vice president's office later proposed revisions to the regulations that Congressman Henry Waxman, Chair of the House Oversight Committee, said "could be construed as retaliation" against Leonard's office and the National Archives.[186] Cheney aide David Addington proposed changes to the original executive order that would have effectively abolished Leonard's office, preventing further oversight of executive agencies' handling of classified documents.

When this controversy became public in June 2007, media attention focused on the vice president's tortured logic in claiming that his office was not part of the executive branch of government, and thus not subject to regulations regarding classified information. Cheney made this claim even though his office had complied with the requirement for disclosure in 2001 and 2002, when it provided this information to the National Archives. The *Washington Post* declared that the "seismic impact" of Cheney's refusal to report on document classification procedures derived from "the combination of so many Cheneyesque attributes: mania for secrecy, resistance to oversight, willingness to twist the law and assertion of unreviewable power."[187] As columnist Leonard Pitts charged, the Bush-Cheney administration had "withdrawn documents from the public sphere, sealed visitors logs from public scrutiny, fought transparency every step of the way." Without access to information, Pitts explained, "people who are not informed cannot ask pertinent questions. They cannot demand accountability. They cannot give informed consent."[188] Congressman Waxman described Cheney's refusal to comply with the executive order as part of a "pattern" of stonewalling to prevent information from reaching the public. Defending the vice president's actions, White House Deputy Press Secretary Dana Perino claimed that President Bush, not the National Archives, was the "sole enforcer" of the classified information requirements.[189] Such a claim would effectively remove any semblance of oversight, bypassing the clearly mandated authority of the National Archives.

On June 24, 2007 *New York Times* op-ed columnist Maureen Dowd described this controversy under the title, "A Vice President Without Borders, Bordering on Lunacy." Depicting Cheney as "dastardly" for blowing off Congress and the public behind a "culture of invisibility," Dowd declared, "Now, in a breathtaking act of arrogance, he's blowing off his own administration." Dowd ended with a backhanded compliment to archivist J. William Leonard (whom she did not name): "I love that Cheney was able to bully Colin Powell, Pentagon generals and George Tenet when drumming up his fake case for war, but when he tried to push around the little guys, the National Archives data collectors—I'm visualizing dedicated 'We the People' wonky types with glasses and pocket protectors—they pushed back. Archivists are the new macho heroes of Washington."[190] The Dutch press quickly picked up this story, with a front-page article in the major newspaper *NRC-Handelsblad,* under the heading, "Archivists Hunt for Cheney's Secrets." The article began, "The American VP Cheney wants to keep everything secret, but now he has found a tough enemy: archivist!"[191]

Simply by fulfilling the requirements of his job, despite strong resistance from the highest levels of the Bush administration, J. William Leonard had become a media hero. Yet even in the act of praising the anonymous archivist who had defied the vice president, Maureen Dowd employed the stereotypes that have so frequently diminished public recognition for archivists. Perhaps the contrast between the determined underdog and the ruthless and powerful politician needed to be enhanced by diminishing the archivist. However, in the one moment in which an archivist could be publicly lauded for defending the rights of the public, this demeaning stereotype helped to undercut the public perception of all archivists.[192]

Beyond the demeaning stereotypes, however, Dowd's article and other press coverage of the Cheney-Archives controversy highlighted the positive contribution that a single archivist could make in asserting the public's right to information and in upholding his professional responsibility in the face of external pressure and threats. This is how an archivist concerned about professional ethics and social responsibility should behave. With the departure of the Bush administration in January 2009, this controversy came to an end. In one of his first actions as president, Barack Obama declared his support for public access to presidential records, and clearly stated that vice-presidential records should be included under the definition of "presidential records."[193]

BLOWING THE WHISTLE

When such external pressures cannot be resisted, archivists and records managers must be willing to become whistle-blowers, speaking out against abuses of power and efforts to manipulate records or limit access to information. This is unlikely to be a common occurrence, but it can happen when least expected and archivists must be prepared to respond forcefully when it does. The personal danger for whistle-blowers is the risk of losing one's job for the sake of informing the public about threats to their rights and interests. "There are serious legal, political and ethical issues implied here that our profession needs to address," Thomas Connors states.[194] It is difficult to confront powerful leaders and to jeopardize one's career. This is one reason that safeguards protecting whistle-blowers need to be enacted or strengthened. Rick Barry argues that archivists and records managers should "be in the forefront of whistleblower protection legislation," which would provide "a needed umbrella for those among us who have the intestinal fortitude to stand up for proper recordkeeping practices when ethics and sound practices are being trashed within their own organizations."[195] The difficulties faced by archivists in such circumstances can be seen in two case studies, which will be summarized briefly here.

The courage shown by Shelley Davis in her heroic but ultimately unsuccessful struggle to prevent "massive document destruction" and to overcome barriers to public access to Internal Revenue Service (IRS) records should be an inspiration to all archivists and records managers. Hired in 1987 as the first historian of the IRS, Davis attempted to accumulate historical records as a basis for her research. She found few such records, because the IRS routinely destroyed most of its records, resulting in "essentially the wholesale loss of the history of one of our most important government agencies."[196] It also "was truly the most secret of all federal agencies," Davis discovered, more secret than the CIA, FBI, or any other government agency. "The IRS shredded, burned, trashed, and destroyed nearly their entire record path." Attempting to fulfill her responsibilities as IRS historian, Davis only occasionally could find small stashes of records, "usually discovered by mistake or because someone wanted to avoid the task of throwing the stuff out themselves." The IRS records management staff remained uninterested in helping her locate records, and "there was no National Archives in sight to protect them." Even though the IRS had created a politically motivated "enemies list" during the Watergate era, it remained unscathed by the Nixon-era scandals and retained complete control over its own records. As Davis discovered, "The IRS had the power to pick and choose what it would let the National Archives look at—a power not even allowed the Central Intelligence Agency!"[197] The IRS effectively wielded its power to audit individual tax returns to force even the most powerful political insiders to acquiesce in its secrecy and control over records.

When Davis discovered that the IRS records management office planned to destroy "nearly an entire room full of documents gathered from the commissioner's office over a period of about thirty years," she informed the assistant to the deputy commissioner that this "insidious plot" to destroy records would violate the law requiring approval of the National Archives for such destruction.

She took this risk as a whistle-blower because the Records Act "declared it illegal for a federal employee not to take action to save records that were known to be in danger of destruction." Once she informed the National Archives of the IRS plans, the Archives "sprang into action" and backed her up by informing the IRS that it could not legally destroy any records not appraised by the National Archives. IRS officials essentially ignored the National Archives warning, and gave Davis a "verbal reprimand" for acting outside her chain of command.[198] Eventually, less than eight years after being hired as the first IRS historian, Davis resigned from the IRS.

Throughout her struggles within the IRS, neither the historical community nor the National Archives offered real support or assistance. "I longed for the power of the archivist of the United States to back me up, support the lone historian inside this powerful agency, but such help remained elusive," Davis complained. The problems with IRS recordkeeping, Davis concluded, would not change until "the National Archives becomes more proactive in demanding that the IRS open its records."[199] Davis's courage in confronting this problem demonstrates the need for archivists, on rare occasions, to become whistle-blowers when confronted by improper recordkeeping. It is also a warning, of course, of the extent to which powerful government agencies can go to protect their secrets.

The second case of an archivist turned whistle-blower comes from the post-apartheid era in South Africa. In July 1993, Verne Harris, a records management archivist in the South African State Archives Service, heard from junior officers in several government departments that "they had received instructions to destroy certain categories of classified record without authorization from the director of archives." Harris briefed the archives director of this proposed "large-scale destruction of sensitive public records" in violation of the Archives Act. When official action through channels failed to prevent the destruction of important records, Harris faced a difficult decision: "Should I allow the official process to take its course, or should I act outside official channels in an attempt to stop the destruction?"[200] Turning to the South African Society of Archivists' *Professional Code* for guidance, Harris found contradictory provisions. On one hand, "the archivist has a moral duty to preserve information about the past and present for the future" and "the archivist must protect the integrity of archives/information against alteration, removal, damage and theft"; yet on the other hand, "At all times the archivist must act within the parameters of the policy laid down by his/her employer."[201] Disclosing what was happening to the press or outside agencies would defy state policy on confidentiality. It would require committing an offense against the Protection of Information Act, which carried a maximum penalty of ten years imprisonment. The ethics code offered "contradictory imperatives and no guidance how to resolve them," Harris declared.[202]

Ultimately, Harris disclosed the unauthorized destruction of records to a journalist and to Lawyers for Human Rights, providing them with supporting documentation. In making this choice, he consciously "did what was wrong in the eyes of the law, my employer, and the last-quoted tenets of the *Professional Code.*" Subsequently, his employer was taken to court and forced to acknowledge that the destruction of records had violated the Archives Act. Harris had become a whistle-blower. "In making my decision I had been forced to reach beyond articulations of right and wrong provided by law and professional ethics," Harris declared. "In the end, my moment of decision was an intensely subjective one. Me and my conscience." From this personal experience, Harris concluded, "There is no knowing of right without giving account to personal morality. For each of us has the right, and the obligation, to be true to ourselves."[203]

Since none of us is impartial, we can only seek to make such difficult decisions in an appropriate manner. Harris argues that this requires four steps: illuminating the web of rights for all parties; weighing competing claims in each specific circumstance; testing one's views and feelings with respected colleagues and friends; and finally, "paying heed to one's conscience." This process ensures some measure of accountability, based on reason, without abandoning our humanity. There can be no blueprint for ethical behavior, no easy or self-evident answer to complex moral choices. "Two archivists confronted by the same moral dilemma can embrace the four elements of process I've outlined and come to different conclusions. And both be right." Harris points out that it is also possible for both archivists "to come to the same conclusion, but one be right and the other wrong." Determination of right and wrong in such cases can be found only "in the deeper spaces of the subject's psyche," he concludes.[204]

As archivists confront ethical dilemmas such as those faced by Shelley Davis and Verne Harris, they each need to weigh the often conflicting obligations of professional requirements, employer demands, constituent interests, and personal values. Ultimately, professional ethics cannot ignore or remain aloof from the individual's sense of morality, civic duty, and social responsibility. These can be difficult choices, but the archivist committed to ethical behavior cannot take shortcuts and easy solutions based on a professional catechism or recipe for proper conduct. The truly ethical archivist must remain true to her or his individual sense of morality, bearing in mind the various claims and interests of other parties and the ultimate good of society.

ARCHIVES FOR ALL

One of the great strengths of the archival profession and of archival repositories is their variety and diversity. In responding to the call of justice—to the ethical imperatives raised by many archivists, historians, and social activists—archivists likewise can follow a variety of approaches. The range of activities and orientations outlined here merely suggest some of these options. Some archivists will be able to undertake most or all of these actions; others will choose one or two steps that they are willing and able to take; still others may not follow any of these paths. As a profession, archivists need to accept all of these approaches as valid responses to the challenges of change. No one should be denounced for following the call of justice in professional work, nor for rejecting it. Traditional archival practices and principles still provide valuable social benefits.

Archivists and archival repositories that do put into practice some or all of the recommendations based on the call of justice will make an even more valuable contribution to society, beyond the inherent value of preserving archival records and making them available for research use. Putting aside the illusion of neutrality, archivists can still maintain professional standards of objectivity, openness, inclusivity, and equal treatment for all users of archival records. By welcoming new perspectives and voices into the archives, they can contribute to tolerance and diversity. Through inclusion of oral testimony archivists open their repositories to new perspectives, and by accepting or sponsoring oral history they can fill gaps in the historical record and document aspects of human experience that would otherwise remain unknown. Embracing the democratic values of new technologies can break down barriers to access and foster collaboration between users and archivists rather than perpetuate the dominance of gatekeepers and guardians of the past.

In order to secure public understanding and awareness, archivists
need to promote advocacy initiatives. This will engage them
in public policy debates, bringing archives into the public
consciousness and showing how archives can contribute to open
government, accountability, and protecting citizens' rights. As
archivists encounter problems in recordkeeping and documentation,
they may need to consider becoming whistle-blowers. When doing
so in defense of the public interest, archivists should expect their
professional colleagues, including organizations such as the Society
of American Archivists, to support their actions. It is important
for the archival profession to foster a social conscience and a
willingness to stand up for people's rights and for the proper
care and management of evidence and the historical record. This
commitment to the public interest and to professional values will
contribute to archival repositories and an archival profession that
provides benefits for all people in society.

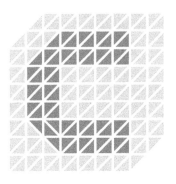

CONCLUSION:
Rethinking Archival Ethics

There is no knowing of right without giving account to personal morality.
For each of us has the right, and the obligation, to be true to ourselves.

- Verne Harris

After the collapse of apartheid, the newly created Nelson
Mandela Foundation focused on using archival memory
to promote social justice. In August 2005 the Mandela
Foundation hosted a colloquium in Johannesburg dedicated to
exploring the theme of "Memory for Justice." Nearly one hundred
participants representing more than thirty institutions attended
sessions focusing on memory as a powerful catalyst for social change,
the social power exercised by archivists, systemic shortcomings in
archival user service, the role of archivists in striving for historical
and contemporary justice, and South African experiences of
memory construction in the wake of the apartheid era. From this
dialogue emerged key propositions and questions, for archival
institutions, for practitioners, and for society as a whole. Among
these statements, summarized in the report of the colloquium, a few
examples illustrate the range of issues examined:

  ◀ Those who work with archives should be guided primarily by a concept of
    and commitment to justice.

- ◗ Prevailing relations of power and influence in societies (even in democracies) tend to disadvantage certain voices. The call of justice sounds two imperatives: 1) to proactively enable participation and access; and 2) to construct the archive beyond the normative assumptions circumscribed by power and the status quo.
- ◗ The archive . . . is best understood as a contested terrain for memory construction shaping contemporary understandings of society.
- ◗ The justice potential of the archive must be identified and fought for in these contexts.
- ◗ Injustice is routinely documented by those who perpetrate it. Such records are systematically hidden, sanitized, neglected, or destroyed. Justice requires resistance to such processes.
- ◗ The archive provides a powerful resource for restorative justice.
- ◗ Disclosing what was hidden (and what remains secret) is but a first step. . . . What is the next step beyond creating a more accurate version of the past? And how does that—can that—shape and connect to contemporary struggles for justice? [1]

The challenges raised in these statements presented a manifesto for a new conception of archival ethics. No longer seen as neutral and passive centers for historical documentation, archives would be reborn as active participants in the social, political, and intellectual struggles to achieve social justice and personal freedom for all peoples. What the Johannesburg conference proposed amounted to a redefinition of archives and of the role of archivists in society.

CHANGING CONCEPTS OF ARCHIVAL ETHICS

In the waning years of the twentieth century, public discourses about memory, accountability, and multiculturalism increasingly focused on aspects of documentation, evidence, and "the archive" as a conceptual framework for recording and preserving information crucial to members of society. Scholars in many disciplines examined "the archive" as a disembodied repository from which they could derive evidence and documentation. Although they considered the societal importance of archives, they often overlooked or ignored the people who work in these repositories, making daily decisions that affect the documentation that will be available for future use, the systems for organizing and accessing records, and the manner in which archival sources are identified and described. The critical role of archivists in managing, selecting, preserving, and shaping the documentary record of society remained largely unexamined and uncontested. By the 1990s, when archivists began joining these intellectual discourses, their attention focused precisely on the implications of these theories and concepts of memory, accountability, and diversity for traditional archival functions and goals. This soon led archivists to examine for themselves the ethical implications of these new perspectives.

The emerging discourse on archival ethics grew directly from the social upheavals of the 1990s. The collapse of the apartheid regime led South African archivists, in particular, to seek responses by which they could contribute to the healing process exemplified by the Truth and Reconciliation Commission. The beginning of the twenty-first century found a small but growing number of archivists questioning archival ethics and seeking a broader conception of what it means to be an ethical archivist in a world of profound societal upheavals. The collapse of communist governments in the former Soviet Union and eastern Europe, the end of apartheid in South Africa, the emergence of China and other nations as economic and political powers, and the technological, economic, and political impact of globalization— to name only a few of these recent upheavals—fundamentally altered many western-based assumptions about social dynamics and national identity. Among many profound changes, these new concepts of archives and the role of archivists in society may seem trivial. However, the importance of documentation and archival memory, as argued in previous chapters, affects many of these central concepts of society's governance, functioning, identity, "memory," and stability. Records and archives support and strengthen important elements of society's infrastructure, culture, and operations. They can contribute to accountability, transparency, multiculturalism, diversity, and social justice. Underlying these connections runs an essential theme of professional ethics and social responsibility.

In order to understand the current discourse on archival ethics, memory construction, and social justice, it is essential to consider the development of concepts of professional ethics, and to explore the implications that these issues could have for archivists and the societies they serve. The previous chapter examined: the diverse types of archives; the distinction between objectivity and neutrality; how the call of justice could affect archivists' responsibilities (such as archival selection and appraisal, organization and control of records, reference, access, and use); documenting underrepresented societal groups; public advocacy on social policy issues; the ethics of whistle-blowing; and the different ways that these issues affect archivists in public, not-for-profit, and corporate archives. This conclusion considers the historical context of professional codes of archival ethics, the limitations of such codes, and the challenges posed by non-western concepts of the archive. It concludes with some thoughts about how archivists can move, individually or collectively, toward accepting an ethics of social justice. These are not prescriptions or recipes for action, but rather a presentation of options for archivists—and those they serve both within institutions and the broader society—to consider as they reconcile their personal and professional obligations with their responsibilities to society.

CODIFYING ARCHIVAL ETHICS

These appeals for archivists to address their own relationship to societal needs raise questions about the very nature of professional ethics and responsibility. Archives represent temples of knowledge, veneration, and authority; prisons of control and security; and service centers engaged in mediation and interpretation. With the growing recognition of this power of archives as institutions and of archivists as power brokers who can limit or expand accessibility of the records, comes social responsibility. Every action taken by the archivist engages questions of ethics and professional conduct. "As gatekeepers of information, information professionals have a greater ethical responsibility than ever before to their users, to themselves, to the profession, and to society," declare Wallace C. Koehler and J. Michael Pemberton.[2] Consideration of these new concepts of professional ethics must take place in the context of ethical theory and traditional views of archival ethics.

Ethics is the branch of philosophy that examines the morality of human behavior. For present purposes, the most relevant aspects of ethics derive from deontological theory and teleological theory. Deontological theories seek to establish the morality of an action based only on the act itself, with no consideration of its consequences. One example is Immanuel Kant's "categorical imperative," which extends the so-called Golden Rule (treat others as you would want them to treat you) into a universal law of behavior. Kant argued that human actions could only be considered moral if the principles could be applicable to all similar situations.[3] Teleological theory reverses this orientation, focusing on ends rather than means. In these formulations, the moral act is that which would produce the most desirable consequences, regardless of the ethical aspects of the actions taken. These results can be judged according to their beneficial consequences for the individual actor (egoism), for everyone but the individual (altruism), or for all parties (utilitarianism).[4] Statements of archival ethics traditionally have emphasized deontological statements (what archivists should do), with less attention to teleological statements (what results are desired). In the latter category, most archival ethics formulations fall under utilitarian or altruistic rather than egoistic concepts.

Another important orientation to consider in evaluating professional ethics is the contrast between what Julia Evetts identifies as organizational and occupational professionalism. Organizational professionalism emphasizes hierarchical structures of authority, standardized work practices, and accountability. By contrast, occupational professionalism focuses on "discretionary decision-making in complex cases, collegial authority, [and] the occupational control of the work"; it is "based on shared education and training, . . . occupational identity, and codes of ethics" established by professional institutes and associations.[5] Organizational professionalism expects employees to align their values with those of the employer or parent institution, which may at times conflict with the occupational professionalism that advocates external criteria for professional conduct.

Archivists seeking to define and clarify their professional roles usually emphasize external characteristics, such as those established in taxonomic models using such criteria as: education based in a body of theory; service orientation to community needs; an organized professional association; common values; and a body of expertise that can be applied freely by members of the profession.[6] An alternative model, proposed by ethics theorist Daryl Koehn, evaluates professionalism on the basis of concepts such as power, trust, and morality. Professionals acknowledge a public pledge of service that binds them in a trust relationship with the clients they purport to serve. As Glenn Dingwall observes, archivists have not fully established "a clearly defined trust relationship between archivists and the public," who remain generally unaware about the purpose of archives and their importance in providing societal benefits, such as defense of democratic rights. However, Dingwall argues that archivists deserve greater recognition as a profession because, "Archivists do important work that no one else does, or is capable of doing, without access to our theoretical base; and, this work contributes to the defense of the democratic rights of individuals and of society as a whole."[7] As archivists seek a clearer social mandate for their public services, this need for greater public awareness and understanding of archives becomes increasingly essential. "The role of archivists in contemporary society is definitely changing," Berndt Fredriksson stated at a 2001 international archival conference in Reykjavik. Archivists need to adopt a proactive role in making their voices heard in society. "First we must define more in detail what we want our role to be," Fredriksson declared. "Having done that we have to convince the rest of the world about our competence, because in the knowledge society archival professionalism has an essential role to play."[8] Without public understanding, this archival role will not gain enough acceptance to be effective.

Professional ethics for archivists in the United States have been codified only since 1980, when the Society of American Archivists (SAA) adopted its first "Code of Ethics for Archivists." This code was revised in 1992, and again in February 2005. The previous codes incorporated both guidelines for ethical conduct in the principal areas of professional activity and also a commentary to explain and provide examples of what these guidelines implied. Because this commentary provided specific applications of the general guidelines, it could "be interpreted to restrict the scope of legitimate responses,"[9] and the 2005 code omitted all commentary. The 1980 and 1992 codes employed a primarily deontological formulation of archival ethics, using terms such as "archivists shall . . ." or "archivists must not . . ." The codes also included a few teleological statements to explain reasons for certain archival practices or the expected consequences of actions.[10]

In addition to the SAA Code of Ethics, archival associations in many other countries have developed guidelines for professional ethics in recent years. These codes provide a common set of ten ethical principles that enjoy worldwide acceptance. As summarized in a recent volume on archival ethics by Karen Benedict, these principles state that archivists:

1. should treat both users and colleagues fairly, without discrimination or preference;
2. must preserve the intellectual and physical integrity of their records;
3. may never alter, manipulate, or destroy data in records;
4. should discourage restricting access to records except for essential reasons of legality, privacy, or confidentiality; and must apply any such restrictions without preference or bias;
5. should protect the privacy of donors, users, and individuals who are the subject of records, and observe all legitimate access restrictions;
6. may never personally profit from privileged information in their records;
7. should use impartial judgment, rather than personal beliefs or biases, when appraising records;
8. should not publicly disparage their colleagues or other archival institutions;
9. should not personally collect manuscripts or archival records in competition with their employers; nor appraise the fiscal value of materials donated to their own institutions;
10. should use their specialized knowledge and expertise for the benefit of society.[11]

These ethical principles outline the archivist's traditional obligations. Foremost among these is the responsibility to protect the integrity of records and to ensure their preservation. The archivist also has to balance responsibility to the records creators and donors, on one hand, and researchers, on the other. In addition, the archivist bears obligations to the parent institution and to the general benefit of society.

THE LIMITATIONS OF ETHICS CODES

Ethical concerns for archivists sometimes have easy answers, but more often require sensitivity to multiple perspectives and balancing of divergent interests. The policies and interests of the larger institutions which archives serve also have to be taken into account. At times the institution's needs will dictate actions that either donors, researchers, or other parties might find unsatisfactory. Above all, however, archivists and those responsible for manuscripts and archival collections should remember their professional obligations to behave ethically in their dealings with all parties. A professional archivist is an ethical archivist.

Access to records can have important political consequences. The archivist plays an essential role in mediating conflicting interests of researchers, donors, and third parties. This is not a passive or neutral position. However, paying close attention to professional ethics can prepare archivists to be "uniquely qualified to balance competing demands for open access and for protection of confidential information."[12] This is a responsibility of profound professional significance. It requires a clear understanding of archival ethics.

Unfortunately, formal codes of ethics do not always provide such clarity for archivists. By emphasizing abstract concepts with little context for analysis, such ethics codes can be interpreted in numerous ways and often provide only the vaguest sort of guidance for archival practitioners. Having examined professional codes of ethics in light of his experiences during and after the apartheid regime in South Africa, Verne Harris concluded that archivists "construct codes of conduct that define their core principles as a defense against the dynamics of power and authority, which is precisely why most professional codes of conduct are entirely useless." Such codes carefully avoid political contexts, which Harris insists must be addressed, because "the making of principle, the defining of ethics, happens in the crucible where principle and power engage, fast and loose, low down and dirty, sublimely and ridiculously." Instead of codifying theory and principle, archivists should be articulating praxis, the combination of theory and practice. Rather than avoid politics, they should ask, "What should our politics be?"[13] Harris contends that ethics codes do not help when applied in practice because they "define tension rather than suggesting an appropriate way of resolving it."[14] Ultimately, he argues, professional ethics must yield to individual values. "There is no knowing of right without giving account to personal morality," he declares. "For each of us has the right, and the obligation, to be true to ourselves."[15]

For the archivist who responds to the call of justice, however, a professional code of ethics may interfere with this obligation to personal morality. According to Norwegian archivist Gudmund Valderhaug, "The archivist may have to respond to the challenges of justice (both as fulfillment of the democratic right to access and the rectifying of former injustice) more or less on a daily basis." The International Council on Archives (ICA) Code of Ethics states that archivists "should offer impartial advice to all, and employ available resources to provide a balanced range of services." Given inequities in who typically benefits from archival services, Valderhaug argues that in such circumstances "the Code of Ethics could be an obstacle to social justice and democratic access to records."[16] In such circumstances, archivists would have to choose between personal values and professional obligations, as defined by consensus-seeking associations. Another problem with ethics codes, archivist David Wallace argues, is that they "largely provide a bureaucratic insular view of our social responsibilities through their focus on procedure and policy and 'professionalism' at the expense of a broader moral calling."[17] The 2005 SAA Code of Ethics, for example, presents the law as an unquestioned social value, stating: "Archivists must uphold all federal, state, and local laws."[18] As Wallace contends, the law can sometimes be a force used to oppress people, to reinforce existing power relationships, with "absolutely no bearing to morality or justice."[19]

These tensions between professional ethics and the competing demands of personal morality and the law have led some archivists to advocate a new conceptualization of archival ethics. David Wallace calls for a code of ethics "based more affirmatively on human morality as our core professional value, and not on what we do and do not do to records from a professional practice orientation or the paramount adherence to the law."[20] Part of the difficulty arises from the contradictions between professional codes, which, according to

Toon van Meijl, depict morality as "non-ambivalent and universal," and the insights of postmodernism, which assumes that morality is "essentially ambivalent and not universalizable." Professionals may be tempted to substitute professional ethics codes for the "moral self."[21] Karl Popper contended that ethics codes provide a form of escape from moral responsibilities, and thus destroy "all personal responsibility and therefore all ethics."[22] Furthermore, according to Peta Bowden and Anne Surma, ethics codes diminish the value of contextuality, and their "determinacy, uniformity, externality and authority" leave no room for consideration of multiple points of view, motivations, or outcomes. Codes can only become meaningful when they "invite interpretation, debate, and discussion . . . in relation to ethics and specific ethical conduct."[23] These limitations of codes of ethics in other professions raise serious concerns for archivists. Awareness of the tools of entrenched power—the controlling mechanisms of those creating and enforcing disciplinary (in both senses of the word) standards—lead many archivists to question codes of ethics and to seek a more open and inviting sense of moral discourse in the profession.

Archival ethics codes thus provide only limited guidance for archival praxis and may inhibit actions to ensure a fully representative and diverse approach to documentation, interpretation, and access to archives. Perhaps more significantly, such codes offer virtually no useful perspectives on the nature of the archival enterprise for those outside the profession. As archivists continue to seek ways to secure broader public understanding of archival programs and services, such internal standards fail to communicate archival perspectives to the rest of society. "Most of the codes fall short when it comes to strengthening public confidence in the profession," Glenn Dingwall concludes.[24] This is a missed opportunity.

A strong professional code of archival ethics could explain the principles that govern archivists' behavior and practice. It could help bridge the gap between the archival profession and the public it strives to serve. As Dingwall argues, professional associations must acknowledge that the public—particularly the "resource allocators" who control funding for archival programs—is one of the primary audiences for their codes of ethics. In making such connections between archivists and society, archival codes of ethics should place greater emphasis on particular categories of actions taken by archivists and on their desired outcomes. Dingwall contrasts this narrow (deontological) statement in the Association of Canadian Archivists code—"Archivists endeavour to protect the intellectual and physical

integrity of the records in their care"—with the more explanatory
(teleological) statement in the ICA code—"Archivists should protect
the integrity of archival material and thus guarantee that it continues
to be reliable evidence of the past."[25] The latter goes beyond a merely
prescriptive injunction of the actions archivists should take to explain
the motive behind such action and the benefits society reaps from
archival actions. In order to make ethics codes accessible to the public,
archivists should incorporate more teleological language to highlight
the consequences they are trying to achieve on behalf of societal
interests. In this way, ethics codes can indicate the moral reasoning
that underlies archival activities and relate such concepts to specific
dilemmas that occur in the workplace. This will not resolve moral
dilemmas, but it will establish a solid basis for individuals to make
ethical choices and to explain the resulting decisions to the rest of
society.[26]

AN ETHICAL IMPERATIVE FOR ARCHIVISTS

Recognizing the distinction between objectivity and neutrality
permits an archivist to engage in moral or political advocacy
without sacrificing his or her professional standards.
However, in promoting accountability and social justice, for
example, archivists should consider developing the framework for
what James O'Toole calls "a moral theology of archives": "When
archivists appraise and acquire records, when they represent them
in various descriptive media, when they make them available for use,
they are engaging in activities that have moral significance beyond
the immediate concerns of managing forms of information,"
O'Toole argues. These archival responsibilities suggest "how a
concern for historical accountability is a part of the archival mission,
a way of elaborating a practical moral theology of archives."[27] Such
a moral vision goes beyond the limited perspective of professional
ethics, but it reaffirms rather than overturns professional principles.
Commitment to honesty, fairness, and truth provides the necessary
grounding in "objectivity." As the postmodernists remind us,
however, these virtues are not absolute, but are contingent and
contested. Even with such cautions archivists can proceed to engage
the public discourse on concerns arising from their professional
responsibilities.

These considerations resonate with the classical concerns of ethics,
and with current debates in such related fields as anthropology.
As van Meijl indicates, the postmodernist perspective toward
anthropology addresses issues of "human rights, social justice, and
tolerance," all topics that have engaged ethicists and philosophers

for millennia.[28] The postmodernist rejection of absolutes and universals is not the first such break with the past, but it signals a shift from traditional efforts to identify universal laws of ethics. Similarly, Ian Harper and Alberto Jiménez call their fellow anthropologists to "embrace broader contemporary issues" more deeply and to recognize that their work is "entangled in complex institutional and political structures." They call anthropologists to be aware of the political conditions under which their knowledge is produced and to embrace ethical uncertainty.[29]

Once professionals engage in political and public policy debates, of course, there is the possibility that ethical arguments can be used to justify authoritarian regimes. This occurred most notably in Nazi Germany, which used the language of ethics to justify social engineering and centralized political power, and in South Africa under apartheid. "The possibility of ethics being used for reactionary, coercive and authoritarian social purposes is real," warns Noel Preston. "Ethics as philosophical reflection is never enough but must interact with a realistic and accurate interpretation of social conditions and the prospects for their transformation."[30] Yet Preston argues that "sound social analysis" can support concerns for social justice and "widen the agenda from process to policy, from the micro to the macro, from parochial interests to social responsibility."[31] Arguing that ethical codes remain inadequate for addressing such concerns, van Meijl states that anthropologists should make a "moral appeal to justice and righteousness" by re-privileging the moral self over a retreat to codes of conduct. This would return the profession to "premodern ethics in which politics and justice were intrinsically interwoven."[32] Taking such steps requires recognition of the significance of context and acceptance of ambiguity. These perspectives from anthropology provide valuable insights for archivists, who contend with similar demands and pressures.

Archives bring critical resources of information, evidence, and identity to members of society, both individually and collectively. In order for such benefits to become available to all citizens there must be adequate representation of their needs, interests, and perspectives in the institutions of societal documentation. "Archives are about memory, continuity, linkages, community, heritage, humanity—about allowing the solace of remembering and the balm of forgetting to move the spirit, to open us evermore sensitively to the possibilities of justice," Terry Cook asserts. "This is not politics as in left wing or right wing, liberal or conservative, Republican or Democrat, but politics as engagement, as committing the archives to societal interventions for justice rather than curatorial passivity under the guise (and illusion) of professional neutrality."[33] Engagement in public policy issues does not liberate the archivist to assert her (or his) personal preferences, but to ensure that as many people as possible find a home—a voice—in the archival records. "The archivist cannot remain isolated in the ivory tower, but must engage in new social circumstances," asserts Gudmund Valderhaug. "Confronted with people who are seeking justice, it is impossible to remain neutral."[34] Following the traditional praxis that focuses attention on the records may "contribute to the continuation of injustice," Valderhaug cautions, whereas responding to the needs of victims of oppression or others marginalized by dominant power structures enables the archivist to be "an instrument of justice."[35] Such responses come from an acceptance of archival ethics rooted in personal morality rather than in legalistic codes that support the status quo.

This ethical imperative, if accepted, challenges archivists to engage in public policy and even in the political debates that continually swirl about them. It does not replace professional responsibilities, but places them in a public context. All actions taken by archivists arise from social pressures and assumptions of one kind or another. How archivists respond has—always has had—repercussions within the societal context, and for future generations. Verne Harris provides valuable suggestions for wrestling with the difficult task of articulating an activist role within the constraints of professional obligations. "There is no knowing of right without giving account to personal morality," he declares. None of us can be truly impartial. "The most we can do is ensure that in making difficult decisions we have done so in an appropriate way," Harris states. This includes understanding "the web of rights" for all parties, "weighing competing claims" within specific circumstances, testing the archivist's "views and feelings with respected colleagues and friends," and "finally, paying heed to one's conscience." Harris cautions:

> If we follow conscience without taking the first three steps, we abandon accountability and risk assuming godlike powers. If we ignore conscience and rely only on the exercise of reason, we deny our humanity and seek to avoid bearing the burden of choice. It is only when we embrace all four elements that we can feel confident about having fulfilled the responsibilities invested in us as professionals.[36]

Harris concedes the dangers of abandoning the archivist's image as a neutral party in ideological or political contexts. "Give up on the notion of the archivist as impartial custodian, as honest broker, and one opens the door to activist archivists pursuing any and every political agenda," Harris warns.[37]

However, the "greater danger" is that in claiming an impartiality that is impossible to achieve archivists will become "pawns in bigger power plays." Challenging those in power carries risks. "To access resources, to secure the status we need, to do what we have to do effectively, we are forced to adopt neat theorizing to a greater or lesser degree," Harris concedes. "My call is simply to remember this. . . . Knowledge is always contingent, always standing above an abyss."[38] It is impossible to escape the context in which we live or the societal structures constraining us. "Archivists cannot avoid complicity," Harris acknowledges. "But we can work against the pull; and for me it is a moral imperative to do so."[39] Archivists always act within a political context, buffeted by the (often unseen) dynamics of power and authority. "The professional acts ethically not when he or she keeps politics at bay, but when he or she finds a just politics in action," Harris contends.[40] The challenge facing archivists—and anyone else weighing the competing demands of morality, politics, professional standards, and funding imperatives—is to articulate a vision that balances these considerations. In doing so, archivists need to heed the call to honesty, fairness, accountability, justice, and transparency in their professional practice.

The hope is that considering such matters openly and mindfully will engage archivists in deeper consideration of *why* they do things in particular ways. This discussion will take archivists, for a time, away from the *what* and *how* of professional praxis in order to envision the ultimate goals and societal benefits of the archival enterprise. In doing so, archivists can consider the fundamental purposes and implications of their professional work. A commitment to ethical practice might lead to a reinvigorated role in modern society.

NATIVE AMERICAN PROTOCOLS: A TEST OF ARCHIVAL ETHICS

The archival profession is currently being challenged to modify its traditional theory and practice to accommodate ethical considerations being raised by Native American peoples. From the first onslaught of Euro-Americans seeking to explore, then colonize, and finally usurp control over the North American landscape, Indians have faced exclusion, annihilation, and discrimination. As with other colonized peoples, they have lost significant portions of their history, culture, and collective memory. These oral tradition cultures produced few written records, and anthropologists, ethnographers, the Bureau of Indian Affairs, and other federal and state agencies have long controlled the archival documentation of their heritage. As William T. Hagan declared in 1978, "to be an Indian is having non-Indians control the documents from which other non-Indians write their version of your history."[41]

In the late 1960s, the rise of Native American consciousness, led by the American Indian Movement, led to demands for regaining control over their heritage, including archival materials. Laws such as the Native American Graves Protection and Repatriation Act (NAGPRA) led to return and restoration of many Indian artifacts and human remains. This significant change in museum practices set a precedent that archives have been slow to follow, despite scattered appeals to apply the concepts of NAGPRA to archival materials.[42] In 2005 the Society of American Archivists secured grant funding to pay for twenty-five Native American archivists and curators to attend the SAA annual meeting and participate in a seminar on tribal archives. This led directly to creating a Native American Archives Roundtable in SAA, with the following mission: "To serve as a forum to educate archivists on the complexities and beauty of Native American archives of the western hemisphere and as a source of communication and inspiration for archivists working with Native American collections."[43]

In April 2006 the First Archivists Circle, an independent group of archivists, librarians, museum curators, historians, and anthropologists representing fifteen Native American, First Nation, and Aboriginal communities—as well as some non-Native Americans—met "to identify best professional practices for culturally responsive care and use of American Indian archival material held by non-tribal organizations."[44] Using the *Aboriginal and Torres Strait Islander Protocols*[45] as a model, this group prepared a document entitled *Protocols for Native American Archival Materials,* which the Native American Archives Roundtable later asked the Society of American Archivists to endorse. Based on the concept that "Native American communities have primary rights for all culturally sensitive materials that are culturally affiliated with them," the *Protocols* call on libraries, archives, museums, and other collecting institutions to "develop new models for shared stewardship and reciprocity" for Native American archival materials.[46] Some of the proposals have become controversial, such as the call to respect Native American principles and practices regarding restricting access to certain aspects of cultural knowledge, the "community ownership of original source information," and the declaration that in matters of ownership and access "the rights of a Native American community must take precedence." In addition to access and use restrictions, the *Protocols* request: repatriation of some Native materials acquired by non-Native repositories; obtaining clearance from Native American communities before permitting access to sensitive materials; adding explanations or removing "offensive terms" from original titles and archival descriptions; and providing culturally sensitive reference service for Native American users of archives.[47]

The SAA Council has reviewed the *Protocols* and, although not endorsing the document, concluded that it offers "the archives profession the chance to examine its practices in light of a new global effort on the part of native populations to reclaim certain ethical and legal rights over property," and to establish new ways to develop relationships between cultural and scholarly communities, according to former SAA president Mark Greene. Greene adds, "the *Protocols* challenge not only traditional archival practice but the heuristics on which it is built. The *Protocols* raise such questions as whether traditional Western norms of study and knowledge are the only legitimate ones."[48] Created by SAA Council in August 2008, a Native American Protocols Forum Working Group, in cooperation with SAA's Diversity Committee, will hold open membership forums at the 2009, 2010, and 2011 SAA annual meetings to create a formal structure through which SAA members can express thoughts and share opinions about the *Protocols.* This honors the request of the Native American Archives Roundtable for a formal discussion of the *Protocols* within SAA, creates a process for educating members about the document and fostering discussion of that document, and establishes a mechanism for sharing the discussion throughout the profession.[49]

The debate on the *Protocols* reflects the controversy inspired by challenges to traditional practices, institutional authority (both of archival repositories and of the SAA as a standard-setting body), and alternative approaches to archival ethics. The *Protocols* specifically call for recognition of a community's moral right to control its own records, documentation, cultural knowledge, and values. Some archivists have objected that the *Protocols for Native American Archival Materials* privilege Indian interests over all others, and that they call for sweeping changes in traditional archival concepts such as public access to records. In one of the most extensive written critiques of the *Protocols,* archivist John Bolcer of the University of Washington raises important concerns. Bolcer points out that the *Protocols* call for non-tribal repositories to conduct extensive procedural operations for their holdings of Indian materials. He estimates that this would require at least one full-time staff member dedicated to responding to these guidelines. Instead of guidelines "for how non-tribal archivists could be culturally responsive to Native American communities," Bolcer argues, the *Protocols* demand that they "operate as though they were agencies or extensions of Native American governments." Bolcer also objects to "the automatic privileging of Native American interests and concerns" over those of other constituencies and stakeholders to whom archivists remain accountable. Bolcer finds the sweeping demands of the *Protocols* "incompatible with our basic professional tenets of open and equitable access to information." Beyond such disagreements with many provisions, Bolcer states that he is "solidly behind" many other concerns, including the concept of "informed and culturally respectful description of culturally affiliated collections in non-tribal archives." He remains open to revisions that could be implemented by non-tribal archivists while still meeting the underlying needs and concerns of Native American communities.[50]

These are significant concerns, both because the *Protocols for Native American Archival Materials* call into question centuries of interaction between Euro-Americans and Indians and because they challenge some central Euro-American archival principles. Yet it is important to recognize that many of these archival values derive from western European traditions that privilege the rights of mainstream culture, values, and practices. American privacy laws already prevent disclosure of personal and institutional information such as Social Security numbers, medical records, student grades, national security information, and business trade secrets. Accepting the *Protocols* would simply recognize the right of Native peoples to control their own records, customs, and cultural practices. It would acknowledge that concepts such as secret information, accessible only to certain members of the community, derive in part from oral traditions and culture.

Archivists should recognize and accept these rights of Native peoples. They should display cultural sensitivity for people from a different tradition. At the very least, archivists should open their minds to these non-western concepts of community, knowledge, access, and identity. Welcoming "the stranger" into the archives—providing the "hospitality" called for by Jacques Derrida and Verne Harris—may require new interpretations of traditional archival concepts and perspectives. Although archivists should uphold their professional principles and practices, as an important component in exercising both conceptual and procedural objectivity (not to be confused with neutrality in values), they need to recognize the cultural boundaries of peoples from different traditions. Insisting on rigid application of western concepts such as provenance and even equal access to cultural information reflects a persistent mentality of the colonizers and conquerors. The current debate over the *Protocols for Native American Archival Materials* represents a complex situation that poses a significant test for the archival profession's tolerance, openness, and acceptance of Native people's rights. This is one instance in which professional archivists need to step back and consider documentation issues from a different cultural perspective. There may be room for some compromises over specific language, but archivists concerned about the ethical dimensions of their professional principles should support the essence of the *Protocols.*

TOWARD AN ETHICS OF SOCIAL JUSTICE

Archivists can perform only a limited range of actions to further the goals of social justice, diversity, accountability, and public service. They cannot achieve these goals or even make significant differences through their own efforts. With a commitment to ethical behavior and purposeful action, however, they can contribute to broader societal interests. Some progress can already be seen in the establishment of human rights archives in the United States and several other countries. Writing about the human rights movement in Chile, Louis Bickford, director of the International Center for Transitional Justice, declares: "By creating human rights archives, [human rights] activists suggest that they can help construct a narrative of the past which gives adequate emphasis to the pain and suffering of victims of human rights abuses. Archives are thus seen as both an activist tool (i.e., because they contain *living* documents: documents that are still relevant to the pursuit of justice) but also as a source of ammunition on a broader and more complex battlefield: the battlefield of historical memory."[51] Grace Lile, archivist for the human rights organization WITNESS, states, "Archives have an important role to play here too, by insuring accurate documentation that will stand up to scrutiny in future contexts, by being advocates for ethical and judicious use of images by their users, by forging strategic alliances and sharing resources, by being diligent preservationists, and by providing access as broadly as ethics, security, and resources allow."[52] Likewise, even archivists in repositories less fully dedicated to a social action agenda can contribute to these goals of inclusiveness, accountability, access, diversity, and social justice. It is an ethical choice that each individual can make, based on personal values, institutional constraints, and willingness to take risks.

Commitment to diversity and inclusiveness must have an international perspective in order to be effective. For example, the British Library has launched an Endangered Archives Program. According to its director, Graham Shaw, "The Program has two principal objectives: to contribute to the preservation of mankind's documentary heritage particularly in those less well-developed regions of the world where collections may be more at risk and where the availability of funding may be limited; and to help foster professional standards in cataloguing, preservation, etc. and so assist in safeguarding the longer term availability and accessibility of heritage collections worldwide." Shaw quotes the UNESCO Memory of the World initiative statement to explain the importance of such efforts: "Documentary heritage reflects the diversity of languages, peoples, and cultures. It is the mirror of the world and its memory, but this memory is fragile. Every day, irreplaceable parts of this memory disappear forever."[53] These concerns are fundamental for archivists as they strive to serve the best interests of all groups in society.

The quest for professional objectivity in meeting these goals will not be easy. Archivists cannot follow a simple recipe to achieve broad documentation of society as their contribution to justice, diversity, and the public good. One example from the field of law illustrates the theoretical and practical challenges facing archivists. Feminist legal scholar Robin West proposed a list of virtues of the "ideal judge," including such characteristics as "a commitment to justice and the social good" and "a heightened sensitivity to the plight of others, particularly the silenced, the outsider, and the subordinate."[54] These traits might also meet criteria for the type of ethical archivist proposed above. Yet even such virtues as these would not guarantee the results West desired, according to Barbara Herrnstein Smith, since any general principle necessarily leaves "the specific determination of justice contingent and contestable." As Smith argues, "the idea of objectively good judgments, as distinct from judgments that are good under certain (ranges of) conditions and good from the perspectives of certain (sets of) people, is fundamentally untenable." However, Smith contends that "the alternative to the dream of objective judgment is not pessimism, cynicism, or torpor but attentiveness, responsiveness, and activity, both intellectual and pragmatic."[55] Ultimately, judges, archivists, and others must continuously work out for themselves how to make the best decisions they can. This offers the best hope we have. Creating a formula or recipe for success would simply invoke a new ("improved") orthodoxy to replace one that has been discredited.

By opening a dialogue concerning their ethical responsibilities, archivists can begin to ask fundamentally important questions about the nature of their professional work, their service to diverse constituencies and stakeholders, and their role in society.

The 2005 Johannesburg colloquium generated ongoing discussions of archival ethics, constructing memory, and promoting social justice. A series of public meetings focused on issues of archival ethics in relation to social constructs including memory, justice, and accountability. Prominent organizers and speakers at these meetings included Verne Harris of the Nelson Mandela Foundation, and two keynote presenters from the Johannesburg colloquium, David Wallace of the University of Michigan and Gudmund Valderhaug of the Norwegian Archive, Library and Museum Authority. In February 2006, Valderhaug organized the "Arkiv, Demokrati Og Rettferd" (Archives, Justice, and Democracy) Conference, sponsored by the Norwegian Archive, Library, and Museum Authority, in Oslo, Norway.

Having examined the themes of archives, memory, and justice in South Africa and Norway, the discourse moved next to the United States. The annual meeting of the Society of American Archivists in Washington, DC, in August 2006, included a seminar, "Archives for Justice," featuring Harris, Valderhaug, Wallace, and Anthea Josias, another South African presenter at the Johannesburg conference. In November 2007 Amy Cooper Cary of the University of Wisconsin–Milwaukee (UWM) hosted a one-day conference, "Archives and Ethics: Reflections on Practice," focusing on: "[s]uch significant ethical issues as social justice, ownership of records, representation in the historical record, accountability, and privacy"; the role of archives as "a particular representation of memory, of voice, and of story"; and "ethical questions revolving around the stewardship of the archival record, and the ownership of image and voice."[56] This conference featured three speakers: Harris, Wallace, and Menzi Behrnd-Klodt, co-editor of *Privacy and Confidentiality Perspectives*.[57] Explaining why the UWM School of Information Studies agreed to host this meeting, Dean Johannes Britz stated, "Budgets, digitization, and other practical things facing archives are important, but underlying everything is ethics."[58] This recognition suggests the beginning of a potentially significant shift of focus from archival techniques to concerns for professional mission and ethics.

The next major venue for this series of discussions included
speakers from the fields of law, sociology, genealogy, libraries,
and museums, as well as archives. David Wallace, Anthea Josias,
and Julie Herrada, archivist of the University of Michigan Labadie
Collection, organized another conference, "Interdisciplinary
Perspectives on Archives and the Ethics of Memory Construction,"
held in Ann Arbor, Michigan on May 2-3, 2008. As the conference
announcement states, "Despite claims to impartiality, archival
responsibilities are increasingly being seen as having broader
social significances beyond records curation and management of
the institutions where they are kept."[59] The conference brought
together interdisciplinary and international perspectives on these
issues. Verne Harris and Gudmund Valderhaug spoke about archival
perspectives on ethics and memory. Other speakers examined
attempts to conceal evidence of the 1915 Armenian genocide in
Turkey, challenges in conducting research in Native American
documents, collecting prisoner memories from the apartheid-
era prison on Robben Island (where Nelson Mandela had been
confined), efforts to resurface the repressed and "forgotten" historic
"yellow peril" archive, and the influence of "Japan-bashing" in the
murder of Chinese-American Vincent Chin in 1982, during the
crisis affecting the Detroit automobile industry.[60] The Ann Arbor
conference provided an important opportunity to engage these
issues with the perspectives of several disciplines and participants
from Europe, South Africa, the Middle East, and the United States.

These examinations of archival ethics have prompted SAA's
Committee on Ethics and Professional Conduct (CEPC) to launch
an initiative to engage all archivists in discussing the intersection
of archival ethics and social justice. At the request of CEPC, SAA
held a Global Issues Forum at its August 2008 annual meeting in
San Francisco. Under the title, "Archival Ethics and Social Justice:
What Is Our Professional Responsibility?" this open forum began by
considering the "Key Propositions and Questions" adopted by the
2005 Johannesburg colloquium. The forum raised these questions:
"What does 'archival ethics' mean in a society beset by challenges
to public accountability, questioning of collective memory and
national/group identity, threats to social justice, and uncertainty
about social diversity and forgotten voices in the archival record?
Do archival ethics require engagement in these processes? What
would this mean for governmental, religious, university, nonprofit,
or business archives? Even if we could define a 'social justice
ethic,' should we? What are the implications of these issues for our
professional identity?" Panelists David Wallace, Anthea Josias, and

Tywanna Whorley, Assistant Professor of Library and Information Science at Simmons College, conducted a lively discussion with more than two hundred audience members. CEPC has recommended ongoing public discussions of these ethical concerns.

The current SAA Code of Ethics represents a substantial revision of the previous code adopted in 1992. To avoid legal limitations posed by the explanatory "Commentary" of previous codes, it omits examples of situations in which ethical precepts were explained in previous codes. The Code of Ethics is thus more aspirational and general, focusing primarily on deontological statements and providing a broad framework for addressing ethical dilemmas within the archival community. In early 2009 CEPC began a review of the SAA Code of Ethics to see what recommendations could be made to strengthen, clarify, or revise its provisions.

Loosely related to the concept of ethics is the idea of values. What essential values do archivists support, endorse, embody, and exemplify? Mark Greene devoted his August 2008 SAA presidential address to considering these questions. His initial suggestions included ten key concepts: professionalism, collectivity, activism, selection, preservation, democracy, service, diversity, use and access, and history.[61] These values suggest important themes in the postmodern world. Greene prepared his list of values as a starting point for discussion, not a final set of criteria. In February 2009, SAA Council established a task force to develop a statement of fundamental archival values. The discussion likely to ensue in this process should help to clarify what archivists—as professionals—consider important about their perspective on society and its needs.

Responding effectively to the challenges of using the power of archives for the public good will require a broad commitment by the archival profession to reflect on underlying assumptions and biases, and to overcome these through a renewed commitment to democratic values. There are risks involved in such changes. It will be difficult to commit archivists and their profession to a more inclusive view of social responsibilities. But the stakes are too high not to accept these challenges. Historical examples of abuses of power, control through manipulation of the archival record, and efforts to limit access to vital information show the dangers of misusing the power of archives and records. Archivists should commit themselves to preventing the archival profession's explicit or implicit support of privileged elites and powerful rulers at the expense of the people's rights and interests. They should commit themselves to the values of public accountability, open government, cultural diversity, and social justice. Then archivists can truly say that they are ensuring archives for all, and employing their professional skills to promote a better society. This will be a valuable application of archives power to secure memory, accountability, and social justice.

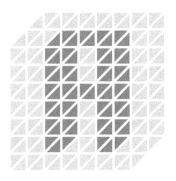

Appendix

Many of the themes, perspectives, and questions examined in *Archives Power* can be discerned in the report of a colloquium sponsored by the Nelson Mandela Foundation in Johannesburg, South Africa, in August 2005. Although addressed most directly in the conclusion to this volume, the report, "Memory for Justice: Report on a Colloquium," provides useful context for the discussion of issues in chapters 3 through 6 of *Archives Power*. The "Key Propositions and Questions" listed here provide an invaluable starting point for the ongoing discussion of memory, accountability, and social justice, in the context of archival ethics. I am grateful to Verne Harris for securing permission to reproduce the "Memory for Justice" report in this appendix. (Note: The report's "Appendix 1" and "Appendix 2" are not included here.)

NELSON MANDELA
FOUNDATION

Living the Legacy

MEMORY FOR JUSTICE

REPORT ON A COLLOQUIUM

18 August 2005

The event

On 18 August 2005 the Nelson Mandela Foundation hosted a colloquium dedicated to exploring the theme of "Memory for Justice". Nearly 100 participants representing more than 30 institutions attended (see Appendix 1). Colloquium activities were grouped around four sessions (see Appendix 2):

- Introduction by Nkosinathi Biko (Founder and Executive Director of the Steve Biko Foundation). Mr. Biko's presentation focused on memory as a powerful catalyst for social change.
- Keynote session addresses by international speakers David A. Wallace (Visiting Assistant Professor, Catholic University of America) and Gudmund Valderhaug (Director of Strategy and Planning, Norwegian Archive, Library and Museum Authority). Dr. Wallace's address focused on the role of archivists in striving for historical and contemporary justice. Mr. Valderhaug's address focused on the social power exercised by archivists, and identified systemic shortcomings in archival user services.
- Panel discussion on the South African terrain, which examined South African experiences of memory construction in the wake of the apartheid era. The panel was chaired by Sibongiseni Mkhize (Director, Market Theatre) and comprised five South Africans:
  - Graham Dominy (National Archivist, National Archives of South Africa);
  - Sello Hatang (Director, Promotion of Access to Information Act Unit, Human Rights Commission);

Founder : Mr N R Mandela   Chairperson : Professor G J Gerwel   Chief Executive : Mr Achmat Dangor

IT Number : 9259/99   PBO Number : 034-681-NPO   Vat Number : 4590213601
PRIVATE BAG X70 000, HOUGHTON, 2041, SOUTH AFRICA
Tel +27 11 728 1000   Fax +27 728 1111
Website : www.nelsonmandela.org

- o Anthea Josias (Senior Project Officer, Centre of Memory and Commemoration, Nelson Mandela Foundation);
- o Khwezi ka Mpumlwana (Director, Nelson Mandela Museum); and
- o Neo Lekgotla laga Ramoupi (Researcher, South African Research and Archival Project, Howard University).
- General discussion led by Ciraj Rassool (Associate Professor, History Department, University of the Western Cape) and the two international speakers.

A key goal of the colloquium's organizers was to ensure a productive balance between formal presentations and open discussion. From this dialogue *emerged key propositions and questions*, for institutions, for practitioners, and for society as a whole. These are detailed below. No attempt has been made to prioritize these propositions or to resolve any tensions or contradictions that may exist between them. References to specific sites and cases have been excluded in favor of propositions carrying general application.

Key Propositions and Questions

Archives and Other Memory Institutions

- The archive must be understood as a social resource that reaches across conventional disciplinary boundaries.

- The archive is a site of ambiguity. It is best understood as a contested terrain for memory construction that in turn shapes contemporary understandings of society.

- Current political landscapes always play a formative role in shaping archives, both in their scope and content, as well as access to them.

- The challenge faced by those who maintain memory institutions is, fundamentally, a structural challenge. Structures of power design, shape, consign and represent the archive. The justice potential of the archive must be identified and fought for in these contexts.

- There are limitations to a document-focused orientation for engaging and understanding the archive. The role and work of documents is one dimension within broader societal memory processes. A wider frame of reference and utilization of resources is necessary.

- Justice as a concept needs to be examined in the context of dissimilar traditions, cultures, and epistemologies, which often compete and contest

N E L S O N   M A N D E L A
F O U N D A T I O N

Living the Legacy

with one another for supremacy. The shaping roles played by memory institutions in these relationships must be explored.

- The dimensions of power at play in all acts of memorialization must be examined and, if necessary, confronted.

Archivists and Other Memory Practitioners

- Those who work with archive should be guided primarily by a concept of, and commitment to, justice.

- A commitment to justice must be made central to the professional education of memory practitioners.

- The "archival profession" is socially constructed, and elements of this construction favor the status quo and impose a spurious philosophy of de-politicized and objective practices and methods.

- The role and work of archivists and other memory practitioners are best understood in terms of individual, institutional, and societal power and influence. The exercise of such power and influence by those who work with the archive must be properly appreciated.

- There are always systemic barriers to participation in, and access to, the archive. Prevailing relations of power and influence in societies (even in democracies) tend to disadvantage certain voices. The call of justice sounds two imperatives: 1) to pro-actively enable participation and access; and 2) to construct the archive beyond the normative assumptions circumscribed by power and the status quo.

- The voices that are absent in the archive can often be filled by imaginative engagement with resources conventionally not regarded as archival, such as oral histories.

Founder : Mr N R Mandela   **Chairperson :** Professor G J Gerwel   **Chief Executive :** Mr Achmat Dangor

IT Number : 9259/99   **PBO Number :** 034-681-NPO   **Vat Number :** 4590213601
PRIVATE BAG X70 000, HOUGHTON, 2041, SOUTH AFRICA
Tel +27 11 728 1000   Fax +27 728 1111
Website : www.nelsonmandela.org

- Archivists and other memory practitioners are relatively weak socially and politically, thus limiting their capacities to serve justice. At the same time, these practitioners are powerful agents in the construction of the past.

- Discussion and debate around the ideas raised and addressed by this colloquium are largely and regrettably absent in professional archival forums. Their inclusion needs to be fostered and nurtured.

Society

- Injustice is routinely documented by those who perpetrate it. Such records are systematically hidden, sanitized, neglected, or destroyed. Justice requires resistance to such processes.

- The archive provides a powerful resource for restorative justice. It can be a catalyst for recognizing previously ignored injustices, as well as a tool to rectify the distortions of the past. At times, even its noted absence can be a catalyst for restoration.

- Disclosing what was hidden (and what remains secret) is but a first step. Questions remain as to how the process of disclosure – moving from not knowing to knowing – can act as the foundation for justice. What is the next step beyond creating a more accurate version of the past? And how does that - can that - shape and connect to contemporary struggles for justice?

- Memory is about the future, a future which we should be making by resisting exclusion and marginalization.

- In moving from oppression to liberation, close attention needs to be paid to the resilience of privilege and inequality.

- Democratization routinely is associated with bureaucratization. The ideals of a liberation struggle must, necessarily, be tempered by the need to manage competing priorities in contexts of limited resources.

Nelson Mandela Foundation
18 September 2005

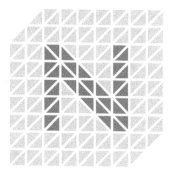

Notes

PREFACE

1. Kurt Vonnegut, *A Man Without a Country* (New York: Seven Stories Press, 2005), 56.
2. For brief glimpses of my father's civil rights work, see: Charles Morgan, Jr., *A Time to Speak* (New York: Harper and Row, 1964), 123–34; Diane McWhorter, *Coming Home: Birmingham, Alabama, The Climactic Battle of the Civil Rights Revolution* (New York: Simon and Schuster, 2001); Andrew M. Manis, *A Fire You Can't Put Out: The Civil Rights Life of Birmingham's Reverend Fred Shuttlesworth* (Tuscaloosa: University of Alabama Press, 1999); Glenn T. Eskew, *But for Birmingham: The Local and National Movements in the Civil Rights Struggle* (Chapel Hill: University of North Carolina Press, 1997). His correspondence and reports can be found in the Southern Regional Council Records at Atlanta-Clark University.
3. Portions of this book previously appeared in my articles, "Embracing the Power of Archives," *American Archivist* 69 (Spring/Summer 2006): 19–32; "Archives for All: Professional Responsibility and Social Justice," *American Archivist* 70 (Fall/Winter 2007): 252–81; "Orwell in the Archives: Memory, Records, and Politics," available at: http://www.dundee.ac.uk/archives/SUV2007/papers/jimerson_randall.htm; and "Archives and Memory," *OCLC Systems & Services* 19:3 (2003): 89–95.

INTRODUCTION

1. Eric Ketelaar, "Archival Temples, Archival Prisons: Modes of Power and Protection," *Archival Science* 2 (2002): 221-38.
2. Ann Curthoys, "The History of Killing and the Killing of History," in *Archive Stories: Facts, Fictions, and the Writing of History*, ed. Antoinette Burton (Durham, NC: Duke University Press, 2005), 369.
3. Laura Mayhall, "Creating the 'Suffragette Spirit,'" in *Archive Stories*, 232.
4. Antoinette Burton, "Introduction," in *Archive Stories*, 2.
5. Burton, in *Archive Stories*, 5.
6. Burton, in *Archive Stories*, 12.
7. Ketelaar, "Archival Temples," 234.
8. Richard Harvey Brown and Beth Davis-Brown, "The Making of Memory: The Politics of Archives, Libraries and Museums in the Construction of National Consciousness," *History of the Human Sciences* 11, no. 4 (1998): 21.
9. Quoted in Ketelaar, "Archival Temples," 233-34.
10. Eric Ketelaar, "The Panoptical Archive," in *Archives, Documentation and Institutions of Social Memory*, ed. Francis X. Blouin, Jr. and William G. Rosenberg (Ann Arbor: University of Michigan Press, 2006), 146-47.

11. Ian E. Wilson, "'The Gift of One Generation to Another': The Real Thing for the Pepsi Generation," in *Archives, Documentation and Institutions of Social Memory*, 335.

12. Lilly Koltun, "The Architecture of Archives: Whose Form, What Functions?" *Archival Science* 2 (2002): 246.

13. Richard J. Cox, *No Innocent Deposits: Forming Archives by Rethinking Appraisal* (Lanham, MD: Scarecrow Press, 2004), 40-41. Trouillot quoted on page 41.

14. David Lowenthal, "Archives, Heritage, and History," in *Archives, Documentation and Institutions of Social Memory*, 199-200.

15. Verne Harris, *Archives and Justice* (Chicago: Society of American Archivists, 2007), 102.

16. Cox, *No Innocent Deposits*, 234.

17. Elisabeth Kaplan, "We Are What We Collect, We Collect What We Are: Archives and the Construction of Identity," *American Archivist* 63 (Spring/Summer 2000): 126-51.

18. Richard White, *Remembering Ahanagran: A History of Stories* (New York: Hill and Wang, 1998), 4.

19. J. K. Rowling, *Harry Potter and the Half-Blood Prince* (New York: Scholastic, 2005), 197.

20. Luciana Duranti, "Diplomatics: New Uses for an Old Science," *Archivaria* 28 (Summer 1989): 7-27.

21. Laurent Dubois, "Maroons in the Archives: The Uses of the Past in the French Caribbean," in *Archives, Documentation and Institutions of Social Memory*, 293.

22. Ketelaar, "Archival Temples," 227.

23. Ketelaar, "The Panoptical Archive," 145.

24. A leading manual on archival security recommends that "every effort should be made to let the researchers know that they are being supervised," and "the layout of tables and chairs should provide the archivist with a clear view of all areas and researchers in the room." It also recommends installing security cameras and circular detection mirrors. Gregor Trinkaus-Randall, *Protecting Your Collections: A Manual of Archival Security* (Chicago: Society of American Archivists, 1995), 26-27.

25. Ketelaar, "Archival Temples," 234, 236.

26. Ketelaar, "The Panoptical Archive," 147.

27. Martha Cooley, *The Archivist: A Novel* (Boston: Little, Brown and Company, 1998), 246.

28. Ketelaar, "Archival Temples," 236-37.

29. These terms are used for categories of information presented in archival finding aids using XML-based Encoded Archival Description. See Daniel V. Pitti and Wendy M. Duff, eds., *Encoded Archival Description on the Internet* (New York: Haworth Press, 2002).

30. Jacques Derrida, *Archive Fever* (Chicago: University of Chicago Press, 1998), 55.

31. Derrida, *Archive Fever*, 75.

32. Francis X. Blouin, Jr. and William G. Rosenberg, "Part I: Archives and Archiving," in *Archives, Documentation and Institutions of Social Memory*, 1. The quoted phrases are the editors' summary of Steedman's remarks, not her own words.

33. Patrick Geary, "Medieval Archivists as Authors: Social Memory and Archival Memory," in *Archives, Documentation and Institutions of Social Memory*, 106.

34. Blouin and Rosenberg, "Part II: Archives in the Production of Knowledge," in *Archives, Documentation and Institutions of Social Memory*, 86.

35. Terry Cook and Joan M. Schwartz, "Archives, Records, and Power: From (Postmodern) Theory to (Archival) Performance," *Archival Science* 2 (2002): 173.

36. Cook and Schwartz, "Archives, Records, and Power," 183.

37. Harris, *Archives and Justice*, 64. The text referred to is: S. Muller, J.A. Feith, and R. Fruin, *Manual for the Arrangement and Description of Archives* (Chicago: Society of American Archivists, 2003; reprint of 1940 English translation).

38. Harris, *Archives and Justice*, 64-65.

39. Timothy L. Ericson, "At the 'rim of creative dissatisfaction': Archivists and Acquisition Development," *Archivaria* 33 (1991-1992): 66-77.

40. Frank Boles, *Archival Appraisal* (New York: Neal-Schuman, 1991); Mary Lynn McCree, "Good Sense and Good Judgment: Defining Collections and Collecting," *Drexel Library Quarterly* 11 (1975): 21-33.

41. William Saffady, *Records and Information Management: Fundamentals of Professional Practice* (Lenexa, KS: ARMA International, 2004), 45-76.

42. Repositories should not acquire manuscripts unless they have adequate staff, space, and funding to protect the materials and provide research access. Faye Phillips, "Developing Collecting Policies for Manuscript Collections," *American Archivist* 47 (1984): 30-42; Frank Boles, *Selecting and Appraising Archives and Manuscripts* (Chicago: Society of American Archivists, 2005).

43. Maynard J. Brichford, *Archives and Manuscripts: Appraisal and Accessioning* (Chicago: Society of American Archivists, 1977), 1.

44. Society of American Archivists, *Planning for the Archival Profession* (Chicago: Society of American Archivists, 1986); Richard J. Cox and Helen W. Samuels, "The Archivist's First Responsibility: A Research Agenda to Improve the Identification and Retention of Records of Enduring Value," *American Archivist* 51 (1988): 28-42.

45. Boles, *Selecting and Appraising Archives and Manuscripts*, 1-10.

46. Hilary Jenkinson, *A Manual of Archive Administration: Including the Problem of War Archives and Archive Making* (Oxford: Clarendon Press, 1922; rev. ed. 1938); Luciana Duranti, "The Concept of Appraisal and Archival Theory," *American Archivist* 57 (1994): 328-44.

47. Boles, *Selecting and Appraising Archives and Manuscripts*, 11-38.

48. S. Muller, J. A. Feith, and R. Fruin, *Manual for the Arrangement and Description of Archives*; T. R. Schellenberg, "Archival Principles of Arrangement," in Maygene F. Daniels and Timothy Walch, *A Modern Archives Reader* (Washington, DC: National Archives and Records Service, 1984), 149–161.

49. James M. O'Toole and Richard J. Cox, *Understanding Archives and Manuscripts* (Chicago: Society of American Archivists, 2006), 100–101.

50. Examples of the latter include the *National Union Catalog of Manuscript Collections*, Chadwyck-Healey's *National Inventory of Documentary Sources in the United States*, as well as electronic catalogs such as RLIN and OCLC.

51. Canadian–U.S. Task Force on Archival Description, "Statement of Principles for the CUSTARD project," Society of American Archivists website (2002), http://www.archivists.org/news/custardproject.asp (accessed 6 August 2002).

52. James Cross, "Archival Reference: State of the Art," *Reference Librarian* 56 (1997): 5-25.

53. Mary Jo Pugh, *Providing Reference Services for Archives and Manuscripts* (Chicago: Society of American Archivists, 2005), 175-208; Trinkaus-Randall, *Protecting Your Collections*, 21-28.

54. Pugh, *Providing Reference Services*, 112-32.

55. Elsie Finch, *Advocating Archives: An Introduction to Public Relations for Archivists* (Metuchen, NJ: Scarecrow Press, 1994), 1.

56. Paul Conway, "Facts and Frameworks: An Approach to Studying the Users of Archives," *American Archivist* 49 (1986): 393-407.

57. Elizabeth Yakel and Laura Bost, "Understanding Administrative Use and Users in University Archives," *American Archivist* 57 (1994): 596-615; Conway, "Facts and Frameworks."

58. Tom Ruller, "Open All Night: Using the Internet to Improve Access to Archives: A Case Study of the New York State Archives and Records Administration," *Reference Librarian* 56 (1997): 161-70.

59. For an intriguing analysis of these images see Arlene Schmuland, "The Archival Image in Fiction: An Analysis and Annotated Bibliography," *American Archivist* 62 (Spring 1999): 24-73.

60. Philip B. Eppard, "Pondering the Archival Image Thing," *American Archivist* 62 (Spring 1999): 5-6.

61. Harris, *Archives and Justice*, 270.
62. Cox, *No Innocent Deposits*, 35.
63. Harris, *Archives and Justice*, 102.
64. Carolyn Steedman, *Dust: The Archive and Cultural History* (New Brunswick, NJ: Rutgers University Press, 2002), 70, 81.
65. Steedman, *Dust*, 150.
66. David Lowenthal, *The Past Is a Foreign Country* (Cambridge: Cambridge University Press, 1985); Michael Kammen, *Mystic Chords of Memory: The Transformation of Tradition in American Culture* (New York: Alfred A. Knopf, 1991); Terry Cook, "The Archives is a Foreign Country: Historians, Archivists, and the Changing Archival Landscape" (unpublished paper provided to the author).
67. Stephen Haycox, "Rely on Documents, Not Memory," *Anchorage Daily News*, December 6, 2002.
68. David Wallace, comments during brown bag luncheon, conference on "Archives and Ethics: Reflections on Practice" (29 November 2007), videotaped presentation available at: www.uwm.edu/Dept/SOIS/cipr/archive.html.

CHAPTER 1

1. Cicero quoted in "The Society of American Archivists: Description and Brief History," http://www.archivists.org/history.asp?prnt=y (accessed 29 February 2008).
2. Bob Marley and N. G. Williams, "Buffalo Soldier" (Island Records, 1983).
3. James M. O'Toole, "Back to the Future: Ernst Posner's *Archives in the Ancient World,*" *American Archivist* 67 (Fall/Winter 2004): 163.
4. Hugh Taylor, "'My Very Act and Deed': Some Reflections on the Role of Textual Records in the Conduct of Affairs," *American Archivist* 51 (Fall 1988): 458.
5. Lionel Casson, *Libraries in the Ancient World* (New Haven: Yale University Press, 2001): 1.
6. M. T. Clanchy, *From Memory to Written Record: England, 1066-1307*, 2nd ed. (Oxford: Blackwell Publishing, 1993), 114.
7. Matthew Battles, *Library: An Unquiet History* (London: Random House Vintage, 2003), 42.
8. M. T. Clanchy, "'Tenacious Letters': Archives and Memory in the Middle Ages," *Archivaria* 11 (Winter 1980/81): 115.
9. J.N. Postgate, "Documents in Government under the Middle Assyrian Kingdom," in *Ancient Archives and Archival Traditions: Concepts of Record-Keeping in the Ancient World*, ed. Maria Brosius (Oxford: Oxford University Press, 2003), 130.
10. Lewis Carroll, *Through the Looking-Glass*, Chapter 1, Project Gutenberg Release 1.5, Millennium Fulcrum Edition, 1991, http://www.cs.indiana.edu/metastuff/looking/looking.txt.gz (accessed 29 November 2007).
11. James M. O'Toole and Richard J. Cox, *Understanding Archives and Manuscripts* (Chicago: Society of American Archivists, 2006), 4.
12. O'Toole and Cox, *Understanding Archives and Manuscripts*, 6.
13. Maria Brosius, "Ancient Archives and Concepts of Record-Keeping: An Introduction," in *Ancient Archives and Archival Traditions*, 1.
14. Nikolaus Schneider (1940), cited in Ernst Posner, *Archives in the Ancient World* (Chicago: Society of American Archivists, 2003), 13-14. However, Posner cautions (page 27) that in the ancient Orient little or no distinction was made between records and literary products or between archives and libraries as we now distinguish the two types of institutions.
15. Brosius, "Introduction," in *Ancient Archives and Archival Traditions*, 10-11.
16. Brosius, "Introduction," in *Ancient Archives and Archival Traditions*, 12.
17. Posner, *Archives in the Ancient World*, 23.
18. Battles, *Library*, 25.
19. Posner, *Archives in the Ancient World*, 29-30, 64.

20. Casson, *Libraries in the Ancient World*, 3-4.
21. Antonio Invernizzi, "They Did Not Write on Clay: Non-Cuneiform Documents and Archives in Seleucid Mesopotamia," in *Ancient Archives and Archival Traditions*, 314-15.
22. Brosius, "Introduction," in *Ancient Archives and Archival Traditions*, 5.
23. Casson, *Libraries in the Ancient World*, 2.
24. Posner, *Archives in the Ancient World*, 46-47.
25. Posner, *Archives in the Ancient World*, 66.
26. Postgate, "Documents in Government," in *Ancient Archives and Archival Traditions*, 136.
27. Heather D. Baker, "Record-Keeping Practices as Revealed by the Neo-Babylonian Private Archival Documents," in *Ancient Archives and Archival Traditions*, 242-43. Baker lists numerous types of transactions recorded on clay tablets, from promissory notes to sales of real estate, slaves, and assets; leases of houses and land; apprentice contracts and manumissions; marriage agreements and gifts, etc. (page 242).
28. Alfonso Archi, "Archival Record-Keeping at Ebla, 2400-2350 BC," in *Ancient Archives and Archival Traditions*, 17.
29. Posner, *Archives in the Ancient World*, 50. The Ebla tablets, for example, were preserved by a fire set by invaders around 2300 or 2250 BCE. See Casson, *Libraries in the Ancient World*, 3.
30. Posner, *Archives in the Ancient World*, 20.
31. Brosius, "Introduction," in *Ancient Archives and Archival Traditions*, 3.
32. Invernizzi, "They Did Not Write on Clay," in *Ancient Archives and Archival Traditions*, 302-3.
33. Posner, *Archives in the Ancient World*, 67-68.
34. Casson, *Libraries in the Ancient World*, 9-10.
35. Invernizzi, "They Did Not Write on Clay," in *Ancient Archives and Archival Traditions*, 303.
36. Brosius, "Introduction," in *Ancient Archives and Archival Traditions*, 15.
37. Posner, *Archives in the Ancient World*, 54-56.
38. Posner, *Archives in the Ancient World*, 71.
39. Posner, *Archives in the Ancient World*, 74.
40. Hermann Kees (1933), quoted in Posner, *Archives in the Ancient World*, 78.
41. Karl Wittfogel, *Oriental Despotism: A Comparative Study of Total Power* (New Haven: Yale University Press, 1957), quoted in Posner, *Archives in the Ancient World*, 79.
42. Posner, *Archives in the Ancient World*, 76-77.
43. Posner, *Archives in the Ancient World*, 84.
44. Posner, *Archives in the Ancient World*, 81-82.
45. Posner, *Archives in the Ancient World*, 84-85.
46. Battles, *Library*, 28-31.
47. Ian F. McNeely and Lisa Wolverton, *Reinventing Knowledge: From Alexandria to the Internet* (New York: W. W. Norton & Company, 2008), 17-18, 35.
48. Battles, *Library*, 32.
49. Posner, *Archives in the Ancient World*, 94.
50. Posner, *Archives in the Ancient World*, 91-93.
51. Luciana Duranti, "The Odyssey of Records Managers," in *Canadian Archival Studies and the Rediscovery of Provenance*, ed. Tom Nesmith (Metuchen, NJ: Scarecrow Press, 1993), 35.
52. On the early development of literacy see, for example, Eric Havelock, *The Literate Revolution in Greece and Its Cultural Consequences* (Princeton: Princeton University Press, 1982); Jack Goody, *The Logic of Writing and the Organization of Society* (Cambridge: Cambridge University Press, 1986); Barry B. Powell, *Homer and the Origin of the Greek Alphabet* (Cambridge: Cambridge University Press, 1991); and Walter Ong, *Orality and Literacy: The Technologizing of the Word* (London: Methuen, 1982).
53. William V. Harris, *Ancient Literacy* (Cambridge, MA: Harvard University Press, 1989), 26-27.
54. McNeely and Wolverton, *Reinventing Knowledge*, 10.

55. Rosalind Thomas, *Literacy and Orality in Ancient Greece* (Cambridge: Cambridge University Press, 1992), 3.

56. James P. Sickinger, *Public Records and Archives in Classical Athens* (Chapel Hill: University of North Carolina Press, 1999), quoted in O'Toole, "Back to the Future: Ernst Posner's *Archives in the Ancient World*," 171.

57. *The Politics of Aristotle*, ed. Sir Ernest Barker (1952), quoted in Posner, *Archives in the Ancient World*, 92.

58. Posner, *Archives in the Ancient World*, 111.

59. John K. Davies, "Greek Archives: From Record to Monument," in *Ancient Archives and Archival Traditions*, 324-27.

60. James Sickinger, "Literacy, Documents, and Archives in the Ancient Athenian Democracy," *American Archivist* 62 (Fall 1999): 232.

61. Posner, *Archives in the Ancient World*, 104-6.

62. James M. O'Toole, "Herodotus and the Written Record," *Archivaria* 33 (Winter 1991-92): 151-52.

63. Sickinger, "Literacy, Documents, and Archives in the Ancient Athenian Democracy," 238-39.

64. Posner, *Archives in the Ancient World*, 108-10.

65. Posner, *Archives in the Ancient World*, 96.

66. Posner, *Archives in the Ancient World*, 114.

67. Duranti, "Odyssey of Records Managers," in *Canadian Archival Studies and the Rediscovery of Provenance*, 35.

68. Sickinger, "Literacy, Documents, and Archives in the Ancient Athenian Democracy," 245.

69. This practice echoes in modern society, with cenotaphs and war memorials honoring the dead, most notably "The Wall," a black marble monument in Washington, DC honoring more than 58,000 Americans killed in the Vietnam War. James M. O'Toole, "Herodotus and the Written Record," 156.

70. Davies, "Greek Archives," in *Ancient Archives and Archival Traditions*, 334.

71. Sickinger, "Literacy, Documents, and Archives in the Ancient Athenian Democracy," 231-32; Posner, *Archives in the Ancient World*, 97-102.

72. Davies, "Greek Archives," in *Ancient Archives and Archival Traditions*, 336-38.

73. Posner, *Archives in the Ancient World*, 127.

74. Posner, *Archives in the Ancient World*, 162-63.

75. Posner, *Archives in the Ancient World*, 184-85.

76. Posner, *Archives in the Ancient World*, 185.

77. Posner, *Archives in the Ancient World*, 165-66.

78. Posner, *Archives in the Ancient World*, 176-80.

79. Posner, *Archives in the Ancient World*, 180-81.

80. Battles, *Library*, 49; Posner, *Archives in the Ancient World*, 182.

81. Posner, *Archives in the Ancient World*, 185-88.

82. Posner, *Archives in the Ancient World*, 222.

83. Posner, *Archives in the Ancient World*, 189-92.

84. Posner, *Archives in the Ancient World*, 186-87.

85. McNeely and Wolverton, *Reinventing Knowledge*, 52.

86. Posner, *Archives in the Ancient World*, 198-99.

87. Battles, *Library*, 53-54.

88. Posner, *Archives in the Ancient World*, 213-15.

89. Posner, *Archives in the Ancient World*, 220-21.

90. Duranti, "Odyssey of Records Managers," in *Canadian Archival Studies and the Rediscovery of Provenance*, 42.

91. Battles, *Library*, 57.

92. Battles, *Library*, 61, 64-65; McNeely and Wolverton, *Reinventing Knowledge*, 32-33.
93. McNeely and Wolverton, *Reinventing Knowledge*, 111-13.
94. Posner, *Archives in the Ancient World*, 230.
95. Posner, *Archives in the Ancient World*, 230.
96. Rosamond McKitterick, *The Carolingians and the Written Word* (Cambridge: Cambridge University Press, 1989), 1-4.
97. McKitterick, *The Carolingians and the Written Word*, 36.
98. McKitterick, *The Carolingians and the Written Word*, 23.
99. McKitterick, *The Carolingians and the Written Word*, 60-66.
100. Taylor, "'My Very Act and Deed,'" 459.
101. McKitterick, *The Carolingians and the Written Word*, 77.
102. McKitterick, *The Carolingians and the Written Word*, 74-75.
103. McKitterick, *The Carolingians and the Written Word*, 82, 89.
104. McKitterick, *The Carolingians and the Written Word*, 125-27.
105. McKitterick, *The Carolingians and the Written Word*, 165.
106. McKitterick, *The Carolingians and the Written Word*, 196.
107. McKitterick, *The Carolingians and the Written Word*, 182.
108. McKitterick, *The Carolingians and the Written Word*, 209-10.
109. McKitterick, *The Carolingians and the Written Word*, 150-51.
110. McKitterick, *The Carolingians and the Written Word*, 222, 227.
111. McKitterick, *The Carolingians and the Written Word*, 272-73.
112. Michael T. Clanchy, *From Memory to Written Record* (Oxford: Blackwell Publishers, 1993), 3, 296 (quoted passages found on page 3).
113. Clanchy, *From Memory to Written Record*, 253-54.
114. Clanchy, *From Memory to Written Record*, 261-62.
115. Clanchy, *From Memory to Written Record*, 1.
116. Clanchy, *From Memory to Written Record*, 247.
117. Clanchy, *From Memory to Written Record*, 29. Bracketed insert in original.
118. Jack Goody, quoted in Clanchy, *From Memory to Written Record*, 7.
119. Clanchy, *From Memory to Written Record*, 6-7.
120. Clanchy, *From Memory to Written Record*, 32-33.
121. Clanchy, *From Memory to Written Record*, 264-65.
122. Clanchy, *From Memory to Written Record*, 164-66.
123. Clanchy, *From Memory to Written Record*, 328-29.
124. Clanchy, *From Memory to Written Record*, 45.
125. Clanchy, *From Memory to Written Record*, 52.
126. Clanchy, *From Memory to Written Record*, 251. For an interesting perspective on scribal culture among monks and its influence on archival recordkeeping, see Robert F. Berkhofer III, *Day of Reckoning: Power and Accountability in Medieval France* (Philadelphia: University of Pennsylvania, 2004).
127. Clanchy, *From Memory to Written Record*, 236-37.
128. Clanchy, *From Memory to Written Record*, 328.
129. Clanchy, *From Memory to Written Record*, 2.
130. Clanchy, *From Memory to Written Record*, 10-11.
131. Clanchy, *From Memory to Written Record*, 146.
132. Clanchy, *From Memory to Written Record*, 148-49.
133. Clanchy, *From Memory to Written Record*, 318.
134. Clanchy, *From Memory to Written Record*, 304-5.
135. Clanchy, *From Memory to Written Record*, 70.
136. Clanchy, *From Memory to Written Record*, 68-69.
137. Clanchy, *From Memory to Written Record*, 70-71.
138. Clanchy, *From Memory to Written Record*, 153-54.

139. Clanchy, *From Memory to Written Record*, 184.
140. Clanchy, *From Memory to Written Record*, 330-31.
141. Ernst Posner, *Archives and the Public Interest: Selected Essays by Ernst Posner*, ed. Ken Munden (Washington, DC: Public Affairs Press, 1967), 24-25.
142. Clanchy, *From Memory to Written Record*, 14-15.
143. Duranti, "Odyssey of Records Managers," in *Canadian Archival Studies and the Rediscovery of Provenance*, 44.
144. Quoted in O'Toole and Cox, *Understanding Archives and Manuscripts*, 8.
145. Battles, *Library*, 67-68, 72-73.
146. Richard Brown, "Death of a Renaissance Record-Keeper: The Murder of Tomasso da Tortona in Ferrara, 1385," *Archivaria* 44 (Fall 1997): 4-7.
147. Brown, "Death of a Renaissance Record-Keeper," 8-16.
148. Brown, "Death of a Renaissance Record-Keeper," 2-3.
149. Brown, "Death of a Renaissance Record-Keeper," 22.
150. Brown, "Death of a Renaissance Record-Keeper," 25-29.
151. Luciana Duranti, *Diplomatics: New Uses for an Old Science* (Lanham, MD: Scarecrow Press, 1998), 36.
152. Duranti, *Diplomatics*, 45.
153. Corcoran Gallery, "Art and Economics: Sienese Paintings from the Dawn of the Modern Financial Age," news release from 2002 exhibit, Corcoran Gallery website, http://www.corcoran.org/exhibitions/press_results.asp?Exhib_ID=51 (accessed 27 December 2007).
154. Corcoran Gallery, "Art and Economics: Sienese Paintings from the Dawn of the Modern Financial Age."
155. "Collezione delle Tavolette di Biccherna e Mostra documentaria," Archivio di Stato di Siena website, http://archiviostato.si.it/archistato_6_01.htm (accessed 27 December 2007). In December 2007 my wife and I enjoyed a private tour of the Siena Archives and the Biccherne exhibit. In several shops in Siena we found postcards depicting *biccherne* illustrations, and at the Duomo gift shop we bought a wooden box replica of a *biccherna* volume.
156. David Lowenthal, "Archives, Heritage, and History," in *Archives, Documentation and Institutions of Social Memory*, ed. Francis X. Blouin, Jr. and William G. Rosenberg (Ann Arbor: University of Michigan Press, 2006), 194.
157. Giorgetta Bonfiglio-Dosio, "Padua Municipal Archives from the 13th to the 20th Centuries: A Case of a Record-keeping System in Italy," *Archivaria* 60 (Fall 2005): 92-95.
158. Bonfiglio-Dosio, "Padua Municipal Archives," 95-102 (quoted passage found on page 102).
159. Michel Duchein, "The History of European Archives and the Development of the Archival Profession in Europe," *American Archivist* 55 (Winter 1992): 14-16.
160. Baldassare Bonifacio, quoted in Duranti, "Odyssey of Records Managers," in *Canadian Archival Studies and the Rediscovery of Provenance*, 49.
161. Benedict Anderson, *Imagined Communities: Reflections on the Origin and Spread of Nationalism*, rev. ed. (London and New York: Verso, 2006), 33-34.
162. Anderson, *Imagined Communities*, 37.
163. McNeely and Wolverton, *Reinventing Knowledge*, 122, 129, 136-37, 147.
164. McNeely and Wolverton, *Reinventing Knowledge*, 158-59.
165. Jacques Le Goff, *History and Memory* (New York: Columbia University Press, 1992), 87-88.
166. Posner, *Archives and the Public Interest*, 25.
167. Judith M. Panitch, "Liberty, Equality, Posterity?: Some Archival Lessons from the Case of the French Revolution," in *American Archival Studies: Readings in Theory and Practice*, ed. Randall C. Jimerson (Chicago: Society of American Archivists, 2000), 110.
168. *Encyclopédie ou Dictionnaire raisonné des sciences, des arts et des métiers* (Paris: Briasson, 1751-1765),

as quoted in Panitch, "Liberty, Equality, Posterity," 104.

169. Panitch, "Liberty, Equality, Posterity," 104.

170. Posner, *Archives and the Public Interest*, 25-26.

171. Philippe Sagnac, *La Législation civile de la Révolution française* (1898), quoted in Panitch, "Liberty, Equality, Posterity," 105.

172. Panitch, "Liberty, Equality, Posterity," 105-6.

173. Panitch, "Liberty, Equality, Posterity," 106-7.

174. McNeely and Wolverton, *Reinventing Knowledge*, 24. See also Battles, *Library*, 33-40. The Spanish conquistadors likewise burned Aztec painted books in order to control the conquered peoples. Battles, *Library*, 43.

175. Panitch, "Liberty, Equality, Posterity," 110-12.

176. Panitch, "Liberty, Equality, Posterity," 121-22.

177. Posner, *Archives and the Public Interest*, 29; Duranti, "Odyssey of Records Managers," in *Canadian Archival Studies and the Rediscovery of Provenance*, 51.

178. Posner, *Archives and the Public Interest*, 30. Nationalists also used public education to forge unified cultures out of fragmented societies, particularly when combining independent states into a new nation. See McNeely and Wolverton, *Reinventing Knowledge*, 165.

179. Kerwin Lee Klein, "On the Emergence of Memory in Historical Discourse," *Representations* 69 (Winter 2000): 130.

180. McNeely and Wolverton, *Reinventing Knowledge*, 209.

181. E. H. Carr, quoted in Le Goff, *History and Memory*, 114.

182. McNeely and Wolverton, *Reinventing Knowledge*, 200.

183. Charles V. Langlois and Charles Seignobos, quoted in Le Goff, *History and Memory*, 179.

184. Allan Megill, *Historical Knowledge, Historical Error: A Contemporary Guide to Practice* (Chicago: University of Chicago Press, 2007), 31.

185. Jeremy Black, *Using History* (London: Hodder Arnold, 2005), 65-66.

186. Jennifer S. Milligan, "The Problem of *Publicité* in the Archives of Second Empire France," in *Archives, Documentation and Institutions of Social Memory*, 21.

187. T. R. Schellenberg, *Modern Archives: Principles and Techniques* (Chicago: University of Chicago Press, 1956; reprinted Chicago: Society of American Archivists, 2003), 170-74; Duchein, "The History of European Archives," 19.

188. Sarah Anita Nelson, *Jared Sparks: A Founding Father of American Archives and Historiography* (Master of Arts thesis, Western Washington University, 2006), 102-3.

189. Milligan, "The Problem of *Publicité* in the Archives of Second Empire France," 20-23.

190. Quoted in Milligan, "The Problem of *Publicité* in the Archives of Second Empire France," 25.

191. Milligan, "The Problem of *Publicité* in the Archives of Second Empire France," 25-26.

192. Milligan, "The Problem of *Publicité* in the Archives of Second Empire France," 30-31.

193. Duchein, "The History of European Archives," 18.

194. Peter J. Horsman, "A French Legacy: The Transition from Collegiate to Bureaucratic Record-keeping in a Dutch Town, 1800-1900," *Archivaria* 60 (Fall 2005): 125-27, 133-43.

195. Peter Horsman, Eric Ketelaar, and Theor Thomassen, "Introduction to the 2003 Reissue," *Manual for the Arrangement and Description of Archives*, by S. Muller, J. A. Feith, and R. Fruin (Chicago: Society of American Archivists, 2003), v-xxv.

196. Marjorie Rabe Barritt, "Coming to America: Dutch *Archivistiek* and American Archival Practice," *Archival Issues* 18, no. 1 (1993): 51-52.

197. Hilary Jenkinson, *A Manual of Archive Administration: Including the Problem of War Archives and Archive Making* (Oxford: Clarendon Press, 1922).

CHAPTER 2

1. Harvey C. Mansfield and Delba Winthrop, "Editors' Introduction," in Alexis de Tocqueville, *Democracy in America* (Chicago: University of Chicago Press, 2000), xl, lxxxvii.
2. Tocqueville, *Democracy in America*, 326n.
3. Mansfield and Winthrop, "Editors' Introduction," in Tocqueville, *Democracy in America*, xvii.
4. Tocqueville, quoted in T. R. Schellenberg, *Modern Archives: Principles and Techniques* (Chicago: University of Chicago, 1956), 33. In this passage Tocqueville did not actually use the term "archives." He wrote, "Nul ne s'inquiète de ce qu'on a fait avant lui. On n'adopte point de méthode; on ne compose point de collection; on ne réunit pas de documents, lors même qu'il serait aisé de le faire." Alexis de Tocqueville, *De La Démocratie en Amerique*, http://classiques.uqac.ca/classiques/De_tocqueville_alexis/democratie_1/democratie_t1_2.rtf#livre_1_p2_ch_05_07_instabilité (accessed 3 March 2008). Schellenberg quoted an earlier translation. Mansfield and Winthrop translate this passage, "No one worries about what has been done before him. No method is adopted; no collection is composed; no documents are gathered, even if it would be easy to do it." Tocqueville, *Democracy in America*, 198.
5. James M. O'Toole, "Democracy—and Documents—in America," *American Archivist* 65 (Spring/Summer 2002): 108.
6. Tocqueville, *Democracy in America*, 35; O'Toole, "Democracy—and Documents—in America," 110.
7. Tocqueville, *Democracy in America*, 37-40 (quoted passage on page 39).
8. Tocqueville, *Democracy in America*, 29.
9. Tocqueville, *Democracy in America*, 41.
10. O'Toole, "Democracy—and Documents—in America," 112.
11. Tocqueville, *Democracy in America*, 251 and 256; O'Toole, "Democracy—and Documents—in America," 113.
12. O'Toole, "Democracy—and Documents—in America," 113.
13. Tocqueville, *Democracy in America*, 683.
14. Tocqueville, *Democracy in America*, 685.
15. For example, he uses such phrases as, " . . . it is enough to cast a glance at the archives of the different states of the Union to be convinced that . . ."; Tocqueville, *Democracy in America*, 238.
16. Tocqueville, *Democracy in America*, 14.
17. Tocqueville, *Democracy in America*, 198.
18. Michael Kraus, *A History of American History* (New York: Farrar and Rinehart, 1937), 171.
19. There is a growing archival literature on these postmodern concepts of power, evidence, and the role of documents. See for example: Francis X. Blouin, Jr., "Archivists, Mediation, and the Constructs of Social Memory," *Archival Issues* 24 (1999): 101-12; Terry Cook, "Fashionable Nonsense or Professional Rebirth: Postmodernism and the Practice of Archives," *Archivaria* 51 (Spring 2001): 126-51; Heather MacNeil, "Trusting Records in a Postmodern World," *Archivaria* 51 (Spring 2001): 36-47; Tom Nesmith, "Seeing Archives: Postmodernism and the Changing Intellectual Place of Archives," *American Archivist* 65 (Spring/Summer 2002): 24-41; Mark Greene, "The Power of Meaning: The Archival Mission in the Postmodern Age," *American Archivist* 65 (Spring/Summer 2002): 42-55.
20. David D. Van Tassel, *Recording America's Past* (Chicago: University of Chicago Press, 1960), 4; J. Franklin Jameson, *The History of Historical Writing in America* (New York: Antiquarian Press, 1961), 13-28; Louis Leonard Tucker, *Clio's Consort* (Boston: Massachusetts Historical Society, 1990), 29-30.
21. Van Tassel, *Recording America's Past*, 19.

22. Albert E. Van Dusen, *Connecticut* (New York: Random House, 1961), 350. The Charter Oak was featured on the Connecticut commemorative quarter issued by the United States Mint in 1999. "Connecticut's roots are deeply steeped in American history, so we are especially proud to feature the 'Charter Oak' on the Connecticut quarter," said John Rowland, governor of Connecticut, at the U.S. Mint ceremony, http://www. usmint.gov/mint_programs/50sq_program/states/CT/index.cfm?flash=yes&action=CT_ strike (accessed 10 March 2008).

23. "Declaration of Independence."

24. Percy Scott Flippin, compiler, "The Archives of the United States Government: A Documentary History, 1774-1934" (1938), Record Group 64, National Archives and Records Administration, volume I:II.

25. James M. O'Toole, "Between Veneration and Loathing: Loving and Hating Documents," in *Archives, Documentation and Institutions of Social Memory*, ed. Francis X. Blouin, Jr. and William G. Rosenberg (Ann Arbor: University of Michigan Press, 2006): 43-45; Donald R. McCoy, *The National Archives: America's Ministry of Documents, 1934-1968* (Chapel Hill: University of North Carolina Press, 1978), 254-56; Milton O. Gustafson, "The Empty Shrine: The Transfer of the Declaration of Independence and the Constitution to the National Archives," *American Archivist* 39 (July 1976): 271-85.

26. Flippin, "The Archives of the United States Government," I:28-30.

27. Tucker, *Clio's Consort*, 32-33; Kraus, *A History of American History*, 87.

28. General Lincoln to Jeremy Belknap, 21 January 1792, Jeremy Belknap Papers, Massachusetts Historical Society.

29. George H. Callcott, *History in the United States, 1800-1860* (Baltimore: Johns Hopkins University Press, 1970), 5-6.

30. Joyce Appleby, Lynn Hunt, and Margaret Jacob, *Telling the Truth About History* (New York: W. W. Norton, 1994), 101-3.

31. Louis Leonard Tucker, *The Massachusetts Historical Society* (Boston: Massachusetts Historical Society, 1995), 3. Tocqueville praised Belknap's *History of New Hampshire*, which contained "more general ideas and more force of thought than other American historians have presented up to the present." Tocqueville, *Democracy in America*, 689.

32. Jeremy Belknap to Ebenezer Hazard, 8 January 1783, "Correspondence Between Jeremy Belknap and Ebenezer Hazard, Part I," *Collections of the Massachusetts Historical Society* (hereafter *MHS Collections*), vol. 42 (Boston, 1877), 178.

33. Belknap to Hazard, 19 February 1791, *MHS Collections*, vol. 43, 245.

34. Van Tassel, *Recording America's Past*, 181-85.

35. William Larsen, "Virginia," in *The Encyclopedia of Southern History*, ed. David C. Roller and Robert W. Twyman (Baton Rouge: Louisiana State University Press, 1979), 1281-83.

36. Virginius Cornick Hall, Jr., "The Virginia Historical Society: An Anniversary Narrative of Its First Century and a Half," *Virginia Magazine of History and Biography* 90 (January 1982): 3.

37. "The Address of the New-York Historical Society," http://www.nyhistory.org (accessed 22 April 2002).

38. Walter Muir Whitehill, *Independent Historical Societies: An Enquiry Into Their Research and Publication Functions and Their Financial Future* (Boston: Boston Athenaeum, 1962), 4.

39. Hazard quoted in Fred Shelley, "Ebenezer Hazard: America's First Historical Editor," *William and Mary Quarterly*, 3rd ser., 12 (January 1955): 44-45.

40. Lester J. Cappon, "American Historical Editors Before Jared Sparks: 'they will plant a forest . . . ,'" *William and Mary Quarterly*, 3rd ser., 30 (July 1973): 380-83; Hazard to Belknap, 6 June 1791, *MHS Collections*, vol. 43, 262. Hazard's *Historical Collections* later earned Tocqueville's praise as the best source for historical documents concerning early American history. Tocqueville, *Democracy in America*, 683.

41. Roland M. Baumann, "Samuel Hazard: Editor and Archivist for the Keystone State,"

Pennsylvania Magazine of History and Biography CVII (April 1983): 195-215.

42. Van Tassel, *Recording America's Past*, 103-10.

43. Matthew St. Clair Clarke to "Dear Sir," 17 April 1834, Peter Force Papers, Library of Congress Manuscript Division.

44. Jared Sparks, quoted in Lyman C. Draper, printed circular, 1 January 1846, in Francis Parkman Papers, Massachusetts Historical Society.

45. Joan M. Schwartz, "'Records of Simple Truth and Precision': Photography, Archives, and the Illusion of Control," in *Archives, Documentation and Institutions of Social Memory*, 68-69.

46. John Higham, *History: Professional Scholarship in America* (Baltimore: Johns Hopkins University Press, 1989), 4-13; Thomas Haskell, *The Emergence of Professional Social Science: The American Social Science Association and the Nineteenth Century Crisis of Authority* (Urbana: University of Illinois Press, 1977), 69.

47. Brantz Mayer to Lyman Draper, 1 October 1853, Lyman Draper Papers, Wisconsin Historical Society.

48. Sparks to Nathaniel Niles, 20 April 1831, Jared Sparks Papers, Harvard University (HU). The best recent account of Sparks's career is Sarah Anita Nelson, *Jared Sparks: A Founding Father of American Archives and Historiography* (Master of Arts thesis, Western Washington University, 2006).

49. Sparks to General Lafayette, 16 April 1830, Sparks Papers, HU.

50. Sparks to General Lafayette, 1 March 1828, Sparks Papers, HU.

51. For an example of Force's contracts, see Daniel Webster to Matthew St. Clair Clarke and Peter Force, 23 August 1841, Peter Force Papers, Library of Congress Manuscript Division.

52. Peter Force to A. Langdon Elwyn, 8 February 1843, Force Papers.

53. Force, "Preface," American Archives Transcripts, Series 4, vol. 1, in Series 7A, Box 1, Force Papers.

54. Peter Force to [Congressional committee], 10 May 1836, Force Papers.

55. Jared Sparks to Clarke and Force, 28 September 1833, Force Papers.

56. Force, "Preface," American Archives Transcripts, Series 4, vol. 1, in Series 7A, Box 1, Force Papers.

57. The best secondary sources on Force are: Carolyn Hoover Sung, *Peter Force: Washington Printer and Creator of the "American Archives"* (PhD dissertation, George Washington University, 1985); and Erin Whitesel-Jones, *Peter Force: An Early American Archivist* (Master of Arts thesis, Western Washington University, 2004).

58. Force to Committee of Congress, 26 June 1840, Force Papers.

59. Peter Charles Hoffer, *Past Imperfect: Facts, Fictions, Fraud—American History from Bancroft and Parkman to Ambrose, Bellesiles, Ellis and Goodwin* (New York: Public Affairs, 2004), 20.

60. Lyman C. Draper, printed circular, 1 January 1846, in Parkman Papers, Massachusetts Historical Society.

61. William B. Hesseltine, *Pioneer's Mission: the Story of Lyman Copeland Draper* (Madison: State Historical Society of Wisconsin, 1954).

62. Higham, *History*, 8; Van Tassel, *Recording America's Past*, 106-7.

63. George Bancroft to Richard H. Dana, 22 October 1864, Richard H. Dana Papers, Massachusetts Historical Society.

64. Francis Parkman to George Bancroft, 26 December 1856, George Bancroft Papers, Massachusetts Historical Society.

65. Hoffer, *Past Imperfect*, 22-24.

66. Hoffer, *Past Imperfect*, 24-28.

67. Sparks to James Madison, 25 August 1827, Sparks Papers, HU.

68. Force, "Preface," American Archives Transcripts, Series 4, vol. 1, in Series 7A, Box 1, Force Papers.

69. Sparks to George Bancroft, 10 March 1829, George Bancroft Papers.

70. Sparks to A. H. Everett, 17 August 1828; Sparks to Henry Wheaton, 29 January 1844, Sparks Papers, HU.

71. Morey Rothberg and Jacqueline Goggin, eds., *John Franklin Jameson and the Development of Humanistic Scholarship in America, vol. 1, Selected Essays* (Athens: University of Georgia Press, 1993), 350-51.

72. Higham, *History*, 168-74; Ellen Fitzpatrick, *History's Memory: Writing America's Past, 1880-1980* (Cambridge, MA: Harvard University Press, 2002), 13.

73. H. B. Adams to S. A. Green, 3 November 1880, S. A. Green Papers, Massachusetts Historical Society.

74. George Bancroft to Leopold von Ranke, 5 December 1885, George Bancroft Papers.

75. Appleby, Hunt, and Jacob, *Telling the Truth About History*, 56.

76. Higham, *History*, 93-96.

77. Appleby, Hunt, and Jacob, *Telling the Truth About History*, 67-68, 73.

78. Henry Adams, quoted in Higham, *History*, 70.

79. Albert Bushnell Hart, quoted in Hoffer, *Past Imperfect*, 33-34.

80. Peter Novick, *That Noble Dream: The "Objectivity Question" and the American Historical Profession* (Cambridge: Cambridge University Press, 1988), 26-28.

81. Richard C. Berner, *Archival Theory and Practice in the United States: A Historical Analysis* (Seattle: University of Washington Press, 1983), 11-23.

82. Berner, *Archival Theory and Practice in the United States*, 13-17. For a useful critique of Berner's interpretation of these two traditions, see Luke J. Gilliland-Swetland, "The Provenance of a Profession: The Permanence of the Public Archives and Historical Manuscripts Traditions in American Archival History," *American Archivist* 54 (Spring 1991): 160-75.

83. Robert J. Jakeman, "Thomas Owen and the Alabama Department of Archives and History" (unpublished paper presented at the annual meeting of the Society of American Archivists, Denver, Colorado, 30 August 2000).

84. Patricia Galloway, "Archives, Power, and History: Dunbar Rowland and the Beginning of the State Archives of Mississippi (1902-1936)," *American Archivist* 69 (Spring/Summer 2006): 86.

85. Thomas McAdory Owen, "State Departments of Archives and History," *Annual Report of the American Historical Association for the Year 1904* (Washington, DC: Government Printing Office, 1905), 238.

86. Jakeman, "Thomas Owen."

87. Owen, "State Departments of Archives and History," 239.

88. Owen to R. D. W. Connor, 4 April 1912, quoted in Jakeman, "Thomas Owen."

89. Report quoted in Jakeman, "Thomas Owen."

90. Galloway, "Archives, Power, and History," 85.

91. Galloway, "Archives, Power, and History," 88.

92. Galloway, "Archives, Power, and History," 86-89.

93. Galloway, "Archives, Power, and History," 97-113.

94. Galloway, "Archives, Power, and History," 91, 94, 98.

95. Galloway, "Archives, Power, and History," 99-100.

96. Galloway, "Archives, Power, and History," 103-104, 115.

97. William F. Birdsall, "The Two Sides of the Desk: The Archivist and the Historian, 1909-1935," *American Archivist* 38 (April 1975): 166-67; Donnelly Faye Lancaster, *Margaret Cross Norton: Dedication to the Development of the American Archival Profession* (Master of Arts thesis, Auburn University, August 2000), 1-2; Thornton W. Mitchell, "Introduction," in *Norton on Archives: The Writings of Margaret Cross Norton on Archival & Records Management*, ed. Thornton W. Mitchell (Chicago: Society of American Archivists, 1975), xviii.

98. Gilliland-Swetland, "The Provenance of a Profession," 160-75.
99. Randall C. Jimerson, "Margaret C. Norton Reconsidered," *Archival Issues* 26, no. 1 (2001): 40-52.
100. Margaret C. Norton to Francis S. Philbrick, 12 November 1939, in *The Margaret Cross Norton Working Papers, 1924-1928*, microfilm edition (Springfield: Illinois State Archives, 1993), roll 4, frame 1341.
101. Norton to William F. Birdsall, 24 May 1973, in *The Margaret Cross Norton Working Papers, 1924-1928*, microfilm edition, roll 3, frame 1206.
102. Norton to Charles C. Williamson, 13 November 1939, in *The Margaret Cross Norton Working Papers, 1924-1928*, microfilm edition, roll 4, frame 364.
103. Ernst Posner, *American State Archives* (Chicago: University of Chicago Press, 1965), 25.
104. Robert H. Wiebe, *The Search for Order, 1877-1920* (New York: Hill and Wang, 1967), 2-4.
105. Wiebe, *The Search for Order*, 28-37.
106. Wiebe, *The Search for Order*, 53-57, 164-95.
107. Victor Gondos, Jr., *J. Franklin Jameson and the Birth of the National Archives, 1906-1926* (Philadelphia: University of Pennsylvania Press, 1981), 3-4.
108. Gondos, *J. Franklin Jameson and the Birth of the National Archives*, 26-27, 92-93. Unfortunately, despite outcry over the loss of many census records in the 1921 fire, thirteen years later the Census Bureau destroyed many remaining records, which the bureau considered not to have historical value. Kellee Blake, "'First in the Path of the Firemen': The Fate of the 1890 Population Census," *Prologue: The Journal of the National Archives* 28, no. 1 (Spring 1996), at: http://www.archives.gov/publications/prologue/1996/spring/1890-census-1.html (accessed 12 February 2009). The most recent examination of the census records fire is Robert L. Dorman, "The Creation and Destruction of the 1890 Federal Census," *American Archivist* 71 (Fall/Winter 2008): 350-83.
109. Thomas McAdory Owen, "State Departments of Archives and History," 239; Higham, *History*, 14-17.
110. Higham, *History*, 35.
111. John Franklin Jameson to Daniel C. Gilman, 14 February 1902, in Elizabeth Donnan and Leo F. Stock, eds., *An Historian's World: Selections from the Correspondence of John Franklin Jameson* (Philadelphia: American Philosophical Society, 1956), 80-81; Higham, *History*, 20-21.
112. Rodney A. Ross, "Waldo Gifford Leland: Archivist by Association," *American Archivist* 46 (Summer 1983): 265-66; Leland, "Reflections of the Man Who Rang the Bell," *American Archivist* 21 (January 1958); Jameson to Fred T. Field, 9 January 1915, Box 104, John Franklin Jameson Papers, Library of Congress Manuscript Division; Leland, transcript of interview, 24 May 1955, pp. 2-3, Waldo G. Leland Papers, Library of Congress Manuscript Division.
113. Ross, "Waldo Gifford Leland: Archivist by Association," 267, 270.
114. Jameson to Fred T. Field, 9 January 1915, Box 107, John Franklin Jameson Papers, Library of Congress Manuscript Division.
115. Theodore Schellenberg, *Archival Principles: Selections from the Writings of Waldo Gifford Leland*, National Archives Staff Information Papers No. 20 (Washington, DC: National Archives, 1955).
116. "Address by Waldo G. Leland, 1956," in Leland Papers. Leland borrowed his opening statement from a Russian guide to the archives of Moscow.
117. Leland, "The First Conference of Archivists," quoted in Ross, "Waldo Gifford Leland: Archivist by Association," 276.
118. Gondos, *J. Franklin Jameson and the Birth of the National Archives*, 29.
119. Gondos, *J. Franklin Jameson and the Birth of the National Archives*, 30.

120. Gondos, J. *Franklin Jameson and the Birth of the National Archives*, 31.
121. Gondos, J. *Franklin Jameson and the Birth of the National Archives*, 32-35.
122. Quoted in Gondos, J. *Franklin Jameson and the Birth of the National Archives*, 82-83.
123. Gondos, J. *Franklin Jameson and the Birth of the National Archives*, 162-66.
124. Gondos, J. *Franklin Jameson and the Birth of the National Archives*, 175.
125. Herbert Hoover quoted in Gondos, J. *Franklin Jameson and the Birth of the National Archives*, 1-2.
126. Gondos, J. *Franklin Jameson and the Birth of the National Archives*, 174.
127. J. Frank Cook, "The Blessings of Providence on an Association of Archivists," in Randall C. Jimerson, ed., *American Archival Studies: Readings in Theory and Practice* (Chicago: Society of American Archivists, 2000), 143-44.
128. Birdsall, "The Two Sides of the Desk," 160-61.
129. Waldo G. Leland, "The National Archives: A Programme," quoted in Birdsall, "The Two Sides of the Desk," 164.
130. Paltsits, quoted in Birdsall, "The Two Sides of the Desk," 169.
131. Jameson to George Burton Adams, 11 November 1908, in Morey Rothberg and Jacqueline Goggin, eds., *John Franklin Jameson and the Development of Humanistic Scholarship in America*, vol. 3, *The Carnegie Institution of Washington and the Library of Congress, 1905-1937* (Athens: University of Georgia Press, 2001), 54.
132. John Franklin Jameson, "Future Uses of History," in Morey Rothberg and Jacqueline Goggin, eds., *John Franklin Jameson and the Development of Humanistic Scholarship in America*, vol. 1, *Selected Essays* (Athens: University of Georgia Press, 1993), 305.
133. Jameson to Henry Adams, 31 October 1910, in Donnan, *An Historian's World*, 136. Peter Charles Hoffer uses the same metaphor to illustrate the later change in perspective when relativism entered the historical discourse, with its central point "that facts were not irreducible bricks that the historian piled up but little arguments that he fabricated from the pieces of evidence he selected." Hoffer, *Past Imperfect*, 38-39.
134. Novick, *That Noble Dream*, 56.
135. Margaret C. Norton to A. R. Newsome, 15 April 1935, American Historical Association Records, Library of Congress Manuscript Division.
136. Leland to Herman V. Ames, 29 May 1909, quoted in Birdsall, "The Two Sides of the Desk," 161.
137. Waldo G. Leland, "American Archival Problems," in American Historical Association, *Annual Report*, 1909, 346.
138. T. R. Schellenberg, *The Management of Archives* (New York: Columbia University Press, 1965), 43.
139. Leland to Jameson, 13 September 1910, Box 104, John Franklin Jameson Papers, Library of Congress Manuscript Division.
140. Leland, "Address by Waldo G. Leland, 1956," (quoting his 1912 address), Waldo Gifford Leland Papers, Library of Congress Manuscript Division.
141. Schellenberg, *Modern Archives*, 181.
142. Marjorie Rabe Barritt, "Coming to America: Dutch *Archivistiek* and American Archival Practice," *Archival Issues* 18, no. 1 (1993): 51-52.
143. J. Frank Cook, "The Blessings of Providence on an Association of Archivists," in Jimerson, ed., *American Archival Studies*, 143-45.
144. Cook, "The Blessings of Providence," 150, 152.
145. Joyce Appleby, *A Restless Past: History and the American Public* (Lanham, MD: Rowan and Littlefield, 2005), 2-3.
146. Howard Zinn and Eugene Genovese, quoted in Hoffer, *Past Imperfect*, 66-67.
147. Appleby, Hunt, and Jacob, *Telling the Truth About History*, 146-49.
148. Howard Zinn, "Secrecy, Archives, and the Public Interest," *Midwestern Archivist* 2, no. 2 (1977): 20-21.

149. Sam Bass Warner, Jr., "The Shame of the Cities: Public Records of the Metropolis," *Midwestern Archivist* (1977): 27-30.
150. F. Gerald Ham, "The Archival Edge," *American Archivist* 38 (January 1975); reprinted in *A Modern Archives Reader*, ed. Maygene Daniels and Timothy Walch (Washington, DC: National Archives Trust Fund Board, 1984), 329-30, 334.
151. Jason D. Viers, *A Willful Transformation: The Incorporation of Professional Ideology in American Archival Development* (Master of Arts thesis, Western Washington University, 2005), 57-60.
152. Archie Motley, "Out of the Hollinger Box: The Archivist as Advocate," *Midwestern Archivist* 9, no. 2 (1984): 65-68.
153. Cook, "The Blessings of Providence," 167-68.
154. Cook, "The Blessings of Providence," 170-71.
155. Cook, "The Blessings of Providence," 171.
156. Viers, "A Willful Transformation," 86.
157. Randall C. Jimerson, "American Archivists and the Search for Professional Identity," in Jimerson, ed., *American Archival Studies*, 1-17; Viers, *A Willful Transformation*, 86-93.
158. Lawrence Dowler, "The Role of Use in Defining Archival Practice and Principles: A Research Agenda for the Availability and Use of Records," *American Archivist* 51 (Winter/Spring 1988): 74-86.
159. J. Rogers Hollingsworth, "American Anti-Intellectualism," *South Atlantic Quarterly* 63, no. 3 (1964): 269. The classic analysis of American individualism was Alexis de Tocqueville, *Democracy in America*.
160. Harold T. Pinkett, "American Archival Theory: the State of the Art," *American Archivist* 44 (Summer 1981): 217, 222.
161. William J. Maher, "Lost in a Disneyfied World: Archivists and Society in Late Twentieth-Century America," *American Archivist* 61 (Fall 1998): 259-65.
162. Society of American Archivists Task Force on Goals and Priorities, *Planning for the Archival Profession: A Report of the SAA Task Force on Goals and Priorities* (Chicago: Society of American Archivists, 1986).
163. Leland, quoted in Higham, *History*, 72.
164. William L. Joyce, "Historical Records Repositories," in Lisa B. Weber, ed., *Documenting America: Assessing the Condition of Historical Records in the United States* (Atlanta: National Association of State Archives and Records Administrators, 1984), 39.
165. Edwin C. Bridges, "State Government Records Programs," in Lisa B. Weber, ed., *Documenting America*, 1-18.
166. David B. Gracy, "Our Future is Now," *American Archivist* 48 (Winter 1985): 13.
167. Sidney J. Levy and Albert G. Robles, *The Image of Archivists: Resource Allocators' Perceptions* (Chicago: Society of American Archivists, 1984), iv-v.
168. Arlene B. Schmuland, *The Image of Archives and Archivists: Fictional Perspectives* (Master of Arts thesis, Western Washington University, 1997), and "The Archival Image in Fiction: An Analysis and Annotated Bibliography," *American Archivist* 62 (Spring 1999): 24-73.
169. "Archivists' Resource Allocators: The Next Step," *SAA Newsletter* (January 1987), 8-9.
170. David B. Gracy II, "Archivists, You Are What People Think You Keep," *American Archivist* 52 (Winter 1989): 78.
171. Gracy, "Archivists, You Are What People Think You Keep," 78.
172. Ian F. McNeely and Lisa Wolverton, *Reinventing Knowledge: From Alexandria to the Internet* (New York: W. W. Norton & Company, 2008), 271-72. Interesting perspectives on these new technologies were introduced in two unpublished papers presented at the conference of the International Council on Archives, Section on University and Research Institution Archives, in Dundee, Scotland, August 2007: Alan Bell, "Content, Creation or Conflict: What Might Web 2.0 Mean for Record Keepers?" and Jane Stevenson, "Web 2.0 for Archivists: Sharing, Participation, and

Collaboration," http://www.dundee.ac.uk/archives/SUV2007/ (accessed 28 March 2008).

173. Charles M. Dollar, *Archival Theory and Information Technologies: The Impact of Information Technologies on Archival Principles and Methods* (Macerata, Italy: University of Macerata, 1992), 35.

174. John Seely Brown and Paul Duguid, *The Social Life of Information* (Boston: Harvard Business School Press, 2002), 17.

175. David M. Levy, *Scrolling Forward: Making Sense of Documents in the Digital Age* (New York: Arcade Publishing, 2001), 141-42.

176. Vannevar Bush, "As We May Think" (1945), as quoted in Abigail J. Sellen and Richard H. R. Harper, *The Myth of the Paperless Office* (Cambridge, MA: MIT Press, 2002), 4.

177. Levy, *Scrolling Forward*, 145-50.

178. Richard E. Barry, "Technology and the Transformation of the Workplace: Lessons Learned Traveling Down the Garden Path," in *Effective Approaches for Managing Electronic Records and Archives*, ed. Bruce W. Dearstyne (Lanham, MD: Scarecrow Press, 2002), 10-11.

179. Roy C. Turnbaugh, "What Is an Electronic Record?" in *Effective Approaches for Managing Electronic Records and Archives*, 24-26.

180. H. Thomas Hickerson, "Ten Challenges for the Archival Profession," *American Archivist* 64 (Spring/Summer 2001): 8.

181. Richard Pearce-Moses, "Janus in Cyberspace: Archives on the Threshold of the Digital Era," *American Archivist* 70 (Spring/Summer 2007): 15. This change in record formats is also noted in Levy, *Scrolling Forward*, 4.

182. Sellen and Harper, *The Myth of the Paperless Office*, 16, 101-3 (quoted phrase on page 63).

183. Levy, *Scrolling Forward*, 56-57.

184. Levy, *Scrolling Forward*, 138-39, 154-55.

185. Catherine O'Sullivan, "Diaries, On-line Diaries, and the Future Loss to Archives; or, Blogs and the Blogging Bloggers Who Blog Them," *American Archivist* 68 (Spring/Summer 2005): 54; Levy, *Scrolling Forward*, 119.

186. Matthew Battles, *Library: An Unquiet History* (London: Random House Vintage, 2003), 212.

187. For examples, see: International Research on Permanent Authentic Records in Electronic Records (InterPARES) Project at http://www.interpares.org/; Philip Bantin, "Electronic Records Management—A Review of the Work of a Decade and a Reflection on Future Directions" at http://www.indiana.edu/~libarch/L597; National Archives and Records Administration, Electronic Records Archives, http://www.archives.gov/era/ (all accessed 28 March 2008).

188. Levy, *Scrolling Forward*, 159.

189. Brown and Duguid, *The Social Life of Information*, 159.

190. Linda Henry, "Schellenberg in Cyberspace," in Jimerson, ed., *American Archival Studies*, 571.

191. Trudy Huskamp Peterson (1988), as quoted in Henry, "Schellenberg in Cyberspace," 587-88.

192. David Bearman and Margaret Hedstrom, "Reinventing Archives for Electronic Records: Alternative Service Delivery Options," in Jimerson, ed., *American Archival Studies*, 549-50, 566-67.

193. Alan S. Kowlowitz, "Playing the Electronic Angles and Working the Digital Seams: The Challenge and Opportunities State Electronic Government Initiatives Present to State Archival and Records Management Programs," in *Effective Approaches for Managing Electronic Records and Archives*, 90-93, 103-4.

194. Steven Lubar, "Information Culture and the Archival Record," *American Archivist* 62

(Spring 1999): 11, 20 (quoted passage found on page 20).

195. Brown and Duguid, *The Social Life of Information*, xii.

196. Brown and Duguid, *The Social Life of Information*, 182-83.

197. Barry, "Technology and the Transformation of the Workplace," 16.

198. Brown and Duguid, *The Social Life of Information*, 187-89.

199. Robert Horton, "Obstacles and Opportunities: A Strategic Approach to Electronic Records," in *Effective Approaches for Managing Electronic Records and Archives*, 64-65. See also Levy, *Scrolling Forward*, 178.

200. International Research on Permanent Authentic Records in Electronic Records (InterPARES) Project at http://www.interpares.org/; Bantin, "Electronic Records Management—A Review of the Work of a Decade and a Reflection on Future Directions"; National Archives and Records Administration, Electronic Records Archives, http://www.archives.gov/era/ (accessed 28 March 2008).

201. Adrian Cunningham, "Digital Curation/Digital Archiving: A View From the National Archives of Australia," *American Archivist* 71 (Fall/Winter 2008): 530-43.

202. For information about the Washington State Digital Archives, see: http://www.digitalarchives.wa.gov/content.aspx?txt=background (accessed 3 December 2008).

203. Anne Gilliland-Swetland, "Digital Communications: Documentary Opportunities Not to Be Missed," in Jimerson, ed., *American Archival Studies*, 590, 602-3.

204. Pearce-Moses, "Janus in Cyberspace," 18.

205. Pearce-Moses, "Janus in Cyberspace," 20-21.

206. O'Toole and Cox, *Understanding Archives and Manuscripts*, 10.

207. Ernst Posner, *Archives in the Ancient World* (Cambridge, MA: Harvard University Press, 1972): 3-4.

208. O'Toole and Cox, *Understanding Archives and Manuscripts*, 12-13.

209. O'Toole and Cox, *Understanding Archives and Manuscripts*, 11. Benedict Anderson provides a compelling account of "imagined" communities; see Anderson, *Imagined Communities: Reflections on the Origin and Spread of Nationalism* (New York: Verson, 2006).

210. O'Toole and Cox, *Understanding Archives and Manuscripts*, 35.

211. O'Toole and Cox, *Understanding Archives and Manuscripts*, 39.

212. O'Toole and Cox, *Understanding Archives and Manuscripts*, xvi-xvii.

213. Stephen Haycox, "Rely on Documents, Not Memory," *Anchorage Daily News*, December 6, 2002.

CHAPTER 3

1. John Ross, "Against Amnesia," available at: http://www.media-alliance.org/article.php?story=2004051402014153 (accessed 18 January 2007); used with permission of John Ross.

2. Jacques Derrida, *Archive Fever: A Freudian Impression* (Chicago: University of Chicago Press, 1995), 2-3.

3. Derrida, *Archive Fever*, 4n.

4. David M. Levy, *Scrolling Forward: Making Sense of Documents in the Digital Age* (New York: Arcade Publishing, 2001), 23.

5. Levy, *Scrolling Forward*, 183-89, 194.

6. Levy, *Scrolling Forward*, 202. For an interesting discussion of diaries, and the online version known as blogs, see: Catherine O'Sullivan, "Diaries, On-line Diaries, and the Future Loss to Archives; or, Blogs and the Blogging Bloggers Who Blog Them," *American Archivist* 68 (Spring/Summer 2005): 53-73.

7. Joyce Appleby, Lynn Hunt, and Margaret Jacob, *Telling the Truth About History* (New York: W.W. Norton, 1994), 73.

8. Terry Cook, "Remembering the Future: Appraisal of Records and the Role of Archives in Constructing Social Memory," in *Archives, Documentation and Institutions of Social Memory*,

ed. Francis X. Blouin, Jr. and William G. Rosenberg (Ann Arbor: University of Michigan Press, 2006), 170.

9. Hilary Jenkinson, quoted in Terry Cook, "What Is Past Is Prologue: A History of Archival Ideas Since 1989, and the Future Paradigm Shift," *Archivaria* 43 (Spring 1997): 23.

10. Elisabeth Kaplan, "'Many Paths to Partial Truths': Archives, Anthropology, and the Power of Representation," *Archival Science* 2, nos. 3-4 (2002): 215-16.

11. Cook, "Remembering the Future," 173.

12. Du Mei, "The Role of Archives in Chinese Society: An Examination from the Perspective of Access," in *Archives, Documentation and Institutions of Social Memory*, 431.

13. Michael Fegan, quoted in Mark Greene, "The Messy Business of Remembering: History, Memory, and Archives," *Archival Issues* 28, no. 2 (2003-04): 95-96.

14. Verne Harris, *Archives and Justice: A South African Perspective* (Chicago: Society of American Archivists, 2007), 186.

15. Harris, *Archives and Justice*, 241.

16. Harris, *Archives and Justice*, 248.

17. Cook, "Remembering the Future," 174.

18. Steven Lubar, "Information Culture and the Archival Record," *American Archivist* 62 (Spring 1999): 15.

19. Howard Zinn, "Secrecy, Archives, and the Public Interest," *Midwestern Archivist* 2, no. 2 (1977): 20-21.

20. Claude Lévi-Strauss, quoted in Lubar, "Information Culture and the Archival Record," 18-19.

21. Carolyn Steedman, *Dust: The Archive and Cultural History* (New Brunswick, NJ: Rutgers University Press, 2002), 69.

22. Jennifer Milligan, "'What Is an Archive?' in the History of Modern France," in *Archive Stories: Facts, Fictions, and the Writing of History*, ed. Antoinette Burton (Durham, NC: Duke University Press, 2005), 160.

23. Jennifer Milligan, "The Problem of *Publicité* in the Archives of Second Empire France," in *Archives, Documentation and Institutions of Social Memory*, 23-24.

24. Matthew Battles, *Library: An Unquiet History* (London: Random House Vintage, 2003), 82, 196.

25. Patrick M. Quinn, "Archivists and Historians: The Times They Are A-Changin,'" *Midwestern Archivist* 2, no. 2 (1977): 8.

26. Terry Cook and Joan M. Schwartz, "Archives, Records, and Power: From (Postmodern) Theory to (Archival) Performance," *Archival Science* 2 (2002): 178.

27. Kaplan, "Many Paths," 211.

28. Derrida, *Archive Fever*, 16-17. Emphasis in original.

29. Derrida, *Archive Fever*, 91.

30. Achille Mbembe, "The Power of the Archive and Its Limits," in *Refiguring the Archive*, ed. Carolyn Hamilton, Verne Harris, Jane Taylor, Michael Pickover, Graeme Reid, and Razia Saleh (Dordrecht, Netherlands: Kluwer Academic Publishers, 2002), 19.

31. Jeff Sahadeo, "Without the Past There Is No Future," in *Archive Stories*, 63.

32. Sahadeo, "Without the Past There Is No Future," 49.

33. Peter Fritzsche, "The Archives and the Case of the German Nation," in *Archive Stories*, 185-86.

34. Abby Smith, "Russian History: Is It in the Archives?" in *Archives, Documentation and Institutions of Social Memory*, 451.

35. Richard Harvey Brown and Beth Davis-Brown, "The Making of Memory: The Politics of Archives, Libraries and Museums in the Construction of National Consciousness," *History of the Human Sciences* 11, no. 4 (1998): 21.

36. Derrida, *Archive Fever*, 40.

37. Wendy M. Duff and Verne Harris, "Stories and Names: Archival Description as Narrating Records and Constructing Meanings," *Archival Science* 2 (2002): 282.

38. George Orwell, *The Road to Wigan Pier* (New York: Berkley Medallion, 1961), 107.

39. George Orwell, quoted in Christopher Hitchens, *Why Orwell Matters* (New York: Basic Books, 2002), 13.

40. Orwell, *Road to Wigan Pier*, 124-26.

41. George Orwell, *Burmese Days* (New York: Signet Classic, 1963), 60.

42. Orwell, *Burmese Days*, 21, 23.

43. Hitchens, *Why Orwell Matters*, 34.

44. George Orwell, *Down and Out in Paris and London* (New York: Berkley Medallion, 1959), 87-88.

45. Orwell, *Road to Wigan Pier*, 128.

46. Orwell, *Road to Wigan Pier*, 28.

47. Orwell, *Road to Wigan Pier*, 98.

48. Orwell, *Road to Wigan Pier*, 100.

49. Orwell, *Road to Wigan Pier*, 182.

50. Orwell, *Road to Wigan Pier*, 178.

51. Hitchens, *Why Orwell Matters*, 25.

52. George Orwell, "Preface to the Ukrainian Edition of Animal Farm," March 1947, available at: http://www.netcharles.com/orwell/articles/ukrainian-af-pref.htm (accessed 3 January 2007).

53. George Orwell, *Homage to Catalonia* (Boston: Beacon, 1952), 149.

54. Orwell, *Homage to Catalonia*, 150.

55. Hitchens, *Why Orwell Matters*, 67.

56. Hitchens, *Why Orwell Matters*, 77, 76.

57. George Orwell, "As I Please" column, *Tribune*, February 4, 1944, available at: http://www.netcharles.com/orwell (accessed 3 January 2007).

58. George Orwell, "Looking Back on the Spanish War," in *A Collection of Essays* (Garden City, NY: Doubleday, 1954), 202-4.

59. Orwell, "Looking Back," 205.

60. John Lewis Gaddis, *The Landscape of History: How Historians Map the Past* (Oxford: Oxford University Press, 2003), 143, as quoted in Jeremy Black, *Using History* (London: Hodder Arnold, 2005), 175.

61. Orwell, "As I Please."

62. Joyce Appleby, *A Restless Past: History and the American Public* (Lanham, MD: Rowan and Littlefield, 2005), 147.

63. George Orwell, "Notes on Nationalism," October 1945, available at: www.netcharles.com/orwell/essays/notes-on-nationalism1.htm (accessed 3 January 2007).

64. George Orwell, "The Prevention of Literature," 1945/46, available at: http://whitewolf.newcastle.edu.au/words/authors/O/OrwellGeorge/essay/prevention.html (accessed 3 January 2007).

65. Orwell, "As I Please."

66. Orwell, "Looking Back," 206. Writing about French Caribbean archives, Laurent Dubois echoes Orwell. Dubois examines "the limits of the archives left by slavery" and "the stories of the slaves themselves—the absences and silences in the archives." Laurent Dubois, "Maroons in the Archives: Uses of the Past in the French Caribbean," in *Archives, Documentation and Institutions of Social Memory*, 292.

67. Orwell, "Notes on Nationalism."

68. Pierre Nora, "Entre mémoire et histoire," in *Lieux de mémoire* (1984), quoted in David Lowenthal, "Archives, Heritage, and History," in *Archives, Documentation and Institutions of Social Memory*, 195.

69. Foucault paraphrased in Blouin and Rosenberg, "Archives and Social Memory," in *Archives, Documentation and Institutions of Social Memory*, 165.

70. Blouin and Rosenberg, "Archives and Social Memory," in *Archives, Documentation and Institutions of Social Memory*, 165.

71. George Orwell, "Raffles and Miss Blandish," in *A Collection of Essays*, 153.

72. Orwell, "The Prevention of Literature."

73. Quoted in Lowenthal, "Archives, Heritage, and History," in *Archives, Documentation and Institutions of Social Memory*, 195.

74. Orwell, "The Prevention of Literature."

75. George Orwell, "Such, Such Were the Joys," in *A Collection of Essays*, 13.

76. Orwell, "The Prevention of Literature."

77. George Orwell, *Animal Farm: A Fairy Story* (New York: Signet Classic, 1996), 76-77.

78. Orwell, *Animal Farm*, 79.

79. Orwell, *Animal Farm*, 98.

80. Orwell, *Animal Farm*, 89-91.

81. Orwell, *Animal Farm*, 103.

82. Orwell, *Animal Farm*, 129.

83. Orwell, *Animal Farm*, 129-30.

84. George Orwell, *Nineteen Eighty-Four* (New York: Signet Classic, 1950), 213.

85. Orwell, *Nineteen Eighty-Four*, 38-39.

86. Orwell, *Nineteen Eighty-Four*, 36.

87. Orwell, *Nineteen Eighty-Four*, 32.

88. Orwell, "You and the Atom Bomb" (1945), quoted in Hitchens, *Why Orwell Matters*, 86. Hitchens states that Orwell "is credited with coining the term 'cold war'" in this passage.

89. E. P. Thompson, *Beyond the Frontier*, quoted and paraphrased in Jeffrey Burds, "Ethnicity, Memory, and Violence: Reflections on Special Problems in Soviet and East European Archives," in *Archives, Documentation and Institutions of Social Memory*, 469.

90. Orwell, *Nineteen Eighty-Four*, 19.

91. Orwell, *Nineteen Eighty-Four*, 34-35.

92. Orwell, *Nineteen Eighty-Four*, 40.

93. Orwell, *Nineteen Eighty-Four*, 42.

94. Orwell, *Nineteen Eighty-Four*, 45.

95. Orwell, *Nineteen Eighty-Four*, 155.

96. Verne Harris, "Redefining Archives in South Africa: Public Archives and Society in Transition, 1990-1996," in *Archives and Justice*, 173-74.

97. Harris, "Redefining Archives in South Africa," 176-77.

98. Verne Harris, "Contesting Remembering and Forgetting: The Archive of South Africa's Truth and Reconciliation Commission," in *Archives and Justice*, 290.

99. Verne Harris, "Toward a Culture of Transparency: Public Rights of Access to Official Records in South Africa," in *Archives and Justice*, 273-74.

100. Jeremy Black, *Using History*, 140-41, 144.

101. Orwell, *Nineteen Eighty-Four*, 32.

102. Orwell, *Nineteen Eighty-Four*, 92-93.

103. Elie Wiesel, *From the Kingdom of Memory: Reminiscences* (New York: Schocken Books, 1990), 222.

104. Nancy Wood, "Memory's Remains: *Les lieux de mémoire*," *History and Memory* 6, no. 1 (1994): 131.

105. Jay Winter and Emmanuel Sivan, eds., *War and Remembrance in the Twentieth Century* (Cambridge: Cambridge University Press, 1999), 29.

106. Orwell, *Nineteen Eighty-Four*, 78.

107. Orwell, *Nineteen Eighty-Four*, 79.

108. Orwell, *Nineteen Eighty-Four*, 80.
109. Allan Megill, *Historical Knowledge, Historical Error: A Contemporary Guide to Practice* (Chicago: University of Chicago Press, 2007), 35
110. Orwell, *Nineteen Eighty-Four*, 246-47.
111. Orwell, *Nineteen Eighty-Four*, 145.
112. Orwell, *Nineteen Eighty-Four*, 97.
113. Megill, *Historical Knowledge, Historical Error*, 34.
114. Orwell, *Nineteen Eighty-Four*, 222-23.
115. Orwell, *Nineteen Eighty-Four*, 155-56.
116. Orwell, *Nineteen Eighty-Four*, 248-49.
117. Orwell, *Nineteen Eighty-Four*, 213.
118. Orwell, *Nineteen Eighty-Four*, 155.
119. Orwell, quoted in Hitchens, *Why Orwell Matters*, 85.
120. George Orwell, "Charles Dickens," in *A Collection of Essays*, 97.
121. Orwell, "The Prevention of Literature."
122. George Orwell, "Writers and Leviathan," *Politics and Letters* (Summer 1948), available at: http://www.netcharles.com/orwell/essays/writers-and-leviathan.htm (accessed 3 January 2007).
123. Orwell, *Homage to Catalonia*, 159-60.
124. George Orwell, "Why I Write," in *A Collection of Essays*, 318.
125. George Orwell, "Politics and the English Language," in *A Collection of Essays*, 163.
126. Orwell, "Politics and the English Language," 171-72.
127. Orwell, *Nineteen Eighty-Four*, 82.
128. Orwell, *Nineteen Eighty-Four*, 298-99.
129. Orwell, *Nineteen Eighty-Four*, 308.
130. Orwell, *Nineteen Eighty-Four*, 212.
131. Orwell, *Nineteen Eighty-Four*, 214.
132. Orwell, *Nineteen Eighty-Four*, 104.
133. Orwell, "Politics and the English Language," 172-76.
134. Noam Chomsky, as paraphrased by Verne Harris, "Archives, Politics, and Justice," in Margaret Procter, Michael Cook, and Caroline Williams, eds., *Political Pressure and the Archival Record* (Chicago: Society of American Archivists, 2005), 175.
135. Derrida, *Archive Fever*, 4.
136. Timothy L. Ericson, "Building Our Own 'Iron Curtain': The Emergence of Secrecy in American Government," *American Archivist* 68 (Spring/Summer 2005): 50.
137. Orwell, *Nineteen Eighty-Four*, 176.
138. Robert Boyers, *Atrocity and Amnesia: The Political Novel Since 1945* (New York: Oxford University Press, 1985), 17.
139. Franz Fanon, *The Wretched of the Earth* (New York: Grove Press, 1963).
140. Milan Kundera, *The Book of Laughter and Forgetting* (New York: Alfred A. Knopf, 1980), 231.
141. Kundera, *The Book of Laughter and Forgetting*, 234-35.
142. Milan Kundera, *The Art of the Novel* (New York: HarperPerennial, 2000), 12, 14, 79.
143. Kundera, *The Book of Laughter and Forgetting*, 237.
144. Milan Kundera, *The Joke* (New York: Harper & Row, 1982), viii.
145. Kundera, *The Joke*, 26.
146. Kundera, *The Joke*, 37.
147. Kundera, *The Joke*, 15-16.
148. Kundera, *The Joke*, 60-61.
149. Kundera, *The Joke*, 140-41.
150. Kundera, *The Joke*, 199.
151. Kundera, *The Joke*, 220-21.

152. Kundera, *The Joke*, 244-45.
153. Kundera, *The Joke*, viii.
154. Milan Kundera, *Immortality* (New York: Grove Weidenfeld, 1990), 29-31.
155. Kundera, *Immortality*, 115-16.
156. Kundera, *Immortality*, 164.
157. Kundera, *Immortality*, 73-74.
158. Milan Kundera, *Ignorance* (New York: HarperCollins, 2000), 122-24.
159. Kundera, *Ignorance*, 126-27.
160. Kundera, *Ignorance*, 128-29.
161. Kundera, *Ignorance*, 129-30.
162. Kundera, *The Art of the Novel*, 143.
163. Kundera, *The Art of the Novel*, 157.
164. Kundera, *The Art of the Novel*, 44.
165. Kundera, *The Art of the Novel*, 164-65.
166. Kundera, *The Art of the Novel*, 36-37.
167. Kundera, *The Art of the Novel*, 39-40.
168. Boyers, *Atrocity and Amnesia*, 226.
169. Milan Kundera, *The Unbearable Lightness of Being* (New York: Harper Perennial Classic, 1999), 133.
170. Kundera, *The Unbearable Lightness of Being*, 72-73.
171. Kundera, *The Unbearable Lightness of Being*, 100.
172. Kundera, *The Unbearable Lightness of Being*, 254.
173. Kundera, *The Unbearable Lightness of Being*, 67.
174. Kundera, *The Unbearable Lightness of Being*, 67.
175. Kundera, *The Unbearable Lightness of Being*, 212.
176. Kundera, *The Unbearable Lightness of Being*, 218.
177. Kundera, *The Unbearable Lightness of Being*, 142.
178. Kundera, *The Unbearable Lightness of Being*, 61. Such access to another person's medical records would not be permitted in the United States or many other countries, due to patient privacy laws and confidentiality policies.
179. Kundera, *The Unbearable Lightness of Being*, 103.
180. Kundera, *The Unbearable Lightness of Being*, 125.
181. Kundera, *The Unbearable Lightness of Being*, 199.
182. Kundera, *The Unbearable Lightness of Being*, 267-68.
183. Kundera, *The Unbearable Lightness of Being*, 222-23.
184. Kundera, *The Book of Laughter and Forgetting*, 235-36.
185. Boyers, *Atrocity and Amnesia*, 226, 229.
186. Kundera, *The Book of Laughter and Forgetting*, 3.
187. Kundera, *The Book of Laughter and Forgetting*, 3-4.
188. Kundera, *The Book of Laughter and Forgetting*, 23.
189. Kundera, *The Art of the Novel*, 130.
190. Kundera, *The Book of Laughter and Forgetting*, 7.
191. Kundera, *The Book of Laughter and Forgetting*, 14.
192. Kundera, *The Book of Laughter and Forgetting*, 18.
193. Kundera, *The Book of Laughter and Forgetting*, 22.
194. Kundera, *The Book of Laughter and Forgetting*, 84-85.
195. Kundera, *The Book of Laughter and Forgetting*, 86-87, 94-95.
196. Kundera, *The Book of Laughter and Forgetting*, 100-1.
197. Kundera, *The Book of Laughter and Forgetting*, 107.
198. Kundera, *The Book of Laughter and Forgetting*, 157-58.
199. Kundera, *The Book of Laughter and Forgetting*, 158-59.
200. Allan Spear, "Politics and the Professions," *Midwestern Archivist* 9, no. 2 (1984): 81.

201. Cook and Schwartz, "Archives, Records, and Power," 181.

202. Eric Ketelaar, *The Archival Image* (Hilversum: Verloren, 1997), 19.

203. Ketelaar, *Archival Image*, 15.

204. John M. Dirks, "Accountability, History, and Archives: Conflicting Priorities or Synthesized Strands?" *Archivaria* 57 (Spring 2004): 35, 49. Spragge quoted on page 35.

205. Tom Nesmith, "What's History Got to Do With It?: Reconsidering the Place of Historical Knowledge in Archival Work," *Archivaria* 57 (Spring 2004): 25-26.

206. Kundera, *The Book of Laughter and Forgetting*, 3. This passage also quoted in David Thelen, "Memory and American History," *Journal of American History* 75 (March 1989): 1126.

207. Kenneth E. Foote, "To Remember and Forget: Archives, Memory, and Culture," *American Archivist* 53 (Summer 1990): 393.

208. "Address by Waldo G. Leland, 1956," in Waldo G. Leland Papers, Library of Congress Manuscript Division.

209. F. Gerald Ham, "The Archival Edge," *American Archivist* 38 (January 1975): 5-13.

210. Zinn, "Secrecy, Archives, and the Public Interest," 25.

211. Dirks, "Accountability, History, and Archives," 38.

212. Eric Ketelaar, "Archival Temples, Archival Prisons: Modes of Power and Protection," *Archival Science* 2 (2002): 230-31; John Fleckner, "'Dear Mary Jane': Some Reflections on Being an Archivist," *American Archivist* 54 (Winter 1991): 8-13; see also the extensive writings by Verne Harris on the archives of South Africa, particularly in *Archives and Justice*.

213. Duff and Harris, "Stories and Names," 278-79.

214. Conversation with Juanita Jefferson, archivist and records manager for Lummi Nation, 5 August 2005. See also Michael F. Brown, *Who Owns Native Culture?* (Cambridge, MA: Harvard University Press, 2003).

215. Jeannette Allis Bastian, *Owning Memory: How a Caribbean Community Lost its Archives and Found its History* (Westport, CT: Libraries Unlimited, 2003).

216. Joel Wurl, "Ethnicity as Provenance: In Search of Values and Principles for Documenting the Immigrant Experience," *Archival Issues* 29, no. 1 (2005): 66.

CHAPTER 4

1. Elie Wiesel, *From the Kingdom of Memory: Reminiscences* (New York: Schocken Books, 1990), 194.

2. Kurt Vonnegut, Jr., *Slaughterhouse-Five, or The Children's Crusade* (New York: Delacorte Press, 1969), 29.

3. Vonnegut, *Slaughterhouse-Five*, 82.

4. William Faulkner, *Requiem For a Nun* (Act I Scene III), available at "William Faulkner on the Web," ed. John B. Padgett, University of Mississippi, http://www.mcsr.olemiss. edu/~egjbp/faulkner/quotes.html (accessed 30 July 2007).

5. John Ross, "Against Amnesia," at: http://www.media-alliance.org/article. php?story=2004051402014153 (accessed 18 January 2007).

6. Buddy Buie, James Cobb, and Emory Gordy, "Traces," http://www.lyricsprofessor. com/four-classics/traces.html (accessed 30 July 2007).

7. Richard White, *Remembering Ahanagran: A History of Stories* (New York: Hill and Wang, 1998), 4.

8. White, *Remembering Ahanagran*, 6.

9. White, *Remembering Ahanagran*, 20-21.

10. White, *Remembering Ahanagran*, 92.

11. White, *Remembering Ahanagran*, 247-48.

12. White, *Remembering Ahanagran*, 49.

13. White, *Remembering Ahanagran*, 50-51.

14. White, *Remembering Ahanagran*, 51-52.

15. Jeff Sahadeo, "'Without the Past There Is No Future': Archives, History, and Authority in Uzbekistan," in *Archive Stories: Facts, Fictions, and the Writing of History*, ed. Antoinette Burton (Durham, NC: Duke University Press, 2005), 45.

16. Maurice Halbwachs, *La mémoire collective*, quoted in Patrick H. Hutton, *History as an Art of Memory* (Hanover: University of Vermont, 1993), 76.

17. Hutton, *History as an Art of Memory*, 76-77.

18. Henri Atlan, quoted in Jacques Le Goff, *History and Memory* (New York: Columbia University Press, 1992), 52-53.

19. Christopher Nolan, "Memento" script, http://www.dailyscript.com/scripts/memento. html (accessed 26 July 2007). Unless otherwise noted, quotations from the film are taken from this version of the script.

20. "Anterograde amnesia is a selective memory deficit, resulting from brain injury, in which the individual is severely impaired in learning new information. Memories for events that occurred before the injury may be largely spared, but events that occurred since the injury may be lost. In practice, this means that an individual with amnesia may have good memory for childhood and for the years before the injury, but may remember little or nothing from the years since. Short-term memory is generally spared, which means that the individual may be able to carry on a conversation; but as soon as he is distracted, the memory of the conversation fades." Catherine E. Myers, "Anterograde Amnesia," *Memory Loss and the Brain* glossary (2006), http://www. memorylossonline.com/glossary/anterogradeamnesia.html (accessed 26 July 2007).

21. Daniel L. Schacter, *Searching for Memory: The Brain, the Mind, and the Past* (New York: Basic Books, 1996), as cited in Harry Ritter, "Memory, Certified History, and Consciousness of the Past," (unpublished paper, 1999), 11. The summation of Schacter's three modes of memory is based on Ritter, pages 11-13.

22. Ritter, "Memory, Certified History," 12.

23. Alison Landsberg, *Prosthetic Memory: The Transformation of American Remembrance in the Age of Mass Culture* (New York: Columbia University Press, 2004), 2.

24. Ritter, "Memory, Certified History," 12.

25. Jay Winter and Emmanuel Sivan, "Setting the Framework," in *War and Remembrance in the Twentieth Century* (Cambridge: Cambridge University Press, 1999), 12.

26. Oliver Sacks, "The Abyss: Music and Amnesia," *The New Yorker*, September 24, 2007, 101-2.

27. Sacks, "The Abyss," 103.

28. Sacks, "The Abyss," 104, 106. Sacks cites the quoted passage from Lawrence Weiskrantz, *Consciousness Lost and Found* (New York: Oxford University Press, 1997).

29. Sacks, "The Abyss," 108.

30. Sacks, "The Abyss," 110.

31. Sacks, "The Abyss," 112. Sacks cites the quoted passage from Victor Zuckerkandl, *Sound and Symbol* (1956).

32. Jack Goody, quoted in Le Goff, *History and Memory*, 53.

33. David Thelen, "Memory and American History," *Journal of American History* 75 (March 1989): 1121.

34. Sigmund Freud, quoted in W. Walter Memminger, "Memory and History: What Can You Believe?" *Archival Issues* 21, no. 2 (1996): 102. For a somewhat different account of Freud's views, see Hutton, *History as an Art of Memory*, 78, and Carolyn Steedman, "'Something She Called a Fever': Michelet, Derrida, and Dust (Or, in the Archives with Michelet and Derrida," in *Archives, Documentation and Institutions of Social Memory*, ed. Francis X. Blouin, Jr. and William G. Rosenberg (Ann Arbor: University of Michigan Press, 2006), 6.

35. Hutton, *History as an Art of Memory*, 64.

36. Memminger, "Memory and History," 101.

37. Elizabeth Loftus, quoted in Memminger, "Memory and History," 102.
38. Israel Rosenfeld, quoted in Brien Brothman, "The Past that Archives Keep: Memory, History, and the Preservation of Archival Records," *Archivaria* 51 (2001): 70n.
39. Brothman, "The Past that Archives Keep," 59.
40. Brothman, "The Past that Archives Keep," 79.
41. Quoted in Le Goff, *History and Memory*, 74-75.
42. André Leroi-Gourhan, quoted in Le Goff, *History and Memory*, 91.
43. Allan Megill, *Historical Knowledge, Historical Error: A Contemporary Guide to Practice* (Chicago: University of Chicago Press, 2007), 28-29.
44. Hutton, *History as an Art of Memory*, 78.
45. Hutton, *History as an Art of Memory*, 73.
46. Le Goff, *History and Memory*, 95.
47. Nancy Wood, "Memory's Remains: Les lieux de mémoire," *History and Memory* 6, no. 1 (1994): 123.
48. Pierre Nora, "Between Memory and History: *Les lieux de mémoire*" (1989), quoted in Wood, "Memory's Remains," 127.
49. Wood, "Memory's Remains," 127.
50. David Lowenthal, *The Past Is a Foreign Country* (Cambridge: Cambridge University Press, 1985), xvi.
51. Michael Kammen, *Mystic Chords of Memory: The Transformation of Tradition in American Culture* (New York: Alfred A. Knopf, 1991), 13.
52. Kenneth E. Foote, "To Remember and Forget: Archives, Memory, and Culture," in *American Archival Studies: Readings in Theory and Practice*, ed. Randall C. Jimerson (Chicago: Society of American Archivists, 2000), 29-46.
53. James W. Loewen, *Lies Across America: What Our Historic Sites Get Wrong* (New York: New Press, 1999), 38.
54. Michael Roth, *Ironist's Cage*, quoted in Kerwin Lee Klein, "On the Emergence of Memory in Historical Discourse," *Representations* 69 (Winter 2000): 135.
55. Jeremy Black, *Using History* (London: Hodder Arnold, 2005), 160.
56. Black, *Using History*, 170.
57. Allan Megill, "History, Memory, Identity," *History of the Human Sciences* 11, no. 3 (1998): 55-56.
58. Megill, *Historical Knowledge, Historical Error*, 48, 58.
59. Kammen, *Mystic Chords of Memory*, 625-26.
60. Kammen, *Mystic Chords of Memory*, 688.
61. Michael Kammen, *In the Past Lane: Historical Perspectives on American Culture* (New York: Oxford University Press, 1997), 204.
62. Wood, "Memory's Remains," 147.
63. Gary B. Nash, *First City: Philadelphia and the Forging of Historical Memory* (Philadelphia: University of Pennsylvania Press, 2002), 8-9.
64. Geoffrey Elton, *The Future of the Past* (1968), and Meg Greenfield, "Chronic Political Amnesia" (1980), both quoted in Kammen, *Mystic Chords of Memory*, 9.
65. Landsberg, *Prosthetic Memory*, 2.
66. Landsberg, *Prosthetic Memory* (quoted passages found on pages 21, 30, and 155).
67. Winter and Sivan, *War and Remembrance*, 16.
68. Le Goff, *History and Memory*, 111.
69. Noa Gedi and Yigal Elam, "Collective Memory—What Is It?" *History and Memory* 8, no. 1 (June 30, 1996), accessed via ProQuest: pg. 9 of 11.
70. Amos Funkenstein, *Perceptions of Jewish History* (Berkeley: University of California Press, 1993), 4.
71. Funkenstein, *Perceptions of Jewish History*, quoted in Klein, "On the Emergence of Memory," 133.

72. Derrida and others make the point that historical memory and archival memory are also "emotional, fluid, dynamic, evocative, etc."; Verne Harris, e-mail to author, 18 May 2008.

73. Hutton, *History as an Art of Memory*, 8.

74. Megill, *Historical Knowledge, Historical Error*, 58.

75. Megill, *Historical Knowledge, Historical Error*, 11.

76. Brothman, "The Past that Archives Keep," 59-60.

77. Herodotus, quoted in Ritter, "Memory, Certified History," 16.

78. Thucydides, quoted in Megill, *Historical Knowledge, Historical Error*, 21.

79. Le Goff, *History and Memory*, 111.

80. Leopold Ranke, *Histories of the Latin and Germanic Nations* (1824), quoted in Megill, *Historical Knowledge, Historical Error*, 209.

81. Megill, *Historical Knowledge, Historical Error*, 28.

82. Hutton, *History as an Art of Memory*, 9, 20.

83. Mark A. Greene, "The Messy Business of Remembering: History, Memory, and Archives," *Archival Issues* 28, no. 2 (2003-2004): 97. There is an extensive historiography on this topic; see, for example, Michel-Rolph Trouillot, *Silencing the Past* (Boston: Beacon Press, 1996).

84. Pierre Nora, quoted in Terry Cook, "Remembering the Future: Appraisal of Records and the Role of Archives in Constructing Social Memory," in *Archives, Documentation and Institutions of Social Memory*, 172.

85. Megill, *Historical Knowledge, Historical Error*, 25-26.

86. Anthony F. Aveni, *Empires of Time: Calendars, Clocks, and Cultures* (New York: Basic Books, 1989), 336, as quoted in Richard J. Cox, *Closing an Era: Historical Perspectives on Modern Archives and Records Management* (Westport, CT: Greenwood Press, 2000), 140.

87. Le Goff, *History and Memory*, 58-60.

88. Ritter, "Memory, Certified History," 10, 24.

89. Maurice Mandelbaum, quoted in Steedman, "Something She Called a Fever," 15.

90. Matt K. Matsuda, *The Memory of the Modern* (New York: Oxford University Press, 1996), 62, as quoted in Cox, *Closing an Era*, 147.

91. Jean-Pierre Wallot, quoted in Cook, "Remembering the Future," 172.

92. Foote, "To Remember and Forget," 30.

93. Michel Foucault, quoted in Le Goff, *History and Memory*, 177.

94. James M. O'Toole, "The Symbolic Significance of Archives," in Jimerson, ed., *American Archival Studies*, 47-72.

95. Le Goff, *History and Memory*, 138.

96. Charles V. Langlois and Charles Seignobos, quoted in Le Goff, *History and Memory*, 179.

97. For a thoughtful examination of the concept of memory as a metaphor for archives, see Joshua J. Zimmerman, *Memory Discourse in Archival Literature: A Semantic History of a Metaphor* (Master's thesis, Western Washington University, 2008).

98. Carolyn Steedman, *Dust: The Archive and Cultural History* (New Brunswick, NJ: Rutgers University Press, 2002), 68.

99. Klein, "On the Emergence of Memory," 135-36. Note the similarity of imagery to the "faded photographs" and "tickets torn in half" in "Traces" by the Classics IV.

100. Albert E. Van Dusen, *Connecticut* (New York: Random House, 1961), 350.

101. Hilary Jenkinson, *A Manual of Archive Administration*, rev. ed. (Oxford: Percy Lund, Humphries, 1937), 12; Luciana Duranti, "The Records: Where Archival Universality Resides," *Archival Issues* 19 (1994): 83-94.

102. W. Ross Winterowd, quoted in Mark Greene, "The Power of Meaning: The Archival Mission in the Postmodern Age," *American Archivist* 65 (2002): 53.

103. Eric Ketelaar, quoted in Greene, "The Power of Meaning," 55.

104. Richard Harvey Brown and Beth Davis-Brown, "The Making of Memory: The Politics

of Archives, Libraries and Museums in the Construction of National Consciousness," *History of the Human Sciences* 11, no. 4 (1998): 22.

105. Verne Harris, quoted in Terry Cook, "Fashionable Nonsense or Professional Rebirth: Postmodernism and the Practice of Archives," *Archivaria* 51 (2001): 35.

106. Du Mei, "The Role of Archives in Chinese Society: An Examination from the Perspective of Access," in *Archives, Documentation and Institutions of Social Memory*, 430-34.

107. Francis X. Blouin, "Archivists, Mediation, and the Constructs of Social Memory," *Archival Issues* 24 (1999): 104-6.

108. Elisabeth Kaplan, "We Are What We Collect, We Collect What We Are: Archives and the Construction of Identity," *American Archivist* 63 (2000): 149.

109. Cook, "Fashionable Nonsense or Professional Rebirth," 23.

110. Adrian Cunningham, quoted in Greene, "The Power of Meaning," 51.

111. Kaplan, "We Are What We Collect," 147.

112. Cook, "Fashionable Nonsense or Professional Rebirth," 25.

113. Brothman, "The Past that Archives Keep," 71.

114. Ian E. Wilson, "'The Gift of One Generation to Another': The Real Thing for the Pepsi Generation," in *Archives, Documentation and Institutions of Social Memory*, 338.

115. Howard Zinn, "Secrecy, Archives, and the Public Interest," *Midwestern Archivist* 2 (1977): 14-26. See also Patrick Quinn, "Archivists and Historians: The Times They Are A-changin'," *Midwestern Archivist* 2 (1977): 5-13.

116. Kaplan, "We Are What We Collect," 150-51.

117. Tom Nesmith, "Seeing Archives: Postmodernism and the Changing Intellectual Place of Archives," *American Archivist* 65 (2002): 27.

118. Nesmith, "Seeing Archives," 32.

119. Nesmith, "Seeing Archives," 37.

120. Blouin, "Archivists, Mediation, and the Constructs of Social Memory," 111.

121. Lesley Richmond, "The Memory of Society: Business," *Comma: International Journal on Archives* 1/2 (2002): 113.

122. James M. O'Toole, "Between Veneration and Loathing: Loving and Hating Documents," in *Archives, Documentation and Institutions of Social Memory*, 48. See also Judith M. Panitch, "Liberty, Equality, Posterity?: Some Archival Lessons from the Case of the French Revolution," in Jimerson, ed., *American Archival Studies*, 101-22.

123. O'Toole, "Between Veneration and Loathing," 48.

124. Verne Harris, "Claiming Less, Delivering More: A Critique of Positivist Formulations on Archives in South Africa," *Archivaria* 44 (Fall 1997): 137.

125. Cook, "Remembering the Future," 169.

126. Plato, *Phaedrus*, quoted by Clara Claiborne Park, "The Mother of the Muses: In Praise of Memory," in *The Anatomy of Memory: An Anthology*, ed. James McConkey (New York: Oxford University Press, 1996), 179-80.

127. Julius Caesar, *Gallic Wars* (VI, 14), quoted in Le Goff, *History and Memory*, 57.

128. Milan Kundera, *The Book of Laughter and Forgetting* (New York: Alfred A. Knopf, 1980), 3.

129. Patricia Hampl, "Memory and Imagination," in *I Could Tell You Stories: Sojourns in the Land of Memory* (New York: W.W. Norton, 1999), 208-11.

130. Megill, *Historical Knowledge, Historical Error*, 54.

131. Peter Fritzsche, "The Archive and the Case of the German Nation," in *Archive Stories*, 186-87.

132. Lowenthal, *The Past Is a Foreign Country*.

133. Brothman, "The Past that Archives Keep," 73, 76.

134. Verne Harris, *Archives and Justice: A South African Perspective* (Chicago: Society of American Archivists, 2007), 47.

135. Harris, *Archives and Justice*, 300-1.

136. "Archive Fever: A Seminar by Jacques Derrida," in *Refiguring the Archive*, ed. Carolyn

Hamilton, Verne Harris, Jane Taylor, Michele Pickover, Graeme Reid, and Razia Saleh (Dordrecht, Netherlands: Kluwer Academic Publishers, 2002), 54.

137. Harris, *Archives and Justice*, 394.
138. Harris, *Archives and Justice*, 300-1.
139. Harris, *Archives and Justice*, 396.
140. Jacques Derrida, *Archive Fever: A Freudian Impression* (Chicago: University of Chicago Press, 1995), 10-11. Italics in the original.
141. Derrida, *Archive Fever*, 12.
142. Megill, *Historical Knowledge, Historical Error*, 73.
143. Wood, "Memory's Remains," 147.
144. Kammen, *Mystic Chords of Memory*, 13.
145. Foote, "To Remember and Forget," 46.
146. Frank Boles, "'Just a Bunch of Bigots': A Case Study in the Acquisition of Controversial Material," *Archival Issues* 19 (1994): 53-65.
147. Ralph Ellison, *Going to the Territory* (New York: Random House, 1986), 123-24, quoted in Kammen, *In the Past Lane*, 164.
148. Inge Bundsgaard, "The Question of Access: The Right to Social Memory versus the Right to Social Oblivion," in *Archives, Documentation and Institutions of Social Memory*, 115.
149. Matthew Battles, *Library: An Unquiet History* (London: Random House Vintage, 2003), 180.
150. Robert J. Donia, "The New Masters of Memory: Libraries, Archives, and Museums in Postcommunist Bosnia-Herzegovina," in *Archives, Documentation and Institutions of Social Memory*, 394-96.
151. Battles, *Library*, 188.
152. Eleanor Robson, "Whose Heritage? National and International Interests in Cultural Property in Post-war Iraq" (undated manuscript provided by Robson to the author, 10 September 2007), 1 of 11.
153. Saad Eskander, quoted in Jeff Spurr, "Iraqi Libraries and Archives in Peril: Survival in a Time of Invasion, Chaos, and Civil Conflict, A Report" (11 April 2007), 16. I am indebted to Steven Garfinkle, Professor of History, Western Washington University, for giving me a copy of this report.
154. Spurr, "Iraqi Libraries and Archives in Peril," 12.
155. Spurr, "Iraqi Libraries and Archives in Peril," 8.
156. Society of American Archivists Council, "Iraq National Library and Archives in Jeopardy" (8 August 2007), http://www.archivists.org/news/iraqi_archives-07.asp (accessed 11 September 2007).
157. Spurr, "Iraqi Libraries and Archives in Peril," 7-8.
158. Robson, "Whose Heritage?" 8 of 11.
159. Harris, *Archives and Justice*, 404.
160. Spurr, "Iraqi Libraries and Archives in Peril," 8.
161. Beatrice S. Bartlett, "Qing Statesmen, Archivists, and Historians and the Question of Memory," in *Archives, Documentation and Institutions of Social Memory*, 418-19.
162. Bartlett, "Qing Statesmen, Archivists, and Historians," 422-23.
163. Du Mei, "The Role of Archives in Chinese Society," 434.
164. George Orwell, "Looking Back on the Spanish War," in *A Collection of Essays* (Garden City, NY: Doubleday, 1954), 206.
165. Laurent Dubois, "Maroons in the Archives: Uses of the Past in the French Caribbean," in *Archives, Documentation and Institutions of Social Memory*, 292.
166. Adele Perry, "The Colonial Archive on Trial: Possession, Dispossession, and History in *Delgamuukw v. British Columbia*," in *Archive Stories*, 345.
167. Wiesel, *From the Kingdom of Memory*, 239.
168. Ann Laura Stoler, "Colonial Archives and the Art of Governance: On the Content of

the Form," in *Archives, Documentation and Institutions of Social Memory*, 271.

169. Steedman, *Dust*, 151.
170. Le Goff, *History and Memory*, 54.
171. Kammen, *In the Past Lane*, 210-11.
172. Harris, *Archives and Justice*, 259.
173. Fritzsche, "The Archive and the Case of the German Nation," 185-86.
174. Achille Mbembe, "The Power of the Archive and Its Limits," in *Refiguring the Archive*, 20.
175. Eric Ketelaar, "Archival Temples, Archival Prisons: Modes of Power and Protection," *Archival Science* 2 (2002): 223.
176. Richard Pearce-Moses, *A Glossary of Archival and Records Teminology*, Archival Fundamentals Series II (Chicago: Society of American Archivists, 2005), 22.
177. Maynard Brichford, *Archives and Manuscripts: Appraisal and Accessioning*, Basic Manual Series (Chicago: Society of American Archivists, 1977), 1.
178. Frank Boles, *Selecting and Appraising Archives and Manuscripts*, Archival Fundamentals Series II (Chicago: Society of American Archivists, 2005), xv.
179. Cook, "Remembering the Future," 169.
180. Cook, "Fashionable Nonsense or Professional Rebirth," 30.
181. Derrida, *Archive Fever*, 70.
182. Ketelaar, "Archival Temples, Archival Prisons," 233.
183. Derrida, *Archive Fever*, 30.
184. Derrida, *Archive Fever*, 33-34.
185. Derrida, *Archive Fever*, 35-36.
186. Derrida, *Archive Fever*, 67-68.
187. There is a large and increasing literature on this topic. For only a few examples, see the following articles reprinted in Jimerson, *American Archival Studies*: Elsie Freeman Finch, "In the Eye of the Beholder: Archives Administration from the User's Point of View" (1984), 417-31; Paul Conway, "Facts and Frameworks: An Approach to Studying the Users of Archives" (1986), 433-48; Elizabeth Yakel and Laura L. Bost Hensey, "Understanding Administrative Use and Users in University Archives" (1994), 449-71; Randall C. Jimerson, "Redefining Archival Identity: Meeting User Needs in the Information Society" (1989), 607-17; John J. Grabowski, "Keepers, Users, and Funders: Building an Awareness of Archival Value" (1992), 619-29; and Mark Greene, "'The Surest Proof: A Utilitarian Approach to Appraisal" (1998), 301-42.
188. Verne Harris and Sello Hatang, "Archives, Identity, and Place: A Dialogue on What It (Might) Mean(s) to be an African Archivist," in *Archives and Justice*, 235, 237.

CHAPTER 5

1. "Address by Former President Nelson Mandela at the launch of the Nelson Mandela Centre of Memory and Commemoration Project" (September 2004), ID # NMS761, Nelson Mandela Foundation website, http://www.nelsonmandela.org/index.php/memory/resources/speeches/ (accessed 4 October 2007).
2. "Address by Former President Nelson Mandela."
3. "Address by Former President Nelson Mandela."
4. "Address by Former President Nelson Mandela." In 2006 the Nelson Mandela Foundation recast its core business as a nongovernmental organization (NGO), renamed "The Nelson Mandela Centre of Memory and Dialogue."
5. "Address by Former President Nelson Mandela."
6. Nelson Mandela, *Long Walk to Freedom: The Autobiography of Nelson Mandela* (Boston: Little, Brown and Company, 1994), 18.
7. Mandela, *Long Walk to Freedom*, 21, 97.
8. *Nelson Mandela in His Own Words*, ed. Kader Asmal, David Chidester, and Wilmot James

(Boston: Little, Brown and Company, 2003), 293-94.

9. *Nelson Mandela in His Own Words*, 42.

10. Nelson Mandela Foundation, *A Prisoner in the Garden* (London: Viking Studio, 2006), 69.

11. *A Prisoner in the Garden*, quotations from pages 69 and 83.

12. *A Prisoner in the Garden*, 51-52, 103-4.

13. *A Prisoner in the Garden*, 174-76; Mandela, *Long Walk to Freedom*, "Acknowledgments" page and 476-84.

14. Mandela, *Long Walk to Freedom*, 470, 489.

15. *A Prisoner in the Garden*, 203.

16. *Nelson Mandela in His Own Words*, 130.

17. *Nelson Mandela in His Own Words*, 294-99.

18. Elie Wiesel, *From the Kingdom of Memory: Reminiscences* (New York: Schocken Books, 1990), 187, 200-1.

19. Chomsky, as paraphrased by Verne Harris, "Archives, Politics, and Justice," in *Political Pressure and the Archival Record*, ed. Margaret Procter, Michael Cook, and Caroline Williams (Chicago: Society of American Archivists, 2005), 175.

20. Peter Fritzsche, "The Archive and the Case of the German Nation," in *Archive Stories: Facts, Fictions, and the Writing of History*, ed. Antoinette Burton (Durham, NC: Duke University Press, 2005), 196.

21. Jacques Derrida, *Archive Fever: A Freudian Impression* (Chicago: University of Chicago Press, 1996), 4n.

22. Eric Ketelaar, "The Panoptical Archive," in *Archives, Documentation and Institutions of Social Memory*, ed. Francis X. Blouin, Jr. and William G. Rosenberg (Ann Arbor: University of Michigan Press, 2006), 145.

23. Verne Harris, "Redefining Archives in South Africa: Public Archives and Society in Transition, 1990–1996," in *Archives and Justice: A South African Perspective* (Chicago: Society of American Archivists, 2007), 173–202.

24. Chris Hurley, "The Evolving Role of Government Archives in Democratic Societies" (unpublished paper, 2001), quoted in Harris, *Archives and Justice*, 245.

25. Ben Kiernan, Yale Center for International and Area Studies Global Resources Network Conference, March 2005, available at http://www.library.yale.edu/mssa/globalrecord/new_web/kiernan_richie.html#text (accessed 6 July 2007). See also Dawne Adam, "The Tuol Seng Archives and the Cambodian Genocide," *Archivaria* 45 (Spring 1998): 5–26.

26. Achille Mbembe, "The Power of the Archive and Its Limits," in *Refiguring the Archive*, ed. Carolyn Hamilton, Verne Harris, Jane Taylor, Michele Pickover, Graeme Reid, and Razia Saleh (Dordrecht, Netherlands: Kluwer Academic Publishers, 2002), 23.

27. F. Gerald Ham, "The Archival Edge," in *A Modern Archives Reader*, ed. Maygene Daniels and Timothy Walch (Washington, DC: National Archives and Records Service, 1984), 335.

28. Richard J. Cox and David A. Wallace, eds., *Archives and the Public Good: Accountability and Records in Modern Society* (Westport, CT: Quorum Books, 2002); Procter, Cook, and Williams, eds., *Political Pressure and the Archival Record*; Hamilton, Harris, Taylor, Pickover, Reid, and Saleh, eds., *Refiguring the Archive*; Blouin and Rosenberg, eds., *Archives, Documentation and Institutions of Social Memory*; and Harris, *Archives and Justice*.

29. John McDonald, "Accountability in Government in an Electronic Age" (1998), available at International Records Management Trust website: http://web.archive.org/web/20010726105930/www.irmt.org/education/malpaper2.html (accessed 11 May 2007).

30. Chris Hurley, "Recordkeeping and Accountability," in Sue McKemmish, Michael Piggott, Barbara Reed, and Frank Upward, eds., *Archives: Recordkeeping in Society* (Wagga Wagga, New South Wales: Charles Sturt University, 2005), 224-25.

31. Hurley, "Recordkeeping and Accountability," 237.
32. Terry Cook, "Archival Music: Verne Harris and the Cracks of Memory," in Harris, *Archives and Justice*, x.
33. Bruce P. Montgomery, "Nixon's Legal Legacy: White House Papers and the Constitution," *American Archivist* 56 (Fall 1993): 609.
34. David A. Wallace, "Implausible Deniability: The Politics of Documents in the Iran-Contra Affair and Its Investigations," in *Archives and the Public Good*, 95–99.
35. Wallace, "Implausible Deniability," 106, 108, 112.
36. Hon. Jack Lee, et al. to Hon. Peter Beattie, Queensland Premier, "The Heiner Affair—A Matter of Concern," August 2007.
37. Kevin Lindeberg, "The Need for a Public Sector Independent Watchdog Commission—Yes or No," Submission to the Joint Select Committee on Ethical Conduct, Parliament of Tasmania (18 August 2008), 6; Kevin Lindeberg, e-mail to author, 11 November 2008.
38. Lindeberg, "The Need for a Public Sector Independent Watchdog Commission," 20-21.
39. Chris Hurley, "Records and the Public Interest: The 'Heiner Affair' in Queensland, Australia," in *Archives and the Public Good*, 313.
40. Hurley, "Evolving Role of Government Archives," 243.
41. Piers Ackerman, "PM Shreds His Own Credibility," Piers Akerman blog, http://blogs.news.com.au/dailytelegraph/piersakerman/index.php/dailytelegraph/comments/pm_shreds_his_own_credibility/P20/ (accessed 10 December 2008); Kevin Lindeberg, e-mail to author, 11 November 2008; Rick Barry, e-mail to author, 11 November 2008.
42. Kevin Lindeberg, e-mail to author, 18 February 2009. See public submission: http://www.parliament.tas.gov.au/ctee/Submissions/24A%20Lindeberg.pdf
43. Rick Barry, e-mail to author, 16 February 2009.
44. Society of American Archivists, Code of Ethics, available at: http://www.archivists.org/governance/handbook/app_ethics.asp (accessed 1 December 2006).
45. "Who's Accountable? Inside the Growing Enron Scandal: How Evidence Was Shredded and Top Executives Fished for a Bailout as the Company Imploded," *Time*, 13 January 2002, available at http://www.commondreams.org/cgi-bin/print.cgi?file=/headlines02/0113-02.htm (accessed 12 May 2007).
46. Patrice Davis, *Some Much Deserved Respect: The Impact of the Sarbanes-Oxley Act from a Records Management Perspective Focusing on Small Businesses* (Master of Arts thesis, Western Washington University, 2006), 62–65.
47. William L. Joyce, "Classified Federal Records and the End of the Cold War: The Experience of the Assassination Records Review Board," in *Archives, Documentation and Institutions of Social Memory*, 242.
48. Ian E. Wilson, "'The Gift of One Generation to Another': The Real Thing for the Pepsi Generation," in *Archives, Documentation and Institutions of Social Memory*, 339.
49. Anne Van Camp, "Trying to Write 'Comprehensive and Accurate' History of the Foreign Relations of the United States: An American Perspective," in *Archives and the Public Good*, 229.
50. Derrida, *Archive Fever*, 4n.
51. Verne Harris, Sello Hatang, and Peter Liberman, "Unveiling South Africa's Nuclear Past," in Harris, *Archives and Justice*, 370.
52. Ernst Posner, "Some Aspects of Archival Development Since the French Revolution," in *Archives and the Public Interest: Selected Essays by Ernst Posner*, ed. Ken Munden (Washington, DC: Public Affairs Press, 1967), 23–35; Judith M. Panitch, "Liberty, Equality, Posterity?: Some Archival Lessons from the Case of the French Revolution," *American Archivist* 59 (Winter 1996): 30–47.

53. Harvey J. Kaye, *"Why Do Ruling Classes Fear History?" and Other Questions* (New York: St. Martin's Griffin, 1997), 14–15.

54. Kaye, *"Why Do Ruling Classes Fear History?"* 19, 23.

55. Timothy L. Ericson, "Building Our Own 'Iron Curtain': The Emergence of Secrecy in American Government," *American Archivist* 68 (Spring/Summer 2005): 50.

56. Ericson, "Building Our Own 'Iron Curtain,'" 24, 38.

57. Ericson, "Building Our Own 'Iron Curtain,'" 43.

58. Thomas James Connors, "The Bush Administration and 'Information Lockdown," in *Political Pressure*, 195.

59. Al Kamen, "Millions of Secrets," *Washington Post,* May 3, 2004, quoted in Ericson, "Building Our Own 'Iron Curtain,'" 20.

60. Ericson, "Building Our Own 'Iron Curtain,'" 44.

61. Ron Wyden testimony, *Congressional Record* 150 (15 July 2004): S8234-S8237, quoted in Ericson, "Building Our Own 'Iron Curtain,'" 50-51.

62. "Government Secrecy on the Rise: New Book Updates 1987 Report on Government Secrecy," OpenTheGovernment.org press release (July 12, 2007), http://www. openthegovernment.org/article/articleview/268/1/68/?TopicID= (accessed 29 September 2007).

63. "Secrecy Report Card 2007: Report Finds Expanded Federal Government Secrecy in 2006," OpenTheGovernment.org press release (September 1, 2007), http://www.openthegovernment.org/article/articleview/275/1/68/?TopicID= (accessed 29 September 2007).

64. Connors, "The Bush Administration," 199.

65. Connors, "The Bush Administration," 202. For further background on the struggle between Congress and the executive branch over control of presidential records, see Bruce P. Montgomery, "Presidential Materials: Politics and the Presidential Records Act," *American Archivist* 66 (Spring/Summer 2003): 102–38.

66. Ericson, "Building Our Own 'Iron Curtain,'" 49.

67. National Coalition for History, "President Obama Revokes Bush Presidential Records Executive Order" (updated 26 January 2009), at: http://historycoalition. org/2009/01/21/president-obama-revokes-bush-presidential-records-executive-order/#more-1033 (accessed 5 February 2009). For the text of the Executive Order see *Federal Register*, Vol. 74, No. 15 (26 January 2009), also at: http://www.whitehouse. gov/the_press_office/ExecutiveOrderPresidentialRecords/ (accessed 12 February 2009).

68. White House Office of the Press Secretary, "Freedom of Information Act" (21 January 2009), at: http://www.archivists.org/news/FOIA_1.21.09.pdf.

69. Mark J. Rozell and Mitchel A. Sollenberger, "Obama Opens the Books," (2 February 2009), http://www.politico.com/news/stories/0209/18266.html (accessed 11 February 2009).

70. Connors, "The Bush Administration," 208.

71. Frank Boles to President Barack Obama, 22 January 2009, at: www.archivists.org/ news/ObamaReEO13233.pdf.

72. David Lowenthal, "Archives, Heritage, and History," in *Archives, Documentation and Institutions of Social Memory*, 194.

73. Jennifer S. Milligan, "'What Is an Archives?' in the History of Modern France," in *Archive Stories*, 167.

74. Milligan, "What Is an Archives?": 169-71.

75. Harris, in *Political Pressure*, 173.

76. Harris, in *Political Pressure*, 181–82.

77. Masahito Ando, "The Asian-Pacific War and the Fate of Archives," in *Political Pressure*, 4.

78. Ando, "The Asian-Pacific War," 17.

79. Quoted in Trudy Huskamp Peterson, "Archives in Service to the State," in *Political Pressure*, 270. See also Agnes Jonker, "Srebenica: A Balkan Tragedy and the Making of a

Dutch Affair," in *Political Pressure*, 277-88.

80. Astrid M. Eckert, "'. . . And Grant German and Foreign Scholars Access at All Times': Archival Access in West Germany During the Cold War," in *Political Pressure*, 75.

81. Eckert, "Access at All Times," 90. Imbedded quotation is cited as "Kostengünstige Resource im Systemkonflict."

82. Friedrich Kahlenberg, "Governmental Rule and Archivists: The Historical Experience of the 20th Century in Central Europe," in *Political Pressure*, 59.

83. Ziva Galili, "Archives and Historical Writing: The Case of the Menshevik Party in 1917," in *Archives, Documentation and Institutions of Social Memory*, 444-45, 449.

84. Kyong Rae Lee, "Political Democracy and Archival Development in the Management of Presidential Records in the Republic of Korea," *American Archivist* 69 (Spring/Summer 2006): 118, 128, 130.

85. Lee, "Political Democracy and Archival Development in . . . Korea," 133–37.

86. Derrida, *Archive Fever*, 76-77.

87. Cook, "Archival Music," x-xi.

88. Truth and Reconciliation Commission of South Africa, Report, vol. 1 (New York: Grove's Dictionaries, Inc., 1998), 201, quoted in Helena Pohlandt-McCormick, "In Good Hands: Researching the 1976 Soweto Uprising in the State Archives of South Africa," in *Archive Stories*, 299.

89. Verne Harris, "'They Should Have Destroyed More': The Destruction of Public Records by the South African State in the Final Years of Apartheid, 1990–1994," in *Archives and the Public Good*, 205.

90. Harris, "Redefining Archives," 173–74.

91. Pohlandt-McCormick, "In Good Hands," 299-300.

92. Harris, *Archives and Justice*, quotations from pages 43 and 259.

93. Pohlandt-McCormick, "In Good Hands," 313.

94. Harris, in *Archives and the Public Good*, 224–25.

95. Pohlandt-McCormick, "In Good Hands," 314.

96. Pohlandt-McCormick, "In Good Hands," 320.

97. Harris, *Political Pressure*, 177–78. For more on SAHA, see Harris, "Using the Promotion of Access to Information Act (PAIA): The Case of the South African History Archive," in *Archives and Justice*, 337–49.

98. Harris, *Political Pressure*, 180–81.

99. Trudy Huskamp Peterson, *Final Acts: A Guide to Preserving the Records of Truth Commissions* (Washington, DC: Woodrow Wilson Center Press, 2005), 1–2.

100. Peterson, *Final Acts*, 8.

101. Greg Bradsher, "Turning History into Justice: The National Archives and Records Administration and Holocaust-Era Assets, 1996–2001," in *Archives and the Public Good*, 178.

102. Bradsher, "Turning History into Justice," 177.

103. Bradsher, "Turning History into Justice," 194.

104. Bradsher, "Turning History into Justice," 199–200.

105. Tywanna Whorley, "The Tuskegee Syphilis Study: Access and Control Over Controversial Records," in *Political Pressure*, 110.

106. Whorley, "The Tuskegee Syphilis Study," 110–11. Haworth is quoted from his article, "The Principles Speak for Themselves: Articulating a Language of Purpose for Archives," in *The Archival Imagination: Essays in Honour of Hugh Taylor*, ed. Barbara L. Craig (Ottawa: Association of Canadian Archivists, 1992).

107. Whorley, "The Tuskegee Syphilis Study," 116–17.

108. Jeff Sahadeo, "'Without the Past There Is No Future': Archives, History, and Authority in Uzbekistan," in *Archive Stories*, 45-47.

109. Sahadeo, "Without the Past There Is No Future," 63-64.

110. Sarah Demb, "Vital Records and Cultural Heritage: The Role of the National Archives in the Governance of Sierra Leone" (unpublished paper presented at the 2006 annual meeting of the Association of Canadian Archivists).
111. Elisabeth Kaplan, "We Are What We Collect, We Collect What We Are: Archives and the Construction of Identity," *American Archivist* 63 (Spring/Summer 2000): 126–51.
112. Diane Vogt-O'Connor, "Is the Record of the Twentieth Century at Risk?" quoted in Lowenthal, "Archives, Heritage, and History," in *Archives, Documentation and Institutions of Social Memory*, 200.
113. Howard Zinn, "The Archivist and Radical Reform," unpublished manuscript quoted in F. Gerald Ham, "The Archival Edge," *American Archivist* 38 (January 1975): 5; Sam Bass Warner, Jr., "The Shame of the Cities: Public Records of the Metropolis," *Midwest Archivist* 2, no. 2 (1977): 27–34; Patrick M. Quinn, "Archivists and Historians: The Times They Are A-Changin'," *Midwest Archivist* 2, no 2 (1977): 513.
114. Joyce Appleby, *A Restless Past: History and the American Public* (Lanham, MD: Rowman and Littlefield, 2005), 139.
115. Kaplan, "We Are What We Collect," 126–51.
116. Gerda Lerner, *The Creation of Patriarchy* (New York: Oxford University Press, 1986): 4–5.
117. Lerner, *Creation of Patriarchy*, 221.
118. Terry Cook, "Remembering the Future: Appraisal of Records and the Role of Archives in Constructing Social Memory," in *Archives, Documentation and Institutions of Social Memory*, 174.
119. Ellen Fitzpatrick, *History's Memory: Writing America's Past, 1880-1980* (Cambridge, MA: Harvard University Press, 2002), 237.
120. Eleanor Flexner, *Century of Struggle: The Woman's Rights Movement in the United States* (Cambridge, MA: Harvard University Press, 1959), 335.
121. Lerner, *Creation of Patriarchy*, 221.
122. Andrea Hinding, ed., *Women's History Sources: A Guide to Archives and Manuscript Collections in the United States* (New York: R. R. Bowker Company, 1979).
123. Laura Mayhall, "Creating the 'Suffragette Spirit': British Feminism and the Historical Imagination," in *Archive Stories*, 232.
124. Suffragette Fellowship Newsletter (1936): 3, quoted in Mayhall, "Creating the 'Suffragette Spirit,'" 245.
125. Mayhall, "Creating the 'Suffragette Spirit,'" 247.
126. Jeannette Allis Bastian, "Whispers in the Archives: Finding the Voices of the Colonized in the Records of the Colonizer," in *Political Pressure*, 27–28, 34. See also Bastian, *Owning Memory: How a Caribbean Community Lost Its Archives and Found Its History* (Westport, CT: Libraries Unlimited, 2003). Laurent Dubois echoes Bastian: "As is the case in many colonial contexts, a large percentage of the documents relating to Guadeloupe are in fact not on the island but in metropolitan France . . ." Laurent Dubois, "Maroons in the Archives: Uses of the Past in the French Caribbean," in *Archives, Documentation and Institutions of Social Memory*, 293.
127. Bastian, "Whispers in the Archives," 26-29, 32.
128. Ann Curthoys, "The History of Killing and the Killing of History," in *Archive Stories*, 363.
129. Ann Laura Stoler, "Colonial Archives and the Art of Governance: On the Content of the Form," in *Archives, Documentation and Institutions of Social Memory*, 268.
130. Stoler, "Colonial Archives and the Art of Governance," 270-71.
131. Stoler, "Colonial Archives and the Art of Governance," 273-74.
132. Ann Laura Stoler, *Along the Archival Grain: Epistemic Anxieties and Colonial Common Sense* (Princeton, NJ: Princeton University Press, 2008), 1.
133. Frederick Cooper, "Memories of Colonization: Commemoration, Preservation, and Erasure in an African Archives," in *Archives, Documentation and Institutions of Social Memory*, 257.

134. Fletcher and Trevor-Roper, quoted in David Lowenthal, "The Timeless Past: Some Anglo-American Historical Preconceptions," *Journal of American History* 75 (March 1989): 1269.

135. Adele Perry, "The Colonial Archive on Trial: Possession, Dispossession, and History in *Delgamuukw v. British Columbia*," in *Archive Stories*, 326-27.

136. McEachern's court judgment, quoted in Perry, "The Colonial Archive on Trial," 336, 339.

137. Perry, "The Colonial Archive on Trial," quoted passages on pages 333, 339-40.

138. Perry, "The Colonial Archive on Trial," 341.

139. Shauna McRanor, "Maintaining the Reliability of Aboriginal Oral Records and Their Material Manifestations: Implications for Archival Practice," *Archivaria* 43 (1997): 81. Similarly, court decisions in Australia have privileged written (white) documents over indigenous oral testimony in title cases over tribal lands. See Michael Piggott, "Archives and Memory," in *Archives: Recordkeeping in Society*, 318.

140. Perry, "The Colonial Archive on Trial," 337.

141. Perry, "The Colonial Archive on Trial," quoted passages on pages 326, 327, 344.

142. Schomburg Center for Research in Black Culture, "History and General Information," http://www.nypl.org/research/sc/about/history.html (accessed 10 May 2007).

143. Thomas C. Battle, "Moorland-Spingarn Research Center," *Library Quarterly* 58, no. 2 (1988): 143–63 and http://www.founders.howard.edu/moorland-spingarn/HIST. HTM (accessed 10 May 2007).

144. "Amistad Research Center," http://www.amistadresearchcenter.org (accessed 10 May 2007).

145. Harold T. Pinkett, "Preserving the Past for the Present," *The Crisis* (February 1944), 57.

146. King Center, "The King Center's Mission," http://www.thekingcenter.com/tkc/mission.asp (accessed 10 May 2007).

147. Birmingham Civil Rights Institute, "Archives Division," http://www.bcri.org/index.html (accessed 10 May 2007).

148. University of Southern Mississippi, "About the Civil Rights in Mississippi Digital Archives," http://www.lib.usm.edu/~spcol/crda/about.htm (accessed 10 May 2007).

149. King Center, "The King Center's Mission," http://www.thekingcenter.com/tkc/mission.asp (accessed 10 May 2007).

150. King Center, "King and the Modern Civil Rights Movement Scholar and Historian Research Program," http://www.thekingcenter.com/prog/research.html (accessed 10 May 2007).

151. Howard Zinn, "Secrecy, Archives, and the Public Interest," *Midwestern Archivist* 2, no. 2 (1977): 25.

152. Harris, *Archives and Justice*, 262.

153. *A Prisoner in the Garden*, 23, 25.

154. *A Prisoner in the Garden*, 9.

155. "Speech delivered by Mr. N. R. Mandela at the launch of '466/64: A Prisoner Working in the Garden Exhibition' at Constitution Hill" (March 2005), ID# NMS757, Nelson Mandela Foundation website, http://www.nelsonmandela.org/index.php/memory/resources/speeches/ (accessed 4 October 2007).

CHAPTER 6

1. http://jillandhal.home.att.net/halqn/w_kelly6.htm (accessed 1 August 2008).

2. Nicholas C. Burckel, "Academic Archives: Retrospect and Prospect," in *College and University Archives*, ed. Christopher J. Prom and Ellen D. Swain (Chicago: Society of American Archivists, 2008), 6-7.

3. August Suelflow, *Religious Archives: An Introduction* (Chicago: Society of American Archivists, 1980), 6-7.
4. James M. O'Toole, "What's Different About Religious Archives?" *Midwestern Archivist* 9, no. 2 (1984): 94-95.
5. O'Toole, "What's Different About Religious Archives?" 94-99.
6. David A. Haury, "The Research Potential of Religious Archives: The Mennonite Experience," *Midwestern Archivist* 11, no. 2 (1986): 136.
7. Lesley Richmond, "The Memory of Society: Business," *Comma: International Journal on Archives* 1/2 (2002): 113-14.
8. Richmond, "The Memory of Society: Business," 115-16.
9. Richmond, "The Memory of Society: Business," 116-18 (quoted passages on page 118).
10. Becky Haglund Tousey and Elizabeth W. Adkins, "Access to Business Archives: U.S. Access Philosophies," in Japan-U.S. Archives Seminar (May 2007): 2 of 6; available at SAA website: www.archivists.org (accessed 9 April 2008).
11. Tousey and Adkins, "Access to Business Archives," 3 of 6.
12. Tousey and Adkins, "Access to Business Archives," 4 of 6.
13. Tousey and Adkins, "Access to Business Archives," 5 of 6.
14. Tousey and Adkins, "Access to Business Archives," 6 of 6.
15. Phil Mooney, Elizabeth Adkins, Bruce Bruemmer, Leslie Simon, Becky Tousey, Jane Nokes, Paul Lasewicz, and Ed Rider, "To the Editor," in "Forum," *American Archivist* 67, no. 2 (Fall/Winter 2004): 152-53. Note: The poster illustration changed "Sun Maid" to "Sun Mad."
16. Mark A. Greene, "To the Editor," in "Forum," *American Archivist* 67, no. 2 (Fall/Winter 2004): 153.
17. Richard J. Cox, "To the Editor," in "Forum," *American Archivist* 68, no. 1 (Spring/Summer 2005): 9-10.
18. Randall C. Jimerson and Richard Pearce-Moses, "To the Editor," in "Forum," *American Archivist* 68, no. 2 (Fall/Winter 2005): 202-3.
19. Corporate Archives Forum e-mail message, cited in Bruce H. Bruemmer, "Brown Shoes in a World of Tuxedos: Corporate Archives and the Archival Profession" (2006), available at: www.mybestdocs.com/bruemmer-b-SAA082006-bizethics.htm (accessed 12 May 2008).
20. Bruemmer, "Brown Shoes in a World of Tuxedos."
21. Independent counsel Simon Reich, quoted in Bruemmer, "Brown Shoes in a World of Tuxedos."
22. Bruemmer, "Brown Shoes in a World of Tuxedos."
23. Andrew V. Abela, "Digesting the Raisins of Wrath: Business, Ethics, and the Archival Profession," *American Archivist* 71 (Spring/Summer 2008): 209.
24. Abela, "Digesting the Raisins of Wrath," 204, 208-9.
25. Harvey J. Kaye, *"Why Do Ruling Classes Fear History?" and Other Questions* (New York: St. Martin's Griffin, 1997), 153.
26. Terry Cook, "The Archive(s) Is a Foreign Country: Historians, Archivists, and the Archival Landscape," *Canadian Historical Review* (forthcoming, fall 2009).
27. Peter Novick, *That Noble Dream: The "Objectivity Question" and the American Historical Profession* (New York: Cambridge University Press, 1988), 1-2.
28. Novick, *That Noble Dream*, 11.
29. Novick, *That Noble Dream*, 37.
30. Novick, *That Noble Dream*, 6.
31. Thomas L. Haskell, *Objectivity Is Not Neutrality: Explanatory Schemes in History* (Baltimore: Johns Hopkins University Press, 1998), 149-50. See also Haskell, "Objectivity: Perspective as Problem and Solution," *History and Theory* 43 (October 2004): 341-59.
32. Haskell, *Objectivity Is Not Neutrality*, 155.

33. Mea culpa. In my 2005 SAA presidential address I fell into the same trap that has ensnared many who have argued that abandoning the "illusion of neutrality" also requires abandoning the ideal of objectivity. Randall C. Jimerson, "Embracing the Power of Archives," *American Archivist* 69 (Spring/Summer 2006): 19-32.

34. Haskell, *Objectivity Is Not Neutrality*, 150-52.

35. Haskell, *Objectivity Is Not Neutrality*, 158-59.

36. Haskell, *Objectivity Is Not Neutrality*, 167-68.

37. Allan Megill, *Historical Knowledge, Historical Error: A Contemporary Guide to Practice* (Chicago: University of Chicago Press, 2007), 109-11.

38. Megill, *Historical Knowledge, Historical Error*, 208.

39. Megill, *Historical Knowledge, Historical Error*, 215. See his detailed examination of these concepts on pages 112-24; and in "Introduction: Four Senses of Objectivity," in *Rethinking Objectivity*, ed. Allan Megill (Durham, NC: Duke University Press, 1994), 1-20.

40. Megill, *Historical Knowledge, Historical Error*, 124.

41. George Orwell, "Writers and Leviathan," *Politics and Letters* (Summer 1948), available at: http://www.netcharles.com/orwell/essays/writers-and-leviathan.htm (accessed 3 January 2007).

42. Elie Wiesel, *From the Kingdom of Memory: Reminiscences* (New York: Schocken Books, 1990), 151.

43. Howard Zinn, *You Can't Be Neutral on a Moving Train: A Personal History of Our Times* (Boston: Beacon Press, 2002).

44. Patrick M. Quinn, "Archivists and Historians: The Times They Are A-Changin'," *Midwestern Archivist* 2, no. 2 (1977): 5.

45. Howard Zinn, "Secrecy, Archives, and the Public Interest," *Midwestern Archivist* 2, no. 2 (1977): 20-21; Quinn, "Archivists and Historians," 8.

46. Ericson, "At the 'rim of creative dissatisfaction': Archivists and Acquisition Development," *Archivaria* 33 (Winter 1991-92): 66-77.

47. In a 1943 essay Orwell wrote, "When I think of antiquity, the detail that frightens me is that those hundreds of millions of slaves on whose backs civilization rested generation after generation have left behind them no record whatever." Orwell, *A Collection of Essays* (Garden City, NY: Doubleday, 1954), 206.

48. David A. Wallace, "Historical and Contemporary Justice and the Role of Archivists," in *Arkiv, Demokrati og Rettferd* (proceedings of Oslo conference, 2005), 25-26, at: http://www.abm-utvikling.no/publisert/abm-skrift/arkiv_demokrati.pdf (accessed 12 May 2008).

49. Jeannette Bastian, *Owning Memory: How a Caribbean Community Lost Its Archives and Found Its History* (Westport, CT: Libraries Unlimited, 2003), 3-5.

50. Paraphrased from Tom Nesmith's commentary on Hugh Taylor, "Transformation in the Archives: Technological Adjustment or Paradigm Shift?" (1970), in Nesmith, ed., *Canadian Archival Studies and the Rediscovery of Provenance* (Metuchen, NJ: Scarecrow Press, 1993), 17.

51. Jeannette Allis Bastian, "Whispers in the Archives: Finding the Voices of the Colonized in the Records of the Colonizer," in *Political Pressure and the Archival Record*, ed. Margaret Procter, Michael G. Cook, and Caroline Williams (Chicago: Society of American Archivists, 2005), 41.

52. Adele Perry, "The Colonial Archive on Trial: Possession, Dispossession, and History in *Delgamuukw v. British Columbia*," in *Archive Stories: Facts, Fictions, and the Writing of History*, ed. Antoinette Burton (Durham, NC: Duke University Press, 2005), 345.

53. Michel-Rolph Trouillot, "Silencing the Past: Layers of Meaning in the Haitian Revolution," in *Between History and Histories: The Making of Silences and Commemorations*, ed. Gerald Sider and Gavin Smith (Toronto: University of Toronto Press, 1997), 42-43.

54. Trouillot, "Silencing the Past," 38, 42.

55. Patricia Galloway, "Archives, Power, and History: Dunbar Rowland and the Beginning of the State Archives of Mississippi (1902-1936)," *American Archivist* 69 (Spring/Summer 2006): 80.

56. Loris Williams, Kirsten Thorpe, and Andrew Wilson, "Identity and Access to Government Records: Empowering the Community," *Archives and Manuscripts* 34, no. 1 (May 2006): 14. See also pages 10-12.

57. Kirsten Thorpe, "Indigenous Knowledge and Archives," in *Australian Indigenous Knowledge and Libraries*, ed. Martin Nakato and Marcia Langton (Sydney: University of Technology, 2006), 189-94.

58. First Archivists Circle, *Protocols for Native American Archival Materials*, http://www2.nau.edu/libnap-p/protocols.html (accessed 12 May 2008). This document is discussed fully in the conclusion of this book.

59. Gerald Sider and Gavin Smith, "Introduction," in *Between History and Histories: The Making of Silences and Commemorations*, 3.

60. Sider and Smith, "Introduction," in *Between History and Histories*, 10-11.

61. Francis Blouin, "Archivists, Mediation, and the Constructs of Social Memory," *Archival Issues* (1999): 101-12.

62. Elisabeth Kaplan, "We are What We Collect, We Collect What We Are: Archives and the Construction of Identity," *American Archivist* 63 (2000): 126-51.

63. Tom Nesmith, "Seeing Archives: Postmodernism and the Changing Intellectual Place of Archives," *American Archivist* 65 (2002): 24-41.

64. Mark Greene, "Not Magic, Not Science, but Art: Comment on 'Archival Appraisal Alchemy,'" Benson Ford Research Center symposium paper (2002), http://www.hfmgv.org/research/events/symposium2002/papers/greene.asp (accessed 5 February 2003).

65. Helen W. Samuels, "Who Controls the Past," *American Archivist* 49 (1986): 109-24; Larry J. Hackman and Joan Warnow-Blewett, "The Documentation Strategy Process: A Model and a Case Study," *American Archivist* 50 (Winter 1987): 12-47.

66. Richard J. Cox, "The Documentation Strategy and Archival Appraisal Principles: A Different Perspective," *Archivaria* 38 (1994): 11-36.

67. Elizabeth Snowden Johnson, "Our Archives, Our Selves: Documentation Strategy and the Re-Appraisal of Professional Identity," *American Archivist* 71 (Spring/Summer 2008): 193-95.

68. Eric Ketelaar, "Tacit Narratives: The Meaning of Archives," *Archival Science* 1 (2001): 136.

69. Terry Cook, "Remembering the Future: Appraisal of Records and the Role of Archives in Constructing Social Memory," in *Archives, Documentation and Institutions of Social Memory*, ed. Francis X. Blouin, Jr. and William G. Rosenberg (Ann Arbor: University of Michigan Press, 2006), 173. See also Verne Harris, "Postmodernism and Archival Appraisal: Seven Theses," in *Archives and Justice* (Chicago: Society of American Archivists, 2007), 101-6.

70. Verne Harris, "Exploratory Thoughts on Current State Archives Service Appraisal Policy and the Conceptual Foundations of Macro-Appraisal," in *Archives and Justice*, 93.

71. Verne Harris, "The Archival Sliver: A Perspective on the Construction of Social Memory in Archives and the Transition from Apartheid to Democracy," in *Refiguring the Archive*, ed. Carolyn Hamilton, Verne Harris, Jane Taylor, Michele Pickover, Graeme Reid, and Razia Saleh (Dordrecht, Netherlands: Kluwer Academic Publishers, 2002): 151.

72. Harris, *Archives and Justice*, 102-4.

73. Gudmund Valderhaug, "Memory, Archives and Justice," revised paper based on a talk at the "Memory for Justice" colloquium, Nelson Mandela Foundation, Johannesburg (2005), available at: http://depotdrengen.wordpress.com/memory-archives-and-justice-article/ (accessed 14 May 2008).

74. Cited in Bastian, *Owning Memory*, 10.

75. Bastian, *Owning Memory*, 11.

76. Dora Schwarzstein, "Oral History Around the World: Present and Future Perspectives," *Comma: International Journal on Archives* 1/2 (2002): 185.

77. Jan Vansina, *Oral Tradition as History* (Madison: University of Wisconsin Press, 1985): xi.

78. Vansina, *Oral Tradition as History*, 147.

79. Vansina, *Oral Tradition as History*, 33-34.

80. Vansina, *Oral Tradition as History*, 177, 185.

81. Vansina, *Oral Tradition as History*, 197-98.

82. Ndiyoi Mutiti, "Re-figuring the Archives: the African Experience," *Comma: International Journal on Archives* 1/2 (2002): 204-5.

83. Williams, quoted in Williams, Thorpe, and Wilson, "Identity and Access to Government Records," 22.

84. Horacio N. Roque Ramirez, "A Living Archive of Desire: Teresita La Campesina and the Embodiment of Queer Latino Community Histories," in *Archive Stories*, 116.

85. Harris, *Archives and Justice*, 189.

86. James E. Fogerty, "Oral History as a Tool in Archival Development," *Comma: International Journal on Archives* 1/2 (2002): 207.

87. Bastian, *Owning Memory*, 5, 11.

88. Verne Harris and Sello Hatang, "Archives, Identity, and Place: A Dialogue on What It (Might) Mean(s) to be an African Archivist," in *Archives and Justice*, 231.

89. Philip P. Mason, "The Society of American Archivists in the Seventies: Report of the Committee for the 1970's," *American Archivist* 35 (April 1972): 205.

90. This historical background was reported in the final report of SAA's Task Force on Diversity in 1999; see http://www.archivists.org/governance/taskforces/diversity-final.asp (accessed 12 May 2008).

91. Michele F. Pacifico, "Founding Mothers: Women in the Society of American Archivists, 1936-1972," *American Archivist* 50 (Summer 1987): 370-89.

92. Elizabeth W. Adkins, "Our Journey Toward Diversity—and a Call to (More) Action," *American Archivist* 71 (Spring/Summer 2008): 32-33. In addition to SAA the committee included the American Association for State and Local History and the American Association of Museums.

93. SAA Council statement on diversity, http://www.archivists.org/statements/diversitystatement.asp (accessed 12 May 2008).

94. Quoted in Adkins, "Our Journey Toward Diversity," 37. Adkins notes that the Committee's charge was revised in August 2006, and now reads, in part: "It functions as a catalyst for new diversity-related initiatives, developed in coordination with various SAA entities, and monitors, evaluates, advocates for, and reports on matters pertaining to the diversity of archival practitioners and documentation."

95. Richard Pearce-Moses and Randall C. Jimerson, "Facing the Future: SAA's 2006-2007 Strategic Priorities," *Archival Outlook* (July/August 2006): 8-9.

96. Adkins, "Our Journey Toward Diversity," 25. Bunch quotation abbreviated by this author.

97. Adkins, "Our Journey Toward Diversity," 48-49.

98. Harris, "The Archival Sliver," 148.

99. Margaret Hedstrom, "Charting the Way Forward: Summation and Sustainability," Archives and the Ethics of Memory Construction conference, Ann Arbor, Michigan, 3 May 2008, author's notes.

100. Michael Kammen, *Mystic Chords of Memory: The Transformation of Tradition in American Culture* (New York: Alfred A. Knopf, 1991), 3.

101. Tom Nesmith, "Still Fuzzy, But More Accurate: Some Thoughts on the 'Ghosts' of Archival Theory," *Archivaria* 47 (Spring 1999): 144-45.

102. Durba Ghosh, "National Narratives and the Politics of Miscegenation," in *Archive Stories*, 38.

103. JoAnne Yates, *Control Through Communication: The Rise of System in American Management* (Baltimore: Johns Hopkins, 1989), 271-75.

104. Benedict Anderson, *Imagined Communities: Reflections on the Origin and Spread of Nationalism* (New York: Verson, 2006), 184-85.

105. David M. Levy, *Scrolling Forward: Making Sense of Documents in the Digital Age* (New York: Arcade Publishing, 2001), 120-28.

106. Laura Millar, "An Obligation of Trust: Speculations on Accountability and Description," *American Archivist* 69 (Spring/Summer 2006): 70-71.

107. Heather MacNeil, "Picking Our Text: Archival Description, Authenticity, and the Archivist as Editor," *American Archivist* 68 (Fall/Winter 2005): 272.

108. MacNeil, "Picking Our Text," 274.

109. Wendy Duff and Verne Harris, "Stories and Names: Archival Description as Narrating Records and Constructing Meanings," *Archival Science* 2 (2002): 275-76.

110. Elizabeth Yakel, "Archival Representation," *Archival Science* 3 (2003): 10-24.

111. Tom Nesmith, "Reopening Archives: Bringing New Contextualities into Archival Theory and Practice," *Archivaria* 60 (Fall 2005): 268.

112. Nancy Ruth Bartlett, "Past Imperfect *(l'imparfait)*: Mediating Meaning in Archives of Art," in *Archives, Documentation and Institutions of Social Memory*, 129.

113. Verne Harris, "'A World Whose Horizon Can Only Be Justice': Toward a Politics of Recordmaking," in *Archives and Justice*, 260.

114. Rainbow L. Koehl, *What Lies Beneath: How Description in Archival Finding Aids Mirrors Our Society's Values: A Case Study of Four Repositories* (Master of Arts thesis, Western Washington University, 2006), 56-58.

115. Koehl, *What Lies Beneath*, 62.

116. Yakel, "Archival Representation," 20-25.

117. Jeff Sahadeo, "'Without the Past There Is No Future': Archives, History, and Authority in Uzbekistan," in *Archive Stories*, 55.

118. MacNeil, "Picking Our Text," 273-78.

119. Michelle Light and Tom Hyry, "Colophons and Annotations: New Directions for the Finding Aid," *American Archivist* 65 (Fall/Winter 2002): 226-27.

120. Nesmith, "Reopening Archives," 271-73.

121. "Testimony of Anne R. Kenney before Senate Subcommittee on Regulation and Government Information" (unpublished typescript, June 11, 1993).

122. Elena S. Danielson, "The Ethics of Access," *American Archivist* 52 (Winter 1989): 60.

123. Charles L. Miller, *Archival Ethics* (Master of Arts thesis, Western Washington University, July 1998), 46-53.

124. "SAA Resolution on Access to the Thurgood Marshall Papers at the Library of Congress," SAA Council, June 13, 1993.

125. *Archives at the Crossroads 2007: Open Report to the Minister of Arts and Culture from the Archival Conference "National System, Public Interest" (April 2007)*: 15, at http://www.nelsonmandela.org.

126. Ann Laura Stoler, "Colonial Archives and the Arts of Governance: On the Content in the Form," in *Refiguring the Archive*, 98-99.

127. Timothy L. Ericson, "Building Our Own 'Iron Curtain': The Emergence of Secrecy in American Government," *American Archivist* 68 (Spring/Summer 2005): 18-52.

128. Koehl, "What Lies Beneath," 63.

129. Nesmith, "Reopening Archives," 266.

130. Nesmith, "Reopening Archives," 266-67.

131. Gudmund Valderhaug, "Memory, Justice and the Public Record," paper presented at the conference "Archives and the Ethics of Memory Construction," Ann Arbor,

Michigan, 2 May 2008; information available at: http://memoryethics.org (accessed 8 May 2008).

132. Gudmund Valderhaug, "The Good Archivist," blog posting of paper presented at Norwegian Archives Meeting, April 2007, http://depotdrengen.wordpress.com/ (accessed 14 May 2008).

133. Gudmund Valderhaug, "Memory, Archives and Justice," revised paper based on a talk at the "Memory for Justice" colloquium, Nelson Mandela Foundation, Johannesburg, 2005, http://depotdrengen.wordpress.com/memory-archives-and-justice-article/ (accessed 14 May 2008).

134. Valderhaug, "Memory, Archives and Justice."

135. Bhekizizwe Peterson, "The Archives and the Political Imaginary," in *Refiguring the Archive*, 33.

136. Harris, "The Archival Sliver,"148.

137. Philip C. Bantin, "The Indiana University Electronic Records Project Revisited," *American Archivist* 62 (Spring 1999): 153-63.

138. Digital Curation Centre, "What Is Digital Curation?" quoted in Adrian Cunningham, "Digital Curation/Digital Archiving: A View from the National Archives of Australia," *American Archivist* 71 (Fall/Winter 2008): 531.

139. Cunningham, "Digital Curation/Digital Archiving," 533.

140. Mary E. Samouelian, *Embracing Web 2.0: Archives and the Newest Generation of Web Applications* (Master of Arts thesis, School of Information and Library Science, University of North Carolina at Chapel Hill, April, 2008), 2.

141. Helen R. Tibbo, "The Impact of Information Technology on Academic Archives in the Twenty-first Century," in *College and University Archives*, 38-39. See also Margaret Hedstrom, "Archives, Memory, and Interfaces with the Past," *Archival Science* 2, nos. 1-2 (2002): 21-41.

142. Richard V. Szary, "Encoded Finding Aids as a Transforming Technology in Archival Reference Service," in *College and University Archives*, 247, 252.

143. Richard Pearce-Moses, "Janus in Cyberspace: Archives on the Threshold of the Digital Era," *American Archivist* 70 (Spring/Summer 2007): 13-22.

144. Quoted in Nicholas C. Burckel, "Academic Archives: Retrospect and Prospect," in *College and University Archives*, 20.

145. Magia Ghetu Krause and Elizabeth Yakel, "Interaction in Virtual Archives: The Polar Bear Expedition Digital Collections Next Generation Finding Aid," *American Archivist* 70 (Spring/Summer 2007): 282.

146. Tim O'Reilly, quoted in Samouelian, *Embracing Web 2.0*, 2-3.

147. Peter Van Garderen, "Web 2.0 and Archival Institutions," Archivematica blog, 8 May 2006, http://archivemati.ca/2006/05/08/web-20-and-archival-institutions/#more-34 (accessed 18 December 2008).

148. See Michelle Springer, Beth Dulabahn, Paul Michel, Barbara Natanson, David Reser, David Woodward, and Helena Zinkham, *For the Common Good: The Library of Congress Flickr Pilot Project* (30 October 2008), http://www.loc.gov/rr/print/flickr_report_final.pdf (accessed 20 December 2008).

149. These categories and examples from Kate Theimer, "Archives & 'new' Technology," ArchivesNext blog, http://www.archivesnext.com/?page_id=62 (accessed 18 December 2008).

150. Samouelian, *Embracing Web 2.0*, 6-7.

151. Samouelian, *Embracing Web 2.0*, 46. Emphasis in original.

152. Krause and Yakel, "Interaction in Virtual Archives," 285-86, 306-12.

153. Hedstrom, "Archives, Memory, and Interfaces with the Past," 21-41.

154. Elizabeth Yakel, "Inviting the User Into the Virtual Archives," *OCLC Systems and Services* 22, no. 3 (2007): 159-63.

155. Elizabeth Yakel, "AI: Archival Intelligence and User Expertise," *American Archivist* 66 (Spring/Summer 2003): 51-78; and Yakel, "Managing Expectations, Expertise, and Effort While Extending Services to Researchers in Academic Archives," in *College and University Archives*, 270.

156. Max J. Evans, "Archives of the People, by the People, for the People," *American Archivist* 70 (Fall/Winter 2007): 387-400.

157. Kate Theimer, "An Archivist's 2.0 Manifesto?" ArchivesNext blog, http://www.archivesnext.com/?p=64 (accessed 18 December 2008).

158. Kate Theimer, "A Different Kind of Web: New Connections between Archives and Our Users with Web 2.0," draft book proposal submitted to Society of American Archivists Publications Board, November 2008.

159. Andrew Keen, *The Cult of the Amateur: How Today's Internet Is Killing Our Culture* (New York: Doubleday, 2007), 1.

160. Keen, *The Cult of the Amateur*, 92.

161. Keen, *The Cult of the Amateur*, 177.

162. Kate Theimer, e-mail to author, 9 January 2009. See also Peter B. Kaufman and Jeff Ubois, "Good Terms—Improving Commercial-Noncommercial Partnerships for Mass Digitization," *D-Lib Magazine* 13 (November/December 2007), at: http://www.dlib.org/dlib/november07/kaufman/11kaufman.html (accessed 9 January 2009).

163. For a thoughtful analysis of advocacy as a means of securing public support for archives, see Leslie Schuyler, *The Wonderful World of Archives: American Archivists and Their Quest for Public Support* (Master's thesis, Western Washington University, 2008).

164. Kaye, *Why Do Ruling Classes Fear History?* 60-61.

165. Verne Harris, "Redefining Archives in South Africa," in *Archives and Justice*, 173-74.

166. William J. Maher, "Society and Archives," (incoming presidential address, 61st annual meeting of the Society of American Archivists, 30 August 1997), www.archivists.org (accessed 12 May 2008).

167. See Randall C. Jimerson, "Secret Discussions," letter to the editor, *US News & World Report*, January 26, 2004.

168. "The Haunted Archives" (Editorial), *The Nation*, April 15, 2004.

169. Ericson, "At the 'rim of creative dissatisfaction,'" 51.

170. John W. Dean, *Worse Than Watergate: The Secret Presidency of George W. Bush* (New York: Little, Brown & Company, 2004), 92.

171. Randall C. Jimerson, "Secret Discussions," letter to the editor, *US News & World Report*, January 26, 2004.

172. White House Office of the Press Secretary, "Freedom of Information Act" (21 January 2009), at: http://www.archivists.org/news/FOIA_1.21.09.pdf.

173. For the text of President Obama's Executive Order see *Federal Register*, Vol. 74, No. 15 (26 January 2009), also at: http://www.whitehouse.gov/the_press_office/ExecutiveOrderPresidentialRecords/ (accessed 12 February 2009); Frank Boles to President Barack Obama, 22 January 2009, at: http://www.archivists.org/news/ObamaReEO13233.pdf.

174. Elena S. Danielson, "The Ethics of Access," *American Archivist* 52 (Winter 1989): 58-59.

175. Christopher H. Schmitt and Edward T. Pound, "Keeping Secrets: The Bush Administration is Doing the Public's Business out of the Public Eye. Here's How—and Why," *US News & World Report*, December 22, 2003.

176. Graham, quoted in Dean, *Worse Than Watergate*, 92.

177. OpenTheGovernment.org, "Statement of Values," http://www.openthegovernment.org/article/subarchive/63 (accessed 29 September 2007).

178. Steve Hensen to Representative Stephen Horn, 6 November 2001, available at: "SAA Responds to Executive Order 13233 on Presidential Papers," www.archivists.org/statements/stephenhorn.asp (accessed 12 May 2008).

179. Steven L. Hensen, "The President's Papers Are the People's Business," *Washington Post*, December 16, 2001, also available at: www.archivists.org/statements/prespapers.asp (accessed 12 May 2008).

180. Robert Weiner, "Orwell in 2007," *The Oregonian*, October 7,2007, also available at www.commondreams.org/archive/2007/10/07/4378/ (accessed 9 April 2008).

181. Society of American Archivists, "Statement on the Renewal of the USA PATRIOT Act" (15 July 2004), www.archivists.org/statements/patriotact.asp (accessed 9 April 2008).

182. Thomas James Connors, "Secrecy vs. Access: Government Information Policy and Politics in the George W. Bush Administration," *Arkiv, Demokrati og Rettferd* (proceedings of Oslo conference, 2005), 56.

183. Truman, quoted by Archivist of the United States Allen Weinstein, in "Progress Toward a Goal of Greater Access," *Prologue: Quarterly of the National Archives and Records Administration* 39, no. 2 (Summer 2007): 5.

184. For further details and more examples, see Meredith Fuchs, "The White House: Off Limits to Historians?" *Passport* (April 2008): 5-9; Connors, "Secrecy vs. Access," 54-67; and Ericson, "Building Our Own 'Iron Curtain,'" 18-52.

185. Elsie Freeman Finch, "Introduction," in *Advocating Archives: An Introduction to Public Relations for Archivists* (Chicago: Society of American Archivists, 1994), 1.

186. Henry A. Waxman to the vice president, 21 June 2007, in Jesse Lee, "Oversight Committee on the Vice President and Classified Information" (21 June 2007), available at Speaker Nancy Pelosi's website, www.speaker.gov (accessed 25 June 2007).

187. Ruth Marcus, "Cheney's Secrets Defy Explanation," reprinted from the *Washington Post* in the Bellingham (WA) *Herald*, June 29, 2007, B3.

188. Leonard Pitts, "Cheney's Obsession With Secrecy, Maniacal, Scary," Bellingham (WA) *Herald*, July 2, 2007.

189. Waxman and Perino quoted in Michael Isikoff, "A New Cheney-Gonzales Mystery," *Newsweek* (July 2–9, 2007): 10.

190. Maureen Dowd, "A Vice President Without Borders, Bordering on Lunacy," *New York Times* op-ed page, June 24, 2007.

191. Quoted in e-mail message, Eric Ketelaar to Randall Jimerson, June 26, 2007.

192. So starved for attention are archivists, however, that they celebrated the positive aspect of Dowd's depiction. Within weeks, archivists attending the 2007 SAA annual meeting received "Macho Hero" ribbons to attach to their nametags and "Macho Hero" temporary tattoo decals.

193. National Coalition for History, "President Obama Revokes Bush Presidential Records Executive Order" (updated 26 January 2009), at: http://historycoalition.org/2009/01/21/president-obama-revokes-bush-presidential-records-executive-order/#more-1033 (accessed 5 February 2009). For the text of the Executive Order see *Federal Register*, Vol. 74, No. 15 (26 January 2009).

194. Connors, "Secrecy vs. Access," 62.

195. Rick Barry, "Thinking About Accountability, Recordkeeping and Shelley Davis' Unbridled Power: A Commentary," (March 2001), 8 of 13, available at: www.mybestdosc.com/barry-r-on%20sdavis.html (accessed 14 May 2008).

196. Shelley Davis, "The Failure of Federal Records Management," in *Archives and the Public Good*, 115. For a more detailed account of Davis's experiences, see her book, *Unbridled Power: Inside the Secret Culture of the IRS* (New York: HarperBusiness, 1997).

197. Davis, "The Failure of Federal Records Management," 117, 120-21, 124.

198. Davis, "The Failure of Federal Records Management," 127-28.

199. Davis, "The Failure of Federal Records Management," 132-33.

200. Verne Harris, "Ethics and the Archive: 'An Incessant Movement of Recontextualisation'" (unpublished paper presented at University of Wisconsin–

Milwaukee Conference on Archival Ethics, 30 November 2007), 12.

201. South African Society of Archivists, Professional Code for South African Archivists, quoted in Harris, "Ethics and the Archive," 12.
202. Harris, "Ethics and the Archive," 12.
203. Harris, "Ethics and the Archive," 12-13.
204. Verne Harris, "Knowing Right from Wrong: The Archivist and the Protection of People's Rights," in *Archives and Justice*, 211-12.

CONCLUSION

1. Nelson Mandela Foundation, "Memory for Justice: Report on a Colloquium," (18 August 2005), http://www.memoryethics.org/resources (accessed 12 May 2008). The full report also can be found in the Appendix.
2. Wallace C. Koehler and J. Michael Pemberton, "A Search for Core Values: Towards a Model Code of Ethics for Information Professionals" (2000), quoted in Eric Ketelaar, "The Ethics of Preserving and Destroying Private Archives," *Argiefnuus/ Archives News* 43/4 (June 2001): 70, http://cf.hum.uva.nl/bai/home/eketelaar/ Ethicspreserving.doc (accessed 14 May 2008).
3. Glenn Dingwall, "Trusting Archivists: The Role of Archival Ethics Codes in Establishing Public Faith," *American Archivist* 67 (Spring/Summer 2004): 12-14.
4. Dingwall, "Trusting Archivists," 15.
5. Julia Evetts, "Short Note: The Sociology of Professional Groups" (2006), as quoted in David Wallace, "Locating Agency: Archivists and the Challenges of Professional Ethics" (unpublished paper, University of Wisconsin–Milwaukee Conference on Archival Ethics, 30 November 2007), 4.
6. Dingwall, "Trusting Archivists," 16; Richard J. Cox, "Professionalism and Archivists in the United States," *American Archivist* 49 (Summer 1986): 238.
7. Dingwall, "Trusting Archivists," 17, 20, 23-24.
8. Berndt Fredriksson, "The Changing Role of Archivists in the Contemporary Society," *Comma: International Journal on Archives* 1/2 (2002): 43.
9. Karen Benedict, *Ethics and the Archival Profession: Introduction and Case Studies* (Chicago: Society of American Archivists, 2003), 5.
10. Dingwall, "Trusting Archivists," 25-26.
11. Benedict, *Ethics and the Archival Profession*, 4-5.
12. "Nixon Papers Controversy," Society of American Archivists Newsletter, July 1986, cited in Elena S. Danielson, "The Ethics of Access," *American Archivist* 52 (Winter 1989): 59.
13. Verne Harris, *Archives and Justice: A South African Perspective* (Chicago: Society of American Archivists, 2007), 254-55.
14. Harris, *Archives and Justice*, 209.
15. Harris, *Archives and Justice*, 211.
16. Gudmund Valderhaug, "Memory, Archives and Justice," revised paper based on a talk at the "Memory for Justice" colloquium, Nelson Mandela Foundation, Johannesburg (2005), http://depotdrengen.wordpress.com/memory-archives-and-justice-article/ (accessed 12 May 2008).
17. David A. Wallace, "Historical and Contemporary Justice and the Role of Archivists," in *Arkiv, Demokrati og Rettferd* (proceedings of Oslo conference, 2005), 23, http://www. abm-utvikling.no/publisert/abm-skrift/arkiv_demokrati.pdf (accessed 12 May 2008).
18. Society of American Archivists, "Code of Ethics," www.archivists.org (accessed 12 May 2008).
19. Wallace, "Historical and Contemporary Justice and the Role of Archivists," 23-24.
20. Wallace, "Historical and Contemporary Justice and the Role of Archivists," 24.

21. Toon van Meijl, "Modern Morals in Postmodernity: A Critical Reflection on Professional Codes of Ethics," *Cultural Dynamics* (2000), quoted in Wallace, "Locating Agency," 5.
22. Wallace, "Locating Agency," 5.
23. Quoted in Wallace, "Locating Agency," 6.
24. Dingwall, "Trusting Archivists," 27.
25. Dingwall, "Trusting Archivists," 27.
26. Dingwall, "Trusting Archivists," 29-30.
27. James O'Toole, "Archives and Historical Accountability: Toward a Moral Theology of Archives," *Archivaria* 58 (Fall 2004): 14.
28. Van Meijl, quoted in Wallace, "Locating Agency," 7.
29. Ian Harper and Alberto Corsín Jiménez, "Towards Interactive Professional Ethics," *Anthropology Today* (2005), as quoted in Wallace, "Locating Agency," 7.
30. Noel Preston, "Applied and Professional Ethics: An Instrument of Social Transformation?" (1996), as quoted in Wallace, "Locating Agency," 8.
31. Preston, quoted in Wallace, "Locating Agency," 12.
32. Van Meijl, quoted in Wallace, "Locating Agency," 12.
33. Terry Cook, "Archival Music: Verne Harris and the Cracks of Memory," in *Archives and Justice*, xiii-xiv.
34. Valderhaug, "Memory, Archives and Justice."
35. Valderhaug, "Memory, Archives and Justice."
36. Verne Harris, "Knowing Right from Wrong: The Archivist and the Protection of People's Rights," in *Archives and Justice*, 211.
37. Verne Harris, "The Archive Is Politics," in *Archives and Justice*, 247.
38. Harris, "The Archive Is Politics," 248-49.
39. Verne Harris, "Ethics and the Archive: An Incessant Movement of Recontextualisation" (unpublished paper presented at University of Wisconsin–Milwaukee Conference on Archival Ethics, 30 November 2007), 3.
40. Harris, "Ethics and the Archive," 5.
41. William T. Hagan, "Archival Captive—The American Indian," *American Archivist* 41 (April 1978): 136.
42. For example, see Caithlin Lynn Frost, *An Examination of the Distinctive Policies and Procedures of Tribal Archives* (Master's thesis, Western Washington University, 2003).
43. See Native American Archives Roundtable website, http://www.archivists.org/saagroups/nat-amer/ (accessed 22 December 2008).
44. "Introduction," in First Archivists Circle, *Protocols for Native American Archival Materials*, http://www2.nau.edu/libnap-p/protocols.html (accessed 12 May 2008).
45. Loris Williams, Kirsten Thorpe, and Andrew Wilson, "Identity and Access to Government Records: Empowering the Community," *Archives and Manuscripts* 34, no. 1 (May 2006): 10-14. See also Kirsten Thorpe, "Indigenous Knowledge and Archives," in *Australian Indigenous Knowledge and Libraries*, ed. Martin Nakato and Marcia Langton (Sydney: University of Technology, 2006), 189-94.
46. "Building Relationships of Mutual Respect," in *Protocols for Native American Archival Materials*.
47. Society of American Archivists, "Report: Task Force to Review Protocols for Native American Archival Materials (February 2008), SAA website, www.archivists.org (accessed 12 May 2008).
48. Mark A. Greene, "Protocols for Native American Materials," *Archival Outlook* (March/April 2008): 25.

49. SAA Native American Protocols Forum Working Group, available at: http://
    saa.archivists.org/Scripts/4Disapi.dll/4DCGI/committees/SAAWG-NAPF.
    html?Action=Show_Comm_Detail&CommCode=SAA**WG-NAPF&Time=-
    291345005&SessionID=327341886r15818v93zxx4q19dl99y57l20xmp2f49xgmq0z4a2
    390lne3q6l700 (accessed 22 December 2008).
50. John Bolcer, "The Protocols for Native American Archival Materials: Considerations
    and Concerns from the Perspective of a Non-Tribal Archivist," *Easy Access* 34, no.4
    (January 2009): 3-6.
51. Louis Bickford, "Preserving Memory: The Past and the Human Rights Movement in
    Chile" (2000), quoted in Grace Lile, "Bearing Witness: Audiovisual Archiving for
    Human Rights Documentation and Advocacy" (unpublished paper presented at the
    annual meeting of the Society of American Archivists, September 2007).
52. Lile, "Bearing Witness."
53. Graham Shaw, presentation on the Endangered Archives Program, Yale Center for
    International and Area Studies Global Resources Network Conference, March 2005,
    http://www.library.yale.edu/mssa/globalrecord/new_web/shaw.html#text (accessed 11
    May 2007).
54. Robin West, quoted in Barbara Herrnstein Smith, "The Unquiet Judge: Activism
    without Objectivism in Law and Politics," in *Rethinking Objectivity*, ed. Allan Megill
    (Durham, NC: Duke University Press, 1994), 307.
55. Smith, "The Unquiet Judge," 307-8.
56. "Archives and Ethics: Reflections on Practice" (30 November 2007), videotaped
    presentations available at: www.uwm.edu/Dept/SOIS/cipr/archive.html (accessed 20
    June 2008).
57. Menzi L. Behrnd-Klodt and Peter J. Wosh, eds., *Privacy and Confidentiality Perspectives:
    Archivists and Archival Records* (Chicago: Society of American Archivists, 2005).
58. Britz, quoted in Katie Blank, "Archives and Ethics Explored in Seminar," *Archival
    Outlook* (January/February 2008): 28.
59. "Interdisciplinary Perspectives on Archives and the Ethics of Memory Construction,"
    www.memoryethics.org (accessed 12 May 2008).
60. Conference program and abstracts of papers are available at www.memoryethics.org
    (accessed 12 May 2008).
61. Mark A. Greene, "The Power of Archives: Archivists' Values and Value in the Post-
    Modern Age," http://www.archivists.org/conference/ (accessed 22 December 2008).
    For another thoughtful discussion of archival values see Scott Cline, "'To the Limit of
    Our Integrity': Reflections on Archival Being" (paper presented at the annual meeting
    of the Society of American Archivists, August 2008).

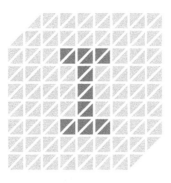

Index

Printed in the USA
CPSIA information can be obtained
at www.ICGtesting.com
LVHW011153150324
774517LV00047B/2073